THE IDEA OF
BIBLICAL INTERPRETATION

Supplements to the
Journal for the Study
of Judaism

Editor
JOHN J. COLLINS
The Divinity School, Yale University

Associate Editor
FLORENTINO GARCÍA MARTÍNEZ
Qumran Institute, University of Groningen

Advisory Board
J. Duhaime
A. Hilhorst
P. W. van der Horst
A. Klostergaard Petersen
M. A. Knibb
J. T. A. G. M. van Ruiten
J. Sievers
G. Stemberger
E. J. C. Tigchelaar
J. Tromp

Volume 83

THE IDEA OF
BIBLICAL INTERPRETATION

THE IDEA OF
BIBLICAL INTERPRETATION

Essays in Honor of James L. Kugel

Edited by
Hindy Najman
Judith H. Newman

SBL

Society of Biblical Literature
Atlanta

Library of Congress Cataloging-in-Publication Data

The idea of biblical interpretation : essays in honor of James L. Kugel /
edited by Hindy Najman and Judith H. Newman.
      p. cm. — (Supplements to the journal for the study of Judaism ; v.83)
   Includes bibliographical references and index.
   ISBN 978-1-58983-387-6 (paper binding : alk. paper)
   1. Bible. O.T.—Criticism, interpretation, etc. I. Kugel, James L. II. Najman,
Hindy. III. Newman, Judith H. (Judith Hood), 1961–
   BS1171.3.I34 2008
   221.6—dc22   2008040684

Printed in the United States of America
on acid-free paper

James L. Kugel

CONTENTS

PART ONE

THE BIBLE AS IT WAS

PART TWO

TRADITIONS OF THE BIBLE IN
SECOND TEMPLE JUDAISM

PART THREE

THE INTERPRETIVE LIFE OF BIBLICAL TEXTS
FROM EARLY JUDAISM TO THE PRESENT

LIST OF CONTRIBUTORS

Moshe J. Bernstein
Professor of Bible
Yeshiva University

Daniel Boyarin
Herman P. and Sophia Taubman Professor of Talmudic Culture
University of California, Berkeley

Gerald L. Bruns
William P. and Hazel B. White Professor of English
University of Notre Dame

Shaye J. D. Cohen
Littauer Professor of Hebrew Literature and Philosophy
Harvard University

John J. Collins
Holmes Professor of Old Testament Criticism and Interpretation
Yale University Divinity School

Peter Enns
Associate Professor of Old Testament
Westminster Theological Seminary

Steven D. Fraade
Mark Taper Professor of the History of Judaism
Yale University

Christine E. Hayes
Professor of Religious Studies in Classical Judaica
Yale University

Jon D. Levenson
Albert A. List Professor of Jewish Studies in the Divinity School and
the Department of Near Eastern Languages and Civilizations
Harvard University

Wayne A. Meeks
Woolsey Professor Emeritus of Biblical Studies
Yale University

Jacob Milgrom
Professor Emeritus of Biblical Studies
University of California, Berkeley

Hindy Najman
Assistant Professor and Jordan Kapson Chair of Jewish Studies
University of Notre Dame

Harry P. Nasuti
Professor of Hebrew Bible/Old Testament
Fordham University

Judith H. Newman
Associate Professor of Old Testament
The General Theological Seminary of the Episcopal Church

Lawrence F. Rhu
Associate Professor of English and Comparative Literature
University of South Carolina

Lawrence H. Schiffman
Ethel and Irvin A. Edelman Professor of Hebrew and Judaic Studies
New York University

Bernard Septimus
Jacob E. Safra Professor of Jewish History and Sephardic Civilization
Harvard University

David Stern
Ruth Meltzer Professor of Classical Hebrew Literature
University of Pennsylvania

Isaiah Teshima
Associate Professor of Hebrew and Jewish Studies
Osaka Sangyo University, Japan

James C. VanderKam
John A. O'Brien Professor of Hebrew Scriptures
University of Notre Dame

Steven Weitzman
Irving M. Glazer Chair in Jewish Studies
Indiana University

Elliot R. Wolfson
Abraham Lieberman Professor of Hebrew and Judaic Studies
New York University

JAMES L. KUGEL
LIST OF PUBLICATIONS

BOOKS

The Techniques of Strangeness. Yale University Press, 1971. Japanese translation, 1981.

The Idea of Biblical Poetry. Yale University Press, 1981. Second edition, Johns Hopkins University Press, 1998.

Early Biblical Interpretation. With R. Greer. Library of Early Christianity. Westminster Press, 1986.

In Potiphar's House: the Interpretive Life of Biblical Texts in Early Judaism and Christianity. HarperCollins, 1990. Paperback edition, Harvard University Press, 1994.

On Being a Jew. HarperCollins, 1990. Paperback edition, Johns Hopkins University Press, 1998.

The Bible As It Was: Biblical Traditions of Late Antiquity. Harvard University Press, 1997.

Traditions of the Bible: A Guide to the Bible as it Was at the Start of the Common Era. Harvard University Press, 1998.

Great Poems of the Bible. The Free Press, 1999.

The God of Old. The Free Press, 2003.

The Ladder of Jacob: Biblical Interpretation in the Apocrypha and Pseudepigrapha. Princeton University Press, 2004.

The Kingly Sanctuary. Forthcoming.

BOOKS EDITED

Poetry and Prophecy. Cornell University Press, 1990.

Studies in Ancient Midrash. Harvard University Press, 2001.

Shem in the Tents of Japhet: Essays on the Encounter of Judaism and Hellenism. Brill, 2002.

Prayers That Cite Scripture. Center for Jewish Studies. Harvard University Press, forthcoming.

ARTICLES

"Some Medieval and Renaissance Writings on the Poetry of the Bible." Pages 57–81 in *Studies in Medieval Jewish History and Literature.* Edited by I. Twersky. Harvard University Press, 1979.

"Adverbial *Kî Tôb.*" *Journal of Biblical Literature* 99 (1980): 433–36.

"On the Bible and Literary Criticism." *Prooftexts* 1 (1981): 217–36; discussion (by A. Berlin), *Prooftexts* 2 (1982): 323–32.

"On *All* of Hebrew Poetry." *Prooftexts* 2 (1982): 209–21.

"Is There But One Song?" *Biblica* 63 (1982): 329–50.

"Song and Poetry in the Mechilta d'R. Yishmael." Pages 141–44 in *Proceedings of the Eighth World Congress of Jewish Studies: Division C.* Magnes Press, 1982 [Hebrew].

"The Influence of Moses ibn Habib's *Darkhei Noʿam.*" Pages 308–25 in *Jewish Thought in the Sixteenth Century.* Edited by B. D. Cooperman. Harvard University Press, 1983.

" 'The Bible as Literature' in Late Antiquity and the Middle Ages." *HSL: Hebrew University Studies in Literature* 11 (1983): 20–70.

"Two Introductions to Midrash." *Prooftexts* 3 (1983): 131–55. Reprinted, pages 77–103 in *Midrash and Literature.* Edited by G. Hartman and S. Budick. Yale University Press, 1986.

"Some Thoughts on Future Research into Biblical Style." *Journal for the Study of the Old Testament* 28 (1984): 107–17.

"Ecclesiastes," "Poetry, Biblical," and "Psalms." Pages 236–37, 804–06, 833–35 in *Harper's Bible Dictionary.* Harper and Row, 1985.

"Topics in the History of the Spirituality of the Psalms." Pages 113–44 in *The History of Jewish Spirituality.* Edited by A. Green. Seabury-Winston, 1986.

"Torah." Pages 995–1005 in *Contemporary Jewish Religious Thought.* Edited by A. Cohen and P. Mendes-Flohr. Scribners, 1986.

"Biblical Studies and Jewish Studies." *AJS Newsletter* 36 (1986): 22–24.

"On Hidden Hatred and Open Reproach: Early Exegesis of Lev. 19:17." *Harvard Theological Review* 80 (1987): 43–61.

"How Should We Teach the Bible?" Pages 1–20 in *The Bible and the Liberal Arts.* Crawfordsville, Ind.: Wabash College, 1987.

"The Bible's Earliest Interpreters." *Prooftexts* 7 (1987): 269–83.

"The Psalms and Wisdom." Pages 396–406 in *Harper Bible Commentary.* Harper and Row, 1989.

"Qohelet and Money." *Catholic Biblical Quarterly* 51 (1989): 32–49.

"The Bible in the University." Pages 143–66 in *The Hebrew Bible and its Interpreters*. Edited by W. H. Propp, B. Halpern, and D. N. Freedman. Eisenbrauns, 1990.

"The Case Against Joseph." Pages 272–87 in *Lingering Over Words: Studies in Ancient Near Eastern Literature in Honor of William L. Moran*. Edited by Tz. Abusch, J. Huehnergard, and P. Steinkeller. Scholars Press, 1990.

"Cain and Abel in Fact and Fable." Pages 167–90 in *Hebrew Bible or Old Testament?* Edited by R. Brooks and J. J. Collins. University of Notre Dame, 1989.

"Why Was Lamech Blind?" *Hebrew Annual Review* 12 (1990): 91–104.

"Poets and Prophets." Pages 1–25 in *Poetry and Prophecy*. Edited by J. L. Kugel. Cornell University Press, 1990.

"David the Prophet." Pages 45–55 in *Poetry and Prophecy*. Edited by J. L. Kugel. Cornell University Press, 1990.

"Midrashim she-Ne'etqu Mimmeqomam [Midrashim That Ended Up in the Wrong Place]." *Publications of the Israel Academy of Science* 8, no. 3 (1991): 49–61 [Hebrew].

"The Story of Dinah in the *Testament of Levi*." *Harvard Theological Review* 85 (1992): 1–34. Hebrew trans., pages 130–40 in *The Bible in the Light of its Interpreters: Sarah Kamin Memorial Volume*. Edited by S. Japhet. Magnes, 1994.

"Levi's Elevation to the Priesthood in Second Temple Writings." *Harvard Theological Review* 86 (1993): 1–64.

"The *Jubilees* Apocalypse." *Dead Sea Discoveries* 1 (1994): 322–37.

"The Ladder of Jacob." *Harvard Theological Review* 88 (1995): 1–24.

"Reuben's Sin with Bilhah in the *Testament of Reuben*." Pages 525–54 in *Pomegranates and Golden Bells: Studies in Biblical, Jewish, and Near Eastern Ritual, Law, and Literature in Honor of Jacob Milgrom*. Edited by D. Wright, D. N. Freedman, and A. Hurvitz. Eisenbrauns, 1995.

"The Holiness of Israel and its Land in Second Temple Times." Pages 21–32 in *Texts, Temples, Traditions: Menahem Haran Festschrift*. Edited by M. Fox et al. Eisenbrauns, 1996.

"Obscurity in Hebrew Liturgical Poetry." *Medievalia: A Journal of Medieval Studies* 19 (1996): 221–38.

"Wisdom and the Anthological Temper." *Prooftexts* 17 (1997): 9–32.

"'4Q369: The Prayer of Enosh' and Ancient Biblical Interpretation." *Dead Sea Discoveries* 5 (1998): 119–48.

"Introduction." Pages ix–xxix in republication of Louis Ginzberg, *The Legends of the Jews*. Johns Hopkins University Press, 1998.

"What the Dead Sea Scrolls Do Not Tell." *Commentary* 106 (Nov 1998): 49–53.

"Biblical Apocrypha and Pseudepigrapha and the Hebrew of the Second Temple Period." Pages 166–77 in *Diggers at the Well: Proceedings of a Third International Symposium on the Hebrew of the Dead Sea Scrolls and Ben Sira*. Edited by T. Muraoka and J. F. Elwolde. Brill, 2000.

"Ancient Biblical Interpretation and the Ancient Israelite Sage." Pages 1–26 in *Studies in Ancient Midrash*. Edited by J. L. Kugel. Harvard University Press, 2001.

"Some Instances of Biblical Interpretation in the Hymns and Wisdom Writings of Qumran." Pages 155–69 in *Studies in Ancient Midrash*. Edited by J. L. Kugel. Harvard University Press, 2001.

"Appendix: The Calendar of the *Book of Jubilees*: A Reexamination." With L. Ravid, in her Ph.D. dissertation, "Issues in the Book of Jubilees," Bar Ilan University, 2002.

"Biblical Authority in Judaism and the Problems of an 'Aging Text'." Pages 139–51 in *L'Ecriture et l'autorité*. Edited by J.-M. Poffet. Cerf, 2002.

"Stephen's Speech in its Exegetical Context." In *The Old Testament in the New Testament*. Edited by P. Enns et al. Zondervan, forthcoming.

"Is *The Testaments of the Twelve Patriarchs* a Jewish or a Christian Work?" Forthcoming.

Reviews

"Remembering the Holocaust" (T. DesPres, *The Survivor*). *Harper's Bookletter* (March, 1976).

"Our Very Own Bluebloods" (S. Birmingham, *The Grandees*). *Midstream* (Sept. 1971).

Pottery, Poetry and Prophecy (D. N. Freedman). *Biblical Archaeology Review* (Spring, 1981).

"Avot Yeshurun in English" (A. Yeshurun, *The Syrian-African Rift*, tr. Harold Schimmel). *Prooftexts* 1 (1981): 326–31.

"Journey into a Vast Landscape" (T. Carmi, *The Penguin Book of Hebrew Verse*). *The Nation* (June 27, 1981): 28–35.

"The Book of the Honeycomb's Flow" (M. Leon, *Nofet Sufim*, tr. I. Rabinowitz). *Journal of Biblical Literature* 105 (1986): 356–57.

Antithetic Structure in Biblical Hebrew Poetry (J. Krasovec). *Journal of Biblical Literature* 105 (1986): 704–05.

"A Feeling of *Déjà Lu*" (R. Alter, *The Art of Biblical Poetry*). *Journal of Religion* 67 (1987): 66–79.

PREFACE

The rich and variegated essays that appear in this volume are gathered to honor the scholarship and teaching of James L. Kugel, Harry Starr Professor of Classical and Modern Jewish and Hebrew Literature and Professor of Comparative Literature at Harvard University and Professor of Bible at Bar Ilan University in Israel. All the contributors engage the honoree's work. It is with great joy that we offer these essays as a tribute to him and as an expression of gratitude for his gifts to the fields of Jewish studies, biblical studies and comparative literature. The contributors may have encountered him in New Haven or Cambridge, in the United States or Israel, as colleagues or as students, but all have in common the lasting impression he has made on their perceptions of biblical interpretation. His brilliance and poetic spirit have transformed our understanding of the Bible and our conceptions of the relationship between Scripture and interpretation.

The title of this volume points to the heart and soul of James Kugel's contribution to scholarship. To be sure, it is difficult to capture in a single phrase the breadth, depth, and nuance of Kugel's interaction with texts of Judaism in antiquity. Among the intellectual gifts that he brings to his work are a highly refined literary sensibility that embraces a knowledge of literature from antiquity to the present; boundless creativity that allows him to challenge established orthodoxies; and a poetic soul that infuses each of his works with stylistic elegance and extraordinary clarity. Kugel's writing has served to illuminate how Judaism became a *textualized* religion by considering anew the interrelationships of text and interpretation, tradition and innovation, and production and reception. His work has significant implications for the historical study of Christian origins and the study of Judaism, as well as for the appropriation of sacred texts by Jews, Christians, and Muslims today.

* * *

There has been a decided shift of emphasis in contemporary biblical studies due in part to Kugel's work. No longer focusing primarily on the study of the origins and prehistory of the biblical text, the field now also encompasses the study of the emergence of Scripture and its role in shaping religious communities throughout the ages. A related movement is visible in Kugel's own work. In his early work, exemplified by *The Idea of Biblical Poetry*, the study of the Bible is juxtaposed to the history of its interpretive afterlife, enforcing the distinction between scripture and interpretation. In later works, however, such as *In Potiphar's House* and *The Bible as it Was* (and in the longer version *Traditions of the Bible*), this distinction is no longer made: the creative work of interpretation is now treated as the life of the biblical text itself.

Combining literary sensitivity, comparative method, and conceptual boldness, *The Idea of Biblical Poetry* challenged biblical scholars to reconsider the long-established application to the Hebrew Bible of a distinction between poetry and prose drawn by analogy from Greek literature. While not all followed Kugel's denial that there is a clear category of writing in the Hebrew Bible that can be termed "poetry," his definition of the rhetorical feature of parallelism successfully overturned the frequently rigid and schematic way in which Robert Lowth's threefold categories of *parallelismus membrorum* had been appropriated by subsequent biblicists. Although scholarly attention has focused primarily on his reassessment of biblical poetry found in the first section of the book, a major contribution of the book to intellectual history and literary studies was made in the second, longer "half" of the book, in which Kugel traced the way in which Hebrew poetry has been conceived in Christianity and Judaism from antiquity to the contemporary period.

In Potiphar's House: the Interpretive Life of Biblical Texts offered a seminal contribution to biblical studies in its treatment of the *Nachleben* of the text. By tracing the early history of interpretation of the Joseph story and other biblical texts, Kugel demonstrated how early exegetes frequently focused on an irregularity or unusual detail in the biblical text itself as a basis for interpretive expansion. His theory of the origin and development of interpretive motifs and their peripatetic ways suggested new frameworks for the study of early biblical exegesis.

The Bible As It Was, for which he was awarded the 2001 Grawemeyer Award in Religion, along with a series of seminal articles in the 1980's and 90's, marked a continuation of this trajectory. The book is accessible and engaging to non-experts yet, along with its more scholarly edition, *The Traditions of the Bible*, valuable for biblical scholars as well. By providing a catalogue of ancient interpretations of the books of the Torah, culled from a diverse selection of Second Temple, early Jewish and Christian texts, he has raised our awareness of the nature of textual interpretation as a phenomenon that is integral to the formation of Scripture itself. The book also points to the hermeneutical gulf between the presuppositions of ancient interpreters about Scripture and the Enlightenment presuppositions that undergird historical-critical scholarship today.

In addition to authoring nine books and editing three, Kugel has written well over forty articles, whose subjects range from a semantic feature of a biblical Hebrew phrase to the conceptualization of Midrash to the questionable effects of the Renaissance and Protestant Reformation on biblical interpretation. Not only biblical studies, but also the fields of Midrash and Qumran studies have been transformed by Kugel's exposure of the textual process that generates biblical interpretation. Nor has Kugel's work been confined to Judaism in antiquity. He has also contributed in his teaching and writing to the study of medieval Jewish exegesis and *piyyut*, and to the study of modern Hebrew, English, and Russian poetry. Most recently, Kugel has turned his attention to matters of religious experience. In his latest book, *The God of Old: Inside the Lost World of the Bible*, his work takes a theological turn, exploring the imagining of the divine in the Bible.

The twenty-two essays in this volume stand as a testimony to James Kugel's influence on many fields in the humanities, as do the thousands of students who have been touched by his teaching at Yale, Harvard, Bar Ilan, and the many other universities where he has lectured with his characteristic urbane wit and charm. The essays are organized in three roughly chronological categories. The essays in the first group treat some part of the Tanakh, ranging from the creation and Abraham stories of Genesis, to the wisdom of Ecclesiastes, to the evolving conception of sacred writing in the prophetic literature. The second set of essays focuses chiefly on the literature of Second Temple Judaism, from the distinctive biblical interpretation found in the Qumran scrolls to the role of scripture in the diaspora apocryphon Wisdom of Solomon. The last group concerns itself with the scriptural imagination at work in rabbinic literature, in Milton's *Paradise Lost*, in the nefarious anti-semitic work of Gerhard Kittel, and up to the present in a treatment of Levinas and the Talmud. There is overlap among categories, but this is inevitable. Indeed, this is the point James Kugel has struggled to communicate in his teaching and writing: in the earliest days of the rise of Scripture and through the emergence of early biblical interpretation, there can be no strict delineation between Scripture and its interpretation. We have abbreviated journal and series titles in accordance with the *SBL Handbook of Style*.

*   *   *

The editors express our deep gratitude and appreciation to John J. Collins and to Florentino García Martínez, the editors of the Brill series Journal of Jewish Studies Supplement Series. John Collins invited this volume for the Journal of Jewish Studies Supplement Series in November of 2000 and since then has enhanced and improved the volume in innumerable ways through his insights and instruction. Our colleague John Kutsko provided valuable assistance in the early stages of the organization of this volume. We wish to thank Jay Harris, Harry Austryn Wolfson, Professor of Jewish Studies and Director of the Center for Jewish Studies at Harvard University and Rachel Rockenmacher, Administrator of the Center, for their gracious assistance in making possible a celebratory event in connection with this volume. We also want to thank our students, who devoted much time and attention to this project: Amy Donaldson, Matthew Gordley, Clare Nesmith, John Jeffrey Purchal, Alison Schofield, and Samuel Thomas. Stu Rosner, whose exceptional photographic portrait of Jim Kugel captures a unique expression, also deserves our thanks. We are grateful for the graduate student support provided by the Jordan Kapson Chair of Jewish Studies, the Philo of Alexandria Project of the University of Notre Dame, the Institute for Scholarship in the Liberal Arts at the University of Notre Dame, the Conant Fund of the Office for Ministry Development at the Episcopal Church Center, and our two home institutions: the Department of Theology at the University of Notre Dame and the General Theological Seminary of the Episcopal Church.

Our final word of thanks goes to our esteemed honoree, Professor James L. Kugel, who continues to inspire and encourage new pathways of inspiration and interpretation. May his light continue to shine brightly and may God grant him אריכות ימים.

Hindy Najman
University of Notre Dame

Judith H. Newman
General Theological Seminary

PART ONE

THE BIBLE AS IT WAS

THE CONVERSION OF ABRAHAM TO JUDAISM, CHRISTIANITY, AND ISLAM

Jon D. Levenson

I

"Judaism, Christianity, and Islam are all children born of the same Father and reared in the bosom of Abraham." So Francis E. Peters begins his insightful little introduction to the three religions that are variously styled "Western," "monotheistic," or "prophetic."[1] Indeed, the common root of the three in Father Abraham has long been a staple of interreligious dialogue; it undergirds the heartfelt hope of many that the Abrahamic traditions will replace their longstanding animosities toward one another with comity and cooperation. It is thus in Abraham that the German Catholic theologian Karl-Josef Kuschel finds the criterion by which each of the three must assess its own authenticity. "Abraham," he writes, "remains a point of reference by which the later traditions of synagogue, church, and Umma can and must be measured critically."[2] Or, to be more precise, the criterion lies not with the historical figure (whom Kuschel frankly acknowledges to be concealed "once and for all in the shadows of history") but in "the normativity of the original Abraham traditions in the book of Genesis."[3] To the extent that Judaism, Christianity, and Islam deviate from the Abraham of Genesis, they not only weaken the basis for their potential good relations with each other, they also undermine their authenticity.

For all the transparently humane intentions behind Kuschel's proposal, however, the problems besetting it are legion. The most immediate is that the narrative about Abraham in Genesis cannot be convincingly detached from the rest of the pentateuchal story. Consider, for example, the brief tale that appears only a few verses after the

---

[1] Francis E. Peters, *Children of Abraham: Judaism, Christianity, Islam* (Princeton: Princeton University Press, 1982), ix.

[2] Karl-Josef Kuschel, *Abraham: Sign of Hope for Jews, Christians and Muslims* (New York: Continuum, 1995), 204.

[3] Ibid., 204–5.

future patriarch is introduced to us. Famine forces Abram and his wife Sarai[4] into Egypt, where a combination of their defenselessness, her beauty, and probably the Egyptians' reputed licentiousness as well[5] leads him to make an extraordinary request of Sarai. She is to claim that she is actually his sister, lest the Egyptians "kill me and let you live."[6] Fortunately, the ruse works, Abram survives, and, in fact, grows immensely wealthy. Moreover, "the LORD afflicted Pharaoh and his household with mighty plagues on account of Sarai, the wife of Abram," and the Egyptian king "sent him off with his wife and all that he possessed."[7]

In recent decades, it has become common to treat this little narrative as a self-contained unit, related, to be sure, to the suspiciously similar wife-sister stories in Gen 20 and 26:6–11 but not to the rest of the pentateuchal narrative in which it appears. Ephraim A. Speiser, for example, thought the narrative attested to a Hurrian institution in which "the bonds of marriage were strongest and most solemn when the wife had simultaneously the judicial status of a sister, regardless of actual blood ties."[8] Hence, the key point is that "the narrators themselves were no longer aware of the full import of their subject matter," thus proving its vestigial and therefore historical character.[9] Whereas Speiser approaches the text as a historian, uninterested in narrative design, Burton L. Visotzky approaches it as a moralist, finding the future patriarch's behavior here a revolting paradigm of moral squalor. Abram was, he suggests at one point, guilty of nothing less than "pimping his wife."[10]

---

[4] Their names are not changed to "Abraham" and "Sarah" until Gen 17.

[5] E.g., see Lev 18:3, which serves as part of an introduction to a set of laws of sexual behavior.

[6] Gen 12:12. Unless otherwise noted, all translations from the Tanakh are taken from *Tanakh: The Holy Scriptures: The New JPS Translation according to the Traditional Hebrew Text* (Philadelphia: Jewish Publication Society, 5746/1985); abbreviated NJPS.

[7] Gen 12:17, 20.

[8] Ephraim A. Speiser, *Genesis* (AB 1; Garden City, N.Y.: Doubleday, 1964), 92. The inadequacy of Speiser's theory is now broadly recognized. See Barry L. Eichler, "On Reading Genesis 12:10–20," in *Tehillah le-Moshe: Biblical and Judaic Studies in Honor of Moshe Greenberg* (ed. M. Cogan et al.; Winona Lake, Ind.: Eisenbrauns, 1997), 25–26.

[9] Speiser, *Genesis*, 91.

[10] Burton L. Visotzky, *The Genesis of Ethics* (New York: Crown, 1996), 27. Later in the same chapter, Visotzky softens the judgment, asking how Abram and Sarai "come to behave in such a morally ambiguous way" (35), but still not questioning the appropriateness of approaching the story as a morality tale. A weakness of Visotzky's reading is his understanding of למען ייטב לי בעבורך in Gen 12:13 as "I'll turn a profit on it" (25). The rendering of the NJPS, "that it may go well with

As different as the historian and the moralist are, they share an instinctive proclivity to treat our tale as if it were independent of the larger pentateuchal story in which it appears. In Visotzky's case, the result is to interpret Abram and Sarai as realistically as figures in a contemporary—and grossly dysfunctional—American family. The most obvious objection to this is that it is unproductive to judge an ancient culture according to modern norms: this exercise is too easy, or, to be more precise, too easy on us, for it enables moderns to win hands down.[11] It condemns the ancient voices to speaking out of context, thus rendering them absurd. But an objection of another sort is more germane to our topic. This one questions whether it is appropriate to treat the figures in a foundational text (like the Torah even before it took its place in a scriptural canon) as if they are realistic characters with a psychological make-up of the sort we might encounter in a contemporary novel, soap opera, or therapy group. On this, as on so many matters biblical, no one has stated the point better than the honoree of this volume, James L. Kugel. Consider this observation about Gen 37–50:

> I have shuddered to hear it said that Joseph is "one of the most believable figures in Western literature," and not just because such a statement puts the Bible on the wrong bookshelf. At such a remark one wants to object—on the model of the vaudevillian's "Who was that lady I seen you with last night?" "That was no lady, that was my wife"—one wants to say that Joseph is no character at all, but someone far more intimately ours. That initial literary act, "Come gather round and let me spin a tale," is not quite the starting-point of even this most tale-like part of the Pentateuch. Its premise—"Let me tell you what happened to Joseph-your-ancestor, let me tell you how things came to be as you know them actually to be"—is significantly different. Not to speak of "Let me tell you how God has saved us," "Let me tell you God's teachings."[12]

---

me," is preferable and keeps open, as Visotzky's does not, the possibility that this clause is exegeted by, or is otherwise synonymous with, the following one, "that I may remain alive thanks to you."

[11] This sort of treatment also requires us to disregard key factors in the text that do not lend themselves to family relations as known in our quotidian experience, especially the fact that Abram acts *in extremis*, to preserve his life in a famine and in a land known for its sexual debauchery. Those who think the future patriarch should have told the truth need to explain how Sarai would have been better off with him dead and herself absorbed indefinitely into the Pharaoh's harem. For an argument that Abram's motivation is benign and in Sarai's interest, see Eichler, "On Reading," 33–38.

[12] James L. Kugel, "On the Bible and Literary Criticism," *Prooftexts* 1 (1981): 217–36, here 219. For a confessional and Christian formulation of a similar point,

It has been long recognized that in the case at hand, Gen 12:10–20, Abram and Sarai's experience foreshadows that of their descendants in the first half of the ensuing book.[13] For the famine forces the Israelites, too, to go down to Egypt,[14] and against them, too, a decree goes forth that threatens the males but not the females:

> The king of Egypt spoke to the Hebrew midwives . . . saying, "When you deliver the Hebrew women, look at the birthstool: if it is a boy, kill him; if it is a girl, let her live." (Exod 1:15–16)

But, though it tarries, deliverance comes when the LORD strikes the offending Egyptians with plagues,[15] and, what is more, sends the couple off[16] with great wealth.[17] These connections are only a few of the many that traditional Jewish interpreters have long made but modern criticism tends to miss. The typological function of Abram to which they eloquently attest indicates that something vital is lost when we detach his story from the larger narrative and treat it as just another witness to the reconstructed customs of the time (Speiser) or as an example of how not to behave (Visotzky). Both the historian and the moralist have their place, to be sure, but "the original Abraham traditions in the book of Genesis," on which they concentrate and which Kuschel sees as normative, are quite incomplete. Minimally, these traditions require the ensuing narrative of the Pentateuch (or Hexateuch, since the promise of land to Abraham comes to fulfillment only with the conquest under Joshua). Maximally, if they are to serve as Scripture, they require a bridge to the community that sees itself as Abrahamic and, therefore, believes that the promises to the patriarch (whatever his personal virtues and flaws) have been made to them as well. Or, to put it differently (and to adapt Kugel's words about Joseph), the maximalist will see in the

---

see Christopher R. Seitz, "Reader Competence and the Offense of Biblical Language," in *Word Without End: The Old Testament as Abiding Theological Witness* (Grand Rapids: Eerdmans, 1998), 292–99, esp. 299: "The chief task before the church is not to sanitize and correct the Bible from the outside, but rather to learn again from the inside the connected universe of the Bible's presentation; to learn to become competent readers again of a scripture whose intention is not only to include, but to address and judge and cleanse and save."

[13] E.g., *Tanḥ. Lek-leka* 12 (Buber ed.). For a causal connection between the two events, see Ramban (Nachmanides) on Gen 12:10.

[14] Gen 42:1; 43:1; 46:5–7.

[15] Cf. וינגע in Gen 12:17 and נגע in Exod 11:1.

[16] Cf. the use of שלח in Gen 12:20 and Exod 4:21.

[17] Cf. Gen 12:16, 20 and Exod 3:21–22; 11:2; 12:35–36.

protagonist of these stories Abraham-our-father and not just evidence for some long-vanished religion or a figure in a work of fiction. The minimal requirement, it must be stressed, is not a postulate of religious identity. It applies even to secular interpreters devoted to understanding the work (whether the completed Pentateuch/Hexateuch or one of the preexistent sources within it) in its literary integrity. The maximal requirement is a somewhat (but not entirely) different matter: it subsumes the minimal but also appropriates the text in question as part of a scriptural canon sacred to a particular community of interpretation defined by normative practice and belief.

II

The inseparability of the story of Abraham from the ensuing pentateuchal narrative, which we have been at pains to demonstrate, renders the discontinuity in religious practice between the two all the more striking. Here I refer to a fact that Walter Moberly, in his insightful (and provocatively titled) volume, *The Old Testament of the Old Testament*, describes in these words:

> We have argued also that the Pentateuch more or less consistently portrays patriarchal religion as distinct from Mosaic Yahwism. Yet we have noted that the biblical text takes for granted that the God of the patriarchs is one and the same as YHWH the God of Israel, so much so that the patriarchal story is told with frequent use of the name YHWH.[18]

A few examples should suffice to communicate the many differences between "patriarchal religion" and "Mosaic Yahwism." Whereas most pentateuchal law demands centralization of sacrifice in a simple locus or simply assumes it,[19] Abraham builds altars in various locales and does so without a hint of condemnation anywhere in the Hebrew Bible.[20] Whereas Deuteronomic law strictly forbids the use of a sacred pole or tree (אשרה) in worship, demanding, in fact, that such be smashed,[21] Abraham, Genesis tells us, "planted a tamarisk at Beersheba, and invoked there"—obviously as the *hieros logos* of the dedication

---

[18] R. W. L. Moberly, *The Old Testament of the Old Testament: Patriarchal Narratives and Mosaic Yahwism* (OBT; Minneapolis: Fortress, 1992), 105.

[19] E.g., Deut 12:1–28; Lev 17:1–7.

[20] Gen 12:8; 13:18.

[21] E.g., Exod 34:13–14; Deut 7:5; 12:3; 16:21.

of a shrine—"the name of the LORD, the Everlasting God."[22] Again,
he meets no condemnation, explicit or implicit, from this or any
other biblical narrator.[23] So much for his doing what later sources
would see as flagrant sins of commission, but what about his sins of
omission, according, that is, to the standards of "Mosaic Yahwism"?
Is it not curious, for example, that a religion that insists upon observance of the Sabbath as a fundamental norm[24]—indeed, one that constitutes an essential aspect of membership in the community and whose
violation entails capital punishment[25]—should claim as its father and
founder a man to whom the Sabbath had never been revealed? A
similar observation holds for the dietary laws. These, according to
both Leviticus and Deuteronomy, follow from the LORD's having set
Israel apart as a consecrated people,[26] yet there is no evidence that
the man who first set himself apart to follow the LORD's call and to
beget that people ever knew or observed these community-marking
norms. Once again we confront the founding father failing to observe
the norms of the community he is thought to have begotten.

There is a simple explanation for these oddities—one that the
altar law of Deuteronomy itself suggests, albeit indirectly:

> You shall not act at all as we now act here [the speaking voice is that
> of Moses, in Transjordan], every man as he pleases, because you have
> not yet come to the allotted haven that the LORD your God is giving
> you. (Deut 12:8–9)

The norms, in other words, are not presented as timeless absolutes.
Rather, they are embedded in the foundational story. Viewed thus,
they apply only to the present order of things, not to its prehistory.
The previous order was legitimate in its own time, to be sure, but
has now been superseded.[27] One is tempted to go further and to
propose that the patriarchs were permitted things prohibited under

---

[22] Gen 21:33.

[23] The omission is all the more glaring in light of the midrashic efforts to interpret the word here translated as "tamarisk" as representing an orchard, an inn for
wayfarers, or even a rabbinic court—anything but a tree (e.g., *Gen. Rab.* 54:6).

[24] E.g., Exod 20:8–11; 23:12; 31:12–17; 35:1–3; Lev 23:3; Deut 5:12–15.

[25] Isa 56:6–7; Exod 31:14; Num 15:32–36.

[26] Lev 20:22–26; Deut 14:1–2.

[27] Traditionally, critical scholars have seen this principle as exemplified and rendered explicit in the notion that the patriarchs knew the Deity not by the
Tetragrammaton, but by other names—אלהים in the case of E (Exod 3:13–15) and
אל שדי in the case of P (Exod 6:2–6).

"Mosaic Yahwism" precisely because they had the spiritual and moral strength—or the direct contact with God—to remain obedient and faithful withal, and not to be seduced into the idolatry that Deuteronomy, in its reformist zeal, reckons inseparable from the practices it proscribes. Whatever its homiletical value, however, this latter proposal faces formidable obstacles, not the least of which is the absence of any hint in Genesis that the forms of worship in which the patriarchs engage pose a danger to anyone. And are we to believe that any of the sources of Genesis held that Israelites at an exceptionally high spiritual and moral level were exempt from and could not benefit from the Sabbath and kindred institutions? (On this last point, the judgment that the patriarchs lived at an elevated spiritual and moral level—though it is, as we shall see, of venerable antiquity—is hardly the univocal plain sense of Genesis).

The inconsistency of the patriarchal narratives with Mosaic religion is a challenge to those interpreters, secular and religious alike, who assume the semantic integrity of the text (whatever its compositional history). To historians of the religion of Israel, on the other hand, it is a godsend, for it provides—or to them often seems to provide—a means to separate the historical periods that the Pentateuch itself conflates and thus to recover the history that redaction has concealed. This is true both of those who see the depiction of patriarchal religion in Genesis (especially in the Priestly source) as deriving from a late and thoroughly artificial schema, and of those who detect within it the vestiges of pre-Yahwistic religion, whether Mesopotamian or Canaanite. To these classic diachronic arguments, succinctly summarized by Moberly,[28] we must now add the sociological approach of Rainer Albertz in his recent *History of Israelite Religion in the Old Testament Period*. For Albertz, "'patriarchal religion' is to be defined not as a preliminary stage but as a substratum of [YHWH] religion," a stratum that evidences "family religion" in contradistinction to the state religion fostered by the monarchy and its centralized royal cultus.[29] Whatever its strengths or limitations, Albertz's approach does make Moberly's "Patriarchal religion" and "Mosaic Yahwism" contemporaneous, unlike the classic historical-critical approach. But it,

---

[28] See the helpful discussion and categorization in *Old Testament*, 107–25.

[29] Rainer Albertz, *A History of Israelite Religion in the Old Testament Period* (2 vols.; OTL; Louisville: Westminster John Knox, 1994), 1:29. See the general discussion on 23–39.

too, no less than they, challenges the integrity of the text, arguing that what the literature has woven together is better understood as separate components belonging, to be sure, not to different periods but to different social sectors.[30] In all these cases, the operative rule is this: what tradition has joined together, let every historian put asunder.

One effect of this reversal of tradition and its corollary undoing of redaction is to call into doubt a point that the historians are oddly inclined to accept unreflectively—the identification of the God of Mosaic Yahwism with the God of patriarchal religion.[31] That the biblical sources make that identification is beyond doubt,[32] but why should hardheaded historians defer to the sources on this one point or allow themselves to believe that the same divine name necessarily denotes the same deity? Surely when the stories about the Deity are quite different, it takes a suspension of disbelief—indeed, an act of faith—to affirm that the divine agent rendered therein remains one and the same.[33]

I can illustrate with an astute observation made in the middle of the last century by Yehezkel Kaufmann in his monumental *History of Israelite Religion*, an observation that, like the book itself, has been under-noticed ever since. The patriarchs, he points out, are not presented as practicing a different religion from the peoples they encounter: "Between Isaac and Ishmael, Jacob and Esau, there is no religious difference. It is not said that Ishmael and Esau worshiped false gods. That gulf between Israel, the people of YHWH, and the nations, worshipers of false gods, which we have found in all of the rest of the books of the Torah, still does not exist."[34] The Assyriologist H. W. F. Saggs, though without reference to Kaufmann and with regrettable caricature and a deficit of subtlety, makes a similar point:

---

[30] On this, see Jon D. Levenson, *The Hebrew Bible, the Old Testament, and Historical Criticism: Jews and Christians in Biblical Studies* (Louisville: Westminster John Knox, 1993), esp. pp. 29–30. Here it is helpful to remember the etymological source of "text" lies in the Latin, *texo*, "to weave." Responsible historical investigation perforce unweaves the text that redaction has produced.

[31] See Moberly, *Old Testament*, 112.

[32] Exod 3:13–15 (E); 6:2–6 (P).

[33] See Michael Goldberg, "God, Action, and Narrative: *Which* Narrative, *Which* Action, *Which* God?" *JR* 68 (1988): 39–56, esp. 51–56.

[34] Yehezkel Kaufmann, *History of Israelite Religion* (8 vols.; Jerusalem: Bialik Institute, 5736/1966), 1:209 [Hebrew] (my translation). This is the tenth printing of a multi-volume work published 1937–1956.

In tradition, therefore, the God of the Patriarchs had quite different qualities from those of the original Mosaic God [YHWH]; a tincture of universalism as against ethnic exclusiveness; mercy and tolerance against intolerance and vindictiveness; a calm prosecution of a predetermined plan as against aggressive self-assertion and *ad hoc* reaction.[35]

This then allows Saggs—clearly no admirer of Mosaic Yahwism— to venture the value judgment that "it is at least a theoretical possibility that the concept of deity attributed to the Mosaic period was a retrogression from that of the Patriarchs." In support of his position, Saggs turns to the Bible itself, observing that "it is nowhere claimed in the Old Testament that the Mosaic revelation was an advance over the patriarchal concept of deity."[36] This is true, of course, but only because neither the idea of "advance" nor that of a "concept of deity" is native to Israelite culture. Rather, these notions are the products of an Enlightenment schema quite alien to the books from which Saggs seeks support (as is the notion of a polarity of universalism and particularism on which he relies).[37] Furthermore, Saggs's Old Testament (to use his term, a more theologically freighted one than he seems to realize) does offer passages that affirm the superiority of Mosaic over all other forms of prophecy.[38] And, as we have seen, it embeds the patriarchs intentionally in a narrative that foreshadows the exodus and conquest, of which Abraham, not coincidentally, happens to be the first to learn.[39] But, most fundamentally, if the Old Testament is to be our guide, we cannot sever the God of Abraham, Isaac, and Jacob from the God of Moses in the least. For however different the "concept of deity" of the varying corpora may be, and whatever valid *historical* conclusions may be consequently drawn, the biblical affirmation (for it is too self-conscious to be a mere presupposition) is that these are one and the same God. This issue, as Moberly points out,[40] is *theological*, and the history of religion is powerless to resolve it.

If we examine Kaufmann's and Saggs's observations with the theology of the redacted Pentateuch (and even of its major documentary

---

[35] H. W. F. Saggs, *The Encounter with the Divine in Mesopotamia and Israel* (Jordan Lectures in Comparative Religion 12; London: Athlone, 1978), 38.

[36] Ibid., 36–37.

[37] See Jon D. Levenson, "The Universal Horizon of Biblical Particularism," in *Ethnicity and the Bible* (ed. M. G. Brett; BIS 19; Leiden: Brill, 1996), 143–69.

[38] Num 12:6–8; Deut 34:10–12.

[39] Gen 15:13–16.

[40] Moberly, *Old Testament*, 112.

sources) as our guide, our attention will perforce be drawn to contextual differences between the patriarchal narrative and the ensuing literature that we might otherwise miss. Kaufmann is correct
that the difference between proto-Israel and everyone else is not the
difference between worshipers of the true God and idolaters.
Throughout Genesis, the unarticulated assumption is that primordial
humankind was monotheistic, even if they did have a plurality of
names for the universally recognized Deity.[41] Thus can Abram accept
the blessing of Melchizedek, priest-king of Salem, in the name of
אל עליון (conventionally rendered "God Most High," or the like),
and even identify the latter with YHWH.[42] Thus can the Philistine
king, Abimelech, communicate in a dream vision with אלהים ("God"),
the same term Abraham then uses in their contentious exchange
afterwards.[43] Similarly, the "Hittites" (probably a Canaanite group
with no connection to the Anatolian people of the same name in
English) with whom Abraham bargains for a grave for Sarah refer
to him as "the elect of God (אלהים) among us."[44] And, to give one
last example, when Joseph tells Pharaoh that the repetition of the
latter's dreams means that "God (אלהים) has told Pharaoh what He
is about to do," the Egyptian king responds with deep appreciation
and in kind: "Since God (אלהים) has made all this known to you,
there is none so discerning and wise as you."[45] The contrast with
the Pharaoh of the exodus could not be sharper.[46]

Despite the differences—and ungrudgingly recognizing their import
for reconstructing the history of the religion of Israel—I submit that
Genesis offers less evidence for the difference between the patriarchal and the Mosaic God than first seems the case. Note that all
the outsiders mentioned above express recognition of "God" (אלהים):
none of them speaks of YHWH's archrival Baal; none belittles the
patriarchs' invocation of YHWH; none attempts to make them or
members of their households defect to any foreign deity or worship;
and none opposes their dwelling in Canaan and acquiring land there.
When the Pharaoh of the exodus, by contrast, disparages YHWH and
contemptuously refuses to allow Israel to depart for the promised

---

[41] The one exception is 35:2–4, usually ascribed to E.
[42] Gen 14:19–20, 22.
[43] Gen 20.
[44] Gen 23:6.
[45] Gen 41:25, 39.
[46] E.g., Exod 5:1–5.

land,[47] the result is all that putative "ethnic exclusivism," "intolerance and vindictiveness," and "aggressive self-assertion" on the part of the Mosaic God that Saggs finds so distasteful and so contrary to the tolerant universalism of the God of the patriarchs. But why should we assume that in the same situation the God of Abraham, Isaac, Jacob, and Joseph would have responded differently? It is one thing to advance the arguable historical claim that Genesis evidences a period when the great conflict of YHWH and the gods of Canaan had not yet begun (or, alternatively, lay in the past). It is an altogether different matter—and far more problematic—to claim that the God of the patriarchs, *as He is presented in Genesis*, would have never come into conflict with the gods of Canaan, or with a Pharaoh addicted to self-deification and magic and contemptuous of Israel's God and their special and unparalleled status in His providential plan. The idea that there is a natural and hence universally available knowledge of God is widespread in the Hebrew Bible and attested even in its supposedly most particularistic sources.[48] That humankind availed itself of this primarily in the primordial, semi-mythical past, but has generally (but not universally) failed to do so since, hardly indicates that God has changed His character. Indeed, to argue the opposite—that the patriarchal and Mosaic/prophetic God were different—raises the formidable question of why the sources themselves did not detect so large a difference.

III

The continuity of the God of Abraham with the God of Mosaic religion, and of the patriarchal narratives with the subsequent pentateuchal story, puts into high relief the outstanding difference between the two blocks of material. Here we must revert to Kaufmann's observation that "between Isaac and Ishmael, Jacob and Esau, there is no religious difference." Kaufmann is at pains to point out that the promises to the patriarchs include a number of defining aspects of Israel as it is to emerge in the ensuing generations—"numerous progeny, the inheritance of land and kingship"—but, he adds, "the

---

[47] Exod 5:1–5.
[48] See Levenson, "Universal Horizon," 145–51; James Barr, *Biblical Faith and Natural Theology* (New York: Oxford University Press, 1993).

Torah of YHWH is not mentioned."[49] Rather, the difference between Isaac and his older half-brother Ishmael, or between Jacob and his older twin brother Esau, has to do with the establishment of a favored lineage and the acquisition of the rights of the firstborn through divine grace and its manifestation on the human level, parental favoritism. It is not a matter of religious practice.[50] If the great contestation between YHWH and the gods of Canaan is not foreshadowed in Genesis, neither is Israel's receipt of law and commandments in the wilderness—the very gravamen of the other four books of the Pentateuch. Or, to put it in a more rabbinic idiom, Genesis gives no hint that the descendants of Isaac and Jacob (but not those of Ishmael or Esau) will stand at Sinai to receive the Torah.

In the mode of constructive Christian theology, Moberly propounds a fascinating analogy by which to understand this critical difference between patriarchal religion and Mosaic Yahwism.[51] Patriarchal religion is to Mosaic Yahwism, he suggests, as Judaism is to Christianity—from the standpoint, that is, of Christians who struggle to relate positively, even reverently, to an understanding of religious life and community very different from their own. At the heart of Moberly's proposal lies the ancient Christian notion of *dispensation*. Thus, unlike most other Christians who are respectful of Judaism and interested in it, he upholds the idea of supersession[52] and argues that "the language of Old/New Testament *is* essential."

> It is as necessary for the Christian that the faith centered on Jesus in some ways supersedes the religion of the Old Testament as it was for the adherents of Mosaic Yahwism that their faith in some ways superseded patriarchal religion. As we have seen, each time a sense of a new beginning introduces a new dispensation. In their new dispensation, the assumptions and structure of the resultant religion have a consistent logic and identity of their own. Although each time there is a deep sense of continuity with what went before, there is nonetheless a major change of ethos and of religious practice. The new religions, respectively centered on Christ and Torah, have normative status for their adherents and relativize the significance of the former dispensation.[53]

---

[49] Kaufmann, *History*, 1:209.

[50] This is not to deny that cultural and typological factors play a role, e.g., the preference for shepherds over hunters and semi-nomads.

[51] Moberly, *Old Testament*, 147–75.

[52] Note his characterization of "supersessionism" as an "unanalyzed bogey word" in *Old Testament*, 162.

[53] Moberly, *Old Testament*, 161. See also Seitz, "Old Testament or Hebrew Bible?"

But unlike most Christians unembarrassed by the theology that Christ supersedes Torah, Moberly is exceedingly eager to spare it the disparagement that Christian supersessionism has traditionally generated:

> ... the force of our analogy is that the Christian should no more denigrate the Torah-centered religion of the Old Testament, or the Judaism that grows out of it and stands in basic continuity with it, than the Torah-centered religion (i.e., Mosaic Yahwism) itself denigrated patriarchal religion. Mosaic Yahwism respected and preserved the distinctiveness of patriarchal religion, saw it as the foundation for its own existence, and reorganized the continuing validity of God's dealings with the patriarchs. In a similar way, therefore, the Christian should respect and recognize both the content of Mosaic Yahwism as its own antecedent of continuing validity and also the religious system of Judaism that in its own different way develops from it.[54]

Moberly's last sentence is, however, as problematic as it is creative. For if "Christ" has superseded "Torah," "introduc[ing] a new dispensation,"[55] why should Christians think their "own antecedent" has "continuing validity?" And, all the more, if the way in which postbiblical Judaism developed from their common antecedent is indeed different from the cause the Church took, why should Christians deem Judaism valid at all? The logic of dispensation and supersession indeed argue for reverence for the old order in its own time but also and equally for its obsolescence and ineffectiveness once the new has dawned. The latter conviction need not lead to the "denigration" that Moberly opposes (though among Christians it usually has), but the rejection of denigration is far from the affirmation of "continuing validity" that Moberly endorses. Thus, the apostle Paul can affirm both that "the law is holy, and the commandment is holy and righteous and good"[56] and that

---

in *Word Without End*, 61–74. I take the point in both cases to be that "Old Testament" is a term constituted by a Christian confessional claim, and the attempt to assimilate the books to which it refers to Christianity without deference to the claim cannot work. The point is not that the term is neutral and without any implied judgment on Judaism. I have attempted to clarify in what sense the term is appropriate and in what sense it is not in Levenson, *Hebrew Bible*, esp. 1–32.

[54] Moberly, *Old Testament*, 163–64.

[55] Ibid., 161.

[56] Rom 7:12. Unless otherwise noted, all New Testament quotations are taken from the New American Bible. The edition I have used is *The Catholic Study Bible* (New York: Oxford University Press, 1990).

the law was our disciplinarian (παιδαγωγός) for Christ (εἰς Χριστόν), that we might be justified by faith. But now that faith has come, we are no longer under a disciplinarian. For through faith you are all children of God in Christ Jesus. . . . And if you belong to Christ, then you are Abraham's descendants, heirs according to the promise. (Gal 3:24–29)

However one interprets the much-discussed phrase παιδαγωγὸς εἰς Χριστόν,[57] it seems clear that, in Hans Dieter Betz's words, "for the Christian this period of the Torah is a matter of the past. The Torah represents the negative backdrop, without which the positive divine redemption would never have come"[58]—which keeps it "holy and righteous and good," to be sure, but also utterly without "continuing validity" in its own right in the new order.

I have here no wish to deny that Christian theologians can plausibly and authentically affirm the continuing validity of Judaism, as many, in fact, have.[59] Rather, my point is that the dispensationalist theology on which Moberly grounds his proposal for so doing falls seriously short of the goal. Moberly seems to sense this when he writes that, "[f]irst and foremost [among the weaknesses of the analogy] is the fact that patriarchal religion has no known continuation other than Mosaic Yahwism, but Mosaic Yahwism led to both Judaism and Christianity," so that "[t]here is therefore no biblical parallel to the phenomenon of Judaism and Christianity as rival claimants to a common tradition"[60] (of course, if by "biblical" he means to refer to the Christian canon, there is more than a parallel; the New Testament is keenly aware of the Jewish claim and, in the main, eminently eager to refute it). For Moberly's analogy to have adequate force, there would need to have been a group of practitioners of patriarchal religion contemporaneous with Mosaic Yahwists and deeply respected by them on religious grounds.

To imagine how the Mosaic Yahwists would have reacted to the survival and vitality of patriarchal religion might make for an interesting thought experiment. Such an experiment would be handicapped,

---

[57] See Hans Dieter Betz, *Galatians* (Hermeneia; Philadelphia: Fortress, 1979), 177–78.

[58] Ibid., 178.

[59] See, e.g., Paul van Buren, *A Theology of the Jewish Christian Reality* (New York: Seabury, 1980–1983); Clemens Thoma, *Die theologischen Beziehungen zwischen Christentum und Judentum* (2nd ed.; Darmstadt: Wissenschaftliche Buchgesellschaft, 1988); and Kendall R. Soulen, *The God of Israel and Christian Theology* (Minneapolis: Fortress, 1996).

[60] Moberly, *Old Testament*, 166, 167.

however, by more than its sheer speculativeness. For the two corpora—the patriarchal narratives of Genesis and the accounts of Mosaic revelation in the four successive books—differ in kind and not merely in content. Genesis is, in fact, one of the least didactic books in the Tanakh. When, in a highly atypical verse to which we shall turn our attention anon, it reports that Abraham kept God's "charge," "commandments," "laws," and "teachings,"[61] we scratch our heads in wonder about what those four categories of norms can possibly comprise. The reason is simple. Whereas the Mosaic corpora purport to specify how the "kingdom of priests and a holy nation"[62] should organize itself (with, of course, numerous lacunae and a dollop of idealization), the specifics of patriarchal society and religion—even as an ideal—can be reconstructed only by conjecture and (among the wise) with great tentativeness. Abraham, we are told, has a slave.[63] Does the unnamed man have, as Sinaitic law requires, the right of emancipation after six years of service? Or has he declined and thus chosen a lifetime of servitude, as the same law allows?[64] To give another scenario, does he belong under the category not of a kinsman who has fallen into distress but of a foreigner to whom the Torah elsewhere (in another documentary source) denies the right of manumission altogether?[65] Or, finally, should we refrain altogether from all these highly traditionalistic efforts to interpret Abraham in light of putatively Mosaic law and substitute in its stead some corpus of Mesopotamian law as the key to understanding the narrative? If so, then here, too, the procedure will perforce be mostly one of guesswork, and this is so precisely because of the nature of Genesis itself.

We can illuminate the difference between Genesis, on the one hand, and the Mosaic legal and ritual corpora, on the other, by reference to an observation of Paul Veyne's in his provocative and instructive little volume, *Did the Greeks Believe in Their Myths?* The point of the analogy, I hasten to say, is not to make any claim that the substance of patriarchal narratives parallels Greek (or any other) mythological material. Rather, I wish to suggest that the relationship

---

[61] Gen 26:5.

[62] Exod 19:6.

[63] Gen 24. Despite the unnamed man's high status in Abraham's household, it is less likely that he is only a hired "servant," contrary to a longstanding translation tradition.

[64] Exod 21:1–6; Deut 15:12–18.

[65] Lev 25:44–46.

of these two diverse sets of materials to quotidian life in their respective societies exhibits some helpful resemblances. Writes Veyne:

> These legendary worlds [of popular medieval Christian hagiographies] were accepted as true in the sense that they were not doubted, but they were not accepted the way that everyday reality is. For the faithful, the lives of the martyrs were filled with marvels situated in an ageless past, defined only in that it was earlier, outside of, and different from the present. It was the 'time of the pagans.' The same was true of the Greek myths. They took place 'earlier,' during the heroic generations, when the gods still took part in human affairs. Mythological space and time were secretly different from our own. A Greek put the gods 'in heaven' but he would have been astounded to see them in the sky.[66]

The Abraham of Genesis, too (whatever his historical reality or lack thereof), lived in a time "defined only in that it was earlier, outside of, and different from the present," when [God] still took [a much more direct and identifiable] part in human affairs." Indeed, as we have seen, it strains the imagination and violates the plain sense of the text to imagine him, or people living like him, as contemporary with groups attempting to live under pentateuchal law in one form or another and comparable to them. The two live not only in different times, but in different realities as well. And that is why, *a fortiori*, all the efforts to absorb Abraham into one of the Abrahamic religions as well—Judaism, Christianity, and Islam alike—seem so awkward.

IV

Yet, however awkward they may be, efforts to refashion Abraham in the image of the religions that claim him have been the norm, and not the exception. Thus has the first patriarch of Genesis become a Torah-observant Jew before Moses, a man of Christian faith before Jesus, and a Muslim prophet before Muhammad.[67] And, in fact, these transformations are, to a large degree, inevitable. Since, as is well-known, practice influences thought (some would say practice determines thought), those whose practice centers on Torah, Gospel, or Islam (even in the restricted sense of submission to God) do not sit lightly with the idea that their revered patriarch lived a very different life from the one to which they aspire.

---

[66] Paul Veyne, *Did the Greeks Believe in their Myths?* (Chicago: University of Chicago Press, 1988), 17–18.
[67] See Kuschel, *Abraham*, 1–169.

In the Hebrew Bible, the refashioning of Abraham in the direction of the observance of pentateuchal law, characteristic of much Jewish tradition, is still scant. Rather, in the biblical documents his significance and that of the other patriarchs lies in relation to two other points. The first is that God has promised the land of Canaan to their descendants. The second, closely connected to the first, is that this unconditional commitment tempers and even overrides the strict conditionality of Sinai, guaranteeing that the promise would be fulfilled even in the face of Israel's most heinous sins.[68] In the Hebrew Bible apart from Genesis, in other words, Abraham appears as the recipient of a revelation. The particularities of the man's life— even his momentous willingness to sacrifice his beloved son[69]—attract no attention whatsoever. The same holds for his routine religious practices or lack thereof. The revelations Abraham received, the irrevocable land grant they include, and the eternal covenant God makes with him (and with his progeny through Isaac and Jacob forever) stand free of the particulars of patriarchal religion that rightly preoccupy modern historians.

Genesis displays, nonetheless, a few harbingers of the refashioning to come. Abraham does receive, after all, one enduring commandment—circumcision. The phrasing in which this detailed law is given in Gen 17:10–14 (universally ascribed to P, the Priestly source) suggests that it may once have been independent of its current placement. Note, for example, that the second person verbs are plural. In any event, that the authorization of a rite of such importance should have come to Abraham and not to Moses—or, to be more precise, to Abraham before Moses[70]—is surely revealing. The standard view among historians is that circumcision became a community-defining rite and the "sign of the covenant"[71] only in the exile, when the Jews needed to reinforce their differentness from their (uncircumcised) Mesopotamian captors.[72] Even if this be so, however, it does not explain why it is Abraham who first receives the *mitzvah*. If the objective of the rite had been to differentiate Jew from non-Jew, would the law not have been better announced from Sinai? Or, if a patriarchal antecedent had been necessary, would not

---

[68] E.g., Exod 32:13–14; Lev 26:39–42; Isa 41:8–14; 51:1–3; Neh 9:7–8.

[69] Gen 22:1–19.

[70] Note that Exod 12:48 and Lev 12:3 speak as if the norm is already known.

[71] Gen 17:11.

[72] See, e.g., Claus Westermann, *Genesis 12–36* (Minneapolis: Augsburg, 1985), 265.

Jacob (*all* of whose offspring fall within the covenant) have been a
more fitting recipient of the new imperative? Part of the answer lies
in P's desire to endow circumcision with what Mircea Eliade termed
"the prestige of origins."[73] Just as the same document retrojects the
Sabbath onto creation itself, where God rests before any human
beings do,[74] so does it place the commandment of circumcision ahead
of Sinai, investing it with special significance. Note that in the process,
P has made Abraham a little less foreign to Moberly's "Mosaic
Yahwism." He becomes, so to speak, "one of us," bearing the national
marking even before the nation to whom it applies has emerged and
observing divine law even when there is almost none to observe.

A much more comprehensive statement occurs in YHWH's oracle
to Isaac to reassure him that the promise made to his deceased father
will devolve to him as well:

> I will make your descendants as numerous as the stars of heaven, and
> give to your descendants all these lands, so that all the nations of the
> earth shall bless themselves by your offspring—inasmuch as Abraham
> obeyed Me and kept (וישמר) My charge (משמרתי): My commandments
> (מצותי), My laws (חקותי), and My teachings (ותורתי). (Gen 26:4–5)

Verse 4 simply stitches together phrases from various texts spoken to
Abraham[75] to reinforce the central idea that they apply no less to
Isaac, his promised and beloved son. The first half of v. 5 is arguably
the only allusion to the *aqedah* (the binding of Isaac) in the Hebrew
Bible outside of Gen 22 itself. It echoes the language of the second
angelic address to Abraham in that fateful chapter,[76] an address
whose objective is to ground the promises to Abraham in the latter's
extraordinary obedience in the supreme test.[77] What is *not* paralleled
in the Abrahamic narratives, however, is the statement that Abraham
"kept My charge: My commandments, My laws, and My teachings."
Indeed, we are hard pressed to find parallels to this chain of no less
than four nouns all indicating (with whatever shades of meaning)
categories of observances. The closest analogy lies in Deut 11:1:

---

[73] See Mircea Eliade, *Myth and Reality* (New York: Harper & Row, 1968), 21–38.
[74] Gen 2:1–3.
[75] Cf. Gen 15:5; 22:17; 12:7; 13:15; 12:3.
[76] Cf. Gen 22:18b.
[77] See R. W. L. Moberly, "The Earliest Commentary on the Akedah," *VT* 38
(1988): 302–23.

Love, therefore, the LORD your God, and always keep (וּשְׁמַרְתָּ) His charge (מִשְׁמַרְתּוֹ), His laws (וְחֻקֹּתָיו), His rules (וּמִשְׁפָּטָיו), and His commandments (וּמִצְוֹתָיו).

In this chain of four items, three are in common with Gen 26:5b.[78] It is hard to resist the common judgment that at least the words, "My commandments, My laws, and My teachings," in Gen 26:5 are, if not "parenthetical," as Bruce Vawter phrases it, then certainly "one of those rare Deuteronomic expansions which have touched Genesis at some state of its development."[79]

Our interest here lies not in the date at which the Deuteronomic gloss entered the text, but in the understanding of Abraham that the interpolation reflects. Truth to tell, modern commentators have not been much interested in this issue, strongly preferring the Abraham of the story over the man whose obedience (this lone gloss suggests) was comprehensive and thoroughgoing. Arnold Ehrlich, who terms the second half of Gen 26:5 "ein äusserst geschmackloser späterer Einsatz,"[80] expresses the common view, though with his own characteristic acerbity. Behind the negative judgment lies the distaste for later sources, redactors, and halakhah typical of much classical historical criticism of the Hebrew Bible.[81]

As is often the case, this distaste quite inverts the traditional rabbinic priorities. The classic statement of the earlier position appears in a homiletical peroration found at the end of the Mishnaic tractate *Qiddushin.* The immediate context is the superiority of Torah over all the other occupations that a man might teach his son. In the case of the others, if one becomes too sick or too old to ply his trade, "look, he dies of hunger":

> But the Torah is not so. Rather, it protects him from all evil in his youth and grants him a future and a hope in his old age. And thus it says about Our Father Abraham (peace be unto him!): "Abraham

---

[78] Note that תּוֹרֹת in Gen 26:5b is unparalleled in Deut 11:1 and מִשְׁפָּטִים in Deut 11:1 does not appear in Gen 26:5b. Leviticus 26:46, Deut 6:1, and Deut 7:11 all have two expressions in common with Gen 26:5b.

[79] Bruce Vawter, *On Genesis* (Garden City, N.Y.: Doubleday, 1977), 291. That שָׁמְרָה מִשְׁמַרְתּוֹ also appears in Deut 11:1 argues against Vawter's effort to separate it from the ensuing four nouns. It is hard to understand why Speiser (among others) attributes the verse to J (*Genesis*, 198).

[80] Arnold B. Ehrlich, *Randglossen zur Hebräischen Bibel* (7 vols.; Leipzig: J. C. Hinrichs, 1908), 1:122.

[81] On this, see Levenson, *Hebrew Bible,* esp. 1–61.

was now old . . . and the LORD had blessed Abraham in all things."[82]
We thus find that Our Father Abraham practiced the whole Torah
in its entirety before it had been given, as it is said, "inasmuch as
Abraham obeyed Me and kept My charge: My commandments, My
laws, and My teachings."[83] (*m. Qidd.* 4:14)

Two words are of special importance in holding this little midrash
together.[84] The first and most basic, of course, is "old" (זקן). Abraham,
who happens to be the first man in the Bible to be described as
old,[85] seems to suffer none of the all too familiar degradations and
deprivations of age, but rather dies "at a good ripe age, old (זקן)
and contented."[86] The other *Leitwort* is "all" (כל). If "the LORD had
blessed Abraham in all things (כל)," surely something so basic to the
life of the faithful Jew as Torah was not omitted.[87] Indeed, one of
the gifts the Torah brings with it is "a future and a hope in [its
practitioner's] old age (זקנות)." This then draws in its train the notion
that Abraham must have observed the Torah, indeed "the whole
(כל) Torah in its entirety (כלה)," even—and this is the truly remarkable part—"before it had been given."

    The result of this intricate weaving of midrashic ideas is to resolve
a number of outstanding oddities in the biblical narrative and to
bring them into conformity with the broad outlines of rabbinic theology. First, the midrash builds upon the change in the interpretation of Abraham first made explicit in the second angelic address
after the *aqedah*.[88] The singling out of Abraham for a special destiny—and thus the chosenness of Israel through all the generations—
is no longer an act of pure grace, unrelated to the character and
accomplishments of the founding father. For just so it certainly seems
to be when the future patriarch first receives his summons and his
promises.[89] Were the theology to remain as it stood at that initial

---

[82] Gen 24:1.
[83] Gen 26:5.
[84] I speak here only of the midrash in this particular wording. For a listing of
the passages in rabbinic literature in which full observance is predicated of Abraham,
see Saul Lieberman, *Tosefta Ki-feshutah* (10 vols.; New York: Jewish Theological
Seminary of America, 5733/1973), 8:986–87.
[85] Gen 18:12. But note that the previous verse describes both him and Sarah as
"old."
[86] Gen 25:8.
[87] Note the midrash that interprets the same verse to mean that Abraham had
a daughter (*Gen. Rab.* 59:7).
[88] Gen 22:15–18. See Moberly, "Akedah," 302–23.
[89] Gen 12:1–3.

moment, then the God of the Jews could fairly be accused of arbitrariness.[90] For, as Dryden said of great wit and madness, grace and arbitrariness are "near alli'd,/And thin partitions do their bounds divide."[91] The effect of Gen 26:5b is to underscore the justice of God's action, which, while remaining altogether gracious, constitutes the condign response to Abraham's extraordinary obedience. Thus, a story that begins, so to speak, in a Lutheran mode—grace without works—ends in a Catholic mode: grace operating conjointly with works, works completing and validating the grace of God.

In the rabbinic mind, however, even the theology of the second angelic address can seem deficient. For surely Abraham's obedience in the *aqedah*, however great in its own right, must have been only a token of a more encompassing and more reproducible pattern of life-practice, one that his descendants, though vastly inferior to him, could yet imitate in their far humbler circumstances. For the author-redactor of Gen 26:5 (or perhaps only of 5b), that life-practice was summarized in the chain of nouns with which the verse ends—"My charge: My commandments, My laws, and My teachings." But for the rabbis, those nouns could be further epitomized by the expression "the whole Torah in its entirety."

The notion of the maximally observant Abraham that we found in the Mishnah is not without challenge in the Gemara. For after the statement of no less revered a figure than Rav (early third century C.E.) that "Abraham carried out the whole Torah," we find a challenge to him by Shimi bar Hiyya: "I can say [that Gen 26:5b refers only to] the seven commandments," i.e., the norms obligatory on all human beings, Jewish and Gentile alike.[92] Another voice enters the discussion to add the one enduring commandment that Abraham personally receives, circumcision, but is then rebutted with the point that this more minimal interpretation does not do justice to the words "My commandments and My laws" in the verse being debated.[93] Despite the impression that the minimalist view has been defeated, these two understandings of Abraham's observance have continued to reverberate through Jewish tradition.[94] The position I am terming

---

[90] This is the main concern of *Gen. Rab.* 55:1.
[91] John Dryden, "Absalom and Achitophel," lines 163–164.
[92] Listed in *b. Sanh.* 56a.
[93] *b. Yoma* 28b.
[94] On this, see Arthur Green, *Devotion and Commandment: The Faith of Abraham in the Hasidic Imagination* (Cincinnati: Hebrew Union College Press, 1989), esp. 24–50.

"minimalist" interprets Abraham's observance strictly within the confines of Genesis, culminating in the patriarch's agonized willingness to sacrifice his beloved son, upon whom his life—and the promise of God—rested. This act betokened the patriarch's disposition to obey divine direction, though the content of the directives could not yet be inferred from the narratives about him. The maximalist position is evident in the Mishnah and in the statement of Rav (and others) in the Gemara. Its biblical adumbration lies perhaps in the laws of circumcision in Gen 17:10–14 and certainly in the string of nouns that closes Gen 26:5b. It connects the obedience of Abraham with the forms of Israelite and Jewish practice as they are known from later sources.

The maximalist view is nicely set forth in Rashi's exegesis of Gen 26:5 (late eleventh century, Northern France):

> *Inasmuch as Abraham obeyed Me*
> when I tested him.
>
> *And kept My charge*:
> The decrees for prevention of wrongdoing regarding the warnings which are in the Torah, such as incest of second degree, and rabbinical prohibitions regarding Sabbath observance.
>
> *My commandments*,
> Those matters which even if they were not written, would be worthy of being taken as commandments, such as the prohibition on robbery and bloodshed.
>
> *My laws*,
> Matters that the Evil Inclination seeks to refute, such as the prohibition on eating swine's flesh and on the wearing of fabrics of mixed wool and linen, for which there is no reason, but (they are simply) the decree of the King and His law for His servants.
>
> *And My teachings*.
> This includes the Oral Torah, the laws (given) to Moses on Sinai.
> (Rashi on Gen 26:5b)

Only Rashi's first comment, which connects Gen 26:5a with 22:18b, falls into the category of *peshat*, the immediate contextual sense of the scriptural words. As for his glosses on the four nouns in Gen 26:5b, each case represents an effort to connect Abraham's observance with one or another category of rabbinic law. "Charge" thus refers to details of laws articulated by the rabbis themselves, unattested in the plain sense of the Torah. "Commandments" denotes universally applicable moral norms that the human intellect can intuit and respect quite without the assistance of special revelation. "Laws," by contrast, refers to norms without evident rational justification, which human beings are, consequently, inclined to doubt and to disobey. Finally, "teachings," which is the plural of תורה, includes, in Rashi's view, the Oral Torah, the deposit of rabbinic teaching that the maximalist school of rabbinic thought considered to have been revealed to Moses on Mount Sinai with all its details. The maximalist view thus interprets Abraham as observing all categories of Jewish law as the classical rabbinic tradition understood them—rational and non-rational, moral and ritual, biblical and rabbinic.

Although the midrashic method by which Rashi and his Talmudic predecessors derived their maximalist position is characteristically rabbinic, its underlying view of Abraham's observance long predates the emergence of rabbinic Judaism. Here again the honoree of this volume has correctly identified the dynamic when he remarked that "like many a modern-day homilist, the midrashist sometimes betrays signs of having first thought of a solution and then having gone out in search of the problem to which it might be applied."[95] In the case at hand, the solution is the longstanding tradition of Abraham's Torah-observance. The problem to which it is applied is the difference in meaning of the last four nouns in Gen 26:5, words that in the biblical idiom are synonymous or close to it, but in the technical vocabulary of rabbinic theology carry distinct denotations.

Over two centuries before the promulgation of the Mishnah, with its maximalist reading of those four nouns, the book of *Jubilees* had already presented an Abraham who was expert in Mosaic law, but without deriving the idea from Gen 26:5. Indeed, in the patriarch's farewell address to Isaac in *Jubilees* 21, he quotes liberally from the last three books of the Pentateuch, urging the proper observance of norms that apply—and in our version of the Pentateuch are first revealed—only long after his death. But how did he acquire this knowledge of them? This the patriarch answers himself, explicitly: "Thus I have found written in the book of my forefathers and in the words of Enoch and in the words of Noah."[96] Elsewhere, *Jubilees* speaks of books handed down from father to son—Enoch to Methusaleh to

---

[95] James L. Kugel, "Two Introductions to Midrash," in *Midrash and Literature* (ed. G. H. Hartman and S. Budick; New Haven: Yale University Press, 1986), 77–103, here 92.

[96] *Jub.* 21:10. Trans. O. S. Wintermute, *OTP* 2:95.

Lamech to Noah—but also of Abraham's supernatural acquisition
of Hebrew, "the tongue of creation," thus enabling him to study his
own father's long neglected books and the primordial law and lore
they presumably contained.[97] In the version of *Jubilees*, Abraham has
studied large parts of the Torah[98] before it is revealed to Moses, and
long before its meaning was perverted by those *Jubilees* regards as
misguided and noxious sectarians.

In the early part of the first century C.E., the Jewish philosopher
Philo of Alexandria also endorsed the maximalist view of Abraham's
observance, but with a completely different view of how he and the
other patriarchs came to know norms that were not explicitly revealed
for several more generations:

> [I]n these men we have laws endowed with life and reason, and Moses
> extolled them for two reasons. First he wished to shew that the enacted
> ordinances are not inconsistent with nature; and secondly that those
> who wish to live in accordance with the laws as they stand have no
> difficult task, seeing that the first generations before any at all of the
> particular statutes was set in writing followed the unwritten law with
> perfect ease, so that one might properly say that the enacted laws are
> nothing else than memorials of the life of the ancients, preserving to
> a later generation their actual words and deeds. For they were not
> scholars or pupils of others, nor did they learn under teachers what
> was right to say or do: they listened to no voice or instruction but
> their own: they gladly accepted conformity with nature, holding that
> nature itself was, as indeed it is, the most venerable of statutes, and
> thus their whole life was one of happy obedience to law. (*Abr.* 5–6)[99]

In Philo's thinking, the patriarchs did not need the Torah; they were
themselves walking Torahs, ἔμψυχοι καὶ λογικοὶ νόμοι, "laws endowed
with life and reason." They learned these laws not from books, as
in *Jubilees*, or from teachers orally transmitting an ancient corpus,
but from their own philosophically enlightened reading of "nature"
(φύσις), the source of the universal "unwritten law."[100] Thus, these
pre-Mosaic figures demonstrate the universal availability of the norms

---

[97] *Jub.* 7:38; 12:25–27.
[98] But probably not all of it. On this, see Gary A. Anderson, "The Status of the
Torah before Sinai," *DSD* 1 (1994): 1–29, esp. 22–23 n. 41.
[99] Colson, LCL.
[100] Elsewhere, however, Philo does see Abraham as learning from a teacher and
thus inferior to Isaac, who, as Ellen Birnbaum puts it, "acquires his self-taught
knowledge from God." See her book, *The Place of Judaism in Philo's Thought* (BJS
290; Studia Philonica Monograph Series 2; Atlanta: Scholars, 1996), 56–57.

set down in the Torah of Moses; the very existence of the patriarchs exonerates the God of Israel of the weighty charge that, by
revealing His will to but one nation, He condemned the others to
walk in darkness.[101] Instead, the universal God has written His universal law into nature itself and demonstrated through the patriarchs
that those deprived of the Torah of Moses can live in felicitous conformity to it nonetheless. Abraham, Isaac, and Jacob constitute walking proof of the ultimate oneness of creation and revelation.

In comparison with *Jubilees* and Philo, the rabbis who continued
the maximalist view of Abraham's observance seem strikingly uninterested in the question of just how this pre-Sinaitic figure came to
know the Torah that he observed so comprehensively and so metic-
ulously.[102] An exception is this comment in the name of Rabbi
Shimon bar Yochai, of the mid-second century C.E.:

> No father taught him, nor did he have a master. From where did he
> learn the Torah? Actually, the Holy One (blessed be He) appointed
> his two kidneys to be like two masters, and these would gush forth
> and teach him wisdom, as it is written, "I bless the LORD who has
> guided me; my kidneys admonish me at night."[103] (*Gen. Rab.* 61:1)

This is, to be sure, not quite the same as the notion that Abraham
could intuit the "enacted laws from nature alone," but the Philonic
resonances are evident nonetheless.[104] For Abraham learns the Torah
not from father, teacher, or book, or even from a personal event of
special revelation. He listens, as Philo had said about a century earlier, "to no voice or instruction but [his] own"—except that his own
instruction here flows from God's implanting within him the equivalent of two rabbinic teachers.

Elsewhere in rabbinic literature, we find something closer to the
answer to our question that we saw in *Jubilees*. Abraham has personal access to an ancient tradition that becomes public at Sinai.

---

[101] See Hindy Najman, "The Law of Nature and the Authority of Mosaic Law,"
SPhilo 11 (1999): 55–73.

[102] See the list of passages in Lieberman, *Tosefta*, 8:986–87.

[103] Ps 16:7. I have rendered the word, "kidneys," in conformity with the understanding of the midrash. The passage is a midrash on Ps 1:2b.

[104] I thank my colleague, Professor Bernard Septimus, for pointing this out to me.
Urbach suggests that Abraham here does not discover Torah on his own but simply studies what God has revealed to him, in Ephraim E. Urbach, *The Sages: Their
Concepts and Beliefs* (trans. I. Abrahams; Cambridge, Mass.: Harvard University Press,
1975), 318–19. But the image of God's implanting sources of Torah within the
patriarch in effect overcomes the dichotomy on which Urbach's position depends.

We find, for example, a midrash that Melchizedek, the priest-king of Salem/Jerusalem, taught Abraham the laws of priesthood, and even that "he revealed Torah to him."[105] Thus can Abraham send Isaac to Shem, son of Noah (whom the midrash identifies with Melchizedek),[106] "to learn Torah from him," thereby continuing the esoteric tradition that becomes the manifest possession of all Israel at Mount Sinai only long after his death.[107]

V

The rabbinic notion that Abraham observed "the whole Torah in its entirety" before it was revealed on Sinai must have gathered importance in response to the opposite claim that Christians were asserting contemporaneously. The source of this Christian reading of Abraham lies in Paul, for whom Abraham's faith in God proves the dispensability of the "works of the law." As the apostle to the Gentiles sees it, the first patriarch of Israel was pronounced righteous before the Torah became known, thus proving that righteousness does not depend upon human deeds but upon divine grace manifest in faith.[108] Indeed, even the one Abrahamic commandment of circumcision is unnecessary—"For in Christ Jesus, neither circumcision nor uncircumcision counts for anything," he writes to the Galatian churches. "Realize then that it is those who have faith who are children of Abraham."[109] This Pauline interpretation of Abraham undergoes, of course, innumerable interpretations and modifications in the long history of Christian theology. Already in the New Testament itself, the stark polarization of faith and works that it assumes meets with the unyielding critique of the Epistle of James. In support of his claim that "faith without works is dead," the author of this letter cites as proof—

---

[105] *Gen. Rab.* 43:6, commenting on Gen 14:18.

[106] *b. Ned.* 32b.

[107] *Gen. Rab.* 56:11, commenting on Isaac's absence from Gen 22:19.

[108] See Gal 3:1–18 and Rom 4.

[109] Gal 5:6; 3:7. Note the implication that the Jews are not the children of Abraham. Paul backtracks on this in Rom 9–11, though even there he does not renounce the supersessionism (see, e.g., 9:6–9). It is fair to say that Paul never arrived at a settled view of the relationship of Christ to the Jewish people. On the difficulty in the view that Paul believed in the continued validity of the Torah, see Brendan Byrne, "Interpreting Romans Theologically in a Post-'New Perspective' Perspective," *HTR* 94 (2001): 227–41, esp. 228 n. 10.

proof, that is, that his or her works are what justifies the person of faith—none other than "Abraham our father."[110] But even there, the point is not that Abraham observed the Mosaic law or that Christians should do likewise, but only that good works in the general sense are the inevitable and indispensable fruit of Christian faith.[111]

We seem, then, to have come to a rather clear schematization of our subject. Originally uninvolved in the observance of laws of the sort that pervade the last four books of the Torah, the Abrahamic narrative in Genesis displays a few harbingers of the new law-observant Abraham who comes into his own in Second Temple Judaism and flowers in rabbinic literature. Early Christianity, by contrast, holds up as the ideal an Abraham who is not Torah-observant, one who was reckoned as righteous without the works of the Law even before he was circumcised in accordance with a divine command. In the Jacobean vision, to be sure, his justification follows from the works that flowed from his faith, but there is no reason to think that those works are the specific ones of the Torah.

This schematization of the material into a Jewish Abraham (i.e., Torah-observant) and a Christian Abraham (i.e., justified by faith) re-calls the observation of H. L. Mencken that, "[t]here is always an easy solution to every human problem—neat, plausible, and wrong."[112] The Torah-observant Abraham, though too often described in scholarly literature as the "rabbinic view"[113] or as the "singular" solution of Jewish authors,[114] or the like, is only one of the rabbinic positions on the matter. The alternative view, alive and well in rabbinic and later Judaism, is that Abraham observed only the seven Noahide command-ments, or those minimal but universally obligatory norms supplemented perhaps by circumcision.[115] If Rashi's exegesis of Gen 26:5b serves

---

[110] Jas 2:14–26. The quoted verses are 26 and 21.

[111] On the general question of Abraham in early Christianity, see Jeffrey S. Siker, *Disinheriting the Jews: Abraham in Early Christian Controversy* (Louisville: Westminster John Knox, 1991).

[112] Henry L. Mencken, "The Divine Afflatus," in *A Mencken Chrestomathy* (New York: Knopf, 1949), 443; repr. from *New York Evening Mail*, 16 November 1917.

[113] Samuel Sandmel, *Philo's Place in Judaism: A Study of Conceptions of Abraham in Jewish Literature* (aug. ed.: New York: KTAV, 1971), 108.

[114] Thus Gary A. Anderson, "The Status of the Torah in the Pre-Sinaitic Period: St. Paul's Epistle to the Romans," in *Biblical Perspectives: Early Use and Interpretation of the Bible in Light of the Dead Sea Scrolls* (ed. M. E. Stone and E. G. Chazon; STDJ 28; Leiden: Brill, 1998), 1–23, here 23.

[115] See above, section IV.

as our parade example of the maximalist view, then that of his grandson, Rabbi Samuel ben Meir (Rashbam, Northern France, ca. 1085–
1174), can play the same role for the minimalist alternative:

> *Inasmuch as Abraham obeyed Me*
> Concerning the Binding of Isaac, as it is written, "inasmuch as you
> have obeyed Me."[116]
>
> *and kept My charge:*
> Such as circumcision, as it is written about it, "And as for you, you
> shall keep my covenant."[117]
>
> *My commandments,*
> Such as the commandment about the eight days [until the father per-
> forms circumcision on the son], as it is written, "As God commanded
> him."[118]
>
> *My laws, and My teachings.*
> According to the essence of its plain sense, [it refers to] all the com-
> mandments that are [generally] recognized, such as the laws against
> robbery, sexual misdeeds, and coveting, and the requirement for legal
> order, and the laws of hospitality. All of these were in force before
> the Torah was given, but they were [then] renewed and explicated to
> Israel, and they made a covenant to practice them.
> (Rashbam on Gen 26:5b)

The guiding principle of Rashbam's interpretation is patent. The half-
verse ostensibly so supportive of the maximalist view actually refers only
to norms that Abraham could have known according to a plain-
sense reading of the narratives about him in Genesis itself. These are
the norms that the human mind can intuit unaided by special revelation and those that were explicitly commanded to the patriarch
himself. The fact that some of these directives were later absorbed
into Mosaic revelation and the covenantal relationship it establishes
does not make Abraham a Mosaic Jew. He remains thoroughly pre-
Sinaitic.

The minimalist position suggests a theological position that is, in
fact, simply the Jewish counterpart to Moberly's analogy about the
respect accorded "patriarchal religion" in "Mosaic Yahwism." Just
as "Mosaic Yahwism has no polemic against patriarchal religion,"
Moberly writes, so "the Christian," living, like the Mosaic Israelite,

---

[116] Gen 22:18. I have changed the NJPS wording so as to bring out Rashbam's
point about the use of the identical Hebrew phrasing.
[117] Gen 17:9.
[118] Gen 21:4.

in a new and different dispensation, "should respect both the content of Mosaic Yahwism and also the religious system of Judaism that in its own different way develops from it."[119] The Jewish counterpart would maintain that just as Abraham in the minimalist view observed only the Noahide commandments (perhaps augmented by whatever few other norms God revealed to him personally) and yet was accorded the deepest respect, indeed veneration, in the ongoing religion of Torah, so should the Jew respect those whose lives manifest the Abrahamic spiritual stance and refrain from judging it inferior to their own Sinaitic religion.

Two objections to this proposal rapidly come to mind, however—one less and one more compelling. The less compelling objection is that this Jewish counterpart suffers from the weakness in Moberly's proposal that we have discussed. Why should we see "continuing validity" in something that has, in fact, been superseded in the new dispensation? The answer comes to mind, however, with equal rapidity. Whereas Christian respect for Judaism must overcome two millennia of supersessionist theology, Jewish respect for observance of the Noahide commandments faces no comparable obstacle. It is, in fact, an important item in the classical rabbinic tradition itself. For the Noahide dispensation is superseded only for that subset of humanity that is the people Israel, and even they—the Jews—must observe those seven fundamental norms along with the 606 others that have traditionally defined the rabbinic enumeration of 613 commandments in the Torah.[120] According to the preponderant theology of rabbinic Judaism,[121] the election of the Jews places upon them greater obligations (and perhaps greater opportunity for intimacy with God), but it does not damn righteous Gentiles or deny them an authentic relationship with the Creator.[122] The old (Noahide) dispensation is thus still universally valid; the new (Mosaic, or Sinaitic) covenant (which

---

[119] Moberly, *Old Testament*, 163–64. See above, section III.

[120] The *locus classicus* is *b. Mak.* 23b. It should not be assumed that the figure was known before the time of Rabbi Simlai or universally shared after him.

[121] This description of rabbinic teaching will be familiar to any traditionally educated student of the literature, but the historical picture, as always, is considerably more complicated and involves a diversity of positions, some of which did not survive the Talmudic period. For the elaboration of another rabbinic position, see Marc Hirshman, *Torah for the Entire World* (Tel Aviv: Hakkibbutz Hameuchad, 1999) [Hebrew].

[122] This makes the term "election," with the soteriological overtones it has in Christendom (especially in Calvinism), problematic for understanding rabbinic Judaism.

is with the Jews alone) has not displaced it. Here, as often in Jewish-Christian relations (in the past or the present), asymmetry reigns, and efforts to create matching structures fail to reckon adequately with the differences in shape and structure of the two religions.

The more substantial objection to the proposal of a Jewish counterpart to Moberly's observes that the Abrahamic minimalism contributes nothing to the standing structure of rabbinic theology, since it makes of the patriarch—whom Christians and Muslims call father no less than Jews—just another Noahide. There is a measure of truth here, but to state the matter this way is to fall into the trap of calling the glass half-empty. For the same observation could be made to the credit of traditional Jewish teaching about Gentiles who observe the seven Noahide commandments: their observance ranks them not merely with the postdiluvian father of all mankind but also, and more importantly, with the father of Israel. For Christians, I should think the minimalist view of Abraham's observance—the fact that in this interpretation he does not keep the Mosaic Torah in its entirety—can hardly be a matter for protest. For, as we have seen, in Pauline and much later Christian literature, Abraham serves (*inter alia*) precisely the purpose of exempting Gentiles from the Mosaic norms—an exemption that rabbinic theology also endorses. To be sure, the minimalist view does not grant Christians all that they would wish on the basis of their religion. It does not, for example, support the idea that "if you belong to Christ, then you are Abraham's descendants, heir according to the promise,"[123] nor does it identify the Torah with slavery.[124] To do so would have constituted a frontal assault on one of the key assertions of rabbinic theology, that Torah liberates.[125] We are speaking, in other words, of the implications of the minimally observant Abraham in *Jewish* theology, and not in Christian theology (which will inevitably differ in major ways), nor in some other system of thought ostensibly independent of Judaism and Christianity but capable of pronouncing judgment on both.[126]

---

[123] Gal 3:29.

[124] E.g., Gal 4:21–5:1, and much Christian literature over the ensuing centuries.

[125] E.g., *m. 'Abot* 6:2.

[126] The underlying theory is that the warrants with which one religion (call it A) pronounces another religion (B) to be valid necessarily derive from A, not from B, and therefore always to some degree privilege A over B. In other words, there is no such thing as autonomous pluralism or a tradition-neutral criterion for evaluating religious claims. On this, see Gavin D'Costa, "The Impossibility of a Pluralist View of Religions," *RelS* 32 (1996): 223–32.

There is one other argument against the objection that the tradition of the minimally observant Abraham contributes nothing beyond what already exists in the Noahide theology. For in the minimalist view, Abraham is not simply a man who observes the norms that rabbinic Judaism deems incumbent on all human beings. He is still the patriarch whose religious devotion extends far beyond the limited (though important) realm of observance. Here, I think, for example, of a statement in an early collection of midrash. The context is the wondrous things that God has brought about in response to faith (אמנה) in Him:

> And so you also find that our father Abraham inherited both this world and the world-to-come only as a reward for the faith that he had, as it is said: "And because he put his trust (האמן) in the Lord [He reckoned it to his merit]."[127] (*Mekilta de Rabbi Ishmael Bešallah* 7)

It is possible, of course, that the statement is not to be taken literally at all. Rather, it may simply be a hyperbole intended to underscore the preciousness and effectiveness of faith, with Abraham as the scriptural *exemplum*. If it is meant as stated, however, it makes a claim even bolder than that of the minimalists. What is noteworthy about Abraham in this case is not his observance of commandments at all, whether "the whole Torah in its entirety," the Noahide commandments (perhaps augmented by circumcision), or whatever. What is noteworthy about Abraham, rather, is his *faith*. Though one should not interpret this comment as opposed to Torah observance, as if its rabbinic author believed in a stark faith-works dichotomy, its Pauline resonance is still unmistakable.[128] The underlying theology is of a piece with that of an observation by Rabbi Nehemiah (second century C.E.) in the same passage: "anyone who accepts one single commandment in faith is worthy to have the Holy Spirit rest upon him."

This high estimation of Abraham's faith and its soteriological efficacy provides ground for a Jewish evaluation of Christians that puts them in a category different from that of other Noahides. Or, to put it more precisely, it puts practicing Christians in a special sub-category of Noahides defined not only by the general observance of the seven commandments but also by the practice of faith of the sort paradigmatically represented in rabbinic tradition by Abraham.

---

[127] Gen 15:6.
[128] See Gal 3:6 and Rom 4:3.

To the extent that Christian faith is directed to the God of Israel, it reflects an Abrahamic dimension not shared by other Gentiles.[129]

In the aggregate, the two views of Abraham's observance that we have been tracing reflect the efforts of the rabbis to do justice to two key dimensions of the religious life, as they understood it. We may term these the "quantitative" and the "qualitative." The quantitative dimension follows from the idea that the religious person will inevitably seek to maximize his or her observance, pursuing every *mitzvah* and refraining from the impious and hubristic temptation to pick and choose according to one's own preferences. From this perspective, the notion that Abraham followed only the seven Noahide commandments, perhaps augmented by the norms of circumcision, and neither knew, sought, nor was given other *mitzvot*, is highly troublesome. Hence the maximalist view, that "our Father Abraham practiced the whole Torah in its entirety before it had been given."[130] Hence also the rare relative judgment on the minimally observant Abraham, as in a midrash that sees in the following familiar verse references to Abraham (among others) and Israel at Sinai, respectively:[131] "Many women have done well, but you surpass them all" (Prov 31:29). In this telling, Abraham observed only eight commandments, the seven Noahide and circumcision: he is among those "who have done well." But at Sinai, Israel receives the full complement of 613: they thus "surpass them all." The Abrahamic is good; the Mosaic is better.

The qualitative dimension places the stress on the spiritual disposition of the practitioner rather than on the corpus of normative practices. Does he or she observe the *mitzvot*—even be they as few as one—from a stance of obedience, service, and faith, or are the operative motives ones of self-interest, fear of punishment, or social conformity, and the practice itself thus based in mindless routine? When these are the critical questions, then the minimally observant Abraham can more easily be seen as the ideal—the person who serves God out of love rather than fear.[132] Hence the presence of the minimal-

---

[129] On the difficulty of simply identifying the Christian God with the Jewish, however, see Goldberg, "God, Action, and Narrative." Over the last millennium or so, Jewish thought has proven supple enough to affirm that Christians worship the true God without implying that the doctrines of Incarnation and Trinity adequately render the truth about Him.

[130] *m. Qidd.* 4:14.

[131] *Pesiq. Rab Kah.* 12:1.

[132] See, e.g., *b. Soṭah* 31a.

ist view even in rabbinic Judaism, with its uncompromising commitment to the practice of the whole Torah, written and oral.

Like the qualitative and quantitative dimensions of the religious life in rabbinic Judaism, the maximalist and minimalist views of Abraham's observance are not, at the deep level, in contradiction. Here, an observation of Moberly is especially helpful. Moberly notes a suggestive correspondence between the *aqedah* and the revelation at Sinai.[133] In the *aqedah*, God "tests" (נסה) Abraham to learn whether he "fears" (ירא) him.[134] At Sinai, after the revelation of the Decalogue, Moses reassures a people fearful for their lives in these words, in the only verse in the Hebrew Bible in which both verbs occur:

> Be not afraid (ירא); for God has come only in order to test (נסה) you, and in order that the fear (ירא) of Him may be ever with you, so that you do not go astray. (Exod 20:20)[135]

Whether or not Moberly is correct in his assessment that Gen 22 displays "a typological molding of the Abraham story in terms of the normative concept of Torah,"[136] it is surely the case that the structure of rabbinic theology and the hermeneutic procedures associated with it encourage such a reading. The point is this: given his spiritual disposition, refined in test after test and definitively proven in the *aqedah*, Abraham, had he stood at Sinai, would surely have accepted the entire Torah. On that, maximalists and minimalists can agree.

VI

The dispute between Jews and Christians over the man that both call father did not go unnoticed by the founder of the third great religion commonly designated Abrahamic. In the Qur'an, we hear a reflection on the whole controversy and an effort to put it into what Muhammad, relaying the word of God, considers to be its proper perspective:

> People of the Book! Why do you dispute concerning Abraham? The Torah was not sent down, neither the Gospel, but after him. What, have you no reason? Ha, you are the ones who dispute on what you

---

[133] Moberly, *Old Testament*, 188–89.
[134] Gen 22:1, 12.
[135] Exod 20:17 NJPS.
[136] Moberly, *Old Testament*, 189.

know; why then dispute you touching a matter of which you know not anything? No, Abraham in truth was not a Jew, neither a Christian; but he was a Muslim and one pure of faith; certainly he was never of the idolaters. Surely the people standing closest to Abraham are those who followed him, and this Prophet, and those who believe; and God is the Protector of the believers. (Sura 3, The House of Imran)[137]

The essential problem with the way the scriptural peoples handle the issue is precisely that they seek to remake the patriarch in the image of their own faiths. Here, the prophet surely refers to the traditions by which a man who lived before the Torah and before Jesus (and Paul) becomes an observant Jew or an example of the Church's good news about righteousness through grace alone, respectively. Against these patent anachronisms, the Qur'an propounds an Abraham independent of Torah and the Gospel alike. His spiritual grandeur lies, rather, in having refused to engage in idolatry and, instead, in having submitted fully to God. The Qur'an calls this "the religion of Abraham" (*millat 'Ibrahim*), but as one who submitted, he practiced the spiritual act from which Islam would derive its name even before the community of the faithful (*Umma*) came into existence. The patriarch was, in other words, the first Muslim. Or, to put it differently, Islam is the religion of Abraham.[138] Thus, as the end of this passage indicates, the people worthy of Abraham are the Muslims— those who follow his prophetic successor, the seal of all prophets, Muhammad himself.

Although the Qur'an presents Abraham in terms of its own claim to be a restoration of a truth long forgotten or spurned, it is not hard to see that Abraham the Muslim is as much a recreation—and a projection—as Abraham the observant Jew and Abraham the man of Christian faith. For the language of "submission" does not occur in Genesis, and there is no more reason to employ it as the cover term for Abraham's religiousness than there was to employ Torah-observance or faith in the same role. Indeed, there is even less, since Gen 26:5 and 15:6 do provide some basis, of whatever worth, for these Jewish and Christian appropriations, respectively.[139] Arguments

---

[137] The translation is from A. J. Arberry, *The Koran Interpreted* (New York: MacMillan, 1955), 82–83.

[138] See "'IBRAHIM," in *The Encyclopaedia of Islam* (ed. B. Lewis et al.; new ed.; Leiden: Brill, 1971), 980–81.

[139] The Qur'anic notion that Abraham was a prophet is similarly based on only one biblical verse (Gen 20:7).

like these, however, will hardly persuade a Muslim who does not accept historical criticism of the Qur'an (almost none do). Here we must also keep in mind that in Islam, the Jewish and Christian Bibles do not have the status of Scripture at all. We cannot, therefore, use the book of Genesis to critique or correct the Qur'an. This alone seriously qualifies the claim of Muslim kinship with Judaism and Christianity, even though it does not destroy it. The latter two communities, by and large, work with the same text of the Tanakh/Old Testament, whereas that text has no sacred status at all in the other great Abrahamic religion.

The quest for the neutral Abraham has failed. The patriarch is too embedded in the Torah, the New Testament, and the Qur'an (and in the normative documents of the traditions they undergird) to be extracted and set in judgment upon the traditions that claim him. Nonetheless, the temptation to minimize these differences and revert to some pre-Jewish, pre-Christian, pre-Muslim Abraham is powerful, especially in light of acts of mass violence done in the name of Abrahamic religions. This brings us back to Karl-Josef Kuschel, the Catholic theologian from Tübingen, for he has tried to develop a means to reclaim Abraham that gives due recognition to the inevitable divisions that I have just mentioned and yet still moves beyond them in quest of an underlying unity:

> [L]ike Abraham, Jews, Christians, and Muslims have to do with a God who calls into being that which is not and expects from human beings only *emuna, pistis, islam*: dedicated trust. In short, any talk of Abrahamic ecumene cannot be a suspension which forgets the origins but is rather a concretion of the faith of Abraham which is relevant to the present—in the light of Torah, Gospel, and Qur'an. Abraham remains a point of reference by which the later traditions of synagogue, church, and Umma, can and must be measured critically. . . .
>
> For faithfulness to Abraham is more than a slogan only if people in all three traditions are still ready to listen to the Abraham of scripture as he has been handed down in all his dimensions, neither in the Talmud nor in the New Testament nor in the Qur'an, but in the book of Genesis.[140]

The problem with this, as I see it, is that Kuschel's Abraham is not really so ecumenical, and the underlying unity that he claims to find, not so shared, as he thinks. For this is (despite Kuschel's own

---

[140] Kuschel, *Abraham*, 204–5.

Catholicism) essentially a Protestant Christian Abraham. Note that the key thing about Abraham is once again, as in Paul, his faith (*emuna, pistis*).[141] Kuschel altogether ignores the tradition that Abraham was obedient to commandments—the Abraham of rabbinic maximalism who "obeyed Me and kept My charge: My commandments, My laws, and My teachings."[142] This is, to be sure, only one verse, but, as we have observed, so is the verse that claims that Abraham had faith. Second, in Kuschel's proposal the standard by which all renderings of Abraham are to be assessed is once again the notion of *sola scriptura,* "by scripture alone," a concept familiar from the Protestant Reformation but by no means authoritative in every scriptural religion, or even in every Abrahamic religion. In Kuschel's case, unlike Luther's or Calvin's, however, the Scripture is limited to Genesis and the renderings of Abraham in the New Testament are relegated to the level of post-biblical tradition, in the manner of the Talmud of rabbinic Judaism or the Qur'an of Islam. I leave it to Christian theologians to assess the adequacy for their tradition of this proposal to locate the authoritative meaning of Abraham in Genesis rather at the expense of the New Testament. But it is surely the case that not many Jews or Muslims are likely to accept the equivalent downplaying of their own traditions and (in the case of Islam) scriptures that this requires. And I find it easy to imagine some Muslims would want to question whether *islam* is really quite the same thing as *pistis* (the New Testament word usually rendered "faith" but which Kuschel translates as "dedicated trust"). That Judaism and Islam give a prominent place to "dedicated trust" need hardly be gainsaid, but the notion that this is the foundation and all else is secondary will justly meet with resistance among practicing Jews and Muslims and among many Christian communities as well. In short, Kuschel's well-intentioned proposal reminds me of a person who says, "We need to stop arguing and agree on a common position: mine."

We are again compelled to the conclusion that there is no master category in which Abraham can be viewed; there is no vantage point independent of the three religions that call him father that those tra-

---

[141] The assumptions that *pistis* and *emuna* are identical and, more fundamentally, that each term always refers to the same spiritual act, are much to be doubted. Martin Buber's doubts that Christian and Jewish "faith" are the same, though dated in many ways, are still worth pondering. See his *Two Types of Faith* (London: Routledge and Kegan Paul, 1951).

[142] Gen 26:5.

ditions can adopt. Abraham's particularism is indeed stubborn and persistent, and efforts to ignore or circumvent it cannot succeed. A skeptic might say that Abraham is a Rorschach card, onto whom each tradition projects its own convictions. I would prefer to put it differently. The material about Abraham in the Hebrew Bible is so elusive, so enigmatic, so suggestive, and so non-didactic, that it calls out, דרשני—"Interpret me!" as the Talmudic rabbis would say.

This is not to claim that all interpretations are equally valid, as hermeneutical relativism would have it. At the same time, however, we must acknowledge that there are in the materials we have studied bases for greater respect than many traditionalists will at first think to be the case. The rabbinic tradition that attributes minimal observance to Abraham, for example, loosens the First Jew a bit from Judaism itself, without in any way undermining the importance of the Torah and its observance for the people Israel. The Pauline resonance of the rabbinic statement that "our father Abraham inherited both this world and the world-to-come only as a reward for the faith that he had" can serve as a basis for Jewish respect of a mode of appropriation of Abraham rather different from the one that dominates the Jewish tradition. Similarly, on the Christian side, the Epistle of James, which attacks the notion that faith and works can be separated and speaks of Abraham as justified by his works, can serve as something of a counterweight to the more prominent and better known Pauline tradition that sees Abraham as justified by faith alone and denies any salvific role to the observance of law and commandments.[143] In other words, each of these two traditions harbors within it a view of Abraham that looks more like the dominant emphasis of the other one.[144] The fact that the exegetical culture of Late Antiquity cuts across religious boundaries offers a more subtle and productive way of thinking about differences than has usually been employed.

---

[143] This is, it must be stressed, a tradition that has given birth to much vicious caricaturing of Judaism over the centuries, no small part of it in works of critical New Testament scholarship. On this, see E. P. Sanders, *Paul and Palestinian Judaism: A Comparison of Patterns of Religion* (Philadelphia: Fortress, 1977), 33–59.

[144] I leave it to scholars more versed in Islam to develop Muslim analogues to these Jewish and Christian examples of traditions that aid rather than undermine respect.

VII

To conclude: Any appropriation of Father Abraham is inevitably particularistic—how could it be different with a figure who is singled out for a special destiny, different from those of all the families on the earth? But the Jewish and Christian traditions have within them notes that develop fully only in the other community, thus providing a basis for empathy without homogenization. A clearer recognition of this two-fold truth holds forth the possibility of better relations among these faiths. Mutual contempt, on the one extreme, and cultural relativism, with its attendant leveling of ultimate differences, on the other, are not the only possibilities for scriptural interpretation in the modern world.

THE ALLEGED "HIDDEN LIGHT"

Jacob Milgrom

R. Eleazar said: The light which the Holy One, blessed be He, created on the first day, one could see thereby from one end of the world to the other; but as soon as the Holy One, blessed be He, beheld the generation of the Flood and the generation of the Dispersion (cf. Gen 11:9), and saw that their actions were corrupt, He arose and hid it (ויגנזו), lit. "reserved it in his treasury,"[1] from them. . . . For whom did he reserve it (גנזו)? For the righteous in the time to come. (b. Ḥag. 12a; cf. Gen. Rab. 3:6; 11:2)

The question answered by this midrash is obvious. It affords a satisfactory answer to an enigma in the text of the creation story. Though God created light on the first day, he created the sun, moon, and stars on the fourth day (Gen 1:14–19). Since we live by the light of the fourth day, what happened to the light of the first day? Philo solves this problem by proposing the light of the first day was an intellectual, invisible light, whereas the light of the fourth day was visible.[2] But this view never took hold in Jewish tradition. Instead, as related in the above midrash, it postulated that the light of the first day was אור גנוז, lit. "light reserved in God's treasury." This struck deep roots in Jewish lore, especially in mystic literature.[3]

Nonetheless, the essential problem remains: Why were the celestial luminaries created on the fourth day and not on the first day? The answer, noticed (partially) by many scholars,[4] is that the wording of

---

[1] The notion that God reserves beams of light in his celestial treasuries is not original to the midrash. It is already found in *4 Ezra* 6:40 (end of first century C.E.), *lumen . . . de thesauris tuis*, "(then you commanded a ray of) light (be brought forth) from your treasuries." Cf. Léon Gry, *Les dires prophétiques d'Esdras (IV. Esdras)* (Paris: Geuthner, 1938), 115.

[2] Philo, *Opif.* 1.8, 18.

[3] E.g., *Zohar* 1.31b; cf. 34a, 45b.

[4] For example Umberto Cassuto, *A Commentary on the Book of Genesis* (trans. I. Abrahams; 2 vols.; Jerusalem: Magnes, 1961), 1:42–47; Gerhard Von Rad, *Genesis: A Commentary* (OTL; trans. J. H. Marks; rev. ed.; London: SCM, 1963), 53–54; Claus Westermann, *Genesis 1–11: A Commentary* (trans. J. J. Scullion; Minneapolis: Augsburg, 1984), 127; idem, *Creation* (trans. J. J. Scullion; Philadelphia: Fortress, 1974), 44–45; Nahum Sarna, *Genesis* (JPS Torah Commentary; Philadelphia: Jewish Publication Society, 1989), 10; Victor P. Hamilton, *The Book of Genesis: Chapters 1–17* (NICOT; Grand Rapids: Eerdmans, 1990), 127.

the fourth day constitutes a polemic against Babylonian mythology. The sun and moon are unnamed; instead they are designated the "greater light" (מאור) and the "lesser light" (Gen 1:16). This was done so that Israel would avoid identifying the sun (Hebrew: שמש shemesh) with the Babylonian sun god with the same name, Shamash. In addition to being the god of light, Shamash was the judge of gods and men: indeed, he was in charge of the entire universe.[5] It was critical for the priestly theologians that the sun not be identified with Shamash. Hence, not only were the sun and moon unnamed but their creation was relegated to the fourth day as the last of the inorganic creatures; indeed, their creation was even preceded by the vegetation, the lowest of the organic creatures. Moreover, the sun's function was reduced to ממשלה, "rule, management." That is, the light previously created was turned over to the sun and moon to regulate the alternation of day and night. Finally, the stars, which were regarded as controllers of human destiny,[6] are mentioned only as an afterthought. They are not included in the Divine command (vv. 14–19) but in its fulfillment as an appendix to v. 16a.

Yet these stages in the demotion of the celestial luminaries to an anonymous status and a minor position in the order of creation (the fourth day) is only a small step in their debasement. The ultimate, and singular, purpose of the text is to demonstrate that the sun, moon, and stars are powerless. They are not the sources of light; the light they shine is not their own. The evidence follows:

First, it should be noted that in P the only object designated as a מאור, aside from the heavenly luminaries, is the luminary of the Tabernacle, located inside the shrine; מנורת המאור means "the lamp-stand[7] of the luminary" (Exod 35:14 bis, 28; 39:27; Num 4:9, 16), and שמן המאור/למאור, "oil of/for the luminary" (Exod 25:6; 27:20; 35:8; Lev 25:2). It is important to note that the Tabernacle luminary (מאור) is not the source of its light. The light, in the form of oil, must be brought to it, placed inside the seven cups atop the luminary and then kindled. So too, it may be surmised, the heavenly luminaries (מאורות) are also not the sources of their light but must derive it from elsewhere.

---

[5] Cf. Tikva Frymer-Kensky, "Utu," *ER* 15:162–63.

[6] Cf. Fabrizio Lelli, "Stars," *DDD* 530–40.

[7] The menorah is only the central branch of the מאור, the luminary, and must be distinguished from the menorah of the present day.

Then, too, there is scriptural evidence that ancient Israel was aware of a light that existed independently of the sun. In 2 Sam 23:4 the rising sun and the "morning light" are named side by side. In Qoh 12:2 light is listed separately from the sun, moon, and stars. Finally, in Isa 30:26 the light of the sun will compare with the light of the seven days of creation (cf. Amos 8:9), implying that the light of the first day shone with the same intensity for all seven days. This could only take place if the sun and moon refracted this light but added to it no light of their own (cf. Pss 74:16; 104:2).

This conclusion is further affirmed by resolving an ancillary question: How could the sun and moon have separated the day from the night (1:14a, 18a) if God had already done so on day one (1:4b)? The answer is that God indeed had separated them. The function of the sun and moon, however, as mentioned above, was only to manage, regulate their alternation (1:14a). This function is defined, by P's apt term, as אתות, "signs" (1:14b), namely, as cosmic clocks for the benefit of humanity. Being regulators and clocks, the source of their power stems from elsewhere. They themselves are inert and impotent.

All these intimations receive definitive affirmation in the very structure of the creation story, Genesis, chapter one.

As is well known, creation is pictured as a two-panel structure where the first three days are diagrammed side by side of the three parallel concluding days.[8] The first three days list the created ele-

	Genesis 1:1–2:3 CREATION			
Day	Element		User	Day
		Introduction (1–2)		
1	Light (3–5)		Luminaries (14–19)	4
2	Sky Waters (6–8)		Fish Birds (20–23)	5
3	Dry Land Vegetation (9–13)		Land Animals Humans (24–31)	6
		Conclusion (2:1–2a)		
		7 Sabbath (2:2b–3)		

[8] To my knowledge, the first to notice this bilateral harmony was Cassuto, *Genesis*, 16–17 n. 1.

ments of the universe, and the final three days, the users of these elements. Thus, moving from the bottom upon the diagram, day three, featuring the elements dry land and vegetation, is balanced by the users of these elements, land animals and humans, who live on the land and use (eat) the vegetation (exclusively, being vegetarians). On day two, the sky and waters are matched chiastically by their users, the fish and birds (chiastic reversal in the middle of a structure is a lock devised by P signifying the structure's permanence).[9] Finally, the light of day one is paralleled by the users of the light, the heavenly luminaries.

The implications of the latter correspondence have thus far gone unnoticed. They imply that the sun, moon, and stars are not the sources of their light. They are only refractors of the light of the first day. This constitutes the most telling diminution of the sun, moon, and stars. They are powerless! They are only tools created by God to funnel the already existing light upon the earth. Thus there is no other light than the light of the first day. The אור גנוז, the light reserved in God's treasury for the righteous in the time to come, is a beautiful but fanciful midrash. It is not grounded in the biblical text.

---

[9] An elaborate example is the insertion of the little chiasm of Lev 24:16aα–bβ into the large chiasm of vv. 13–23; cf. Jacob Milgrom, *Leviticus 23–27* (AB 3B; New York: Doubleday, 2001), 2128–33.

GOLDEN CALF STORIES: THE RELATIONSHIP OF EXODUS 32 AND DEUTERONOMY 9–10

Christine E. Hayes

I. Introduction

Exodus 32 contains the story of Israel's apostasy with the golden calf at the base of Mount Sinai. The infamous event is also described by Moses in Deut 9–10. The relationship between these two accounts—one a third-person narrative, the other a first-person exhortation—has occupied pre-modern commentators and critical scholars alike. Despite a broad consensus that a relation of literary dependence exists between Exod 32:1–34:28 and Deut 9:7b–10:11, there is some difference of opinion over the direction of the dependence. While most scholars assume a dependence running from Exodus to Deuteronomy, some recent works have argued the reverse.[1]

A case for the dependence of Deuteronomy on Exodus is made by Christopher Begg.[2] Begg bases his argument, however, on limited evidence, viz., the close analysis of a single verse in each account (Exod 32:20 and the corresponding Deut 9:21). The two verses are largely parallel, but minor variations do occur. Begg concludes that Deut 9:21 is an amplifying and disambiguating expansion of Exod 32:20. More important, Begg presents evidence for the claim that Deut 9:21's modification of Exod 32:20 is undertaken in order to set up or foreshadow other significant moments in Israel's cultic history as presented by the Deuteronomistic Historian (DtrH).

That the unique elements in Deut 9:21 can be plausibly explained as purposeful modifications of the text in Exod 32:20 in line with the goals of a (or the) Deuteronomist suggests that Deut 9–10 is

---

[1] For the Exodus account as secondary, see John Van Seters's work, "Histories and Historians of the Ancient Near East: The Israelites," *Orientalia* 50 (1981): 137–85; "Law and the Wilderness Rebellion Tradition: Ex 32," *SBLSP* 27 (1990): 583–91; *The Life of Moses: The Yahwist as Historian in Exodus-Numbers* (Kampen: Kok Pharos, 1994), 290–318.

[2] Christopher Begg, "The Destruction of the Calf (Exod 32,20/Deut 9,21)," in *Das Deuteronomium: Entstehung, Gestalt und Botschaft* (ed. N. Lohfink; BETL 68; Leuven: Leuven University Press, 1985), 208–51.

dependent on Exod 32, rather than the reverse.[3] Begg proposes that
this conclusion holds not only for the isolated verses analyzed by
him but also for their respective contexts (Exod 32:1–34:28 and Deut
9:7b–10:11). Begg acknowledges that the resolution of this question
would require a detailed comparison of many more elements in the
two accounts than the single verse that is the focus of his study. This
paper is, *inter alia*, a limited attempt to answer Begg's call for a fuller
investigation of the golden calf accounts in Exodus and Deuteronomy
in order to determine the direction of literary dependence.

What is at stake in determining the direction of literary dependence? Consider the following observation by Begg:

> The verbal affinities between Deut 9,21 and a whole series of formu-
> lations relating to subsequent moments in Israel's cultic history . . . sev-
> eral of these being quite distinctive within the language of the OT as
> a whole . . . do lend credence to an authorship of the verse by the
> Deuteronomist, that writer who, in the conception of M. Noth, expanded
> an earlier form of the book of Deuteronomy with material of his own
> composition with a view to thereby preparing subsequent events in
> Israel's history as he would relate these in the books of Joshua-Kings.[4]

If Deut 9:21 and the unit within which it appears is the work of the
Deuteronomist, and if the literary dependence of Deut 9:7b–10:11
on Exod 32:1–34:28 can be established, then it follows that the
golden calf account in Exod 32 is pre-Deuteronomistic in origin. As
Begg points out, this conclusion flies in the face of a continuing tendency to view Exod 32 as Deuteronomistic or even, in the case of
Van Seters, as a post-Deuteronomistic composition from the late
post-exilic period.[5]

There are several reasons for the scholarly assertion that Exod 32
is Deuteronomistic, or at least heavily interpolated by a Deuteronomistic
editor. First, inadequate attention to the literary structure and narrative devices employed in the composition of Exod 32 has led some
scholars to imagine a slew of inconsistencies and redundancies signaling disparate sources and interpolation.[6] Second, some sections

---

[3] Ibid., 247.

[4] Ibid., 247–48.

[5] Ibid., 249; Van Seters, "Law and the Wilderness Rebellion Tradition," 591.

[6] See, for example, Immanuel Lewy, "The Story of the Golden Calf Reanalysed,"
VT 9 (1959): 318–22, who assumes a basic J groundwork plus four annotators (a J
reviser, a northern E reviser, a southern priestly E reviser, and D); see also J. Philip
Hyatt, *Exodus* (NCBC; Grand Rapids: Eerdmans, 1971), 301, and the summary of
scholarship in Brevard Childs, *The Book of Exodus: A Critical, Theological Commentary*
(OTL; Philadelphia: Westminster, 1974), 558. Childs notes that many of these so-

(e.g., vv. 7–14 in which God tells Moses of the Israelites' sin and Moses implores God to refrain from immediately destroying the Israelites in his blazing anger) appear to contain Deuteronomistic language and themes.[7] Third, and most important, are the parallels that obtain between Exod 32 and the account of Jeroboam's cultic sin in 1 Kgs 12. This latter point warrants further discussion.

As Moses Aberbach and Leivy Smolar demonstrated decades ago, there are many points of identity or contact between the Exodus golden calf account and the story of Jeroboam in 1 Kgs 12.[8] The most obvious parallels are: the production of a golden calf (Aaron) or calves (Jeroboam) at the behest of others; the description of the calves as molten; the identical declaration, "These are your gods, O Israel, that brought you up out of the land of Egypt"; the construction of altars for calf worship and the proclamation of a feast; and the opposition (Exod 32) or non-participation (1 Kgs 12) of Levites in the calf cult. On the basis of these parallels, many scholars regard Exod 32 as a disguised polemic against Jeroboam's cultic reform. However, the question arises: Did Exod 32 attain its final form in response to the activities of the *historical* Jeroboam in the 10th century B.C.E. (in which case it may be pre-Deuteronomistic), or did Exod 32 attain its final form in response to the DtrH's literary representation (or fabrication) of those events in 1 Kgs 12, centuries later (in which case Exod 32 reached its final form rather late)?

A wide variety of views may be found. Some argue that an original golden calf tradition at the core of Exod 32 was modified by a later editor as part of an anti-northern, or specifically anti-Jeroboam, polemic.[9] For some, that later editor is the Deuteronomist. So, for

---

called inconsistencies and doublets are the result of a literary scheme of contrasting scenes, but even he holds that an underlying chronological sequence (preserved, presumably, in Deuteronomy) has been disrupted by the addition of vv. 7–14 and later by vv. 25–29—an independent tradition that is pro-Levite and anti-Aaronide (559). For an attempt to read Exod 32 as an integral narrative employing episodic narrative techniques in its construction, see Herbert Chanan Brichto, "The Worship of the Golden Calf: A Literary Analysis of a Fable on Idolatry," *HUCA* 54 (1983): 1–44.

[7] Lewy states that Hezekian editors (his D) inserted vv. 7–14 as well as v. 34's veiled allusion to the fall of the northern kingdom in 722 ("Story of the Golden Calf," 321). For the view that Exod 32:7–14 is a D-block inserted into a J, or JE narrative, see J. Clinton McCann, "Exodus 32:1–14," *Int* 44 (1990): 277–80; and Childs, *Exodus*, 559.

[8] See Moses Aberbach and Leivy Smolar, "Aaron, Jeroboam and the Golden Calves," *JBL* 86 (1967): 129–40.

[9] See Aberbach and Smolar, "Aaron, Jeroboam and the Golden Calves," 140. See also Sigo Lehming, "Versuch zu Ex XXXII," *VT* 10 (1960): 1–50, for the notion of a many-layered narrative with additions responding to Jeroboam's cultic violation.

example, Brevard Childs holds that the Deuteronomistic editor of 1 Kings adjusted an existing golden calf story (probably J's) to place his polemic against Jeroboam at the heart of the Sinai narrative.[10] In this view, the *core* tradition of Exod 32 is pre-Deuteronomistic, but the story took on its final form in conjunction with the finalization of the Deuteronomistic history (including 1 Kgs 12). Many scholars, however, draw stronger conclusions from the literary similarities between Exod 32 and 1 Kgs 12. These scholars argue that the Deuteronomistic editor of Kings *created* the golden calf story in its entirety, inserting it into the Pentateuchal traditions to establish the opposition of Moses, the Levites, and God to the cultic activities of Jeroboam.[11] Implicit in this view is the idea that Exod 32 cannot be earlier than the Deuteronomistic history (and cannot be the model for Deut 9–10). The most extreme variation of this view is held by Van Seters, according to whom the Exodus account post-dates even the Deuteronomist.[12] Thus, establishing the priority of Exod 32 to Deut 9–10 requires that we establish the priority of Exod 32 to 1 Kgs 12. If we argue that Exod 32 in its entirety preceded and was the foundation for Deut 9–10 (i.e., Exod 32 is pre-D), then we will have to be able to argue plausibly that 1 Kgs 12, which postdates Deut 9–10, is also literarily dependent on Exod 32, rather than the reverse (and more widely accepted) position.

In this paper, I will argue:

a   that the Exod 32 narrative has a basic literary unity;
b   that literary unity neither requires nor assumes the lack of ambiguity, ambivalence, contradiction, and tension since these are tools of the narrative artist's trade;

---

[10] Childs, *Exodus*, 560.

[11] See Marvin A. Sweeney, "The Wilderness Traditions of the Pentateuch: A Reassessment of Their Function and Intent in Relation to Exodus 32–34," *SBLSP* 26 (1989): 291–99, esp. 294. See also Frederick Victor Winnett, *The Mosaic Tradition* (Toronto: University of Toronto Press, 1949). These scholars are making a claim of *literary* dependence rather than historical dependence: Exodus 32 as a *narrative account* attained its final form in response to the *narrative account* of Jeroboam's sin, as found in the Deuteronomistic History. For the simultaneity of Exod 32 and 1 Kgs 12 see also Lothar Perlitt, *Bundestheologie im Alten Testament* (WMANT 36; Neukirchen-Vluyn: Neukirchener, 1969), who views both Exod 32 and 1 Kgs 12 as compositions from the time of King Josiah (208).

[12] Van Seters, "Law and the Wilderness Rebellion Tradition"; and idem, *Life of Moses*, 290–318.

c   that Exod 32 in basically its current form was known by the
    author of Deut 9–10 and by the Deuteronomistic historian respon-
    sible for 1 Kgs 12 since both appropriate the story for distinct
    and diverse purposes;
d   that these claims can be supported by detailed textual evidence;
e   that these claims are further supported by post-biblical traditions
    of interpretation of Exod 32, whose similarities to Deut 9–10
    justify our characterization of the latter as the earliest midrash
    on Exod 32.

II. Exodus 32 as a Literary Unit

The golden calf story of Exod 32 is told in thirty-five verses. As
noted above, many critical scholars have been quick to point out
apparent contradictions, inconsistencies, and stylistic, thematic, and
ideological divergences in Exod 32; they are even quicker to conclude that these infelicities are symptomatic of a compositional patch-
work.[13] A more or less complete list of the phenomena seen as
disrupting the chapter's narrative unity and signaling distinct sources
would contain the following:[14]

a   *Verses 7–14 appear to anticipate subsequent events.* In these verses, Moses
    is told of the people's sin by God, but he later appears to "dis-
    cover" the sin, prompting a (delayed) reaction of anger. Why this
    furious outburst over a sin of which he has already been informed?
b   *Two prayers for forgiveness.* Moses petitions God successfully on
    Israel's behalf in v. 14. Why, then, must he petition God again
    in vv. 30–34? Moreover, on the first occasion, his prayer appears
    to be accepted while on the second occasion it is not.
c   *Forgiveness stands in tension with punishment.* Verses 14 and 15 depict
    Moses as successful in his first petition; yet punishment is meted
    out at the hands of the Levites in vv. 25ff. and later by God.
d   *Multiple punishments.* Three distinct punishments appear in the story:
    the slaughter by the Levites (vv. 25ff.), the plague (v. 35), and
    an unspecified future punishment (v. 34). If the forced drinking

---

[13] For a summary of various scholarly views see John I. Durham, *Exodus* (WBC
3; Waco, Tex.: Word, 1987), 417, 427–28, 435.
[14] This list is a conflation of items noted by a variety of scholars as disrupting
the narrative unity of Exod 32.

of the dust-strewn water (v. 20) is understood as a punishment
then the number is four.[15] These multiple punishments are construed as a sign of multiple sources.

e   *Two contradictory views of Aaron.* The role of Aaron is ambiguous
    in the story as a whole. Certain verses adopt a condemnatory
    stance toward Aaron, others are rather more neutral, and still
    others appear to exculpate him entirely.

f   *Two contradictory views of Moses.* Moses appears in some verses as
    a benign and patient leader pleading for mercy, and in others
    as an angry and impassioned prophet who vehemently punishes
    the Israelites and grudgingly intercedes for them.

g   *Two contradictory views of God.* In some verses, God appears to be
    benign and forgiving, while in others he is punitive and jealous,
    bent on the destruction of the people.[16]

h   *God's double speech in vv. 7–14.* Why would God's speech to Moses
    be divided into two sections, each introduced by a distinct verb
    of speaking, unless it consisted of two sources set side by side?

i   *Sequence of events contradicts the parallel account in Deuteronomy.* In the
    Exodus account, (i) God tells Moses of Israel's sin and of his plan
    of destruction; (ii) Moses prays; (iii) Moses descends from the
    mountain and sees the people sinning; (iv) Moses destroys the
    calf; and (v) Moses prays a second time. In the Deuteronomy
    account, the events are reported in the following order: (i) God
    reveals Israel's sin and his plan of destruction; (ii) Moses descends
    from the mountain (without first praying) and sees the people
    sinning; (iii) Moses prays forty days and nights; and (iv) Moses
    destroys the calf.

These phenomena are generally taken as evidence of a core text with
interpolations: a Deuteronomistic addition in vv. 7–14 based on the
prayer in Deut 9:26–29, and an independent tradition of a later period
in vv. 25–29 (the Levite episode).[17] Some scholars identify even more
strata,[18] while others posit the creation of the entire account by a

---

[15] See Brichto for a complex and ultimately unconvincing theory of the various
punishments and the different degrees of guilt punished by each ("Worship of the
Golden Calf," 15–16, 18–19).

[16] For these latter three items, see Lewy, "Story of the Golden Calf," 318–20.

[17] See, for example, Childs, *Exodus*, 559.

[18] See, for example, Lewy, "Story of the Golden Calf," 318; and Jacques Vermeylen,
"Les Sections Narratives de Deut 5–11 et leur relation à Ex 19–34," in *Das
Deuteronomium*, 174–207.

Deuteronomistic writer (e.g., Perlitt) or by a post-Deuteronomistic author (e.g., Van Seters). Despite their many differences, these scholarly accounts share the conviction that Exod 32 reached its *final* form in conjunction with or after the Deuteronomistic redaction of Deut 9–10.

None of the phenomena taken as evidence of narrative disunity and interpolation is probative. Close analysis reveals that Exod 32 functions well as a narrative unit, that putative interpolations are integral to the overall context and are not likely of late composition, and that the chronological sequence of Exod 32 has not been disrupted.

We begin with an examination of the narrative sequence of our story which extends from Exod 32:1 to Exod 33:6, then proceed to a consideration of the story's overall literary structure, before responding to each of points (a) through (i) above.

A. *Narrative sequence*

The story unfolds in a clear progression of shifting scenes reported through the perspectives of those present at or participating in each scene. Immediately (in a narrative sense) preceding our story, Moses ascends the mountain to receive God's teaching and commandments (Exod 24:12). Before leaving the people, Moses entrusts the leadership of the people to Aaron and Hur: "You have Aaron and Hur with you; let anyone who has a legal matter approach them" (Exod 24:14).

Exodus 25–31 contains the content of God's teaching and instructions. Exodus 31 ends with God's conclusion of the covenant with Moses on Mount Sinai and Moses' receipt of the two stone tablets of the covenant, inscribed by God—a sublime moment. Exodus 32:1 takes us from the peak of the mountain to its base. The reader may be privy to Moses' activity on behalf of Israel, but the Israelites are not. Moses has been gone some forty days, and this lengthy absence does not sit well with the people. The precise emotional state of the people (fear, anxiety, opportunistic treachery) is not revealed by the narrator. We learn only that, *from the people's point of view*, Moses appears to be long in coming down and that his prolonged absence leads to action on their part. They gather "against" Aaron—the preposition 'al implies a hostile and rebellious mob (cf. Num 16:3, 17:7, 20:2)—and charge him to make *'elohim* who shall go before them, since they do not know what has become of "that man" Moses who brought them out of Egypt.

The opening scene suggests that a central theme of this story is leadership. The people perceive that their leader is gone and may never return. They desire a new leader and turn to the interim authority designated by Moses in Exod 24:12–14 with their demand for *'elohim* to go before them now that Moses is gone. Scholars differ on the exact nature of the people's request. Do they request a new *human* leader or judge to replace Moses (cf. *'elohim* in Exod 21:6)? Or do they request some kind of divine being (cf. *'elohim* in Gen 1:27; Ps 8:6), angel (Gen 6:2, 4), or gods (Exod 18:11, 22:19; Deut 4:28; 2 Kgs 18:33) to replace YHWH? Quite apart from the fact that rebellion against Moses is, in the end, equivalent to rebellion against the God for whom he speaks, an answer to these questions would require a degree of precision that the text simply does not provide. On the contrary, the text hints equally at both possibilities. Moreover, the power and pathos of the request lies in its very ambiguity which suggests that this is a people that does not know what it wants or what is in its best interest. One gets the distinct impression that any *'elohim* will do. The reader hopes that a minimal rejection of Moses in favor of some other human leader is all that is intended, but our worst fears are confirmed when an idol is crafted and worshiped. We realize that rejection of Moses and rejection of God as the exclusive object of worship go hand in hand.

Aaron responds to those who have gathered against him by charging them to tear the gold rings from the ears of their wives and children and to deliver the rings to him. Aaron's motivations and intentions are not revealed to us (and more and less charitable interpretations are certainly possible)—again building suspense as we hope against hope that he will somehow thwart rather than fulfill the people's request. The wording of Aaron's command implies that he is addressing male heads of household only, telling them to plunder the gold from their own families. But in the fulfillment verse that follows, all the people tear off their own gold earrings and deliver them to Aaron, a subtle indication of the unseemly willingness of the entire community to participate in the construction of an idol. Verse 4 describing Aaron's activity with the gold is an exegetical crux that need not detain us.[19] Whether he fashioned the gold with

---

[19] For possible meanings of the phrase *vayyaṣar 'oto baḥereṭ*, see Childs, *Exodus*, 555–56; and Samuel E. Loewenstamm, "The Making and Destruction of the Golden Calf," *Bib* 48 (1967): 481–90.

an engraving tool or placed it in a cloak or bag to be deposited in a fire, one thing is clear: the narrator attributes the calf's manufacture to him—"he made it into a molten calf" (v. 4). Aaron is responsible for the existence of the calf.

It appears that the calf is then formally presented to the people, though by whom is not clear. The text states simply that "they" exclaimed: "These are your gods, O Israel, who brought you out of the land of Egypt." That Aaron is not among those making the presentation is implied by the following verse, which depicts him as something of an observer ("When Aaron saw this . . ."). The exclusion of Aaron from the presentation and declaration raises an interesting possibility. The group that presents the calf to the people may be pointing to Aaron and his calf jointly. Thus the plural form, *'elohim*, is entirely appropriate: These two, Aaron and his visible deity, rather than Moses and his invisible deity, are Israel's *'elohim*, who brought them out of Egypt. Once again, the overlordship of a deity and his chief "spokesman" go hand in hand.

For the second time, Aaron acts decisively, and for the second time his intentions and motivations are obscure to us. When Aaron sees what has happened—that the calf and possibly Aaron himself have been acclaimed leaders in place of Moses—he builds an altar before it (presumably the calf). This action suggests that he accedes to the people's acclamation of the calf and is ready to initiate a cult in its honor. After building the altar he announces that there will be a festival to YHWH on the morrow. Is this an effort to redirect the people away from the calf toward the worship of YHWH?[20] Again one senses that the narrator is stringing us along, raising the hope that all will yet be well. But alas, in the verse that follows, Aaron's feast to YHWH appears to be identical with the sacrifices, feasting, and dancing that occur before the calf (see also v. 19).[21] Thus, the more

---

[20] For interpretive traditions and critical scholarship vindicating Aaron see Leivy Smolar and Moshe Aberbach, "The Golden Calf Episode in Postbiblical Literature," *HUCA* 39 (1968): 91–116, esp. 109–12; Thomas Dozeman, "Moses: Divine Servant and Israelite Hero," *HAR* 8 (1984): 45–61, esp. 52–53; Roy L. Honeycutt, Jr., "Aaron, the Priesthood, and the Golden Calf," *RevExp* 74 (1977): 523–35, esp. 526–28; Brichto, "Worship of the Golden Calf," 11–15.

[21] Childs argues that Aaron is not evil so much as he is cultically confused, believing that the calf can be incorporated in a YHWH festival (*Exodus*, 556). However, according to the narrative, Aaron, like the other Israelites, heard the Ten Commandments not forty days earlier, including the prohibitions spelled out in Exod 20:3–5. That Aaron is strong-armed (or opportunistically drawn) into something he knows is wrong is consistent with a central theme of the story: leadership. Aaron fails to

likely interpretation is that Aaron is riding his calf to power, giving the people what they think they want—a version of YHWH they can see and touch.

There is nothing implausible about the suggestion that Aaron and the people do not seek to overthrow YHWH but instead associate the calf with YHWH in some way. Significantly, there has been no *conscious* rejection of YHWH in these opening verses. The people feel the absence of *Moses* who has walked before them until now, and they want another leader in *his* place. Aaron and his calf fit the bill, and if Aaron should choose to associate the calf with YHWH, why should anyone care? This is no less a sin, of course, and Aaron and the Israelites should have known better: they have heard explicit prohibitions against having other *'elohim* before God (Exod 20:3), against making and bowing down to the image of any creature in heaven, earth, or sea (Exod 20:4–5), and against the manufacture of *'elohim* of silver or gold (Exod 20:20). Thus, whatever their intentions toward YHWH, the people sin by violating his most basic and publicly declared stipulations against co-worship and against the manufacture and worship of images and idols. Scholarly attempts to rationalize the calf as simply an alternative vision of the legitimate worship of YHWH, whatever their *historical* merit, make no sense within the larger *narrative* context of our story.[22] According to the narrative, God has already clearly told the people that the actions undertaken in Exod 32 are prohibited.

This distressing scene leaves the reader in a state of high anxiety. We know that the actions of Aaron and the people are a serious breach of the terms of the covenant so painstakingly set forth by God in previous chapters and we immediately wonder: How will God respond? It is not jarring, then, to be returned to the mountaintop in v. 7 and to learn of God's reaction to the disastrous events that have just transpired. God tells Moses to hurry down from the mountain because—and here he almost petulantly mimics the people's mistaken conception—the people that *Moses brought out of Egypt* have acted corruptly. He details their sin—they have turned aside

---

exercise leadership, with disastrous consequences. Efforts to mitigate Aaron's guilt weaken a major thrust of the story.

[22] See Lloyd R. Bailey, "The Golden Calf," *HUCA* 42 (1971): 97–115 for a review of the scholarly assertion that (the historical) Aaron intended his calves as a "pedestal" for YHWH (like the cherubim) and that his actions reflect an ancient legitimate Yahwistic practice.

from the way that God enjoined upon them, violating God's specific prohibitions in chapter 20 by making a molten calf, worshiping and acclaiming it. God makes no mention of Aaron, thus setting up an information deficit that will motivate Moses' bitter "interrogation" of Aaron in vv. 21–24.

God's first speech (vv. 7–8) is followed by a second (vv. 9–10). Double speech of this type is rare in biblical dialogue, leading some critical scholars to posit a textual suture at this juncture. However, double speech is employed here, as elsewhere, to great rhetorical effect.[23] Moses' failure to respond between God's two speeches suggests a kind of paralysis. Moses' forty days of divine instruction end with a harsh dismissal because the very people for whom the instruction is intended have corrupted themselves and are worshiping a molten calf! Could Moses be anything but dumbstruck, shocked into inaction by the nightmarish news? And so God speaks again, perhaps in an effort to prompt Moses into action.[24] Denouncing the Israelites as a stiff-necked people, he announces his intention to destroy them utterly and to begin again with Moses. Significantly, however, God prefaces this announcement with a directive to Moses to leave him (God) alone—a directive that requires further scrutiny.

Why does God say, "*Now let me be* that my anger may blaze forth against them and I may destroy them, and make of you a great nation?" God surely does not *need* to ask leave of Moses before destroying the Israelites, nor presumably can he be constrained by Moses' efforts to block him. Perhaps the words, "Now let me be," signal to Moses that he does have some say in the matter. If he does indeed let God be—if he does not in some way interfere or argue—then Moses will in effect signal his implicit acceptance of God's plan to

---

[23] See, for example, 1 Sam 17:34–37, where David seeks Saul's consent to fight Goliath by bragging that he will kill the Philistine just as he used to strike down the wild bears and lions that threatened his father's flock. David's unseemly arrogance is met by a deafening silence. David adjusts his line of argument and speaks a second time, more humbly: "The Lord who saved me from lion and bear will also save me from that Philistine," to which Saul responds, "Then go and may the Lord be with you." Employing double speech with no intervening response on the part of David's interlocutor, the narrator subtly signals Saul's initial disapproval and David's subsequent realization that humility would serve him better than bravado. For a discussion of this passage and other instances of double speech in biblical and rabbinic texts, see Bernard Septimus, "Iterated Quotation Formulae in Talmudic Narrative and Exegesis," in the present volume.

[24] This understanding of God's second speech is widespread in rabbinic literature (see, for example, *Exod. Rab.* 42:2, 9).

do away with the Israelites and to begin again with Moses himself. Another man might have been tempted; Moses is not.

In short, the double speech of God is not the result of two carelessly juxtaposed sources. The two speeches function together to generate the dramatic highpoint of the entire story, for in the interstice between these two speeches, we sense that Israel's fate hangs in the balance and Moses—the only hope for Israel's salvation—stands frozen and unresponding. God's hint that the very survival of the nation depends on Moses ("Now let me be so that I can destroy them!") is enough to rouse him to action after his initial shock, and indeed in v. 11 we read, "But Moses implored the LORD his God, saying 'Let not your anger, O LORD, blaze forth against your people. . . .'" Moses argues at length and in the end he succeeds. Precisely by *not* letting God be, Moses ensures the survival of the nation—for the nonce. God renounces his plan of *immediate and total* destruction of the Israelites.

It must be emphasized that we are very far from any kind of resolution at this point in the story. Moses has done no more than secure a stay of immediate execution. He has not asked for, nor obtained, forgiveness, nor has he secured a promise that the Israelites will not be punished for their deed. He has simply stopped God from the furious and wholesale destruction of the people while they are engaged in their sin. He does this by appealing to God's vanity (if you kill them, others will view you as an evil God who planned all along to destroy the Israelites) and conscience (if you kill them, you will not be able to fulfill your promise to the patriarchs). Like a parent calming an angry spouse ready to lash out at a disobedient child, Moses seeks to assuage God's anger so that a more reasonable and fitting course of action can be decided upon in a quieter moment.

Having secured this stay of execution, Moses has bought the time he needs to deal with the situation first hand. On the mountaintop, Moses experienced only shock and then panic at the thought that God might indeed destroy the people. He played the role appropriate to him in God's presence—assuaging God's anger and pleading for constraint. Now he turns from God to face the people and, carrying the tablets, descends from the mountain. Verses 15–18 continue the narrative suspense characteristic of the opening episodes. During his descent, Moses first hears the sounds of the people's revelry, then sees their folly with his own eyes. Freed from the pacifying role forced upon him on the mountaintop, his own anger, which grew with his perception of the situation, bursts forth. He casts the tablets from his hand, and in v. 20, seizes and utterly destroys the calf—forcing the Israelites to drink water upon which the calf's dust has been strewn.[25]

Moses' first and most immediate task—to halt the sin by destroying the calf—has been accomplished. But before he can seek God's forgiveness and reconciliation, he must restore order and ensure that such a sin will not happen again. If a failure in leadership contributed to the problem, that failure will have to be addressed. Moses seeks out Aaron, the leader designated in Moses' absence.

Verses 21–24 are the second dramatic highpoint of the story as the spotlight shifts to Aaron. Aaron, whose intentions and motivations in the opening scene were obscure, must explain himself and answer for his actions. In v. 21 Moses asks: "What did this people do to you that you have brought such great sin upon them?" Moses is not conducting an investigation, seeking information that will enable him to determine whether or not Aaron is culpable, as many commentators suppose.[26] Aaron's culpability is clearly a *foregone conclusion* for Moses (he believes that Aaron has brought a "great sin upon them"), and thus his words are more accusatory than interrogative: What possible excuse can there be for your having jeopardized everything? As the leader of the moment, Aaron should have done whatever was necessary to prevent the sin. The only motivation Moses can conjure for Aaron's failure to stop the people is vengeance, hence his angry and disgusted question: What evil did they do to you that you repaid them in this fashion, allowing them to sin so seriously that they will surely be destroyed? One senses that the query is rhetorical—there can be no justification for endangering the lives of those in one's charge.

Aaron's response holds the interpretative key to his character in the opening scene: "Let not my LORD be enraged; you know that this people is bent on evil." Offering no apology and assuming no responsibility for his failure to prevent the sin, Aaron places the blame squarely on the people. There *is* no stopping this people, Aaron avers, ironically echoing God's pronouncement that the Israelites are a stiff-necked people deserving destruction. In vv. 23 and 24, Aaron recounts the events that transpired while Moses was on the mountaintop. The similarities and differences between Aaron's account

---

[25] For a full discussion of this verse and its ancient Near Eastern parallels, see the excellent article by Begg, "The Destruction of the Calf."

[26] See, for example, Lewy, "Story of the Golden Calf"; Brichto, "Worship of the Golden Calf"; and Honeycutt, "Aaron, the Priesthood, and the Golden Calf."

and the narrator's account of the opening scene are significant and help to bring interpretative closure to the ambiguity surrounding Aaron's activities in vv. 1–6. Childs writes:

> When Aaron relates the role of the people, he repeats *verbatim* the entire dialogue as recorded in v. 1 along with its demand for other gods and the abusive reference to Moses. When he comes then to his own role in gathering the gold, the account is considerably abbreviated and minimizes Aaron's own role. The people bring the gold of their own accord, as if it had not been requested by him. When he reaches the crucial point on the actual construction of the calf, Aaron's story diverges completely from the original account. He pictures himself uninvolved. The calf came out all by itself.[27]

This truncated version downplays Aaron's agency. Omitted are any references to the altar and the feast—all instigated by Aaron. In short, Aaron seeks to exonerate himself while condemning the people, and we are led to suspect that his intentions were dishonorable from the outset. A sympathetic reading of Aaron's activity in vv. 1–6 is all but precluded following his pusillanimous effort at self-defense in vv. 22–24. Our hopes for Aaron die in this speech and the contrast between Aaron and Moses is extreme, as Childs discerns:

> Moreover, the fact that Aaron commences his defense with a broad condemnation of the people as evil by nature and ends up disavowing any responsibility for himself, hardly speaks well for Aaron . . . [and] serves merely to highlight by contrast the role of the true mediator. Aaron saw the people "bent on evil;" Moses defended them before God's hot anger (v. 11). Aaron exonerated himself from all active involvement; Moses put his own life on the line for Israel's sake. Aaron was too weak to restrain the people; Moses was strong enough to restrain even God.[28]

Moses is not fooled—he sees that Aaron is a weak and unfit leader who has brought a great sin on the people. Verse 25 captures the triangulation of false leadership, illicit cult-images, and mass chaos leading to self-destruction so central to our story:[29] "Moses saw that the people were out of control—since Aaron had let them get out of control—so that they were a menace to any who might oppose

---

[27] Childs, *Exodus*, 570.
[28] Ibid.
[29] So Stuart Lasine, "Reading Jeroboam's Intentions: Intertextuality, Rhetoric, and History in 1 Kings 12," in *Reading Between Texts: Intertextuality and the Hebrew Bible* (ed. D. N. Fewell; Louisville: Westminster John Knox, 1992), 133–52, esp. 146.

them."[30] The people are out of control because Aaron their leader allowed them to get out of control, creating a situation of extra-ordinary danger for any who might now try to quell the crowd and exert control. And yet this is precisely what Moses undertakes to do in vv. 26–29.

Moses needs assistance and rallies to his side all those who are "for the LORD." The Levites come running, and Moses issues a ter-rible command (v. 27): "He said to them, 'Thus says the LORD, the God of Israel: Each of you put sword on thigh, go back and forth from gate to gate throughout the camp, and slay brother, neighbor, and kin.'" The idiom, "Thus says the LORD," occurs rarely in the Penta-teuch and is generally reserved for prophetic pronouncements that fol-low upon a direct revelation to the prophet by God. Yet here we have no record of God's instructions to Moses; indeed, the quick transition from Moses' shrewd assessment of the danger he faces (v. 25) to the emergency measure spelled out in vv. 26–27 implies that Moses has hatched this plan on his own. This suspicion is confirmed by the narrator's statement in v. 28: "The Levites did as *Moses* had bid-den." The command, it would appear, issues from Moses, not God.

What is the purpose of the slaughter? Pre-modern and modern commentators alike have interpreted the Levites' slaughter as a pun-ishment of the guilty. For example:

> [The command is to] come from all directions hither and thither, pass-ing to and fro ... from one end of the camp to the other ... [to] put to death all those who, you know of a certainty sinned, in connection with the calf, either because you were actually witnesses, or because they were found guilty by the ordeal of drinking; spare no one, even if he be your brother, or companion, or neighbour. It is better that a few Israelites lose their lives than that the entire people should perish.[31]

There is no indication in the text that the purpose of the slaughter is punitive. Moses does not charge the Levites to kill those who are surely guilty, *even* one's close kin and neighbor. He simply charges the Levites to kill brother, neighbor, and kin. In all likelihood, Moses

---

[30] The phrase *lešimṣah beqamehem* is an exegetical crux. *Beqamehem* refers to those who would "stand against" or "oppose" them. The root *šmṣ* means "to whisper"; the noun *šimṣah* may refer to derision. The idea, perhaps, is that the people are so unruly as (foolishly) to deride any who oppose them.

[31] Umberto Cassuto, *A Commentary on the Book of Exodus* (trans. I. Abrahams; Jeru-salem: Magnes, 1967), 421.

seeks to identify persons zealous for God and so capable of imposing order on the chaotic mob.[32]

If this reading seems odd, consider again the scene immediately preceding the Levite episode. Moses has confronted Aaron with his culpability for the dreadful sin and mass rioting of the people, only to find that even now he cannot rely on Aaron for assistance. Moreover, Moses observes that the people will oppose any who might try to quell them. Clearly he will need help to impose order on the unruly mob, and that help will have to come from persons of a fierce and fearless nature. And so his plan: whoever is for the LORD come to me, he cries, and simultaneously prove yourselves and bring an end to the anarchy with a demonstration of zeal in God's name— a deadly and random slaughter of your own flesh and blood. The gruesome deed done, Moses acclaims and installs the Levites as the true servants of God. In short, the Levite episode is not simply a punishment inflicted upon the guilty, as is widely assumed. It is a desperate—and apparently successful—effort by Moses at crowd control.[33] And it is the central episode in what turns out to be a cautionary tale regarding the critical importance of fit leaders: without effective leaders the slide toward moral chaos and mob rule is inevitable, a slide halted only by the extreme and brutal violence of zealots. The Levites may be blessed for their deed (v. 29), but the reader senses that any society that has fallen so far into riotous abandon as to require the violent imposition of order by leaders of this type is more cursed than blessed.[34]

The violence brings an end to the people's riotous behavior. With the calf eliminated, Aaron rebuked, and order reimposed, the task of reconciliation can begin. On the following day, Moses addresses the

---

[32] Leslie Brisman observes that Moses has not specified the guilty as the object of slaughter and suggests that the Levites are being asked to display their zeal for God ("Sacred Butchery: Exodus 32:25–29," in *Theological Exegesis: Essays in honor of Brevard S. Childs* [ed. C. Seitz and K. Greene-McCreight; Grand Rapids: Eerdmans, 1999], 166).

[33] It is possible that the interpretation of the Levite episode as a punishment of the guilty is influenced by Num 25:1–13. But the differences between this story and our own are important. In Numbers, the narrator clearly informs us that God commands Moses to have the ringleaders killed. Moses then turns to the officials, or elders, and tells each to slay those of his men who are guilty of attaching themselves to Baal-Peor. In Exod 32, there is no instruction from God and no reference to guilt or innocence, suggesting again that a display of violence—more effective if random—is intended.

[34] For a critique of standard readings of the Levite episode as a positive piece of propaganda written to promote Levite interests, see Brisman, "Sacred Butchery," 178–81.

people: "You have been guilty of a great sin. Yet I will now go up to the LORD; perhaps I may win forgiveness for your sin." Verses 31–34 contain the dialogue between Moses and God over the appropriate course of action with regard to the Israelites. Moses plays the part of intercessor confessing the people's sin openly and honestly (v. 31: "Alas, this people is guilty of a great sin in making for themselves a god of gold") but asking for forbearance. Indeed, he would strike a bargain with God: "Now, if you will forgive their sin [well and good]; but if not, erase me from the record which You have written" (v. 32). Moses' words here are a masterful inversion of God's own proposal to destroy the Israelites and save Moses alive. Moses makes it clear that he is no Aaron—exonerating himself at the expense of the people. Knowing that the people have sinned terribly, he attempts no apology or defense (indeed there is none), but neither does he conclude that the people are incorrigibly stiff-necked (v. 9) or, with Aaron, that the people are disposed to evil (v. 22). Israel's only chance is forgiveness, and Moses stakes his life on that single chance.

Moses' prayer for total forgiveness does not, in fact, succeed. God will not forgive but neither will he destroy the people wholesale: "He who has sinned against Me, him only will I erase from My record" (v. 33). A just enough resolution—death for the guilty, resumption of the covenant relationship with those who remain—and Moses rests his case. God promises to settle accounts at some future date (v. 34). Although some scholars read the promise of a future punishment as a veiled allusion to the destruction of the northern kingdom, the immediate *narrative* fulfillment of this promise is spelled out in the very next verse—God sent a plague to punish the people (v. 35).

But God is not finished. In an ironic reversal of the people's illicit desire for 'elohim to go before them (Exod 32:1), God announces that he will no longer go before the people himself but will appoint an angel for the task (v. 34). God's withdrawal from the Israelites is the central theme of the next two chapters in Exodus. In Exod 33:4 the news is greeted with mourning and removal of ornaments, prompting repeated efforts by Moses to regain God's direct and unmediated leadership (33:12–34:9). Ultimately God relents (34:10–12), but in so doing he makes it clear that his presence requires complete and total abstinence from the gods and cultic practices of other peoples, lest the blessing of that presence be rendered a curse.

The preceding analysis reveals a tightly organized and coherent unity. The story unfolds in an orderly fashion: (1) the appointment

of an interim leader (Exod 24:12–14); (2) the failure of that leader
to thwart the people's sinful activity (32:1–6); (3) God's impassioned
threat to destroy the entire nation for their sin (vv. 7–10); and (4)
Moses' success in securing a stay of execution (vv. 11–14) prior to
returning to deal with the people (vv. 15–18), halt their idolatry (vv.
19–20), ascertain the failure of leadership (vv. 21–25), and reassert
control over the menacing mob through a display of violence (vv.
26–29)—a less than ideal course of action but one that threatens
inevitably when leaders fail to prevent anarchy. In the ensuing quiet,
(5) Moses reaches a negotiated settlement (vv. 30–32) that includes
punishment of the guilty and God's partial withdrawal from those
remaining (32:33–35; 33:1–3), now chastened and stripped of their
finery (33:4–6). (6) After subsequent intense negotiations, God resumes
his place at the head of the community (34:10–12).

The unity of the story is reinforced by recurring motifs and literary
linkages between the story's episodes. The motif of the Exodus from
Egypt recurs seven times (32:1, 4, 7, 8, 11, 23; 33:1). In addition,
as Dozeman observes, the verb of seeing (r'y) is used in connection
with each of the *dramatis personae* in order to present the point of
view of each throughout the narrative (32:1, the people; 32:5, Aaron;
32:9, God; 32:19 and 25, Moses), and an overall chronological framework is provided by temporal indicators: tomorrow (32:5), the next
morning (32:6), this/that day (32:28, 29), and the next day (32:30).[35]

B. *Overall literary structure*

I have argued that the narrative elements of our story signal a concern with the theme of leadership and the devastating consequences
of failed leadership—a point that is not fully appreciated by most
commentators. Further support for the claim that leadership is a central theme in Exod 32 may be adduced from an examination of the
overall literary structure of the chapter. As Ralph Hendrix has shown,
our chapter can be viewed as a chiastic series of units, whose pivot
point is none other than the Levite episode.[36]

---

[35] Dozeman, "Moses: Divine Servant and Israelite Hero," 48–49.
[36] Ralph E. Hendrix, "A Literary Structural Analysis of the Golden-Calf Episode
in Ex 32:1–33:6," *AUSS* 28 (1990): 211–17.

A   32:1–6 People act, and Aaron (YHWH's High Priest) reacts
   B   32:7–10 God's two utterances *vayedabber, vayyo'mer*
     C   32:11–14 Moses intercedes
       D   32:15–20 Moses goes down the mountain
         E   32:21–25 Judgment: investigative phase
           F   32:26a OPPORTUNITY FOR REPENTANCE
         E`   32:26b–29 Judgment: executive phase
       D`   32:30 Moses goes up the mountain
     C`   32:31–32 Moses intercedes
   B`   32:33–33:3 God's two utterances *vayyo'mer, vayeddaber*
A`   33:4–6 God acts and People react[37]

According to Hendrix, action and reaction are inverted in A and A`.[38] In A the people request *'elohim*, and Aaron, God's priest, reacts by taking their ornaments and making a calf. In A` God warns the people of the dangers of a jealous *'elohim* in their midst and tells them to remove their ornaments. Sections B and B` contain double speeches by God which are parallel both formally and substantively. The formal parallelism occurs with the inversion of two verbs of speech (*vayeddaber, vayyo'mer* of B becomes *vayyo'mer, vayeddaber* in B`). Substantively, both *vayeddaber* speeches refer to "the people whom you brought from the land of Egypt" and both *vayyo'mer* speeches concern the destruction/punishment God will mete out upon the people. In sections C and C`, Moses intercedes for the people before God, the first time requesting a stay of execution, the second time requesting total forgiveness. Sections D and D` feature an inverse parallelism. In D, Moses goes down the mountain and breaks the tablets. In D`, Moses goes up the mountain in the hope of restoring the people to God.

    Hendrix describes the three central sections (E, E`, and the pivot point F) as forming a unit of judgment consisting of an investigative stage (E) in which Moses seeks information in order to assess the sin of the people, and an executive stage (E`) in which Moses instigates the punishment of execution. Sandwiched between these phases (F) is his call for those faithful to God. Thus, the pivot point of the entire chapter is Moses' cry, "Whoever is for the LORD, come

---

[37] Ibid., 212.
[38] This summary is based on, but is not a full representation of, Hendrix's analysis.

to me!" which Hendrix reads as an implicit assertion of the opportunity for repentance in the midst of the judgment process.

While I accept Hendrix's analysis of the literary structure of our story, I do not agree with his interpretation of sections E, F and E`. Hendrix's reading assumes that (1) Moses' question in v. 21 is genuinely investigative; (2) Moses' question is directed at assessing the sin of the people; and (3) the Levites' action is punitive. However, Moses is not seeking to determine whether, or why, the people have sinned. He has no doubt that the people have sinned and, as argued above, he equally has no doubt that Aaron is responsible. His words in v. 21 are more *cri-de-coeur* than question—What could they possibly have done to you, Aaron, that would provoke you to such irresponsible endangerment of their lives!? Aaron's response makes it clear that he will be of no assistance in restoring order, and Moses turns to fierce zealots to halt the anarchy by a show of force. Restoring order, not punishing the guilty, is the primary narrative function of the Levites' actions.[39] Understood in this way, Moses' cry in v. 26a is not a call for repentance but a call for reinforcements in his struggle against the mob. Below is a modified description of E, F, and E` to replace that of Hendrix.

> E 32:21–25 Failure of Aaron's leadership confirmed—total anarchy observed
>   F 32:26a Call for those zealous for the Lord
> E` 32:26b–29 Reassertion of control through brutality—anarchy ceases

Hendrix is absolutely correct in identifying Exod 32:26a ("Whoever is for the LORD, come to me!") as the central element and turning point in our story. However, whether this "turning point" is acme or nadir is precisely the question. Those who interpret the Levites' action as an execution of the guilty have with rare exception argued for a positive interpretation of the deed:[40] the Levites display a heroic fortitude in their execution of the guilty—including friends and family

---

[39] That the Levites killed only guilty persons is not inconceivable and certainly not inconsistent with my claim that the *primary* narrative function of this episode is the reassertion of authority in a state of anarchy. However, in my view there is no clear textual evidence for interpreting the Levite episode as punitive. The narrator's ambiguity—or silence—on this point suggests that it is not a significant feature of the episode.

[40] For a negative interpretation, see Brisman, "Sacred Butchery."

members—and by eliminating the guilty they pave the way for reconciliation with God. I have already suggested that this reading of the Levites' activity is not persuasive, if only because (a) Moses (not God) commands the killing of friends and family without reference to guilt, and (b) the punishment of the people occurs later in v. 35. I am inclined to understand this "turning point" as a nadir—toward which the story has inexorably tended from the very first. The failure of a community's legitimate leaders to exercise authority responsibly results in anarchy, which can be ended only by resort to brutality and violence. The Levites may indeed be heroes, blessed for their role in restoring the community to order, but they are dark heroes whose services—one hopes—will not be required in the future.

Thus, from the point of view of both narrative structure and overall literary structure, Exod 32:1–33:6 forms a tightly organized and coherent unity that thematizes the connection between false leadership, illicit cult images, and social anarchy.[41] The narratological and structural coherence of the chapter makes the identification of interpolations a dubious endeavor. Moreover, linguistic resonances with material in Deuteronomy are not determinative of Deuteronomistic provenance. As Anthony Phillips has argued, the Tetrateuch contains material that foreshadows what comes to be known as Deuteronomistic but should itself be identified as proto-Deuteronomistic (e.g., the hortatory anti-Canaanite epilogue in Exod 23:20–33 anticipates rather than presupposes Deuteronomistic theology).[42] Thus, Exod 32:7–14, often assigned to the Deuteronomistic school, contains language and themes scattered throughout the Tetrateuch (cf. Num 14:13–19) and is simply not demonstrably Deuteronomistic. Finally, our literary analysis suggests that the structural and narrative focal point of the story is 32:26a. Yet v. 26a occurs in the very unit (vv. 25–29, the Levite episode) perceived by the vast majority of scholars as a late addition inserted to justify the role of the Levites in the later Judean state, or as propaganda against the northern kingdom. Against this widespread perception, the structural and narrative centrality of this unit must be asserted. Far from being a late insertion, the Levite episode may well have been an integral component of the story from its inception.[43]

---

[41] On this connection see Lasine, "Reading Jeroboam's Intentions," 146–47.

[42] See Anthony Phillips, "A Fresh Look at the Sinai Pericope," *VT* 39 (1984): 282–94, esp. 292.

[43] Supporting this claim is the parallelism that obtains between the Levites' zealous

C. *Response to points (a) through (i) in Section II above*

We are now in a position to address those features of the text construed by scholars as symptoms of narrative disunity and interpolation.

a. *Verses 7–14 do not anticipate subsequent events*
God's revelation of the people's sin does not anticipate Moses' first-
hand witnessing of the people's activity in vv. 15–19 nor is Moses'
outburst of anger in vv. 19–20 jarring and unmotivated. On the
mountaintop, Moses is shocked by the news of Israel's sin, but in the
face of God's destructive fury he has but one clear course of action—
he must contain God's raging anger long enough to turn the people
around and effect a reconciliation. Once this goal is achieved he leaves
God and turns toward the people. When confronted with the full vision
of the people's folly he, like God, is outraged and acts accordingly.

b. *There are not two prayers for forgiveness, one apparently successful and*
one not
Moses' two prayers serve entirely different functions. Only the second prayer is a prayer for forgiveness. Indeed, only the second prayer
could be a prayer for forgiveness, since the people are still actively
sinning at the time of Moses' first conversation with God. In his first
conversation Moses seeks no more than a stay of execution before
restoring order and returning to God to petition for forgiveness.

c. *Forgiveness does not stand in tension with punishment*
Since vv. 14 and 15 do not constitute a prayer for forgiveness, there
is no tension between forgiveness and punishment in the story. God
does not forgive Israel in v. 15 only to retract this forgiveness in
v. 33 and execute punishment in v. 35 as some scholars claim. In
v. 15 God merely renounces his plan to summarily obliterate the
entire nation and begin again with Moses.

d. *The story does not feature multiple punishments*
As argued above, two of the punishments identified by scholars are
not best understood as punishments. As Begg has shown, the forced
drinking of the dust-strewn water (v. 20) is the final step in a series

---

response to Moses' call for supporters and the people's zealous response to Aaron's
call for a feast. See further Perlitt, who also disputes the view of Exod 32:25–29
as an addition (*Bundestheologie*, 209).

of eliminative acts attested in cognate literatures and may be viewed
as something of an ancient literary topos.[44] Moreover, as I have
argued, the slaughter by the Levites is not clearly a slaughter of the
guilty but a demonstration of zeal that serves to bring the anarchists
to order. Finally, the unspecified punishment mentioned in v. 34 ("I
will bring them to account for their sins") is in all likelihood identical with, rather than distinct from, the plague mentioned in v. 35.

Nevertheless, to play devil's advocate for a moment, let us suppose that we do have four discrete punishments in our story. Does
the existence of multiple punishments point to disparate sources? Not
necessarily. There is biblical precedent for multiple punishments. In
Num 25:1–13, some sinners are put to the sword, while others are
killed by a plague. The integration of the two punishments (the
plague is halted by the zealot Phineas's slaughter) suggests that they
do not derive from juxtaposed sources. Moreover, in Num 25, the
two punishments serve distinct purposes: the slaughter is directed at
the ringleaders while the plague smites the people generally (a distinction imported into Exod 32 by commentators).

e. *Although Aaron's intentions are ambiguous, there are not here two contradictory
views of Aaron—one innocent and exonerated, the other guilty and condemned*
Many scholars are misled by the narrator's suspenseful suppression
of detail in vv. 1–6 into supposing that Aaron is blameless or even
righteous. Thus, Honeycutt refers to certain suggestions of innocence
in vv. 1–6, which imply that the sin was caused by Moses' delay
and was initiated by the people, and that Aaron may even have
remained faithful to God.[45] Likewise, Lewy reads v. 5, in which
Aaron builds an altar and calls for a festival to YHWH, as an excul-
pation of Aaron inserted by a later hand. Moreover, Lewy describes
Moses as asking Aaron in balanced language why he committed this
great sin and Aaron as providing a factual account of the responsibility of the people.[46] Brichto construes Moses' silence after Aaron's
explanation as consent: Moses accepts Aaron's story as factual and
so must the reader—the calf miraculously emerged from the fire
with no effort on Aaron's part (despite the narrator's ascription of
the manufacture of the calf to Aaron in vv. 4 and 35).[47] Honeycutt

---

[44] Begg, "Destruction of the Calf," 231–33.
[45] Honeycutt, "Aaron, the Priesthood, and the Golden Calf," 527.
[46] Lewy, "Story of the Golden Calf," 319.
[47] Brichto, "Worship of the Golden Calf," 13.

even claims that the phrasing of Moses' question in v. 20 projects Aaron's innocence because it assumes instigation by the people and that v. 35 blames the people rather than Aaron for the sin.[48]

Such interpretations are difficult to sustain. There is nothing balanced about Moses' speech to Aaron in v. 21, as indicated by Aaron's immediate plea that Moses not be angry. Moreover, far from projecting Aaron's innocence and the people's guilt, Moses *assumes* Aaron's guilt. As for the opening scene, Aaron builds his altar before "it," i.e., the calf, so that the subsequent declaration of a feast to YHWH implicitly associates YHWH with the calf in some way (an act clearly prohibited in the recent narrative past). To argue that Aaron was merely engaged in an alternative and once-normative practice of YHWH worship through a bull-calf is to construe a narrative question as a historical question. The question is not whether the *historical* ancient Israelites once employed bulls in their worship of God, and whether this story might reflect the *historical* Aaron's innocent desire to continue this practice. The question before us is whether the *narrative* Israelites who have been prohibited from such practices can be understood as doing anything other than following their basest instincts in total disregard of these prohibitions, and whether the *narrative* Aaron, who is also fully cognizant of the prohibited nature of these acts, can be understood as doing anything other than facilitating the people in their sin. In the context of the *narrative*, the answer must be negative; the context makes it extraordinarily difficult to argue the *legitimacy* of Aaron's behavior.[49]

Nevertheless, the narrator allows a high degree of ambiguity regarding Aaron's intentions and motivations—hence the tendency of so many commentators to construe Aaron's actions as innocently as possible—and so creates a state of suspense that is resolved only later, in the critical encounter between Moses and Aaron (vv. 21–24).[50] In the light of vv. 21–25, the ambiguity of vv. 1–6 evaporates: Aaron's actions can no longer be construed as efforts to thwart, stall, or redirect the people. Though the narrator teases us into hoping that Aaron's actions will be explained in due time, *ultimately* there is

---

[48] Honeycutt, "Aaron, the Priesthood, and the Golden Calf," 527.

[49] For a critique of the claim that our story reflects an older and once-normative practice of YHWH worship through a bull-calf, see Bailey, "The Golden Calf," 98–101.

[50] Cf. Brichto, "Worship of the Golden Calf," 5 n. 2.

only Aaron, weak and misguided, acceding to, and facilitating the fulfillment of, the people's demands.

Efforts to vindicate Aaron are generally driven by extra-textual considerations. It is often assumed that since Aaron goes on to become high priest of Israel, the biblical writer is compelled to exonerate him. Thus Brichto writes:

> The logic of Aaron's role in history and the logic of the narrator's placement within the account of how he attained that role, require that Aaron emerge from this narrative as its hero, at best, or blameless, at the least, and it is as such that the narrator contrives to present him.[51]

Moreover, some argue that since Aaron escapes punishment he must have been innocent after all and thus his words in vv. 22–24 must be read as a genuine apology. Neither of these two assumptions is correct. First, there are no flawless heroes in the biblical corpus, and future greatness does not serve retrospectively to justify the actions of biblical heroes. Judah, Saul, David, Simeon, Levi, and Moses himself, are guilty of error and in some cases egregious sin. King David, who founds the line of Israel's kings, is guilty of the capital crimes of adultery and murder. The biblical narrator demonstrates no consistent propensity to cover up the sins of Israel's heroes. Moreover, that Aaron is not executed is no guarantee that the narrator or even God holds him blameless (as is clear from the case of David). If we free ourselves from the prejudice (i.e., the dogma) that Israel's future high priest must be virtuous and from the idea that the absence of punishment means innocence and read the textual clues provided by the narrator, we see that Aaron stands condemned and shamed.

f. *There are not here two contradictory views of Moses*
Moses' character is complex but far from contradictory. As in so many pentateuchal stories, Moses plays the dual role incumbent upon him as the people's defender and intercessor and as God's servant charged with carrying his covenant to the recalcitrant Israelites. True to this dual role, Moses rails against the people for their sinful rejection of YHWH only to plead on their behalf for total forgiveness a few verses later. Dozeman writes:

---

[51] Ibid., 13.

[Exodus 32's] narrative focuses on Moses as ideal mediator. The contradictory functions of Moses, pleading to Yahweh for Israel's survival and purging Israel for Yahweh, are not to be explained simply as the result of separate narratives. On the contrary, Ex 32 accentuates these conflicting roles by presenting the devotion of Moses to Yahweh and to Israel with equal intensity through the qualities of justice, violence, and prudence.[52]

g. *There are not here two contradictory views of God*

The idea that Exod 32 contains two contradictory views of God, one punitive and destructive and the other benign and forgiving, stems from a misreading of vv. 7–14 as a prayer for forgiveness. The declaration in v. 14 that God renounced the evil he planned to do to the people is therefore construed as God's having forgiven the Israelites. But Moses' prayer for forgiveness occurs at the end of the story, after the sinful calf has been destroyed and order restored. In vv. 7–14 Moses intercedes in order to secure a stay of execution. It is *this* "evil"—the summary destruction of the entire nation except for Moses—that God renounces. He has not, however, forgiven the people, nor has he renounced the idea of punishment for the guilty. He simply agrees to wait while Moses descends from the mountain to deal with the situation as best he can. Thus there is no portrait of God as benign and forgiving in this story at all.

However, God is not entirely static in this narrative either. His attitude to the Israelites shifts in predictable ways in response to the actions taken by Moses and the people. Thus we see God move from a deity provoked to destroy his people because of their great sin to a deity who destroys only the guilty. This is not a great contrast, or even a contradiction, but a natural evolution, well-motivated by the narrative events of Moses' intercession and refusal to abandon the people, the elimination of the sin and restoration of order, and the display of zeal by certain loyalists.

h. *God's double speech in vv. 7–14 creates the first, and more powerful, of two dramatic highpoints in our chapter*

The double speech of God is not the result of carelessly juxtaposed sources. The two speeches function together to generate a dramatic highpoint by underscoring Moses' paralysis as the nation stands on

---

[52] Dozeman, "Moses: Divine Servant and Israelite Hero," 59.

the brink of destruction. Moreover, from a literary perspective these verses seem to function as a well-crafted unit, balancing God's double speech in 32:33–33:3.

i. *Differences in the sequence of events reported in the Exodus and Deuteronomy accounts are due to non-chronological organizational principles at work in Deuteronomy*

The context of the golden calf story in Deuteronomy makes it clear that chronological sequence is deliberately disturbed for reasons having to do with the larger argument attributed to Moses at this juncture in the nation's history. Independent of any comparison with Exodus, the sequence of events in Deuteronomy is illogical (e.g., is it reasonable to suppose that Moses destroys the calf only after his forty-day prostration in prayer?). Scholars have erred in privileging the chronological sequence evidenced in Deuteronomy so as to identify interpolations in the Exodus account. For example, scholars have asserted that the prayer represented in Exod 32:7–14 must be a later (Deuteronomistic) interpolation into an original narrative which, like the Deuteronomy account, lacked any prayer at this point. However, once we acknowledge that the Deuteronomy account is not chronologically organized and does not preserve a more original narrative core, and that the omission/modification of this prayer serves the hortatory agenda of the Deuteronomist, we realize that the sequence of events depicted in Deuteronomy should not be taken as the standard in comparison to which the Exodus account may be deemed a deviation (see below).

In sum, the narratological and literary evidence adduced by scholars in support of the claim that Exod 32 is a pastiche of diverse sources, including interpolations that are Deuteronomistic or post-Deuteronomistic, is not probative. Instead, this evidence points to a strongly unified and coherently structured account in which each episode plays an integral role in advancing the narrative themes of the story and in creating a balanced literary structure. While narrative and literary unity are not to be mistaken for compositional unity (disparate elements may have been joined together in the construction of this narrative), there is no narratological or literary reason to suppose that the story did not take its present form in a single redaction.

III. Deuteronomy 9–10

I have just argued that there is no internal evidence for the claim that Exod 32 consists of a core narrative with Deuteronomistic or even post-Deuteronomistic interpolations. However, some argue that a comparison of our story with certain biblical parallels—specifically Deut 9–10 and 1 Kgs 12—yields evidence of the interpolated character of Exod 32. Van Seters draws the more radical conclusion that Exod 32 is a secondary creation literarily dependant on both Deut 9–10 and 1 Kgs 12. In this section, I examine Deut 9–10, and in the next section, 1 Kgs 12, in order to argue the literary priority of Exod 32.

My argument for Deut 9–10's literary dependence on Exod 32 in its present form is based on the following observation: the divergences between Deut 9–10 and Exod 32 are best (often, only) explicable in terms of the modification of the Exodus account by the author of Deuteronomy rather than the reverse.[53] Deuteronomy's divergences from Exodus are of three distinct types: (1) divergences determined by the immediate hortatory context; (2) divergences undertaken to establish resonances with other parts of the Deuteronomistic History; and (3) divergences emerging from an exegetical posture toward Exod 32.

A. *Divergences determined by the immediate hortatory context*

Eep Talstra divides Deut 9:1–10:22 into three sections on discursive grounds: 9:1–6 (Section I), 9:7–10:11 (Section II, the narrative section), and 10:12–22 (Section III).[54] Talstra observes that many critical analyses isolate the narrative section II from its immediate context in order to effect a comparison with Exod 32–34, without first analyzing the text of Deuteronomy on its own terms.[55] According to Talstra the separate treatment of this section is incorrect given the

---

[53] See Begg ("Destruction of the Calf") who makes his argument for the literary dependence of Deut 9:21 on Exod 32:20 in precisely these terms.

[54] Eep Talstra, "Deuteronomy 9 and 10: Synchronic and Diachronic Observations," in *Synchronic or Diachronic? A Debate on Method in Old Testament Exegesis* (ed. J. C. de Moor; OTS 34; Leiden: Brill, 1995), 187–210, esp. 195.

[55] Talstra, "Deuteronomy 9 and 10," 189. See Brian Peckham, "The Composition of Deuteronomy 9:1–10:11," in *Word and Spirit* (ed. J. Plevnik; Willowdale, Ont.: Regis College Press, 1975), 3–59, esp. 3–8, for various views on the stratification of 9:1–10:11 and the separation of the narrative unit from vv. 1–6/7 in particular.

syntactic integration into the surrounding materials (e.g., the continuation of first- and second-person verbs and suffixes). Reading the
narrative in its full context (Sections I and III) reveals that Deut
9:7–10:11 is not simply a Deuteronomistic comment on Exod 32–34
but rather a set of background narratives that bears the status of
argumentation within the chapter's discourse.[56] For this reason, the text
should be treated not in terms of any narrative plot but rather in
terms of the line of argumentation advanced in the overall pericope.[57]

To what end is the argumentation aimed? While complex form-
critical studies are sometimes employed to determine the purpose of
these chapters,[58] Moses' goal in retelling the golden calf story is
explicit in the story's immediate context, particularly Section I (9:1–6):
Moses paints a portrait of Israel as perpetually rebellious and incorrigibly disloyal, sustained only by Moses' strenuous intercession and
God's grace, in order to discredit the false historiographic conceptions and arrogant self-reliance that may arise in the wake of Israel's
conquest of the Promised Land, jeopardizing all she has gained.[59]

In chapter 9, Moses speaks to the Israelites on the east side of
the Jordan. He reminds them that they will have to dispossess nations
greater and more populous than they (vv. 1–2). Such a formidable
task can only be accomplished by the God who is crossing at their
head (v. 3). But God's action on Israel's behalf must not lead to the
arrogant assumption that victory is a proof of virtue.[60] When peace-
ably settled in your land, Moses warns, do not suppose that God
has acted for you only as you deserved, for it is not on account of
any special merit or virtue that God has brought you into the land
but because of the wickedness of the current inhabitants and God's
former promise to the patriarchs (vv. 4–6). Indeed, Moses continues,
far from being a people of virtue or merit, you have been particularly

---

[56] See Talstra, "Deuteronomy 9 and 10," 197. Whether Deut 9–10 is *also* a
Deuteronomistic comment on Exod 32–34 will be discussed below.

[57] Talstra, "Deuteronomy 9 and 10," 200.

[58] As an example, Talstra cites Norbert Lohfink, *Das Hauptegebot: Einer Untersuchung
literarischer Einleitungsfragen zu Dtn 5–11* (AnBib 20; Rome: Pontifical Biblical Institute,
1963), 207ff. Talstra is critical (perhaps overly so) of Lohfink's work for its too psychological reflection as to why and how the author expanded an original story of
a covenant break at Horeb ("Deuteronomy 9 and 10," 190).

[59] So Moshe A. Zipor, "The Deuteronomic Account of the Golden Calf and its
Reverberation in Other Parts of the Book of Deuteronomy," *ZAW* 108 (1996): 20–33,
here 21.

[60] Jeffrey Tigay, *Deuteronomy* (JPS Torah Commentary; Philadelphia: Jewish Publication Society, 1996), 96.

stiff-necked and rebellious, provoking in God a murderous fury on
more than one occasion. It is in support of this last claim that Moses
recounts incidents from the wilderness history, beginning with the
most egregious example of Israel's rebellious disloyalty—the golden
calf incident.

If the golden calf story is to serve as evidence for the claim that
the Israelites are undeserving recipients of God's bounty, then it will
have to be told in a manner that stresses those two themes: Israel's
unmitigated and sinful rebelliousness on the one hand, and God's
total forbearance and forgiveness on the other.[61] An examination of
Deuteronomy's version of the golden calf story reveals that it indeed
contains only those details that stress one or both of these themes,
while omitting details that would work against them.

We must be cognizant not only of the larger purpose our story
serves in Deuteronomy, but also of the perspective from which our
story is told. As Peckham observes, in contrast to the Exodus account
where the drama revolves around the people and Aaron, the narrative pivots in the Deuteronomist's account are Moses and God.[62]
Moses does not tell the people what they already know, viz., what
they and Aaron did. He harps on how angry they made God and
how close they came to destruction. Thus, we do not have in Deuteronomy a complete narrative account of the golden calf incident
told by an omniscient narrator (as in Exodus), but a retelling of the
incident from the perspective of one of the players—Moses. This
retelling is partial in both senses of the word: whole scenes at which
Moses was not present are, logically enough, not included (he does
not report what he has not witnessed), while other scenes and details
are reported and reinterpreted from Moses' particular (i.e., partial)
perspective.

Bearing in mind, then, the explicit purpose for the retelling of our
story in Deut 9–10 *and* the perspective from which it is told, let us
examine Deuteronomy's version of the golden calf incident in greater
detail. The account opens with Moses' ascent up the mountain to

---

[61] As Robert H. O'Connell points out, Deut 9–10 frequently repeats God's intention to destroy Israel and the intensity of Moses' intercession and his success in
securing God's total forgiveness ("Deuteronomy IX 7–X 7, 10–11: Panelled Structure,
Double Rehearsal and the Rhetoric of Covenant Rebuke," *VT* 42 [1992]: 492–509,
esp. 499).

[62] Peckham, "The Composition of Deuteronomy 9:1–10:11," 31.

receive the tablets of the covenant while fasting forty days and nights (vv. 9–11). Moses tells the people what they would not otherwise know and may not in fact ever have learned—that as Moses was poised to return, God reported the dreadful news of Israel's corruption; that God was so enraged by this act that he fully intended to destroy Israel (vv. 12–14). In these verses we have only the perspective of Moses (the scene on the mountaintop) and not the perspective of the people or Aaron (the scene at the foot of the mountain). Even God's description of the people's sin is brief and to the point (they made a molten calf) with no mention of the cultic activities surrounding the calf as in Exod 32. Moses can assume that the people are only too aware of the events in which they participated. In short, the omission of any parallel to Exod 32:1–6 makes perfect sense: Moses did not witness these actions, and he is reporting on *his* experiences at the time.

Other differences between the Deuteronomist's account and Exod 32 are explicable in terms of Moses' immediate purpose. Instead of Exod 32:10's "Now, let Me be, that my anger may blaze forth against them and that I may destroy them, and make of you a great nation," Deut 9:14 reads, "Let Me alone and I will destroy them and blot out their name from under heaven, and I will make you a nation far more numerous than they." This version underscores both the extent of God's wrath and Moses' virtue in declining such a stunningly tempting offer. A more important difference between the two accounts is Deuteronomy's omission of Moses' first intercession. Any mention of Moses' intervention at this juncture, any reference to his success in calming God and removing the threat of extinction, would undermine Moses' argument. For that argument to work the people must believe at this point in the retelling that their lives hung by a thread.

In Deuteronomy, the narrative impulse is not paramount. Thus, Deut 9:15–17, describing Moses' descent, his sighting of the people *in flagrante delicto*, and his destruction of the tablets, is a telescoped version of Exod 32:15–19 that focuses on those elements most supportive of Moses' purpose: I had the tablets, but when I saw you had sinned, I flung the tablets away and smashed them *before your very eyes*. The addition of this last phrase converts what was perhaps merely an uncontrolled burst of destructive rage in Exodus into a public display calculated to have a particular effect on the people. No subtlety here—the covenant was within your grasp, Moses scolds, but because of *your* sin it was destroyed.

Moses continues with an account of his immediate prostration before God. Terrified that God would utterly destroy you, I threw myself down before him forty days and nights, fasting and drinking no water (vv. 18–19). The effort was successful: "and that time, too, the LORD gave heed to me." There are significant differences between this account and that in Exodus. In Exodus, God has already renounced his plan of total annihilation; Moses returns up the mountain to plead for forgiveness and meets with only partial success. None of these details serves the explicit goals of Moses' speech in Deuteronomy. Moses wants the Israelites to believe that all would have been lost were it not for his strenuous self-affliction (hence he does not reveal to them that God had already renounced his plan of total destruction). Moreover, he says that the Lord heeded him, implying that total forgiveness was secured.

Thus, in Deut 9:9–19, Moses uses the golden calf story as evidence of Israel's rebellious sinfulness. He assumes the details of the events are known to his (narrative) audience and so provides a streamlined version that highlights those points supportive of his argument while obscuring or suppressing those points that would weaken his argument: (a) I ascended the mountain and was given the tablets; (b) God told me you had sinned; (c) I came down and found it was so and therefore I smashed the tablets before your eyes; (d) I threw myself down before God for forty days and nights to save you from utter annihilation; (e) God heeded me, forgiving you completely. Nothing is allowed to distract from this detailing of the sinful provocation, the utter alienation it forced between God and Israel, and God's gracious and undeserved forgiveness in response to Moses' intercession. The diverse perspectives offered by Exod 32:1–6, the suspense added by the drawn-out account of Moses' descent and dialogue with Joshua in Exod 32:17–18, the tense confrontation between Aaron and Moses, Moses' brutal efforts to restore order to the camp by means of Levite zealots, and the detailed negotiations between God and Moses over the fate of Israel may be excellent narratological touches; but they have no place in Deut 9–10 whose interest in the golden calf story is forensic rather than narratological.

Having adduced the golden calf incident as evidence of Israel's extreme sin and God's unmerited forgiveness, Moses takes up the theme of reconciliation (vv. 25–29).[63] Here again, earlier events are

---

[63] I defer until section III.C.1 a consideration of vv. 20–21, the motivation for which is—I will argue—exegetical.

packaged for public consumption in line with Moses' stated purpose—to emphasize the people's wickedness and the undeserved
nature of God's kindness toward them. Divergences from the prayers
presented in Exodus (32:11 13, 31–32) are explicable in this light.
In Exod 32:13, Moses mentions the patriarchs to remind God of his
promise to give the land to their numerous descendents. But the
idea of an eternal promise that survives even the most grievous apostasy would only support the kind of self-assured arrogance Moses
explicitly seeks to discredit. Thus, in Deut 9:27 the three patriarchs
are invoked for an entirely different reason: "Give thought to your
servants Abraham, Isaac, and Jacob, and pay no heed to the stubbornness of this people, its wickedness, and its sinfulness." Here the
patriarchs are mentioned not to remind God of his obligation, but
precisely to underscore the unworthiness of the current generation
in contrast to its ancestors. Remember the patriarchs whom you did
love, act in accordance with that love, and pay no heed to this
wicked nation. This modified use of the patriarchal theme underscores Moses' central point: it is not through any virtue of your own
that you have been brought to this day, for you are utterly wicked;
nor does a promise to your ancestors shield you from the consequences of your actions.

Scholars have been troubled by the fact that the prayer described
in Deut 9:25–29 seems to coincide in timing with the second prayer
in the Exodus account (Exod 32:31–32) while coinciding in substance
with the first account (Exod 32:11–13).[64] But if we bear in mind the
explicit goals of the literary character Moses, we can easily explain
this state of affairs. Moses would work against his stated purpose if,
in the midst of this rebuke, he were to mention the removal of the
threat of immediate and wholesale destruction by an earlier petition
(Exod 32:11–14), his devotion to the people (Exod 32:31–32), or
God's punishment of the guilty (Exod 32:33–35). In short, Moses'
prayer in Deuteronomy reveals precisely and only what is supportive of his purpose: you sinned horribly, God was ready to destroy
you, I managed to obtain total forgiveness by asking God to avert
his eyes from your wickedness and to focus on your virtuous ancestors. In the future, avoid those behaviors (apostasy and sin) that will
assuredly be your destruction in my absence. In the same vein, Moses

---

[64] See, for example, Samuel R. Driver, *A Critical and Exegetical Commentary on
Deuteronomy* (ICC 5; New York: Scribner, 1895), 116.

would work at cross-purposes to his stated purpose if he were to mention any suffering on the part of the people. Remembrances of their suffering would not support the claim that the people have been treated with forgiving beneficence, and have been relieved of the punishment they really deserved. Thus Moses quite understandably makes no mention of his own rough treatment of the people by forcing them to drink the remains of the idol,[65] nor does he refer to the slaughter by the Levites.

The foregoing analysis reveals that a full retelling of the incident of the golden calf in chronological sequence is not to be found in Deut 9–10. In Deuteronomy the character Moses rebukes the people with evidence of their past provocation of God. Chronology is a casualty of his polemical argument right from the outset: of the four incidents mentioned in 9:22 (Horeb, Taberah, Massah, and Kibroth-hattaavah), the golden calf incident was not temporally first; it is mentioned first by Moses because it is the most egregious example of rebellion.[66] Chronology continues to be sacrificed as Moses presents only those elements of the event supportive of the larger portrait he is painting of sin, mortal danger, intercession, and total forgiveness. Since chronology is clearly unimportant to the forensic treatment of the golden calf incident in Deuteronomy, and since chronology is so clearly central to the narrative structure of the story in Exod 32, the sequence of events depicted in Deuteronomy should not be privileged over the sequence depicted in Exodus. The identification of interpolations in the Exodus account because of corresponding absences in the Deuteronomy account is particularly suspect. The claim that Exod 32:11–13 is an interpolation based on the petition presented in Deut 9:25–29 and that, originally, the Exodus story contained only one prayer (for total forgiveness) at the end of the chapter is unfounded.[67] On the contrary, the prayer in Exod 32:11–13, which is not a prayer for forgiveness, finds its natural home at this point in the narrative (before Moses' descent); moreover, its omission from Deuteronomy is well motivated. Similarly, we have seen that Moses' failure to mention in Deuteronomy the substance of his second dialogue with God (Exod 32:31–34) is well

---

[65] See David Hoffmann, *Das Buch Deuteronomium* (Berlin: M. Poppelauer, 1913), 109. Cf. Begg for a discussion of Deuteronomy's omission of the drinking of the calf's remains ("Destruction of the Calf," 241–42).

[66] Tigay, *Deuteronomy*, 98.

[67] See, for example, Childs, *Exodus*, 559.

motivated—because of its mixed success, presenting this dialogue here would undermine his assertion of total forgiveness by God. If the inclusion of Exodus material in Deut 9–10's account would clearly undermine the explicit purpose of Moses' speech, we have strong grounds for the assumption that Deuteronomy has deliberately excluded that material, rather than the reverse assumption—that Exodus has added it to an account that lacked a prayer at this point, and has done so under the influence of the Deuteronomist's account.[68]

The foregoing analysis suggests that the author of Deut 9–10 presents Moses as providing a partial reading of the golden calf story known to his audience from Exod 32. Moses is represented as mining this account for evidence in support of the charge that Israel has provoked God to the point of utter alienation and imminent destruction, and yet has been forgiven and favored, a situation that should lead to humility and moral reform.

B. *Divergences establishing resonances with other parts of the Deuteronomistic History*

Deuteronomy 9–10's literary dependence on Exod 32 is also suggested by divergences that establish resonances between Deuteronomy and other parts of the Deuteronomistic History. Begg has already shown that when its wording diverges from Exod 32:20, Deut 9:21 (on the elimination of the idol) evidences verbal links with a wide range of texts in Kings recounting significant moments (both positive and negative) in the cultic history of Israel.[69] Deuteronomy 9:21 "appears as a very deliberate rewriting of the text of Exodus with a view to setting up and foreshadowing those various later moments."[70] For example, Deuteronomy refers to the calf as "your sin," the term repeatedly applied to the calves of Jeroboam in Kings,[71] and the

---

[68] That an argumentative text lacking chronological organization (Deut 9–10) might serve as the source for a text (Exod 32) that almost miraculously manages to make a coherent narrative sequence out of its chronological jumble strikes me as absurd. The reverse idea of a structurally coherent narrative (Exod 32) being mined for material that is then crafted into a polemical witness of past wrongs and present unworthiness without regard for narrative sequence or full disclosure (Deut 9–10) strikes me as far more intuitively plausible. Cf. O'Connell, "Deuteronomy IX 7–X 7, 10–11," 506.

[69] Begg, "Destruction of the Calf," 236–43.

[70] Ibid., 236.

[71] Thus, Van Seters's claim that Deuteronomy has no connection to the story of Jeroboam is false. The conclusion based upon that claim—that since Exodus has

word *le'afar* added to the phrase *'ad 'ašer daq* links Deut 9:21 to 2 Kgs 23:4ff. concerning Josiah's reforms, the only two uses of *'afar* with reference to the dust of illicit cultic objects.

In short, Deut 9:21's unique terminology and formulations are not random or capricious, but establish verbal contacts between Deuteronomy and later cultic developments: Jeroboam's fatal offense (1 Kgs 12:26ff.) and the four major Judean cultic reforms in 1 Kgs 15:13; 2 Kgs 11:18b, 18:4b, and 23:4ff.[72]

The divergences between Exod 32:20 and Deut 9:21 can be plausibly accounted for on the assumption that Deut 9:21 is dependent on Exod 32:20; on the reverse assumption (Exod 32:20's dependence on Deut 9:21), these divergences find no ready explanation.

C. *Divergences emerging from an exegetical posture toward Exodus 32*

I have argued that Deuteronomy's account of the golden calf story is an appropriation and reworking of material from Exodus selected in accordance with the specific purpose and perspective of the literary character Moses at this juncture in the Pentateuchal narrative. Nevertheless, Deut 9–10 does contain a few details that seem to bear no relation to the argument put forward by Moses in these chapters. Two of these details—God's anger toward Aaron and Moses' destruction of the calf—follow Moses' description of the golden calf incident (9:20–21). Two others—the death of Aaron and the setting apart of the Levites—appear toward the end of the entire unit (10:6–9). The latter are particularly jarring, couched as they are in the third-person voice of the narrator. If there is no narrative or rhetorical reason to include these details, why are they here, and what is the nature of their relation to the parallel portions of Exod 32?

That these miscellaneous details tend to occur at the end of major rhetorical units suggests that they stand outside the rhetorical compositions as additions that serve some other purpose. A cursory examination of these details reveals their common denominator: each reflects upon and resolves an exegetical problem or ambiguity in the

---

connections with both Deuteronomy and 1 Kings, and Deuteronomy and 1 Kings have no connection with each other, then Exodus must draw from and post-date both of the other texts—is therefore called into question. See the full discussion of this issue below.

[72] Begg, "Destruction of the Calf," 241.

Exodus account. Indeed, these passages address the major interpretive cruxes that dominate so much of the post-biblical tradition of exegesis of Exod 32—namely, the intentions, relative guilt or innocence, and fate of Aaron, the meaning of the forced drinking of the idol's ashes, and the Levite episode. It may be argued, then, that in these passages Deut 9–10 is engaged in exegesis of Exod 32. That Deut 9–10 adopts an exegetical posture toward Exod 32 on numerous occasions is a strong argument for Deut 9–10's literary dependence on Exod 32. Moreover, in none of the cases adduced below can it be argued plausibly that dependence runs in the other direction, i.e., that Exod 32 is interpreting, disambiguating, and filling gaps in Deut 9–10. Below is an examination of material suggestive of a relationship of exegesis between Deut 9–10 and Exod 32.

1. *Interpreting Aaron*

Ambiguity surrounds Aaron's behavior in the opening scene of Exod 32. Although Moses is clearly angry with Aaron later in the story, some doubt about Aaron's sinfulness and culpability linger. After all, Aaron is not killed by the plague and later he is honored with the office of high priest in Israel. The question of Aaron's guilt plagues any reader of Exod 32, as evidenced by the attention it receives in post-biblical tradition. The Deuteronomist avails himself of the opportunity to bring interpretive closure to the riddle of Aaron.

Deuteronomy is completely unambiguous—Aaron was guilty of a great sin and provoked God to great fury: "Moreover, the LORD was angry enough with Aaron to have destroyed him" (Deut 9:20a). Why, then, was he not punished? According to Deuteronomy, Aaron was spared not for any virtue of his own but on account of the aggressive intercession of Moses: "so I also interceded for Aaron at that time" (Deut 9:20b). But this is not the end of his story. In a miscellaneous and seemingly irrelevant interpolation by the narrator we read: "From Beeroth-bene-jaakan the Israelites marched to Moserah. Aaron died there and was buried there, and his son Eleazar became priest in his stead. From there they marched to Gudgod, and from Gudgod to Jotbath, a region of running brooks" (Deut 10:6–7). There is certainly no *narrative* reason to include this itinerary tradition, momentarily wrenching the reader into the future. Might it be included precisely and only for the notification it contains of Aaron's death? Might not *Aaron's* death, like Moses', be construed as a punishment for sin?[73] In short, Deut 9:20 and 10:6–7 provide all the information we need to solve the riddle of Aaron in Exod 32: Aaron sinned terribly, God wanted to destroy him immediately, Moses won a reprieve, and Aaron went on to fulfill his allotted destiny but ultimately died a premature death as just punishment for his role in the golden calf incident. Deuteronomy's additions concerning the guilt and fate of Aaron foreclose the ambiguity inherent in Exod 32 and point to Deuteronomy's literary dependence on Exod 32. I see no way to account for these phenomena on the view that Exodus is literarily dependent on Deuteronomy.

2. *Moses' anger and the forced drinking of the idol's ashes*
Exodus 32:19b reads: "He [Moses] became enraged and hurled the tablets from his hands and shattered them at the foot of the mountain." The explicit reference to Moses' anger suggests that the tablets were destroyed in an embarrassing lapse into raw emotion on the part of Israel's great leader. In Deut 9:17, we read: "Thereupon I gripped the two tablets and flung them away with both my hands, smashing them before your eyes." Deuteronomy replaces Moses' anger with a methodical determination ("I gripped . . . and flung . . . with both my hands") and highlights the public dimension of his action. It seems likely that Deuteronomy is engaging in apologetics here, recasting this one detail of the Exodus account in order to shed a more positive light on Moses. That Exodus's description of Moses' anger had an unsettling effect on ancient readers is apparent in early interpretations that echo Deuteronomy's desire to distance Moses from anger and to assign a rational purpose to his destruction of the tablets (see, for example, Philo, *Mos.* 2.167 and Pseudo-Philo 12–13).

   Similarly, the forced drinking of the idol's ashes (Exod 32:20) reflects poorly on Moses who seems again to succumb to an almost vindictive anger. It may occasion little surprise, then, that according to Deut 9:21 there is no forced drinking. Begg offers several possible explanations for Deuteronomy's divergence from Exodus at this point.[74] My own inclination is to see here a second attempt to distance Moses from unseemly emotions of anger, vindictiveness, and cruelty. That the forced drinking of the idol's ashes had an unsettling effect on ancient readers is borne out by early interpretations

---

[73] See Peckham, "The Composition of Deuteronomy 9:1–10:11," 52.
[74] Begg, "Destruction of the Calf," 241–43.

that seek to identify a rational purpose for Moses' action (e.g., to identify the guilty).[75]

3. *The Levite episode*

The Levite episode in Exod 32:25–29 raises many questions, as demonstrated by diverse interpretative traditions from earliest times forward.[76] Did God really command the slaughter? Who is being slaughtered and for what reason? Are the Levites executing the guilty or zealously demonstrating their passion for the LORD by wielding their sword against neighbor, brother, and kin? Do they fill a leadership vacuum in the wake of Aaron's disgrace, helping Moses reassert control, for which they then receive an eternal reward? Or are they God's avengers, plain and simple? And what precisely is the nature of their reward—this blessing of which Moses speaks?

The Levite episode is not mentioned in Moses' recounting of the golden calf incident in Deuteronomy (Section II). Any reference to zealous retribution or to suffering on the part of the Israelites would work against Moses' larger argument that the people have sinned greatly but suffered little. Nevertheless, the Levites are mentioned toward the very end of our passage (10:8–9). Interrupting Moses' first-person speech for a moment, the narrator first informs us of Aaron's death years later and then reports on God's separation of the tribe of Levi "at that time." Following this interruption we are returned to Moses' first-person account of his prostration before God.

There is neither a narrative nor a rhetorical reason to interrupt Moses' speech to provide information about the Levites. No effort is made to integrate this material into its context (by converting it, for example, into the first person and attributing it to Moses). Like the notification of Aaron's death, this reference to the Levites is best seen as a symptom of the exegetical orientation of Deuteronomy toward Exodus.

The opening assertion (Deut 10:8) that *the LORD* set the tribe of Levi apart at that time obliquely addresses the question that has

---

[75] Pre-modern interpretations of our story describe the drinking of the idol's ashes as a punishment (in Pseudo-Philo, it causes the tongues of the guilty to be cut off) or as a kind of trial by ordeal (*Num. Rab.* 9:46–48) that causes a mark to appear on the bodies of the guilty, thereby identifying them for execution by the Levites (*Tg. Ps.-J.* to Exod 22:20, 28).

[76] See Michael Walzer, "Exodus 32 and the Theory of Holy War: The History of a Citation," *HTR* 61 (1968): 1–14; and Brisman, "Sacred Butchery."

puzzled interpreters of Exod 32:25–29 from earliest times: Did Moses act alone when he summoned and charged the Levites, or at God's behest? According to the Deuteronomist, at least, the separation and dedication of the Levites "at that time" was God's idea, not Moses'. Second, the Deuteronomist mentions the incident in order *not* to mention it. In other words, he refers to the separation of the Levites, their dedication to serve God, and their blessing without referring to the bloody butchery by which they earned this special status. This silence may denote a certain hesitation or discomfort with the activity of the Levites, so clearly evidenced in even the earliest interpretative traditions (Josephus, Philo, Pseudo-Philo, *Targum Pseudo-Jonathan, b. Yoma* 66b).[77] The apologetic impulse attested in these traditions may lie behind the Deuteronomist's silence on the slaughter.

Third, the Deuteronomist divorces the dedication of the Levites from any role the latter may have played in the golden calf story and represents their selection as a positive act of dedication initiated by God. Moreover, by mentioning the dedication of the Levites immediately after the notification of Aaron's death, the Deuteronomist subtly implies that continuity of leadership is the primary concern in the appointment of the Levites. Indeed, the ambiguity of the temporal phrase, "at that time," allows the reader to associate the dedication of the Levites with the death of Aaron mentioned in the preceding verse rather than the golden calf incident. If this association is the Deuteronomist's intent, then we have an attempt at revisionist history: with the passing of Aaron, the Levite class was elevated to authority. The feasibility of this interpretation is strengthened when we consider that Deuteronomy's description of the Levites' responsibilities is itself revisionist. At least two of the duties assigned to the Levites in Deut 10 are assigned exclusively to priests (i.e., Aaronides) in the Priestly source. Thus, Deut 10:8–9 may be a polemical assertion that priestly functions are the prerogatives of the Levites generally, and not merely the descendants of Aaron. The Levites as a class, and not merely the Aaronides, inherited Aaron's mantle after his death.

In short, from Exod 32:25–29, the Deuteronomist selects and expands upon only one element—the installation of the Levites as cultic leaders in Israel—and considerably weakens that element's connection to the story of the calf. The expansion that occurs is exegetical in nature, answering the question: What is the nature of the

---

[77] See Walzer, "Exodus 32 and the Theory of Holy War," 4, 10–11.

Levites' "dedication" and blessing in Exod 32? The answer provided is consistent with Deuteronomy's view of the relative prerogatives of Levites and priests. Thus, we see a revisionist exegetical motivation for Deuteronomy's selective and adaptive use of material in Exod 32, suggestive of literary dependence.

4. *The restoration of the covenant*
Section II of our passage also contains a brief description of the restoration of the covenant that contrasts sharply with the account in Exod 33–34. In Exodus, God withdraws from the people to consider what he will do (Exod 33:5). The people strip themselves of their finery and wait in a tense state of mourning while Moses carries out a series of intense negotiations. While ultimately God is reconciled to his people, and a new set of tablets is carved, the process is tortuously slow.

This is not the sense conveyed by Deuteronomy's five brief verses, and understandably so. A central peg upon which Moses' argument hangs is that God has been unstinting in his grace and favor. Moses' argument would hardly be served by reminding the people of the lengthy cooling-off period and intense intercessions needed before God finally, and almost grudgingly, agreed to return to the *status quo ante*. In Deuteronomy, God initiates a full reconciliation, responding to Moses' prayer with instructions regarding the creation of a second and explicitly identical set of tablets (10:2–4). There is no suggestion that God withdraws from the community to consider what is to be done, no dire warning of the danger of God's presence within such a wicked community.

We have explained the omissions in Deuteronomy's account, but how are we to understand the details selected for *inclusion*? For all its brevity, Deuteronomy's summary contains details that are not found in, or directly contradict, the longer reconciliation account in Exodus, and these details require some explanation.

If we examine the explicit emphases of Deut 9–10, the answer becomes apparent. Twice it is stated that the second set of tablets is identical to the first and the contents of the tablets are the Ten Commandments. Four times Moses' construction of the ark to house the tablets is mentioned, as well as an additional notification that the tablets remain deposited in the ark. The Deuteronomist is emphasizing that the restored covenant was in no way different from the original, that the content of the tablets was the Ten Commandments and that the tablets were immediately stored in an ark manufactured by Moses himself. This is not entirely consistent with the Exodus account. In Exodus, although we read that the second set of tablets is inscribed with the Ten Commandments, these Commandments do not appear to be identical with the earlier list of ten (see Exod 34:1–28 and cf. Exod 20:1–14), generating an exegetical crux that has exercised commentators for centuries. Moreover, according to Exod 37 it is Bezalel who makes the ark and at a slightly later time. When one biblical source offers a telescoped version of events receiving lengthy treatment elsewhere, and emphasizes within that brief version specific details that resolve exegetical difficulties in the longer text, the likelihood is great that the brief version is functioning at least in part as a gloss on the longer text—revising or resolving problems in an *earlier* account. I would argue that in Deut 10:1–5, the Deuteronomist engages in a revisionist kind of exegesis yet again. The Deuteronomist presents a summary account of the restoration of the covenant not only to serve the rhetorical argument of these chapters (God has been totally forgiving and eager for reconciliation despite your utter wickedness) but also in order to create the occasion for a revised understanding of that event. As noted above, revisionist exegesis of this kind is strongly suggestive of literary dependence.

The examples of gap-filling and revisionist exegesis discussed in sections III.C.1–4 underscore an important phenomenon that strongly supports the presumption of Deut 9–10's literary dependence on Exod 32: on more than one occasion the author of Deut 9–10 assumes the reader's familiarity with the story of the golden calf as presented in Exod 32 and therefore recounts it selectively or with his own particular, and at times revisionist, emphases.[78]

IV. Is Exodus 32 Literarily Dependent on Deuteronomy 9–10? The Evidence of 1 Kings 12

Van Seters rejects the claim that Deut 9–10 is literarily dependent on Exod 32 and argues the reverse, in support of his theory that J (the author of Exod 32) is a post-exilic and post-Deuteronomistic

---

[78] The best example of this phenomenon is Deut 9:20 in which Moses refers to God's anger against Aaron, although he has said nothing about Aaron's misdeed at all (Zipor, "Deuteronomic Account of the Golden Calf," 22 n. 6). A second example may be the reference to the Levites in 10:8–9.

writer. According to Van Seters, Deuteronomy's account is spare in comparison with the Exodus account, and since Van Seters sees no convincing reason for Deuteronomy to excise whole passages from the Exodus story, he assumes that Deut 9–10 did not know Exod 32.[79] Van Seters provides three examples of what he would consider to be unmotivated "excisions." First, why would D omit Exod 32:1–6 detailing the actual construction and worship of the idol?[80] Second, why would D omit any mention of the forced drinking of the idol, referring only to the scattering of its dust on the brook that descended from the mountain?[81] Finally, why would DtrH, for whom Joshua is a major figure, ignore Joshua if he were working from a prevenient source that mentioned Joshua?[82]

Van Seters's questions betray a general insensitivity to the rhetorical purposes of Deut 9–10. Van Seters focuses instead on what he *assumes* to be the underlying purpose of the editors of Deuteronomy as a whole: the polemic against idolatry. He cannot, therefore, understand why the author of Deut 9–10 would omit in his retelling any passage that reflects badly on idolatry (Exod 32:1–6, 20b). Likewise, he cannot understand why the author would pass up the opportunity to include any favorite theme (e.g., Joshua).

Because he isolates the narrative Section II from its immediate context, Van Seters fails to note the clearly articulated rhetorical purpose that guides the selection and adaptation of material from Exod 32. Had he noted this purpose, he would have seen that a general polemic against idolatry is not the guiding theme of these chapters. On the contrary, in Deut 9–10 the literary character Moses adduces, from his own perspective, evidence of the utter wickedness of the Israelites and the total forgiveness and beneficence of God. He excludes events he did not witness (Exod 32:1–6) and information that is irrelevant (e.g., the presence of Joshua, which is not even central to Exod 32's account) or counter-productive to his argument (e.g., any reference to punishment or suffering on the part of the Israelites, such as the forced drinking of the idol's ashes). Far from having "no reason" to excise these passages, the literary character Moses, as drawn by the author or redactor of Deuteronomy, has

---

[79] Van Seters, *Life of Moses*, 302–3.
[80] Ibid., 307.
[81] Ibid., 306–7.
[82] Ibid., 310.

multiple good reasons for omitting precisely the passages that puzzle Van Seters.

Nevertheless, Van Seters contends that Exodus is an expansion of Deuteronomy and that the source of the details that Exodus adds to the basic Deuteronomic account is 1 Kgs 12. Van Seters asserts that the Jeroboam account is so thoroughly anachronistic and propagandistic that one must judge it a complete fabrication—a framework for the interpretation of the history of the northern kingdom invented by the Deuteronomistic Historian and having no basis in historical fact.[83] Deuteronomy 9–10 cannot, therefore, refer or allude to a purported cultic violation by Jeroboam since it predates its redactor, DtrH, and Jeroboam's activity is the invention of this redactor. However, while nothing in Deut 9–10 reflects the story in 1 Kgs 12, several details in Exod 32 appear to draw on the Jeroboam story. Specifically, making a golden calf, ascribing the Exodus to it, and establishing a festival for it are elements taken by Exod 32 from the Deuteronomistic History. This assertion is supported by little more than Van Seters's sense that the plural form "these are your gods" is incongruous in Exodus, and that the mention of an altar and a feast does not fit well with a god who is to lead people through a wilderness.[84] Van Seters concludes that Exod 32 uses the Jeroboam apostasy in 1 Kgs 12 as a model for its polemic against the entire people and shapes that polemic in accordance with Deut 9–10. Thus, Exod 32 postdates and is literarily dependent on both 1 Kgs 12 and Deut 9–10. This is all the more likely, Van Seters contends, since it is hard to imagine that Deut 9–10 and 1 Kgs 12 could both draw on Exod 32 and at the same time avoid having anything in common with each other.

However, it is not at all hard to imagine that Deut 9–10 and 1 Kgs 12 would draw on Exod 32 and yet have nothing in common with each other, given the radically diverse purposes of these texts. We have discussed the purpose of Deut 9–10 at some length and have seen that there are powerful rhetorical and literary (perspectival) reasons to excise Exod 32:1–6 from the account in Deut 9–10. By contrast, the entire purpose of 1 Kgs 12 is to vilify a king for establishing an illicit cult and for leading the people astray—to rep-

---

[83] Ibid., 296.
[84] Ibid., 300. The logic of Van Seters's second claim regarding the altar and feast escapes me.

resent this king as a new Aaron. The one part of Exod 32 of greatest use to DtrH in 1 Kgs 12 is the description in Exod 32:1–6 of
Aaron's activity, precisely that section of Exod 32 that was of no
use to the author of Deut 9–10. Given their radically different purposes, it is no surprise that Deut 9–10 and 1 Kgs 12 draw on com-
plementary elements of Exod 32.

Moreover, it is not true that Deut 9–10 and 1 Kgs 12 are as radically divorced as Van Seters claims. Indeed, an examination of 1
Kings's construction of the sin of Jeroboam suggests that the author
of 1 Kgs 12 drew upon and combined material from both Exod 32
and Deut 9–10. As Aberbach and Smolar have pointed out, there
are numerous similarities between Aaron in the golden calf story and
Jeroboam in 1 Kgs 12.[85] What these scholars do not make explicit,
however, is that Jeroboam resembles Aaron not merely as he appears
in Exod 32 but *also as he appears in Deuteronomy*. Jeroboam, like Aaron
in Deut 9:10, is said to come under divine displeasure and is threatened with annihilation, but then comes ultimately to a natural end
(see 1 Kgs 13:34, 14:20). In other words, the description of Jeroboam
in 1 Kings appears to combine material found only in Exod 32
(Aaron's actions as instigator of an illicit cult) with material found
only in Deut 9 (the unambiguous condemnation of Aaron as having provoked God's anger and incurring a threat of annihilation).
By Van Seters's own lights, then, we may conclude: if Exod 32 and
Deut 9–10 have unique traditions regarding Aaron, and if 1 Kings
combines both of these traditions in its representation of Aaron, the
most plausible conclusion is that 1 Kings is literarily dependent on
both Exod 32 and Deut 9–10. Moreover, since Deuteronomy's tradition regarding Aaron's guilt and ultimate fate assumes details of
his behavior related only in Exod 32, then the most plausible conclusion is that Exod 32 predates and is the source for Deut 9–10,
which predates and, with Exod 32, is the source for 1 Kings.

Nevertheless, it must be said that the relationship of 1 Kgs 12 to
Exod 32 is a matter of some controversy that requires further con-
sideration. First Kings 12 describes the cultic reform initiated by
Jeroboam following the northern tribes' secession from the Davidide
King Rehoboam and does so in terms reminiscent of Exod 32. The
attempt to determine the direction of dependence between the two

---

[85] Aberbach and Smolar, "Aaron, Jeroboam and the Golden Calves."

accounts is often guided by historical rather than literary considerations. Many scholars assert that the *historical* Jeroboam would never have been foolish enough to set up a cult on the model of Aaron's sinful cult, repeating verbatim the notorious declaration, "These are your gods, O Israel," were Aaron's act widely known and understood to be a sinful deviation. Nor would the author of 1 Kgs 12 be foolish enough to depict Jeroboam as seeking to establish a cult like Aaron's were that cult already discredited by Exod 32. These considerations lead some scholars to conclude that the historical Jeroboam's intentions (not to mention Aaron's) were honorable and based on an older tradition of Yahwistic calf-symbolism.[86] Therefore, (1) the *literary* Jeroboam of 1 Kgs 12 is a polemical distortion at the hands of DtrH; and (2) Exod 32, which is probably contemporaneous with or postdates 1 Kgs 12, creates a negative precedent in an attempt to discredit the northern kingdom by representing Moses, God, and the Levites as opposed to it.[87] The plural form, "these are your gods," is thought to support this view since it is correct for Jeroboam's dual calves but not for Aaron's single calf.[88] However, as we have seen, the term *'elohim* may be applied by the speakers to Aaron and his calf jointly (or it may be the plural of majesty). Moreover, it is no more appropriate for 1 Kings, since Jeroboam must have been situated at the shrine of one calf or the other when making the deictic declaration, "These are your calves," and so employed a plural when pointing at a single calf.[89] Thus, there are scholars who maintain the priority of the Exodus account (Aberbach and Smolar, Beyerlin, and Albright) but still see in Exod 32 a pointed polemic against the northern cult, or Deuteronomistic interpolations that convert an existing story into just such a polemic.

A literary question cannot be answered by recourse to historical speculation. What the historical Jeroboam might have done and whether he inherited some ancient and legitimate Aaronide practice are questions that are not only unanswerable but also irrelevant. All that we have is 1 Kgs 12's representation of the *literary* Jeroboam initiating a cultic reform in terms reminiscent of the *literary* Aaron's primordial cultic sin. The question before us, then, is first and fore-

---

[86] For scholars holding some version of these views (including Morgenstern, De Vries, Jenks, Kaufmann, Janzen, Sarna), see Lasine, "Reading Jeroboam's Intentions," 136 and Bailey, "The Golden Calf," 97–98 nn. 2–6.

[87] So Noth, Gray, Waterman, de Vaux, Pfeiffer.

[88] Bailey, "The Golden Calf," 97 n. 2.

[89] Ibid.

most a literary one and must be answered in literary terms: would a Deuteronomistic writer polemicizing against Jeroboam's cultic activity be likely to express his condemnation of that activity by casting Jeroboam as a latter-day Aaron? The answer is yes.

Stuart Lasine has argued persuasively that "historians who assume that the ancient audience of 1 Kings 12 was incapable of recognizing the ludicrous and reductive nature of the polemic against Jeroboam have misconstrued the authorial audience."[90] Citing Booth, Lasine notes that

> when authors make glaring errors of historical fact and have speakers betray "foolishness that is 'simply incredible'" they may be signaling readers to view such elements as indicators of an ironic intent. . . . The authorial audience will recognize that the narrator's picture of Jeroboam attempting to attract pious Yahwists by alluding to the apostasy at Sinai is so startling and incredible (historically as well as intertextually) that the point must be that the king was actually foolish and self-destructive enough to use such an absurd strategy. Only the *ideal narrative audience* could accept the narrator's report of Jeroboam's allusion to Exodus 32 at face value and not be confounded.[91]

Noting the Bible's use of caricature and irony, especially in its representation of idols and image worship, Lasine notes:

> [i]n biblical polemics against idolatry, the astonishing and fatal self-deception and obtuseness of idolators is often revealed by presenting their private thoughts and intentions in an ironic manner [e.g., Isa 28:15; 44:9–20]. . . . In 1 Kgs 12:28, the narrator exposes the king's idolatrous mentality by directly "quoting" his speech and thoughts in the same way that the prophets ironically "quote" idolators as saying what they would actually *never* say or even acknowledge. For the narrative audience familiar with Exodus 32 as well as 1 Kings 12, calf-worship is so foolish, and so obviously doomed to disaster, that it is as though the king had actually been so mad as to declare "Behold your gods, Israel, who brought you up out of the land of Egypt," in spite of the apostasy at Sinai and its consequences. In addition, the narrative audience which appraises Jeroboam's other cult reforms (1 Kgs 12:31–32) in terms of the standards set up by the speaker Moses in Deuteronomy 12, 16, and 18, will again be astounded by the overwhelming folly and self-defeating nature of his actions.[92]

---

[90] Lasine, "Reading Jeroboam's Intentions," 138.

[91] Ibid., 138; cf. Wayne C. Booth, *A Rhetoric of Irony* (Chicago: University of Chicago Press, 1974), 57–58.

[92] Lasine, "Reading Jeroboam's Intentions," 141–42.

In short, 1 Kgs 12 bears the rhetorical earmarks of an ironic exposé of idolators and other malefactors. The likelihood is great that DtrH chose to model Jeroboam on Aaron, the leader responsible for the primordial cultic sin that brought Israel to the brink of total annihilation, not despite the fact that Jeroboam would appear foolish and self-deluded but precisely *because* of that fact. Jeroboam is satirized, like a cartoon villain, and his ancient Israelite audience would have had enough knowledge and literary sophistication "to recognize that the narrator's account of Jeroboam intentionally reproducing the fiasco at Sinai is a blatant misrepresentation designed to expose the king's self-defeating willfulness through the use of irony and the absurd."[93] Of course, the irony works only if we assume the pre-existence of Exod 32's presentation of Aaron, and 1 Kgs 12's literary dependence on Exod 32.

V. Conclusion

Expanding on Christopher Begg's observation that all of the distinctive features of Deut 9:21 can be readily and satisfactorily accounted for in terms of a rewriting of Exod 32:20, I have argued that Deut 9–10 in general is a reworking of its parallel in Exodus in accordance with three distinct principles. First, Deut 9–10 selects and modifies material from Exod 32 in accordance with explicit hortatory goals of the character Moses set out in the opening verses of chapter 9. Second, Deuteronomy's distinctive formulations and treatment of parallel material is on occasion motivated by the historiographic goals of the Deuteronomistic redactor who conforms that material to Deuteronomistic accounts of later cultic reforms. Third, several of the divergences between Exodus and Deuteronomy are the function of the exegetical stance of the latter toward the former as suggested by the continued attention paid to precisely these points in later interpretative tradition. The combined weight of this evidence, and the absence of persuasive evidence to the contrary, lends strong support to the claim that Deut 9–10 is literarily dependent on Exod 32. This claim is in no way disabled by the existence of 1 Kgs 12 since the latter is best understood as a lampooning of Jeroboam that

---

[93] Ibid., 148.

relies on audience familiarity with the portrait of Aaron in Exod 32 and the brief mention of his sinfulness in Deut 9. In short, the likelihood is strong that Exod 32 as a literary unit stood before the author of Deut 9–10 and that both Exod 32 and Deut 9–10 stood before the Deuteronomistic Historian responsible for 1 Kgs 12.

PLUMBING THE DEPTHS:
GENRE AMBIGUITY AND THEOLOGICAL CREATIVITY IN THE INTERPRETATION OF PSALM 130

Harry P. Nasuti

Psalm 130 has long resisted attempts to classify it in form-critical terms. Modern scholars vary widely as to how they define its genre, and they often claim that the psalm deviates in significant ways from the standard genre categories. Certainly, the diversity that one finds in the scholarly literature lends considerable support to the statement that "it is by no means clear to which genre this psalm should be assigned."[1]

Despite this lack of genre clarity, Ps 130 has had a rather eventful history of reception. Both in its own right and as one of the Songs of Ascents, this psalm has played a prominent role in the liturgical and interpretive traditions of both Judaism and Christianity from the late biblical period onwards. Its additional designation as one of the seven penitential psalms meant that Ps 130 was one of the most prominent psalm texts in the western Christianity of the medieval period. It retained this prominence as one of the central texts of the Reformation. Even today, Ps 130 remains one of the most widely recognized and commented upon psalms.[2]

This essay will explore the possibility that it is precisely those elements in Ps 130 that are responsible for its form-critical ambiguity that have contributed to its exceptional theological fruitfulness. In so doing, it will also suggest that both individual interpreters and the interpretive tradition as a whole have been enriched by the necessity of coming to terms with this psalm's ambiguous and even competing elements. Finally, it will argue that an awareness of the complexity of the tradition can still be a valuable resource for the modern appropriation of this important psalm.

---

[1] Leslie C. Allen, *Psalms 101–150* (WBC 21; Waco, Tex.: Word, 1983), 192.

[2] See, for example, the title of Bernhard W. Anderson's popular handbook on the Psalms: *Out of the Depths: The Psalms Speak for Us Today* (with S. Bishop; 3rd ed.; Louisville: Westminster John Knox, 2000).

I. Elements of Genre Ambiguity in Psalm 130:
The Form-Critical Debate

Any discussion of the genre of Ps 130 must begin with its dramatic opening phrase, מִמַּעֲמַקִּים קְרָאתִיךָ יְהוָה. Critical scholars are in substantial agreement that the מַעֲמַקִּים image is part of a larger motif cluster that refers to the waters of the underworld and the primordial chaos. In the biblical material, these waters represent the realm and power of death that threatens to break forth into individual and communal life.[3] This imagery is especially prominent in the psalms of lament, where it helps to describe the dire situation of those praying. It is also part of the narrative description of past distress and deliverance that one finds in the thanksgiving psalms.[4]

The fact that the image of the depths is at home in the genres of both the lament and the thanksgiving means that the unavoidable decision about the time value of the next word (קְרָאתִיךָ) has form-critical implications. As is also the case with the קִוִּיתִי in v. 5, the perfect form of קְרָאתִיךָ could be taken as either a past or an iterative present. A strictly past sense would place the distress at a time previous to the present act of praying. Scholars who have taken the term in this way have argued for understanding Ps 130 as a thanksgiving psalm, since a description of past distress is a standard part of that genre.[5] Usually, however, the term is taken as an iterative present, a time value more in keeping with the imperatives that follow.[6] This would mean that the situation in the depths is a continuing one.

Such a view led Gunkel and others to classify Ps 130 under the general category of the individual lament.[7] However, not every scholar

---

[3] So Christoph Barth, *Die Errettung vom Tode: Leben und Tod in den Klage- und Dankliedern des Alten Testaments* (ed. B. Janowski; Stuttgart: W. Kohlhammer, 1997). Cf. also Manfred Görg, *Ein Haus im Totenreich: Jenseitsvorstellungen im Israel und Ägypten* (Düsseldorf: Patmos, 1998), 151–53.

[4] Or, as Claus Westermann describes them, the declarative psalms of praise. See his *Praise and Lament in the Psalms* (Atlanta: John Knox, 1981).

[5] So, for example, Artur Weiser, *The Psalms: A Commentary* (OTL; Philadelphia: Westminster, 1962), 772–76.

[6] See Loren D. Crow, *The Songs of Ascents (Psalms 120–134): Their Place in Israelite History and Religion* (SBLDS 148; Atlanta: Scholars Press, 1996), 85.

[7] Hermann Gunkel and Joachim Begrich, *Introduction to the Psalms: The Genres of the Religious Lyric of Israel* (trans. J. D. Nogalski; Macon, Ga.: Mercer University Press, 1998), 121. Gunkel is followed in this classification by, among others, Claus Westermann, "Psalm 130," in *Herr, tue meine Lippen auf: Eine Predigthilfe* (ed. G. Eichholz; Wuppertal-

who accepts a present interpretation of קְרָאתִיךְ has followed Gunkel in this respect. Part of the reason for this disagreement is that despite the commonly acknowledged connection of the depths with the lament, the מַעֲמַקִּים of v. 1 is unusual in ways that complicate the form-critical definition of Ps 130. First of all, one should note that מַעֲמַקִּים is not the most common term to refer to the waters of death and chaos.[8] Even more significant is the fact that the present example is the only absolute use of this term with this meaning. In all the other examples, מַעֲמַקִּים is used in the construct with either מִים or יָם, which makes the reference explicit.

Augmenting the ambiguity of the depths in Ps 130 is the fact that there is no further description of the psalmist's situation after the opening phrase. Most individual laments contain such an extended description of the psalmist's physical and/or social state. While this description is usually general enough to allow the use of the psalm in a variety of situations, its presence is an important way in which the psalm attempts to move God to pity and action.[9] The fact that Ps 130 does not have any such description has led a number of scholars to question its classification as a standard individual lament psalm.[10]

Another usual feature of the individual lament missing from Ps 130 is the description of the psalmist's human enemies. While there is never any doubt in the laments that God is ultimately behind the psalmist's present suffering, these psalms usually contain extended

---

Barmen: Emil Müller, 1961), 606–12; idem, *The Living Psalms* (Edinburgh: T&T Clark, 1989), 117–22; and Erhard Gerstenberger, *Psalms, Part 2, and Lamentations* (FOTL 15; Grand Rapids: Eerdmans, 2001), 355–59. As noted below, the peculiar nature of this psalm led Gunkel to assign it to a particular subcategory of the lament. Both Westermann and Gerstenberger also note the genre difficulties presented by this psalm's distinctive features.

[8] The word is used in this respect in Ps 69:3, 15 with מַים; cf. also Isa 51:10 and Ezek 27:34, where it is used with יָם and מַים, respectively. The more usual words to refer to the mythological deep are תְּהוֹם, מְצוּלָה, and their related forms.

[9] See Gunkel, *Introduction*, 155. Gunkel sees the situation of the psalmist in Ps 130 as probably one of life-threatening illness, though without basing this in the details of the text. See his *Die Psalmen* (5th ed.; Göttingen: Vandenhoeck & Ruprecht, 1968), 561.

[10] So, for example, Jörg Jeremias, "'Aus tiefer Not schrei ich zu dir' Ps 130 und Luthers Psalmlied," in *Von Wittenberg nach Memphis: Festschrift R. Schwarz* (Göttingen: Vandenhoeck & Ruprecht, 1989), 122–25; Werner H. Schmidt, "Gott und Mensch in Ps. 130: Formgeschichtliche Erwägungen," *TZ* 22 (1966): 241–53, esp. 243. Schmidt explicitly notes the fact that Gunkel's life-threatening illness is not to be found in the psalm itself. These scholars also note the lack of reference to enemies and explicit petition described in the following paragraphs.

and passionate descriptions of those who are the more immediate agents of this suffering (or who take advantage of it in some way). As with the self-description of the psalmist, the purpose of such a feature is apparently to move God to pity and action.[11] Again, the lack of any reference to such enemies has led a number of scholars to question the classification of Ps 130 as an individual lament.

Connected with the lack of such descriptions is the absence of any specific petition beyond the petition to hear the psalmist's prayer found in v. 2. While the call for God to hear is a standard part of the lament genre, it is usually supplemented by a more specific request for God's action. This is not the case in Ps 130. Just as there is no description of the psalmist's concrete situation, there is no specific request for a remedying of that situation. Indeed, while the psalmist would obviously like to be rescued from the depths, even that action is never requested directly.

Instead of such concrete concerns, the psalm raises the issue of human sinfulness in vv. 3–4. A confession of sin is clearly not out of place in the individual lament genre, where it often signals the psalmist's acknowledgment that his/her current situation of distress is, at least to some degree, deserved. At the same time, the very fact that the psalmist admits his/her guilt can function as a motivation for God to end the difficult situation. It should be noted that the individual lament genre also admits the other possibility, that the psalmist could assert his/her innocence, thus implying that his/her suffering is undeserved.[12]

While such a concern with sin is a standard element in the lament, its expression in Ps 130 is distinctive in a number of ways. First of all, the issue of sinfulness is especially prominent in this psalm, in part because of the lack of more concrete descriptions of the psalmist's distress. The prominence of this issue has led Gunkel to see this psalm as one of the few pure examples of a penitential song (*Busslied*), which he sees as a subcategory of the individual lament in which the confession of sins appears dominantly in the foreground.[13]

The issue of sin is not only especially prominent in Ps 130; it is also framed in unusually far-reaching terms. Other lament psalms

---

[11] Gunkel, *Introduction*, 155–56.

[12] Ibid., 176–77.

[13] Ibid., 187. The other pure examples of this subcategory are Ps 51 and the Prayer of Manasseh.

are concerned with particular sins that could have been avoided.[14] Psalm 130, on the other hand, raises the possibility that it is impossible for anyone to claim innocence before God, even as it asserts confidence in God's forgiveness. The result of this combination is that the psalm does not contain any explicit confession of sin.[15]

Finally, the form in which Ps 130 raises the issue of sin is also unusual. As a number of scholars have noted, the question in v. 3 has a certain similarity to the questions found in such entrance liturgies as Pss 15 and 24.[16] In these liturgies, the question functions to determine whether its addressee is able to participate in the Temple festivities. Those who have committed the ritual and/or moral sins mentioned in these psalms are excluded. In the present case, however, the question is rhetorical, since no one can stand if God decides to keep track of sins.

The distinctive way that Ps 130 treats the issue of sin raises a number of form-critical questions. Several scholars have argued that the psalm's approach to sin moves it beyond the genre of the individual lament and even beyond the subcategory of the penitential psalm, at least as that subcategory was envisioned by Gunkel.[17] Instead, such scholars see this psalm as engaging in a more general theological reflection, similar to that found in wisdom circles.[18] For these scholars, the fact of human sinfulness is in itself the cause of the psalmist's distress.

Scholars who view Ps 130 more along the lines of a lament see v. 3 as a motive clause that attempts to move God to act on the psalmist's behalf.[19] For these scholars, reminding God that human sinfulness is inevitable is meant to convince God that the psalmist's sins should not stand in the way of God's coming to his/her rescue. In such a view, pardoning the psalmist's sins is the first step towards resolving the concrete situation that is the cause of the lament.

---

[14] This is apparently the case even in Ps 51, the only other psalm that Gunkel sees as fully "penitential."

[15] Westermann, *Living Psalms*, 118.

[16] Schmidt, "Gott und Mensch," 246; Jeremias, "Aus tiefer Not," 124–25.

[17] So Schmidt, "Gott und Mensch," 241.

[18] Schmidt, "Gott und Mensch," 245 and passim; Jeremias, "Aus tiefer Not," 123–24; cf. also Franz Sedlmeier, " 'Bei dir, da ist die Vergebung, damit du gefürchtet werdest': Überlegungen zu Psalm 130," *Bib* 73 (1992): 473–95, esp. 482.

[19] Westermann, "Psalm 130," 607–8. In keeping with this view, Westermann does not see vv. 3–4 as the most important part of this psalm.

How one understands the verses that follow will depend on the genre decisions that one has made to this point in the psalm. Thus, vv. 5–6 detail the psalmist's hopes and expectations in moving terms, though it is not entirely clear what the psalmist is hoping for or expecting. Some scholars see the hoped-for divine word in v. 5 in terms of a word of divine forgiveness of sin, while others also see it as a more concrete word of assurance about the psalmist's distress.[20] Some scholars even see a specific reference to a salvation oracle of some sort, such as might be delivered by a priest or a temple prophet.[21]

The final two lines of the psalm also contain a number of genre ambiguities, especially in connection with the move from an individual to a communal reference. Some have seen the allusion to Israel as an explicitly national or political reference that is at odds with the first six verses of the psalm. Because of this, a number of scholars have seen most or all of these final verses as a later addition.[22]

Even if one accepts the present form of the psalm, these verses raise a number of form-critical questions. Particularly important in this respect is the question of who is speaking in these verses. If one agrees with those scholars who see the divine "word" of v. 5 as a reference to a specific salvation oracle, it is possible to see vv. 7–8 as such an oracle that assures the psalmist that his/her prayer has been heard.[23] If, on the other hand, the psalmist continues to speak in these verses, it is possible to see them as an example of the call to praise that often concludes the individual lament.[24] Such a call to praise could be a response to an oracle that was received between vv. 6 and 7, or it might be simply a testimony to the psalmist's confidence in God's faithfulness and mercy. All of these possibilities fit well with a view of this psalm as some form of an individual lament.

---

[20] Thus, for Schmidt, "das Wort is nur das vergebende, nicht das erlösende Wort" ("Gott und Mensch," 249). For Westermann, on the other hand, "Vergebung und Erlösung gehören zusammen" ("Psalm 130," 609).

[21] So, for example, Hans-Joachim Kraus, *Psalms 60–150: A Commentary* (5th ed.; Minneapolis: Augsburg, 1989), 467; also Allen, *Psalms 101–150*, 194.

[22] For an overview of the arguments for and against the originality of vv. 7–8, see Allen, *Psalms 101–150*, 193–94. Opposed to those who emphasize the distinction between the individual concerns of vv. 1–6 and the communal emphasis of vv. 7–8 are those who stress the fact that the entire psalm shares a common vocabulary, similar theology, and chiastic structure.

[23] Thus, for example, Kraus, *Psalms 60–150*, 468.

[24] So Allen, *Psalms 101–150*, 194; cf. Gunkel, *Psalmen*, 562.

On the other hand, it is possible to see vv. 7–8 as an attempt to broaden the theological insight of vv. 3–4 to the wider community of Israel.[25] In support of such a view is the fact that the exhortation of the opening phrase of v. 7 is followed by the same type of theological affirmations of God's forgiving nature that one finds in those earlier verses. Scholars who emphasize this aspect of the psalm often argue that the final verse's redemption of Israel from all its sins has an "eschatological" weight.[26]

Other scholars are inclined to see the "redemption" of these verses in more concrete terms.[27] Such scholars note that the standard usage of פדות usually has to do with specific deliverance from physical distress and danger. They also note that עון can refer to the punishment for sins as well as to the sins themselves. Obviously, how one sees the distress in the first half of the psalm helps to determine how one decides these issues.

The diversity of critical opinion just described would seem to confirm the view that Ps 130 contains a fair amount of ambiguity that makes its form-critical classification difficult. It also seems clear that much of this ambiguity is centered in the relatively unspecified nature of the psalm's opening image. Scholars who interpret the depths in the context of a specific situation of distress from which the psalmist is seeking relief tend to define this psalm as some form of individual lament.[28] Those who see the depths in terms of some sort of general human condition tend to see the psalm as a more wisdom-oriented theological reflection.[29]

The next part of this paper will examine how the Jewish and Christian traditions have come to terms with those aspects of Ps 130 that have caused difficulties for modern scholars. Since the psalm's opening image of the depths is at the heart of many of these difficulties, the following survey will focus on how Jewish and Christian interpreters have understood that image. It will be seen that much of these interpreters' theological creativity stems from the very ambiguity that makes the form-critical classification of this psalm so difficult.

[25] Schmidt, "Gott und Mensch," 251–52.
[26] Jeremias, "Aus tiefer Not," 130.
[27] So Westermann, "Psalm 130," 610; Allen, *Psalms 101–150*, 192.
[28] So, for example, Gunkel and Westermann.
[29] So, for example, Schmidt and Jeremias.

II. The Depths in the Jewish Tradition

Ironically, one needs to begin this survey of the Jewish interpretation of the depths in Ps 130:1 by taking note of this psalm's designation as a Song of Ascents (שיר המעלות). Indeed, it would not be
incorrect to see the designation of Ps 130 as one of the Songs of
Ascents as the earliest interpretation of that psalm.[30] Neither ancient
nor modern scholars completely agree as to the precise significance
of this superscription.[31] Nevertheless, interpreters from an early age
clearly saw this superscription as significant for understanding these
psalms both as a group and as individual texts.

Of particular interest in the present case is the way the Targum
has rendered the superscription of these psalms: שירא דאתאמר על מסוקין
דתהומא. In this rendering, the "ascents" of the MT is explicitly connected with the "rise" of the "deep." While the Targum renders the
superscription of all the Songs of Ascents in the same way, this rendering obviously has a special resonance in the case of Ps 130 in
light of the usual connection between the תהום and the מעמקים.

The significance of the Targum's rendering of the superscription
is underlined by a story about the Songs of Ascents that is found
(in somewhat different versions and in different places) in the
Babylonian and Jerusalem Talmuds. The setting of the story in both
accounts is David's digging of the pits, apparently in preparation for
the building of the Temple. This excavation project results (in different
ways) in a welling up of the waters of the deep, which threaten to
flood the world. This in turn necessitates David's actions to save the
world and (for different reasons) the praying of the Songs of Ascents.
It is worth looking at the particulars in the different versions.

In *b. Sukkah* 53a-b, David's digging directly results in a welling up
of the waters of the deep. David responds to this threat by asking
whether it is permitted to write the divine name on a piece of pottery and toss it into the deep so that the waters will subside. After
being threatened by David and engaging in some legal reasoning,
Ahithophel informs David that such an action was permitted. David

---

[30] That is, of the psalm as it now stands. As noted above, some scholars see the
redactional addition of either all or part of vv. 7–8 as an interpretation of vv. 1–6.
For some of these scholars, this addition took place as part of Ps 130's incorporation
into the group of the Songs of Ascents. See, for example, Crow, *Songs of Ascents*, 142.

[31] For a representative survey, see ibid., 1–27.

tosses the inscribed pottery into the water, and the deep subsides 16,000 cubits, a distance that is then seen as less than desirable for the watering of the earth. At this point, David says the fifteen Songs of Ascents, which raises the water 15,000 cubits to a more acceptable level.[32]

The story in *y. Sanh.* 29a is somewhat different. In that version, David dug down to a depth of 1,500 cubits, where he found a pot that he wanted to remove. The pot spoke to David, denying him permission to proceed further and identifying itself as the cover of the great deep.[33] Despite this warning, David removed the pot and the deep surged up to flood the world. As in the Babylonian account, David threatens Ahithophel who then speaks (אמר מה דאמר) to stop the flood.[34] At this point, David begins to say the Songs of Ascents, with each song corresponding to one hundred cubits.[35]

These accounts are similar in that they both see a connection between David's excavation activities, a threat from the deep, advice from Ahithophel, and the Songs of Ascents. On the other hand, they differ in that the Jerusalem Talmud sees David's removal of the pot as the cause of the welling up of the deep, while the Babylonian version sees David's making of such a pot (inscribed with the divine name) as the cause of the deep's (overly effective) subsidence.

These versions also differ in that the Jerusalem Talmud sees the Songs of Ascents as corresponding to the lowering of the deep to its previous position, while the Babylonian Talmud sees these Songs as the means by which David raised the waters after the latter had sunk to an unacceptable level. It should, however, be noted that the Babylonian version has an introduction in which it is first claimed that David made the waters of the flood subside by saying the fifteen Songs of Ascents. Only after the objection is raised that they should then be called "Songs of Descent" is the above story remembered and recounted.[36]

---

[32] At this point in the text, the implication that the earth's crust is a thousand cubits thick is noted, and the apparent contradiction of being able to find water without digging to that depth is explained by the high level of the Euphrates.

[33] In this text, the pot claims to have been at this spot from the time of the earthquake connected with the divine revelation at Mount Sinai.

[34] In this version, Ahithophel at first apparently sees the danger of the flood as specific to David and comments that as a result he will himself become king.

[35] This equivalence is explained by seeing each Song of Ascents (שיר המעלות) as being for a hundred (מאה) ascents (עולות).

[36] Later versions of this story also speak of the threat of the rising of the deep.

The connection of the deep with the Temple has a particular
significance for the water-drawing ritual that took place during the
Feast of Tabernacles. This ritual seems to have had the purpose of
helping to ensure the coming year's rains by a raising of the waters
of the deep.[37] Significantly, the levitical singing of the Songs of Ascents
seems to have been a part of this ritual.[38]

In view of this apparent role of the Songs of Ascents in the water-
drawing ritual, it is significant that Ps 130 has an even more specific
role when the rain does not come. In the latter circumstance, *m.
Ta'an.* 2.2–3 specifies a number of days of fasting, during some of
which six special benedictions are added to the eighteen of daily use.

(For a discussion of such versions, cf. Raphael Patai, *Man and Temple in Ancient Jewish
Myth and Ritual* [2nd ed.; New York: KTAV, 1967], 55–58.) Of particular interest
is the version cited by Patai in which a stone has a role similar to that of the pot
that contains the deep in the Talmudic accounts (Sode Raza, *Yalqut Reubeni* ad Gen
1:1). In this version, God made the stone at the time of the creation, inscribed it
with the divine name, and set it as a seal on the deep. Because of human sinfulness, God removed this stone at the time of the flood. David disturbed this stone
in his excavation and then returned it to its place to contain the deep once again.

This tradition of the inscribed stone that holds the deep in check is found in a
number of much earlier sources. Some of these see this stone as both the first solid
thing created and the foundation stone of the Temple; cf. Patai, *Man and Temple*,
85. (For a discussion of the Near Eastern background of this, cf. Richard J. Clifford,
The Cosmic Mountain in Canaan and the Old Testament [HSM 4; Cambridge, Mass.:
Harvard University Press, 1972]. For its theological significance, cf. Jon D. Levenson,
Sinai and Zion: An Entry into the Jewish Bible [San Francisco: Harper & Row, 1985]).
See, for example, *Targum Pseudo-Jonathan* to Exod 28:30 which refers to the "great
and holy name . . . which was clearly inscribed on the foundation stone with which
the LORD of the world sealed the mouth of the great deep from the beginning"
(*Targum Neofiti 1: Exodus; Targum Pseudo-Jonathan: Exodus* [trans. M. Maher; Collegeville,
Minn.: Liturgical Press, 1994]). The same stone is also mentioned in *Tg. Qoh.* 3:11
and *Tg. Cant.* 4:12.

This tradition seems to combine three elements: the widespread biblical motif
that God's name dwells in the Temple (cf. among other places Deuteronomy, and
Jdt 9:8), the biblical (and widespread ancient Near Eastern) connection between the
subjugation of the chaos waters and the building of a divine dwelling place (cf. Isa
44:24–28; also Clifford), and the motif of the enemies sinking in or being cast into
the deeps of the exodus like a stone (Exod 15:5; Neh 9:11). One sees partial com-
ings together of these motifs in the Prayer of Manasseh 3, (where God confines the
deep and seals it with God's name) and 3 Macc 2:9 (where at the creation God
sanctifies Jerusalem and makes it a firm foundation for God's name).

[37] For a detailed analysis of this ritual and its significance, cf. Patai, *Man and Temple*.

[38] So Patai, *Man and Temple*, 29, 54–60, 86; cf. *m. Sukkah* 5.4; *t. Sukkah* 4.7; *m.
Mid.* 2.5. According to these passages, the fifteen Temple steps on which the Levites
stood and sang during the water-drawing ritual correspond to the fifteen Songs of
Ascents. As such, these texts do not explicitly state that the Levites sang the Songs
of Ascents on these steps, though that seems to be the implication. Patai and others
accept it as such.

These additional benedictions begin with either the remembrance and the shofar verses from the Rosh Hashanah service or 1 Kgs 8:37ff. and Jer 14:1ff.[39] They then continue with three Songs of Ascents (Pss 120, 121, and 130) and Ps 102 (in that order). Each of these additional benedictions is "sealed" with its own prayer that refers to a particular biblical narrative in which God answers prayer.[40] The seal for Ps 130 refers to God's answering of Jonah's prayer.[41]

These references obviously do not provide us with reliable information about the original settings and use of Ps 130 and the other Songs of Ascents. They may, however, show the later use of these psalms in the Second Temple period, and they certainly give an indication of how these psalms were viewed in that period and the early centuries of the common era. It is worth considering the genre implications of these references.

Perhaps the most important aspect of these references from a genre perspective is their consistent view that these psalms are at home in a situation of specific and concrete need. For the Songs of Ascents as a whole, this need is the normal need for the annual rains.[42] The use of Ps 130 in times of drought obviously reflects an even more specific situation of need.

Also significant from a genre perspective is the way these references provide groupings of texts that are meant to be used together. This is perhaps especially noteworthy in the case of the *m. Taʿan.* 2.2–3, where Ps 130 is grouped with other texts that are felt to be either similar or at least compatible in some way. From the perspective of modern form criticism, the nature of this grouping is to some extent, but not entirely, clear.

As noted above, six texts are added to the Benedictions during the fast days in times of drought. The psalms added, along with Ps 130, are Pss 120, 121, and 102. Of these, Ps 102 is clearly an individual lament, as is Ps 120. In both of these texts, the psalmist calls

---

[39] For the remembrance and shofar verses, cf. *m. Roš Haš.* 4.5–6. R. Judah argues for the substitution of the 1 Kings and Jeremiah passages for these verses.

[40] Cf. *m. Taʿan.* 2.4.

[41] "The one who answered Jonah from the belly of the fish, he will answer you and hearken to the voice of your crying this day. Blessed are you, LORD, who answers in time of trouble!"

[42] The Talmudic stories about David's disturbing of the deep also reflect a situation of need, as well as a concern for the watering of the earth (at least in the Babylonian version).

to God out of a situation of distress.[43] Psalm 121 also begins with the psalmist's looking for help, though it then continues with an assertion of confidence and a blessing. One finds a similar expression of confidence in Ps 102.

The other two texts added to the benedictions are either the remembrance and the shofar verses or 1 Kgs 8:37ff. and Jer 14:1ff. The former pairing emphasizes the need for God to remember the covenant with Israel and act on its behalf.[44] The latter pairing adds to this an emphasis on the need for God to forgive Israel's sins.[45]

Most of these texts have at least some connection with the modern form-critical category of the lament.[46] This, of course, fits well with the way *m. Ta'an.* 2.2–3 situates these psalms in a time of communal distress.[47] The fact that Ps 130 is grouped with these texts would seem to indicate that the tradition saw this text as at home with laments arising out of a situation of specific need.[48]

---

[43] It is noteworthy that in neither of these psalms is the distress connected with drought. It is instead enemies that seem to be the problem in these psalms, a fact that obviously does not keep them from being used for the present situation of specific need.

[44] Although these verses become fixed at a later date, there seems to be some flexibility about their nature (and even their number) in *m. Roš Haš.* 4.5–6.

[45] The Kings passage is from Solomon's prayer at the dedication of the Temple. In it, Solomon asks that God hear both individual and communal prayers in future times of famine, plague, and other disasters (though not specifically lack of rain, as in 1 Kgs 8:35–36). As such, it might be seen as an "anticipatory lament," in which Solomon plays the role of intermediary or intercessor. Included in his prayer is a plea that God will "forgive" (סלח) those future petitioners "so that they may fear you" (למען יראוך), which has suggestive parallels with Ps 130:4. One might also note that the parallel to this passage in 2 Chr 6:31 adds "to walk in your ways" (ללכת בדרכיך) to the latter phrase. This parallel is little noted in the literature on Ps 130. Nevertheless, it might well provide some insight as to one way in which Ps 130:4 was understood in the post-exilic period that is usually seen as the time of its origins.

The Jeremiah passage specifically concerns a drought, as that chapter's opening description makes clear. Israel's petition includes a confession of sin as well as a petition for God to act. In Jer 14, of course, this petition is not successful.

[46] Again, this is less clear with the remembrance and shofar verses.

[47] Within this larger context of the lament, one can also discern a number of other prominent motifs, including confidence in God's mercy and a focus on the role of Jerusalem. Confidence is especially prominent in Ps 121, but it is also present in Ps 102. Jerusalem is a focus in Ps 102, as well as in the Kings and Jeremiah passages. One may also note that the psalms are all basically psalms of the individual (though they do have some communal elements). The Kings and Jeremiah passages are more strictly communal.

[48] Psalm 130 clearly shares with these other psalms an expression of confidence (vv. 4–8). It may also share a connection with Jerusalem by virtue of its status as one of the Songs of Ascents, though this is less clear. Such a connection with Jerusalem may also be implied by its reference to watching for the morning and even by its reference to the depths.

On the other hand, it is worth noting that psalms such as 120 and 102 supply some important elements of the lament that are missing in Ps 130. Thus, Ps 120 is very much concerned with human enemies, while Ps 102 has an extended description of the psalmist's desperate condition. As noted above, it was precisely the absence of these elements that helped to make the genre definition of Ps 130 so difficult.

One further way that Ps 130 differs from the other psalms in this grouping is in its emphasis on human sinfulness. It may be that this element was simply assumed for all the psalms by virtue of the situation of the fast itself[49] or that this was the distinctive contribution of Ps 130 to the ceremony. Nevertheless, it is perhaps significant that it is precisely this motif that is especially prominent in R. Judah's substitutions of the Kings and Jeremiah passages for the remembrance and the shofar verses. Whether or not such an emphasis on sinfulness is the reason for these substitutions, the latter certainly underline that aspect of Ps 130—without downplaying the concrete nature of the situation of need.

All of this indicates that the rabbinic tradition did not see the concern with sinfulness in vv. 3–4 as in any way compromising an understanding of the depths as a concrete situation of need. This is borne out by the explicit statements on the depths that one finds in the later tradition. Thus, for example, in *Cant. Rab.* 2.1 the עמקים are explicitly equated with Israel's sorrows on the basis of Ps 130:1. A number of later commentators move in a similar direction.

Among these commentators, one may cite David Qimḥi who makes a specific comparison between the depths (which he specifies as depths of waters, מים) and Israel's exile. For Qimḥi, this exile does not simply refer to Israel's ancient history. It is rather a present reality from which his contemporaries need to be redeemed, just as Israel was redeemed from Egypt, Babylon, and many other times of distress.[50] In his comments on v. 8, Qimḥi explicitly sees this redemption as a two step process, a process he ties to Deut 30. First, God redeems Israel from its sins by forgiving its iniquities and putting a desire to repent in its heart. God then rescues Israel from its captivity.

A similar connection between the depths and exile may be seen in Ibn Ezra's comments on Ps 130:1. It is, however, significant that for Ibn Ezra exile is not the only possible understanding of the depths. He also sees the depths as signifying poverty and disgrace,

---

[49] Cf. the citation of Jonah 3:10 and Joel 2:13 in *m. Taʿan.* 2.1.

[50] So his comments on v. 7.

both of which are not necessarily limited to exile. In all of these, the depths are connected with concrete situations of need.

Ibn Ezra has one further understanding of the depths alongside his first three interpretations of them as exile, poverty, and disgrace, namely, as שפלות. This may be understood in a way similar to the first three terms if one sees it as "humiliation." However, it seems more likely that one should understand it in a positive sense, as "humility."[51] Such an understanding would fit well with another, quite widespread strand of the traditional interpretation of this verse.

To see this other understanding of the depths in Ps 130:1, one may turn first of all to *b. Ber.* 10b. There one finds R. Jose b. Ḥanina (in the name of R. Eliezer b. Jacob) using this verse to argue that one should pray in a low place. This prescription is further specified as a means of ensuring that there is no "elevation" (נבהות) in the presence of the LORD. This same tradition is cited in *Midrash Tehillim* on Ps 130:1. An abbreviated form is found in *Qoh. Rab.* 4:17, where it is attributed to R. Adda b. R. Simeon (in the name of R. Nathan). Also relevant in this respect is the citation of Ps 130:1 in *b. Taʿan.* 23b in connection with the practice of R. Jonah the father of R. Mani who went to pray in a low-lying place in times when rain was needed.

It is of interest that both the *b. Berakot* and the *Midrash Tehillim* passages just cited also defend this tradition with a reference to Ps 102:1. One finds a similar link between Pss 130 and 102 in *Lev. Rab.* 3.7. That passage cites Ps 130:1 with reference to the situating of the Torah within the scholar, on the basis of the comparison of counsel in the human heart with the "deep waters" (מים עמקים) in Prov 20:5.

In all of these passages, the relevance of the connection between Pss 130 and 102 is not immediately apparent. Certainly, Ps 102 seems to be more concerned with the specific distress of the psalmist than with the latter's humble stance before God.[52] Nevertheless, it hardly seems coincidental that Ps 102 also immediately follows Ps 130 in the fast service for times of drought in *m. Taʿan.* 2.3 or that *b. Taʿan.* 23b is also concerned with the need for rain. One suspects

---

[51] One sees this sense of שפלות in David Qimḥi's comments on Ps 131, where he sees David as giving an example of the way that Israel should act in exile. For the translation of "humility" in the Ibn Ezra passage, see Arnold J. Rosenberg, *Psalms: A New English Translation* (3 vols.; New York: Judaica, 1991), 3:495.

[52] Though it is interesting that *Midrash Tehillim* sees Ps 102:3 as referring to the prayer of Manassah who was destitute in good deeds.

that the connection of Pss 130 and 102 (in that order) in the expanded drought benedictions has played a role in keeping them together here. The reference in *Leviticus Rabbah* to the deep waters in Prov 20:5 is also suggestive in this sense.[53]

The connection of עמק with Torah and wisdom that one sees in *Leviticus Rabbah* and Prov 20:5 reflects a more widespread usage of that root in the biblical and post-biblical periods. A number of texts from the Second Temple and rabbinic periods use this root to describe the depths of divine or human thought, as well as both matters difficult to understand and the deep mysteries of the world.[54] Also of interest are those passages that see either a mythological or an historical connection between wisdom and the depths of the sea.[55]

Before concluding this section, one should mention the role of Ps 130 in the ongoing Jewish liturgical tradition. Given *m. Taʿan.* 2.2–3, it is no surprise to find that penitential psalms are to be found in settings associated with fast days, such as *Selihot*.[56] Psalm 130 plays a specific role during the Ten Days of Penitence between Rosh Hashanah and Yom Kippur, as well as in the *Seder Tashlik* on Rosh Hashanah. In the Sephardic tradition, it is said after *Selihot* in the month of Elul in preparation for these Holy Days, as well as in the *minchah* service before Yom Kippur.[57] The psalm's concern with human sinfulness obviously makes it appropriate for such ceremonies of repentance, though it is less clear how this affects an understanding of the psalm's image of the depths.

In this respect, it is suggestive that depths imagery plays a recurring role in the Holy Days of Rosh Hashanah and Yom Kippur, even beyond the use of Ps 130. Thus, the *Tashlik* ceremony on Rosh Hashanah recalls the sending of sins to the depths of the sea (במצלות ים)

---

[53] It is intriguing that Ps 102 is also linked with Ps 130 as one of the seven penitential psalms in the Christian tradition.

[54] See the survey in *TDOT* 11:207–8.

[55] Thus, Sir 24:5 describes wisdom's role at creation when it walked in the "depth of the abyss." Cf. Sir 24:29 where wisdom (now identified with Torah) is seen to have counsel more profound than the great abyss. Wisdom 10:18–19 describes how wisdom led the Israelites through "much water," drowned their enemies, and cast them out of the "depth (βάθους) of the abyss."

[56] On the role of penitential psalms in *Selihot*, cf. Ismar Elbogen, *Jewish Liturgy: A Comprehensive History* (Philadelphia: Jewish Publication Society, 1993), 178.

[57] See Macy Nulman, *The Encyclopedia of Jewish Prayer* (Northvale, N.J.: Jason Aronson, 1993), 304–5. Cf. Elbogen, *Jewish Liturgy*, 181. One might also note that *Midrash Tehillim* to Ps 130:4 relates the withholding of forgiveness during the Days of Penitence to the fear of God on Yom Kippur.

in Mic 7:19. That same passage plays a role in the "sabbath of
return" between Rosh Hashanah and Yom Kippur, and it is also
found after the Jonah reading in the *minchah* service on Yom Kippur.
The depths obviously play a prominent role in that Jonah reading
itself, though as in the Micah passage, the word is not the same as
in Ps 130. It is perhaps significant that in the Micah passage the
depths are where God will ultimately send Israel's sins after freeing
Israel from them, while in Jonah the depths are the locus of Jonah's
distress. In neither place do the depths seem to be directly identified
with Israel's sins.

One may conclude this section by recalling that a large part of
the ambiguity surrounding the genre of Ps 130 was related to the
unique use of the absolute מעמקים in v. 1, as well as to the fact that
there is no further specification of the nature of the depths elsewhere
in the psalm. The preceding overview suggests that the resulting
ambiguity has allowed for a flexible and creative usage of this image
in the Jewish tradition, one that includes both a negative and a positive approach to the depths. The next section will note a similarly
flexible and creative usage in the Christian tradition.

III. The Depths in the Christian Tradition

Psalm 130 is perhaps especially known in the Christian tradition for
being one of Martin Luther's favorite psalms and the basis of one
of his most famous hymns. Nevertheless, this psalm had a prominent place in that tradition well before Luther. Contributing to this
prominence, at least in western Christianity, was its inclusion as one
of the seven penitential psalms, though it also played an important
role in the interpretive and liturgical traditions of Christianity in its
own right.

In order to understand the role of the depths in this tradition, it
is necessary to note that the מעמקים was usually translated into the
LXX by some form of βάθος, the same way that מצולה and (more
rarely) תהום were translated. This meant that for Greek-speaking Jews
and Christians Ps 130:1 was easily linked with such passages as Mic
7:19 and Jonah 2:4. In addition, this translation brought these texts
into conversation with certain New Testament texts that also used
the term βάθος.

Particularly influential along these lines was the usage of Paul in
his Epistle to the Romans. In Rom 8:38–39 Paul mentions "depth"

(βάθος) as one element in a list of things which will not be able to separate the believer from the love of God. On the other hand, in Rom 11:33, Paul extols the "depth of the riches and wisdom and knowledge of God." In this negative and positive use of βάθος, Paul is very much in keeping with the Jewish tradition noted above.

One early Christian father who was influenced by Paul's use of "depth" was Origen of Alexandria. Thus, in the midst of his discussion of the hardening of Pharaoh's heart, Origen cites Paul's arguments concerning the human inability to understand the subtleties of God's plan. For Origen, it is in the face of those things that have been "submerged" (*demersa*) in such "deep mysteries" that one prays, as in Ps 130:1.[58] One finds a similar argument in his commentary on Ps 130:1, where he notes that the person who searches the depths of God is one who cries to the LORD out of the depths. In that work Origen also makes a distinction between a superficial crying out with one's lips and a crying out from one's depths, which he ties to the Spirit's crying out in one's heart.[59]

This interpretation of the depths as a positive attribute of the person praying is also to be found in such Antiochene fathers as John Chrysostom and Theodoret of Cyrus. Like Origen, Chrysostom sees the depths as indicative of an intense prayer that arises from the depths of one's heart and mind, "with great zeal and enthusiasm," rather than from one's mouth and lips alone. For Chrysostom, this type of intense prayer provides great spiritual benefits to the one praying, even before that person receives what is being requested.[60] Theodoret likewise sees the depths as referring to prayer that arises from the bottom of one's heart rather than one's mouth alone. He describes those who pray in such a fashion as "a chorus of the righteous," (Τῶν δικαίων χορὸς) despite the fact that v. 3 describes everyone as sinful.[61]

One finds similar interpretations of the depths in the Latin fathers. The comments of Hilary on Ps 130:1 are particularly instructive.[62]

---

[58] Origen, *Hom. Exod.* IV.2 (PG 12:318).

[59] Origen, *Sel. Ps.* on Ps 130 (PG 12:1648).

[60] These spiritual benefits include control of such passions as anger, envy, desire, and lust for the things of this life (PG 55:373–77); cf. John Chrysostom, *Commentary on the Psalms* (trans. R. C. Hill; 2 vols.; Brookline, Mass.: Holy Cross Orthodox Press, 1998), 2:180–87.

[61] Theodoret of Cyrus, PG 80:1899–1902; cf. Theodoret of Cyrus, *Commentary on the Psalms* (trans. R. C. Hill; 2 vols.; Washington D.C.: Catholic University of America Press, 2001), 2:302–3.

[62] Hilary, *Tractatus super Psalmos* (CCSL 61:647–57).

Like the Greek fathers, Hilary contrasts prayer of the heart with that
of the lips, citing the Gospel command to pray inwardly rather than
outwardly. He also offers a very specific connection with the inscrutable
depths of God's wisdom in Rom 11:33, even beginning his discussion of Ps 130 with a quotation of that passage. It is, however,
Hilary's third interpretation of the depths that is of particular interest, since it places the depths in the context of human loss, anxiety,
and suffering.[63] Thus, for Hilary, the depths could bear a number
of interpretations at the same time, both positive and negative.

It is, of course, Augustine that is the major figure in the western
interpretation of the psalms, and it is with Augustine that one finds
both a continuation of the patristic tradition noted so far and a
somewhat different approach to the depths.[64] Thus, at the beginning
of his comments on Ps 130:1, Augustine agrees with many of the
above authors that the voice in this psalm is that of one who is
faithful and who prays with the heart. For Augustine, this is the
voice of one ascending, in keeping with his understanding of the
psalm's superscription. Indeed, for Augustine, in the very act of crying from the deep this person rises from the deep. As in the Jewish
tradition, Augustine cites Jonah as an example of one whose prayer
arises from the deep and reaches the ears of God.

Augustine also, however, is concerned that his audience understand the nature of the deep from which one cries to God. For him,
it is the deep of this mortal life, a mortal life that has worn away
the divine image so as to submerge a person under "the deep of
evils" (de profundo malorum).[65] It is with this understanding of the deep
as sinful human nature that Augustine's argument takes a characteristically Pauline turn. For Augustine, those who are in this deep
have two choices. If they are "really in the deep" (valde in profundo),
they will despair, continue in their sins, and not cry out from the
deep.[66] On the other hand, they may be "very frightened" (expauescens)
and cry out, recognizing that their only hope is the fact that Jesus

---

[63] Hilary supports this by quoting Ps 69:3, with its more explicit reference to the
profundum maris.

[64] Augustine, Enarrationes in Psalmos (CCSL 40:1189–898).

[65] As Augustine notes in his comments on v. 5, this includes not just former sins
but human weakness itself, sins of the heart, not just major sins. At this stage of
his argument, Augustine again quotes all of vv. 1–3 as the song of one who recognizes his sinfulness and so is rising from the depths.

[66] Augustine sees this possibility especially if they are otherwise prosperous. As
such, he clearly does not see the deep as indicative of worldly distress.

has "despised not our deeps" and "come to this life, promising remission of all sins." It is this act that has "raised man even from the deep so that he might cry out from the deep, beneath the mass of his sins, and that the sinner's voice might come to God: crying from where, if not from the depth of evils."

Augustine's argument is also characteristically Pauline in its eschatology. Augustine situates his audience between the "already" of their past remission of sins and the "not yet" of the future kingdom of heaven, between the blotting out of debts and pardon, on the one hand, and the reward of eternal life, on the other.[67] In this situation, one cannot hope to fulfill the "law of Christ," as this is set forth in the stringent terms of the Sermon on the Mount.[68] As a result, the proper response is one of hope and trust in the certainty of God's promises, which is exactly how Augustine interprets the second half of this psalm.

Cassiodorus provides an appropriate conclusion to this consideration of ancient commentaries on Ps 130, as well as a useful transition to the medieval era.[69] As usual, his interpretation is heavily dependent on that of Augustine, even while it mitigates some of the more radically Pauline aspects of the latter's analysis. In this, Cassiodorus sets the stage for the medieval reception of Augustine.

Like Augustine, Cassiodorus notes this psalm's status as a "canticle of steps." In keeping with what was by his time a well-established tradition, Cassiodorus sees these psalms as an upward development in the spiritual life. Cassiodorus is, however, especially expansive on the question of why someone so far along in this process (on the eleventh step) prostrates himself in the depths. His answer is that the more one ascends on this spiritual path the more one needs to "bend low" in "greater humility" and with "devoted prayers, so that despite our inability to be free from guilt, we may deserve to be pardoned (*mereamur absolui*) through the kind offices of devotion." This greater humility comes from an "awareness of the human condition, though he had long subdued it." Cassiodorus also sees the

---

[67] See his comments on the reasons for waiting in v. 6.

[68] One will recall that Augustine's text has "law" in v. 4 (as does the LXX). Augustine takes a Pauline approach to law here, seeing it as a means of bringing one to trust in God's mercy.

[69] Cassiodorus, *Expositio Psalmorum* (CCSL 98:1185–90). For the English translation in the text, see Cassiodorus, *Explanation of the Psalms* (trans. P. G. Walsh; ACS 53; New York: Paulist Press, 1991), 311–16.

psalmist as "asking to be freed from the depth of sins and imploring the kindly deliverance of the goodly Judge from the disasters which he has recounted."

Cassiodorus follows Augustine in citing Jonah as an example of someone who prays from the depths. Once again, however, Cassiodorus goes further than Augustine in praising Jonah's "outstandingly and wholly glorious repentance" and "humility." Jonah is a testimony to the power of "holy prayer," which is heard more quickly the deeper the depths from which one cries to God.[70] Despite his agreement with Augustine that one does not merit forgiveness by one's own actions, Cassiodorus also sees the waiting of v. 4 in terms of charity, "which awaits all, suffers all, and longingly anticipates its hope."[71] Charity also "wholesomely fires the hearts of the faithful, and achieves nothing less than the perfection of Christians." Such statements may well suggest a more "realized" eschatology than that found in Augustine.

In his conclusions, Cassiodorus describes how this psalm "begins from the depths, but like the advancing sun mounts to a great height, enabling us to realise how beneficial is the repentance which we see residing at such a lofty eminence." Also important for Cassiodorus's entire analysis is his view of this psalm as one of the seven penitential psalms.[72] Along these lines, he notes that in this psalm, the "evil of pride is struck with the sixth axe of repentance." Cassiodorus concludes by counseling his reader to "love the humility which has raised the faithful to heaven" and to "swiftly confess our evil deeds so that we may not meet our deserts."

As noted above, one sees in Cassiodorus the transition to the medieval period and the medieval appropriation of Augustine. Certainly, both Cassiodorus and his medieval successors agree with Augustine that v. 3 rules out any human merit that would enable one to stand before God. (To do otherwise would compromise the redemptive nature of the Christ event.) In this vein, they emphasize the depths as the depths of human sinfulness. Thus, for example, Gregory the Great

---

[70] Cassiodorus also sees Peter and the tax collector as two other examples of those who had need to pray from the depths because they had fallen so deeply into sin.

[71] One will recall that Cassiodorus's v. 4 both contained a reference to the law and had a different verse division than the MT.

[72] Cassiodorus is the first known source to enumerate these psalms, though he speaks of them as an earlier tradition. It is probable that Augustine is the source of this tradition.

sees this verse in terms of Jonah's crying out of the depths of his dis-obedience.[73] At a later period, John Fisher also connects the psalm to Jonah and details a seven-step journey of sin into the depths of hell.[74]

At the same time, Cassiodorus and his successors also build upon those elements in Augustine (and Paul) that emphasize the need for human effort and the possibility of spiritual advancement. To this end, they emphasize the place of this psalm in two sequential group-ings, the Songs of Ascents and the seven penitential psalms. In this perspective, the depths retain the positive sense that was seen espe-cially in the earlier fathers. In contrast to Augustine's emphasis on trust and hope, the emphasis here tends to fall on intense prayer, humility, and charity in conformity with the law of love. Thus, in keeping with Ps 130's status as a Song of Ascents, Gregory sees the psalmist as a zealous person who is ascending to God.[75] Also echo-ing this tradition, Fisher cites the need for contrition from the depths of the heart and humility coming from the heart-root.[76]

The importance of Ps 130 for Luther and the Reformation has already been noted. Luther saw it as the height of the Old Testament gospel and commented on it in a number of contexts. Psalm 130 also formed the basis of "Aus tiefer Not," one of Luther's most influential hymns.[77] As his designation of it as a "Pauline psalm" implies, Luther's understanding of Ps 130 was part of his larger retrieval of Paul, a retrieval that resulted in his different under-standing of faith, repentance, and Christian virtue.[78]

---

[73] Gregory the Great, *Expositio in Septem Psalmos Poenitentiales* (PL 79:632).

[74] John Fisher, *Exposition of the Seven Penitential Psalms* (San Francisco: Ignatius, 1998), 204–12.

[75] Gregory the Great, *Expositio in Septem Psalmos Poenitentiales* (PL 79:633). In answer to the question of why such a person is praying a psalm out of the depths, Gregory notes how the nearer holy men come to God the more they feel weak and lowly, defending this with the examples of Abraham and Jacob in Gen 18 and 32.

[76] Fisher, *Exposition*, 214–15.

[77] Many scholars have analyzed the way that Luther's adaptation of Ps 130 in this hymn (especially in his later five stanza version) illustrates his theological con-cerns. Cf., among others, Jeremias, "Aus tiefer Not"; Hermann Kurzke, "Säkularisation oder Realisation? Zur Wirkungsgeschichte von Psalm 130 ('De profundis') in der deutschen Literatur von Luther bis zur Gegenwart," in *Liturgie und Dichtung* (ed. H. Becker et al.; 2 vols.; St. Ottilien: EOS, 1983), 2:67–89. These authors also note the way that the reception (and revision) of this hymn has continued to be theo-logically significant right up the present.

[78] For the Pauline designation of Ps 130, cf. *Weimarer Ausgabe der Werke Luthers Tischreden* (WA TR) 1:374–75 nn. 390–91.

How then does Luther's new understanding affect his view of the depths in v. 1? According to his revised commentary on the seven penitential psalms, v. 1 contains the "noble, passionate, and very profound words of a truly penitent heart that is most deeply moved in its distress."[79] For Luther, "we are all in deep and great misery, but we do not all feel our condition." This condition is further spelled out in his comments on v. 3 (and Ps 143:2), which Luther sees as giving "the contents of this psalm: a consideration of the severe judgment of God, who cannot and will not let even one sin go unpunished." He continues: "Whoever, therefore, does not consider the judgment of God, does not fear; and whoever does not fear, does not cry out; and whoever does not cry out, finds no grace."

Luther's understanding of the depths is similar to that of Augustine in a number of respects. First of all, both Luther and Augustine note the passionate nature of the psalmist's plea. Secondly, both authors see the depths as a situation common to all of humanity rather than a specific situation of need. Even more specifically, both see the inescapably sinful nature of humanity before God as that which results in the psalmist's terror and the resulting passionate plea.[80] Like Augustine, Luther expounds at length upon the need to wait and trust in the LORD.[81]

It is perhaps not without significance that Luther abandons the traditional view in which the Songs of Ascents constitute a progression of some sort.[82] One will recall that even though Augustine

---

[79] *Weimarer Ausgabe der Werke Luthers* (WA) 18:517–21. This is Luther's 1525 revision of his 1517 commentary. For the English translation, see vol. 14 of *Luther's Works* (ed. J. Pelikan; 55 vols.; St. Louis: Concordia/Philadelphia: Fortress, 1955–1986).

[80] In his later commentary on the gradual psalms, Luther explicitly excludes David's earthly troubles (such as the dangers connected with Saul, Absalom, or false prophets) as the reason for his being in the depths. For Luther, these and other worldly troubles can be overcome with patience; the real problem here is a "sickness of conscience" and a "deathly anxiety" in the face of one's sin and unworthiness. Cf. WA 4:2817–21.

[81] Thus, although Luther also mentions (in his comments on v. 6) the need to live in the three supreme virtues of faith, hope, and love, his main emphasis is on the first two of these. On this shift in emphasis from the medieval period, cf. James S. Preus, *From Shadow to Promise: Old Testament Interpretation from Augustine to the Young Luther* (Cambridge, Mass: Belknap, 1969).

[82] Thus, when Luther discusses the title of these psalms at the beginning of his later commentary on the gradual psalms, he deals strictly with historical matters of their performance in ancient Israel. Although he ultimately explains their title as deriving from their being sung in an elevated place, he does not think that the matter is of much importance for interpreting these psalms. It might also be noted that Luther does not follow the traditional placement of Ps 130 in the story of Jonah.

does not expound upon this aspect of the present psalm as much as
his successors, the superscription does play at least some role in his
interpretation of Ps 130. Thus, he notes that this is the voice of one
who is ascending and that the psalmist's crying out is already indicative of a rising from the deep made possible by God's previous action.

For Luther, on the other hand, the psalmist is not someone who
is moving from one state to another as much as he is someone who
despairs and hopes at the same time.[83] Rather than adopting the
traditional view of Ps 130 as a particular stage in a fifteen-step spiritual ascent, Luther sees it as the fundamental stance that defines
the psalmist's (and the Christian's) faith.[84] Given his view that it is
impossible for anyone to have merit before God, Luther clearly sees
this psalm more in terms of the need to rely completely on divine
mercy rather than in terms of any form of spiritual progress.

Calvin is similar to Luther in the way that he sounds a number
of central Reformation themes in his interpretation of Ps 130.[85] Calvin
does, however, differ somewhat in that he describes the depths as
specific historical adversity facing the psalmist. To be sure, Calvin sees
this adversity as a divine chastisement or punishment occasioned by
human sinfulness and intended to bring about repentance and obedience. Nevertheless, Calvin's description of the psalm's concrete situation retrieves an important element that was present earlier in the
tradition.[86] Along these lines, Calvin also sees the redemption of the

---

[83] As he notes in his comments on v. 5:

For God deals strangely with His children. He blesses them with contradictory
and disharmonious things, for hope and despair are opposites. Yet His children
must hope in despair; for fear is nothing else than the beginning of despair,
and hope is the beginning of recovery. And these two things, direct opposites
by nature, must be in us, because in us two natures are opposed to each other,
the old man and the new man. The old man must fear, despair and perish;
the new man must hope, be raised up, and stand. Both of these are in one
person and even in one handiwork at the same time.

[84] It has been suggested that Luther's view of this psalm (at least as reflected in
his hymn) is temporal rather than spatial. The psalmist does not look up out of
the deeps for help but forward to that help in the future. So Daniel Olivier and
Ulrich Weisgarber, "Aus tiefer Not Schrei Ich zu dir: Eine gemeinsame Besinnung
auf Martin Luthers Lied," in *Dank an Luther* (ed. A. Aarflot et al.; Göttingen:
Vandenhoeck & Ruprecht, 1984), 90–98, who see this as a safeguard against the
temptation of contempt for or flight from the world.

[85] John Calvin, *Comentarii in Librum Psalmorum, Pars Posterior, Opera Exegetica et
Homiletica*, 10.333–39 (*Commentary on the Book of Psalms* [trans. J. Anderson; Grand
Rapids: Baker, 1989], 127–38).

[86] It also anticipates one strand of the later form-critical analysis of this psalm,
though Calvin specifically cautions against seeing v. 3 as an argument that in any
way mitigates the psalmist's guilt in the eyes of God.

final verses as a two-step process including first the remission of sins and then the moderating of the chastisements arising from those sins.

Like Luther, Calvin breaks with earlier tradition and attributes little interpretive significance to the designation of this psalm as a Song of Ascents.[87] As was also the case with Luther, the reason for this seems to be that Calvin sees the stance of the psalmist primarily as one of reliance on God's mercy rather than spiritual progress. Thus, Calvin understands humility not as a means of imitating Christ but rather as the recognition of the fundamental absence of human righteousness in the face of the majesty and judgment of God.[88]

Later Christian interpretation of Ps 130:1 was heavily influenced by these reformers' emphasis on the Augustinian understanding of the depths in terms of human sinfulness. Nevertheless, a number of other elements of the patristic and medieval traditions continue into the post-Reformation period. Not surprisingly, this is especially the case in the Catholic tradition, though it is not exclusive to that tradition.

Representative in this respect is the interpretation of the depths by the noted Jesuit theologian and cardinal, Robert Bellarmine.[89] Bellarmine continues the older tradition of bringing this psalm into conversation with Jonah, whom he sees as disobedient but fervent in prayer. He also notes the immense distance between God and the sinner, which is terrifying and can only be bridged by God's mercy.

Of special interest is Bellarmine's view that the plural form of "depths" indicates the need for the true penitent to cry from two depths, the depth of misery and the depth of one's heart. The latter reflects the traditional understanding of the depths in terms of the intensity of prayer, as well as the need to reflect deeply on one's misery in one's heart. What Bellarmine means by the depth of misery is a bit more complex. On the one hand, he uses this term to refer to the state of the sinner who "is always bad and miserable," even though Bellarmine (echoing Augustine) also notes that the sinner is not always aware of his own misery. On the other hand, he uses this term to refer not only to the misery of one's sins but also to the suffering that results from them. Particularly informative along

---

[87] He also abandons the traditional link with Jonah here.

[88] "*Si quis serio iudicii Dei sensu expergefiat, pudore et metu humiliari necesse erit*" (Calvin, *Comentarii* 10.335).

[89] Cf. Robert Bellarmine, *Commentaria in Psalmos; Opera Omnia XI* (Frankfurt am Main: Minerva, 1965), 370–74.

these lines is Bellarmine's situating of this psalm in the life of David who was "in the depths of misery" both in terms of his fault (*culpam*) and his punishment (*poenam*).[90]

Like Bellarmine, a number of authors from the later Protestant tradition also have an understanding of the depths that reflects the multifaceted interpretation of the earlier tradition. Thus, for example, Sir Richard Baker details a number of depths out of which David cried in this psalm. These include the depths of sin, misery (by reason of sin), sorrow (by reason of misery), danger (of both body and soul), and devotion.[91] Other authors remark upon the way that God uses the depths of temporal affliction to prod sinners to the depths of more fervent prayer.[92] In keeping with the earlier tradition, such authors often see Jonah as an example of someone praying from these depths.

As in the previous section, it is useful to conclude with a brief look at the role of Ps 130 in Christian liturgical usage. Several aspects of this psalm helped to give it a prominent place in a number of liturgical settings. Thus, for example, its reference to waiting for the morning made it a natural choice for the night offices of Vespers and Compline in both eastern and western Christianity. A specifically christological interpretation of the "word" and redemption resulted in a role for the psalm in the Christmas office. Further, as one of the seven penitential psalms, Ps 130 had a prominent role in the office and liturgies of western Christianity, especially during Lent. It also had an important role in the office of the dead and the funeral liturgy of western Christianity, a role that was, of course, severely criticized by the reformers.[93]

---

[90] It is of interest that Bellarmine is concerned with specific sins of David (adultery, murder, ingratitude) rather than his general human condition. He also names specific examples of his suffering (his persecutions by Saul and the threats on his life). It is unclear how Bellarmine sees the persecutions by Saul as David's sufferings for his sins. In his preliminary remarks, Bellarmine also notes that as one of the gradual psalms, Ps 130 laments the misery of the exile.

[91] See Sir Richard Baker, "*Meditations and Disquisitions upon the Three Last Psalmes of David*" (1639); cited in Charles H. Spurgeon, *The Treasury of David* (3 vols.; McLean, Va.: MacDonald, n.d.), 3.2:122.

[92] So, for example, Archibald Symson (*A Sacred Septenarie* [1638]; cited in Spurgeon, *Treasury*, 3.2:122–23), who argues that God uses such adversity to move us away from prayer with our lips to prayer from our hearts.

[93] On the last usage, cf. Richard J. Pettey, "Psalm 130, A Song of Sorrow," in *The Psalms and Other Studies on the Old Testament: Festschrift J. I. Hunt* (ed. J. Knight

This section has found the Christian interpretation of Ps 130 to
be similar to that of the Jewish tradition in its witness to both the
power and flexibility of that text's opening image. Like their Jewish
counterparts, Christian interpreters have been capable of seeing the
depths as either positive or negative, and individual authors frequently have seen them as both. As will be seen below, such tendencies are suggestive in a number of respects.

IV. CONCLUSIONS

While the preceding survey is by no means exhaustive, it may be
said to describe some of the most important ways in which the Jewish
and Christian traditions have understood the depths of Ps 130's opening verse. It remains to summarize these different understandings
and then to discuss some of the implications of this interpretive history for both the genre definition and the theological interpretation
of Ps 130.

Traditional interpretations of the depths seem to fall into four
broad approaches: mythological, historical, sin-oriented, and virtue-
oriented. These approaches are not mutually exclusive, and individual
interpreters often make use of more than one approach. The choice
of approaches also does not entirely divide along confessional lines.
Interpreters from different theological traditions make use of all of
these approaches, though there are certain differences in emphasis.

The mythological approach usually understands the depths of Ps
130:1 with reference to the primordial waters of chaos and the ever-
present threat of death. These waters are in opposition both to God
and to human life, and they are only kept in check by divine power.
As such, the tradition sees the divine containment of the depths as
the foundational example of God's continuing care for humanity.
Paradoxically, the tradition also relates these threatening waters to
the waters that are necessary for human life.[94]

---

et al.; Nashotah: Nashotah House Seminary Press, 1990), 51–52. Pettey discusses
whether the predominant liturgical usage of the psalm reflects purgatory, judgment,
or penitence, opting for the last of these possibilities. One wonders whether the traditional connection of the depths with purgatory preserves an echo of their earlier
mythological association with the realm of the dead.

[94] As noted above, it is possible that the Christian use of this psalm in the office
of the dead and the funeral liturgy is an echo of the mythological approach to the
image of the depths.

The second approach to the depths is the historical counterpart of the first. This approach sees the depths as indicating a variety of difficulties that threaten the person praying. Some interpreters have identified these difficulties with specific historical events, such as Saul's persecution of David, Jonah's being thrown overboard, or Israel's exile (either that of Babylon or that of subsequent eras). Other inter- preters see the depths as recurring individual situations, such as poverty or sickness. In either case, this approach sees the depths in terms of concrete afflictions of the person praying, as an individual or as a member of a larger community.[95]

The third approach to the depths sees them as referring to the depths of human sinfulness. Not surprisingly, this approach is espe- cially common in the Augustinian tradition of western Christianity, which has tended to define the opening image in light of the rhetor- ical question in v. 3. Nevertheless, at least some relationship between the depths and sin is also apparent in the liturgical usage of Ps 130 in both Judaism and Christianity. Within this approach, one can dis- tinguish further between interpreters that see sin as a general aspect of human nature and those that see it in terms of specific individ- ual or communal offenses.

Finally, the fourth approach to the depths sees them as indicative of certain positive virtues of the person praying. These virtues include the intensity or sincerity of prayer, the humility (in a number of senses) of the person praying, and that person's commitment to Torah. Interpreters who adopt this approach tend to see the person praying as in some sense (or to some degree) "righteous" and even advanced in God's ways (though still in need of humility). This way of seeing the depths seems to be particularly, though not exclusively, associated with those who see Ps 130 as part of a larger sequence of psalms (such as the Songs of Ascents or the seven penitential psalms).

It is clear that some of these approaches lend themselves to par- ticular genre definitions. Thus, an historical understanding of the depths is at least to a certain degree more consistent with a view of Ps 130 as a lament or a psalm of thanksgiving. Sin-oriented under- standings that emphasize human sinfulness favor a more strictly theo- logical genre definition, while those that focus on individual sins favor its definition as a penitential psalm. Certain types of virtue

---

[95] One will recall that for Christoph Barth (*Errettung vom Tode*), such afflictions were indicative of the realm or forces of death impinging on the life of the psalmist.

approaches also lend themselves to a definition of this psalm as a penitential psalm, though they also are compatible with seeing Ps 130 as a psalm of trust or confidence.

It is, however, important to recognize that both the tradition as a whole and many individual interpreters do not opt for any one approach to the depths along such lines. Instead, most of these interpreters respond to the psalm's genre ambiguity by adopting multiple approaches to the image of the depths. This carries with it a certain cost in the precision of their genre definitions, though it also seems to stimulate their theological creativity. While the tradition is extremely diverse in this respect, one can see a number of characteristic tendencies in its theological appropriation of this psalm.

First of all, it seems significant that both the tradition as a whole and a number of the individual interpreters of Ps 130 tend in some way to hold together a negative and a positive interpretation of the depths. As a negative, the depths are often particularly associated with the *occasion* of the psalm, whether that is seen in mythological, historical, spiritual, or psychological terms. In many interpretations, however, it is this negative occasion that either brings about or goes hand in hand with the more positive response of the person praying. There are a number of ways in which this negative to positive connection is made.

One common way of connecting negative and positive may be seen in those interpreters who combine an historical and a sin-oriented approach to the depths. Such interpreters often see the concrete historical difficulties facing the individual or community as divine chastisements or punishments meant to make these believers aware of their sinfulness and promote their repentance. As such, the depths are paradoxically both negative (in that they involve real suffering and danger) and positive (in that they are also the means by which God is working for the greater good of those involved).

A different relationship of negative and positive is evident in those interpreters who see the depths as both sin- and virtue-oriented. Not surprisingly, there is considerable variety here in the way that this relationship is seen, depending on the interpreters' different views of sin and virtue. Some interpreters, for example, emphasize the need to repent one's sins and "ascend" to holiness by greater humility and more fervent prayer. Other interpreters emphasize the need to acknowledge humbly one's sinful nature and trust in the mercy of God's forgiveness. While there are obviously similarities here, there are also important differences as to how the depths of human sin are to be counterbalanced by the depths of human virtue.

Many of these examples point to another recurring feature in the interpretive tradition, namely, an emphasis on the theological significance of the act of praying itself. Interpreters often stress the importance of the fact that even though the psalmist is in the depths he/she is also crying out from those depths (especially with passion, intensity, and humility).[96] These interpreters then encourage their audiences to recognize their similar situation and to pray in a similar manner. As part of their argument, these authors often relate this psalm to specific models of prayer (such as David, Jonah, or Peter) that they encourage their audiences to imitate.

Once again, there is considerable variety in the tradition as to how the act of praying this psalm is understood, depending on how particular interpreters see the depths of the first verse and their relationship to the situation of those praying the psalm.[97] Thus, for example, interpreters who see the depths in terms of specific historical afflictions often see this psalm as performing an expressive function. That is to say, the psalm functions as the means by which the persons praying express their sense of misery before God. Similarly, interpreters that see the depths in terms of human sinfulness sometimes see those praying as expressing their sorrow or terror in the face of that sinfulness.

Interpreters that adopt a sin-oriented approach also often see the psalm as functioning to help those praying come to an awareness of their true situation before God. Many interpreters (such as Augustine) note the possibility that a person might not realize the gravity of this situation. For such interpreters, the praying of Ps 130 can be the means of coming to a better understanding of the way things really are.

Finally, interpreters that see the depths in a virtue-oriented way often see Ps 130 as having a transformative (or sacramental) function.

---

[96] See Patrick D. Miller, Jr., "Psalm 130," *Int* 33 (1979): 176–81. "The human being who speaks in and through and with this psalm is a lamenter, a fact which signifies a dual reality: He or she is in the depths but also is one who prays" (177).

[97] On the different types of functions that follow, cf. my *Defining the Sacred Songs: Genre, Tradition and the Post-Critical Interpretation of the Psalms* (Sheffield: Sheffield Academic, 1999), 84–107; and "The Sacramental Function of the Psalms in Contemporary Scholarship and Liturgical Practice," in *Psalms and Practice: Worship, Virtue, and Authority* (ed. S. B. Reid; Collegeville, Minn.: Liturgical Press, 2001), 78–89.

For such interpreters, the praying of the psalm acts as the means by which one is transformed into a particular type of person with a particular set of virtues. Thus, the psalm enables one to become passionate in prayer or to rely on God's mercy. These virtues are brought into being by the performative act of praying this particular psalm.

Recognizing the different ways Ps 130 can function helps to explain another tendency in this psalm's interpretive history, the way (or, more accurately, the variety of ways) that interpreters tend to situate the person praying "in the middle." The fact that Ps 130 situates the person praying in the depths means that that person is not where he/she should be, either historically or spiritually (in terms of sinfulness). Nevertheless, the fact that someone is praying this particular psalm means that that person is also not in as bad a state as he/she could be (in virtue terms), since he/she at least recognizes his/her shortcomings and is open to adopting a more positive stance.[98] In other words, praying this psalm situates a person in a state of expectation and hope that is rooted in both the concrete difficulties of individual and communal life and a real but imperfect relationship with God.[99]

Those who take the interpretive history of Ps 130 seriously find themselves plumbing the depths of some of the most important aspects of human existence. This interpretive history is especially useful in its insistence that one come to terms with both sin and suffering, rather than too quickly defining this psalm in terms of one or the other. It also enables one to engage these issues in conversation with a tradition whose wisdom continues to both inform and challenge.[100]

---

[98] Or, in Luther's case, one is not simply in despair, but one despairs and hopes at the same time.

[99] Those interpreters who see this psalm as part of a larger sequence of psalms (such as the seven penitential psalms or the Songs of Ascents) underscore its "middle" setting in yet another way.

[100] It is a pleasure to dedicate this paper to Professor James Kugel, someone whose own wisdom has so deeply informed and challenged both the field as a whole and my own work in particular. I was first exposed to Jim's groundbreaking approach to biblical studies when I served as his teaching assistant in a Yale College course over twenty years ago. My appreciation for his brilliant scholarship on the relationship between the biblical text and the traditions that treasure it has grown with every passing year. For his work and for his friendship, I remain most grateful.

כל־האדם AND THE EVALUATION OF QOHELET'S WISDOM IN QOH 12:13 OR "THE 'A IS SO, AND *WHAT'S MORE,* B' THEOLOGY OF ECCLESIASTES"

Peter Enns

I. Introduction

I am very pleased to offer this essay in honor of my teacher, Professor James Kugel. My first doctoral course with Professor Kugel was on Ecclesiastes. This course was also my first exposure to reading the Hebrew Scriptures under the eye of one whose own Jewish heritage gave him an intimacy with the text that I had not experienced before. As a hardworking and well-intentioned Protestant, I was nonetheless thoroughly intimidated. Not only were we expected to translate, but read aloud—and well. His classes were the closest I have ever come to being in a synagogue, and his questions (from which there was no escape) were designed to move us away from the comfort of a superficial handling of the text to ask questions that, if left to ourselves, we would not have asked. "Well, you've told us what the words are, but what does it *mean?*" "What would this construction look like in Standard Biblical Hebrew?" "Where else in the Bible do you find an expression like this?" Our class structure was simple. There were no overheads, handouts, or Powerpoint presentations, only students with Bibles and notebooks open, sitting around a table, interacting with a master teacher who had internalized the twists and turns of Ecclesiastes. Professor Kugel's teaching has influenced me deeply, and his approach to pedagogy is one I try to emulate.

Perhaps my one frustration with that class, however, was that, even after twelve weeks, we barely made it into chapter 5. (Was it Professor Kugel's attention to detail or our inability to maintain a faster pace?) Hence, in this essay, I would like to finish in a certain sense what Professor Kugel left unfinished. I would like to jump directly to the closing verses of Ecclesiastes 12:13–14, not simply to gain a sense of closure to my graduate school years, but to see what these crucial words tell us about the book as a whole. Such also was a theme of Professor Kugel's teaching: to balance the meaning of the whole and the meaning of its constituent parts, to see the forest *and* the trees.

Ecclesiastes is an enigmatic book. Discussions, reaching back at least to rabbinic times,[1] continue today not only as to the meaning of verses here and there, but as to the basic message of the book as a whole. An overview of the secondary literature will quickly demonstrate the diverse opinions on Qohelet's basic psychological state and the overall purpose of the book. Perhaps no other book of the Hebrew Scriptures has had the history of "counter-understandings" as Ecclesiastes. Of nearly any other biblical book one can make coherent statements as to its basic content and purpose, which would find general agreement (Song of Songs being one notable exception). If any ten knowledgeable people were asked what Genesis is about, you might get ten different answers, but those answers would still accent *legitimate* aspects of the book. But no one capable of coherent thought would say, "Genesis is about God's destruction of the universe, his blessing of the Tower of Babel project, and his rejection of the Patriarchs." Yet, Ecclesiastes is a book that is amenable to conflicting and contradictory interpretations: Is Qohelet coherent or incoherent, insightful or confused? Is he a stark realist or merely faithless? Is he orthodox or heterodox? Is he an optimist or pessimist? Is the final message of the book "be like Qohelet, the wise man" or "Qohelet is wrong"? Discovering the meaning and purpose of Ecclesiastes will likely continue as a back-and-forth journey between overarching concepts and smaller exegetical details, balancing the forest and the trees. In the end, the theory that presents the most cohesive picture of Ecclesiastes will gain assent, at least for the time being.

As everyone acknowledges, how one understands the message of the book of Ecclesiastes as a whole is bound up with how one interprets the function of the frame.[2] The purpose of this article is to offer one

---

[1] On whether Ecclesiastes "made the hands unclean" (was inspired) in early rabbinic years (*m. Yad.* 3:5, *m. 'Ed.* 5:3), see the summary of the debate in Roger Beckwith, *The Old Testament Canon of the New Testament Church* (Grand Rapids: Eerdmans, 1985), 274–304. At issue were the contradictory (e.g., 7:3, 8:15) and heretical (compare 2:10 to Num 15:39) statements in Ecclesiastes. See also the recent treatment by Marc Hirshman, "Qohelet's Reception and Interpretation in Early Rabbinic Literature," in *Studies in Ancient Midrash* (ed. J. L. Kugel; Cambridge, Mass.: Harvard University Press, 2001), 87–99.

[2] That Ecclesiastes is a 1st-person discourse with a 3rd-person frame is the consensus position. See Michael V. Fox, "Frame-Narrative and Composition in the Book of Qohelet," *HUCA* 48 (1977): 83–106. More recently, see Michael V. Fox,

brief contribution to the scholarly conversation concerning the relationship of the closing verses of Ecclesiastes to the book as a whole, and I would like to do so by focusing on one phrase, כל־האדם, which occurs at the end of 12:13, and which I leave untranslated for the moment: סוף דבר הכל נשמע את־האלהים ירא ואת־מצותיו שמור כי־זה כל־האדם. An assumption that buttresses my argument is the widely recognized notion that the frame narrator's comments in the epilogue intentionally pick up on the language and themes of Qohelet's discourse.[3] The phrase כל־האדם, which concludes 12:13, is found three other times in Ecclesiastes, in 3:13, 5:18, and 7:2. Strangely enough, the four-fold recurrence of this phrase in Ecclesiastes and its relevance for the discussion of the meaning of book have remained relatively unexplored in the secondary literature.

My suspicion is that the frame narrator's use of this phrase in 12:13 was meant by him to be read in light of its previous uses in Qohelet's discourse. 3:13 and 5:18 are found in so-called *carpe diem* passages, where Qohelet affirms that כל־האדם, "everyone," is to enjoy pleasure amid their daily existence. Then in 7:2, Qohelet observes that death is the end (סוף) of כל־האדם. Pleasure and death are two important themes in Qohelet's discourse. As I hope to show below, the use of the emphatic phrase כי־זה כל־האדם in 12:13 as a description of humanity's "duty" (as it is often translated, see below) to "fear God and keep his commandments" (12:13b) seems to suggest that 12:13 is intended to direct the reader's attention toward a higher goal that sums up humanity's quest for meaning. If I may paraphrase what I understand 12:13 to mean in the context of the epilogue as a whole: "Qohelet is wise, to be sure. As he says, pleasure and death are real and are the portion of כל־האדם. But there is a deeper, more fundamental obligation, amid these realities, which is to fear God and keep his commandments. *This* is *truly* כל־האדם."

In evaluating Qohelet's words this way, the frame narrator neither corrects Qohelet nor points out his lapse into heterodoxy.[4] He

---

A Time to Tear Down and a Time to Build Up: A Rereading of Ecclesiastes (Grand Rapids: Eerdmans, 1999), 363–77; Tremper Longman III, The Book of Ecclesiastes (Grand Rapids: Eerdmans, 1998), 15–20.

[3] For example, see Andrew G. Shead, "Reading Ecclesiastes 'Epilogically,'" TynBul 48 (1997): 67–91; Craig G. Bartholomew, Reading Ecclesiastes: Old Testament Exegesis and Hermeneutical Theory (AnBib 139; Rome: Pontifical Biblical Institute, 1998), 237–53.

[4] I agree with the growing consensus that the frame narrator does not simply contradict the words of Qohelet. Bartholomew goes so far as to say that it is "naïve" to think otherwise (Reading Ecclesiastes, 95–96). As Fox puts it:

is, rather, sympathetically evaluating Qohelet's observations. He is saying, to employ Professor Kugel's summary of the "idea of biblical poetry" cited in the title of this essay: "*Qohelet's observations are correct, but there is more.*"

II. כל־האדם IN QOH 3:13 AND 5:18: PLEASURE

At various points in his argument, Qohelet counsels his readers concerning the matter of pleasure. We meet this topic first in 2:1–11 where Qohelet determines that pleasure (שמחה) and amusement (שחוק) are ultimately הבל (see also 7:4).[5] Elsewhere, however, he gives a

---

[T]he author of the epilogue basically supports Qohelet's teachings. Otherwise he could have refrained from writing, editing, or transmitting the book. . . . In my view, the epilogue does not undermine the persona [i.e., Qohelet], but only takes a cautious and cautionary stance toward him. The book's ending does not invalidate Qohelet's complaints or observations. These are never said or shown to be wrong. . . . The book's ending does not contradict Qohelet, but only changes the emphasis. . . . [There is no] ideological conflict between Qohelet's teachings and the epilogue. Both express the author's views, but with different tones and emphases. (*Time to Tear Down*, 371, 373)

See also Choon L. Seow: ". . . the perspective of the book is one and the same as the framework" (*Ecclesiastes* [AB 18C; New York: Doubleday, 1997], 38). Moreover, whether 12:13–14 are from the hand of a later glossator does not come into play here. The closing verses of Ecclesiastes give the book its theological shape and it is the theology of the book as a whole that is the object of study here. For a recently articulated contrasting view, see Martin A. Shields, "Ecclesiastes and the End of Wisdom," *TynBul* 50 (1999): 117–39. He states:

In essence, Qohelet is the epilogist's 'straw man'. But the epilogist does not go to great lengths to knock down the straw man, for—to employ a different illustration—the epilogist has given Qohelet sufficient rope, and he has hung himself. To the reader familiar with the remainder of the Old Testament, it is clear that the wisdom of Qohelet has gone astray—much as Solomon himself had gone astray—and is ultimately incompatible with the message of the remainder of the canon. (138–39)

Although this is not the place to engage Shields's argument in any detail, it is my opinion that such a summary of Ecclesiastes fails to address a number of important questions surrounding any explanation of the book, namely, how a book that is "critical of the wisdom movement" (138), which itself assumes a rather flat understanding of Israel's wisdom tradition, could have been embraced in the Jewish canon.

[5] The precise meaning of הבל in Ecclesiastes has been a matter of debate in modern scholarship and will not detain us here (see Eric Christianson, *A Time to Tell: Narrative Strategies in Ecclesiastes* [JSOTSup 280; Sheffield: Sheffield Academic, 1998], 79–91; Fox, *Time to Tear Down*, 27–49). Suffice it to say, I do not think "meaningless" is a helpful translation, as it seems that Qohelet's observations on life are intended to expose the "collapse of meaning." The *carpe diem* passages represent Qohelet's attempts to "reconstruct meaning" (Fox, *Time to Tear Down*, 133). Fox's translation of הבל as "absurd" helps alleviate misconceptions (ibid., 30–35).

more positive evaluation of the role of pleasure in life (2:24–26;
3:12–14, 22; 5:18–20; 6:1–6; 8:15; 9:7–10; 11:8–9). I am not suggesting, however, that Qohelet's observations in these instances are
free from the ambiguity that pervades so much of the book. After
all, he nowhere suggests that pleasure brings all questioning to a
close. Rather, the recurring phrase, "there is nothing better than . . ."
(אין־טוב; 2:24; 3:12, 22; 8:15), suggests a degree of resignation.

That Qohelet considers his observations to be of universal value
is made clear by his use of כל־האדם in 3:13 and 5:18. Excluding
Ecclesiastes, the phrase כל־האדם occurs fourteen times in thirteen
verses in the Hebrew Scriptures: Gen 7:21; Exod 9:19; Num 12:3;
16:29 (2x), 32; Josh 11:14; Judg 16:17; 1 Kgs 8:38; Jer 31:30; Ezek
38:20; Zech 8:10; Ps 116:11; 2 Chr 6:29. In all of these instances,
the meaning is typically (and rather unambiguously) rendered "every
man/everyone," "any man/anyone," "all mankind/humanity," or
something similar. The phrase is found as the object of a preposition (e.g., Num 12:3; Judg 16:17; 1 Kgs 8:38), the subject of a clause
(e.g., Ezek 38:20), and the object of the verb (e.g., Zech 8:10).

Commentators routinely agree that "anyone," "everyone," or the like
render well כל־האדם in Ecclesiastes. To be sure, the fact that the
phrase occurs in a verbless clause גם כל־האדם in 3:13 and 5:18 (וגם
in 3:13), followed by the relative pronouns ש in 3:13 and אשר in 5:18,[6]
offers some challenges, and the commentaries take good note of these
factors. In the final analysis, however, the syntax of this phrase in
3:13 and 5:18 is not a problem. The syntax of כל־האדם in 7:2 (to
be discussed below) is straightforward in that it occurs in the phrase
סוף כל־האדם, "end of everyone." Although there are some syntactical
similarities with 3:13 and 5:18, 12:13 is unique in that the phrase
appears at the end of an independent, verbless clause (כי־זה כל־האדם).

The first instance of כל־האדם is found in 3:13, where Qohelet
considers the value of pleasure and enjoyment. Verses 12–13 read
as follows:

---

[6] Bo Isaksson argues, however, that ש/אשר do not function as relative pronouns
in 3:13 and 5:18 but as demonstratives marking out "the following sentence as
being the subject of a nominal clause" (*Studies in the Language of Qoheleth, with Special
Emphasis on the Verbal System* [Acta Universitatis Upsaliensis Studia Semitica Upsaliensia
10; Stockholm: Almqvist & Wiksell, 1997], 120). His translation, however, does not
differ significantly from conventional translations.

ידעתי כי אין טוב בם כי אם־לשמוח ולעשות טוב בחייו:
וגם כל־האדם שיאכל ושתה וראה טוב בכל־עמלו מתת אלהים היא:

I know that there is nothing better for them[7] than to have pleasure and do what is enjoyable[8] in one's life. Moreover, that anyone should eat, drink, and experience[9] pleasure in all his labor, it is a gift from God.

The meaning of כל־האדם in Qoh 3:13 depends to a certain extent on the context in which the phrase is found. The immediate context of 3:13 is 3:10–15. We are justified in demarcating this passage thus on the basis of the marker ראיתי which appears in 3:10 and 3:16 and is regularly used in Ecclesiastes to introduce a new or subsequent observation, or to summarize an evaluation for an observation just made.[10] This section follows 3:1–9, in which, despite the Byrds' optimistic interpretation, Qohelet resigns himself to the inevitability of the cycles of life, thus understood on the basis of the "pessimistic" evaluation in 3:9 of the previous eight verses (מה־יתרון העושה באשר הוא עמל). Qohelet is revisiting here the theme introduced by the frame narrator in 1:1–11: the recurring cycles of life demonstrate that there is no יתרון, no surplus or profit.[11] The terms הבל and יתרון are closely related concepts in Ecclesiastes. All human activity is ultimately הבל because no human activity produces יתרון. This is the life lesson so clearly illustrated in 1:5–7. The sun, wind, and streams labor, but in the end, they are no better off than when they started. There is no profit or surplus to their struggles. The

---

[7] Fox emends בם to באדם (*Time to Tear Down*, 192) whereas Seow prefers בם as the more difficult reading (*Ecclesiastes*, 164). See also Longman, *Ecclesiastes*, 112; James L. Crenshaw, *Ecclesiastes* (OTL; Philadelphia: Westminster, 1987), 98. I have opted to follow the consonantal tradition reflected in the MT, although, for our purposes, it does not matter.

[8] The phrase לעשות טוב does not imply moral behavior, i.e., the doing of what is right. The same goes for the use of טוב in v. 13.

[9] ראה means more than simply optical activity in Ecclesiastes. Qohelet often uses the verb to speak of things he has experienced, or, as in this case, things that one should experience. See also Antoon Schoors, "Words Typical of Qohelet," in *Qohelet in the Context of Wisdom* (BETL 136; ed. A. Schoors; Leuven: Leuven University Press, 1998), 26–33.

[10] See 1:14; 2:13; 3:22; 4:4, 15; 5:12, 17; 6:1; 7:15; 8:9, 10, 17; 9:13; 10:5, 7. The perfect ראה is also used in this way (2:3; 4:1, 7).

[11] Seow discusses יתרון as one of several examples in Ecclesiastes which indicate that the author "presumes an audience that is deeply concerned with economic terms" ("The Socioeconomic Context of 'The Preacher's' Hermeneutic," *PSB* 17, no. 2 [1996]: 168–95, here 173). See also the more detailed discussion in Seow, *Ecclesiastes*, 21–36.

same holds for human activity. Since death levels the playing field for all, and since you can't take it with you, it is the inevitability of death that insures that no human activity will provide anyone with a profit or surplus. It is this fact that renders life under the sun הבל.

Verses 10–15 continue this mood of resignation. Echoing 1:13, Qohelet remarks that God has given humans a "task" or "occupation" (ענין) to occupy them (v. 10). The specific nature of that task is not made explicitly clear, but the sentiment of v. 11 is certainly to be understood as commenting on it in some sense: God has made everything "fitting" or "appropriate" (יפה) in its "time" (עת). To be sure, the use of עת in v. 11 is to be understood in light of the recurrent use of this word in 3:1–8, which, as mentioned above, is a statement of resignation (hence, the translation "fitting" or "appropriate" for יפה rather than the more positively construed "beautiful").[12] Moreover, not only has God ordered the times in such a way, but he has also given to humanity the ability to ponder the fact that such order extends throughout all earthly time (עולם—not "eternity"),[13] even though they cannot understand (ponder, plan, predict, control) what God does "from beginning to end" (מראש ועד־סוף). In view of such observations, Qohelet concludes that there is nothing better than the experience of enjoyment (לשמוח ולעשות טוב) in this life (v. 12).

In v. 13, where we find the phrase כל־האדם, Qohelet further resigns himself to the fact that eating, drinking, and "experiencing what is good" (ראה טוב) are what God gives everyone to do; it is God's "gift" (מתת). Of course, by gift, Qohelet does not imply that it is God's "present," wrapped in festive paper and tied in a bow, putting joy in the heart of humanity. Rather, the procurement of mundane benefits, such as eating, drinking, and getting some simple pleasures out of life, *these* are the things that everyone can and should do throughout the days of one's existence. These are the activities that counter, albeit ultimately unsuccessfully, the absurdity of life under the sun in the face of death's inexorable final blow. Finally, vv. 14–15 continue Qohelet's rather pessimistic appraisal of the human situation. What God has done, the recurring cycle of times and humanity's meager lot in life, are God's doing and cannot be changed.

---

[12] Bartholomew, *Reading Ecclesiastes*, 243–44.
[13] Ibid., 243.

They are for a lifetime (עוֹלָם) and cannot be added to (יֹסֵף) or taken away from (נִרַע). The purpose for which God has done it so is "so that they [humanity] will fear him" (שֶׁיָּרְאוּ מִלְּפָנָיו). Precisely what Qohelet means by "fear" is a matter of some discussion, but it certainly seems to be bound up in the frustrating incomprehensibility of the inevitability that there is nothing new under the sun,[14] a point aptly made in v. 15a: מַה־שֶּׁהָיָה כְּבָר הוּא וַאֲשֶׁר לִהְיוֹת כְּבָר הָיָה ("That which is already was, and what will be already was").

The rhythm of life under the sun does not change, which is the frame narrator's own summation of Qohelet's thoughts (1:1–11). Amid the timing of the circumstances of life, scrutable only to God, the summation of humanity's existence is to accept as God's gift the simple pleasures that come from one's labor. *This* is what is for "everyone," כָּל־הָאָדָם.

5:18 is also a *carpe diem* passage set within a larger context.

גַּם כָּל־הָאָדָם אֲשֶׁר נָתַן־לוֹ הָאֱלֹהִים עֹשֶׁר וּנְכָסִים וְהִשְׁלִיטוֹ לֶאֱכֹל מִמֶּנּוּ וְלָשֵׂאת
אֶת־חֶלְקוֹ וְלִשְׂמֹחַ בַּעֲמָלוֹ זֹה מַתַּת אֱלֹהִים הִיא׃

> Moreover, everyone to whom God gives wealth and possessions,[15] he gives him the ability to partake of them, to accept his lot, and rejoice in his labors. This is a gift from God.

5:17–19 is likewise set off by the marker רָאָה in 5:17 and 6:1. The sentiment expressed here is very similar to that of 3:10–15, a point borne out by a number of similarities in wording. Verse 17 repeats the triad "eat, drink, experience good" of 3:13. Moreover, this activity is what Qohelet calls "fitting" (עָת), thus echoing the notion of God's fitting activity of ordering the rhythms of life (3:11). This pas-

---

[14] On this see L. M. Muntingh, "Fear of Yahweh and Fear of the Gods according to the Books of Qohelet and Isaiah," in *Studies in Isaiah: Old Testament Essays* (Ou-Testamentiese Werkgemeenskap in Suid-Afrika 22–23; ed. W. C. van Wyk; Pretoria West, South Africa: NHW Press, 1981), 143–58, esp. 143–44. Muntingh cites Egon Pfeiffer, "Die Gottesfurcht im Buche Kohelet," in *Gottes Wort und Gottes Land: Hans-Wilhelm Hertzberg zum 70. Geburtstag am 16. Januar 1965 dargebracht von Kollegen, Freunden und Schülern* (ed. H. G. Reventlow; Göttingen: Vandenhoeck & Ruprecht, 1965), 133–58, here 133.

[15] Fox (*Time to Tear Down*, 111) and Isaksson (*Studies in the Language of Qoheleth*, 96) treat this as a conditional sentence. Although my translation does not make this explicit, a sense of conditionality is still evident: "If God should give to anyone wealth and possessions, he gives them. . . ."

sage also speaks of what God has given (מתח) to humanity (5:18), although here it is summed up a bit differently. Whereas 3:13 speaks simply of eating, drinking, and experiencing good as humanity's כל האדם, in 5:18 the thought is added that God gives humanity wealth (עשר), possessions (נכסים), and the ability (והשליטו) (1) to partake of these things (לאכל ממנו), (2) to accept one's lot (ולשאת את־חלקו), and (3) to rejoice in one's labor (ולשמח בעמלו).

Qohelet's admonition to his readers to content themselves with the pleasures of this life as their portion (חלק) is his attempt to construct meaning in a world where meaning, at least for him, has collapsed. But his calls to seize the day, however sincere, are repeatedly relativized by the universal inevitability of death, for it is death that renders all human activity without יתרון, without profit. There is no payoff ultimately to anything we do, since we, like the animals, will die (3:19). The juxtaposition of death and *carpe diem* in Ecclesiastes creates a tension that is not resolved until the end of the book.

III. כל־האדם IN QOH 7:2: DEATH

As mentioned above, the use of כל־האדם in 7:2 presents no syntactical challenges. כל־האדם is joined to סוף by the conjunctive accent *mûnach*, and should be translated "end of everyone."

טוב ללכת אל־בית־אבל מלכת אל־בית משתה באשר הוא סוף כל־האדם והחי
יתן אל־לבו:

> It is better to go to the house of mourning than to the house of feasting, because[16] that is the end of everyone; the living should take this to heart.

Death, as Shannon Burkes puts it, is the "driving theme and main concern of Qohelet."[17] This is not an exaggeration, for it is the specter of death that routinely nullifies whatever positive conclusions Qohelet might draw. Burkes attempts to locate Qohelet's preoccupation with death in the context of larger paradigm shifts in the post-exilic world. Specifically, she focuses on Egyptian biographies

---

[16] Although not true for every instance, אשר preceded by the preposition ב in 7:2 is causal (Isaksson, *Studies in the Language of Qohelet*, 152). See also 8:4.

[17] Shannon Burkes, *Death in Qohelet and Egyptian Biographies of the Late Period* (SBLDS 170; Atlanta: SBL, 1999), 1.

that share certain themes with Ecclesiastes. Both Ecclesiastes and these Egyptian biographies are part of a larger paradigm shift (Burkes is very careful not to argue for any direct dependence) fueled by "permutations" in the "power structures of the ancient world . . . that were felt far and wide."[18] For the author of Ecclesiastes, who passed his days in such a time of upheaval, death "represents the chief flaw that embraces and subsumes all other problems in the world."[19]

There are a number of explicit references to death in Ecclesiastes: 2:14–16; 3:2, 19–21; 4:2–3; 5:15–16; 6:3–6; 7:1–2, 4, 17, 26; 8:8; 9:2–12; 11:8. It is not simply in 7:2 where Qohelet laments that death is כל־האדם; this is implied throughout the book. Qohelet's focus on death is out of proportion with what is found elsewhere in the Hebrew Scriptures. As Burkes puts it, "With Qohelet . . . death makes its entrance into the Hebrew traditions as a phenomenon to be reckoned with."[20] This is a result, Burkes argues, of this ancient paradigm shift felt by the Israelites in the form of the Babylonian exile and subsequent struggles to reclaim their past glory while under the thumb of the Persians and, later, the Greeks. The exile brought a heretofore subdued emphasis on the individual (such as one finds in Proverbs) to the fore. The status of the group was uncertain and so the question of the individual's fate began to present itself. To put it another way, whatever national hope there might have been for Israel is transferred to the individual.[21] Perpetual covenant fidelity to a *nation* had been demonstrated (indeed, promised; see 2 Sam 7:5–16) in the form of possession of land, performance of cult, and an unbroken line of kings. Such things ceased for Israel in the early 6th century B.C.E. But to transfer these promises to the individual is no easy task, for how can an individual experience the perpetual covenant? The reality and finality of death call into question the applicability of God's ancient promises to the individual. Moreover, "The symbolic immortalities offered elsewhere in the Bible, the memory and endurance of a good name, survival through one's children and people, even the qualitative good life that negates the 'death'

---

[18] Ibid., 6.
[19] Ibid., 2.
[20] Ibid., 75.
[21] Burkes (Ibid., 111) cites Fox (*Qohelet and His Contradictions* [JSOTSup 18; Sheffield: Almond, 1989], 294) that Qohelet has "no sense of the nation or community."

of folly and unrighteousness, fail utterly in Qohelet's opinion."[22]

Death is that which ultimately renders futile humanity's "quest for meaning." All, human and animal alike, come to the same end. What punctuates, then, Qohelet's theology is that which is the activity of "everyone": to enjoy the pleasures that God has given (3:13 and 5:18) and then to die (7:2). The book as a whole, however, does not let the matter rest there. A solution to the tension is provided.

IV. כל־האדם IN QOH 12:13 AS AN ECHO OF PREVIOUS USES

It seems highly unlikely to me that כל־האדם in 12:13 can be treated in isolation from the theology espoused in the previous uses of the phrase. I propose that כל־האדם contributes to our understanding of the epilogue as a mild corrective to the teachings of Qohelet, by taking Qohelet's observation and "going one further."

I should make it clear once again that I do not see the epilogist as contradicting Qohelet, and in this view I align myself with what is becoming an increasingly popular point of view. It seems an almost absurd logic to think that the teachings of Qohelet, which are expressed very intentionally over the span of roughly twelve chapters, are there merely to be dismissed by the frame narrator in the closing verses of the book. Moreover, the frame narrator's evaluation of Qohelet has a decidedly positive flavor. Despite legitimate ambiguities in the closing section of the book, it is clear to me that the frame narrator thinks of Qohelet as a wise teacher (12:9).[23] There is no indication that the frame narrator wishes his comments to be seen in fundamental contrast to Qohelet's. I do suggest, however, that in 12:13–14 the frame narrator puts Qohelet's observations in a broader perspective. It is, perhaps, a gentle critique, although the epilogist falls far short of condemning or chastising him. A window into the nature of this critique is the phrase כל־האדם.

Two things are worth noting concerning the use of כל־האדם in 12:13. First, this phrase seems to be emphatic: כי־זה כל־האדם. Throughout Ecclesiastes the demonstrative pronoun זה is used in a number

---

[22] Burkes, *Death in Qohelet*, 111.

[23] I do not think that the epilogue exposes the ironic use of הכמה throughout the book, as Bartholomew argues (*Reading Ecclesiastes*, 236).

of climactic statements.[24] In fourteen instances it is used to introduce Qohelet's conclusion זה הבל: 2:15, 19, 21, 23, 26; 4:4, 8, 16; 5:9; 6:2, 9; 7:6; 8:10, 14. Similarly, it is used as a concluding statement of some sort in twelve other instances: זה הוא רעיון (1:10); זה חדש (1:10); זה רעה חולה (1:17); וזה־היה חלקי (2:10); זה ראיתי (2:24; 8:9; 9:13); זה מצאתי (5:15); זה אלהים היא (5:18); זה מתת (7:23); זה נסיתי (7:27, 29); זה רע (9:3). When we keep in mind the rather obvious fact that 12:13–14 are themselves the concluding verses of the concluding section of Ecclesiastes, the "concluding" force of זה in 12:13 seems self-evident. Further, in light of these observations, it is likely that we should assign asseverative force to כי. It is not too much to expect the writer to want to drive home his point emphatically in the closing thought of the book. "Fear God and keep his commandments. Indeed, *this* is כל־האדם."[25]

Also important is the syntax of 12:13. Whereas נם כל־האדם in 3:13 and 5:18 is followed by the relative ש/אשר, in 12:13 the phrase concludes the sentence. This has led to a number of suggestions for its translation, the most common of which is "this is the (whole) duty of man."[26] Of all the suggestions I have come across, however, the one offered by Fox comes closest to reading 12:13 as an intentional echo of 3:13, 5:18, and 7:2: fearing God and keeping his commandments are ". . . the substance, the 'material' of every person. There should be no alloy."[27] If I may put it differently, fearing God and keeping his commandments, *this* (כי־זה) is what should summarize the human experience. Although taking to heart the pleasures

---

[24] T. Anthony Perry argues, somewhat tersely, that the demonstrative זה "is intended to denigrate . . . what follows" (*Dialogues with Kohelet* [University Park, Pa.: Pennsylvania State University Press, 1993], 173). He cites Job 14:3 in support. It is not entirely clear to me what Perry means by this comment, but I would prefer to assign to זה an emphatic force.

[25] The use of כי in Ecclesiastes is outlined in Diethelm Michel, *Untersuchungen zur Eigenart des Buches Qohelet* (Berlin: de Gruyter, 1989), 200–212. Unfortunately, he does not consider 12:13 in his investigation.

[26] In discussing this phrase, the comment by Robert Gordis is commonly cited. He states that זה כל־האדם is "a pregnant idiom, characteristically Hebrew, for 'this is the whole duty of man'" (*Kohelet—The Man and His World: A Study of Ecclesiastes* [3rd ed.; New York: Schocken, 1968], 355). It is not immediately clear what Gordis means by a "pregnant idiom." Moreover, to suggest that the idiom is "characteristically Hebrew, for 'this is the whole duty of man'" does not seem to square with the fact that this specific phrase in Qoh 12:13 is unique to the Hebrew Bible. The examples he cites (Pss 109:4; 110:3; 120:7; Isa 28:12; Job 5:25; 8:9; 29:15; Num 10:31) do not seem to clarify the matter.

[27] Fox, *Time to Tear Down*, 362.

and rewards of life (3:13 and 5:18) and facing the stern reality of death (7:2) are central components of the human drama for each Israelite, more foundational and central is each Israelite's fear of God and obedience to God's law.

I would argue strongly that such a conclusion to the book does not pit the frame narrator against Qohelet, but rather places Qohelet's flesh and blood struggles into their larger and theologically ultimate context and perspective. Qohelet was indeed wise in his observations (12:9–11), but the frame narrator encourages his readers to view their daily struggles, which are a legitimate and expected element of life, in view of a broader perspective.

To refer back to Burkes's categories, Qoh 12:13–14 is an attempt to answer the crisis of Israel's exile and the resulting paradigm shift. But the epilogue does not answer this crisis by engaging it in debate. Rather, it acknowledges the true wisdom of Qohelet's observations while at the same time *reiterating Israel's central tradition of fear of God and obedience to Torah.* To be sure, times have changed, paradigms have shifted, but Israel's responsibility, at the individual as well as the corporate level, remains the same. In other words, despite the reality of the struggles so eloquently outlined by Qohelet, the answer is still as it always was. Qohelet was right, but there is a "what's more." And the "what's more" is not a new twist, but the tried and true formula of "fear and obedience." Such a solution to the newer problems that beset post-exilic Israelites also serves as an appeal to see Israel's historical vicissitudes from the point of view of traditional categories, thus encouraging a sense of continuity between Israel past and present, despite the circumstances.[28]

[28] I would like to thank Profs. C.-L. Seow, R. Van Leeuwen, and T. Longman III for their encouragement in the initial stages of this project in pursuing the line of reasoning represented here.

THE SYMBOLIC SIGNIFICANCE OF WRITING IN ANCIENT JUDAISM

Hindy Najman

> Writing holds for me an indescribable magic, perhaps because of the glimmer of eternity that hovers around it. Yes, I confess to you, I wonder what mysterious power lies hidden in these dead pen strokes and how the simplest of expressions that seem to be nothing but true and accurate can be so meaningful that they stare as if from clear eyes, or speak to us like accents without artifice coming from the depths of the soul. It is as if one can hear what one reads, yet the only thing one who recites these beautiful passages can do is attempt not to spoil them. The silent characters seem to me a more proper cloak for these most profound, most immediate expressions of the mind than the sound made by lips. I would almost like to say . . . Life is writing; the sole purpose of mankind is to engrave the thoughts of the divinity onto the tablets of Nature with the stylus of the formative spirit.
>
> Friedrich Schlegel[1]

I. The Rise of Sacred Writing

This essay develops an insight expressed by James Kugel in the following passage about the rise of Scripture in ancient Judaism:

> God's part in the divine-human discourse, it will be remembered, was not alone mediated by live human beings; it was also carried by texts. Long before the Babylonian exile, the word of God and his messengers had been committed to memory and to writing, and Israel had cherished these words; even in preexilic times, the record of ancient deeds and ancient legislation had constituted an important part of God's "speech" to humans. But as time went on, the significance of

---

[1] Friedrich Schlegel, "On Philosophy. To Dorothea," in *Theory as Practice: A Critical Anthology of Early German Romantic Writings* (ed. and trans. J. Schulte-Sasse et al.; Minneapolis: University of Minnesota Press, 1997), 420.

these texts increased, and with it the importance of those who copied
and expounded them. This change, certainly characteristic of post-
exilic life, is probably not a mere reflex of events of the exile—its
causes, tied up in part with the career of literacy and education in
earlier times, need not detain us here. But something of the growing
independent life of texts may perhaps be glimpsed even among writings that preceded the Return.[2]

Kugel's discussion is rich with implications for the study of sacred
writing in ancient Judaism. This essay explores some of those implications by considering the symbol of writing in biblical prophecy.

There is scholarly consensus that at an earlier stage, Israelite religion was first and foremost a matter of oral tradition and orally
transmitted laws and narratives.[3] But when, if ever, did orality begin
to cede its primacy to writing? While there was certainly no decisive rupture, one determining moment for the rise in the authority
of writtenness came with the return from the Babylonian exile and
Ezra's reconstitution of Jewish life centered on a body of sacred texts
known as the Mosaic Torah. This Torah-centered society was of
immense importance. However, as Kugel remarks in the above passage, the innovation was preceded by a long and gradual prehistory,
in which writing had steadily come to possess greater prominence
and, specifically, an authority greater than, or at the very least equal
to, oral discourse. Indeed, authoritative writing had already played

---

[2] James L. Kugel, "Early Interpretation: The Common Background of Late Forms
of Biblical Exegesis," in James L. Kugel and Rowan A. Greer, *Early Biblical Interpretation*
(LEC 3; Philadelphia: Westminster, 1986), 11–106, here 17.

[3] See Frank Moore Cross, *Canaanite Myth and Hebrew Epic: Essays in the History of
the Religion of Israel* (Cambridge, Mass.: Harvard University Press, 1973), 112, 117,
127; Simon B. Parker, *Stories in Scripture and Inscriptions: Comparative Studies on Narratives
in Northwest Semitic Inscriptions and the Hebrew Bible* (Oxford: Oxford University Press,
1997), 8–12, 145 n. 15; Albert I. Baumgarten, *The Flourishing of Jewish Sects in the
Maccabean Era: An Interpretation* (JSJSup 55; Leiden: Brill, 1997), 116–17. Compare
Jeffrey H. Tigay, who states:
> The main form of publication in the ancient world was oral presentation. This
> is Moses' method as well. He stores the tablets of the Decalogue in the
> Ark . . . and reads the Book of the Covenant to the people. . . . Although he
> ordains that the Teaching be written on the doorposts of homes, on city gates,
> on steles on Mount Ebal, and apparently in *tefillin* . . ., he does not have copies
> made on parchment or papyrus, a form convenient for study. . . . All of this
> points to the fact that even in Deuteronomy the dissemination of the Teaching
> remains primarily oral, with teachers either reciting it from memory or read-
> ing aloud from the written text. . . . Doubtless, in the First Temple period the
> written text of Scripture was used primarily for preservation, copying and
> verification, memorization, and for reading to others, as in Mesopotamia, early
> Greece, and Arabia. (*Deuteronomy* [JPS Torah Commentary: Philadelphia: Jewish
> Publication Society, 1996], 500)

a part in interactions between the divine and the human, along with oral discourse, in pre-exilic times.

I will uncover traces of writing's rise to prominence in both pre-exilic and exilic passages, traces that are discernible sometimes between passages and sometimes between the lines of redacted traditions. Although the changes are gradual, they add up to a profound shift, in which sacred writing—although not, before the return, any particular body of writings—became a repository of religious authority, and in which authoritative prophecy itself came to be seen as the revelation of written texts.

How should we understand this shift in the rise of references to writtenness? One familiar explanation goes as follows: written traditions are more precise and durable than oral traditions, and these factors may have become particularly important in the exile. Furthermore, the exile had a negative impact upon the institution of prophecy, which apparently lost some of the authority that people had previously accorded it before the exile. This explanation seems correct, as far as it goes. In fact, however, the durability of writing came to stand for the inalterability of the covenant even *before the exile*, at a time when, after the destruction of the northern kingdom, the southern monarchy seemed precarious. Moreover, as we shall see, the durability of writing is only part of the explanation for its rise to prominence. Writing was also understood, from an early period, to have a special symbolic significance and efficacy, promise, or consolation; it was to set events in motion, to realize what was written in a preliminary or anticipatory fashion. At times God Himself was depicted as a writer, and the portrayal of someone writing on God's behalf became a pre-eminent way of claiming authority for that person.

In what follows, I will focus on a group of biblical passages and their shifting portrayals of the authority of sacred writing. I should state at the outset, however, that this focus on the biblical evidence is in no way to suggest that extrabiblical evidence is irrelevant. The increasing prominence of sacred writing should be considered against the backdrop of the Assyrian, Babylonian, and Persian influences on biblical authors and their audiences, whether while living in their homeland or in exile. As may be seen from the material finds of the pre-exilic period, the Assyrians made great use of sacred writings in the form of monuments, royal inscriptions, and palace reliefs.[4]

---

[4] P. Gerardi, "Epigraphs and Assyrian Palace Reliefs: The Development of the Epigraphic Text," *JCS* 40 (1988): 1–35; Irene J. Winter, "Royal Rhetoric and the

Closer to Israel, material evidence such as the Mesha Stele from Moab attests to the use of writing as a means of memorializing history, a way of making the record of events survive to future generations and so preserve the king's name.[5] Such uses of writing continued and even increased during the Babylonian and Persian periods.[6] Arguably such a circumstance might have affected Israelite conceptions of writing and its uses.

In considering biblical texts, however, my main concern is the connection of writing and the Israelite imagination. I will raise such questions as: How was the work of writing imagined? What was the symbolic significance of sacred writing? How was the authority of writing conceived at different times? Certainly, long before the biblical period, writing had been a way of recording things in a permanent, or at least enduring, fashion, and also of preserving an exact and verifiable version of the wording. Thus, from pre-biblical times, we have written inventories, deeds, manumissions, and other legal documents such as treatises, law codes, and the like. This part of writing's function of course influenced its "reputation" as well, and writing soon came to acquire less practical or immediately necessary roles. Perhaps this expanded function had something to do with, for example, the writing down of mythical texts (such as those of ancient Babylon or Ugarit), texts whose enduring importance was, as it were, embodied by their being written down.

It is also tempting to consider whether a background increase in literacy rates was a factor. However, at this point in the study of

---

Development of Historical Narrative in Neo-Assyrian Reliefs," *Studies in Visual Communication* 7 (1981): 2–38; Piotr Michalowski, "Early Mesopotamian Communicative Systems: Art, Literature, and Writing," in *Investigating Artistic Environments in the Ancient Near East* (ed. A. Gunter; Washington, D.C.: Smithsonian Institute, 1990); Jack M. Sasson, "On Idrimi and Sarruwa, the Scribe," in *Studies on the Civilization and Culture of Nuzi and the Hurrians in Honor of Ernest R. Lacheman* (ed. D. I. Owen and M. A. Morrison; Winona Lake, Ind.: Eisenbrauns, 1981), 309–24. For a very helpful study of ancient Near Eastern inscriptions, see Klaas A. D. Smelik, *Writings from Ancient Israel: A Handbook of Historical and Religious Documents* (trans. G. I. Davies; Louisville: Westminster/John Knox, 1991). On the development of writing and reasoning, see Peter Machinist, "On Self-Consciousness in Mesopotamia," in *The Origins and Diversity of Axial Age Civilizations* (ed. S. N. Eisenstadt; New York: State University of New York Press, 1986), 183–202, 511–18; Jean Bottéro, "Writing and Dialectics, or the Progress of Knowledge," in *Mesopotamia: Writing, Reasoning, and the Gods* (trans. Z. Bahrani and M. Van de Mieroop; Chicago: University of Chicago Press, 1992), 87–102.

[5] For further discussion of the Mesha Stele, see Smelik, *Writings from Ancient Israel*, 29–50; James L. Kugel, *The Idea of Biblical Poetry: Parallelism and Its History* (New Haven: Yale University Press, 1981), 62.

[6] Michalowski, "Early Mesopotamian Communicative Systems," 64.

literacy it is impossible to draw significant conclusions. Some scholars have gone to great lengths to argue for widespread literacy in even the pre-exilic period,[7] while others offer far more reserved conclusions. Here, for example, is the assessment of Simon B. Parker:

> Writing was thus almost certainly restricted to people in the service of the government and, judging by the context of the inscriptions, was used largely for official business. The only substantial literary narrative recovered from these communities is the Balaam inscription from Tell Deir 'Alla, east of the Jordan, which is both too damaged and too little understood to justify its inclusion in this volume. Most written texts dated to the period of the kingdoms of Israel and Judah either served some immediate practical purpose, such as communication (witness the letters written on ostraca found at Lachish and Arad) or short-term record-keeping (such as the administrative notes written on ostraca found at Samaria), or more emblematic purposes (such as inscriptions on seals, which abound outside Israel).[8]

The biblical traditions themselves offer little direct evidence on this score. In the texts I will examine, references are made to prophetic ability to read and, in certain cases, even to write down divine revelation. Occasionally, a reader is invoked who, it seems, is supposed to be a member of the general Israelite community, but that community is mostly portrayed as hearing a text that is read aloud. Very rarely do we see texts being read by non-prophetic or non-scribal figures. This lack of documentation cannot contribute to either side of the literacy debate.

Indeed, even if there were more conclusive evidence about the numbers of potential readers at any given time, it would still be necessary to examine the internal evidence, presented by the biblical

---

[7] A. R. Millard, "Literacy," *ABD* 4:337–40; Andrè Lemaire, *Les écoles et la formation de la Bible dans l'ancien Israel* (Göttingen: Vandenhoeck & Ruprecht, 1981); idem, "Sagesse et écoles," *VT* 34 (1984): 270–81; J. van der Ploeg, "La rôle de la tradition orale dans la transmission du texte de l'Ancien Testament," *RB* 54 (1947): 5–41; James L. Crenshaw, *Education in Ancient Israel: Across the Deadening Silence* (New York: Doubleday, 1998), 29–49.

[8] Parker, *Stories in Scripture and Inscriptions*, 9. See also Parker's discussion of literacy and writing on pages 8–12, 145 n. 15. For a more skeptical view about the possibility of widespread literacy, see Anthony Phillips, "The Ecstatics' Father," in *Words and Meanings: Essays Presented to David Winston Thomas* (ed. P. R. Ackroyd and B. Lindars; London: Cambridge University Press, 1968), 183–94. See also Baumgarten, *Flourishing of Jewish Sects*, 114–36; Aaron Demsky, "Scribes and Books in the Late Second Commonwealth and Rabbinic Period," in *Mikra: Text, Translation, Reading and Interpretation of the Hebrew Bible in Ancient Judaism and Early Christianity* (ed. M. J. Mulder; CRINT 2.1; Assen: Van Gorcum and Minneapolis: Fortress, 1990), 2–20.

traditions themselves, concerning the ways in which the authority of
writing was conceived and the shifts in those conceptions over time.
Even if we knew how many literate Israelites existed at every moment,
we would still need to know what reading and writing meant to
them and how texts might have played especially authoritative roles
in their lives. After all, we are concerned here not with a dichotomy
between an oral culture and a literate culture, but with complex
economies of orality and literacy that shifted subtly over time. As
Ellen Davis writes:

> Biblical scholars have worked so hard in this century to overcome their
> own writing-bound biases, crystallized into theories of documents and
> authors which came to dominate the field, that it may seem a step
> backward to reassert the peculiar contribution of writing. Yet the
> achievement of those who have studied writing as a cultural and
> hermeneutical phenomenon has been to clarify the difference between
> orality and writing as primary modes of creating and transmitting dis-
> course. There is no question of going back to a naïve assumption that
> the bulk of Israel's traditions were produced in a mode of authorial
> composition resembling that prevalent in the modern world. Nor is it
> satisfactory, on the other hand, to see writing merely at the end of
> the creative process, either for individual pieces or for the tradition as
> a whole, with attendant implications of failure of nerve, lapse of inspi-
> ration, or both. Rather than setting oral and literary processes over
> against one another, with the implication that the literary historian
> must choose between these alternatives or at least rank them evalua-
> tively, the task and the opportunity which modern research places
> before biblical scholars is to refine our appreciation of the gradual
> transition between the two.[9]

What is called for, then, is a study, informed by the historical and
cultural context, of biblical traditions in which the sacred literary
process is portrayed, so that we can understand how, at various
moments, the work and authority of writing were conceived.

Of course, there are many societies in which written documents
play an authoritative role in various legal interactions. In our own
society, as the joke goes (if it is still a joke), an oral contract is not
worth the paper on which it is written. How were such functions
invoked and elaborated in biblical traditions? Although Israelite society may not have attained such an exalted state of text-dependence,
legal practice surely conferred a variety of authoritative functions

---

[9] Ellen F. Davis, *Swallowing the Scroll: Textuality and the Dynamics of Discourse in
Ezekiel's Prophecy* (BLS 21; JSOTSup 78; Sheffield: Almond, 1989), 38.

upon writing, and these functions were sometimes transferred from the social realm of human interaction to the sacred realm of the interaction between Israel and God.

In some biblical passages, the *testimonial* role of writing is specifically invoked, a role that is by no means unique to ancient Israel.[10] Testimony can serve numerous functions in social interactions. To name two that are important here: a witness may attest to the performance of a legally significant deed, such as a contract or covenant, hence to the responsibilities undertaken by both parties; and a witness may warn a prospective transgressor of the severity of his or her action, rendering the transgressor liable for punishment.[11] In both cases, human witnesses may offer their testimony either in oral or written fashion. The permanence and portability of written testimony—its availability even if the original witness is absent, unwilling, or dead—would privilege it over oral testimony in a society with a certain degree of literacy. If we turn from legal relations between humans to those between humans and God, the same basic rules seem to apply. Some biblical texts, for example, represent heaven and earth as witnesses to divine-human covenants or warnings,[12] and once such transfer of legal conventions had occurred, it is not difficult

---

[10] For a helpful discussion of biblical testimony, see H. G. M. Williamson, "On Writing and Witnesses," in *The Book Called Isaiah: Deutero-Isaiah's Role in Composition and Redaction* (Oxford: Clarendon, 1994), 94–115; Mary A. Loisier, "Witnesses in Israel of the Hebrew Scriptures in the Context of the Ancient Near East" (Ph.D. diss., University of Notre Dame, 1973). The claim that sacred writing can function, as it were, as a live witness is very central to the import and impact of writing in the pre-exilic period throughout the ancient Near East. See Bottéro's discussion of the role of writing in the ancient Near East in *Mesopotamia*, esp. 166–70.

[11] See the following comment by James L. Kugel:
Numerous Jewish writings from the second temple period bear witness to a common assumption that punishment could not properly be imposed unless some prior act of warning had taken place. This principle, which found expression in human jurisprudence, applied as well to divine-human interaction: God had thus dispatched prophets for the purpose of *warning* human beings of the consequences of disobedience. (The technical term used in biblical Hebrew for such acts of warning was *hēʿîd bĕ-* [often translated as "testify to" or "against," though "warn" would be a more straightforward equivalent] . . .). A proper warning required explicit condemnation of the act or behavior in question and equally explicit threat of punishment for continued infraction. ("The Jubilees Apocalypse," *DSD* 1 [1994]: 322–37, here 328)
For additional examples and discussion of this phenomenon in exilic biblical traditions, see Sara Japhet, *The Ideology of the Book of Chronicles and Its Place in Biblical Thought* (BEATAJ 9; Frankfurt am Main: Peter Lang, 1989), 183–91.

[12] E.g., Deut 32:1–3; Isa 1:2.

to see how the secular privilege of written testimony might also be
adapted to the sacred realm. Writing can record attestations to the
covenant between God and Israel, or warnings of punishments to
be incurred by transgressors, or promises of redemption for the faithful. Writing would then provide a valuable complement to oral testimony. It would supply a permanence and portability that oral
discourse could never attain. Yet it would not undo the need for
oral testimony, without which it would have nothing to record.

As already noted, there was more to writing's role in Israel's imagination than its permanence and portability. In this essay, I will claim
that writing was thought from pre-exilic times to be symbolically
significant and efficacious.[13] Furthermore, I will show that this efficacy—
variously imagined as, for example, birth and digestion—was connected to the testimonial function in a way that made writing far
more than a valuable complement to oral discourse between God
and Israel.[14] Even as early as First Isaiah, as I will show in my discussion below, written texts became not merely the records of testimony by other agents but the witnesses themselves.[15] Taking over
the role played by heaven and earth, written texts came to stand
for the permanence and inalterability of the covenantal relationship,
especially when that relationship appeared to be in jeopardy. Through
their special efficacy, written texts were thought to set in motion the
prophesied events of punishment or redemption, thus actualizing the
covenant when its reality seemed questionable. Thus, it was not simply that written texts could be carried into exile, although that was
both true and important. By the time the exile came, a way of thinking existed, according to which both exilic punishment and promised
redemption could be seen as having been initiated by sacred writing.[16]
Meanwhile, God's communications with prophets took the form,
more and more, of written texts, and prophetic activity itself focused
increasingly on the symbolic significance, the efficacy, and the authority
of acts of writing. Writtenness became a sign of authority. All this
set the stage for the text-based Judaism instituted by Ezra with his
public reading of Mosaic Torah.[17]

---

[13] For the development and argument of this claim, see my discussions below on
Hab 2, Jer 36, Ezek 4, and Zech 5.
[14] On this point, see my discussions below of Isa 8:1–4 and Ezek 2:8–3:3.
[15] See my discussions below of Isa 8:1–4, 16–20; 30:8–11. See also my discussion of Hab 2:2–4 later in this essay.
[16] See my discussions below of Jer 17 and Ezek 37.
[17] See, e.g., Neh 8:1–8.

A. *Isaiah 8:1–4*

I will begin by considering a passage from First Isaiah in which the prophet is instructed to inscribe a prophecy (Isa 8:1–4):

> The LORD said to me: "Get yourself a large table and write on it in ordinary script 'concerning *Mahĕr-Shālāl-Ḥāsh-Baz*.'" I appointed[18] reliable witnesses: Uriah the priest and Zechariah son of Jeberechiah.[19] I approached the prophetess, she became pregnant and bore a son. The LORD said to me, "Name him *Mahĕr-Shālāl-Hāsh-Baz*. For before the boy learns to call out 'my father' and 'my mother' the wealth of Damascus and the spoils of Samaria will be carried away in the presence of the king of Assyria."

The text of Isa 8:1–4 presents two ways of causing the divine promise to be, as it were, embodied, hence irreversible: writing down the text and naming the child. Two types of witnesses are invoked: human witnesses who attest to a text closely connected to a child, and a text that itself serves as a witness. Isaiah 8 is riddled with textual and interpretive difficulties, but it provides us with some fascinating insights into ways in which the authority of writing could be conceived. Indeed, the difficulties are themselves illuminating because they appear to arise in part from the fact that the text has more than one stratum, and the differences between the strata provide evidence of the shifting role of writing in Israel's imagination.

I will begin with the strikingly connected text and child. At the outset of the chapter, Isaiah is told to write a scroll and then to

---

[18] There are a number of variants for וְאָעִידָה. 4QIsaᶜ reads וֹהָעֵד; the LXX reads καὶ μάρτυράς μοι ποίησον; the Targum reads וְאַסְהִיד; the Peshitta reads *washed lî shāhdê*. All of this evidence might suggest an emendation in the MT from וְאָעִידָה to וְהָעִידָה. However, the Vulgate reads *et adhibui* supporting the MT. Based on this evidence (of course, excluding that from Qumran), Bernhard Stade suggests only a slight emendation to the pointing of the MT in his article, "Zu Jes. 8.1f.," *ZAW* 26 (1906): 129–41, esp. 136. See Hans Wildberger, who accepts Stade's emendation, in *Isaiah: A Commentary* (trans. T. H. Trapp; 2 vols.; CC; Minneapolis: Fortress, 1991), 1:332–33 n. 2a. As my translation indicates, I also accept Stade's suggestion of "I appointed witnesses for myself." Thus, the verb is pointed with a causative stem but also preserves the first person form as reflected in the MT and the Vulgate. I have preserved the first person consecutive preterite (as in Isa 8:3). Here, in Isa 8:2, the prophet is recounting his activity, and this verse should not be seen as part of God's command to him.

[19] There is a general consensus that the two witnesses are to be identified with the priest Uriah in 2 Kgs 16:10–16 and Zechariah, the father of Ahaz's wife in 2 Kgs 18:2 // 2 Chr 29:1. See Wildberger, *Isaiah*, 1:336. For further discussion concerning these two human witnesses in chapter 8 of Isaiah, see Williamson, *Book Called Isaiah*, 101.

write down the following: מַהֵר שָׁלָל חָשׁ בַּז. This נִּלְיוֹן, of text, is affirmed by two reliable witnesses, who apparently testify to the authenticity of the prophecy. The resulting child is to be named with the four-word phrase already recorded in the text: מַהֵר שָׁלָל חָשׁ בַּז. Thus in Isa 8:1–4 the attested text and the child share, as it were, the same revealed content.

What does this tell us about the role of writing in First Isaiah's prophecy? Prophetic writing is more, it seems, than a sign of things to come. For the pregnant prophetess does not merely signify the coming child; the child already grows inside her. On the other hand, prophetic writing is not performative.[20] It does not directly bring about the event it signifies, any more than impregnation directly brings about birth. Rather, it seems that Isaiah's prophetic writing is something like an *anticipatory realization* of what it symbolically signifies, just as the prophetess's pregnancy is the anticipatory realization of the child that will be born. In other words, the act of writing is more than a mere recording or making permanent. It seems to have the power to realize—if not fully, then in an anticipatory fashion—the very event it names. Like the fetus in the womb, the seed of the similarly named event grows in the attested text. Destruction may yet miscarry, but it is already in gestation.

Thus, what is striking in this passage is the peculiarly intimate relationship between written texts and the reality they signify. A written text—perhaps in distinction to an oral discourse, although this cannot be said with certainty—is symbolically significant insofar as it is pregnant with the future events it describes. Testimony is not invoked here as the authoritative function of the written word; rather,

---

[20] John L. Austin invented and employed the notion of a performative utterance that brings about the truth of what is said (e.g., "I name this ship the Titanic," said by an appropriate speaker in appropriate circumstances) in the development of his theory of speech acts; see his *How to Do Things with Words* (William James Lectures delivered at Harvard University, 1955; ed. J. O. Urmson and Marina Sbisà; 2nd ed.; Oxford: Oxford University Press, 1975). For further discussion of Austin on performatives, see the seminal discussion of Jacques Derrida, "Signature Event Context," in *Limited, Inc.* (ed. G. Graff; Evanston, Ill.: Northwestern University Press, 1988), 1–23; and the trenchant criticism of Stanley Cavell, "What did Derrida Want of Austin?," in *Philosophical Passages: Wittgenstein, Emerson, Austin, Derrida* (Oxford: Blackwell, 1995), 42–65; idem, "Derrida's Austin and the Stake of Positivism," in *A Pitch of Philosophy: Autobiographical Exercises* (Cambridge, Mass.: Harvard University Press, 1994), 77–86. For an interesting critique of how speech act theory has been applied to biblical texts, see Walter Houston, "What Did the Prophets Think They Were Doing?: Speech Acts and Prophetic Discourse in the Old Testament," *BibInt* 1 (1993): 167–88.

human testimony is required to authenticate the text, so that it can do—or be known to do—its seminal work.

Moreover, the written text itself is depicted as the female who receives the inscription from the male prophet.[21] The text itself is the child that grows within the woman; she is the protected and preserved text. As text, the woman is the only hope for the future. As prophet, the male inscribes his message for the future through the process of impregnating the woman with his message. The future depends on the inscription and efficacy of that inscription through the birth of a live child, that is a text that can survive the turmoil and challenges of the times, of birth, of survival.

B. *Isaiah 8:16–20*

However, in Isa 8:16–20, the idea of testimony *is* invoked to describe the work of the text:

> "Bind up the testimony, seal the instruction with my [God's] disci-
> ples." I will wait for the LORD, who is hiding his face from the house
> of Jacob, and long for him. Here I am with the children that the LORD
> has given me as signs and symbols in Israel from the LORD of Hosts
> who dwells on Mount Zion. "People will say to you: 'Inquire of the
> ancestral ghosts and the familial spirits that peep and growl; may not
> a nation inquire of its gods and of the dead on behalf of the living
> for teaching and testimony?'[22] Surely, for one who speaks thus there
> shall be no dawn."

Here testimony is directly evoked: "Bind up the law and testimony with my disciples." Although some scholars have thought that the testimony

---

[21] The association of the female with the image of the Torah can be traced in later rabbinic and mystical sources in the history of Jewish interpretation. See Elliot R. Wolfson, "Female Imaging of the Torah: From Literary Metaphor to Religious Symbol," in *Circle in the Square: Studies in the Use of Gender in Kabbalistic Symbolism* (Albany, N.Y.: State University Press, 1995), 1–28.

[22] This is the only place in the Hebrew Bible where the phrase "Torah and testimony" appears. The phrase appears again in the prologue to the Book of *Jubilees*. In the context of *Jubilees*'s use of this term, James L. Kugel writes:

> The "Torah and the testimony" is a phrase that occurs in Isa 8:20. The author of *Jubilees* liked it because it suited well his own purpose: he took "Torah" to be a reference to the written text of the Pentateuch, and used "testimony" (he actually understood this word more in the sense of "solemn writing") to refer to his own book. *Jubilees* was presented as the solemn warning that God's angel delivered to Moses on Mt. Sinai, a warning about, among other things, the dire consequences of failing to observe the proper calendar ("the divisions of all the times"). (*The Bible As It Was: Biblical Traditions of Late Antiquity* [Cambridge, Mass.: Harvard University Press, 1997], 405–6 n. 23)

in this passage is not the text but, as before, the authenticating testimony of the disciples, it seems to me that here the testimony is
textual and the disciples are charged with its preservation.[23] To what,
however, does the text testify? Recent scholarship has convincingly
argued that the text testifies to the preceding collection of prophecies
from 6:1–8:15, and that these four verses (8:16–20) are a later addition
referring back to the earlier passage.[24] Thus, First Isaiah illustrates
a slight transformation in the depiction of sacred writing described
in the earlier section of the chapter (8:1–4). In Isa 8:16–20, writing,
whose work is conceived of as efficacious, becomes the warning itself:
if the people adhere to the laws they will return to Israel; if not,
the exile of 722/721 B.C.E. will be permanent.

Thus, in what has been generally viewed as the earlier stratum
of Isaiah 8 (in vv. 1–15, but for our discussion vv. 1–4), the act of
writing and the conceiving of the child both appear to function as
warnings and promises for the future. In this depiction sacred writing is associated with childbirth, perhaps suggesting an association
with divine production and human conception. But in the second
stage, it is writing's role as testimony—testimony that may outweigh
the living human witnesses (either literal witnesses or the child as
the testimony to God's prophecy)—that emerges. In both stages,
however, writing is distinctly female, and once it is inscribed, it is
preserved by male tradents. The process calls upon the male as the
force that inscribes and the woman as the force that receives the
tradition and keeps it, preserves it.[25]

C. *Isaiah 30:8–11*

The idea that a text can itself be a witness to divine revelation is
not unique to Isa 8:16. Indeed, God instructs Isaiah to inscribe the
punishment of the Israelites upon a tablet in Isa 30:8–11:[26]

---

[23] In a similar vein, the Levites are put in charge of protecting the Sinaitic tablets
or the written song in Deut 31:25–26.

[24] Joseph Jensen, *The Use of tôrâ by Isaiah: His Debate with the Wisdom Tradition*
(CBQMS 3; Washington, D.C.: Catholic Biblical Association of America, 1973),
108; Williamson, *Book Called Isaiah*, 101–3.

[25] The association of the male with writing and the woman with the subject of
inscription has a long and interesting trajectory well into the later rabbinic and
Jewish mystical traditions. See Elliot R. Wolfson, "Erasing the Erasure/Gender and
the Writing of God's Body in Kabbalistic Symbolism," in *Circle in the Square*, 49–78.

[26] For a summary of scholarship on Isa 30:8–11, see Jensen, *Use of tôrâ by Isaiah*,
112–20.

Now, go write it down on a tablet and inscribe it in a book so that it may be with them for the final day as a witness forever. For it is a rebellious people, deceptive children; children not willing to obey the Torah of the LORD, who said to the seers "do not see" and to the visionaries "do not prophesy true things to us, promise us flattering things, prophesy delusions. Forsake the road, turn from the path, stop [any talk of] the Holy One of Israel in front of us."

Here the writing is intended to last and continue to be with the Israelite people forever. Revelation that involves writing has a special permanence that oral revelation lacks. Here, the idea of permanence should be understood in light of the prophesied exile of the northern Israelite kingdom. Thus, in the face of impending doom and destruction, the prophet is instructed to record *some* word of God[27] that will outlive this generation of Israelites. As an enduring witness, the text will continue to offer its testimony, namely, a divine warning, to listeners. Having abandoned all hope for his own generation, Isaiah inscribes the tablet for an audience of the future.[28]

Comparing Isa 8:16–18 with the above passage from Isa 30:8, Joseph Jensen writes:

> There are some surprising similarities between this passage and 8:16–18, the one just studied. In each case there is a probable real document which serves the purpose of attestation or witness. In the present passage the people are blamed for forsaking the tôrâ of [YHWH], while in the earlier one the tôrâ which Isaiah preserves among his disciples has been rejected. Both texts can be referred to broader contexts in which Isaiah warns against foreign alliances and calls for quiet trust in [YHWH] alone (7:4; 29:12, 16; 30:15). And in each case, it can be argued, his polemic is directed primarily against the royal advisers who advocate the expedient course of seeking outside military aid.[29]

---

[27] Here, too, as in the case of Isa 8:16–18, the actual contents of the prophetic text are not referred to in any clear manner. See Jensen, *Use of tôrâ by Isaiah,* 113–14.

[28] See Williamson's comments:

We may confidently assume that Isaiah is here reflecting on his own experience during the time of crisis. This being the case, God's word through the prophet is to be recorded as a witness for those who in the future may be more willing to listen to it. . . . Although a decision about whether the document explicitly included words of hope as well as judgement will depend on the unresolved question discussed above, we may agree that such a notion is implicit in the action itself. The phraseology of verse 8 presupposes that the text will be read in some unspecified future time, and, if it is to function then as a witness, it must imply a circle of readers who are more sympathetic to its contents than the present generation. (*Book Called Isaiah,* 105)

[29] Jensen, *Use of tôrâ by Isaiah,* 113.

Jensen's comparison of the two passages suggests that in both cases a written copy was made for the same reason: the royal advisors were not listening to Isaiah's warning. As a result, it became necessary to record the prophecies for a future time, after the destruction that will result from the present generation's refusal to listen. As enduring records of divine revelation and of the consequences of human disobedience, these texts testify both to God's special relationship with Israel and to Israel's resulting responsibilities.[30]

What emerges from the textually problematic Isa 8, then, is not a single systematically articulated conception of the authority of writing, but rather at least two distinct conceptions. The difference between the two conceptions may suggest an historical development. In the first, earlier conception (8:1–4), the testimony is provided by human witnesses while, in the second, testimony is provided by the text itself. In the first conception, the authority of writing is related to the peculiarly intimate relationship between a prophetically written text and the events it foretells (in the form of a legally binding warning) while, in the second, later strata in Isa 8:16–20 and 30:8–11, the authority of writing is related to the permanence of written documents. It is important to note that this authority of writing as permanent testimony appears to be a later development of the idea that writing has an efficacy—a capacity for anticipatory realization. This special efficacy may explain why writing became not merely the permanent record of heavenly testimony, but the witness *par excellence* to the covenant between God and Israel.[31]

---

[30] Another interesting example which illustrates the relationship between warning (עד) and the authority of writing can be seen in Deut 31:19–22. After the song is revealed to Moses, God instructs Moses to write it down and teach it to the Israelites. God explains the function of this act of writing: the song should be written down so that "this song will be a witness for me against the Israelites." The people are not called upon to function as witnesses to the revelation. Instead, an inanimate written copy of a divine revelation is to serve as a witness or testimony against the people, i.e., as a warning. One may note, however, that the song itself invokes heaven and earth as witnesses to its original, oral revelation (Deut 32:1). Why is this testimony insufficient? Clearly, written testimony (to divine revelation), which can be reenacted through the act of reading, has an authority that unwritten testimony lacks. What is new here is that the written version of the song is intended to bear witness *against* the Israelites if they transgress. Sacred writing thus serves not only to warn the people against transgression but also to testify against those who disobey the law. Finally, the text is handed over to the Levites for safekeeping. The success and efficacy of the biblical written traditions depends upon their preservation. Only if they are preserved can they continue to be called upon as authentic testimonial texts through public readings.

[31] This privileging of writing over speech can be traced further into the rabbinic period. See Wolfson, "Erasing the Erasure," 54.

D. *Isaiah 10:1–4*

The emergence of sacred writing in ancient Israel is deeply related to the widespread use of writing and in particular sacred writing in other contemporaneous cultures. Given the increasing authority attached to writing, it was very important for Israelite prophets to distinguish sharply between authentic sacred writing and the sacred writings of other peoples. Occasional biblical passages refer with grave concern to the fact that people are inscribing laws into stone and upon walls and are calling their inscriptions sacred. These public displays of laws could lead astray a people impressed with writing and could thus lead to disastrous consequences.

For example, First Isaiah refers to the "inscribers of sin" in Isa 10:1–4:

> Woe to those who inscribe evil inscriptions and those who write sinful writings [and] who neglect the case of the poor and treat the claims of the indigent oppressively so that widows are their spoil and they may plunder orphans. What will you do on the day of punishment when devastation arrives from a distant place? To whom will you flee for assistance, and how will you save your carcasses from collapsing under the bondman and from falling under the slain? With all of this, his anger has not withdrawn and his arm is still outstretched.

These inscribers may be associated with the Assyrians who are oppressing the Israelites and have many impressive texts inscribed upon their palace walls.[32] We also know that the Assyrians had monuments of written laws which they claimed had a divine status. Here the misleading inscription has the effect of oppressing the widow and the orphan. One must beware of false inscriptions and one must learn to distinguish between authentic and inauthentic sacred writing.[33] Writing can undermine divine authority and Israelite law.

---

[32] See Gerardi, "Epigraphs and Assyrian Palace Reliefs," 1–35; and Winter, "Royal Rhetoric and the Development of Historical Narrative in Neo-Assyrian Reliefs," 2–38. For the impact of Assyrian culture on First Isaiah, see Peter Machinist, "Assyria and Its Image in the First Isaiah," *JAOS* 103 (1983): 719–37.

[33] This tradition continues in later extrabiblical traditions. For example, in the Book of *Jubilees* (8:1–4), Kainan seems to have known that there was something transgressive about the writing he discovered. Why else would he have feared Noah's anger? Yet, Kainan took it to be an authoritative record. Why would he have made such an error? Surely, the fact that it was an ancient writing was sufficient. It appears that the writings of the ancients were considered authoritative enough to copy. Hence the danger of writing is inextricably linked to its authoritative function: as well as the correct, divinely-sanctioned texts, there are also dangerous texts, which may claim a certain authority on the basis of their status as ancient writings, and these may lead the reader astray, with world-historical consequences:

E. *Exodus 32–34*

I now turn to Exod 32–34. This pericope preserves pre-exilic traditions, yet in its final redacted form, it is a product of the editors of the late First Temple and early exilic times. Through such acts of editing, we can perceive the gradual transition from a conception of writing as testimony accompanying oral revelation to a conception of writing as the authoritative medium of revelation. As in the case of Isa 8:16–20 and 30:8–11, the traditions of Exod 32–34 depict sacred writing, this time in the form of covenantal tablets. According to divine instruction, these commandments must be recorded in writing. Even if they are destroyed, they must be rewritten and remain permanent and inalterable instruction of divine commands. Thus, they stand as a covenant of eternal warning to those who dare to transgress the sacred written tradition. The fact that these laws were written by God on stone tablets was a statement fraught with meaning about their permanence and exactitude, indeed, their inalterability. The fact that tablets were rewritten by Moses (Exod 34:27–28), acting on God's behalf, was full of implications for the authority of the scribe, and especially for the authority of Moses himself.

1. *Exodus 32:15–19*

The first set of covenantal tablets—לחת העדת—is the only text described in biblical traditions as written directly by the finger of God (Exod 31:18).[34] The tablets also have the unusual feature, mark-

---

In the twenty-ninth jubilee, in the first week—at its beginning [1373]—Arpachshad married a woman named Rasueya, the daughter of Susan, the daughter of Elam. She gave birth to a son for him in the third year of this week [1375], and he named him Kainan. When the boy grew up, his father taught him (the art of) writing. He went to look for a place of his own where he could possess his own city. He found an inscription which the ancients had incised in a rock. He read what was in it, copied it, and sinned on the basis of what was in it, since in it was the Watchers' teaching by which they used to observe the omens of the sun, moon, and stars, and every heavenly sign. He wrote (it) down but told no one about it because he was afraid to tell Noah about it lest he become angry at him about it. (*Jub.* 8:1–4)

[34] On the terms used to describe the tablets, see: Sigo Lehming, "Versuch zu Ex. xxxii," *VT* 19 (1960): 16–50; Lothar Perlitt, *Bundestheologie im Alten Testament* (WMANT 36; Neukirchen Vluyn: Neukirchener, 1969), 203ff.; Brevard S. Childs, *The Book of Exodus: A Critical, Theological Commentary* (OTL; Louisville: Westminster, 1976), 364–75; for references to scholarly discussion regarding the claim that the covenant embodied by the Sinaitic tablets is the same as the covenant in Deuteronomy, see Childs's discussion at 374 n. 5; for a review of earlier scholarship on the divisions of sources in light of the way the Sinaitic tablets were described in J, E, D, and P, see ibid., 572 n. 15. See also, Moshe Weinfeld, "Berit," in *ThWAT* 1:782–808.

ing their divine provenance, of being written on both sides (Exod 32:15–16). Although God's revelation was itself oral, this written record is linked in an especially intimate fashion to that revelation, sharing its divine origin. It is the role of writing in the revelation of the covenantal process that concerns me here, not the much-discussed question of what was actually written on the first and on the second set of tablets. The description of the first tablets and their fate can be found in Exod 32:15–19:

> Moses turned and descended from the mountain with the two tablets of law in his hand—tablets inscribed on both sides; on one [side] and on the other [side] they were inscribed. Now the tablets were the divine creation of God and the writing was divine writing engraved upon the tablets. When Joshua heard the uproar which the people were making, he said to Moses, "There is the sound of war in the camp." Moses replied,[35] "It is not the sound of strength, nor is it the sound of weakness, rather it is the sound of song[36] that I hear." As he approached the camp, and saw the calf and the dancing, Moses became enraged and he threw the tablets from his hands and shattered them at the foot[37] of the mountain.

Thus, the tablets, unique in having been written directly by God, were rendered forever inaccessible to the Israelites.[38] "He (Moses) threw

---

On the covenant in ancient Israel and ancient Near Eastern parallels, see the important discussions by George E. Mendenhall, "Covenant Forms in Israelite Tradition," in *The Biblical Archaeologist Reader 3* (ed. E. F. Campbell, Jr., and D. N. Freedman; Garden City, N.Y.: Doubleday, 1970), 25–53; idem, *The Tenth Generation* (Baltimore: Johns Hopkins University Press, 1973), 174–97; Dennis J. McCarthy, *Treaty and Covenant* (Rome: Pontifical Biblical Institute, 1978); Delbert R. Hillers, *Covenant: The History of a Biblical Idea* (Baltimore: Johns Hopkins University Press, 1969), 25–97; Ronald E. Clements, *Abraham and David* (London: SCM Press, 1967); Moshe Weinfeld, "The Covenant Grant in the Old Testament and in the Ancient Near East," *JAOS* 90 (1970): 184–203; Jon D. Levenson, "Sinai, The Mountain of the Covenant," in *Sinai and Zion: An Entry into the Jewish Bible* (San Francisco: Harper & Row, 1985), 15–86; James Nohrnberg, "The Text of the Law," in *Like Unto Moses: The Constituting of an Interruption* (Bloomington, Ind.: Indiana University Press, 1995), 43–61 and notes on 352–58.

[35] The LXX, some of the Latin manuscripts, and the Peshitta insert the name of Moses immediately after the verb.

[36] Here the LXX adds "wine," so that the phrase reads φωνὴν ἐξαρχόντων οἴνου. This should be understood as an interpretation of the MT and not as an independent, more authentic, or earlier version of the Hebrew text. This interpretation attempts to explain the character of the song. Thus, the LXX suggests that it is a song of wine, i.e., drunkenness. For a similar position, see Childs, *Book of Exodus*, 557.

[37] The Targum, the Samaritan Pentateuch, and the Peshitta reflect the reading בתחתית ההר instead of the MT reading תחת ההר. In my translation, I have emended the MT to reflect the versional evidence, translating as "at the foot of the mountain."

[38] The question of whether Moses had the right to shatter divine tablets is debated extensively in the rabbinic literature. See, e.g., *'Abot R. Nat.* 2(A); see the editions

down the tablets and shattered them . . . to dramatize the end of the covenant."[39] Henceforth, there would be no opportunity for general Israelite access to a divinely-written record of the divine oral tradition.

2. *Exodus 34:1–4*

But the covenant was not, in fact, at an end. Access to the content of divine revelation therefore had to be granted anew, and this, it seems, required yet another written text: a second set of tablets. This time, it was not God but Moses who inscribed the tablets at God's command. Having broken the tablets, symbolically abrogating the treaty, Moses did not merely arrange for Israel to be forgiven and then transmit the contents of the original tablets orally. Instead, he had to go back to the mountain top and rewrite the tablets in order to re-enact the covenant.

According to divine instruction, these tablets were to be like the first, the oral revelation that Moses received on Sinai and that marked the terms of the covenant with Israel:

> The LORD said to Moses, "Cut yourself two stone tablets like the first [tablets] so that I may write upon the tablets the words which were upon the first tablets which you shattered. Be ready by morning and come up in the morning to Mount Sinai and present yourself there to me, at the top of the mountain. No one [else] should come up with you and no one [else] should be seen anywhere on the mountain. Furthermore, the flocks and the cattle should not graze in front of that mountain." Moses cut two tablets like the first and he arose early in the morning and went up to Mount Sinai just as the LORD had instructed him, taking the two stone tablets in his hand.

This second set of tablets has three aspects. First, the tablets attest to the *fact* of revelation and covenant, specifically to the privileged position of Moses as immediate audience for God's speech and as enacting the covenant between God and Israel. Second, the tablets embody the actual *contents* of the revelation or the terms of the covenant and preserve them in a pristine and authentic form. In

---

of Solomon Schechter, ed., *Aboth de Rabbi Nathan* (1887; repr., New York: Shulsinger Bros. Linotyping and Publishing Co., 1945), 10–11; and Judah Goldin, trans., *The Fathers According to Rabbi Nathan* (ed. J. Obermann; Yale Judaica Series 10; New Haven: Yale University Press, 1955), 20–22. On Moses' shattering, see Kugel, *The Bible As It Was*, 426–27, where two motifs are isolated—"The Letters Flew Off" and "Tablets Became Too Heavy"—in response to how Moses could have shattered the divinely-inscribed tablets.

[39] Childs, *Book of Exodus*, 569.

these two respects, writing remains ancillary to the oral dimension of the revelation or covenant itself. However, the third aspect of the tablets adds a further feature to writing's significance. Since Moses is the only figure portrayed as authorized to repeat a divine act of inscription, the tablets may also be said to bolster the sacred authority of Moses himself, the prophet *in loco Dei*.

This authority would later attach to the whole of Mosaic Torah—which certainly exceeded the Ten Commandments, whatever else it may be thought to have included—and would ultimately attach to the whole of what came to be known as the Pentateuch. One important way to authorize a law or interpretation in Second Temple literature, from Ezra on, is to portray that law or interpretation as written by Moses.[40]

In the passages considered so far, both oral discourse and writing have played roles in the revelatory establishments of covenants. Writing is more than a mere record of an oral covenant and more than a record of oral testimony. It can attest to the very existence of the covenant in Exod 32–34 (the destruction of the writing thus effecting the abrogation of the covenant, and the rewriting there, its re-enactment) and a witness issuing fair warning to those who transgress it (Isa 8 and 30). It has even become a product of God's own inscription. All this has prepared writing for a career of its own, gradually increasing its independence from the oral discourse between God and a prophet.

F. *2 Kings 22–23*

Around the year 620 B.C.E. a series of religious, political, and possibly also economic reforms were imposed upon the Judean kingdom under the reign of King Josiah.[41] What is remarkable is that, according to the account in 2 Kings, the Josianic Reform was a result of an allegedly *discovered scroll*. Upon Josiah's hearing the contents of the

---

[40] For further discussion on this point, see my recent study, *Seconding Sinai: the Development of Mosaic Discourse in Second Temple Judaism* (JSJSup 77; Leiden: Brill, 2003).

[41] The nature and impact of these reforms have been debated. See, e.g., Frank Moore Cross and David Noel Freedman, "Josiah's Revolt Against Assyria," *JNES* 12 (1953): 56–58; W. Eugene Claburn, "The Fiscal Basis of Josiah's Reforms," *JBL* 92 (1953): 11–22; Norbert Lohfink, "The Cult Reform of Josiah of Judah: 2 Kings 22–23 as a Source for the History of Israelite Religion," in *Ancient Israelite Religion: Essays in Honor of Frank Moore Cross* (ed. P. D. Miller, Jr., P. D. Hanson, and S. D. McBride; Philadelphia: Fortress, 1987), 459–76.

scroll and the divine warnings of curses as a result of idolatrous transgression, he tore his clothes in mourning and cried. As an immediate result of hearing the contents of the discovered text, Josiah imposed a series of religious reforms upon the nation and consulted the prophetess Huldah concerning the nation's punishment for their past transgressions. The importance of the scroll is not said to depend on any oral revelation to which it attests. Yet Josiah could not assess the implications of the text without consulting a living prophet. In the text below, 2 Kgs 22:18–20, Huldah responded by telling Josiah that it was too late to cancel the inevitable destruction, yet the destruction would be postponed and would not be witnessed by Josiah himself because of his repentance and role in returning the people to the worship of God:

> To the king of Judah, who sent you to inquire of the LORD, say thus to him: "Thus said the LORD the God of Israel concerning the words which you have heard. 'Since your heart is soft and you humbled yourself before the LORD upon your hearing what I said concerning this place and concerning its inhabitants, that it would become a wasteland and a curse, and [since] you rent your clothes and you wept before me, I have surely taken heed,' declares the LORD. 'Therefore, I will bring you to your fathers and you will be brought to your burial place in peace. Your eyes will not see all of the evil that I will bring upon this place.'" They returned the message to the king.

The discovered text of Torah was able to generate repentance among the king and the people. Although the movement of repentance and spiritual cleansing was not powerful enough to eradicate the written text, nevertheless, Josiah's repentance succeeded in delaying the destruction of Jerusalem. The scroll had the power that it had because it was recognized and accepted by a prophet as an authentic piece of sacred writing, inspired by God. As we will see, this theme became combined with the idea of writing's special efficacy, so that the fate of the people—especially their punishment with exile and the hope of their return—came to be seen as intertwined with the fate of sacred writing.

Interestingly, what one does not find in the above examples (nor very much elsewhere in pre-exilic texts) is a claim that eventually became quite common in Second Temple times: that a certain text was actually authored or dictated by this or that human figure and transmitted in writing to later times, and consequently that it has authoritative status. In the Second Temple period, a text's being authored or dictated (rather than, for example, an idea, vision, or law being orally communicated) by this or that figure, and a text's being transmitted by a line of faithful tridents, became marks of its authority. This focus on authorship and faithful transmission contrasts with pre-exilic conceptions of the authority of sacred writing. For example, the pericope of Exod 32–34 described Moses' involvement in the production of the Sinaitic tablets. However, despite Moses' reception and actual rewriting of the tablets, the Exodus narrative did not suggest that Moses was the author of the testimonial tablets. Rather, the author of the Torah was God. Furthermore, although the Torah was to be transmitted through the Levites, we are told remarkably little about how they served as faithful tradents.[42] However, the claim that traditions had been transmitted without alteration and the association of texts with specific authors would become two crucial aspects of the authority of sacred writing in the Second Temple period.

II. The Textualization of Prophecy

When the long threatened exile finally came, sacred writing was well-prepared for a still more prominent role. Prophets could no longer speak to kings. But they could still provide permanent and portable written testimony about the covenantal relationship between God and Israel. And such writings were not merely prophetic predictions of exile or redemption. They were agents setting in motion the events of either exile or redemption, depending upon the responses of their audience.

There are some biblical texts that suggest that if only the Israelites sincerely changed their ways, there would be some hope for redemption and even alteration of a divinely-inspired *written* prophecy.[43] This would depend on some sort of perceptible transformation of the people which would demonstrate their belief in God and their commitment to fulfill the divine commands through repentance and

---

[42] The special status of Levi or the Levites is mentioned in Exod 32:25–29; Num 8:14–19; Mal 2:4–9; the Torah is explicitly associated with them in Deut 17:18–20; 31:9–13, 24–29; 33:8–11; 2 Chr 17:7–9. However, none of these texts contains explicit details about how the Levites administered their special position or their responsibility to promulgate the Torah.

[43] One of the most powerful examples of this phenomenon may be found in Jer 36, esp. vv. 3 and 7. See also my discussion of Jer 36 in this essay.

consistent adherence to the Law. Their fate could be averted through
the proper response to the texts: in a sense, the people could be
redeemed through the texts.

A. *Habakkuk 2:2–4*

Habakkuk records his prophecies at a time of impending doom, at
the time of the Babylonian exile. Yet, he offers a vision of comfort
and of a promise for return. In addition to warning those who read
of the consequences of their transgressive actions, sacred writing is
also represented as a testimony which offers consolation. In Hab
2:2–4, the prophet's capacity to offer such a vision of consolation
depends on the idea that sacred texts have the power not only to
bring about destruction but also to effect redemption:

> The LORD answered me and said, "Write the vision legibly on the
> tablets so that the one reading from it can read quickly. For the vision
> is a witness for a set time; it is a testifier[44] to the end, and it does not
> lie. Even if it seems slow, wait for it. For it will come and it will not
> be late. The arrogant one, he will not walk in it but the righteous one
> will live by his faithfulness."

As in the case of Isa 30:8–9 (above) and Jer 32 (below), this prophecy
was recorded for a generation that the prophet would never see.
Habakkuk's text is intended to offer divine comfort to future readers. J. J. M. Roberts suggests understanding the "deeper meaning"
of Hab 2:2 in the following way: "write the vision on the tablets
and make its import plain so that the one reading can take refuge
in it."[45] It should also be noted that the text is a witness that redemption will come. The Jews are thus taken through the various stages
of exile, accompanied by a series of sacred texts which serve to transform and rebuild the Judahite community in exile. These are some

---

[44] I understand יפח as "a testifier." This understanding is based on a Ugaritic
noun *yph* meaning "witness." This suggestion was first made by Samuel Loewenstamm,
"*yāpîaḥ, yāpiaḥ, yāpēaḥ*," *Leš* 26 (1962): 205–8 [Hebrew]. See also the commentary
of J. J. M. Roberts, who follows this suggestion by Loewenstamm (*Nahum, Habakkuk,
and Zephaniah: A Commentary* [OTL; Louisville: Westminster/John Knox, 1991], 106).
There are a number of occasions in the Hebrew Bible where this root יפח is
employed in a verbal capacity. Roberts notes that it is often paired with עד ("witness"), which should further support Loewenstamm's original suggestion; see, e.g.,
Ps 27:12; Prov 6:19; 14:5; 19:5.
[45] Roberts, *Nahum, Habakkuk, and Zephaniah*, 110. See also his detailed and insightful discussion of Hab 2:2 on 109–11.

of the intended effects of sacred writing. Roberts compares the texts we saw earlier from Isaiah (chapters 8 and 30) with Hab 2 and claims that this parallel of writing

> . . . shows that the practice of writing down the prophetic message as a witness or testimony had two purposes. On the one hand, it was done because of the disbelief of the people who did not want to hear the message (Isa 30:8–11). When the word was fulfilled, its testimony would leave the unprepared without excuse. On the other hand, the written word would serve in the meantime as a source of reassurance and guidance for those who believed (Isa 8:16–17). It is this latter function which is highlighted in Habakkuk's use of the motif. Habakkuk is assured that the vision is a safe guide for the present, because its testimony about the future was true. The vision was not a lying witness; its fulfillment would come at the appropriate time. . . . The word *môʿēd* is used for the end term for a woman's pregnancy (Gen 18:14), and, just as the nine-month term for a pregnancy is fixed, though it may often seem to the pregnant woman that her condition will never change, so the vision will be fulfilled at its appointed time. If it seems slow in coming, wait for it, for like the birth of a child it cannot be delayed.[46]

B. *Jeremiah 36 and 17*

Although these are some of the *intended effects*, they did not always come about. An example of the failure of a written text which was intended to generate repentance can be found in Jer 36:1–8:

> In the fourth year of Jehoiakim, the son of Josiah, king of Judah, this word came to Jeremiah from the LORD: "Take a scroll[47] and write upon it all of the words that I have spoken to you concerning Israel, concerning Judah, and concerning all of the nations from the day I spoke to you, from the days of Josiah until this day. Perhaps the house of Judah will hear all of the evil that I intend to do to them, so that each person will turn back from his evil path and then I will forgive their iniquity and their sin." Then Jeremiah called Baruch the son of Neriah, and Baruch recorded onto a scroll Jeremiah's dictation, all the words of the LORD that he had spoken to him. Jeremiah commanded Baruch, saying: "I am debarred from entering the House of the LORD. You go and read the scroll which you recorded from my dictation, the words of the LORD, in the earshot of the people in the House of the LORD on the fast day. You should read it in the earshot of all of the people of Judah who come in from their cities. Perhaps their supplication

---

[46] Ibid., 110.

[47] This phrase, מגלת ספר, appears four times in the Hebrew Bible: Jer 36:2, 4; Ps 40:8; Ezek 2:9.

will be accepted before the LORD and each person will turn back from his evil path, for great is the anger and wrath that the LORD has spoken against this people." And Baruch the son of Neriah did everything that Jeremiah the prophet commanded him concerning the reading from the scroll, the words of the LORD in the House of the LORD.

Here God instructs Jeremiah to record in writing prophecies he has already received, in the hope that the Israelites might hear the words and repent in response to them.

But repentance is not the only way to respond to a sacred text with acknowledged potency. In Jer 36:21–25, the king Jehoiakim decided not to respond to the warning transmitted by a sacred text but instead to destroy the text:

> Then the king sent Jehudi to get the scroll and he took it from the chamber of Elishama the scribe. Jehudi read it in the earshot of the king and all of the officials who attended the king. The king was staying at his winter house, it was the ninth month, and there was a fire burning in the brazier before him. As Jehudi read three or four columns,[18] he [the king] would cut it with a scribe's knife and throw it into the fire in the brazier until the entire scroll was consumed by the fire in the brazier. The king and all of his servants who heard all these words did not fear and did not rend their clothes. Even when Elnathan and Delaiah and Gemariah urged the king not to burn the scroll, still he would not listen to them.

Clearly, Jehoiakim could not merely ignore the written prophecy. If the prophecy's efficacy was conceived as dependent on its material representation, then the king's destruction of the sacred text may have been a genuine attempt to inhibit the effect of the recorded prophecy.

As the text is read, Jehoiakim tears and burns each section of the scroll (Jer 36:22). But God instructs Jeremiah to *rewrite* the prophecies and to record additional prophecies of doom against Jehoiakim (Jer 36:27–29, 32). Why was it so important to have a written record of the prophecy? Robert Carroll writes: "With the disintegration of the nation brought about by the fall of the king, city, and land and the development of the prophetic word in a written form, it becomes possible to discern the emergence of the idea of the word over against society. Committed to writing, the word has a permanence beyond the exigencies of human existence and can survive even the absence

---

[18] On דלת as a column of a scroll and its relation to the מגלה, see R. Lansing Hicks, "DELET AND MᶜGILLĀH: A Fresh Approach to Jeremiah xxxvi," *VT* 33 (1983): 46–66.

of its original bearer."[49] These enduring written prophecies appear to have been important, not only as affirmations in the time of Jeremiah but also as testimony for a future audience. "Writing the oracles is here a supplement to oral prophecy and, in the last analysis, a counsel of despair."[50] The Jews could consult and find the right path through these prophecies at a later time in history, and thus the text could exercise its transformative power at a future date. But as far as the fate of the Judahites is concerned, ". . . the fate of Jerusalem and Judah is determined by the ashes of that scroll lying under the king's brazier. . . . When the king dismisses its claims by burning it, he seals the fate of himself and his people. The threats and curses in the scroll are not destroyed by the king's apotropaic act but released by it."[51]

Jeremiah lived at a time when he might have expected a different reaction from Jehoiakim. As we learn from the very first chapter of Jeremiah, the prophet would have been a boy of about twelve years old when Josiah implemented his reforms.[52] He might have heard of Josiah's respect and deference to the prophetess Huldah and of Josiah's willingness to transform himself and his people in response to a divinely-authorized prophetic text.

There is a striking contrast between 2 Kgs 22–23 and Jer 36. Despite the similarity of setting, the responses of the Judahite kings could not be more different. Robert Carroll's comparison is both insightful and compelling:

> The story of king Josiah's response to the finding of the book of the law in the temple is the counterpart to the tale of Jehoiakim's burning of the scroll. Both stories belong together and, Deuteronomistic editing apart, provide paradigms of how to respond to the hearing of the divine word (or not as the case may be). Josiah's reaction to the

---

[49] Robert P. Carroll, *Jeremiah: A Commentary* (OTL; Philadelphia: Westminster, 1986), 668.

[50] Davis, *Swallowing the Scroll*, 51.

[51] Carroll, *Jeremiah*, 663.

[52] The relationship between Jeremiah and Josiah's reform is a complex one. The Book of Jeremiah does not provide much evidence of Josiah's reforms. That Jeremiah could have been preaching during the reforms and their aftermath but not at least allude to them seems odd. The issue has thus centered on whether the "thirteenth year of Josiah" in Jer 1:2 refers to the date of Jeremiah's birth or to his prophetic call in 1:4–10. See the differing positions of John Bright, *Jeremiah* (AB 21; Garden City, N.Y.: Doubleday, 1965), lxxviii–lxxxviii; Carroll, *Jeremiah*, 89–93; and William L. Holladay, *Jeremiah 1: A Commentary on the Book of Jeremiah Chapters 1–25* (Hermeneia; Philadelphia: Fortress, 1986), 1, 17.

reading of the book by Shaphan the scribe (hence Baruch in Jer. 36) is to rend his garments. . . . His next response is to send his servant to inquire of [YHWH] on behalf of himself, the people and all of Judah because the nation is in dire trouble over their failure to obey the words of the book. This inquiry takes the form of a consultation with the prophet Huldah who assures the delegation that the words mean what they say and that the nation is doomed (II Kings 22:14–17). She also conveys an individual message for king Josiah which promises him a peaceful death because of his reaction to the curses of the book (II Kings 22:18–20). Josiah's weeping and torn garments, his concern for the nation and his consultation with a prophet represent the correct way to respond to the divine word in its written form. That story cannot be ignored in reading the account of the scroll of Jeremiah's words delivered by Baruch to the people, the princes and, finally, to the king. In spite of the apparent concern of the princes for the safety of Baruch and Jeremiah (vv. 16–19), they do not respond to the actual words read out to them. Throughout [Jeremiah] 36 there is no response to the scroll's contents: people, princes, king and courtiers *all* are represented as ignoring the contents of the scroll. Thus [Jeremiah] 36 reverses the paradigmatic response of Josiah to the words of the book.[53]

This reversal is jarring and frightening. As a result of Jehoiakim's destruction of the scroll, his punishment is intensified. To destroy a sacred text is to reject God and God's messengers. We are left with a fading glimmer of hope: what if the people had listened to the prophetic warnings and repented, as God had hoped?

The actions of Jehoiakim made it impossible for the glimmer of hope to be realized. Instead, a new text emerged, leaving no option for repentance and even adding extensive punishment for the perpetrator Jehoiakim. Of course, Jer 36 was written during the exile, after Jehoiakim's downfall and the destruction of Jerusalem in 587 B.C.E. But this enables us to see how important it was, after the fact, to view the destruction as the direct result of responding wrongly to a sacred text.[54] So great had the symbolic significance of sacred writing become in Israel's imagination that it rendered the destruction more intelligible to view it as the effect of a text.

In light of writing's increasing prominence as witness and agent, it is perhaps not surprising that later biblical prophecies exhibit

---

[53] Ibid., 663–64.

[54] On the exilic editing of the Jeremianic traditions, see Christopher R. Seitz, "The Crisis of Interpretation Over the Meaning and Purpose of the Exile," *VT* 35 (1985): 78–97.

greater fascination with the production and materiality of writing than earlier passages, and that they insist more on their own writtenness. To inscribe or write the divine word upon bricks or trees was to represent—or even to participate in—the effectiveness of that word in the earthly realm. This was particularly important during a period of approaching disaster or in the midst of exile, when the efficacy of the covenant could have appeared to be questionable.

Jeremiah 17:1–4 emphasizes the permanence of God's decision to destroy Jerusalem by describing it as having been written with an iron stylus:

> The sin of Judah is written with an iron stylus; with a diamond point it is engraved on the tablet of their heart and on the horns of their altars. While their children remember their altars and their *Asherim* beside green trees on the high hills, on the mountains in the open country, your wealth and all your treasures I will give away as spoil because of the sin of your high places throughout your borders. You will loosen your hold from your inheritance which I gave to you and I will make you serve your enemies in a land which you do not know for you have lit the fire of my anger; it will burn forever.[55]

Furthermore, the text in Jeremiah states that their sins were also carved out on the horns of the altars. Robert Carroll writes: "Judah's sin (unspecified) is so deep that it is engraved on the nation's heart and altars. That engraving is permanent and deep because it is made with an iron tool, a flint point. . . . The carving of Judah's sin on the altars mocks the sanctity of such objects by making them expressions of the nation's corrupt state and reminders to [YHWH] of their sinfulness."[56] In Jeremiah 17, writing with an iron stylus signified the stubbornness of the Judahites and the inevitability of their punishment.

C. *Ezekiel 4 and 37*

Another example of biblical fascination with the materiality and inalterability of writing can be seen in the writings of another exilic prophet, Ezekiel. In the text below from Ezek 4:1–3, the prophet is instructed to effect national punishment by means of an act of writing whose materiality is emphasized:

---

[55] These verses do not appear in the main manuscripts of the LXX. Carroll and Bright suggest that Jer 15:12–14 (which is intact, both in the LXX and the MT) may reflect the tradition in Jer 17:1–4; see Carroll, *Jeremiah*, 325; and Bright, *Jeremiah*, 114.

[56] Carroll, *Jeremiah*, 349.

You, man, take a brick[57] and place it in front of you and engrave
upon it a city, Jerusalem. Place a siege against it and build a ramp
against it, pour out a mound against it, place camps around it, and
place battering-rams against it on all sides. Take an iron plate and set
it as an iron wall between yourself and the city. Set yourself towards
it; let it be under siege, you will make a siege against it. It is a sign
for the house of Israel.

Ezekiel receives a vision and is instructed to write upon a brick,
"Jerusalem." This brick is then set up as if it were the city of
Jerusalem itself, and Ezekiel constructs a siege and a surrounding
enemy encampment against it. Once inscribed with the city's name,
its fate is the anticipatory realization of Jerusalem's fate. Thus, the
act of writing is an integral part of the revelation itself. But, of course,
the inscription is intended not only to set an event in motion, but
to do so in a way that is understandable, that is legible, by an audience. The brick and the various siege tactics mounted against the
"brick," namely Jerusalem, seem to function symbolically as a "sign"
for the Israelite nation: אות היא לבית ישראל.[58] This sign warns the
Israelite nation of their inevitable destruction. Johannes Lindblom
writes:

> As a divine word, the word uttered by a prophet had an effective
> power. The same is true of the visible word. . . . Such an action served
> not only to represent and make evident a particular fact, but also to
> make this fact a reality. . . . The effect . . . upon the onlookers was con-
> sequently not only to present visibly what the prophet had to say, but
> also to convince them that the events . . . would really take place. They
> were also intended to arouse the emotions of fear or hope. . . . Thus
> what was done powerfully reinforced what was said.[59]

Both Jer 17 and Ezek 4 describe a process of inscription which is
inalterable and resistant to erasure.[60] This permanence is meant to
reflect the stubbornness and permanence of the Israelite nation. Yet,
in Ezek 4, as we have seen previously, the inscription is also a sign
of warning. Thus, the Israelites are granted the possibility of repentance and transformation through the efficacy of sacred writing.

---

[57] See the comments of Moshe Greenberg, *Ezekiel 1–20* (AB 22; New York:
Doubleday, 1983), 103.
[58] Note also the language of "sign," אות, in Isa 8 as a reference to a written text
for future use.
[59] Johannes Lindblom, *Prophecy in Ancient Israel* (Philadelphia: Fortress, 1965), 172.
[60] On the possibility of erasure on inscribed papyrus, see Menahem Haran, "Book-
Scrolls in Israel in Pre-Exilic Times," *JJS* 33 (1982): 161–73.

The act of inscribing can also generate hope for national security and a return to Zion. In the text of Ezek 37:15–22 below, Ezekiel is instructed to carve out a received prophecy upon two sticks, signifying the future unification of northern and southern Israel:

> The word of the LORD came to me saying: "You, man, take one stick for yourself and write upon it 'to Judah and to the children of Israel their associate.' Then take one stick and write upon it 'to Joseph, the stick of Ephraim, and all of the house of Israel their associates.' Bring them close to one another, as one stick and so that they may become one in your hand. And when your fellow countrymen ask you: 'Won't you tell us what these are to you?' tell them, 'Thus says the LORD God: "I am taking the stick of Joseph which is in the hand of Ephraim and the tribes of Israel their associates from among the nations to which they have gone, and I will gather them from all around and I will bring them to their country. I will make them a unified nation in the land, in the mountains of Israel, and a single king will be a king for all of them, and they will no longer be two nations and they will no longer be divided into two kingdoms."' "

Ezekiel is instructed to prepare the only tree-graft referred to in the Hebrew Bible.[61] Ezekiel writes, "to Judah and to the children of Israel, their associate" on one branch, and on the second branch he writes, "to Joseph, the stick of Ephraim, and all of the house of Israel, their associates." Ezekiel then combines the two branches together. He attaches the second branch to the tree of the first branch and they are now as one. This time, the writing is a symbol of the promise of restoration. The two parts of the house of Israel will be united and will be one people. Here, as in the case of Ezek 4, the act of inscribing upon a tree or stick is part of the prophecy itself. The very act of inscription seems intended to generate a hope of restoration for those in exile.[62] Although there is no act of restoration or return that accomplishes the tree graft, the very inscription, as a divinely-inspired prophecy, symbolically anticipates a return to Judah and a reconstruction of the Davidic monarchy.[63] In fact, Ezekiel's

---

[61] See the use of the grafting metaphor in its only occurrence in the NT in Rom 11:13–32.

[62] The choice of the stick itself, and the staff (שבט), can refer both to the leader and to the leadership which is granted to Judah (in Gen 49:10) or more generally to a descendant of Judah through the Davidic line (in Ezek 37). See 4Q252, the LXX, and the Vulgate for textual variants. On this double meaning of שבט in Gen 49:10, see Ze'ev Falk, "Sophet and Shebet," Leš 30 (1966): 243–47 [Hebrew].

[63] At the conclusion of Ezek 37, a promise is made to reconstitute the Davidic monarchy and to insure eternal peace in the form of a covenant (ברית עולם and ברית שלום).

choice of עץ further emphasizes the hope of reconstituting the Israelite nation under Davidic rule. "The choice of ʿṣ seems to have been dictated by its ambiguity, symbolizing both king and kingdom."[64]

D. Jeremiah 32

I will now turn to an example which is less obviously an example of *sacred* writing. Here, the divine instruction does not refer to the act of writing; rather, God instructs Jeremiah to acquire his uncle's property.[65] But, in Jer 32:6–15, Jeremiah obeys God's command by composing a deed of ownership in order to secure land for the future:

> Jeremiah said: The word of the LORD came to me saying: "Hanamel the son of Shallum your uncle, will come to you and say, 'Buy my field which is in Anatoth, for the right of redemption is yours to buy.'" Just as the LORD spoke, Hanamel, the son of my uncle, came to me to the court of the guard and he said to me, "Purchase my field in Anatoth which is in the territory of Benjamin, for the right of inheritance and of redemption is yours. Purchase it." Then I knew it was the word of the LORD. So I purchased the field from Hanamel, the son of my uncle, which was in Anatoth and I weighed out the money for him, seventeen shekels of silver. I wrote and sealed the deed and I got witnesses and I weighed out the money on a scale. Then I took the sealed deed of purchase, the law and the enactments, and the open copy. I gave the deed of purchase to Baruch, son of Neriah, son of

---

[64] Moshe Greenberg, *Ezekiel 21–37* (AB 22A; New York: Doubleday, 1997), 753.

[65] Carroll points to an interesting parallel between Jer 32 and Gen 23 and emphasizes the significance of the transaction in Jer 32:

> The family land bought by Jeremiah is like the field of Ephron which Abraham bought in order to bury his dead (Gen 23), an earnest of the future and a land claim legitimately acquired. The small plot of land in Anathoth will become a symbol of the whole land and the prophet is the first man to own property in the new age when [YHWH] restores the fortunes of Israel. Ironically Jeremiah will be dead by then, and as a childless man (the conventional interpretation of 16.1–2) his piece of property will have passed on to others. However, the niceties of legal requirements have been observed and the act is more important than the fact that Jeremiah will never see that land. Its purchase by *the* prophet is what matters because it stakes a claim to the future *in the land* for the people. The future is not in Babylon (*contra* 24.4–7; 29.4–7) but here in Judah—which is why the story is set in the period of Jeremiah's arrest during the siege of Babylon. The terrifying present is reversed by his act in buying Palestinian land. Zedekiah may go to Babylon ... but [YHWH] has a future for the land of Judah (cf. 42.7–12). The jar containing the title deeds to that field in Anathoth, wherever it may be hidden ..., contains Judah's future and the divine word acting through *the prophet* has already created that future. The Babylonians may lay siege to the city, take it and raze it to the ground, but the future has been secured. (*Jeremiah*, 623)

Mahseiah, in front of Hanamel my cousin and in front of all of the Jews sitting in the court of the guard. I instructed Baruch before them saying, "Thus says the LORD of Hosts, the God of Israel: 'Take these deeds, this deed of purchase, the sealed one, and this open copy, and place them into an earthen vessel, so that they will last for a long time.' For thus said the LORD of Hosts, the God of Israel: 'Houses and fields and vineyards will once again be purchased in this land.'"

At a time of political stability, Jeremiah's document would have been considered an unremarkable deed of ownership of land. But, in light of the impending destruction and exile by Nebuchadnezzar, the composition of this document could only seem absurd to onlookers. Consequently, the deed of ownership is a public document signifying the divine promise of the return to the land of Israel.

In addition to the composition of the deed of ownership, an intricate process of preservation is also recorded. The text itself is preserved in a ceramic container and a copy of that text is inscribed on the container's exterior.[66] Only through this process is the preservation of the deed of ownership insured. Although human witnesses are present at the transfer of ownership, the text itself—and the divine promise it signifies—will most certainly outlive them.

E. *Ezekiel 2:8–3:3*

In some of the earlier passages examined above, the transcription from a divinely-produced text was portrayed as important and authoritative, yet revelation itself was still, to some degree, oral. However, so great had writing's authority become—along with the symbolic significances associated with writing—during the exile, that some later exilic and post-exilic passages portray writing as the medium of revelation itself. Thus, in the opening chapters of Ezekiel, God presents the prophet with a text apparently composed by God. Ezekiel sees that the text is filled with words of woe. God instructs him to eat it and thus to internalize the prophecy (Ezek 2:8–3:3):

> "You, man, listen to what I tell you: do not be rebellious like the rebellious house; open your mouth and eat what I give to you." Behold! I saw a hand extended towards me and in it was a written scroll. He unrolled it before me, and it was inscribed on both the front and the

---

[66] See the comment of Carroll: "The legal terminology may indicate the rule governing contracts: the sealed copy was for a permanent record and the open copy was for consultation" (*Jeremiah*, 620).

back;[67] and upon it were written lamentations, moaning, and woe. He said to me, "Man, what you find, eat. Eat this scroll, and go speak to the house of Israel." I opened my mouth and he fed me this scroll. He said to me, "Man, feed your stomach and fill your belly with this scroll which I am giving to you." I ate and it became like sweet honey in my mouth.

Like the first set of divine testimonial tablets in Exodus, this divinely-written text will not be directly accessible to the Israelite readers. Instead, Ezekiel must internalize the text and then present the material which he has now, quite literally, digested. Ellen Davis writes:

> The metaphor of ingestion has progressed greatly by the time of its appearance as the prominent figure in Ezekiel's call narrative, coloring any conception of his life as prophet. This time verbal consumption is not a casual, voluntary gesture; it is the precondition for public service. These words are not merely encountered; their authenticity and authority are unmistakable, for they come directly from the hand of God. But most strikingly, there is no longer any ambiguity about the form in which the prophet receives the edible revelation. It comes to Ezekiel *as a text*. This is the form in which he must claim his inheritance and the basis on which he must make his own contribution to the tradition of faithful witness.[68]

Although sacred writing was so important for Moses and Jeremiah that they were both divinely instructed to rewrite sacred texts which had been destroyed, nevertheless they received revelation in the form of divine speech. The fact that God communicates with Ezekiel through a heavenly text reflects the important role that writing had come to play for the exilic community. In the case of Ezekiel, the written text *is the prophecy* and is no longer ancillary to oral discourse. James Kugel writes:

> But how significant it is that, in Ezekiel, God's speech has already become a *text*; and the very act of eating God's word now demands impossible "obedience" and self-control, swallowing up an actual scroll, and then *not* (in both senses) "spitting it back," not just being the messenger and vehicle before the people, but, on the contrary, digesting the twice uneaten thing, a scroll, and one of lamentation and mourning and woe, to find it—how obedience pays off!—not bitter but sweeter than honey.[69]

---

[67] See Haran, "Book-Scrolls," 161–73.
[68] Davis, *Swallowing the Scroll*, 51.
[69] Kugel, "Early Interpretation," 19.

Like the first set of testimonial tablets, the divine text eaten by Ezekiel has writing on both front and back. These are the only texts mentioned in biblical traditions as clearly possessing this feature.[70] Unlike the tablets, however, Ezekiel's text is apparently written upon papyrus, which no doubt makes eating them somewhat easier.

F. Zechariah 5:1–4

In Zech 5:1–4, the prophet sees an image of a flying scroll. Kugel calls this image "a symbol of the presence of texts in the minds of restored Judea as well as of the texts' growing independence and power."[71]

> I looked up again and I saw a flying scroll. He [God] asked me, "What do you see?" I responded, "I see a flying scroll, twenty cubits long and ten cubits wide." He said to me, "This is the curse which is going out across the face of the entire earth;[72] for anyone who steals shall be henceforth cut off according to it, and every one who swears falsely shall be cut off henceforth according to it. I have sent it out," declares the LORD of Hosts. "It will enter the house of the thief and the house of him who swears falsely by my name. It will lodge in his house and it will consume it, both the timber and the stones."

---

[70] However, it is possible that Zech 5:1–4 also refers to a scroll with writing on both sides. The key phrase beginning כל הגנב מזה is difficult to translate and the text does not explicitly state that writing was on both sides of the flying scroll. For more on this passage, see my further discussion below.

On the use of papyrus in the biblical period, see Haran, "Book-Scrolls," 161–73. Haran argues that the scrolls in the biblical period were made of papyrus (171–72). This is supported by biblical descriptions of the writing, erasing, and cutting of texts which would have been possible only with papyrus. For example, see Jer 36 where a scroll of prophecies is cut with a scribal knife and then subsequently burnt; these processes presuppose that the material of the scroll was papyrus.

Also, the above passage from Ezek 2 depicts a scroll which is written both on the front and on the back. Although the art of writing on the front and back of skins was not perfected until the beginning of the Christian era, writing on the front and back of *papyrus* was already done in Egypt in the New Kingdom period. Haran also addresses the question of whether prophets wrote only on papyrus or whether there is some evidence for tablet writing: "As a rule, the classical prophets used papyrus for their writing material except where other substances are expressly mentioned or alluded to. (Employment of wooden tablets by prophets, mainly for testimonial or ceremonial display, is referred to in Isa 30:8; Hab 2:2; Ezek 37:16–20)" ("Book-Scrolls," 168). For a discussion of the production of Torah scrolls, see Étan Levine, "The Transcription of the Torah Scroll," ZAW 94 (1982): 99–105.

[71] Kugel, "Early Interpretation," 21.

[72] This phrase, "the entire earth," appears elsewhere in Zechariah; see 1:11; 4:10.

This prophecy employs a formula familiar from earlier prophetic traditions: a prophet sees an object, God asks the prophet what he sees, the prophet reports "I see X," then God explains the sign.[73] Yet here the sign that demands prophetic interpretation and divine instruction is a written text: "To see a scroll . . . for a Judahite in the Persian period was not an impossible thing. To see it floating up in the air was quite another matter. Scrolls are normally in someone's hands, lying on the table, placed in storage jars or the like. They are always touching something. The scroll that Zechariah sees is touching nothing; it is between heaven and earth, disconnected from the scribe or lector."[74] That the text has been written and is publicly accessible seems more important than the text's actual content, which remains obscure. As Kugel notes, this passage shows the extent to which the authoritative status of divine writing seems to have attained prominence in the prophetic visions during the Second Temple period:

> Here the prophet is not even given to touch the divine word. It does not enter his mouth even in the form of food, but he sees it passing by, a giant scroll—what greater literalization of "God in action"?—to which he can only bear witness: Its mission will be to destroy the house of thieves and perjurers, to avenge the transgression of that which is also, and most often, written, the Decalogue. But if this text represents in some form the disappearance, or mediation, of the prophet's own powerful speech, it also has a positive side: as Actor, the written word which flies like an angel to carry out God's decrees and indeed, like the "angel of the LORD" in the Pentateuch, is even able to wreak physical destruction on those who have incurred the divine wrath.[75]

It is also worth noting that in Zech 5, the text is more than a witness testifying to a potent event. Rather, the text is itself the potent agent.

The effects of the prophecy are inscribed in the form of an earthly (Ezek 2:8–3:3) or heavenly (Zech 5:1–4) written revelation, both apparently made of the same material: papyrus. However, there is

---

[73] For example, Amos 7–9; Zech 4:2; Jer 1.

[74] David L. Petersen, *Haggai and Zechariah 1–8: A Commentary* (OTL; Philadelphia: Westminster, 1984), 246.

[75] Kugel, "Early Interpretation," 19. In this passage, Kugel is comparing his earlier discussion of Ezek 2:7–3:3 with Zech 5:1–4. Kugel's reference to the laws of the Decalogue may suggest another means of connecting the two-sided written tablets from Exod 32–34 and the possibly two-sided flying scroll of Zech 5. In addition, although he does not discuss the issue of writing on two sides, Petersen notes the connection with the Decalogue and with the first set of tablets in particular (*Haggai and Zechariah 1–8*, 250, esp. n. 10).

no independent oral revelation that precedes the written revelation. Rather the prophecy itself is revealed as sacred writing and the power, inalterability, and efficacious warning are all part of such a written revelation. The fate of Israel was already determined through the heavenly inscription of these texts. The warning was communicated to the prophet, and it becomes the responsibility of the prophet to insure the circulation of this written prophecy.

III. Conclusion

Although we have seen that sacred writing was already symbolically significant in the pre-exilic period,[76] we have also seen a gradual rise in writing's prominence as an authoritative medium for covenantal testimony and even for revelation itself. When the monarchy was terminated through the exile, and when many of the exiles were disillusioned with the prophetic traditions and distrustful of new prophetic hope, sacred writing was well-prepared to fill the authority vacuum.

The text-based Judaism of books like Ezra-Nehemiah and Chronicles constitutes a dramatic shift in Israel's conception of religious authority, which would now be vested in a central body of text, and their authoritative interpretations, designated as Mosaic Torah.[77] From now on, authority did not have to rely on the oral recitation of unmediated revelation but could be claimed primarily through the demonstration that one stood in the appropriate relation—of reading or reciting or interpreting—to the sacred writings of Mosaic Torah. Yet this profound shift could hardly have occurred without the long prehistory I have traced in this essay.

---

[76] See the comments of Davis: "From the eighth century, writing was a feature of prophecy, not only for transmission and publication at scribal hands (Isa 8:16; Jer 36), but also apparently as a means of illustration and emphasis within the original act of pronouncement (Isa 8:1; Hab 2:2; cf. Jer 17:1)" (*Swallowing the Scroll*, 38).

[77] See my discussion of this tradition in "Torah of Moses: Pseudonymous Attribution in Second Temple Writings," in *The Interpretation of Scripture in Early Judaism and Christianity: Studies in Language and Tradition* (ed. C. A. Evans; JSPS 33; SSEJC 7; Sheffield: Sheffield Academic, 2000), 202–16; and the subsequent development of the authority of Moses and of his Torah after the time of Ezra-Nehemiah and the Chronicler in my *Seconding Sinai*.

PART TWO

TRADITIONS OF THE BIBLE IN
SECOND TEMPLE JUDAISM

SEVEN MYSTERIES OF KNOWLEDGE: QUMRAN E/SOTERICISM RECOVERED

Elliot R. Wolfson

> Kakuseba iyo-iyo arawaru.
> The more you hide it, the more it is exposed.
>
> Rinzai Zen Kôan

In this study, I offer a modest contribution to Qumran studies in particular and to the history of esotericism in late Second Temple Palestinian Judaism more generally.[1] As is well known to experts in this field, notwithstanding the fact that the extant corpus of primary documents, the so-called "Qumran library,"[2] is relatively small, in great measure restored on the basis of highly technical, and at times boldly imaginative, modes of textual reconstruction, the bibliography of scholarly studies on that corpus is quite sizeable. One might posit an inverse correlation at work here: the more fragmentary the textual evidence, the greater the propagation of interpretative stratagems.[3]

The specific focus of this essay is a reconsideration of the notion of mystery, *raz*, a Persian loanword, as it is employed in select sectarian texts.[4] Needless to say, there have been important observa-

---

[1] The core of this study took shape in the seminar I led on heavenly ascents in late antique Judaism and Christianity at the University of Notre Dame, Fall 2002. I am grateful to the students who attended for their thoughtful engagement, and a special note of thanks to Hindy Najman for immeasurably enriching the seminar by her faithful attendance and participation. This study, in no small measure, was inspired by our conversations. It is an honor to publish this study in a volume honoring the scholarly achievement of Professor James Kugel, a man of considerable literary sensibility and exegetical acumen.

[2] Geza Vermes, *The Dead Sea Scrolls: Qumran in Perspective* (with the collaboration of Pamela Vermes; rev. ed.; Philadelphia: Fortress, 1977), 45–86.

[3] For a thoughtful discussion of this issue, see Hartmut Stegemann, "Methods for the Reconstruction of Scrolls from Scattered Fragments," in *Archaeology and History in the Dead Sea Scrolls: The New York University Conference in Memory of Yigael Yadin* (ed. L. H. Schiffman; Sheffield: Sheffield Academic, 1990), 189–220.

[4] On the philological and conceptual implications of the term *raz*, especially in the Sassanian period, see Shaul Shaked, "Esoteric Trends in Zoroastrianism," PIASH 3 (1969): 193: "The word *râz* is used several times in the Pahlavi books in connection with a group of religious mysteries, which seem to be usually related to the

tions regarding this term elicited from the various genres of what is considered the canon of Qumran literature, a canon determined by scholarly consensus formed, with more than a little political intrigue and drama, over several decades.[5] A recent opportunity to teach *4Q*

fields of creation and eschatology as well as to the knowledge of the proper way of fighting the demons. It should, however, be remarked that this word does not necessarily designate in many of its occurrences a secret piece of knowledge or a doctrine which must be kept hidden; it seems often to denote a hidden cause, a latent factor, a connection which is not immediately evident." A selection of relevant texts are cited and translated by Shaked, "Esoteric Trends," 206–13, whence he draws the conclusion that there are "two main characteristics of the mystery designated by the word *râz*: the secret of the battle of the gods with the demons . . . and the secret of eschatology." My gratitude to Maria Subtelny for drawing my attention to Shaked's study. The meaning he ascribes to the word *raz* in the Zoroastrian context resonates well with the semantic range of this term in the Qumran literature, a matter worthy of a separate analysis. On the possible links between Qumran and Zoroastrianism, see David Winston, "The Iranian Component in the Bible, Apocrypha, and Qumran: A Review of the Evidence," *HR* 5 (1966): 183–216; Shaul Shaked, "Qumran and Iran: Further Considerations," *IOS* 2 (1972): 433–46.

[5] On "mystery" (*raz, sod*) in Qumran texts, see the list compiled by E. Vogt, "'Mysteria' in textibus Qumran," *Bib* 37 (1956): 247–57; and the study by Raymond E. Brown, *The Semitic Background of the Term "Mystery" in the New Testament* (Philadelphia: Fortress, 1968), 22–30. Brown utilizes the following categories: (1) mysteries of divine providence—the secret is thus related to the providence that God shows vis-à-vis angels, humankind, and Israel; (2) mysteries of the sect's interpretation of the law— the members of the community are entrusted with special understanding of Torah; (3) cosmic mysteries; and (4) evil mysteries. See also Matthew Black, *The Scrolls and Christian Origins: Studies in the Jewish Background of the New Testament* (New York: Scribner, 1961), 142–44. Black focuses on the expression "mysteries of redemption" and its link to *mysterion* in the NT as it is applied to the mystery of redemption in the suffering of Christ (Col 1:24–26). Black mentions 1 QH IX, 6–8 (1QHᵃ XVII, 6–8) where the soul is described as being brought low in the marvels or wonders of God (*nifle'otekha*) and 23–27 where the soul is said to be chastised in the mystery of divine wisdom (*beraz ḥokhmatekha*). It does seem that here the mystery of wisdom involves the element of divine providence. Black also mentions 1 QH IV, 27–28 (1QHᵃ XII, 27–28) where God is said to illumine the face of the many through the one who has become acquainted with the secrets of God's mysteries (*ki hoda'atani berazei pela'ekhah*)—in this case it seems a theosophic intent is implied. To know the divine nature results in an illumination. I do not discern support for Black's contention that these texts espouse the idea of the mystery of redemptive suffering. For other attempts to compare the use of "mystery" in the New Testament, particularly in the Christology of Paul, and Qumran, see Béda Rigàux, "Révélation des mystères et perfection a Qumrân et dans le Nouveau Testament," *NTS* 4 (1958): 237–62; Joseph Coppens, "Le 'Mystère' dans la théologie paulinienne et ses parallèles qumrâniens," *RechBib* 5 (1960): 142–65; trans. "'Mystery' in the Theology of Saint Paul and Its Parallels at Qumran," in *Paul and Qumran: Studies in New Testament Exegesis* (ed. J. Murphy-O'Connor; Chicago: Priory, 1968), 132–58; and Heinz-Wolfgang Kuhn, "The Wisdom Passage in 1 Corinthians 2:6–16: Between Qumran and Proto-Gnosticism," in *Sapiential, Liturgical and Poetical Texts from Qumran: Proceedings of the Third Meeting of the International Organization for Qumran Studies, Oslo, 1998—Published in Memory of Maurice Baillet* (ed. D. K. Falk, F. G. Martínez, and E. Schuller; Leiden: Brill, 2000), 240–53, esp. 251–53. For the use of the term *raz* in the sapiential

Širot ʿOlat Haššabbat, the *Songs of the Sabbath Sacrifice*, occasioned a reconsideration on my part of the term and some of its philosophical ramifications yet to be disclosed in academic treatments.

I. *IMAGO TEMPLI* AND RECIPROCAL RECIPROCITY

To state my hypothesis at the outset: I begin with the seemingly trivial assumption that *raz* is multivalent in its range of semantic insinuation. This assertion, needless to say, is hardly unique to this term, but it is nonetheless relevant for me to make the point, as it underscores the fact that what I shall present is consciously acknowledged to be only one of many indexical possibilities. I shall focus on a trajectory of meaning that, for lack of a better term, I call onto-theosophic. This admittedly awkward (and to some readers, no doubt, anachronistic) locution suggests that the nature of mystery is not merely epistemological, understood either as a matter of marking the spot where intellect falters before its own limit and thus yields to a higher revelation as the ultimate source of knowledge, or as a social mechanism to create an inner circle, a group distinguishing itself from a larger cohort and claiming supremacy for its own agenda.[6]

---

works known as the *Mysteries*, see Lawrence H. Schiffman, *Reclaiming the Dead Sea Scrolls: The History of Judaism, the Background of Christianity, the Lost Library of Qumran* (Philadelphia/Jerusalem: The Jewish Publication Society, 1994), 206. According to Schiffman, *raz* "refers to the mysteries of creation, that is, the natural order of things, and to the mysteries of the divine role in historical processes." The source of both kinds of cosmological and providential mysteries, the secrets of nature and history, is divine wisdom. For another useful survey of the different terminological signposts to denote mystery or secret in Qumran texts, see Markus Bockmuehl, *Revelation and Mystery in Ancient Judaism and Pauline Christianity* (Tübingen: Mohr, 1990), 53–56. Commenting specifically on the connotation of *raz* in the depiction of the worship of the "seven exalted angelic princes" in the *Songs of the Sabbath Sacrifice*, Bockmuehl remarks that we cannot make a distinction between "cosmological and soteriological concerns. . . . Revelation of both kinds of mysteries illustrates and derives from God's wisdom and understanding" (55). While acknowledging the source of the two kinds of mystery in the divine, Bockmuehl does not go far enough in appreciating the onto-theosophic implication of *raz*, as I have argued in the body of this study.

[6] A useful discussion to reflect on the esotericism in Qumran is the account of the "mysteries of God" in John J. Collins, *Between Athens and Jerusalem: Jewish Identity in the Hellenistic Diaspora* (2nd ed.; Grand Rapids: Eerdmans, 2000), 210–60. Admittedly, Collins focuses on a different geographical area with its cultural distinctiveness, but we well know that Palestine in the period that corresponds to the Qumran community and the evolution of its practices and teachings was influenced by Hellenic trends of thinking. For specific discussion of this issue, see Martin Hengel, "Qumrân und der Hellenismus," in *Qumrân: sa piété, sa théologie et son milieu* (ed. M. Delcor; BETL 46; Paris: Duculot, 1978), 333–72.

I readily admit that both of these features are attested in the use of *raz* in the Scrolls, but there is an additional connotation, which I take to be ontological, a technical philosophical expression that I employ to convey the sense of confronting that which is yet to be confronted, a meaning epitomized in the signature denotation of divine mystery that appears in the sapiential works 1Q/4QInstruction and 1Q/4QMysteries as well as in 1QS XI, 3–4, *raz nihyeh*,[7] rendered most often as "mystery of being"[8] or "mystery of existence,"[9] and applied generally to God's mysterious plan for human history from beginning to end, creation to the eschaton.[10] This technical

---

[7] For a brief but useful account of the different scholarly renderings, see Daniel J. Harrington, "The *Râz Nihyeh* in a Qumran Wisdom Text (1Q26, 4Q415–418, 423)," *RevQ* 17 (1996): 549–53, esp. 551; see also Daryl F. Jefferies, *Wisdom At Qumran: A Form-Critical Analysis of the Admonitions in 4QInstruction* (Piscataway, N.J.: Gorgias, 2002), 64–67.

[8] Ben Zion Wacholder and Martin G. Abegg, *A Preliminary Edition of the Unpublished Dead Sea Scrolls: The Hebrew and Aramaic Texts from Cave Four* (2 fasc.; Washington, D.C.: Biblical Archaeology Society, 1991–1992), 2:xii–xiv. The authors propose that *raz nihyeh* in the Qumran sapiential fragments is to be interpreted textually, that is, the term "refers to a work, or works, that had been available to the author(s) and readers of these compositions but has since perished," or it is "the sectarian title for many of the works found in this fascicle" (xiii). Wacholder and Abegg speculate, moreover, that alternative names for the compositions referred to as *raz nihyeh* are "book of memory," *sefer zikkaron*, and the "vision of meditation," *ḥazon haguy* (4Q417 2 I, 16). On the possibility that *raz nihyeh* is a body of teaching or a vehicle of transmission of divine wisdom, see Harrington, "*Râz Nihyeh*," 552; Jefferies, *Wisdom At Qumran*, 67, 299–305. I have appropriated the translation "vision of meditation" from *The Dead Sea Scrolls Study Edition* (ed. and trans. F. G. Martínez and E. J. C. Tigchelaar; 2 vols.; Leiden: Brill, 1997–1998), 2:859. Support for this rendering may be elicited from an earlier passage in this fragment, based partially on Josh 1:8, [. . . *yom wa-laylah hagah beraz ni*]*hyeh wedoreš tamid we'az teda' 'emet we'awwal ḥokhmah*, "[. . . day and night meditate on the mystery of ex]istence, and seek continuously. And then you will know truth and injustice, wisdom" (4Q417 2 I, 6; *Dead Sea Scrolls Study Edition*, 2:858–59). The *ḥazon haguy* is linked by them to the *sefer hagu* mentioned in CD X, 6; XIII, 2. See the rich note offered by Rabin in the apparatus (*The Zadokite Documents* [2nd ed.; Oxford: Clarendon, 1958] 50, 6.3). He suggests a possible emendation, *hehaghi*, and notes the etymological derivation from a verb that means "to study."

[9] *Dead Sea Scrolls Study Edition*, 1:66–67 (1Q26 1+2 2; 1Q27 1 I, 2), 1:96–97 (1QS XI, 3–4), 2:662–63 (4Q300 3 3, 4), 2:846–47 (4Q415 6 4), 2:850–53 (4Q416 2 III, 9, 14, 18), 2:854–55 (4Q416 7 1), 2:858–59 (4Q417 2 I, 6, 18), 2:870–71 (4Q418 77 2), 2:886–87 (4Q423 3+4 2), 2:888–89 (4Q423 5 2).

[10] Torleif Elgvin, "An Analysis of 4QInstruction" (Ph.D. diss., Hebrew University of Jerusalem, 1997), 80–81 (cited in Jefferies, *Wisdom At Qumran*, 66): "*raz nihyeh* is a comprehensive word for God's mysterious plan for creation and history. His plan for man and for redemption of the elect. . . . The translation 'mystery to come' better catches the historical and eschatological connotation of *raz nihyeh* than 'mystery of being.'" See also John J. Collins, *Jewish Wisdom in the Hellenistic Ages* (Edinburgh: T&T Clark, 1997), 122, and references to other scholars cited below, n. 12.

term substantiates the hermeneutical point I was making above, to
wit, attested in Qumran literature is an ontological connotation of
the word *raz*, as it denotes the "being" of the divine image,[11] a mystery that consists in the fact that the "being" of this image is in the
image of being (be)coming what it is to be.[12] Without denying the
cosmological and eschatological implications, I would argue there is
another dimension to consider as *raz* relates to the mystery of divine
becoming; the cosmological and eschatological are grounded in this

---

[11] Another example to substantiate this philological claim is the expression *razei
'el lešaḥet rišʿah*, "God's mysteries will destroy wickedness" (1QM III, 9). This sentence is meaningful only if we interpret *razei 'el* ontologically, that is, as referring
to the powers of the divine nature, which will, in the end, exact justice and destroy
the wicked. I would suggest a similar interpretation for the expression *razei ʿormato*,
"the mysteries of his cunningness" (1QpHab VII, 14), used in conjunction with the
eschatological promise that in the end the righteous will prosper and the wicked
will suffer. In this connection, mention should also be made of the expression *ʿormat
daʿat*, the "cunningness of knowledge," in 1QS X, 25. See also CD II, 3–4: *'el 'ohev
daʿat ḥokhmah wetušiyyah hiṣṣiv lefanaw ʿormah wedaʿat hem yešartuhu*.

[12] Harrington, *"Râz Nihyeh,"* 551, remarks that he and Strugnell followed Milik's
lead, *le mystère futur*, and thus translated *raz nihyeh* as "the mystery that is to be/come."
The future tense is reflective of the mystery in a "body of teaching," whether written or oral, that "concerns behavior and eschatology" (552). See also Daniel J.
Harrington, *Wisdom Texts from Qumran* (London/New York: Routledge, 1996), 60,
64. For a similar approach, which emphasizes that *raz nihyeh* is an apocalyptic reinterpretation of the earlier concept of divine wisdom, see Torleif Elgvin, "The Mystery
To Come: Early Essene Theology of Revelation," in *Qumran Between the Old and New
Testaments* (ed. F. H. Cryer and T. L. Thompson; Sheffield: Sheffield Academic,
1998), 113–50; idem, "Wisdom With and Without Apocalyptic," in *Sapiential, Liturgical
and Poetical Texts*, 24–25, 37. See also the translation of *raz nihyeh* as "the mystery
that is to be" in Collins, *Jewish Wisdom*, 121–25. Schiffman, *Reclaiming*, 207, renders
raz nihyeh as "the mystery that was coming into being," which he also relates to
divine wisdom, the source of the "mysteries of creation, that is the natural order
of things," and "the mysteries of the divine role in historical processes" (206). In a
similar vein, A. Klostergaard Petersen, "Wisdom As Cognition: Creating the Others
in the Book of Mysteries and 1 Cor 1–2," in *The Wisdom Texts from Qumran and the
Development of Sapiential Thought* (ed. C. Hempel, A. Lange, and H. Lichtenberger;
Leuven: Leuven University Press, 2002), 415, translates *raz nihyeh* as the "mystery
of that which was coming into being" and suggests that it "is apparently connected
to the eschaton. It includes a body of teaching involving creation, ethical activity,
and eschatology." Crispin H. T. Fletcher-Louis, *All the Glory of Adam: Liturgical
Anthropology in the Dead Sea Scrolls* (Leiden: Brill, 2002), 116, submits that *raz nihyeh*
refers to the "original order of creation." See also John I. Kampen, "The Diverse
Aspects of Wisdom in the Qumran Texts," in *The Dead Sea Scrolls After Fifty Years:
A Comprehensive Assessment* (ed. P. W. Flint and J. C. Vanderkam, with the assistance
of A. E. Alvarez; 2 vols.; Leiden: Brill, 1998–1999), 1:228–30. Finally, Bilhah Nitzan,
"The Idea of Creation and Its Implications in Qumran Literature," in *Creation in
Jewish and Christian Tradition* (ed. H. G. Reventlow and Y. Hoffman; London: Sheffield
Academic, 2002), 250–52, renders *raz nihyeh* as "the mystery of what is to come
into being," which she relates to the cosmological and eschatological secrets of God's
hidden wisdom beyond human knowledge.

other dimension that I shall call the ontological. The key to open this door, and perhaps, for some, to go through, is to think of the juxtaposition of *raz* and *da'at*, "mystery" and "knowledge."[13] By uncovering this conjunction we hope to begin to recover the soteric nature of esotericism promulgated by some of the priests in what is prudently referred to as the Qumran community (*yaḥad*).

The text that has inspired my reflections inscribed herein appears in what is believed to be the eighth in the sequence of thirteen *Sabbath Songs*,[14] presumed to have been recited during the thirteen Sabbaths of the first quarter of the annual calendar[15] or repeated once in each of the four quarters.[16] In my judgment, a symbolic significance can be ascribed to each of these possibilities, as the numbers thirteen and four are both sacred markers of an underlying unity. Be that as it may, these angelic hymns, as scholars of the Scrolls have duly noted,[17] provide critical information about the liturgical piety cultivated by the priestly defectors from the Jerusalem Temple responsible for the formation of the *yaḥad* in the desert, even if one casts doubt about the composition of the hymns by members alleged to represent the communal viewpoint.[18] Central to that piety is a liturgical synchro-

---

[13] For a still useful survey of the various applications of the term *da'at* in Qumran literature, see William D. Davies, "'Knowledge' in the Dead Sea Scrolls and Matthew 11:25–30," *HTR* 46 (1953): 113–39, and esp. 121–22 for analysis of passages dealing with secret knowledge.

[14] The fullest account of these angelic hymns remains Carol Newsom's *Songs of the Sabbath Sacrifice: A Critical Edition* (Atlanta: Scholars Press, 1985), which served as the basis for her critical edition in J. VanderKam and M. Brady, consulting eds., *Qumran Cave 4.VI: Poetical and Liturgical Texts, Part 1* (DJD 11; Oxford: Clarendon Press, 1998), 173–401. See also Adiel M. Schwemer, "Gott aus König und seine Königsherrschaft in den Sabbathliedern aus Qumran," in *Königsherrschaft Gottes und himmlischer Kult in Judentum, Urchristentum und in der hellenistischen Welt* (ed. M. Hengel and A. M. Schwemer; Tübingen: Mohr, 1991), 45–118; Bilhah Nitzan, *Qumran Prayer and Religious Poetry* (trans. J. Chipman; Leiden: Brill, 1994), 273–318; Fletcher-Louis, *Glory of Adam*, 252–394. For a concise summary, see Schiffman, *Reclaiming*, 355–60, and particularly his suggestion (359) on the basis of 11Q5 XXVII, 5–7 that the sect believed David composed the *Sabbath Songs*.

[15] Johann Maier, "*Shîrê 'Ôlat hash-Shabbat*. Some Observations on their Calendric Implications and on their Style," in *The Madrid Qumran Congress: Proceedings of the International Congress on the Dead Sea Scrolls, Madrid, 18–21 March, 1991* (ed. J. Trebolle Barrera and L. Vegas Montaner; 2 vols.; STDJ 11; Leiden: Brill, 1992), 2:546–52.

[16] Newsom, *Songs*, 19–20.

[17] For a somewhat more reserved approach, see the careful weighing of the philological and textual evidence in Daniel K. Falk, *Daily, Sabbath, and Festival Prayers in the Dead Sea Scrolls* (Leiden: Brill, 1998), 126–39.

[18] Carol Newsom, "'Sectually Explicit' Literature from Qumran," in *The Hebrew Bible and Its Interpreters* (ed. W. H. Propp, B. Halpern, and D. N. Freedman; Winona

nism[19] or what may be called reciprocal reciprocity, double mirroring of heaven and earth, Jerusalem Temple and celestial throne.[20] To speak of double mirroring—as below above, as above below[21]—

Lake, Ind.: Eisenbrauns, 1990), 179–85; and see the cautionary remarks of Ra'anan Abusch, "Sevenfold Hymns in the *Songs of the Sabbath Sacrifice* and the Hekhalot Literature: Formalism, Hierarchy and the Limits of Human Participation," in *The Dead Sea Scrolls as Background to Postbiblical Judaism and Early Christianity: Papers from an International Conference at St. Andrews in 2001* (ed. J. R. Davila; Leiden: Brill, 2003), 225. It should be noted that in earlier studies, Newsom argued that the Qumran community was the probable *Sitz im Leben* for the composition of the angelic hymns; see *Songs*, 1–4, 59–74; idem, " 'He Has Established for Himself Priests': Human and Angelic Priesthood in the Qumran Sabbath *Shirot*," in *Archaeology and History*, 103–4. Much controversy still surrounds the precise sociological identification of the community. For what appears to me to be a balanced and sensible account, see Shemaryahu Talmon, *The World of Qumran from Within: Collected Studies* (Jerusalem: Magnes, 1989), 11–52. According to Talmon, it is best to avoid the approach of seeking a single identity from without and imposing it on the community as opposed to examining the contours from within. Talmon assumes that the small band of priests who left Jerusalem is a *sui generis* phenomenon of the Second Temple period. See idem, "Between the Bible and the Mishna—the World of Qumran from Within," in *The Scrolls of the Judaean Desert: Forty Years of Research* (ed. M. Broshi et al.; Jerusalem: Bialik Institute and Israel Exploration Society, 1992), 10–48 [Hebrew]; and for an alternative review of the issue, see James C. Vanderkam, "Identity and History of the Community," in *Dead Sea Scrolls After Fifty Years*, 2:487–533.

[19] Henry Corbin, *Le paradoxe du monothéisme* (Paris: Éditions de l'Herne, 1981), 110, 126–27, utilizes the expression *synchronisme liturgique* to describe the relationship between heaven and earth in the Qumran angelology.

[20] Many worthy studies have been written on the mythopoeic theme of the correspondence between the earthly and heavenly Temples. As a selective list, I note Victor Aptowitzer, "The Celestial Temple as Viewed in the Aggadah," *Tarbiz* 2 (1931): 137–53, 257–77 [Hebrew], abridged English translation in *Studies in Jewish Thought* (vol. 2 of *Binah: Studies in Jewish History, Thought, and Culture*; ed. J. Dan; New York: Praeger, 1989), 1–29; M. Barker, *The Gate of Heaven: The History and Symbolism of the Temple in Jerusalem* (London: SPCK, 1991). For studies related more specifically to this theme in the Qumran Scrolls, see Bertil Gärtner, *The Temple and the Community in Qumran and the New Testament: A Comparative Study in the Temple Symbolism of the Qumran Texts and the New Testament* (Cambridge: Cambridge University Press, 1965); James R. Davila, "The Macrocosmic Temple, Scriptural Exegesis, and the Songs of the Sabbath Sacrifice," *DSD* 9 (2002): 1–19.

[21] This sensibility is an integral aspect of ancient mythologies based on a presumed parallelism between heaven and earth, the pantheon and royal court. This archaic principle evolved into an elemental hermetic principle articulated in the beginning of *Tabula Smaragdina*, the "Emerald Tablet," a series of gnomic utterances attributed to the legendary Hermes Trimegistus, cited in John Read, *Prelude to Chemistry: An Outline of Alchemy, Its Literature and Relationships* (Cambridge: MIT Press, 1966), 54: "I speak not fictitious things, but that which is certain and true. What is below is like that which is above, and what is above is like that which is below, to accomplish the miracles of one thing." For a learned discussion of the development of this theme in later hermetic literature, see Gilles Quispel, "Gnosis and Alchemy: the Tabula Smaragdina," in *From Poimandres to Jacob Böhme: Gnosis, Hermetism and the Christian Tradition* (ed. R. van den Broek and C. van Heertum; Amsterdam: Bibliotheca Philosophica Hermetica, 2000), 304–33. See further below, n. 59.

suggests something of a challenge to the hierarchical alignment of heavenly and mundane; mirrored and mirror are indistinguishable when the mirror is mirrored as the mirrored of the mirror. The play of (dis)semblance is not dependent on linear causality, whether charted vertically or horizontally, and hence even in the absence of an earthly temple the correlation of upper and lower is not severed in the imagination; quite to the contrary, the correlation seems to be strengthened and its horizons expanded to the extent that there is no concrete instantiation of the symbolic paradigm. Scholars of Jewish literature in the Second Temple period, what is sometimes referred to (in what strikes me as an overly determined historiographical taxon) as "early Judaism," have not generally appreciated the full mythopoeic import of the imaginal symbol of the celestial temple,[22] a transcendent reality supposedly envisioned contemplatively in the heart of the worshiper, the organ of apperception that corresponds to the throne upon which the glory sits.[23] The symbolic correlation of heart and throne implies that the imaginal faculty, the vehicle that provides the showground wherein the theophanic image appears, is engendered as feminine, the veil through which the hidden becomes manifest and the manifest, hidden, speculum of the other, lucidly dense, densely lucid, sapphire stone whence the throne is hewn.

When the matter is examined from a perspective beholden to an empiricist epistemology, it is obviously the case that images depicting the heavenly temple are contrived on the basis of the concrete reality of an earthly temple. It would be foolish to think otherwise; however, there is no compelling intellectual reason to privilege this angle of vision, which, I suspect, has attained prominence in the academy in large measure due to the dominance of social scientific method in the study of history and other disciplines included in the rubric of the humanities.[24] It is entirely possible from a conceptual

---

[22] Henry Corbin, *Temple and Contemplation* (London: Routledge & Kegan Paul, 1986), 263–390. Although I have utilized Corbin's thinking in a number of studies, the one most relevant for this analysis is Elliot R. Wolfson, "Sacred Space and Mental Iconography: *Imago Templi* and Contemplation in Rhineland Jewish Pietism," in *Ki Baruch Hu: Ancient Near Eastern, Biblical, and Judaic Studies in Honor of Baruch A. Levine* (ed. R. Chazan, W. Hallo, and L. H. Schiffman; Winona Lake, Ind.: Eisenbrauns, 1999), 593–634.

[23] A notable exception is Christopher Morray-Jones, "The Temple Within: The Embodied Divine Image and its Worship in the Dead Sea Scrolls and Other Early Jewish and Christian Sources," *SBLSP* 37 (1998): 399–431.

[24] A poignant example of this methodological flaw is found in the arguments made about temple imagery in *Sefer Yeṣirah* by Yehuda Liebes, *Ars Poetica in Sefer*

standpoint to reverse the causal relation, impelling one to consider the architectural construction of the earthly temple in light of the mythical *imago templi*.[25] This point, which has ramifications for a wider understanding of the symbolic fabric of ritual, mediated always by and through the prism of a socio-political community, the conduit to past tradition that calls forth incessantly for reappropriation, is especially pertinent in the case of the priests who absconded from their temple duties[26] and deserted the city to establish a priestly order[27] in the wilderness based not on the offering of sacrifices but on upholding purity laws,[28] fostering poetic forms of liturgical devotion,[29] and sponsoring oracular study of Torah, a form of visionary

---

Yetsira (Tel-Aviv: Schocken, 2000), 205–8 [Hebrew]. The relevancy of this reference is enhanced by the fact that Liebes dates the textual core of *Sefer Yeṣirah* to the Second Temple period. The somewhat unconventional and, to my mind, misguided approach to this textual aggregate deserves to be treated in more detail, but suffice it to say here that the methodological confusion displayed by Liebes on this point has to do with approaching the dual temples, celestial and earthly, in a binary and hierarchical fashion, according priority to the latter as the ground upon which the former is to be constructed.

[25] A clear-cut illustration of the failure to apprehend this point is found in Abusch, "Sevenfold Hymns," 236. The author criticizes the angelomorphic reading of the *Sabbath Songs* offered by Fletcher-Louis (see reference below, n. 61), which presumes an ontological identification of human and angelic based on a common semantic field: "This assumption, however, is especially problematic in the *Songs*, in which language functions primarily as a mode of representation and the imagined realms are perforce described as mirroring the earthly reality of the author(s)." In the first instance, it is not obvious to me why mirroring would preclude ontological identity, and, secondly, I am not convinced that the imagined, heavenly realms mirror the earthly reality. It is equally plausible—indeed, from my vantage point, preferable—to suggest that the reverse is the case, the earthly mirroring the heavenly, the veridical reflecting the imaginal.

[26] On the segregation of the priests to form the desert community, see 4Q397 14–21 7 (in E. Qimron and J. Strugnell, *Qumran Cave 4.V: Miqṣat Maʿaśe ha-Torah* [DJD 10; Oxford: Clarendon, 1994], 27, 58, 111); CD VIII, 16; Craig A. Evans, "Opposition to the Temple: Jesus and the Dead Sea Scrolls," in *Jesus and the Dead Sea Scrolls* (ed. J. H. Charlesworth; New York: Doubleday, 1992), 235–53; Schiffman, *Reclaiming*, 84–85. In 1QS VIII, 13–14; IX, 19–20, the physical withdrawal is expressed in the image of clearing a path, linked exegetically to Isa 40:3.

[27] On the priestly nature of the sectarian community, see the survey by Robert A. Kugler, "Priesthood at Qumran," in *Dead Sea Scrolls After Fifty Years*, 2:93–116.

[28] See Florentino García Martínez and Julio Trebolle Barrera, *The People of the Dead Sea Scrolls: Their Writings, Beliefs, and Practices* (Leiden: Brill, 1993), 139–57; Schiffman, *Reclaiming*, 97–112; Hannah K. Harrington, *The Impurity Systems of Qumran and the Rabbis: Biblical Foundations* (Atlanta: Scholars Press, 1993).

[29] There has been a profusion of studies written on the liturgical dimensions of Qumran piety, so here I offer but a modest sampling: Talmon, *World of Qumran*, 200–243; Moshe Weinfeld, "Prayer and Liturgical Practice in the Qumran Sect," in *The Dead Sea Scrolls: Forty Years of Research* (ed. D. Dimant and U. Rappaport; Leiden: Brill, 1992), 241–58; Eileen Schuller, "Prayer, Hymnic and Liturgical Texts

midrash,[30] or, as some scholars have put it, inspired biblical exegesis,[31] an effort goaded by the determination to determine the will of YHWH in accord with the demands of each and every moment.[32]

from Qumran," in *The Community of the Renewed Covenant* (ed. E. Ulrich and J. C. Vanderkam; Notre Dame, Ind.: University of Notre Dame Press, 1993), 153–71; Nitzan, *Qumran Prayer*; idem, "The Dead Sea Scrolls and the Jewish Liturgy," in *Dead Sea Scrolls as Background*, 195–219; Esther G. Chazon, "Prayers from Qumran and Their Historical Implications," *DSD* 1 (1994): 265–84; idem, "Hymns and Prayers in the Dead Sea Scrolls," in *Dead Sea Scrolls After Fifty Years*, 1:244–70.

[30] As has often been noted in scholarly literature, the root *drš* appears prominently in the Scrolls; the community's "righteous teacher" (*moreh ṣedeq*) bears the honorific title *doreš hattorah*, "interpreter of the teaching" (CD VI, 7; VII, 18). See Philip R. Davies, *The Damascus Covenant: An Interpretation of the "Damascus Document"* (Sheffield: JSOT Press, 1982), 123–24. The exegetical proficiency of the priestly leader is affirmed in a number of places; see 1QS V, 2–3; VIII, 1–2; CD XIII, 1–2. It is worthy to recall as well the expression *midraš hattorah* in CD XX, 6, which parallels *midraš yaḥad* in 1QS VI, 24, as noted by Joseph M. Baumgarten, "Corrigenda to the 4Q MSS of the Damascus Document," *RevQ* 19 (1999–2000): 221. The word *midraš* occurs as well in 1QS VIII, 15 (see below, n. 32), 26; 4Q174 1–2 I, 14. On the revelatory nature of the exegetical enterprise in sectarian literature, see Bockmuehl, *Revelation and Mystery*, 42–49; Aharon Shemesh and Cana Werman, "Hidden Things and Their Revelation," *RevQ* 18 (1998): 409–27. On revelation as the source of authoritative interpretation of the written text, see also A. R. C. Leaney, *The Rule of Qumran and Its Meaning: Introduction, Translation and Commentary* (Philadelphia: Westminster Press, 1966), 63–75; Michael Mach, "The Social Implication of Scripture-Interpretation in Second Temple Judaism," in *The Sociology of Sacred Texts* (ed. J. Davies and I. Wollaston; Sheffield: Sheffield Academic, 1993), 166–79. For discussion of this theme linked especially to angelic mediation, see Hindy Najman, "Angels At Sinai: Exegesis, Theology, and Interpretive Authority," *DSD* 7 (2000): 313–33. The philological and conceptual implications of the terms *pesher* and *midrash* are discussed by George J. Brooke, *Exegesis At Qumran: 4QFlorilegium in its Jewish Context* (Sheffield: JSOT Press, 1985), 149–56. On affinities between the midrashic character of sectarian *pesher* and later rabbinic hermeneutical principles, see Eliezer Slomovic, "Toward an Understanding of the Exegesis in the Dead Sea Scrolls," *RevQ* 7 (1969): 3–15; Paul Mandel, "Midrashic Exegesis and Its Precedents in the Dead Sea Scrolls," *DSD* 8 (2001): 149–68.

[31] Ithamar Gruenwald, *Apocalyptic and Merkavah Mysticism* (Leiden: Brill, 1980), 19–23; Lawrence H. Schiffman, *Sectarian Law in the Dead Sea Scrolls: Courts, Testimony, and the Penal Code* (Chico, Calif.: Scholars Press, 1983), 15–16; Michael Fishbane, "Use, Authority and Interpretation of Mikra at Qumran," in *Mikra: Text, Translation, Reading and Interpretation of the Hebrew Bible in Ancient Judaism and Early Christianity* (ed. M. J. Mulder; Assen: Van Gorcum, 1988), 345–46, 364–66. For an attempt to view the emphasis on study of Torah advocated in the Scrolls as part of a larger "return to the text" in Second Temple Judaism, a move that had a great impact on subsequent rabbinic Judaism, see Adiel Schremer, " '[T]he[y] Did Not Read in the Sealed Book': Qumran Halakhic Revolution and the Emergence of Torah Study in Second Temple Judaism," in *Historical Perspectives: From the Hasmoneans to Bar Kokhba in Light of the Dead Sea Scrolls. Proceedings of the Fourth International Symposium of the Orion Center for the Study of the Dead Sea Scrolls and Associated Literature, 27–31 January, 1999* (ed. D. Goodblatt, A. Pinnick, and D. R. Schwartz; Leiden: Brill, 2001), 105–26.

[32] 1QS VIII, 15: *hi'h midraš hattorah 'a[š]er ṣiwwah beyad mošeh la'aśot kekhol hannigleh 'et be'et*, "This is the study of the Torah that he commanded through Moses in order

Indeed, the poetic compositions betray a complicated hermeneutical pattern that suggests it may not be wise to distinguish too sharply between liturgical and exegetical activities on the part of the priestly scribes.[33] From the same ranks came forth visionary poet and inspired exegete, *maśkil* and *moreh ṣedeq*, entrusted with knowledge of the mysteries of the prophets that pertained especially to the "appointed time," the eschatological end, *ḥazon lammoʿed weyafeaḥ laqqeṣ* (Hab 2:3), the final terminus, *haqqeṣ haʾaharon* (1QpHab VII, 7).[34]

Members of the "sacred community," *yaḥad qodeš*,[35] "community of the sons of Zadok," *yaḥad benei ṣadoq*,[36] community of "those who enter the renewed covenant," *boʾei berit hahadašah*,[37] defined themselves as the "elect ones of Israel" (*beḥirei yiśraʾel*),[38] the "righteous remnant,"[39] "his chosen assembly" (*ʿadat beḥiro*), which is compared

---

to act in compliance with all that is revealed at each and every moment." For analysis of this passage, see Gershon Brin, *The Concept of Time in the Bible and the Dead Sea Scrolls* (Leiden: Brill, 2001), 308. In 1QS V, 9, the priests, sons of Zadok, are described as "guardians of the covenant and interpreters of his will," *šomrei habberit wedoršei reṣono*. See 1QS VIII, 6 where the community council is said to be *beḥirei raṣon*, that is, the elect "chosen by the will" of God. The members of the community are designated *benei raṣon*, "sons of favor," in 1QHᵃ XII, 32–33; XIX, 9. The idiom *ʾanšei raṣon*, "men of will," occurs in 4Q298 I, 3–4; 4Q418 81 10.

[33] On the exegetical-meditative aspects of the liturgical compositions, see Carol Newsom, "Merkabah Exegesis in the Qumran Sabbath Shirot," *JJS* 38 (1987): 11–30.

[34] Vermes, *Dead Sea Scrolls*, 167–68; Bilhah Nitzan, *Pesher Habakkuk: A Scroll from the Wilderness of Judaea (1QpHab)* (Jerusalem: Bialik Institute, 1986), 27–28, 172–73.

[35] Many scholars have noted the centrality of cultic purity in the sectarian's understanding of self-identity. For a relatively recent study that takes into account previous discussions, see Hannah K. Harrington, "Holiness and Law in the Dead Sea Scrolls," *DSD* 8 (2001): 124–35.

[36] This title is derived from Ezekiel's depiction of the priests who will serve in the future Temple (44:15). See 1QS V, 2, 9; CD III, 20–IV, 3; Kugler, "Priesthood," 97–100. On the figure of Zadok, see Ben Zion Wacholder, *The Dawn of Qumran: The Sectarian Torah and the Teacher of Righteousness* (Cincinnati: Hebrew Union College Press, 1983), 99–140.

[37] Howard C. Kee, "Membership in the Covenant People at Qumran and in the Teaching of Jesus," in *Jesus and the Dead Sea Scrolls*, 104–22.

[38] 4Q174 1 I, 21, 2 19; CD IV, 3–4. In 1QpHab X, 13, the sectarians are referred to as *beḥirei ʾel*, the "elect ones of God." See also the expression *beḥirei raṣon*, "chosen by the will," in 1QS VIII, 6, and *beḥirei haʿet*, "chosen ones of the moment," in 1QS IX, 14 (= 4Q259 III, 11), discussed by Brin, *Concept of Time*, 303–4; and *beḥirei ṣedeq*, the "just chosen ones," in 1QHᵃ X, 13.

[39] Members of the *yaḥad* viewed themselves as the holy remnant of Israel (Jer 6:9; 31:7; Ezek 9:8; 11:13; Mic 2:12; Zeph 3:13; 2 Chr 34:9) with whom God would renew the covenant and effect the restoration to the days of glory past (CD I, 4–5); the community thus understood its destiny in terms of receiving the "new covenant," *berit hadašah*, inscribed on the heart (Deut 10:16; 30:6; Jer 31:31–33; Ezek 36:26). *Berit* connotes the covenant with God that must be renewed through reenactment of biblical ceremony (Deut 27–28; Josh 8:30–35). See Davies, *Damascus*

to "sapphire amidst the stones" (*ke'even hassappir betokh ha'avanim*),[40] whose primary task was to establish a priestly regimen without temple or sacrificial cult.[41] Hence, one should not be surprised that by their own account the liturgical rite, "offering of the lips" (*terumat śefatayim*),[42] is trumpeted as a substitute for the "flesh of burnt offerings" and the "fat of sacrifices" (1QS IX, 4–5); prayer as an instrument of theurgic power, which in this context denotes bestowal of praise upon, that is, glorifying, the "glorious king," *melekh hakkavod*,[43] tem-

---

Covenant, 173–97; Bilhah Nitzan, "The Concept of the Covenant in Qumran Literature," in *Historical Perspectives*, 85–104. The Scrolls have also yielded evidence that circumcision of the flesh and circumcision of the heart both play a role in the formation of the community's pietistic ideal. Regarding the latter, see, for example, 1QS V, 5 where those in the *yaḥad* are described as circumcising the "foreskin of the inclination and the stiff neck" (echoing Deut 10:16) and 4Q434 1 I, 2–4 where circumcising the foreskin of the heart is attributed to God (cf. *Jub.* 1:22); and the depiction of the wicked priest "whose disgrace exceeded his glory because he did not circumcise the foreskin of his heart" in 1QpHab XI, 12–13. See R. Le Déaut, "La thème de la circoncision du cœur (Dt. 30:6; Jer. 4:4) dans les versions anciennes (LXX et Targum) et à Qumrân," *VT* 32 (1982): 178–205; David R. Seely, "The 'Circumcised Heart' in *4Q434 Barki Nafshi*," *RevQ* 17 (1999): 527–35.

[40] 4Q164 1 3 (interpreting Isa 54:11).

[41] Many scholars have emphasized this character of the sectarian worldview. For several relatively recent discussions and substantial bibliographies of other relevant studies, see Israel Knohl, "Between Voice and Silence: The Relationship between Prayer and Temple Cult," *JBL* 115 (1996): 17–30; Philip R. Davies, *Sects and Scrolls: Essays on Qumran and Related Topics* (Atlanta: Scholars Press, 1996), 45–60; Lawrence H. Schiffman, "Community Without Temple: The Qumran Community's Withdrawal from the Jerusalem Temple," in *Gemeinde ohne Tempel: Zur Substituierung und Transformation der Jerusalemer Tempels und seines Kults im Alten Testament, antiken Judentum und frühen Christentum* (ed. B. Ego, A. Lange, and P. Pilhofer, in collaboration with K. Ehlers; Tübingen: Mohr Siebeck, 1999), 267–84, and Florentino García Martínez, "Priestly Functions in a Community without Temple," op. cit., 303–19.

[42] Compare 1QS X, 6, 14. A parallel locution for the prayers of the priestly community, *terumat lašon*, "offering of the tongue," appears in 4Q400 2 7, whereas the angelic hymns are referred to as *terumat lešoneihem* in 4Q403 1 II, 26—a philological support to the theoretical claim that the liturgical gesture blurs the ontic line separating human and angelic. For discussion of this theme, see Devorah Dimant, "Men as Angels: The Self-Image of the Qumran Community," in *Religion and Politics in the Ancient Near East* (ed. A. Berlin; Bethesda, Md.: University Press of Maryland, 1996), 93–103; and the somewhat different perspective offered by Esther G. Chazon, "Liturgical Communion with Angels at Qumran," in *Sapiential, Liturgical and Poetical Texts*, 95–105. A related expression, *bero'šei terumot lešonei da'at*, occurs in 4Q405 23 II, 12, and see Newsom's note (DJD 11:365) where she suggests, relying in part on Elisha Qimron ("A Review Article of Songs of the Sabbath Sacrifice: A Critical Edition by Carol Newsom," *HTR* 79 [1986]: 349–71, esp. 356–57), that the word *terumot* in the angelic songs may be translated as "praise-offerings" rather than simply "offerings," since it is developed independently from the verb *rwm*, which means "exaltation," and thus is not linked exclusively to the scriptural *terumah*, "heave offering." See as well Newsom's note, DJD 11:190, but see Nitzan, *Qumran Prayer*, 291 n. 59.

[43] A commonplace epithet for God in the sectarian nomenclature derived from

porarily supplants sacrifice,[44] even as the physical temple still stood and daily sacrifices continued to be offered.[45] From this we may conclude that the temple imagined by the *maśkil*, poet-sage,[46] "spiritual

---

Ps 24:7–10. See 1QH[a] XXVI, 9; 4Q403 1 1, 3, 31; 4Q403 1 II, 25; 4Q511 52 4; 11Q17 V, 5–6.

[44] The qualification "temporarily" is intended to underscore the fact that while there is no evidence for a sacrificial rite in the desert community, the belief on the part of the Qumranites was that they would return to the "New Jerusalem" and reconstitute the offering of sacrifices in the future Temple. Hence, prayer, including the angelic liturgy, cannot be seen as a permanent substitution for sacrifice on the part of the sectarian religious philosophy. See Vermes, *Dead Sea Scrolls*, 129–30, 180–81; Lawrence H. Schiffman, *The Eschatological Community of the Dead Sea Scrolls: A Study of the Rule of Congregation* (Atlanta: Scholars Press, 1989), 64–67. On sacrifice and worship among the Qumran sectarians, see as well Joseph M. Baumgarten, *Studies in Qumran Law* (Leiden: Brill, 1977), 39–56.

[45] Talmon, *World of Qumran*, 209; Lawrence H. Schiffman, "The Qumran Scrolls and Rabbinic Judaism," in *Dead Sea Scrolls After Fifty Years*, 563–64; Maier, "Shîrê 'Ôlat hash-Shabbat," 543–60; Falk, *Daily, Sabbath, and Festival Prayers*, 137–38; idem, "Qumran Prayer Texts and the Temple," in *Sapiential, Liturgical and Poetical Texts*, 106–26. On the image of the New Jerusalem and the future Temple, see Florentino Garcia Martínez, *Qumran and Apocalyptic: Studies on the Aramaic Texts from Qumran* (Leiden: Brill, 1992), 180–213; idem, "The *Temple Scroll* and the *New Jerusalem*," in *Dead Sea Scrolls After Fifty Years*, 2:431–60.

[46] The heading of the individual angelic hymns is *lemaśkil šir 'olat haššabbat*; 4Q400 1 I, 1; 4Q401 1–2 1; 4Q403 1 I, 30; 4Q403 1 II, 18; 4Q405 8–9 1; 4Q405 20 II-21–22 6; Mas1k I, 8. For a similar use of *maśkil* as the one to whom the song is ascribed, see 4Q511 2 I, 1; 8 4; 1Q28b I, 1; III, 22; V, 20. Newsom, DJD 11:179, conjectures that the formulaic introduction is modeled on the psalm heading *lemaśkil*. See also Newsom, " 'Sectually Explicit,' " 180; Bilhah Nitzan, "Hymns from Qumran—4Q510–4Q511," in *Dead Sea Scrolls: Forty Years*, 53–63. I would add that *maśkil* echoes as well the apocalyptic connotation of the term as we find in Dan 12:3. Regarding the latter, see Michael Fishbane, *Biblical Interpretation in Ancient Israel* (Oxford: Clarendon Press, 1985), 492–93. The liturgical-poetical qualities of the *maśkil* are appreciated, albeit with different nuances than my own, by Nitzan, *Qumran Prayer*, 265–72; and idem, "Dead Sea Scrolls and the Jewish Liturgy," 206 n. 40 (mention is made there of Amos 5:13 where *maśkil* denotes one who recites songs). The term *maśkil* appears elsewhere in the sectarian material, for example, as the official title of the instructor of the sons of light according to *Manual of Discipline*; see 1QS1 I, 1; III, 13; IX, 12, 21; 1QM I, 1; 4Q421 1 II, 10, 12; 4Q298 I, 1. In CD XIII, 7–8, the leader of the camp is depicted as one who will "enlighten the multitude in the ways of God," *yaśkil 'et harabbim bema'aśei 'el*. Mention should also be made of the description of the Israelite people in 1QM X, 10 as *maśkilei binah*, "enlightened in understanding." Wacholder, *Dawn of Qumran*, 81, notes that *maśkilei binah* is based on the expressions *lehaśkilekha vinah* (Dan 9:22) and *maśkilei 'am yavinu* (Dan 11:33). On the critical term *maśkil* in Qumran literature, see Rigàux, "Révélation des mystères," 242–44; Hans Kosmala, "Maskil," *JANESCU* 5 (1973): 235–41; Newsom, *Songs of the Sabbath Sacrifice*, 3–4; idem, "The Sage in the Literature of Qumran: The Functions of the Maskil," in *The Sage in Israel and the Ancient Near East* (ed. J. G. Gammie and L. G. Perdue; Winona Lake, Ind.: Eisenbrauns, 1990), 373–82; Schiffman, *Reclaiming*, 123–25, 456; Kampen, "Diverse Aspects," 238–39; James E. Harding, "The Wordplay Between the Roots כשל and שכל in the Literature of the Yahad," *RevQ* 19 (1999): 71–74; Jefferies, *Wisdom at Qumran*, 38–41. Finally,

guide,"[47] luminous and illuminating, obfuscated any unequivocal demarcation between celestial and mundane, angelic and human; indeed, one can even say the blueprint for construction of the community below was what the priests imagined with respect to the realm above.[48]

One of "pure heart," *lev tahor*,[49] is capable of envisioning the imaginary topography of the "king of purity," *melekh hattahor* (4Q403 1 II, 26),[50] the heavenly temple, whilst residing in the desert, a place where one is less encumbered by sensory stimuli. We may conjecture that the desolate and barren terrain was deemed especially worthy of the visionary journey, provided the sojourner's heart was purged of carnal desire,[51] and he attained, perhaps "appropriated" would be the better word, the image of God within, the priestly conception of *selem 'elohim*, luminous presence shared by angel and human, radiance of the divine glory beheld in the prophetic vision uniquely linked to Israel, and of the latter, the priests, and of the priests, the

---

mention should be made of the textual evidence that an alternative version to the formulation *wezeh hasserekh le'ansei hayyahad* in the *Manual of Discipline* (1QS V, 1) was *midras lemaskil 'al 'ansei hattorah* (4Q256 IX, 1; 4Q258 I, 1). See Geza Vermes, "Preliminary Remarks on Unpublished Fragments of the Community Rule from Qumran Cave 4," *JJS* 42 (1991): 251; Hartmut Stegemann, "Some Remarks to 1QSa, to 1QSb, and to Qumran Messianism," *RevQ* 17 (1996): 481–82, 486.

[47] Harrington, *Wisdom Texts*, 65.

[48] This point has been noted in previous scholarship. See Michael Knibb, *The Qumran Community* (Cambridge/New York: Cambridge University Press, 1987), 90; Ben-Zion Wacholder, "Ezekiel and Ezekielianism as Progenitors of Essenianism," in *Dead Sea Scrolls: Forty Years*, 188; and Elliot R. Wolfson, "Mysticism and the Poetic-Liturgical Compositions from Qumran," *JQR* 85 (1994): 195–96. See also John Strugnell, "The Angelic Liturgy at Qumrân—4QSerek Šîrôt 'Ôlat Haššabat," VTSup 8 (1959): 320: "This is no angelic liturgy, no visionary work where a seer hears the praise of the angels, but a Maskîl's composition for an earthly liturgy in which the presence of the angels is in a sense invoked and in which the Heavenly Temple is portrayed on the model of the earthly one and in some way its service is considered the pattern of what is being done below."

[49] The expression occurs at 4Q436 1 I, 10.

[50] Cf. what seems to be a description of the angelic priests as *tehorei 'olamim*, "eternally pure ones," in 4Q403 1 I, 13, and the apparent description of the firmament (*raqi'a*) associated with the inner sanctum as *tohar tehorim*, the "purest of the pure" (4Q403 1 I, 42) and the reconstructed *raqi'a tohar* at 4Q405 6 3. It stands to reason, as Newsom notes (DJD 11:276), that this description of the heavenly sphere was inspired by the words *ukh'esem hassamayim lattohar* (Exod 24:10).

[51] My suggestion accords with a well-attested phenomenon in the history of religions, the emptying of oneself through ascetic practices, including fasting and sexual restraint, as preparation for divine possession, visitation, and the visionary encounter. See David Martinez, " 'May She Neither Eat Nor Drink': Love Magic and Vows of Abstinence," in *Ancient Magic and Ritual Power* (ed. M. Meyer and P. Mirecki; Leiden: Brill, 1995), 343–44 and references to other scholars cited in nn. 31–36.

elite group assembled in the desert. In the angelic/divine state, the *maśkil* is illumined by *ruaḥ haqqodeš*, the holy spirit, and thereby conjures theophanic images of the heavenly chariot (*merkavah*),[52] the "holy dwelling" (*maʿon qadoš*) described in graphic detail in several of the Sabbath hymns, reaching an ocular crescendo in the last three.[53]

---

[52] There have been many commendable studies on *merkavah* imagery and the theological-angelological speculations of the sectarian community related especially to the Sabbath hymns. See Lawrence H. Schiffman, "*Merkavah* Speculation at Qumran: the 4Q *Serekh Shirot ʿOlat ha-Shabbat*," in *Mystics, Philosophers, and Politicians: Essays in Jewish Intellectual History in Honor of Alexander Altmann* (ed. J. Reinharz, D. Swetschinski, and K. Bland; Durham: Duke University Press, 1982), 15–47; idem, "Hekhalot Mysticism and the Qumran Literature," *Jerusalem Studies in Jewish Thought* 6:1–2 (1987): 121–38 [Hebrew]; Newsom, "Merkabah Exegesis"; Joseph M. Baumgarten, "The Qumran Sabbath Shirot and Rabbinic Merkabah Traditions," *RevQ* 13 (1988): 199–213; Devorah Dimant and John Strugnell, "The Merkabah Vision in Second Ezekiel (4Q385 4)," *RevQ* 14 (1990): 331–48; Devorah Dimant, "The Apocalyptic Interpretation of Ezekiel at Qumran," in *Messiah and Christos: Studies in the Jewish Origins of Christianity Presented to David Flusser* (ed. I. Gruenwald, S. Shaked, and G. G. Stroumsa; Tübingen: Mohr Siebeck, 1992), 31–51, esp. 42–43; Elisabeth Hamacher, "Die Sabbatopferlieder im Streit um Ursprung und Anfänge der Jüdischen Mystik," *JSJ* 27 (1996): 119–54; James R. Davila, "The *Hodayot* Hymnist and the Four Who Entered Paradise," *RevQ* 17 (1996): 457–78; idem, "4QMESS AR (4Q534) and Merkavah Mysticism," *DSD* 5 (1998): 367–81; idem, "The Dead Sea Scrolls and Merkavah Mysticism," in *The Dead Sea Scrolls in Their Historical Context* (ed. T. H. Lim; Edinburgh: T&T Clark, 2000), 249–64; James M. Scott, "Throne-Chariot Mysticism in Qumran and in Paul," in *Eschatology, Messianism, and the Dead Sea Scrolls* (ed. C. A. Evans and P. W. Flint; Grand Rapids: Eerdmans, 1997), 101–19; Rachel Elior, "The Merkavah Tradition and the Emergence of Jewish Mysticism: From Temple to Merkavah, from Hekhal to Hekhalot, from Priestly Opposition to Gazing upon the Merkavah," in *Sino-Judaica: Jews and Chinese in Historical Dialogue* (ed. A. Oppenheimer; Tel-Aviv: Tel-Aviv University Press, 1999), 101–58; idem, *Temple and Chariot, Priests and Angels, Sanctuary and Heavenly Sanctuaries in Early Jewish Mysticism* (Jerusalem: Magnes, 2002), 174–211 [Hebrew]; Michael D. Swartz, "The Dead Sea Scrolls and Later Jewish Magic and Mysticism," *DSD* 8 (2001): 182–93; Abusch, "Sevenfold Hymns," 220–47.

[53] Bilhah Nitzan, "The Idea of Holiness in Qumran Poetry and Liturgy," in *Sapiential, Liturgical and Poetical Texts*, 143–45. Nitzan describes the experience encoded in the thirteen Sabbath hymns as an "ascent" leading to a "mystical experience," a continuation of the thesis she has promulgated elsewhere. See idem, "Harmonic and Mystical Characteristics in Poetic and Liturgical Writings from Qumran," *JQR* 85 (1994): 163–83. For a critical assessment of Nitzan's argument, see Wolfson, "Mysticism." What is worth pointing out here is that there is no definitive philological marker in the text to validate the conjecture that there is an ascent experience preserved in the Sabbath hymns, though I acknowledge that continued study of the texts has convinced me that some such experience may indeed be alluded to in some critical passages. Nevertheless, from a conceptual standpoint it is unnecessary to press this point inasmuch as the distinction between upper and lower is significantly blurred for the one who envisions the imaginal in the mirror of the heart; in this visual field, below is above and above, below; angelic, human (that is, according to the ideal thought to be embodied in the priestly ascetics; see n. 56) and human, angelic.

We would do well at this juncture to pause and consider a bit more carefully the nexus of revelatory experience and angelification.[54] To envision the glory, a term that signifies in Qumran fragments the world of the chariot in its totality, which encompasses angelic forms, cherubim-thrones,[55] and the enthroned king, one must become glorious, aglow with the glimmer of the divine image, the angelic splendor in whose likeness Adam was created.[56] Though not stated explicitly, at work here are two independent but related epistemological principles, one traceable in the Greek philosophical tradition to Anaxagoras, "like sees like,"[57] and the other to the occult wisdom of hermetic alchemy,[58] "like mirrors like," expressed succinctly in the second precept of the *Emerald Tablet* (*Tabula Smaragdina*) attributed to Hermes Trismegistus,[59] "I speak not fictitious things, but that which is certain and true. What is below is like that which is above, and what is above is like that which is below, to accomplish the miracles

---

[54] Peter W. van der Horst, *Japheth in the Tents of Shem: Studies on Jewish Hellenism in Antiquity* (Leuven: Peeters, 2002), 195–96.

[55] See reference to *merkavot kevodekhah*, "chariots of your glory," in 4Q286 1 II, 2; Schiffman, "*Merkavah* Speculation," 42–43.

[56] Stephen N. Lambden, "From Fig Leaves to Fingernails: Some Notes on the Garments of Adam and Eve in the Hebrew Bible and Select Early Postbiblical Jewish Writings," in *A Walk in the Garden: Biblical, Iconographical and Literary Images of Eden* (ed. P. Morris and D. Sawyer; Sheffield: Sheffield Academic, 1992), 74–90, esp. 80–82; John J. Collins, "In the Likeness of the Holy Ones: The Creation of Humankind in a Wisdom Text from Qumran," in *The Provo International Conference on the Dead Sea Scrolls: Technological Innovations, New Texts, and Reformulated Issues* (ed. D. W. Parry and E. Ulrich; Leiden: Brill, 1999), 609–18; Fletcher-Louis, *Glory of Adam*, 113–22.

[57] Particularly important for the point I am making is the exegesis of Anaxagoras offered by Plotinus in *Enneades* I, 6.9.

[58] A lucid account of alchemy in the manner that I am employing it is offered by Richard Goldard, *Remembering Heraclitus* (Hudson, N.Y.: Lindisfarne Books, 2000), 11, who notes that in a "strict sense" alchemy consists of delving "into secrets of nature for the purpose of understanding the relationship between human and divine nature." See ibid., 73–74.

[59] There are various legends intended to procure the antiquity of *Tabula Smaragdina*, the alchemical fragment purportedly engraved on an emerald slab. Critical historians are skeptical of the antiquity and prefer to pick the story up from the thirteenth century when the text, though modest in size, exerted an impressive influence on the development of western alchemy. See Titus Burckhardt, *Alchemy: Science of the Cosmos, Science of the Soul* (trans. W. Stoddart; London: Stuart & Watkins, 1967), 196–97; Allison Coudert, *Alchemy: The Philosopher's Stone* (London: Wildwood House, 1980), 27–28; Gareth Roberts, *The Mirror of Alchemy: Alchemical Idea and Images in Manuscripts and Books from Antiquity to the Seventeenth Century* (Toronto/Buffalo: University of Toronto Press, 1994), 68–70. The issue of dating the composition of this fragment is not central to my argument as it seems beyond question that the homology between heaven and earth is a belief that stretches far back in time.

of one thing."[60] In the particular case of the sectarian priests, the *maśkil* can behold the glorious light without only when he has become that light within, a transformation facilitated by faithful adherence to ascetic practices, especially sexual renunciation, intended to realize the ideal of ritual purity incumbent on members of the community.[61]

The transformation, however, would not be imaginable if one did not presume that the design of the community was patterned in the likeness of the paradigmatic image, the symbolic constellation configured in the visionary's heart. From the textual remains of the *yahad*, we can infer that this image—at once virtually real and really virtual—set the purview of the historical phenomenon, and not vice-versa, the temple above laying the groundwork for the sacred space of the community below. Tellingly, in one passage the community is designated *beit qodeš le'aharon lehayyahad qodeš qodašim*, "the holy house for Aaron, the holy of holies for the community" (1QS IX, 6); according to the elocution of another passage, the *yahad* is simply called *miqdaš 'adam*, "sanctuary of man" (4Q174 1–2 I, 6). As George Brooke suggested, this expression lends philological support to the idea that the community described in the fragments recovered from the caves at Qumran anticipated in its own existence the eschatological sanctuary without denying belief in a future rebuilding of the temple.[62] I would add that the prolepsis renders future present, albeit present as the future that is to come, an imaginal bridging of time that parallels the bridging of space implied in the homology between the encampment of the community below and the elaborate workings of the temple above.

---

[60] See reference cited above, n. 21.

[61] On angelomorphism and celibate abstention, see Fletcher-Louis, *Glory of Adam*, 131–34. Also pertinent is the comparative analysis of Alexander Golitzin, "Recovering the 'Glory of Adam': 'Divine Light' Traditions in the Dead Sea Scrolls and the Christian Ascetical Literature of Fourth-Century Syro-Mesopotamia," in *Dead Sea Scrolls as Background to Postbiblical Judaism*, 275–308. In this connection, it is relevant to recall the prohibition of sexual intercourse in Jerusalem, the "city of the sanctuary," *'ir hammiqdaš*, according to CD XII, 1–2, lest it be rendered unclean. The unequivocal implication of this injunction, whether or not it was ever instantiated in an actual community, is that sexual intercourse defiles the ritual purity appropriate for the holy city. See Baumgarten, *Studies in Qumran Law*, 41, 43–44.

[62] Brooke, *Exegesis At Qumran*, 212, and see his comments (ibid., 276 n. 357) about the link between the attitude of CD toward the temple and the implication of the phrase *miqdaš 'adam* in 4Q174 1–2 I, 6. See also Dimant, "Apocalyptic Interpretation," 38, 40, 45; Fletcher-Louis, *Glory of Adam*, 167 n. 52.

II. Re/Covering Knowledge of Mystery

The poetic utterance that opened the path of inquiry, the pathmark in the Heideggerian idiom, occurs in the eighth of the thirteen songs:

> Ševa' razei da'at
> beraz happele'
> lešiv'at gevulei
> qode[š qodašim . . .]

> Seven mysteries of knowledge
> in wondrous mystery,
> corresponding to seven boundaries
> of the ho[ly of holies . . .] (4Q 403 1 II, 27)[63]

To explicate this passage responsibly, and particularly the key expression *razei da'at*, it is obviously necessary to consider the meaning of two terms, *raz*, "mystery," and *da'at*, "knowledge." What kind of knowledge, what kind of mystery? How does knowledge impart mystery, how does mystery impart knowledge? Before approaching these philological and philosophical clarifications, it would be beneficial to situate the text better in its literary setting, a move that will shed light on the symbolic significance of the number seven, which will, in turn, facilitate a better understanding of the mysteries of knowledge.

At the outset of the eighth song there appears to be a correlation between seven celestial priests, "seven priesthoods of the inner sanctum," *ševa' kehunat qorvo* (4Q403 1 II, 20; 4Q405 8–9, 4–5),[64] "priests of the highest heaven," *kohanei merommei rom* (4Q400 1 I, 20), and another sevenfold angelic division:

---

[63] I have availed myself of the text critically prepared by Newsom in DJD 11:280, but all translations are my own unless otherwise noted.

[64] See DJD 11:279 and 325. The idea of seven chief angels, closely linked to the notion of seven archangels attested in pseudepigraphic and later gnostic texts, may have been derived from Ezek 9:1–2, as suggested by James R. Davila, *Liturgical Works* (Grand Rapids: Eerdmans, 2000), 120. On the apocalyptic conception of the seven archangels, and especially in the context of the septenary symbolism in the book of Revelation, see Adela Yarbro Collins, *Cosmology and Eschatology in Jewish and Christian Apocalypticism* (Leiden: Brill, 1996), 105–6, 111, 113, 115, 119, 174; and Ralph J. Korner, "'And I Saw . . .': An Apocalyptic Literary Convention for Structural Identification in the Apocalypse," *NovT* 42 (2000): 179–80 and relevant notes. See also Abusch, "Sevenfold Hymns," 227 n. 21. I note, parenthetically, that the number of seven priests presents something of a different model than the composition of the council of the community (*'aṣat hayyaḥad*) according to 1QS VIII, 1, which consists of three unblemished priests (*kohanim temimim*) and twelve men (*'iš*).

koha[not] ševaʿ bamiqdaš peleʾ
lešivʿat sodei qodeš

seven priest[hoods] in the wondrous sanctuary
corresponding to seven holy councils (4Q403 1 II, 22)[65]

In the song restored as the first of the cycle, the angelic priesthood
is described as the "god-like ones of all the holiest of the holy ones
(*ʾelohei kol qedošei qedošim*); and in divinity (*uveʾelohut*)[66] . . . among the
eternally holy (*qedošei ʿad*),[67] the holiest of the holy ones (*qedošei qedošim*),
and they have become for him priests of (*kohanei*) . . . ministers of the
presence in the shrine of his glory (*mešartei panim bidevir kevodo*)" (4Q400
1 I, 2–4).[68] Just as below the priestly elite had exclusive access to
the inner chamber of the temple, so above, there is a distinguished
class of angels, the "seven exalted holy ones," *šivʿat qodšei rom* (4Q
403 1 II, 11), that ministers before the presence enthroned in the
innermost of the "seven boundaries[69] of the hol[y of holies]," *šivʿat
gevulei qode[š qedošim]* (4Q 403 1 II, 27), also referred to as the "seven
wondrous boundaries," *šivʿat gevulei peleʾ* (4Q403 1 II, 21),[70] or the
"[se]ven priestly shrines," *[šiv]ʿat devirei kehuno[t]* (4Q405 7 7).[71] The
seventh of these palaces is the "sanctuary of his holiness," *miqdaš*

---

[65] DJD 11:279.

[66] It is of interest to note that initially the scribe wrote *uveʾelohuto*, that is, "in his
divinity," but in the scroll the suffixed *waw* is marked for deletion, yielding *uveʾelohut*,
"in divinity." See Newsom's brief, but informative, note on this matter (DJD 11:179).

[67] The unusual use of *ʿad* as an adjective follows the scriptural precedent in Isa
9:5 and Hab 3:6.

[68] Here I have availed myself of Newsom's translation in DJD 11:178, but I have
made some emendations.

[69] As Newsom suggests (DJD 11:287), the word *gevul* may be indebted to Ezek
43:12 where "it refers to the territory of the temple mount." Given this meaning
of *gevul*, it is obvious why the author(s) of the Sabbath hymns chose it to demarcate the seven palaces in the celestial temple.

[70] This reading is restored at 4Q405 8–9 5 and 11Q17 II, 6. See Nitzan, *Qumran
Prayer*, 315 n. 132.

[71] Note the reference in 4Q405 14–15 I, 7 to the "[sanctuary of the ho]ly of
holies, in the inner shrines of the king," [*miqdaš qo]deš qedošim bidevirei melekh*. Christopher
Morray-Jones suggests the seven sanctuaries (*devirim*) of the celestial temple in the
Songs of the Sabbath Sacrifice "are evidently identical with the seven heavens" (*A
Transparent Illusion: The Dangerous Vision of Water in Hekhalot Mysticism. A Source-Critical
and Tradition-Historical Inquiry* [Leiden: Brill, 2002], 31). It seems to me more sensible to assume that the seven sanctuaries refer to chambers of the celestial temple
rather than the heavenly spheres. For a comprehensive survey of the notion of seven
heavens in Jewish and Christian apocalyptic sources, see Collins, *Cosmology and
Eschatology*, 21–54.

qodšo (4Q403 1 I, 42), "tabernacle of the most high," *miškan ro'š rom*, "glory of his kingdom," *kevod malkhuto* (4Q403 1 II, 10).[72]

Before progressing deeper, or higher, as the case may be, into the labyrinth of symbols—in the *mundus imaginalis*, there is no significant difference between ascent/descent and entry/exit, as going up is going in, going down going out, and hence the two metaphorical templates coalesce—a cautionary note is in order. One must be careful not to lapse, even if inadvertently, into a binary logic that presumes a unilateral relation of upper mirroring lower, a stance that implies further that the symbolic is constructed on the basis of the historical. Is it not equally plausible to view the historical as reflective of the symbolic, the tangible construed on the basis of the imaginal? Is the Qumran material not exemplary of a society wherein the fantastic served as the vehicle of implementation of the real? Consider the assertion, "they are glorified amongst all the camps of angels and venerated in the council of men," *hemmah nikhbadim bekhol maḥanei 'elohim wenora'im lemosdei 'anašim* (4Q400 2 2). Newsom notes the terminological derivation of *maḥanei 'elohim* from Gen 32:2 and also its recurrence in 4Q405 22 13, a context wherein it clearly refers to the camps of angels who utter hymns before the glory. She suggests further the angelic elite is "probably to be identified with the angelic princes."[73]

I would argue that the expression *maḥanei 'elohim* in this context also refers, in part, to the camps of angels stationed in the throne chamber. To support this interpretation I must say more about an admittedly ambiguous passage, but it is precisely by marking the ambiguity that one can see the clarity of the ontic confusion. The beginning of the text in question reads *lehallel kevodekhah pele' be'elei da'at wetišboḥot malkhutekhah biqedošei qe[došim]*, "to praise your wondrous glory with the gods of knowledge, and the praises of your kingship with the holy of h[olies]" (4Q400 2 1). The textual lacuna in the beginning of the fragment opens the interpretative space: I suggest that the subject of the statement is the *maśkilim*, the enlightened priests, who join together through poetic envisioning with the angelic elite, the "gods of knowledge," *'elei da'at*,[74] the "holy of holies," *qedošei qedošim*, to praise the divine glory (*kavod*) and his kingship (*malkhut*). After this

---

[72] See Newsom's comments, DJD 11:287 and 332. See also Esther Eshel, "Prayer in Qumran and the Synagogue," in *Gemeinde ohne Tempel*, 323–34, esp. 327–28. Davila, "Macrocosmic Temple," 12–17, attempts to explain this locution on the basis of Exod 23:20–23 and Isa 63:7–14.
[73] DJD 11:189.
[74] 4Q403 1 I, 38.

line comes the aforecited remark, "they are glorified amongst all the camps of angels and venerated in the councils of wondrous men," *hemmah nikhbadim bekhol mahanei 'elohim wenora'im lemosdei 'anasim pe[le']* (4Q400 2 2). If my supposition is correct, then it is the *maskilim* who are accorded this high honor; they are simultaneously rendered glorious above in the angelic realm and acclaimed below in their congregation. The key term *nikhbadim* denotes transformation, which here does not imply becoming something new but rather actualizing the latent glory, the *kavod*, the image of God (*selem 'elohim*) by which the true Adam was created, believed by the sectarians to be embodied in the perfect ones of Israel, that is, the priestly elite of the *yahad*.

Proof for this reading may be elicited from the continuation of the text, "from gods and men," *me'elohim wa'anasim*. It seems plausible to suggest that this expression refers to the *maskilim* of whom it can be said that they belong both to the angelic pantheon (*'elohim*)[75] and to the human elite (*'anasim*). It is they who "will narrate the splen-

---

[75] The reference to the angels collectively as *'elohim* underscores the lack of clear demarcation between angelic and divine to the point that monotheism, strictly speaking, cannot be applied to these texts unless one understands that term to mean that in the host of divine beings there is one who stands out from the rest and is considered the supreme deity, *'el 'elim, melekh hattahor*, "God of gods, the king of splendour" (4Q403 1 II, 26). The point is underscored as well by angelic epithets such as *'elei da'at, 'elei 'or, 'elei hod*, and *'elei rom*, as noted by Newsom, DJD 11:243. Regarding the question of monotheism as an appropriate classification in the period to which the Qumran scrolls refer, see James H. Charlesworth, "The Dead Sea Scrolls and the Historical Jesus," in *Jesus and the Dead Sea Scrolls*, 47 n. 65. See also Peter Hayman, "Monotheism—A Misused Word in Jewish Studies?" *JJS* 42 (1991): 1–15, esp. 4–9. The word *tahor*, which means "purity," occasionally is indistinguishable from *zohar*, "splendor"—on this see the remark of Nitzan, DJD 11:52–53, in her note to 4Q287 2 5. However, if one assumes that monotheism ontically rules out all but one divine being, then the term is a misnomer if used to describe the theological picture that emerges from these fragments. We would do well to think here of a corporate sense of the deity, composed of the king and his servants, which consists of angels and the priestly elite who join the heavenly host to tell the story, to render its imaginaries visually acoustic and acoustically visual. For discussion of the older roots for this corporate notion of divine unity, see E. Theodore Mullen, Jr., *The Divine Council in Canaanite and Early Hebrew Literature* (Chico, Calif.: Scholars Press, 1980). A useful terminology is Corbin's distinction (*Le paradoxe du monothéisme*, 7–18) between "exoteric monotheism" and "esoteric and gnostic theomonism," the former insisting on a unity without multiplicity, a tendency that can lead to "metaphysical idolatry"—that is, reification of the one God as the being to whom anthropomorphic qualities are invariably ascribed—and the latter, which is predicated on a vision of multiplicity in the unity, a multiplicity that consists of names and attributes that emerge from and return to the undifferentiated oneness of the Infinite. I was reminded of this dimension of Corbin's thought by Maria Subtelny who makes mention of it in her "The Four Sages who Entered the Pardes: A Talmudic Enigma from a Persian Perspective" (forthcoming). I am grateful to the author for sharing an early draft of her study, from which I have benefited.

dor of his kingship according to their knowledge," *yesapperu hod malkhuto keda'atam* (4Q400 2 3). Let us heed these words carefully: the priest-poets have the task of recounting the splendor of his kingship (*hod malkhuto*) in accord with their knowledge (*keda'atam*). Three points are worthy of note to draw forth the full implications of this passage. First, *hod malkhuto* signifies the heavenly abode and all of its luminous components, to wit, glory, chariot-thrones, and various groups of angelic beings who minister before the enthroned king.[76] Thus, in another fragment, the hymns are extolled as the activity that empowers the divine, *ki behadar tišbaḥot kevod malkhuto bah tišbaḥot kol ʾelohim ʿim hadar kol malkh[uto]*, "for in the grandeur of the praises is the glory of his kingship, in it are the praises of all the gods together with the magnificence of all [his] kingship" (4Q403 1 I, 32–33).[77] Second, the specific task is to recount the experience, *lesapper*, to render it narrato-logically and thereby "glorify the splendor of divine kingship."[78] The *sippur*, narration, refers, more specifically, to the poetic depiction of the imaginal realm preserved in the hymns. Third, the narration must be in accord with knowledge, *da'at*, a word that calls to mind the title of the angelic elite, *ʾelei da'at*, "gods of knowledge," as well as the "seven mysteries of knowledge," *ševa' razei da'at*, which are said to correspond to the "seven boundaries of the holy of holies," *ševa' gevulei qodeš qodašim*, the decoding of which sent us on our way. At this juncture we must consider more carefully the word *da'at*, a con-sideration that will enable us to go further along the path to ascer-tain the knowledge of mystery embedded in the mystery of knowledge.

---

[76] Compare 4Q286 1 II, 2.

[77] On the semantic equivalence of *hod* and *hadar*, and especially the scriptural expressions *hod malkhut* (1 Chr 29:25) and *hadar malkhut* (Dan 11:20), see Newsom, DJD 11:273.

[78] The locution is based on scriptural precedent; see Isa 43:21; Jer 51:10; Pss 9:2, 15; 79:13; 96:3; 107:22; 145:6; 1 Chr 16:24. See Ben Sira 1:24, *'ad 'et yastir devaraw wesiftei ne'emanim tesappernah ḥokhmato*; 1QH^a VII, 4–5: *lo' ya'aṣru koaḥ lada'at bekhavod [ulesappe]r nifle'[otekha] [. . .] . . . lefi sikhlam ukhefi da'atam*, "they will not gather the strength to know your glory [or to recou]nt [your] wonders [. . .] . . . according to their intelligence and in accordance with their knowledge." See also 1QH^a VII, 8: *uwehafle' nesapperah yaḥad beda'a[t 'el]*, "and wondrously we shall recount together the knowledge of God."

III. Un/Covering Mystery of Knowledge

In the *Manual of Discipline*, God is described as follows: *me'el hadde'ot kol huyah weniheyyeh welifnei heyotam hekhin kol mahšavtam/uveheyotam lite'udotam kemahševet kevodo yemall'u pe'ulotam we'ein lehiššanot*, "From the God of knowledge comes everything that is and that shall be, and before they were he prepared all their designs/And when they have come into being in their appointed times, they fulfill their actions in accord with his glorious design, and there is nothing to be changed" (1QS III, 15–16). The title *'el de'ot* is applied to God in 1 Sam 2:3,[79] and it would appear that it is used by the author of the Qumran text to express the theological belief in divine omniscience.[80] An almost identical formulation appears to have been utilized in one passage from the *Sabbath Songs* synoptically reconstructed as follows: *ki' me'elohei da'at nihyu kol [hawwei 'ad umidda'ato umizzimotaw hayu kol te'udot 'olam]im*, "For from the God of knowledge came into being every [everlasting existent, and from his knowledge and from his plans all predestined things exist eterna]lly" (4Q402 4 12–13, restored on the basis of Mas1k 1 2–3). Assuming the validity of an admittedly questionable textual reconstruction, we can assert that the philosophical idea expressed herein runs parallel to the aforecited comment in the *Manual of Discipline*: the existence of all beings is predestined by and in the knowledge of God;[81] all things proceed from that knowledge, *da'at*; in the mind of God are laid the schemes and plans of all that is to become in the spatio-temporal world.[82] Confirmation of this interpretation may be adduced from other passages in the *Manual of Discipline*: *wehu'h yada' pe'ulat ma'aseihen lekhol qiṣṣei ['olami]m*, "and he knows the consequences of their actions for all times

---

[79] On the designation *'el hadde'ot*, see 1QH[a] IX, 26.

[80] Jacob Licht, *The Rule Scroll: A Scroll from the Wilderness of Judaea—1QS, 1QSa, 1QSb: Text, Introduction and Commentary* (Jerusalem: Bialik Institute, 1965), 90 n. 15 [Hebrew].

[81] In 1QH[a] IX, 23–25, the matter is expressed in the image of everything being engraved before God with the "engraving of memory," *hakkol haquq lefaneikhah beheret zikkaron*.

[82] Attested in the Scrolls are seemingly contradictory positions, predestinarianism, on the one hand, and voluntarism, on the other; the belief that all things are predestined in divine knowledge did not mitigate against the conviction that human agents are free and responsible for their actions. For a brief but incisive discussion of this matter, see David Winston, *The Wisdom of Solomon: A New Translation with Introduction and Commentary* (AB 43; Garden City, N.Y.: Doubleday, 1979), 50–51.

[everlast]ing" (1QS IV, 25–26); *uveda'ato nihyeh kol wekhol hawwayah bemaḥšavto yakhinu umibbal'adaw lo' ya'aseh*, "everything shall come into being through his knowledge, and every being is established in his thought, and apart from him it is not realized" (1QS XI, 11). A slightly different formulation appears in the *Thanksgiving Scroll: uveḥokhmat da'atekhah hakh[i]notah te'[o]datam beṭerem heyotam we'al pi reṣ[onekhah yih]yeh kol umibbal'adekha lo' ya'aseh*, "through the wisdom of your knowledge you have established their course prior to their existence and according to [your] wi[ll] everything will be and without you nothing comes to be" (1QH^a IX, 19–20). In another passage from this scroll, we learn that members of the *yaḥad*, labeled "sons of your truth," *benei 'amittekhah*,[83] are accorded *sekhel*, usually translated as "intelligence," but, in my judgment, denoting in this context a form of visionary knowledge, the gnosis in virtue of which one assumes the comportment of *maskil*, the enlightened sage-poet. In the continuation, we read that "in accord with their knowledge they are glorified," *ulefi da'atam yekhabbdu* (1QH^a XVIII, 27). I think it reasonable to assume that *sekhel* and *da'at* are interchangeable,[84] and both refer to the cognitive faculty by means of which the enlightened priest apprehends divine truth (*'emet*).[85]

Support for this conjecture may be elicited from other passages, such as, *hiskaltani be'amittekhah uverazei peli'akhah hoda'atani*, "You have enlightened me in your truth and made me know your wondrous mysteries" (1QH^a XV, 26–27). In virtue of that vision, the priest is glorified, that is, he is transfigured into an angelic body and becomes part of the celestial retinue while remaining a leader of the *yaḥad* below. According to another fragment belonging to one of the community songs of the *Hodayot*, a more explicit connection is made between knowledge (*da'at*), inspiration of the holy spirit (*ruaḥ haqqodeš*), and discernment of divine mystery (*raz*), though in this instance the

---

[83] Compare the expression *'ansei ha'emet*, "men of the truth," in 1QpHab VII, 10. It should be noted that *benei 'amittekha* also appears as a designation of the angels in 1QH^a XIX, 11. In 1QS III, 24–25, reference is made to the "angel of his truth," *mal'akh 'amitto*, who will assist the "sons of light," *benei 'or*. In 1QS II, 24, the congregation at large is designated *yaḥad 'emet*, the "community of truth."

[84] See, for instance, 1QH^a XIX, 28: *sekhel de'ah lehavin benifle'otekhah*.

[85] See 1QH^a XVIII, 29: *beda'at 'amittekhah ulefi da'ato*, "in the knowledge of your truth and in accord with his knowledge." On the link between truth and secrecy, see, for instance, the instruction to the *maskil* in 1QS IX, 18: *lehaskilam berazei fele' we'emet*, "to enlighten them in the wondrous secrets and in the truth."

auditory, as opposed to the visual, imagery[86] is summoned to depict the attainment of esoteric knowledge: *wa'ani maśkil yeda'tikhah 'eli beruah 'aśer natattah bi wene'emanah šama'ti lesod pela'ekhah beruah qodšekhah [pa]tahtah letokhi da'at beraz śikhlekhah uma'ayan gevurote[khah]*, "I, the enlightened one, know you, my God, through the spirit that you placed in me, and I have listened faithfully to your wondrous secret through your holy spirit. You have [op]ened within me knowledge of the mystery of your intelligence and the spring of [your] power" (1QH[a] XX, 11–13).[87] In this extremely important and revealing text, the reader is afforded an opportunity to grasp something of the ecstatic experience of the priest acquiring knowledge (*da'at*) of God. Significantly, that knowledge is connected to the mystery (*raz*) drawn from the spirit (*ruah*) opened up within the enlightened one (*maśkil*), an internal awakening that facilitates listening (*šemi'ah*) to the "wondrous secret" by means of which the divine intelligence (*śekhel*) and spring of power (*ma'ayan gevurah*) are accessed.

On the basis of careful attunement to these sources, collectively and individually, I would suggest that *da'at* should be understood in a more technical theosophic manner than has been appreciated hithertofore by Qumran scholars. In my judgment, it appears that this is the best way to account for all the occurrences of this term and grammatically related expressions in the extant fragments, as they apply to God, angels, and priestly elite. I begin with the credible assumption that the imaginal configurations of *da'at* on the part of the Qumran priests were influenced by scriptural connotations of the term. To note the examples most relevant to this study: "divine knowledge," *da'at 'elohim* (Hos 4:1, 6:6; Prov 2:5); "supernal knowledge," *da'at 'elyon* (Num 24:16); "knowledge of the holy ones," *da'at qedośim* (Prov 9:10, 30:3); "For the lips of the priest guard knowledge," *ki śiftei kohen yiśmeru da'at* (Mal 2:7); "and those enlightened in all wisdom, knowers of knowledge, intelligently insightful," *umaśkilim bekhol hokhmah weyod'ei da'at umevinei madda'* (Dan 1:4).

In addition to these, we must add the obvious reference to the "tree of knowledge of good and evil," *'es hadda'at tov wara'* (Gen 2:17), in

---

[86] For another example of the auditory, see 1QH[a] IX, 21: *ki galitah 'oznai lerazei fele'*, "you opened my ears to the wondrous mysteries"; and 4Q416 2 III, 18: *galeh 'oznekhah beraz nihyeh*, "he opened your ears to the mystery of what is becoming."

[87] Similar language of knowledge being attained through the spirit appears in 1QH[a] V, 24–25.

the mythical garden of Eden; the curious response of the serpent to the woman's reiteration of the punishment of death subsequent to transgressing the divine command not to eat of the fruit of the tree of knowledge, "for God knows that on the day you eat from it, your eyes will be opened, and you will be like the gods, knowers of good and evil," *ki yodeʿa ʾelohim ki beyom ʾakholkhem mimmennu wenifqeḥu ʿeineikhem wiheyiytem keʾlohim yodeʿei ṭov waraʿ* (Gen 3:5); and the account of man and woman after they transgressed, "And the eyes of both of them were opened and they knew that they were naked," *wattippaqaḥnah ʿeinei šeneihem wayyedʿu ki ʿerummim hem* (v. 7)—the knowledge of their nakedness seemingly accentuates their mortality, quite the obverse of the serpent's claim, though it is also likely that there is wordplay of the description of the serpent as "cunning," *ʿarum* (v. 1) and the expression "naked," *ʿerom*, applied to the human pair following their disobedience (vv. 7, 11).[88] Confirmation of the latter does come a bit later in the narrative, "The LORD God said, 'Behold Adam has become like one of us, knowing good and evil,'" *wayyoʾmer* YHWH *ʾelohim hen haʾadam hayah keʾaḥad mimmennu ladaʿat ṭov waraʿ* (v. 22), which is immediately followed by the concern that Adam would taste of the fruit of the tree of life and thereby attain immortality, and thus he is cast out of the garden (vv. 22–24). Finally, there is the figurative meaning of *daʿat* as carnal knowledge that ensues from engaging in intercourse, a connotation attested, interestingly enough, in the verse that immediately succeeds the tale of Adam's eviction from Eden, "And Adam knew Eve, his wife," *wehaʾadam yadaʿ et ḥawwah ʾišto* (Gen 4:1), as well as in several other scriptural contexts (Gen 4:17, 25; 24:16; 38:26; Judg 19:25; 1 Sam 1:19; 1 Kgs 1:4). Needless to say, the scriptural text cleverly weaves together these terminological threads to forge an intricate conceptual mesh of knowledge, sexuality, and immortality: Adam knows his wife; the engendering of progeny is conceived as a substitute for the immortality that would have been acquired had the first human pair eaten of the tree of life.[89]

The sense of intimacy conveyed by the use of *yadaʿ* to denote a man's cohabiting with his wife was utilized to depict man's relationship to the divine, as is attested, for instance, in the prophetic decree reaffirming God's covenantal promise to Israel: "I will espouse

---

[88] James Barr, *The Garden of Eden and the Hope of Immortality* (Minneapolis: Fortress, 1993), 69–70.

[89] Barr, *Garden of Eden*, 57–73; Ronald A. Veenker, "Forbidden Fruit: Ancient Near Eastern Sexual Metaphors," *HUCA* 70–71 (1999–2000): 57–73, esp. 69–73.

you forever; I will espouse you with righteousness and justice, and with goodness and mercy. And I will espouse you with faithfulness; then you will know the LORD," *we᾽eraśtikh li le῾olam we᾽eraśtikh li beṣedeq uwemišpaṭ uweḥesed uweraḥamim we᾽eraśtikh li he᾽emunah weyada῾at ᾽et* YWHW (Hos 2:21–22). Knowledge *(da῾at)* is consequent to espousal *(᾽eruśim)*; to know God one must be bound to God in a monogamous relationship, a theme that is central to the conception of piety cultivated in ancient Israel and embellished in sundry ways through the course of Jewish history. The linkage of this theme to the Genesis narrative implies, more specifically, that the knowledge of God consequent to erotic engagement is salvific inasmuch as it restores to man the primal state of enlightenment, an opening of the eyes that is not connected to the shamefulness of the indecent exposure of the naked body.

With the scriptural background in mind, one may conjecture that the priestly *literati* in the desert community placed at the center of their visionary landscape God's knowledge, *da῾at ᾽elohim*, the ultimate object of imaginal representation and contemplative meditation. In the language of a crucial passage in the *Manual of Discipline, lehavin yešarim beda῾at ῾elyon weḥokhmat benei šamayim lehaśkil temimei derekh ki᾽ bam bahar ᾽el liverit ῾olamim welahem kol kavod ᾽adam,* "to instruct the upright in the supernal knowledge and to enlighten those whose way is perfect in the wisdom of the sons of heaven, for God has chosen them for an everlasting covenant and to them belong all the glory of Adam" (1QS IV, 22).[90] Comprehension of the "supernal knowledge," which is parallel to the "wisdom of the sons of heaven," occasions

---

[90] Consider the following comment on 1QS IV, 22 by Ithamar Gruenwald, *From Apocalypticism to Gnosticism: Studies in Apocalypticism, Merkavah Mysticism and Gnosticism* (Frankfurt am Main: Peter Lang, 1988), 78: "the word דעת ('knowledge') may be taken to imply every aspect of divine wisdom: historical and ethical on the one hand, and cosmological and 'scientific' on the other." The passage is adduced by Gruenwald to support his argument that the "preoccupation of Gnosticism with cosmogonical, or cosmological, matters could well be the contribution of Jewish Apocalypticism" (79). The contrast between the use of *da῾at* in apocalyptic literature and *gnosis* in Gnosticism is drawn explicitly by Gruenwald (84). Davies, "'Knowledge' in the Dead Sea Scrolls," 131, similarly distinguishes unequivocally between the *gnosis* of Gnosticism and the knowledge of the Qumran scrolls. See also Helmut Ringgren, "Qumran and Gnosticism," in *Le Origini dello Gnosticismo: Colloquio di Messina 13–18 Aprile 1966*, edited by Ugo Bianchi (Leiden: E. J. Brill, 1970), 379–388, and Menahem Mansoor, "The Nature of Gnosticism in Qumran," op. cit., 389–400, esp. 395–397. By contrast, according to my onto-theosophic interpretation of *da῾at* in Qumran literature, the link to Gnosticism is more pronounced, for I am proposing a mythopoeic conception of the divine mind that encompasses a multiplicity of hypostatic potencies, the esoteric knowledge of which affords one salvation through a transformative experience of ascending upward by turning inward.

the incorporation of the knower into the known, not in the Plotinian sense of union that effaces all difference, but in the ancient Near Eastern mythopoeic conception of angelification whereby the superior human being can join the ranks of the angels chanting hymns before the glory in the heavenly realm.[91] Plainly stated, I propose that *ševa' razei da'at* should be interpreted as seven potencies that constitute the substance of *da'at 'elyon*. Philological support for my contention may be drawn from the expression *ševa' gevurot peli'ah*, "seven wondrous powers" (4Q403 1 I, 2). In the continuation of that passage, God is designated *'elohei gevurot*, "God of the powers" (4Q403 1 I, 2–3), which I assume is an abbreviated allusion to the seven powers that constitute the fullness of God, and, in my estimation, are synonymous with the seven mysteries of knowledge.

To place the matter in a broader context, it should be noted that the number seven occupies a central place in the *Sabbath Songs*, and especially in the seventh of the cycle, plausibly thought by some to be the centerpiece of the poetic architectonic displayed in the hymns, wherein one encounters the supernal tabernacle, the chariot-throne, portrayed as the "pure light," *'ortom*,[92] of the glory refracted through the "variegated[93] spirit of the holy of holies," *roqemet ruah qodeš qodašim* (4Q403 1 II, 1). Without delineating all the permutations of this numerical symbolism, which, needless to say, is deeply

---

[91] Wolfson, "Mysticism," 192–94. On the motif of the song of heavenly beings in ancient Near Eastern literature, see Moshe Weinfeld, "Sumerian Literature and the Book of Psalms—An Introduction to a Comparative Analysis," *Beit Miqra* 57 (1974): 136–60 [Hebrew].

[92] On the form *'ortom*, obviously a composite of the two words *'or*, "light," and *tom*, "unblemished," see 1QH^a XXI, 14 and the restored *be'or 'ortam da'at*, "in light of the perfect light of knowledge," in 4Q403 1 I, 45 (= 4Q404 5 4). Newsom, DJD 11:283, suggests that in the *Sabbath Songs* this expression "refers to a peculiarly celestial light, associated with the inner shrine of the heavenly sanctuary and perhaps with the appearance of the throne of Glory itself." In my judgment, the "pure light" refers to the light of the glory (*kavod*), an identification substantiated by the reference to the polymorphic nature (see following note) of the holy spirit (*ruah haqqodeš*), that is, the purity of the light of the glory is expressed in the kaleidoscope of colors through which the holy spirit appears.

[93] The translation of *roqemet* as "variegated" is based on the word *riqmah* (1 Chr 29:2), following the suggestion of Newsom, DJD 11:283, who draws the reader's attention to 1QM V, 6. See also Schiffman, "*Merkavah* Speculation," 41. One must bear in mind that *roqemet* also has the connotation of "embroidered." The spectral dimension is thus threaded to the image of something woven, a multicolored garment, as it were. Also noteworthy is the use of *roqmah* in 4Q270 7 II, 14, analyzed by George J. Brooke, "Between Qumran and Corinth: Embroidered Allusions to Women's Authority," in *Dead Sea Scrolls as Background*, 157–76.

entrenched in the Jewish literary imagination,[94] let me state that, in my judgment, the significance of this number in this particular literary context stems from the conception of the divine as a corporate body composed of seven potencies.[95] There appears to be an alternative enumeration of these potencies in the account of the songs of praise uttered by the seventh of the chief princes: *yevarekh bešem qodšo lekhol qedošim mimmeyasdei*[96] *da['at] bešiv['ah] divrei qodeš pela'[o]*, "he will bless in his holy name all the holy ones who establish know[ledge] with sev[en] words of [his] wondrous holiness" (4Q403 1 I, 24), a reference to the highest angelic beings, *haramim bekhol 'elei da'at*, "the exalted ones of all the gods of knowledge" (4Q403 1 I, 30–31), the ones "who illumine knowledge among all the divinities of light," *me'irei da'at bekhol 'elei 'or* (4Q403 1 II, 35). We may conclude, therefore, that "knowledge" functions as a technical designation of the divine

---

[94] For a still useful survey of some of the relevant images associated with the number seven cast in a comparative light, see Maurice H. Farbridge, *Studies in Biblical and Semitic Symbolism* (Prolegomenon by H. G. May; New York: Ktav, 1970), 119–39.

[95] If my interpretation stands the test of critical scrutiny, we would have in the *Sabbath Songs* the first reference in a Jewish text to a portrayal of God consisting of seven potencies, an idea that became more prominent in later sources, such as the Pseudo-Clementine *Homilies*, traces of which are discernible in *Sefer ha-Bahir*, an anthology of older traditions that served as the wellspring for many kabbalists in the late middle ages and beyond to the present. See Elliot R. Wolfson, *Along the Path: Studies in Kabbalistic Myth, Symbolism, and Hermeneutics* (Albany: State University of New York Press, 1995), 80–83, and references cited in 217 n. 135, 218 n. 142, 219 n. 146. A particularly important text, which I neglected to mention in the aforementioned reference, appears in the later rabbinic anthology of aggadic dicta, *Avot de Rabbi Natan* A 37 (Schechter ed., 110):

Seven attributes (*middot*) serve before the throne of glory and they are wisdom, righteousness, justice, mercy, compassion, truth, and peace, as it says "I will espouse you forever; I will espouse you with righteousness and justice, and with goodness and mercy. And I will espouse you with faithfulness; then you will know the LORD" (Hos 2:21–22). R. Meir said, What can be deduced from "then you will know the LORD?" This is to teach that every man who has within him all these attributes knows the divine mind (*da'ato šel maqom*).

For discussion of the literary context in which this statement appears, see Menahem Kister, *Studies in Avot de-Rabbi Nathan: Text, Redaction and Interpretation* (Jerusalem: Yad Izhak Ben-Zvi, 1998), 54–56 [Hebrew]. Also relevant to this discussion is the study of Gedaliahu G. Stroumsa, "A Zoroastrian Origin to the *Sefirot?*" *Irano-Judaica* 3 (1994): 17–33, which attempts to trace the origin of seven spirits, connected to the seven heavenly spheres, to Zoroastrianism. Stroumsa conjectures that the latter rabbinic notion regarding the seven hypostatic attributes in front of the throne may be an echo of this earlier tradition (20). On the ancient Zoroastrian notion of seven archangels, see the instructive observations of Corbin, *Le paradoxe du monothéisme*, 100–110.

[96] See Schiffman, "*Merkavah* Speculation," 32, and especially the suggestion that the root *ysd* can mean "to compose a liturgical hymn."

pleroma, the imaginal world of the chariot-throne, a conception conveyed by the expression *bamotei daʿat*, the "high places of knowledge,"
which are associated with the footstool of God (4Q403 1 II, 2).

IV. POIESIS AND RE/COUNTING THE GLORY

On the basis of the textual-philological arguments mounted above,
I would venture that the priests responsible for the imaginal conception of the chariot realm laid out in the Sabbath hymns believed
they were capable of knowing, following the biblical expressions,
"divine knowledge," *daʿat ʾelohim*, "supernal knowledge," *daʿat ʿelyon*,
"knowledge of the holy ones," *daʿat qedošim*. By means of acquiring
that knowledge, moreover, they fulfilled the verse, "For the lips of
the priest guard knowledge," *ki śiftei kohen yišmeru daʿat* (Mal 2:7), and
identified with the eschatological state of "those enlightened in all
wisdom, knowers of knowledge, intelligently insightful," *umaśkilim bekhol
ḥokhmah weyodʿei daʿat umevinei maddaʿ* (Dan 1:4). Scholars have previously suggested the possibility that the recitation of the songs may
have served as a vehicle for ascent to the heavenly throne and communion with the angels. What has not been sufficiently noted is that
the composition of these songs likely ensued from a similar imaginal transport by which spatial and temporal barriers were traversed
by the initiates who viewed themselves as being shaped by God into
"vessels of knowledge" (*kelei daʿat*) to contemplate the ancient mysteries of wisdom (4Q436 1 I, 2).[97] The tenor of the ecstasy underlying the experience of poiesis was well captured by the author of
the *Manual of Discipline*, *ʾazammerah vedaʿat wekhol neginati likhvod ʾel*, "I
will sing with knowledge and all my music shall be for the glory of
God" (1QS X, 9), or again, *mimmeqor daʿato pataḥ ʾori uveniflẹʾotaw
habbiṭah ʿeinai weʾorat levavi beraz nihyeh*, "from the spring of his knowledge he opened my light, and my eyes gazed on his wonders, and
the light of my heart the mystery of what is to be" (1QS XI, 3–4).

Now we can understand more fully the text discussed above, which
assigned to priests the task of recounting what they experienced in
the chariot realm in accord with their knowledge. One can surely

---

[97] See David R. Seely, "The Barkhi Nafshi Texts (4Q434–439)," in *Current Research
and Technological Developments of the Dead Sea Scrolls: Conference on the Texts from the Judaean
Desert, Jerusalem, 30 April 1995* (ed. D. W. Parry and S. D. Ricks; Leiden: Brill,
1996), 194–214, esp. 201–2.

interpret that remark in a general way, that is, knowledge is required so that the narration is informative and accurate. There is, however, another and more esoteric interpretation of the expression *yesapperu hod malkhuto keda'atam*, that is, their knowledge is the glorious element that accords them a divine-angelic status; they come to know the seven mysteries of divine knowledge through the exercise of their own knowledge though the actualization of their own knowledge is facilitated by apprehension of the seven mysteries of knowledge.[98] The duty to discourse poetically about the splendor of divine kingship is predicated on being incorporated into this kingship, to become god-like and glorious, to be illumined by the soteric esotericism that affords one the opportunity to be assimilated into the divine potencies. This possibility is affirmed explicitly in the following passage: *rannenu merannenei [da'ato be]ronen be'elohei fele' wehagu khevodo belašon kol hogei da'at rinnot pela'o*, "Sing with joy, those of you enjoying [his knowledge with] the exultation among the wondrous gods, and proclaim his glory in the language of those who proclaim knowledge of his wondrous songs" (4Q403 1 I, 36).

To apprehend the God of knowledge (*'el hadde'ot*), one must join company with the gods of knowledge (*'elei da'at*) who declare his glory through the chanting of songs. Two predicates are used to demarcate the activity ascribed to the enlightened priest, *rannenu* and *hagu*, which I have rendered respectively as "sing" and "proclaim." It is important to note, however, that the root of the latter term, *hgh*, in scriptural usage can mean "to make a sound" or "to articulate" (Isa 8:19, 31:4, 38:14, 59:11; Pss 35:28, 71:24, 115:7; Prov 8:7; Job 27:4) as well as "to ruminate" (Josh 1:8; Isa 16:7; 33:18; 59:3, 13; Jer 48:31; Pss 1:2, 2:1, 37:30, 38:13, 63:7, 77:13, 143:5; Prov 15:28, 24:2). It is plausible to suppose that both connotations are implied in the aforecited text, and hence the mandate is for the priest to contemplate and proclaim the glory in the language of the angels who are called *hogei da'at*. As the matter is expressed in another fragment from these hymns, *bero'šei terumot lešonei da'at [u]varekhu le'lohei da'at bekhol ma'asei kevodo*, "In the chief of the offerings of the tongues of knowledge [and] they bless the God of knowledge in all of the works of his glory" (4Q405 23 II, 12). Lamentably, the beginning

---

[98] In this respect, I concur with Gruenwald's observation, *From Apocalypticism to Gnosticism*, 83, regarding the reciprocal relationship between knowledge and salvation: "Knowledge brings salvation, and, *mutatis mutandis*, salvation leads to knowledge."

of this passage is not decipherable, but from what has survived we
can confidently assume that the reference is to the angelic elite who
bless the "God of knowledge" with "tongues of knowledge." In the
state of liturgical ecstasy, the poet urges himself and others who shall
read his poem to participate in this process of angelification.

The ideal is set forth in the *Thanksgiving Scroll* in language that is
consonant with the intent of the *Širot ʿOlat Haššabbat*: *weruaḥ naʿaweh
ṭihartah mippešaʿ rav lehityaṣṣev bemaʿamad ʿim ṣevaʾ qodašim welavoʾ beyaḥad
ʿim ʿadat benei šamayim wetappel leʾiš goral ʿolam ʿim ruḥot daʿat lehallel
šimkhah beyaḥad rinnah ulesapper nifleʾotekhah leneged kol maʿaśekhah*, "And
you have purified the depraved spirit[99] from great transgression to
take its place with the host of the holy ones and to enter in communion with the congregation of the sons of heaven, and you cast
a lot for man with the spirits of knowledge, to praise your name in
the community of song and to recount your wonders before all of
your creation" (1QHᵃ XI, 21–23). Jacob Licht noted in his edition
of the *Hodayot* that this passage indicates that the participation of
the sect with the angels was related specifically to the utterance of
praise before God in the heavenly abode.[100] What is particularly
noteworthy for our purposes is the designation of the angels as *ruḥot
daʿat*, an obvious parallel to the expression *ʾelei daʿat* that appears in
the *Sabbath Songs*. The angels are designated in this way not because
they apprehend the inner knowledge of God but because they are
manifestations of the divine mind (*maḥšavah*) wherein all knowledge
inheres.[101] As a consequence of attaining the angelic status—troped
in the image of casting one's lot—the sectarian priest praises the
name of God and narrates the divine wonders. The matter is expressed
elsewhere in these hymns in a manner that is especially pertinent to
our discussion, *waʾani lefi daʿati beʾami[ttekhah . . .] uwehabbiṭi bikhevodekhah
ʾasapperah nifleʾotekhah*, "And I, in accordance with my knowledge of
[your] tru[th . . .] and in my contemplating your glory, I will recount
your wonders" (1QHᵃ XVIII, 20–21). Knowledge of divine truth is
equated with visually gazing at the glory, which occasions the recitation of God's mysteries.[102]

---

[99] An uncommon expression probably inspired by *naʿaweh lev* in Prov 12:8.

[100] Jacob Licht, *The Thanksgiving Scroll—A Scroll from the Wilderness of Judaea: Text, Intro-
duction, Commentary and Glossary* (Jerusalem: The Bialik Institute, 1957), 84 n. 22
[Hebrew]. For extensive philological analysis of this passage, see Bonnie Kittel, *The
Hymns of Qumran: Translation and Commentary* (Chico, Calif.: Scholars Press, 1981), 56–80.

[101] 1QHᵃ XIX, 7–8: *uwemaḥšavtekhah kol deʿah*.

[102] This concurs with the expression *daʿat ʾamitto*, "his true knowledge," which

In what is perhaps the most evocative language depicting the transformative experience, the hymnist thanks God in the following terms:

> [*ho*]*daʿatani besod ʾamittekhah wetaśkileni bemaʿaśei peliʾekhah wattitten befi hodot uveleśoni tehilah. . . . tamid ʾuwarkhah śimkhah waʾasapperah kevodekhah betokh benei ʾadam. . . . ulemaʿan kevodekhah ṭihartah ʾenoś mippeśaʿ lehitqaddeś lekhah . . . lehiyyaḥed ʿi[m] benei ʾamittekha uwegoral ʿim qedośeikhah . . . ulehityaṣṣev bemaʿamad lefaneikhah ʿim ṣevaʾ ʿad weruḥei [daʿat]*[103]* *lehithaddeś ʿim kol nihyeh weʿim yodʿim beyaḥad rinnah.*

> You have made me knowledgeable of the secret of your truth, and you have enlightened me in your wondrous works, and you have placed in my mouth thanksgiving and on my tongue praise. . . . I will bless your name constantly and recount your glory amongst the sons of man. . . . For the sake of your glory you purified man from sin to sanctify himself for you . . . to be united wi[th] the sons of your truth and in the lot of your holy ones . . . and to stand before you together with the everlasting host and spirits [of knowledge] to be renewed in all that will exist and with those who know in the communion of song. (1QHᵃ XIX, 4–6, 10–14)

Once again we see the clearly delineated nexus linking gnosis of the divine secret, transformation into the angelic elite who stand before the throne ("sons of truth," "everlasting host," and "spirits of knowledge"), blessing the divine name, and utterance of hymns through which the supernal glory is recounted. I would suggest that the narrative recounting refers, more specifically, to the composition of liturgical poetry, which is predicated on the imaginal excursion into the theophanic realm, an excursion that breaks down the barrier of angelic and human, celestial and mundane. Thus the poet, who serves the role of "mediator of knowledge in the wondrous mysteries," *meliṣ daʿat berazei feleʾ* (1QHᵃ X, 13), speaks of being renewed in "all that will exist," *kol nihyeh*, with "those who know in the communion of song." I propose that *kol nihyeh* is not simply a rhetorical flourish but is rather a technical term that is synonymous with *raz nihyeh*, the "mystery of what will be." If my surmise is correct, then the reference here is to the experience of ontic incorporation into the divine mystery.

The point I am raising is affirmed as well in a passage from the "Rule of Benedictions"[104] that is addressed, in all likelihood, to the

---

appears in conjunction with the recitation of angelic praise before the throne; that is, in virtue of the knowledge of divine truth, the heavenly mysteries can be recounted. See 4Q403 1 I, 16, 18; Schiffman, "*Merkavah* Speculation," 27.

[103] I have accepted the suggested reconstruction of Licht, *Thanksgiving Scroll*, 163.

[104] Here I am following a lead suggested by Newsom, DJD 11:180.

high priest:[105] "May [everlas]ting blessings be the crown of your head . . . he has chosen you . . . to raise above the heads of the holy ones. . . . May you be like the angel of presence in the holy residence for the glory of the God of the hos[ts. . . . You shall] be around, serving in the temple of the kingship, casting the lot with the angels of presence and the council of the community" (1Q28b IV, 3, 22–26).[106] The blessing bestowed on the high priest underscores the blurring of ontological boundaries, as he is impelled to become "like the angel of presence," *kemal'akh panim*,[107] so that he may take his place in the "holy abode," *ma'on qodeš*, "temple of the kingship," *heikhal malkhut*.[108] The obfuscation is reiterated in the end of the pas-

---

[105] Licht, *Rule Scroll*, 283; Lawrence H. Schiffman, *The Eschatological Community of the Dead Sea Scrolls: A Study of the Rule of Congregation* (Atlanta: Scholars Press, 1989), 72–76; Fletcher-Louis, *Glory of Adam*, 151–58.

[106] *Dead Sea Scrolls Study Edition*, 1:106–7, translation slightly modified.

[107] A possible scriptural basis for the term *mal'akh panim*, an expression attested in *Jubilees* and several Qumran sources, is *umal'akh panaw*, "and the angel of his face," in Isa 63:9, which most likely served as the basis for *ṣar happanim*, the "archon of the face," a term applied to the highest angels, which includes predominantly Yahoel, Michael, and Metatron, according to a strand of Jewish angelology attested in later rabbinic and Hekhalot literature. On the exegetical linking of *mal'akh happanim* and *ṣar happanim* as technical theophanic expressions and the aforementioned verse from Isaiah, see Saul M. Olyan, *A Thousand Thousands Served Him: Exegesis and the Naming of Angels in Ancient Judaism* (Tübingen: Mohr, 1993), 105–9; and Moshe Idel, "Metatron—Notes on the Evolution of Myth in Judaism," in *Myth and Judaism* (ed. H. Pedayah; Negev: Ben-Gurion University of the Negev Press, 1996), 29–44, esp. 36–41 [Hebrew]. For a select list of other scholarly discussions of the relevant terms, see *3 Enoch or the Hebrew Book of Enoch* (ed. and trans. H. Odeberg; Cambridge: Cambridge University Press, 1928), 83, 118–19; Gershom Scholem, *Jewish Gnosticism, Merkabah Mysticism, and Talmudic Tradition* (New York: The Jewish Theological Seminary of America, 1965), 52, 63; Jarl E. Fossum, *The Name of God and the Angel of the LORD: Samaritan and Jewish Concepts of Intermediation and the Origin of Gnosticism* (Tübingen: Mohr, 1985), 189, 220–38, 307–24; Peter Schäfer, *The Hidden and Manifest God: Some Major Themes in Early Jewish Mysticism* (trans. A. Pomerance; Albany: State University of New York Press, 1992), 36; Michael Mach, *Entwicklungsstadien des jüdischen Engelglaubens in vorrabbinischer Zeit* (Tübingen: Mohr, 1992), 3–4, 14, 40, 55, 95–96, 204, 238; Nathaniel Deutsch, *The Gnostic Imagination: Gnosticism, Mandaeism, and Merkabah Mysticism* (Leiden: Brill, 1995), 99–111; idem, *Guardians of the Gate: Angelic Vice Regency in Late Antiquity* (Leiden: Brill, 1999), 43, 152–57; James C. VanderKam, "The Angel of the Presence in the Book of Jubilees," *DSD* 7 (2000): 378–93.

[108] The angelic status of priests, a central tenet of the Qumran sectarian piety, is suggested by earlier sources, for example, Mal 2:7; *Jub.* 31:13–15. On the angelic configuration of the high priest in particular, see Sir 45:7; 50:6–7. For a detailed analysis of priestly angelomorphism in Qumran material, see Fletcher-Louis, *Glory of Adam*, 150–221. For a later echo of this theme in rabbinic literature, see especially *Sifre Num.* 119 (Horovitz ed., 143), cited and discussed in Ephraim E. Urbach, *The Sages: Their Concepts and Beliefs* (trans. I. Abrahams; Jerusalem: Magnes, 1975), 156–57. According to that homily, as one would expect from a rabbinic source, the angelic standing of the priest is dependent on his dispersing words of Torah.

sage where the high priest is said "to cast his lot with the angels of presence," but this is followed immediately by the additional claim that he casts his lot as well with the "council of the community, *'aṣat yaḥad*. In light of the way that this expression is generally used in the Scrolls, it would stand to reason that the transfigured high priest is still part of the priestly sect below. While this is surely a plausible interpretation, and indeed on one level incontestable, the conventional reading is misleading inasmuch as it obscures the apperception that the angelic camp and the priestly congregation are indifferently the same, that is, the same precisely in virtue of being different—the experience of transformation, which is ongoing and repeated rather than intermittent and singular,[109] requires that the two parties are identical and disparate, for if human and angel were not the latter, how could they be the former?

Have we not met this model of the priest-sage, the *kohen doreš hattorah*, according to the community's portrayal of the ideal teacher and leader? On the probable identification of the priest (*kohen*) and expert in the law (*doreš hattorah*) as the same person, see Falk, *Daily, Sabbath, and Festival Prayers*, 120 n. 79; Géza G. Xeravits, *King, Priest, Prophet: Positive Eschatological Protagonists of the Qumran Community* (Leiden: Brill, 2003), 169–71, 187. It is also pertinent to recall the depiction of Moses as an "angel" through whose mouth the divine speaks, *ukhemal'akh yedabber mippihu*, in 4Q377 1 II, 11, transcribed and analyzed by Najman, "Angels At Sinai," 319. The portrayal of Moses in this fragment is an interpretative gloss on the scriptural expression associated with him *'iš ha'elohim*, "man of God" (Deut 33:1; Josh 14:6), which is rendered in the Qumran fragment *'im 'elohim*, that is, "with God." To be sure, the exegesis is suggested by other verses that describe Moses as being with God in an intimate way, but it seems to be an innovation on the part of the author of this text to combine this theme with the designation *'iš 'elohim*, one of the technical labels for a prophet (Judg 13:6, 8; 1 Sam 2:27; 9:6, 10; 1 Kgs 13:1; 17:24; 2 Kgs 1:10; 4:9). See Joseph Blenkinsopp, *Sage, Priest, Prophet: Religious and Intellectual Leadership in Ancient Israel* (Louisville: Westminster John Knox, 1995), 125–26. As the text continues, the reference is to Moses and God being together in the cloud. To the roles of priest and hermeneut, we might add that of the poet, the *maśkil*, responsible for the composition of the liturgical hymns. On the divine/angelic status of Moses in Qumran literature, see also Crispin H. T. Fletcher-Louis, "4Q374: A Discourse on the Sinai Tradition: The Deification of Moses and Early Christology," *DSD* 3 (1996): 236–52; idem, *Glory of Adam*, 136–49; Xeravits, *King, Priest, Prophet*, 174–83. On the divinization of Moses in Hellenistic sources, see Hindy Najman, *Seconding Sinai: The Development of Mosaic Discourse in Second Temple Judaism* (Leiden: Brill, 2003), 95–98. For discussion of this theme in Scripture, see Jack M. Sasson, "Bovine Symbolism in the Exodus Narrative," *VT* 18 (1968): 380–87; and the different view of the image of the shining face of Moses (Exod 34:29–35) proffered by John Van Seters, *The Life of Moses: The Yahwist as Historian in Exodus-Numbers* (Louisville: John Knox, 1994), 356–60. On the avoidance of the apotheosis of Moses in Scripture, see James Nohrnberg, *Like Unto Moses: The Constituting of an Interruption* (Bloomington/Indianapolis: Indiana University Press, 1995), 36.

[109] It seems to me that this point has not been properly emphasized in the scholarly literature. If time permits, I shall return to this theme in a separate study.

In and by imagining the angel of presence adorned in priestly garb, the priest dons the cloak of the angel of presence, which is patterned on the model of the priestly garb, a double mirroring that renders the same different by the different remaining the same. This seems to be the intent of the following passage in the *Manual of Discipline*: "To those whom God has selected he has given them an everlasting possession; and he has given them an inheritance in the lot of the holy ones. He unites their assembly to the sons of heaven in order (to form) the council of the Community and a foundation of the building of holiness to be an everlasting plantation throughout all future ages" (1QS XI, 7–9). The council of the community, *ʿaṣat yaḥad*, is formed when the assembly of those whom God has chosen are united with the angels, the "holy ones," *qedošim*, "sons of heaven," *benei šamayim*, an alliance that is possible only because of the in/difference—that is, the sameness that is the ground for the ontic difference that binds members of the community and angelic beings in the mind/heart of the visionary.

As scholars of Qumran have long noted, the holiness of the desert enclave was expressed in terms of angels joining members of the community and members of the community conceiving of their own angelic identity.[110] The angelomorphic status seems to have implied as well the possibility of transport to the imaginal realm,[111] the incor-

---

[110] The angelomorphic status accorded members of the *yaḥad* is thematically related to the broader portrayal of the righteous as angels, a motif well attested in Second Temple sources. See James H. Charlesworth, "The Portrayal of the Righteous as an Angel," in *Ideal Figures in Ancient Judaism* (ed. G. W. E. Nickelsburg and J. J. Collins; Chico, Calif.: Scholars Press, 1980), 135–51; William F. Smelik, "On Mystical Transformation of the Righteous into Light in Judaism," *JSJ* 26 (1995):122–44; Crispin H. T. Fletcher-Louis, *Luke-Acts: Angels, Christology, and Soteriology* (Tübingen: Mohr Siebeck, 1997), 184–205; idem, "Some Reflections on Angelomorphic Humanity Texts Among the Dead Sea Scrolls," *DSD* 7 (2001): 292–312; idem, *Glory of Adam*, 88–135. See also Christopher R. A. Morray-Jones, "Transformational Mysticism in the Apocalyptic-Merkabah Tradition," *JJS* 43 (1992): 1–31; Elliot R. Wolfson, "*Yeridah la-Merkavah*: Typology of Ecstasy and Enthronement in Early Jewish Mysticism," in *Mystics of the Book: Themes, Topics, and Typologies* (ed. R. Herrera; New York: Peter Lang, 1993), 13–44, esp. 23–26; Daniel L. Bock, *Blasphemy and Exaltation in Judaism and the Final Examination of Jesus* (Tübingen: Mohr Siebeck, 1998), 113–83.

[111] For review of this topic, see James R. Davila, "Heavenly Ascents in the Dead Sea Scrolls," in *Dead Sea Scrolls After Fifty Years*, 2:461–85. Also pertinent here are the studies dedicated to fragments that have been reconstructed and interpreted as referring to an enthroned being, as we find, for example, in the self-glorification fragments. On this topic, see Morton Smith, "Ascent to the Heavens and Deification in 4QMᵃ," in *Archaeology and History*, 181–88; idem, "Two Ascended to Heaven— Jesus and the Author of 4Q491," in *Jesus and the Dead Sea Scrolls*, 290–301; Martin

poration of priests below with priests above into one liturgical congregation, which, I propose, is the intent in this context of the juxtaposition of the expressions "angels of presence," *maĺakhei panim*, and "council of the community," *ʿaṣat yaḥad*.[112] The seeing of the divine face through the deflection of the angelic faces by the pure heart facilitates the twofold membership—the poetic envisioning inscripted in the hymnal compositions—that renders what is above within and what is within above, a fundamental tenet of the theophanic imagination. From this perspective heavenly ascent and incarnational presence may be viewed as two ways of considering the selfsame phenomenon.[113]

G. Abegg, Jr., "Who Ascended to Heaven? 4Q491, 4Q427, and the Teacher of Righteousness," in *Eschatology, Messianism, and the Dead Sea Scrolls*, 61–73; Devorah Dimant, "A Synoptic Comparison of Parallel Sections in 4Q427 7, 4Q491 11 and 4Q471B," *JQR* 85 (1994): 157–62; Esther Eshel, "The Identification of the 'Speaker' of the Self-Glorification Hymn," in *Provo International Conference*, 619–35; Israel Knohl, *The Messiah Before Jesus: The Suffering Servant of the Dead Sea Scrolls* (trans. D. Maisel; Berkeley: University of California Press, 2000), 15–21; J. C. O'Neill, "'Who Is Comparable to Me in My Glory?': 4Q491 Fragment 11 (4Q491C) and the New Testament," *NovT* 42 (2000): 24–38.

[112] Newsom, "Established," 101–20, esp. 108–9.

[113] I thus concur with the thesis of Crispin H. T. Fletcher-Louis, "Heavenly Ascent or Incarnational Presence? A Revisionist Reading of the *Songs of the Sabbath Sacrifice*," *SBLSP* 37 (1998): 367–99.

THE CONTRIBUTION OF THE QUMRAN DISCOVERIES TO THE HISTORY OF EARLY BIBLICAL INTERPRETATION

MOSHE J. BERNSTEIN

I. INTRODUCTION

The discovery and publication of the Qumran texts have marked a watershed in the study of virtually all aspects of Judaism in antiquity.[1] Two aspects of their importance need to be stressed: first, these are primary documents which come down to us "directly" from the classical period, often as the only surviving textual material from certain segments of that era; second, these manuscripts have not been subject to editing and rewriting through the intervening centuries in the way that other texts which owe their survival to transmission within Jewish or Christian tradition often were. The scrolls often fill in gaps which had existed in our sources previously and surpass the quality of many of those already known sources by virtue of being unaffected by the biases of subsequent transmission. Access to the Dead Sea Scrolls now allows more direct, unfiltered light than was heretofore possible to be shed on this critical epoch in the development of Judaism and, later on, Christianity, spanning roughly the third century B.C.E. to the first century C.E.

One major impact which these texts have had is in their contribution to the literary history of the Second Temple era (still labeled by some Christian scholars as the "intertestamental" era). Today, in discussions of the literature of Judaism in antiquity, we expect to

---

[1] Early versions of this paper were delivered as "Biblical Interpretation Before and After Qumran," at the First International Symposium, Orion Center for the Study of the Dead Sea Scrolls and Associated Literature, Institute of Jewish Studies, The Hebrew University of Jerusalem, Jerusalem, Israel, May 1996 and as "The Impact of the Qumran Discoveries on the History of Early Biblical Interpretation," at the Fiftieth Anniversary International Jubilee Celebration on the Dead Sea Scrolls, Princeton Theological Seminary, Princeton, N.J., November 1997 (at the invitation of Professor James H. Charlesworth). It gives me great pleasure to dedicate this essay to James L. Kugel, one of the foremost scholars of early Jewish biblical interpretation in our generation.

find chapters such as "Palestinian Adaptations of Biblical Narratives and Prophecies" in Kraft and Nickelsburg, *Early Judaism and Its Modern Interpreters*, and "Stories of Biblical and Early Post-Biblical Times" and "The Bible Rewritten and Expanded" in Stone, *Jewish Writings of the Second Temple Period.*[2] Mulder's *Mikra* contains chapters on the use, authority, interpretation, and exegesis of Scripture in Qumran, Apocrypha, and Pseudepigrapha, as well as the minor Hellenistic Jewish authors and in Philo, Josephus, rabbinic literature, and the church fathers.[3] Before the Qumran discoveries, such syntheses would not have been and, in fact, were not written. In that sense, the very subdiscipline of Jewish biblical interpretation in antiquity has been reshaped, virtually reinvented, by the discovery of the Dead Sea Scrolls.

II. Early Jewish Biblical Interpretation Before the Qumran Discoveries

In order to get a sense of how early Jewish biblical interpretation was portrayed before the Qumran discoveries it is useful to examine reference works dating to before 1950. For example, in Emil Schürer's classic *Geschichte* of the late 19th–early 20th century (the suitably titled *History of the Jewish People in the Age of Jesus Christ*),[4] Palestinian Jewish literature is divided into historical writing, psalmodic poetry, wisdom literature, hortatory narrative, prophetic pseudepigrapha, and

---

[2] The chapter "Palestinian Adaptations of Biblical Narratives and Prophecies" consists of the following: Daniel J. Harrington, "The Bible Rewritten (Narratives)," and Maurya P. Horgan, "The Bible Explained (Prophecies)," in *Early Judaism and Its Modern Interpreters* (ed. R. A. Kraft and G. W. E. Nickelsburg; Atlanta: Scholars Press, 1986), 239–47 and 247–53, respectively; George W. E. Nickelsburg, "Stories of Biblical and Post-Biblical Times," and "The Bible Rewritten and Expanded," in *Jewish Writings of the Second Temple Period: Apocrypha, Pseudepigrapha, Qumran Sectarian Writings, Philo, Josephus* (CRINT 2.2; ed. M. E. Stone; Assen: Van Gorcum; Philadelphia: Fortress, 1984), 33–87 and 89–156, respectively.

[3] Martin J. Mulder, ed., *Mikra: Text, Translation, Reading and Interpretation of the Hebrew Bible in Ancient Judaism and Early Christianity* (CRINT 2.1; Assen: Van Gorcum; Philadelphia: Fortress, 1990). Mulder's volume and Magne Saebø, ed., *Hebrew Bible/Old Testament: The History of Its Interpretation: From the Beginnings to the Middle Ages* (vol. 1; Göttingen: Vandenhoeck & Ruprecht, 1996), which is the first of a series of volumes on the history of biblical interpretation, are indicative of the growing importance of the history of interpretation as a subdiscipline of biblical studies.

[4] Emil Schürer, *Geschichte des jüdischen Volkes im Zeitalter Jesu Christi* (3 volumes; 4th edition; Leipzig: Hinrichs'sche Buchhandlung, 1901–1909), 3:188–406 (§32). E.T. of volume 3, §§32–34 = E. Schürer, *The Literature of the Jewish People in the Time of Jesus* (ed., with an introduction, N. N. Glatzer; New York: Schocken, 1972).

sacred legends. There is no chapter titled "Biblical Interpretation" or "Biblical Exegesis." By way of contrast, the same section in the Vermes-Millar-Goodman revision of the 1970s and 1980s contains a chapter on "Biblical Midrash," aside from the completely new chapter on the "Writings of the Qumran Community" which has a long sub-chapter on "Bible Interpretation."[5] This is not to say that many of the works which were composed during this period were not acknowledged to be interpretations of Scripture, but that biblical interpretation seems not to have been acknowledged as a genre or a discipline. Similarly, Pfeiffer's catalogue of Jewish literary history in Eretz Yisrael from 200 b.c.e. to 100 c.e. in his *History of New Testament Times* (1949) included terms such as lyric poetry, wisdom poetry, history, fiction, legends and exhortations, apocalypse, and polemic, but the realm of biblical interpretation went unnoticed.[6]

What caused this area of ancient Jewish intellectual endeavor to be ignored as an independent unit or element worthy of consideration? The apparent scholarly neglect of the discipline of early Jewish biblical interpretation in the pre-Qumran era, by which I mean the first half of the twentieth century, the period before the Qumran discoveries, was due only in part to the paucity of relevant material. That deficiency could be, and eventually was, remedied by the discovery of new texts. More significant, however, was probably the failure to recognize the variety of generic forms which biblical interpretation could adopt. It led to the classification of a variety of works which are basically exegetical or interpretive under a variety of generic rubrics, thus placing in diverse pigeonholes material which should have been juxtaposed for analysis. These two concomitant phenomena prevented the recognition of the major role which biblical interpretation, defined loosely, played in Judaism in its various manifestations during this crucial era.

---

[5] Emil Schürer, *The History of the Jewish People in the Age of Jesus Christ (175 b.c.–a.d. 135)* (rev. and ed. G. Vermes, F. Millar, and M. Goodman; Edinburgh: T&T Clark, 1973–1986), 3.1:308–41 and 420–51, respectively.

[6] Robert H. Pfeiffer, *History of New Testament Times with an Introduction to the Apocrypha* (New York: Harper & Brothers, 1949), 60–61. If we include his categories for Jewish-Hellenistic writings, we add legendary history, epic and drama, philosophy, propaganda, autobiography and apologetics. Robert H. Charles, *The Apocrypha and Pseudepigrapha of the Old Testament in English: Pseudepigrapha* (vol. 2; Oxford: Clarendon, 1913), likewise classifies the Pseudepigrapha as "primitive history written from the standpoint of the Law," "sacred legends," "apocalypses," "psalms," "ethics and wisdom literature," and "history."

Furthermore, the works which constituted the corpus of early Jewish
biblical interpretation, formally speaking, were scattered over centuries,
among languages, and across diverse forms of Judaism. Until recently,
we lacked any ancient textual material in their original languages for
many works, including such apocryphal texts as Ben Sira (Ecclesiasticus)
and Tobit, and pseudepigraphical ones like *Jubilees*, *1 Enoch*, and the
Testament of Levi.[7] Definition by arbitrary or artificial collection, such
as the Apocrypha, and according to hypothetical sectarian source,
such as Pharisee, Judeo-Christian, or the like, rather than by literary
category, also hindered the emphasis on biblical interpretation as a
category worthy of investigation. Under the constraints of prevailing
historiographical currents, there was little intrinsic interest in the
period of the Second Temple except as the ground from which rabbinic Judaism and early Christianity sprang. Early treatments of post-
biblical Jewish literature sought therefore merely to bridge the historical
gap between Jewish literature of the *Tanakh* and the *mishnah*, or between the two testaments of which Christian Scripture is composed.
The systematic study of Jewish literature in antiquity, a significant
portion of which constitutes early Jewish biblical interpretation, seems
not to have piqued academic interest.

A further deterrent to scholarly interest in Jewish biblical interpretation in antiquity was the fact that the form of biblical commentary with which we are most familiar and which is most
recognizable as commentary, i.e., the lemmatized type which cites a
biblical text and supplies a comment upon it, appeared to be lacking
from Jewish antiquity. To be sure, it existed in Philo and, later on,
in rabbinic midrash, but each of these had a quality which allowed
them to be further discounted or ignored. Philo's interpretations of
scripture from a philosophical perspective could easily be considered
idiosyncratic and atypical because they represent commentary written
with a goal in mind (Philo's dressing the pentateuchal story in the
garb of Neoplatonism) other than the exegesis and interpretation of
the text. Furthermore, his works represent a Diaspora perspective,
differing geographically (Alexandria) and linguistically (Greek) from
the primary objects of our investigation which happen to be works
written in Hebrew or in Aramaic in Eretz Yisrael. Rabbinic material had the obvious disadvantage of being later, and often in final

---

[7] Several of these works survive in "original" languages in medieval manuscripts.
We are not always certain whether the medieval versions are original or re-translations.

form *much* later, than the Second Temple period on which we are focusing. Although it has much stronger links than Philo to the earlier documents of biblical interpretation from this period, as has been demonstrated by scholars from Vermes to Kugel, rabbinic literature nevertheless appeared to stand much more in virtual isolation before the Qumran discoveries.[8] There was rarely an attempt, with Louis Ginzberg's monumental *Legends of the Jews* being a notable exception, to locate rabbinic treatments of Scripture in the context of any other ancient interpretation.[9]

As we have noted, the "commentary form" of interpretation is largely lacking from Jewish antiquity. Much early biblical interpretation achieved its goal by rewriting the biblical story as Josephus did, introducing material which solved real or perceived exegetical difficulties, and sometimes giving an ideological twist to the narrative. "Offensive" material, in a like fashion, was omitted or de-emphasized. Generically, then, the literary form named by Vermes "rewritten Bible" constituted one of the major pieces in the uncomplicated puzzle of early biblical interpretation which existed before the Qumran discoveries (although Vermes's use of the terminology actually postdates the Qumran discoveries).[10]

---

[8] Compare, for example, Geza Vermes, *Scripture and Tradition in Judaism* (2nd ed.; Leiden: Brill, 1973); and James L. Kugel, *In Potiphar's House: The Interpretive Life of Biblical Texts* (San Francisco: HarperCollins, 1990); idem, *The Bible as It Was* (Cambridge, Mass.: Belknap Press of Harvard University Press, 1997); idem, *Traditions of the Bible: A Guide to the Bible as It Was at the Start of the Common Era* (Cambridge, Mass.: Belknap Press of Harvard University Press, 1998).

[9] Louis Ginzberg, *Legends of the Jews* (7 vols.; Philadelphia: Jewish Publication Society, 1909–1938).

[10] On the genre "rewritten Bible," see (among many others) Vermes, *Scripture and Tradition*, 95; Philip S. Alexander, "Retelling the Old Testament," in *It is Written: Scripture Citing Scripture: Essays in Honour of Barnabas Lindars, SSF* (ed. D. A. Carson and H. G. M. Williamson; Cambridge: Cambridge University Press, 1987), 99–121; Emanuel Tov, "Biblical Texts as Reworked in Some Qumran Manuscripts with Special Attention to 4QRP and 4QParaphrase of Gen and Exod," in *The Community of the Renewed Covenant: The Notre Dame Symposium on the Dead Sea Scrolls* (CJAS 10; ed. E. Ulrich and J. C. VanderKam; Notre Dame: University of Notre Dame Press, 1994), 111–34; Sidnie White Crawford, "The 'Rewritten' Bible at Qumran: A Look at Three Texts," *ErIsr* 26 (1999): *1–*8; George J. Brooke, "Rewritten Bible," in *The Encyclopedia of the Dead Sea Scrolls* (ed. L. H. Schiffman and J. C. VanderKam; 2 vols.; New York: Oxford University Press, 2000), 2:777–81, and my forthcoming treatment "'Rewritten Bible': A Generic Category Which Has Outlived Its Usefulness?" Although there are some scholars who forbear to use this term because of the implications it appears to have regarding the canonicity and authority of the "Bible" during this period, I believe that it is too useful to give up provided that it is used with care.

What representatives of this genre did pre-Qumran scholars have available? Josephus's *Antiquities* 1–11 in the first century C.E. furnishes an outstanding example of this type, as he rewrites the biblical story, adding and subtracting as he sees fit. This detailed retelling of virtually the whole of the narrative of the Hebrew Bible is probably the most extensive example of this genre of biblical commentary. In the collection called the Apocrypha, which is scriptural for certain Christian churches, the Greek version of Esther with its additions similarly shapes and revises our understanding of the story as told in the Hebrew text. The story is given a more Jewish cast, in an attempt to override the "unjewish" atmosphere of the Persian court which prevails in the original. In a somewhat different vein, the Wisdom of Solomon, in its second half, contains a retelling of the Exodus from a sapiential perspective which can often be seen as commentary on or interpretation of the Hebrew (or Greek) text of the book of Exodus.[11] It should be stressed that all of these examples were preserved in their Greek originals and that only Josephus can be said to have a connection with the center of Jewish life in Palestine, even though his *Antiquities* was written in Greek.

Pre-Qumran scholarship also had available two other works which belong to the same genre of rewritten Bible: *Jubilees*, now known from the Qumran texts to have been written originally in Hebrew, and the less well known *Liber antiquitatum biblicarum* ("Book of Biblical Antiquities"), whose author goes by the name Pseudo-Philo and which is generally also held to have had a Hebrew original and to have been written probably in Palestine.[12] Each of them covers less ground than Josephus does, yet more than any of the apocryphal material mentioned earlier, although neither of them attracted much attention

---

[11] There are two recent treatments of the Wisdom of Solomon material as interpretive: Peter Enns, *Exodus Retold: Ancient Exegesis of the Departure from Egypt in Wis 10:15–21 and 19:1–9* (HSM 57; Atlanta: Scholars Press, 1997); and Samuel Cheon, *The Exodus Story in the Wisdom of Solomon: A Study in Biblical Interpretation* (JSPSup 23; Sheffield: Sheffield Academic, 1997). The apocryphal additions to Jeremiah and Daniel, on the other hand, cannot be so easily categorized as interpretation, even though they employ the figures of the biblical story. In this area, there will always be disagreement regarding certain works as to whether their expansions of stories about biblical figures in ways which do not explicitly interpret the biblical text are to be adjudged biblical interpretation.

[12] Compare Howard Jacobson, *A Commentary on Pseudo-Philo's* Liber Antiquitatum Biblicarum *with Latin Text and English Translation* (2 vols.; AGAJU 31; Leiden: Brill, 1996); and Daniel J. Harrington, trans., "Pseudo-Philo," in *The Old Testament Pseudepigrapha* (ed. J. H. Charlesworth; 2 vols.; Garden City, N.Y.: Doubleday, 1985), 2:297–378.

at all. The fact that both existed only in translation, and in the case of *Jubilees* only in a secondary translation into Ethiopic, probably did nothing to appeal to scholarly interest.

In the pre-Qumran period of scholarship, therefore, there was no impetus to integrate the study all of these disparate documents under the single rubric of biblical interpretation. Philo and rabbinic midrash, Josephus and *Jubilees* were points on a plane which did not beg to be connected. The phenomenon of biblical interpretation, if we may so describe it, was simply too multi-dimensional to be perceived easily. The discovery of the Qumran texts therefore had far broader implications for the literary history of the Second Temple period, particularly in the area we are discussing, than merely the availability of the documents preserved in the caves per se.

III. The Qumran Contribution to the History of Early Jewish Biblical Interpretation[13]

A. *Stage One: 1947–1968*

The period after the Qumran discoveries can be divided into two parts from the perspective of the history of early biblical interpretation, although the line of demarcation between them is not completely clear. I should place the break roughly in the decade between Allegro's publication of the first volume of Cave 4 fragments in 1968 and Yadin's publication of the Temple Scroll in 1978.[14] The significance of this separation will be discussed later.

---

[13] Most of the works we shall discuss in our review of the Qumran contribution to the history of biblical interpretation are those which, employing a variety of literary forms, interpret or retell the Bible overtly, and whose exegetical or interpretive aspect is therefore overt to the reader. We should be remiss, however, if we were not to mention, at least in passing, a variety of genres at Qumran which have furnished the contemporary student of early biblical interpretation with forms and examples of exegesis that are more subtly expressed. The Qumran authors were thoroughly imbued with the text and spirit of the Hebrew Bible, and their stylistic and literary borrowings from biblical texts therefore often possess an interpretive dimension. Among the genres in which implicit interpretations may be found are the recensions of the *Hodayot*, the Thanksgiving Hymns found in both Caves 1 and 4, and the wisdom and prayer texts found scattered throughout the Qumran corpus. Even among those Qumran writings which do not reflect explicit or implicit exegesis of the Bible, there is hardly one among them whose literary form and style does not owe a great deal to the Hebrew Bible, even when not interpreting it.

[14] J. M. Allegro, with A. A. Anderson, *Qumrân Cave 4.I (4Q158–4Q186)* (DJD 5; Oxford: Clarendon, 1968); Yigael Yadin, ed., *The Temple Scroll (Megillat haMiqdash)* (3 vols.; Jerusalem: Israel Exploration Society, 1978 [Hebrew] and 1984 [English]).

Already upon the discovery and publication of the scrolls from Cave 1, it was eminently clear that Qumran would force us to reconsider our picture of early biblical interpretation. The lion's share of attention was focused on the *pesharim* from Caves 1 and 4, particularly 1QpHab. They furnished a new type of ancient exegesis, new in form, in exegetical method, and in content. The Qumran *pesharim* now provided an earlier example of the formal commentary genre than anything that we had possessed before their discovery. While it may be argued that they, like the commentaries of Philo, are very different from what passes for commentary in the twentieth century, the employment of the lemma + comment technique made it clear that from a formal standpoint we were dealing with the genre "commentary." Scholars began to compare and contrast the hermeneutics of these newly discovered documents with those of the New Testament, targum, and rabbinic midrash.[15] We were blessed with a corpus of new texts but had not yet realized that we also needed new paradigms, and so we continued to read Qumran documents as if they still fitted into our preconceived literary patterns, not realizing that new models had to, and indeed were beginning to, emerge.

Soon the *pesharim*, too, were found not to be as uncomplicated as they first appeared to be. Texts were published by Allegro from Cave 4 with names appended to them like *Florilegium* (4Q174), *Catena* (4Q177), and *Pesher on the Periods* (4Q180–181), and by van der Woude from Cave 11 called *11QMelchizedek*, all of which exhibited the familiar lemma + comment form, but in which not all biblical citations derived from the same book.[16] Regardless of whether we accept, wholly or partially, and with some or much modification, Carmignac's classic distinction among types of *pesharim*—*thématique* (based on verses

[15] Typical titles of such early scholarship: William H. Brownlee, "Biblical Interpretation among the Sectaries of the Dead Sea Scrolls," *BA* 14 (1951): 54–75; Frederick F. Bruce, *Biblical Exegesis in the Qumran Texts* (London: Tyndale, 1960); Eliezer Slomovic, "Toward an Understanding of the Exegesis in the Dead Sea Scrolls," *RevQ* 7 (1969–71): 3–15.

[16] Allegro's texts are to be found in DJD 5; Adam S. van der Woude's in "Melchisedek als himmlische Erlösergestalt in den neugefundenen eschatologischen Midraschim aus Qumran Höhle XI," *OTS* 14 (1965): 354–73. Not only these "thematic" *pesharim*, but the "continuous" *pesher* 4QpIsa^c as well, cite more than one biblical book. For a broad discussion of the various types of *pesharim*, based on the way in which they do or do not introduce citations of the biblical text with fixed formulas, cf. my "Introductory Formulas for Citation and Re-Citation of Biblical Verses in the Qumran Pesharim: Observations on a Pesher Technique," *DSD* 1 (1994): 30–70.

collected from different books in support of a single theme) and *continu* (following a single biblical book more or less continuously)—the texts which are subsumed broadly under the category *pesher* really subdivide themselves into narrower classifications.[17] It is now possible to distinguish among even the continuous *pesharim* from a variety of perspectives, but what they have in common is the citation of biblical text followed by remarks upon it. Even if the comments frequently do not really explicate the text at all but merely apply it to contemporary circumstances, the form is indubitably that of commentary. We can observe, at times, sensitivity to biblical intertextuality in the association of verses from different parts of the Bible in some of these texts, a technique which alerts us to the author's broader knowledge and comprehension of Scripture.

The other major contribution of Cave 1 to early biblical interpretation was not a new genre, like the *pesharim*, but a new representative of the genre "rewritten Bible." The *Genesis Apocryphon*, from which substantial material of previously unpublished columns has recently been published, covers, in its extant portions, no greater range than Genesis 5–15.[18] It retells the biblical "story," sometimes ranging far beyond the outlines of the biblical text with insertion of large chunks of extra-biblical material, and sometimes hewing fairly close to the words of the Bible and presenting us with a virtual translation into Aramaic. Early discussion of it focused on whether it belonged to the genre of targum or of midrash; so much were old categories still shaping our analysis.[19] Rabbinic literature and its forms still set the terms of the discussion, even though the connections of the *Apocryphon* to non-rabbinic texts like *1 Enoch* and *Jubilees* were

---

[17] Jean Carmignac, "Le document de Qumran sur Melkisédeq," *RevQ* 7 (1969–71): 360–61, cited approvingly by Maurya P. Horgan, *Pesharim: Qumran Interpretation of Biblical Books* (CBQMS 8; Washington, D.C.: Catholic Biblical Association, 1979), 3.

[18] *Editio princeps*: Nahman Avigad and Yigael Yadin, *A Genesis Apocryphon* (Jerusalem: Magnes, 1956); Joseph A. Fitzmyer, *The Genesis Apocryphon of Qumran Cave I: A Commentary* (Rome: Pontifical Biblical Institute, 1971); Jonas C. Greenfield and Elisha Qimron, "The Genesis Apocryphon Col. XII," AbrNSup 3 (1992): 70–77; Matthew Morgenstern et al., "The Hitherto Unpublished Columns of the Genesis Apocryphon," *AbrN* 33 (1995): 30–52. Together with Dr. Esti Eshel of Bar Ilan University, I am in the process of preparing a new edition of the *Apocryphon* with commentary.

[19] The following may serve as typical titles of articles on the *Apocryphon* at this time: Manfred R. Lehmann, "1Q Genesis Apocryphon in the Light of the Targumim and Midrashim," *RevQ* 1 (1958–59): 249–63; and Gerard J. Kuiper, "A Study of the Relationship between *A Genesis Apocryphon* and the Pentateuchal Targumim in Genesis 14:1–12," in *In Memoriam Paul Kahle* (BZAW 103; ed. M. Black and G. Fohrer; Berlin: Töpelmann, 1968), 149–61.

recognized from the beginning. As more research was done on this badly-preserved document, scholars gradually became more independent of the earlier classifications and began to read it on its own and in the light of other Second Temple texts with which it shared exegetical, narrative, and stylistic features.

Having mentioned the connections of the *Genesis Apocryphon* with the Enochic literature and *Jubilees*, I should note that James Charlesworth has made the point on several occasions that the kind of limited vision which I described in pre-Qumran discussions of early Jewish biblical interpretation caused the "Pseudepigraphical Literature," as a whole, to be overlooked as biblical exegesis as well. A great many of the texts belonging to that amorphous collection, in fact, convey, in different ways, insights into the way their authors read and understood Scripture. But I do not think that I am exaggerating in suggesting that a good deal of this renewed interest in the Pseudepigrapha in the last half-century is due directly to the attention which the Qumran scrolls focused on Jewish literature in antiquity, even though the publication of Charles's massive volume and its German analogues had already begun the job of rescuing the Pseudepigrapha from oblivion.[20] Qumran was more than a little responsible for the resurgence of study of the Pseudepigrapha, and the Qumran texts, now taken together with the Pseudepigrapha, forced us to deal with a genre (or genres) which had not been acknowledged properly before, and to expand the definition of what we meant by biblical interpretation in the Second Temple era. In a sense, Qumran presented background, parallels, and connection which helped give context to the previously "unconnected" works of the Pseudepigrapha.

A turning-point in our evaluation of Qumran biblical interpretation and, with it, Second Temple biblical exegesis more generally, came with Yadin's publication of the Temple Scroll in 1978. This text differed radically from earlier Qumran documents, and in a great many ways: in its considerable length, in its genre—rewritten

---

[20] James H. Charlesworth presents six "misconceptions" which "hinder the perception of the Pseudepigrapha as exegetical works" ("In the Crucible: The Pseudepigrapha as Biblical Interpretation," in *The Pseudepigrapha and Early Biblical Interpretation* [JSPSup 14; ed. J. H. Charlesworth and C. A. Evans; Sheffield: Sheffield Academic, 1993], 21–27). In note 2 he anticipated the point which I observed above independently employing Schürer as evidence that the definition of exegesis held in the early part of the century was excessively narrow. The interpretive aspect of texts which are not commentaries or translations, strictly speaking, was not seen or stressed.

Bible of a legal nature (as opposed to the earlier examples which were all primarily narrative)—and in its relative completeness. It therefore furnished an impetus for analysis from a variety of scholarly perspectives. One of those, of course, was the question of its relationship to the Hebrew Bible, not textually, but exegetically.[21] Legal exegesis at Qumran had been fairly neglected on the whole for two reasons: first, outside of CD (Damascus Document or Zadokite Fragment), found in the Cairo Genizah by Solomon Schechter and later in about ten copies in the Qumran caves, not many texts provided legal material and second, most (Christian) Qumran scholars had little interest in *halakhah*, Jewish law in its various manifestations.

As a result of our knowledge of the Temple Scroll, *Jubilees* now demanded renewed attention from a legal perspective (attention which it still has not yet fully received), and CD, that pre-Qumranic Qumran document, now had a possible relative with which to be compared. Some of the laws in CD, which had seemed strange to students of that text in the first half of the 20th century because they did not conform to the prevalent notion that all Jewish legal texts were assumed to be rabbinic, and these clearly were not, now had parallels in the scripturally formulated laws of the Temple Scroll. Looking forward from the last pre-Christian centuries of the Qumran corpus, rabbinic *midrash halakhah* now had something with which it might be correlated, not formally, but from the perspective of comparative legal exegesis.[22] We could even look into the Qumran texts and see a (the?) legal system against which the rabbis, at times, were struggling.

The publication of the Aramaic text of *1 Enoch* by Milik stimulated further interest in that pseudepigraphic apocalyptic work which, although it is related directly to only a few verses in Genesis 5–6, should probably be considered to represent one extreme boundary

---

[21] See, in addition to Yadin's introduction and commentary (Yadin, *Temple Scroll*), Jacob Milgrom, "The Qumran Cult: Its Exegetical Principles," in *Temple Scroll Studies* (JSPSup 7; ed. G. J. Brooke; Sheffield: Sheffield Academic, 1989), 165–80; idem, "The Scriptural Foundations and Deviations in the Laws of Purity of the Temple Scroll," in *Archaeology and History in the Dead Sea Scrolls* (JSPSup 8; JSOT/ASORM 2; ed. L. H. Schiffman; Sheffield: JSOT Press, 1990), 83–99. Lawrence H. Schiffman, in an extended series of articles on specific texts within the Temple Scroll, has attempted to analyze systematically the relationship of the Qumran material to the underlying biblical text.

[22] Compare Moshe J. Bernstein and Shlomo A. Koyfman, "The Interpretation of Biblical Law in the Dead Sea Scrolls: Forms and Methods," in *Biblical Interpretation at Qumran* (ed. M. Henze; Grand Rapids: Eerdmans, forthcoming).

of the exegetical process.[23] The availability of the Qumran fragments influenced the study of Ethiopic *Enoch*, stirring up renewed interest in the Enochic literature as a whole. Discussions of the Qumran Enoch material, which is not limited to the book of *1 Enoch*, but which is part of a large complex of literary material which highlights the antediluvian period, are also to be considered among the important ways in which Qumran stimulated the study of the Pseudepigrapha and its biblical interpretation.

B. *Stage Two: 1978–present*

In the long run, however, I believe that despite the significant contributions which the first three decades of Qumran scholarship made to our understanding of ancient biblical interpretation, it is the more recent publications of fragmentary scrolls from Qumran which will make the largest contribution to our study of biblical interpretation in antiquity. This is the case despite the fact that, in so many ways, the more recently published documents are more fragmentary and more enigmatic. There has been a rapid expansion in the recent past of the volume of new documents from Qumran related to the Bible. The "parabiblical" texts published in DJD 13, 19, 22, and 30 taken together supply a range of textual material which will affect our picture of early biblical interpretation on at least two levels.[24] On the first, more elementary, plane, the sheer number of texts which have been published furnishes considerable grist for the scholarly mill; the part of the picture which we have already drawn can be made more clear.

More significantly, however, these newly published documents represent more literary types, a greater variety of the genres which belong to the broad category, "biblical interpretation"; this variety in the recent Cave 4 material contrasts somewhat with the earlier period when the new texts, the *pesharim*, were all cut from rather similar cloth. It is difficult to think of significant work on early biblical interpretation in that first period of Qumran studies which did not focus on the *pesharim*, the *Genesis Apocryphon*, or variant biblical

---

[23] Josef T. Milik, ed., *The Books of Enoch: Aramaic Fragments of Qumrân Cave 4* (Oxford: Oxford University Press, 1976).

[24] J. VanderKam, consulting ed., *Qumran Cave 4.VIII: Parabiblical Texts, Part 1* (DJD 13; Oxford: Clarendon, 1994); idem, *Qumran Cave 4.XIV: Parabiblical Texts, Part 2* (DJD 19; Oxford: Clarendon, 1995); idem, *Qumran Cave 4.XVII: Parabiblical Texts, Part 3* (DJD 22; Oxford: Clarendon, 1996); D. Dimant, *Qumran Cave 4.XXI: Parabiblical Texts, Part 4: Pseudo-Prophetic Texts* (DJD 30; Oxford: Clarendon, 2001).

texts. A good example of the scholarly neglect to which I allude might be 4Q158, published by Allegro as "Biblical Paraphrase," which did not get the attention it probably deserved until the publication, less than a decade ago, of the 4QReworked Pentateuch (4Q364–367) material, which some scholars believe to represent the same text as 4Q158.

To begin at one generic extreme, the Reworked Pentateuch texts, which make up the lion's share of DJD 13, are new texts which raise the issue of biblical interpretation in antiquity at almost the most elemental level. I am not certain that we are even ready yet to respond to some of the questions which they raise, but the issues are far-reaching and touch upon areas of biblical studies beyond biblical interpretation: When does the writing of a biblical text cease and when does interpretation begin? When and where do we stop talking about Bible and begin talking about rewritten Bible?[25] There is inconsistency in the fact that we continue to refer to the Samaritan Pentateuch as a biblical text, but to 4Q364–367 as Reworked Pentateuch.[26] Sanderson's very important remarks in her book on the paleo-Hebrew Exodus scroll about the writing and editing of the biblical text in the Second Temple period have established useful parameters to begin the discussion of these questions, but the Reworked Pentateuch texts present us with some apparently paradoxical material.[27]

---

[25] Compare the arguments of Michael Segal, "4QReworked Pentateuch or 4QPentateuch?" in *The Dead Sea Scrolls Fifty Years After their Discovery: Proceedings of the Jerusalem Congress, July 20–25, 1997* (ed. L. H. Schiffman et al.; Jerusalem: Israel Exploration Society and the Shrine of the Book, 2000), 391–99.

[26] Eugene Ulrich maintains that "it is possible that yet a third edition [other than MT and SP] of the Pentateuch was circulating within Judaism in the late Second Temple period. It is arguable that the so-called '4QRP' (4Q364–367 plus 4Q158) is mislabelled and should be seen as simply another edition of the Pentateuch." Ulrich is of the opinion that the variants between MT and SP are "exactly the types of variants occurring between the MT and '4QRP'" ("The Qumran Biblical Scrolls— The Scriptures of Late Second Temple Judaism," in *The Dead Sea Scrolls in Their Historical Context* [ed. T. H. Lim et al.; Edinburgh: T&T Clark, 2000], 67–87, here 76). I have argued, in an as-yet unpublished article, that, from the standpoint of the legal material in 4QRP, at least, 4QRP goes well beyond the method and guidelines of SP, making it very unlikely that it, too, is to be considered an edition of the Pentateuch.

[27] Judith E. Sanderson, "Editorial and Scribal Processes in the Late Second Temple Period as Exhibited in the Text of Exodus," in *An Exodus Scroll from Qumran: 4QpaleoExod^m and the Samaritan Tradition* (HSS 30; Atlanta: Scholars Press, 1986), 261–306. Compare also, Crawford, "The 'Rewritten' Bible at Qumran"; eadem, "Reworked Pentateuch," in *The Encyclopedia of the Dead Sea Scrolls* (ed. L. H. Schiffman and J. C. VanderKam; 2 vols.; New York: Oxford University Press, 2000), 2:775–77; and Brooke, "Rewritten Bible," 2:778.

Tov has characterized the Reworked Pentateuch material as "a running text of the Pentateuch interspersed with exegetical additions and omissions."[28] On the one hand, the rewriting, rearranging, and supplementation which is found in these texts falls far short of the classical examples of rewritten Bible—*Jubilees*, Josephus, Pseudo-Philo, and the *Genesis Apocryphon*—but they also seem beyond the boundaries which define the Samaritan and proto-Samaritan texts as texts of the Bible. Either the scope needed to qualify for the title "rewritten Bible" has been narrowed, or the spectrum of re-edited biblical texts has been broadened. Regardless, the resolution of the major problems deriving from the Reworked Pentateuch texts may have a ripple effect on the way in which we discuss genres to either side of it on the textual/exegetical spectrum. I leave aside for now the question of the purpose of these texts, which Tov elsewhere called "a literary exercise."[29] I am perplexed by the nature of the literary exercise but have no more constructive suggestion to offer. Further study is certainly demanded.

But it is not only the Reworked Pentateuch texts which force us to rethink so much about the rewritten Bible in antiquity. DJD 13 also contains a wealth of *Jubilees* texts in their Hebrew original, the remains of eight manuscripts. It is by now a truism that *Jubilees* must have played a significant role at Qumran, but further thought must be given, in light of the many texts of *Jubilees*, as to the relationship between Genesis and *Jubilees*, on the one hand, and between those two texts and other Qumran and Second Temple interpretation of Genesis, on the other. As we are enriched by discovery and publication of such texts from Cave 4, constant re-evaluation of earlier texts and their interrelationship must continue. *Jubilees* may be considered rewritten Bible from one perspective, but is a quasi-canonical text, perhaps itself the object of commentary or the source of exegesis, from another.

Just as we have seen that the boundary between biblical text and rewritten Bible cannot always easily be discerned, it is also hard to tell where rewritten Bible ends and some other, harder to define, genre begins. When we move away from the Reworked Pentateuch texts and *Jubilees*, we leave the realm of those texts which I am com-

---

[28] Tov, DJD 13:191.
[29] Tov, "Biblical Texts as Reworked," 134.

fortable characterizing as "rewritten Bible"[30] and turn our attention to a group of texts which possess certain similarity to that genre, but which do not have the continuity or scope which I believe that that term demands. They have been given names like "pseudo-Jubilees" (4Q225–227), "Exposition on the Flood" (4Q370), "Exposition on the Patriarchs" (4Q464), "4QApocryphal Pentateuch A and B" (4Q368 and 4Q377), and "Paraphrase of Genesis-Exodus" (4Q422). As I have noted elsewhere, the names which these texts have been given in the course of their publication often promise more than the fragments actually deliver in terms of the scope and contents of the text.

4Q464 is a rather summary type of narrative touching on a variety of events in the patriarchal period, as far as we can tell from its sparse fragments. Although I have not made this point earlier in my discussion, I believe that we should always be more than a little interested in just which portions of the Bible recur in the treatments of early interpretation. Such delineations can aid us in our being able to focus on the exegetical interests of the early interpreters. 4Q464 stands out from many of the other Qumran texts of this kind which focus on the pre-patriarchal period and certain specific events in the lives of the patriarchs, particularly Abraham, by virtue of its more complete coverage of a broader range of details drawn from the whole patriarchal narrative. I have examined this issue of the distribution of the narrative Genesis material in the interpretive literature of Qumran elsewhere, and I believe that it may contain one of many keys giving us insight into the interests of the exegete-rewriter.[31]

A text like 4Q422 illustrates further by its selectivity in rewriting how the genre "interpretation" intersects with others. Its surviving material contains two columns of material from Genesis 1–3 and 6–8 and one describing the plagues of Egypt. Once again, the issue

---

[30] In the forthcoming article referred to above ("'Rewritten Bible': A Generic Category Which Has Outlived Its Usefulness?"), I argue for a return to the fairly narrow definition of rewritten Bible which was employed by Vermes when he first used the term in *Scripture and Tradition*, a substantial narrative where "the midrashist inserts haggadic development into the biblical narrative—an exegetical process which is probably as ancient as scriptural interpretation itself" (95). Texts which do not fulfill fairly narrow criteria should be subsumed, in my view, under a different rubric, perhaps employing the term "parabiblical."

[31] Moshe J. Bernstein, "The Contours of Genesis Interpretation at Qumran: Contents, Contexts and Nomenclature," in *Studies in Ancient Midrash* (ed. J. L. Kugel; Cambridge, Mass.: Harvard University Press, 2001), 57–85, esp. 73–74 and 81–82.

of scope is raised by the distribution of the material. This does not appear to be rewritten Bible of a consecutive narrative type, although it does not resemble 4Q464 as far as I can tell, and I believe strongly that all cases of selectively rewritten Bible need to be analyzed together to determine what they have in common, and whether, because not every detail of the biblical text or story is replicated in them, they represent in any sense strides toward biblical commentary.

The narrative of 4Q422 has overtones of what has been called psalmodic wisdom and perhaps should sensitize us to biblical interpretation from a sapiential vantage point. Creation, the first sin of man, the flood, and the plagues of Egypt are selected from the pentateuchal narrative because their subject matter conforms to the didactic goals of the interpreter. As has been shown by Chazon, Collins, and Elgvin, there may be connections between the biblical interpretation in a work like 4Q422 and such generically different texts as Ben Sira, *Dibre Hame'orot*, and the recently published sapiential works from Cave 4.[32]

The tone of a work such as 4Q370, "an admonition based on the flood," resembles that of 4Q422 in the interests of its author in the disobedience-punishment cycle but does not have even the resemblance to a rewritten narrative possessed by the latter text. In a few lines, the author contrasts God's bestowal of bounty on the earth in the antediluvian era with the rebelliousness of man at that time which led to the flood, followed by an allusion to the rainbow and the covenant which accompanied it. It is quite clear, particularly from the remains of the next column, that the story has been told for a didactic purpose and not in order to interpret its narrative. Such retelling, needless to say, also reflects interpretation. This material from Qumran points toward the existence of a trend in biblical interpretation of wisdom retelling, and we would do well to re-examine

---

[32] Esther G. Chazon, "The Creation and Fall of Adam in the Dead Sea Scrolls," in *The Book of Genesis in Jewish and Oriental Christian Interpretation: A Collection of Essays* (ed. J. Frishman and L. Van Rompay; Traditio Exegetica Graeca 5; Louvain: Peeters, 1997), 13–24; John J. Collins, "Wisdom, Apocalypticism and the Dead Sea Scrolls," in *"Jedes Ding hat seine Zeit..."*: *Studien zur israelitischen und altorientalischen Weisheit Diethelm Michel zum 65. Geburtstag* (ed. A. A. Diesel et al.; Berlin: de Gruyter, 1996), 19–32, esp. 26–27; and Torleif Elgvin, "Admonition Texts from Qumran Cave 4," in *Methods of Investigation of the Dead Sea Scrolls and the Khirbet Qumran Site: Present Realities and Future Prospects* (Annals of the New York Academy of Sciences 722; ed. M. O. Wise et al.; New York: New York Academy of Sciences, 1994), 179–96, esp. 188.

pre- and extra-Qumranic wisdom texts and texts with wisdom overtones in order to determine whether the Qumran material is to be
located in a larger Second Temple context.

Although the lion's share of Qumran rewriting or retelling of the
Pentateuch relates the stories in Genesis, particularly through the
Aqedah, there is a group of texts that center on portions of the biblical narrative which focus on Moses. Among them are "Words of
Moses" (1Q22), "Apocryphal Pentateuch A" (4Q368), and "Apocryphal
Pentateuch B" (4Q377).[33] They all contain, in various proportions, text
which is based on the pentateuchal narratives of Exodus, Numbers,
and Deuteronomy and freely composed material integrated into the
biblical story. But each of these texts is so fragmentary that we can
have no sense of any sweeping narrative in any of them: 1Q22
reflects several passages in Deuteronomy, the remains of 4Q368 contain material from Exodus and Numbers, and 4Q377 seems to refer
to events in the wilderness, including the revelation at Sinai, although
the state of the text does not allow us to say much more than that.
These texts, among others, should reinforce the *caveat* that we cannot make the Qumran fragments say more than they actually do,
and, although it is fascinating to note that there were apparently
documents which dealt with the wanderings of the Israelites in the
desert, focusing on Moses, we know almost nothing about their scope,
their nature, or their balance between biblical and extra-biblical
material. Their contribution, then, to the history of early biblical
interpretation is both limited and frustrating.

Several texts described by VanderKam, somewhat reluctantly I
believe, as pseudo-Jubilees clearly belong to the area of biblical interpretation, although their genre is unclear.[34] They are not rewritten

---

[33] 1Q22 in D. Barthélemy and J. T. Milik, *Qumran Cave 1* (DJD 1; Oxford:
Clarendon, 1955), 91–97; 4Q368 and 4Q377 in D. M. Gropp, *Wadi Daliyeh II: The
Samaria Papyri from Wadi Daliyeh*; J. VanderKam and M. Brady, consulting eds.,
Qumran Cave 4.XXVIII: Miscellanea, Part 2 (DJD 28; Oxford: Clarendon, 2001), 131–49
and 205–17, respectively.

[34] "The texts employ language that is familiar from and to some extent characteristic of *Jubilees*, but the documents themselves are not actual copies of *Jubilees*"
(VanderKam, DJD 13:142). Subsequently, VanderKam moved to a different sort
of description of the relationship between *Jubilees* and pseudo-Jubilees: "*Jubilees* and
4Q225 appear to be markedly different kinds of compositions. For all we know, they
could be two largely independent embodiments of exegetical traditions, or, if the author
of 4Q225 knew *Jubilees*, he manifestly altered it in his retelling of Genesis 22. There
appears to be no justification for classifying the cave 4 text as 'pseudo-Jubilees'
because it is not, as nearly as we can tell, pretending to be the work of this author,
nor is there any indication that anyone thought it was. 4Q225 seems to be another,

Bible, since their goal seems not to be the retelling of the extended
biblical narrative, unless we expand further the range of that already
strained genre. It is not clear even that all of these belong to a single category, and they thus highlight one of the problems which the
wealth of new material from Qumran poses to the student of early
biblical interpretation. We operated before Qumran with few examples, relatively speaking, of biblical interpretation, even after we
include texts which we can now consider to be exegetical, but which
were not acknowledged as such in the early part of the century.
These pre-Qumran texts possess insufficient generic variety to be
able to provide classifications or categories for so much of the new
exegetical material from Qumran. It is possible that the association
of the new texts on the grounds of occasional linguistic similarity
with the previously known work, *Jubilees*, is not strongly justified and
may even be misleading at times. But the temporary association is
understandable as we struggle to make sense out of the newly discovered corpus in light of earlier material.

The distribution of biblical material in these Qumran texts also
appears to break new ground when compared with already known
documents. Thus whereas 4Q225, pseudo-Jubilees[a], seems to retell
with supplementation a small selection of the stories of Genesis and
Exodus, 4Q226, pseudo-Jubilees[b], contains a reference to the Aqedah,
but also references to Moses' not crossing the Jordan, while 4Q227,
pseudo-Jubilees[c], has one text referring to Moses and another one
to Enoch. We cannot easily classify these documents generically in
the light of earlier material, and perhaps we need to look for fresh
terminology and categories in order to make our overall pattern of
early biblical interpretation a coherent one. I have suggested elsewhere that these works which resemble rewritten Bible, but with very
limited scope, may represent the first steps toward recognizable biblical commentary.[35]

Cave 4, additionally, does provide works which genuinely merit
the designation commentary, and this is the nomenclature which
their editor, George Brooke, has decided upon for them (4Q252–
253–253a–254–254a), replacing their former, less appropriate,

---

extra-Jubilean interpretation of Genesis passages, another more independent witness
to the importance of Genesis at Qumran" ("The *Aqedah*, *Jubilees* and PseudoJubilees,"
in *Quest for Context and Meaning: Studies in Biblical Intertextuality in Honor of James A. Sanders*
[BIS 28; ed. C. A. Evans and S. Talmon; Leiden: Brill, 1997], 241–61, here 261).
[35] Bernstein, "Contours of Genesis Interpretation," 66 and 84.

classification as *pesharim* on Genesis.[36] This redefinition also serves to point up how our conceptions about biblical interpretation which developed in the early days of Qumran scholarship are now subject to the same sort of re-evaluation that our pre-Qumranic views were. In the 1950s and early 1960s, the only kind of commentary which Qumran offered was *pesher*, Qumran's new contribution, and in the classification process these commentaries were likewise assigned that name.[37] Our growing familiarity with the broader range of material from the caves, which may have differed both from pre-Qumran texts and from the Qumran documents which were published early, forces us to maintain a more flexible stance in classifying the new in light of the old.

Just what kind of commentary 4Q252 (Genesis Commentary A) is has been the subject of a running discussion between George Brooke and myself, and there is no need to repeat it here.[38] What is important is that we both see it as differing generically from anything we possessed before, either within or outside of Qumran material.[39] The other Genesis "commentaries" bear their classification less easily, and, although it is clear that they belong to the broad genre of biblical interpretation and that they pertain in parts to Genesis, they do not resemble Commentary A at all.[40] Some of the fragments of 4Q254 (Genesis Commentary C) seem unconnected with Genesis, raising the kind of scope problem which we saw also regarding pseudo-Jubilees. In the case of the pre-Qumran material, at least,

---

[36] These five texts have been published in DJD 22:185–236; 4Q253a is a "commentary" on Malachi, not Genesis.

[37] It should be admitted that the first publication of material from the final columns of 4Q252 Genesis Commentary A by Allegro under the name "4Qpesher Patriarchal Blessings" misled scholars. That portion of the text, commenting on Jacob's blessings in Genesis 49, is more "*pesher*-like" than anything else in the document, and the word פשרו ("its interpretation") actually occurs in column 4, line 5.

[38] See George J. Brooke's articles, "The Genre of 4Q252: From Poetry to Pesher," *DSD* 1 (1994): 160–79; "The Thematic Content of 4Q252," *JQR* 85 (1994–95): 33–59; and "4Q252 as Early Jewish Commentary," *RevQ* 17 (1996): 385–401. Compare my treatments, "4Q252: From Re-Written Bible to Biblical Commentary," *JJS* 45 (1994): 1–27; and "4Q252: Method and Context, Genre and Sources. A Response to George J. Brooke," *JQR* 85 (1994–95): 61–79. Our positions on the interpretation of this text have grown closer in the course of our vigorous dialogue on the topic.

[39] I find it very difficult to accept Tov's inclusion of this text in the category "rewritten and rephrased Bible texts from Qumran" (DJD 13:187).

[40] I have discussed these issues in a bit more detail in "Contours of Genesis Interpretation," 69–70.

we could look at whole works which we were able to classify in
known genres. We should always be cognizant of the fact that the
fragmentary nature of the Qumran texts may preclude clear generic
identification, but at the same time we must realize that our knowledge of the field is still insufficient for us to be able to recognize
what we see.

In addition to the range of genres represented in the works which
contain pentateuchal interpretation at Qumran, the Dead Sea Scrolls
have expanded the range of the known treatments in Jewish antiquity of material from the section of the Hebrew Bible known as the
Prophets.[41] While before the Qumran discoveries there was a very
limited amount of early Jewish exegesis which focused on the prophets,
such as the narrative material in Josephus (*Ant.* 5–11.303) and in
Pseudo-Philo (*L.A.B.* 20–65), the scrolls present several new genres
based on the prophets, in addition to the *pesharim* discussed earlier.[42]
Granted the very limited number of texts previously available which
pertain to the prophets, the two or three works of which we are
about to take notice are equivalent to several times that number of
works pertaining to the Pentateuch.

One of them, the *Apocryphon of Joshua*, is a work which has been
reconstructed by Emanuel Tov on the basis of a variety of texts
which had originally been given diverse names.[43] He "cautiously suggests" that these "six manuscripts cover different themes and episodes
from the book of Joshua" and comments further that "the term
'apocryphon' is probably not the most appropriate name for this
composition and, in fact, a term like 'paraphrase of Joshua' would
be more appropriate."[44] Tov argues that 4Q522, formerly known as
"Work with Place Names," is connected to 4Q378–379, originally

---

[41] In order not to enter into a discussion about the possible anachronistic use of
the term, I merely refer to the implicit division of the Bible which is implied in
4QMMT[d] (4Q397 14–21 10), the translator's prologue to Ben Sira, Luke 24:44,
and Josephus *C. Ap.* 1.37–43, regardless of whether a tripartite division is implied
in any of them.

[42] For a survey of some of this material, as well as other texts related in different
ways to the prophets, see George J. Brooke, "Parabiblical Prophetic Narratives," in
The Dead Sea Scrolls After Fifty Years: A Comprehensive Assessment (ed. P. W. Flint and
J. C. VanderKam; 2 vols.; Leiden: Brill, 1998), 1:271–301.

[43] Emanuel Tov, "The Rewritten Book of Joshua as Found at Qumran and
Masada," in *Biblical Perspectives: Early Use and Interpretation of the Bible in Light of the
Dead Sea Scrolls* (STDJ 28; ed. M. E. Stone and E. Chazon; Leiden: Brill, 1998),
233–56. Earlier studies are cited by Tov in nn. 1–8 on pp. 234–37.

[44] Ibid., 233.

published as 4QPsalms of Joshua and now named 4QapocrJosh[a,b].[45] He compares the nature of the biblical paraphrase to "that of the Book of Jubilees, the second half of the Temple Scroll, 4QparaGen-Exod (4Q422) and several other fragmentary compositions" in the way the text sometimes follows and sometimes moves away from the biblical text. In summarizing the "coverage" of the hypothetical document, Tov points out that "segments of most of the chapters of the book of Joshua are represented."[46] In the likely event that Tov's reconstruction is correct, and despite the fragmentary nature of the text, this new Qumran text expands the range of Second Temple treatments of the biblical story much more than another treatment of the Pentateuch would.

The other two major recent Qumran contributions to the "interpretation" of the prophets in antiquity are the texts published by Devorah Dimant in DJD 30 under the rubrics 4QPseudo-Ezekiel and 4QApocryphon of Jeremiah. The delay in their publication was due significantly to the fact that they were among the most difficult of the Qumran documents to sort and classify, and the ultimate assignment of the names by which they are now known was the result of a long process.[47] These heretofore unknown texts rewrite and interpret the prophecies of Jeremiah and Ezekiel, and it should be (and has been) noted that neither of these books is represented by dedicated *pesharim* in the surviving manuscripts at Qumran,[48] while the prophetic works which do have *pesharim*, notably Isaiah, do not seem to have been treated in the fashion of Jeremiah and Ezekiel.

According to Dimant, "The two compositions differ noticeably with regard to style and content."[49] Other than the obvious distinctions in content, such as the fact that pseudo-Ezekiel mentions Ezekiel by name and rewrites some of his canonical prophecies while pseudo-

---

[45] Ibid., 247–49. The other texts which Tov attempts to integrate into this "apocryphon" are 5Q9 ("Ouvrage avec toponymes"), Mas 11 (MasParaJosh=Mas 1039–211), and possibly 4Q123 (4QpaleoParaJosh).

[46] Ibid., 253.

[47] Dimant's publication of this material in DJD 30 must be the starting point for any study. For a compact review of these and some related texts, written before the final DJD edition, see Brooke, "Parabiblical Prophetic Narratives," 278–90.

[48] Dimant notes that there are *pesher* interpretations of Ezekiel in CD III, 21–IV, 2 and XIX, 11–13, in 4QFlorilegium 1–2 I, 16–17, and perhaps in 4Q177 (4QCatena A) 7 3–5, despite the fact that there is no surviving continuous *pesher* on Ezekiel (DJD 30:13).

[49] Dimant, DJD 30:7.

Jeremiah is modeled primarily on Deuteronomy and Jeremiah,[50] it is striking to note that "the extant passages from *Pseudo-Ezekiel* deal with eschatological issues, while *Apocryphon of Jeremiah* C produces a review of history. *Pseudo-Ezekiel* reveals no trace of sectarian terminology, while *Apocryphon of Jeremiah* C betrays many stylistic and ideological affinities with sectarian literature."[51] Of particular interest is the concern of pseudo-Ezekiel to interpret Ezekiel's vision of the "Dry Bones" (preserved in three copies of the text) as "presenting the future reward for the righteous in the form of resurrection ... the most ancient witness to such an exegesis of Ezek 37:1–14, later popular with Jewish and Christian authors."[52]

Unlike pseudo-Ezekiel, the newly published "Apocryphon of Jeremiah C" is a review of history, addressed to the prophet Jeremiah, running through the Second Temple era and ultimately reaching the eschaton.[53] Dimant has presented a coherent reconstruction of the six fragmentary manuscripts which she believes belong to this apocalyptic work, including a narrative frame into which the historical vision of Jeremiah is inserted.[54] Differing from other Jeremiah material surviving from antiquity, it stretches from the desert wanderings of the Israelites to the monarchy to the destruction of the First Temple in the past of "Jeremiah" and proceeds into the future depicting Israel's sin and further domination by the "angels of Mastemot," until the eschaton which seems to be alluded to in several fragments.

The substance of the Jeremiah Apocryphon is much less anchored in the biblical book of Jeremiah than the pseudo-Ezekiel texts are in the book of Ezekiel. As a result, the student of early biblical interpretation is presented with two types of expansion of biblical prophetic books. This should lead students of these two documents in the near future to consider the following question: How do the differing genres of these works deriving from biblical prophetic works affect the way in which we evaluate them as interpretation of the Bible, as

---

[50] Ibid.

[51] Ibid.

[52] Ibid., 9. Dimant attempts to locate the pseudo-Ezekiel material in the broader context of ancient Jewish and Christian literature (9–12).

[53] Ibid., 91. Dimant labels 4Q383 "Apocryphon of Jeremiah A," but rejects 4Q384 ("papApocryphon of Jeremiah B?") published by Mark Smith in DJD 19:153–93, from belonging together with these two MSS (95).

[54] Dimant summarizes the contexts (ibid., 96–99) and presents a schematic outline (ibid., 99–100).

opposed to stories which adopt a biblical framework but do not put much effort into the elucidation or the comprehension of the biblical text? It would appear upon cursory examination that pseudo-Ezekiel offers more overt opportunity for its author to reflect upon the meaning of the Bible than does the Apocryphon of Jeremiah. To refer to the latter, then, as biblical interpretation is to stretch our spectrum of works which we feel interpret the Bible, but we include it in our survey as a reminder that at Qumran, as in the Second Temple period more broadly, there is often no sharp dividing line between works which offer interpretation of the biblical text and those which use the Bible as a springboard for what are in effect freestanding, often ideologically motivated, compositions.

IV. Conclusions

How then have the Qumran discoveries changed the picture of early biblical interpretation? In general, the Dead Sea Scrolls have enabled us to develop a more profound understanding of the roles—and not merely the role—which the Bible played in all aspects of Jewish intellectual life and creativity in Second Temple times. In particular, they have contributed in at least four specific ways: first, they have aided in putting interpretation on the map as an independent discipline; second, they have provided us with a substantial body of new texts involving biblical interpretation which can be dated within fairly narrow chronological boundaries, relatively speaking; third, they have added new works, like the *Genesis Apocryphon*, to genres already known; and fourth, by furnishing examples of new genres, beginning with the *pesharim* and extending to the generically problematic parabiblical texts from Cave 4 with a variety of texts in between, they have broadened the range of the genres which constitute biblical interpretation. The material which existed before the Qumran discoveries—whether already the object of academic inquiry, then, like rabbinic literature, Philo, or Josephus, or relatively neglected, like the Pseudepigrapha—now can be read as part of a much broader body of literature, and not in isolation from one another. Together with the Pseudepigrapha, Qumran has driven home the message that commentary is not the only form of biblical interpretation and that such interpretation in Second Temple Judaism took a heretofore unimaginable number of forms.

So what could be bad? As I stressed earlier, Qumran does not
furnish only solutions; it furnishes problems as well. The major problem presented may be the very ease of focusing all of our scholarly
attention on Qumran because it is exciting and (relatively) new. There
is a slight danger of a pan-Qumranism if we allow Qumran and its
texts to dominate our understanding of early biblical interpretation
too much. It is an attractive temptation; scholars, like the public,
can be seduced by the lure of Qumran. As we read these new and
unusual Qumran texts, we must go back and re-read long-known
Qumran texts, as well as biblical interpretation of which we were
aware before the Qumran discoveries. It is probably wrong to let
any form, time-period, or corpus dominate our conception of the
variegated field of early biblical interpretation. Qumran, although
clearly an independent subdiscipline from certain perspectives, must
be acknowledged to be only a piece of a much larger composite of
early biblical interpretation which begins with material within the
Hebrew Bible itself and includes the Apocrypha, Pseudepigrapha,
hellenistic Jewish writers, Josephus, Philo, New Testament, and rabbinic literature.

We must acknowledge what the Qumran texts can and cannot
contribute to drawing the picture of early Jewish biblical interpretation. The texts from Qumran, as challenging and fascinating as
we find them, must be admitted to be only what they are and not
more: fragments of works of uncertain scope, function, and context.
As such, they can only be dots on the lines which connect the
Hebrew Bible to later Jewish literature, and since those dots can be
connected in many different ways, they do not form a clear continuum, either within the Qumran writings or with other works of
interpretation outside of Qumran. We also are limited to the genres which these texts preserve; we should like to have more explicit
legal texts, for example, to contrast with rabbinic material; we should
like more whole texts of any genre, but we are stuck with what survived, and not more. Only if we are able to maintain a propor-
tioned focus on Qumran interpretation as only a part of a broader
collection of corpora will our comprehension of both the microstruc-
ture of Qumran exegesis and the macrostructure of Jewish biblical
interpretation in antiquity as a whole be enhanced.

MYTH, HISTORY, AND MYSTERY IN THE COPPER SCROLL

STEVEN P. WEITZMAN

For those who like a good mystery, it is hard to do better than the *Copper Scroll*. Found in a remote desert cave, the *Copper Scroll* took some three years to open. What scholars found inscribed on its two copper tablets was a kind of treasure map, an itemization of specific quantities of hidden coins and other objects with brief instructions for where to look for them. Here are a few lines from the beginning of the scroll:

> In the ruin which is in the valley of Achor, under the steps leading to the East, forty long cubits: a chest of silver and its vessels with a weight of forty talents. KEN. In the sepulchral monument, in the third course: one hundred gold ingots. In the great cistern of the courtyard of the peristyle in a hollow in the floor covered with sediment, in front of the upper opening: nine hundred talents. (I, 1–8)[1]

One cannot help but wonder where these treasures are, but that is only one of many enigmas posed by the scroll. Who hid the treasures and why? What circumstances led to their concealment, and who was intended to find them? These questions may remain unanswered forever, alas, because the scroll itself discloses no information about the circumstances in which it was composed. It does not begin with any kind of explanatory preamble that might help to identify its author or the origins of the treasure, and nothing in the scroll links it or its

---

[1] I draw on the text and translation in *The Dead Sea Scrolls Study Edition* (ed. F. García Martínez and E. Tigchelaar; 2 vols.; Leiden: Brill, 1997). For the *Copper Scroll* in particular, see also Al Wolters, *The Copper Scroll: Overview, Text and Translation* (Sheffield: Sheffield Academic, 1996). The text was originally made public by J. T. Milik in M. Baillet, J. T. Milik, and R. de Vaux, *Les 'petites grottes' de Qumrân* (DJD 3; Oxford: Clarendon, 1962), 201–302. Recent restoration efforts between 1993 and 1996 now allow for more precise readings (suggesting, for instance, that there may only be 61 items listed in the scroll, not 64 as most scholars thought previously). See Emile Puech, "Some Results of the Restoration of the Copper Scroll by EDF Mécénat," in *The Dead Sea Scrolls: Fifty Years after their Discovery: Proceedings of the Jerusalem Congress, July 20–25, 1997* (ed. L. Schiffman, E. Tov, and J. VanderKam; Jerusalem: IES, 2000), 889–94. For commentary, see Judah Lefkovits, *The Copper Scroll-3Q15: A Reevaluation* (Leiden: Brill, 2000).

treasures clearly to the Qumran sect or any other specific community.

Some mysteries are too tantalizing to resist, however. Despite the paucity of evidence, scholars have tried to use what few clues there are to reconstruct where the treasures came from and why they were hidden. They have made one discovery that seems fairly certain: a good portion of the *Copper Scroll*'s treasures is cultic in nature—tithe vessels, libation bowls, sacred garments. By one count, approximately twenty-five percent of the list's sixty-one or so hiding places contain religious materials, and this does not exclude a cultic provenance for the rest of the treasure as well, mostly coin hoards that could have come from the Temple treasury or been intended for deposit there.[2] Even the *Copper Scroll* itself may have had some cultic significance, for the only other mention of a copper tablet in the Dead Sea Scrolls, a fragmentary reference in the *Temple Scroll*, associates it with the Temple.[3] Apparently, the scroll and its contents have some connection to Jewish ritual practice.

The nature of this connection is the subject of endless debate. The most popular hypothesis is that the treasures come from the Temple itself, having been concealed during or shortly after the Jewish Revolt to protect it from the Romans.[4] According to Josephus, Jews in this period hid much treasure underground (*J.W.* 7.114–115). Josephus also reports that many of the treasures that were in the Temple at the time of Jerusalem's conquest did not escape in this way, having been handed over to the Romans by two priests named Jesus and Phinehas (6.390–391), but this does not preclude the possibility that some objects were smuggled out of Jerusalem before-

---

[2] See Manfred Lehmann, "Identification of the Copper Scroll Based on its Technical Terms," *RevQ* 5 (1964): 97–105; P. Kyle McCarter, "The Copper Scroll Treasure as an Accumulation of Religious Offerings," in *Methods of Investigation of the Dead Sea Scrolls and the Khirbet Qumran Site: Present Realities and Future Prospects* (ed. M. Wise et al.; Annals of the New York Academy of Sciences 722; New York: New York Academy of Sciences, 1994), 133–48; Al Wolters, "History and the Copper Scroll," in ibid., 285–98, esp. 292 (which identifies cultic terms in 32 places in the scroll); Lefkovits, *Copper Scroll*, 505–45.

[3] 11Q19 XXXIII, 5–XXXIV, 1: "when they finish burning . . . in a cop[per] tablet . . . and between column and col[umn]."

[4] See, for instance, Cecil Roth, *The Historical Background of the Dead Sea Scrolls* (Oxford: Blackwell, 1958), 44–45, 67; John Allegro, *The Treasure of the Copper Scroll* (Garden City, N.Y.; Doubleday, 1960), 120–29; Norman Golb, "The Problem of the Origin and Identification of the Dead Sea Scrolls," *APSP* 124 (1980): 1–24; McCarter, "Copper Scroll," 140 (as one of two scenarios he considers possible); Wolters, "History and the Copper Scroll," 292.

hand or without Josephus's knowledge. Such seems to be the view of those who read the *Copper Scroll* as a guide to where those treasures were buried, a view that has in its favor the fact that many of the hiding places listed in the scroll are in Jerusalem or its vicinity.[5] This is not the only possibility, however. The treasures may have been going in the opposite direction at the time of their concealment, on their way to Jerusalem as a collection of cultic offerings but obstructed by the Roman siege of the city or the destruction of the Temple.[6] Other scholars suggest that the treasure belonged to the Qumran sect, set aside for eventual deposit in the eschatological Temple.[7] Yet another theory assigns the treasure to the Bar Kochba rebels, serving their putative attempt to restore the Temple.[8] Although these reconstructions differ from one another in many ways, they do share some things in common. All attempt to historicize the treasures, to read their concealment as a response to real events. Also, because the treasures seem religious in nature, most see the act of hiding them as religious as well, preserving some aspect of ritual activity in the absence of a working Temple.

---

[5] For a comparison with other temple inventories in this period, note David Wilmot, "The Copper Scroll of Qumran (3Q15) and the Graeco-Roman Temple Inventories (Abstract)," *AAR/SBL Abstracts* (Atlanta: Scholars Press, 1984), 214. For hiding places with "priestly" names, note (1) the ford of the high priest in VI.14–VII.1; (2) the name Zadok, the most influential priestly clan in Jerusalem, in XI.3 (Zadok's tomb) and XI.5–6 (Zadok's garden); and (3) mention of "Haqqos" in VII.9, the name of another priestly family (cf. 1 Chr 24:10). Milik, (DJD 3:258) cites evidence that the latter may have been entrusted with guarding the Temple treasury in the Second Temple.

[6] P. Kyle McCarter considers the first a possibility in "The Mysterious Copper Scroll: Clues to Hidden Temple Treasure?" *BAR* 18 (1992): 34–41, 63–64; and "Copper Scroll," 140–41. For the second, see Lehmann, "Identification of the Copper Scroll"; idem, "Where the Temple Tax was Buried: The Key to Understanding the Copper Scroll," *BAR* 19 (1993): 38–43. These and other theories have been reviewed by Al Wolters, "The Copper Scroll," in *The Dead Sea Scrolls After Fifty Years: A Comprehensive Assessment* (ed. P. Flint and J. VanderKam; 2 vols.; Leiden: Brill, 1998), 1:302–23; Lefkovits, *Copper Scroll*, 455–59.

[7] See Bargil Pixner, "Unraveling the Copper Scroll Code: A Study of the Topography of 3Q15," *RevQ* 11 (1983): 323–58, esp. 339–40. Others who associate it with Qumran include Puech, "Results," 893–94 (who reexamined Cave 3 together with Pixner); and Stephen Goranson, "Sectarianism, Geography, and the Copper Scroll," *JJS* 43 (1992): 282–87, esp. 282. The chief argument for this view is that the *Copper Scroll* was found with other texts identified as sectarian.

[8] Ben-Zion Luria (*The Copper Scroll from the Desert of Judea* [Jerusalem: Kiryath Sepher, 1963] [Hebrew]) identifies the treasure as the property of a hypothetical third Temple that Luria believes existed briefly during the Bar Kochba period; Ernest-Marie Laperrousaz, "Remarques sur l'origine des rouleaux de cuivre découvertes dans la grotte 3 de Qumran," *RHR* 159 (1961): 157–72.

The assumption that the *Copper Scroll* records a real treasure is what distinguishes these hypotheses from another way of reading the scroll first proposed by J. T. Milik. Milik argued that the scroll was not a record of actual buried wealth but a collection of legendary treasures inspired by the story of the hidden ark attested in 2 Maccabees and other early Jewish sources.[9] According to this story, the contents of Solomon's Temple had been concealed just before the Babylonian exile, remaining somewhere within the land of Israel or nearby until such time as the Jews could return from exile.[10] In 2 Maccabees, for instance, Jeremiah hides the ark of the covenant and the tent of meeting, the two most important objects in the First Temple, in a cave in the mountain where Moses had viewed the promised land (2 Macc 2:4–8). Their location was to remain a secret until God decided to have mercy on his people and return them to the land. As *Syriac Baruch* tells the story, it was God's angels who hid the Temple's contents, consisting in this version of the Temple veil, the ephod, the priestly vestments, precious stones that adorned the priests, and other Temple vessels, and they did so by burying them underground (*2 Bar.* 6:7–9). Noting that the scroll does not list items like the ark, Milik acknowledged that its author might have adapted this legend in light of the Second Temple, but he nonetheless maintained that the treasure itself was imaginary, something one would never find if one looked for it, as some scholars have attempted to do, because it was never there to begin with.

Since this essay is dedicated to James Kugel, a master at digging up biblical exegesis buried in Second Temple literature, I cannot resist a brief digression on the hidden ark legend as a response to the biblical text. The hidden ark legend obviously constitutes biblical exegesis in the sense that it addresses one of the great unsolved mysteries of biblical narrative: whatever became of the ark of the covenant and other objects featured in the Pentateuchal cult?[11]

---

[9] Milik, DJD 3:275–84. Others who shared this view were L. H. Silberman, "A Note on the Copper Scroll," *VT* 10 (1960): 77–79; and Sigmund Mowinckel, "The Copper Scroll—An Apocryphon?" *JBL* 76 (1957): 261–65.

[10] For studies of the Ark legend as manifest in these sources, see George Nickelsburg, "Narrative Traditions in the Paralipomena of Jeremiah and 2 Baruch," *CBQ* 35 (1973): 60–67; Marilyn F. Collins, "The Hidden Vessels in Samaritan Traditions," *JSJ* 3 (1972): 97–116.

[11] See Menahem Haran, "The Disappearance of the Ark," *IEJ* 13 (1963): 46–58; idem, *Temples and Temple Service in Ancient Israel: An Inquiry into the Character of Cult Phenomena and the Historical Setting of the Priestly School* (Oxford: Clarendon, 1978), 276–88.

Although supposedly central to the Temple cult, the ark, the tent of meeting and other important items are missing from the list of cult vessels plundered by the Babylonians when they destroyed the Temple (2 Kgs 24–25), and nowhere does the Hebrew Bible disclose what became of them or their present whereabouts. The hidden ark legend answers these questions by asserting that the ark and other missing objects were hidden before the Temple's destruction. As Kugel has shown, what early interpreters said about the Bible often arose from a particular place in the biblical text, a mystifying or suggestive phrase within a specific verse.[12] The hidden ark legend may reflect this characteristic of early exegesis as well. In 2 Maccabees, which preserves one of the earliest extant versions of the legend, it is Jeremiah who hides the ark and the tent. Why is the prophet given this task? His role may have been suggested by a verse in the book of Jeremiah:

> In those days, says the LORD, they shall no longer say "the ark of the covenant of the LORD." It shall not come to mind, or be remembered, or missed; nor shall another one be made. (Jer 3:16)

With some tugging, the Hebrew of this passage can be read not as a prophecy but as a divine command, God telling Jeremiah: "Let the ark not come to mind, or be remembered or sought out." In the light of this reinterpretation, the Jeremiah of 2 Maccabees appears to be following the divine order in Jer 3:16, placing the ark out of sight and preventing others from finding it. Now it is true that 2 Maccabees does not cite this verse explicitly—if it did, what I am arguing would be obvious—but it may refer to it obliquely: "the prophet, *having received an oracle*, ordered that the tent and the ark should follow with him" (2 Macc 2:4). To what oracle can 2 Maccabees be referring other than Jer 3:16? If there is anything to this suggestion, the hidden ark legend arose in much the same way that other early Jewish exegetical motifs did, generated through an engagement with a specific verse. It is because of the work of James Kugel that we know as much about this process as we do.

Whatever specific connection the hidden ark motif had to the book of Jeremiah, the link became obscure over time, and the story developed into a full-fledged legend of its own, eventually inspiring the

---

[12] See, for instance, James L. Kugel, *In Potiphar's House: the Interpretive Life of Biblical Texts* (San Francisco: HarperCollins, 1990), 253–55.

Copper Scroll, according to Milik. Since the scroll itself does not refer to the legend in any obvious way, Milik had to look for circumstantial evidence to support his position, settling on two main arguments in the end. The first concerned the amount of treasure in the scroll, some 4,630 talents of gold and silver. In Milik's reckoning, this sum was simply too large to be plausible. The second argument involved an intriguing parallel, a Hebrew text known as *Masseket Kelim* known in a medieval version and (re)discovered in Beirut inscribed on two marble plaques.[13] A kind of mishnaic pseudepigraphon, *Masseket Kelim* enumerates a long list of vessels and treasures hidden in various locales at the time of the First Temple's destruction not by Jeremiah but by a Levite named Shimmur along with other biblical notables from this period. There they were to remain hidden until the messiah appeared to lead the exiles back to Israel. *Masseket Kelim* obviously reflects the hidden ark legend, but it also shares traits in common with the *Copper Scroll*, not only recording a detailed list of hidden cult vessels but even referring to a "copper tablet" inscribed as a record of the Temple's contents. As far as Milik was concerned, *Masseket Kelim* clinched his argument that what we have in the *Copper Scroll* is a fantasy of religious survival, not a record of real treasure.

Since this parallel seems rather remarkable, why do the vast majority of contemporary scholars give it little or no weight in understanding the *Copper Scroll*? In fact, the whole issue of whether the scroll is fact or fiction has become a moot one in contemporary research which takes its authenticity or factuality as the starting point for its investigations. Scholars today vigorously debate who hid the scroll and why, the nature of its treasures, and the location of their hiding places, but I have found no study from the last two decades willing to endorse Milik's hypothesis.[14] There are reasons for this consensus as Al Wolters makes clear in a recent review of *Copper Scroll* scholarship.[15] The amount of treasure listed in the scroll may

---

[13] Milik himself republished a critical edition of *Masseket Kelim* in support of his thesis. See J. T. Milik, "Notes d'épigraphie et de topographie palestiniennes," *RB* 66 (1959): 567–75.

[14] In fact, one recent scholar even argues that some of the treasure has already been found on the basis of a computer program which identifies several matches between the hiding places and weights of the *Copper Scroll* treasures and the location and weights of actual shekel hoards deposited in Palestine prior to 73 c.e. See Robert Leonard, "Numismatic Evidence for the Authenticity of the Copper Scroll," in *XII. Internationaler Numismatischer Kongress Berlin 1997: Akten–Proceedings–Actes* (ed. I. Kluge and B. Weisser; Berlin: Staatliche Museen zu Berlin, 2000), 683–92.

[15] Al Wolters, "Apocalyptic and the Copper Scroll," *JNES* 49 (1990): 145–54.

not be as implausible as Milik suggests, for other temple inventories are supposedly of comparable size (it is also possible that scholars have misread the scroll's abbreviated units of measurement, making them too large).[16] It may be true that no treasure has ever been found, but why would someone take the trouble to compose such a dry and precisely detailed record, and do so on such costly material, if they did not believe it existed? The *Scroll* does not read like myth, lacking any kind of narrative, nor does it list the ark or any other prop from the hidden ark legend. As for *Masseket Kelim*, it may appear to be a missing link between the scroll and the legend, but its testimony is arguably irrelevant, coming as it does from centuries after the *Copper Scroll.* This has been enough to convince the vast majority of contemporary scholars that there is no link between the story of the hidden ark and the copper scroll; one belongs to the realm of fantasy; the other, to history.

I want to unsettle this consensus a bit by introducing into the discussion an intriguing datum which scholars of the *Scroll* have not taken into account: Pausanias's description of the Messenian mysteries. The Messenians were a Greek people defeated by the Spartans and sent into exile where they languished until the fourth century B.C.E., when they were able to resettle their homeland. During the war, the Messenian leader Aristomenes learned from a prophecy that his people were destined to be defeated and that the survival of their culture depended upon the safeguarding of their mysteries, a "secret thing" that Pausanias never describes clearly but which seems to have consisted of rules for religious practice. Here is how Pausanias tells the story in his description of Greece (*Descr.* 4.20.4):

> For the Messenians possessed a secret thing. If it were destroyed, Messene would be overwhelmed and lost for ever, but if it were kept, the oracles of Lycus the son of Pandion said that after lapse of time the Messenians would recover their country. Aristomenes, knowing the oracles, took it towards nightfall, and coming to the most deserted part of Ithome, buried it on the mountain, calling on Zeus who keeps Ithome and the gods who hitherto protected the Messenians to remain guardians of the pledge, and not to put their only hope of return into the power of the Lacedaemonians.[17]

---

[16] See Al Wolters, "The Last Treasure of the Copper Scroll," *JBL* 107 (1988): 419–29, esp. 421; James Harper, "26 Tons of Gold and 65 Tons of Silver: Too Much to Believe?" *BAR* 19 (1993): 44–45, 70; Lefkovits, *Copper Scroll*, 460–62, 471–88; Leonard, "Numismatic Evidence."

[17] Ormerod, LCL.

I refer to the story of the Messenian mysteries as a myth because that is how it is viewed by recent classicists. The age of Aristomenes probably never happened, constituting a pseudo-history or at least a heavily mythologized one fabricated in the fourth century B.C.E. to ground a newly emergent Messenian state in the heroic past.[18] The books of the mysteries themselves, on the other hand, appear to have been real enough, venerated as a sacred relic in the city of Messene, then resurfacing along with the urn in which they were hidden as the centerpiece of a mystery cult in the nearby town of Andania where they were apparently kept in some kind of wooden chest (*Descr.* 4.33.5).[19] The story of Aristomenes cast these objects as key symbols of identity, the link to what the Messenians used to be before war displaced them from their land and disrupted their traditions. The Messenian mysteries made this mythic past manifest in the present-day, supplying physical evidence that the lost traditions of Messenia had been recovered.

The myth of the Messenian mysteries shares so many elements in common with the hidden ark legend—the hiding of a cherished cult object on the eve of conquest; the choice of a mountain as a place of concealment, the association of that object's recovery with a return from exile—that some scholars believe it was the original model for the hidden Ark story.[20] It is only when the mysteries were retrieved many centuries later that we can see the connection to the *Copper Scroll*. At the time when the Messenians were finally restored to their homeland by the Theban general Epaminondas in 369 B.C.E., the Messenian leader Epiteles had a vision revealing where the lost mysteries were hidden. Digging there, he discovered a bronze urn which he took to Epaminondas, and when the latter opened its lid, he

---

[18] See Andrea Jördens and Gercon Becht-Jördens, "Ein Eberunterkiefer als 'Staatssymbol' des Aitolischen Bundes (IG XII 2,15), Politische Identitätssuche im Mythos nach dem Ende der spartanischen Hegemonie," *Klio* 76 (1994): 172–84; Susan Alcock, "The Pseudo-History of Messenia Unplugged," *TAPA* 129 (1999): 333–41.

[19] In addition to Pausanias's testimony, the mysteries are also referred to in the Rule of the Andanian Mysteries, a record of the regulations to be followed in the celebration of the mysteries. The inscription, dated to 92/91 B.C.E., associates the books of the mysteries with a "chest." For an English translation, see Marvin Meyer, *The Ancient Mysteries: a Sourcebook* (San Francisco: HarperSanFrancisco, 1987), 51–59. For the original text, see *Sylloge inscriptionum graecarum* (ed. W. Dittenberger; 4 vols.; 3rd ed.; Leipzig: Hirzel, 1915–1924), 2:401–11 (#736).

[20] See Yoshua Gutman, "Philo the Epic Poet," in *Studies in Classics and Jewish Hellenism* (ed. R. Koebner; ScrHier 1; Jerusalem: Magnes, 1954), 36–63, esp. 59–63; Jonathan Goldstein, *II Maccabees* (AB 41A; New York: Doubleday, 1983), 182–83.

found the mysteries inscribed on "some tin foil, very thin, rolled up like a book" (*Descr.* 4.26.8).

The story of the Messenian mysteries has already been recognized as a possible precursor to the hidden ark myth as it appears in 2 Maccabees. What makes this parallel also relevant for understanding the *Copper Scroll* is its mention of a metallic scroll, hidden in a cave to protect it from the enemy. Short of finding a direct link between the *Copper Scroll* and the hidden ark legend in an ancient Jewish text, the story of the Messenian mysteries is the next best thing, connecting an artifact that resembles the *Copper Scroll* with a mythic narrative that resembles the hidden ark legend. I would argue that this evidence does much to shore up *Masseket Kelim* as a viable analogue for the *Copper Scroll*. *Masseket Kelim* makes a strikingly similar connection between object and story, mentioning a copper scroll among the treasures hidden in the time of the First Temple's destruction, but it is so remote chronologically that it has proven easy to discount. The story of the Messenian mysteries, embedding a similar object within a similar narrative, pushes such a connection back into Hellenistic antiquity.[21] This is not to discount the many differences between the Messenian mysteries themselves and the contents of the *Copper Scroll*, although, as I shall argue shortly, these may not be as great as they might appear. It is to reassert a relationship between the scroll and the hidden ark legend against a scholarly consensus which would disconnect them.

If we are to return to Milik's reading of the scroll as a legend, however, what are we to do with all the arguments that the scroll records a real treasure hidden in Roman times? The comparison with the myth of the Messenian mysteries may be enough to revive the question of whether it reflects fact or fiction; it does not make it a fiction. As we struggle with this problem, it may offer some solace to note the difficulty that ancient people had in distinguishing mythical buried treasures from the real thing. In 65 C.E., a Carthaginian named Bassus informed Nero that he had had a dream which revealed the location of an immense treasure of gold buried in a deep cave on his estate (Tacitus, *Ann.* 16.1–3; cf. Suetonius, *Nero* 31.4). Where did

---

[21] Pausanius's description of Greece, a work completed between 143 and 161 C.E., is less than a century removed from the time of the *Copper Scroll*, and the myth of the Messenian mystery, drawn from authors living in the fourth century B.C.E. (see *Descr.* 4.6.1), predates it by centuries.

such a treasure come from? Dido had hidden the treasure when she founded Carthage, Bassus explained, to prevent its wealth from corrupting her subjects and to discourage attacks by covetous Numidian kings. Desperate for funds, Nero immediately dispatched warships in pursuit of the treasure. All of Rome was abuzz with expectation, rhetoricians making it a central theme in their panegyrics. Nero himself began spending the treasure on credit, so confident was he of its eventual discovery. Unfortunately, the treasure proved to be a figment of Bassus's imagination. With the help of Nero's men, he dug up his whole property, declaring this or that place to be the site of the cave, but he never found the gold and, discredited, he killed himself or, according to some, was arrested and had his property confiscated. What is instructive about this incident for understanding the *Copper Scroll*, I think, is not that Dido's treasure proved illusory but that its fictiveness was not apparent to the Romans or even to Bassus himself, who could only profess astonishment "that, after all his other hallucinations had come true, this one alone had deceived him." Apparently, the first century was an age in which mythical treasure could seem real even to the person imagining it.

In the light of this incident, I have come to wonder whether the way in which the debate over the *Copper Scroll* has been framed—is it real or is it mythical?—simplifies a more complex situation. Perhaps what we have reflected in the *Scroll* cannot be neatly categorized as real or mythical but reflects what anthropologist Marshall Sahlins calls a "mythical reality."[22] What Sahlins is referring to by this oxymoron is the dialectical relationship that can develop between myth and reality; myth shaping the way people act in history and being reshaped by historical experience at the same time. Sahlins's own research focuses on Hawaii where, he argues, the inhabitants experienced the unexpected arrival of Captain Cook as a realization of one of their myths and acted accordingly, treating Cook as a god. We have evidence of such a dialectic between the myth of the hidden ark and history in first century Palestine. During the administration of Pontius Pilate, a certain man rallied a Samaritan mob to go with him to Mount Gerizim, their sacred mountain, where he promised to reveal vessels hidden there by Moses. The Samaritans followed him to the mountain only to find their way blocked by

---

[22] Marshall Sahlins, *Historical Metaphors and Mythical Realities: Structure in the Early History of the Sandwich Islands* (Ann Arbor, Mich.: University of Michigan, 1981).

Pilate's forces. A battle ensued, and Pilate was eventually able to quell the uprising (*Ant.* 18.85–87).[23] Somewhere in the background of this incident, revised in light of Samaritan belief, is a legend similar to the hidden ark myth and the story of the Messenian mysteries.[24] The teller of this tale, Josephus, finds it implausible, accusing the Samaritan leader of mendacity (one problem that would have discredited the claim for Jews was the question of how Moses could have hidden vessels in Palestine if he had died before entering Canaan), but he speaks as a hostile outsider to Samaritan culture.[25] The Samaritans in the story clearly believed in the myth, so much so that, like Bassus, they were ready to stake their lives on the belief that what they were looking for would be where the story called for it to be. In this incident, the hidden ark myth becomes a mythical reality, or at least strove to do so before Roman rule stepped in the way.

The hidden ark myth also reflects the other side of Sahlin's dialectic, the reshaping of myth in light of historical experience. Perhaps our best evidence for how Jews in the Roman period construed the hidden ark myth is *2 Baruch*, a text composed within a few decades of the Second Temple's destruction; the story it tells differs from earlier versions of the hidden ark myth in ways that suggest that it was adapted in light of the Roman destruction of the Temple.[26] An example appears at the beginning of the narrative when God reveals to Baruch his plans to destroy Jerusalem. The scribe protests that the enemy will be able to use the Temple's destruction to boast of its power: "they will go away to the land of their idols, and boast before them" (5:1). It is to deprive the enemy of boasting rights that

---

[23] The Samaritans later complained to the governor of Syria about Pilate's behavior, and he was called back to Rome to explain his actions (*Ant.* 18.88–89).

[24] See M. Collins, "The Hidden Vessels in Samaritan Traditions," *JSJ* 3 (1972): 97–116; Isaac Kalimi and James Purvis, "The Hiding of the Temple Vessels in Jewish and Samaritan Literature," *CBQ* (1994): 679–85. Although Collins's reconstruction of this myth is different from that of Kalimi and Purvis, both suppose that, like its Jewish counterparts, it originally included a prediction of some eschatological figure coming to reveal the vessels. Cf. John 4:25 where a Samaritan woman speaks of a messiah who will come and "show us all things." By claiming to know where these vessels were, then, the leader in Josephus's story may have been promising the onset of the eschatological age.

[25] Interestingly, however, Jews did not deny that there was something buried on Mt. Gerizim; they differed only in identifying those objects as idols. See *L.A.B.* 25:10 and *Gen. Rab.* 81:4. The former text identifies the objects hidden on Mt. "Sychem" with seven golden images hidden by the tribe of Asher; the latter identifies them with the idols hidden by Jacob under an oak tree near Shechem (Gen 34:2–4).

[26] See F. Murphy, "*2 Baruch* and the Romans," *JBL* 104 (1985): 663–69.

God sends his angels down to earth, ordering them to hide the Temple's contents and dismantle the Temple itself "so that the enemies do not boast and say, 'We have overthrown the wall of Zion and we have burnt down the place of the mighty God'" (7:1; 80:3). This consideration is not mentioned as a motive in the earlier version of the myth in 2 Maccabees, composed before the Roman period, and its introduction seems to register what actually happened to the contents of the Holy of Holies after the Second Temple's destruction when Rome used the table of the show-bread, the golden menorah, and other sacred objects to celebrate its victory over the Jews. Removing these from the Temple, Titus brought them back to Rome where they were exhibited in a triumph as trophies of Roman might (*J.W.* 7.148–150; 158–162), a display still visible on the so-called Arch of Titus above the Forum which features an image of soldiers carrying the table of show-bread, two long trumpets, a cup and the seven-branched menorah in the triumph.[27] Mythical realities are generated by two mutually transformative processes: Myth can shape the experience of reality, framing historical events within a pre-given structure determined by native legend and belief, but it also adapts to reality, adjusting its plotline and absorbing new levels of significance. History's effect on myth is all too obvious in the Samaritan incident where the expected denouement of a native legend is violently obstructed by a very real Roman intervention. In *2 Baruch*, Rome has a subtler effect on myth, insinuating into the legend of the hidden ark a new understanding of why the Temple's contents were concealed that reflects what really happened after the Second Temple's destruction.

What I am suggesting is that the distinction between myth and reality that has polarized our understanding of the *Copper Scroll* may be somewhat artificial. The two can bleed into one another in various ways, myth conditioning the way some Jews and Samaritans interacted with Roman rule, the imposition of that rule reshaping the articulation of the myth. This is why I do not feel compelled by the comparison with the story of the Messenian mysteries to argue that the treasure never existed. For all the reasons mentioned above, in fact,

---

[27] For this and other ways in which the Romans used booty from the Jews and their temple to celebrate their power, see Douglas Edwards, "Religion, Power and Politics: Jewish Defeats by the Romans in Iconography and Josephus," in *Disapora Jews and Judaism: Essays in Honor of and in Dialogue with A. Thomas Kraabel* (ed. J. Overman and R. MacLennan; SFSHJ 41; Atlanta: Scholars Press, 1992), 293–310.

I find myself agreeing with scholars that the treasures were probably genuine, hidden in fear of Roman conquest. What I am proposing is that the historical motive for their concealment is best understood in dialectic with Jewish myth. With Jerusalem under siege or already destroyed by that point, Jews faced the challenge of how to sustain their cultic traditions at a time when the tangible symbols of its practice were lost. The hidden ark myth suggests a way to survive this crisis: hide the contents of the Temple as seedlings for an eventual replanting of cultic tradition. In the *Copper Scroll* we may have evidence of this myth put into practice as it were, a real attempt to preserve cult objects from Rome modeled on an imaginary precedent.

Before concluding, it is important to address an obvious weakness in the hypothesis that I am proposing here: the analogy between the *Copper Scroll* and the Messenian mysteries is not exact. We do not know much about the content of the Messenian mysteries, but there is no reason to think that they were composed of cult vessels and other treasure as we have in the scroll. Nor is there any evidence within the *Copper Scroll* itself that its contents were considered essential to cultural survival as the Messenian mysteries were. The *Copper Scroll* treasures seem generic and even interchangeable, the sorts of objects one imagines flowing regularly in and out of the Temple coffers as part of its regular sacrificial routine. This does not deflate the economic value or religious significance of what is enumerated in the scroll, but it is to concede that its contents do not appear to constitute the sorts of objects one would single out as vital links to a pre-conquest past.

While conceding this difference as a vulnerability in my argument, I by no means see it as grounds for rejecting the comparison. If, as I suspect, the hidden ark legend arose under the influence of a Hellenistic pagan precedent, one would not expect it to penetrate Judaism without adapting to its native myths and ritual traditions, and the objects most closely analogous to the mysteries within this tradition were the sacred objects kept within the Temple, not just the ark or the tent of meeting but the priestly vestments, precious stones, and other vessels featured in the variants of the hidden ark legend known from *Syriac Baruch* (6:7) and other texts composed in the same general period of the *Copper Scroll*. The Temple vessels share with the Messenian mysteries two traits that are especially salient.

The first is that both constitute "secret things." We know so little about the Messenian mysteries in large part because Pausanius's description keeps them veiled (*Descr.* 4.20.4). The contents of Solomon's Temple were also hidden from view. According to biblical law, lay Israelites and even the Levites were forbidden from seeing the sacred objects kept within the Temple's inner-sanctum (see Num 4:20; 1 Sam 6:19 [MT]). Such a prohibition was derived, Daniel Schwartz has suggested, by analogy with the sanction against humans seeing God himself, an experience thought to be lethal: "for man shall not see me and live" (Exod 33:20; cf. Gen 32:31; Exod 19:21; Judg 6:22–23; 13:22; Isa 6:5).[28] Schwartz also cites an intriguing piece of evidence which shows this taboo was applied to the Second Temple, a fragment of a non-canonical gospel (*P. Ox.* V.840) composed before 200 C.E., where Jesus is rebuked by a high priest for viewing the holy vessels:

> A certain Pharisee, a chief priest, whose name was Levi (?), met them and said to the Savior, Who gave you leave to walk in this place of purification and to see these holy vessels, when you have not washed nor have your disciples bathed their feet? You have walked into the Temple defiled, a pure place, wherein no other man walks without washing himself and changing his garments, nor does he venture to see these holy vessels. . . .[29]

According to this incident, Jesus was thought by at least one ritual expert to have infringed on the purity of the Temple by entering it to see the holy vessels while in a state of ritual impurity. The scene suggests that visual access to the Second Temple's contents, not just those objects kept within the Holy of Holies but even the vessels within the outer sanctuary where lay Israelites were allowed, was limited to those in a state of ritual purity. In the light of this episode, the Temple appears as something of a mystery cult in its own right, if by that we mean a cult that contained secrets that were not to be divulged to uninitiated outsiders—only these secrets were not esoteric rites or knowledge, but the sacred objects used in the performance of the Temple cult.

---

[28] Daniel Schwartz, "Viewing the Holy Utensils (*P. Ox.* V.840)," *NTS* 32 (1986): 153–59. For more on the danger of seeing God (or parts thereof), see Haran, *Temples and Temple Service*, 178; Howard Eilberg-Schwartz, *God's Phallus and Other Problems for Men and Monotheism* (Boston: Beacon, 1994); Ronald Hendel, "Aniconism and Anthropomorphism in Ancient Israel," in *Image and the Book: Iconic Cults, Aniconism and the Rise of Book Religion in Israel and the Ancient Near East* (ed. K. van der Toorn; Leuven: Peeters, 1997), 204–28.

[29] Adapted from the translation in Bernard Grenfell and Arthur Hunt, *Fragment of an Uncanonical Gospel* (London: Oxford University, 1908), 16–17.

Apparently, it was important to preserve the visual inaccessibility of the Temple's contents even in the absence of the Temple itself. The priest's rebuke of Jesus recalls Jeremiah's rebuke of his followers when they attempt to find the cave where he had hidden the ark and the tent: "the place shall remain unknown until God gathers his people together again and shows his mercy" (*2 Bar.* 2:6–7). The prophet's behavior here is not unlike that of initiates of Hellenistic mysteries who vowed not to tell others about the holy secrets of the cults to which they were devoted—a rule that, in a sense, Pausanias himself honors in his description of the Messenian mysteries by remaining tight-lipped about the mysteries' appearance and content. The *Copper Scroll* does not describe its contents as a secret or a mystery, but if scholars are correct in identifying these objects as sacred vessels removed from the Temple or intended as sacred offerings, they may very well have partaken of the traditional secrecy that seems to have shrouded the Temple's contents in general. For someone to see the Temple vessels without submitting to the necessary ritual procedures was to transgress the Temple's sanctity, which is why those entrusted with guarding that sanctity, its priests, would have seen it as their duty to prevent uninitiated outsiders from seeing them. What we know about the Temple vessels and the importance of protecting them from visual violation suggests that what may have been at stake in the concealment of the *Copper Scroll* treasures was not just the objects themselves but religious secrets considered essential to the preservation of ritual tradition.

Apart from their esoteric character, the mysteries and the legendary contents of the First Temple also share a similar revitalizing power. Aristomenes hastens to preserve the mysteries because he knows his people cannot survive without them. "If it were destroyed, Messene would be overwhelmed and lost for ever, but if it were kept, the oracles of Lycus the son of Pandion said that after lapse of time the Messenians would recover their country."[30] The rediscovery of the Temple's contents is invested with the same significance in the hidden ark myth: when the people return from exile, "then, the LORD will disclose these things, and the glory of the LORD and the cloud will appear, as they were shown in the case of Moses" (2 Macc 2:8). The "glory of the LORD" and the "cloud," biblical terms used to indicate God's presence in the Temple, suggest that not only will

---

[30] *Descr.* 4.20.4 (Ormerod, LCL).

the ark and other lost objects be recovered in this age but the Temple itself will resume the lustrous form that it had in biblical times as a place where God's presence was manifest.[31] Both the mysteries and the Temple's contents function as metonyms of an idealized past thought to have existed before the present age of defeat and dislocation. Their retrieval makes only a fragment of the past present again, but that is enough to initiate a more complete restoration—the recovery of a lost homeland and the revival of an ancient religious tradition.

Were the objects listed in the *Copper Scroll* invested with a similar significance? At first glance, they do not seem to be the kinds of objects one would use to seed a restoration of Jewish religious tradition. But should we assume that only the most important objects in the Temple could serve as agents of cultural revival? There is evidence to suggest otherwise. Consider a story that appears adjacent to the hidden ark myth in 2 Maccabees (1:19–36). As they were being taken captive, some priests in the time of the First Temple's destruction took some fire from the altar and hid it in the hollow of a dry cistern. When the Jews returned from exile, the descendants of the priests were unable to retrieve the fire, but they did find some "thick liquid" which proved sufficient to re-ignite the sacrifice. That some oil, a dormant residue of cultic practice, could have this effect suggests that any object or substance connected with the Temple had the power to revitalize cultic tradition: what mattered was not the nature of the object itself but the mere fact that it was associated with the First Temple before its destruction. A similar metonymic process can be observed in the Messenian cult. The mysteries were central because of their divine origins and mysterious contents, but what of the urn in which they were found, also venerated as a sacred object according to Pausanias? Its status seems to have resulted from a kind of spill-over effect that transferred the mythic resonance of the mysteries to the otherwise undistinguished vessel in which they happened to be stored.

Something similar could be true of the treasures listed in the *Copper Scroll*. At the time of its composition during the Jewish revolt or after, Jews were faced with a predicament not unlike that facing Jews in 2 Maccabees, not only deprived of the Temple itself, but of its most important objects, those in the Holy of Holies. In the absence of

---

[31] Cf. Exod 40:34, which describes the Tabernacle at its completion: "Then the cloud covered the tent of meeting, and the glory of the LORD filled the tabernacle."

such objects, how would Jews be able to revive the cult later on? I would argue that an imagination that could rekindle the Temple cult from just a bit of sacrificial oil could in theory revive the Temple cult from any object, however generic or peripheral, provided that it had some physical connection with the Temple prior to its disruption. Scholars suspect that the treasures of the *Copper Scroll* had just such a connection, coming from the Temple or having been set aside for sacred purposes. It is that association rather than the nature or role of the objects themselves that makes them potential vehicles of cultic continuity.

If there is anything to what I am suggesting here, the analogy of the Messenian mysteries does more than complicate the relationship between myth and reality in the *Copper Scroll*; it suggests that this mysterious text was composed precisely in order to assert a relationship between myth and reality. That reality was one in which the connection with the mythic past had been or was in danger of being fractured by Roman rule which, among its disruptive effects, threatened to dislodge the ancient and secret core of Jewish ritual tradition, the Temple vessels, not just from the Temple but from the religious mindset which gave them meaning. Within this context, these objects resonated as symbols of Jewish tradition and divine presence; ripped from it by the rapacious hands of strangers, they were only so much inert loot. The anxiety this caused Jews may explain why the hidden ark legend became popular again just after the Second Temple's destruction as reflected in narratives like *Syriac Baruch*. For through it, Jews could articulate their yearning not just to hang on to the Temple's contents physically, but to keep the mythic significance of these objects intact. The *Copper Scroll* as I read it is the product of this same aspiration, providing its readers with a way to recover not just treasure, but a tradition interrupted by foreign conquest and dislocation. If its role as a catalyst for religious revitalization is no longer apparent, this might be because the scroll has been cut off from the myth which invested it with its power. Reconnect them, as the Messenian mysteries allows us to do, and the scroll radiates as an attempt to sustain the link between myth and reality at a time when this link was in danger of rupture.

THE CONCEPT OF COVENANT IN THE QUMRAN SCROLLS AND RABBINIC LITERATURE

Lawrence H. Schiffman

The Hebrew scriptures speak of a series of covenants made by God with Israel or its forebears. These covenantal relationships are seen in the Bible to underlie Israel's relationship to God. Indeed, these covenants are axiomatic to Second Temple literature and talmudic texts and to their respective views of the place of Israel in the world and its unique place in history. This study will seek to compare the approaches taken to the concept of covenant and its role in Qumran texts[1] and rabbinic literature,[2] in the hope that we can make a modest contribution to the study of this idea and its role in the history of Judaism. The primary stress within the Qumran corpus will be on texts associated with the life and ideology of the Qumran sectarians.

It is certainly tempting to begin this paper with a lengthy discussion of the important conclusions of modern biblical studies regarding the notion of covenant in the ancient Near East, the literary form of suzerain treaties, and their relevance to the Bible.[3] Suffice it to say here that the study of these materials has yielded the unanimous conclusion that the biblical covenantal formulations follow accepted ancient Near Eastern literary patterns and, therefore, that the biblical covenants are to be seen as statements of contractual relationship. The vassal binds himself to keep faith with the suzerain. If the vassal keeps faith, so must the suzerain. If Israel keeps the Torah, God must keep His pledges. If Israel does not, it will suffer the consequences stipulated in the curse section of the contract. While such treaties or covenants were common in the ancient Near East, it was the

---

[1] See Ed P. Sanders, *Paul and Palestinian Judaism* (Philadelphia: Fortress, 1997), 240–57; Mark A. Elliott, *The Survivors of Israel: A Reconsideration of the Theology of Pre-Christian Judaism* (Grand Rapids: Eerdmans, 2000), 245–81; Alex Deasley, *The Shape of Qumran Theology* (Carlisle: Paternoster, 2000), 138–64, dealing with the implications of covenant for the Qumran sect; and the thorough study of James C. VanderKam, "Covenant," *Encyclopedia of the Dead Sea Scrolls* 1:151–55.

[2] Sanders, *Paul and Palestinian Judaism*, 84–107.

[3] Delbert Hillers, *Covenant: The History of a Biblical Idea* (Baltimore: Johns Hopkins University Press, 1969).

unique contribution of Israel that such contracts could be made with
God himself. Only in Israelite religion was the constancy of the
covenant between God and humanity possible.[4]

We will define the corpus under study as those materials in which
the term *berit*, "covenant," actually appears. We will let the ancient
teachers speak for themselves. What did they consider to be the notion
of covenant in the context of their specific approach to Judaism?

I. THE COVENANT OF NOAH

The *Genesis Apocryphon* (1QapGen XI, 15–XII, 6) originally contained
an account of God's covenant with Noah, even though the passage
is fragmentary and the word for "covenant" does not occur.[5] Column
XIV may also be part of the account of this covenant. This covenant
is also mentioned directly in 4Q370 (*Admonition Based on the Flood*) I,
7–8, which explicitly mentioned the rainbow as the symbol (*le*]*ma‘an
yizkor*) of God's promise not to destroy the world again by a flood
(Gen 8:8–17).[6] *Jub.* 6:1–14 describes God's covenant with Noah,
which entails His promise not to bring another flood, and Noah and
his sons' promise to abstain from eating blood. The text notes that
this covenant was renewed at Sinai where the obligation to sprinkle
the blood of sacrifices was commanded. Here again, the rainbow is
the sign of God's promise. These materials, we should note, are not
part of the mainstream Qumranic sectarian compositions but indicate that the Qumran sectarians were heir to a pre-sectarian tradition regarding this venerable ancestor of Israel. The brief allusion
to this covenant in the *Zadokite Fragments* (CD III, 1–4) reflects this
pre-sectarian tradition.

Rabbinic texts do not contain extensive discussion of a covenant with
Noah. Yet this covenant gives rise to the benediction to be recited
upon seeing a rainbow. The Tosefta, *Ber.* 6(7):5, provides that one who
sees a rainbow recite: "Blessed [art Thou O LORD our God, King of
the Universe] Who is faithful to his covenant, who remembers the

---

[4] See the convenient summary of Moshe Weinfeld, "Covenant," *EncJud* 5:1012–22;
idem, "B'rith," *TDOT* 2:253–79.
[5] *The Dead Sea Scrolls Study Edition* (ed. F. García Martínez and E. J. C. Tigchelaar;
2 vols.; Leiden: Brill, 1997), 1:34–35.
[6] Carol A. Newsom, "4Q370: An Admonition Based on the Flood," *RevQ* 13
(1988): 23–43; Newsom, in J. VanderKam, consulting ed., *Qumran Cave 4.XIV:
Parabiblical Texts, Part 2* (DJD 19; Oxford: Clarendon, 1995), 85–97.

covenant" (*ne'eman biverito zokher habberit*).[7] This covenant with Noah extends God's promise to all humanity that He will not again destroy the world because of the transgressions of mankind (Gen 9:8–17).

Whereas the Qumran materials see Noah as occupying a central place in the chain of covenants leading to the formation of God's people of Israel,[8] the Rabbis see him more as a transitional figure with whom a limited covenant was made. To the pre-sectarian heritage, Noah was a great religious sage, but even to those Rabbis who interpreted Gen 6:9 ("Noah was a righteous man, perfect in his generations") in a positive sense, he was not seen as an anachronistic tradent of the Jewish tradition in the pre-Abrahamic period. Such ideas are common in books like *Jubilees* and *1 Enoch* but had only limited influence on rabbinic aggadah. No significant Noahide covenant was recognized by the Rabbis.

Even the extensive Noahide laws, the rabbinic equivalent of natural law—the basic ethical and moral laws, the observance of which was expected of all humanity—were actually understood to apply even from the time of Adam and Eve. Violation of these commandments led to the eradication of ante-diluvian society. Even where some of these laws were learned from verses connected with Adam, there was no sense of dependence on a two-sided covenant; rather, these natural laws were expressed as one-sided divine commands inherent in creation.[9]

II. The Covenant of Abraham

The *Genesis Apocryphon* contains an allusion to God's covenant with Abraham. In view of the fragmentary nature of this text, additional allusions may have stood in the text. In any case, **XXI**, 8–14 describes God's appearance to Abraham (still called Abram), and his promise to him and his descendants of the Land of Israel as an eternal inheritance, and his assurance that Abraham's descendants will be innumerable. This text represents an expanded version of Gen 13:14–17

---

[7] *Tosefta* (Lieberman ed., 1:34). Cf. Saul Lieberman, *Tosefta Ki-Feshuṭah, Seder Zera'im* (10 vols.; New York: Jewish Theological Seminary of America, 1955), 1:108–9.

[8] Cf. Michael E. Stone, "Noah," *Encyclopedia of the Dead Sea Scrolls* 2:613–14.

[9] See David Novak, *The Image of the Non-Jew in Judaism* (Toronto Studies in Theology 14; Lewiston, N.Y.: Mellen, 1983), especially 3–35, 257–68; and Aaron Lichtenstein, *The Seven Laws of Noah* (Brooklyn, N.Y.: Z. Berman, 1995).

which has been expanded harmonistically with details from other visions of Abraham, as is the method of the author of this text.

To be considered here as well is the concept of a covenant with the forefathers (*rishonim*, literally "first ones") mentioned in the *Zadokite Fragments* (CD I, 4–5; cf. VI, 2) as the reason God chose to leave a remnant of Israel (the forerunners of the sectarians) when he brought destruction on the First Temple. This covenant is also mentioned in CD III, 1–4, which indicates that although Noah and his sons failed in this covenant, Abraham was able to pass it on to Isaac and Jacob. They fulfilled God's commandments, but Jacob's children did not keep the covenant and went into exile in Egypt. Because Israel did not follow the way of these forefathers, God brought upon them the punishments catalogued in the covenantal curses of the Bible (I, 16–18; cf. III, 10–11;[10] see also 4Q463 [Narrative D] 1 1),[11] leading to the destruction of the Temple (cf. CD VIII, 1). As one of their transgressions, Israel caused others to violate the covenant (I, 20). Because of the transgressions of Israel, God transferred His covenant to those who held fast to the commandments (III, 12–13). This remnant continued in the ways of the forefathers and their transgressions were forgiven (IV, 7–10). Since the covenant of God with Abraham and the Sinaitic covenant were both violated, God's covenant was then effectively transferred to the sect. An assumption of this text is that the laws of the Torah actually predated the Sinaitic revelation, a claim made consistently in *Jubilees* as well.

The Abrahamic covenant has one further ingredient, the practice of circumcision. This fact, which we will encounter so extensively in rabbinic literature, is attested rarely in the scrolls. However, CD XII, 11 uses the phrase "covenant of Abraham" as a direct reference to circumcision, so closely associated with Abraham in Gen 17:10–15, 23–27. This covenant may be mentioned in 4Q378 (4QapocrJosh^a) 22 I, 4 (restoring *habber*]*it*),[12] or this passage may only be a general allusion to the covenant with Abraham.

The Mishnah, *B. Qam.* 1:2–3, makes use of the phrase *bene berit*, literally, "sons of the covenant," as a term for Israelites. Indeed, this usage is found throughout the entire rabbinic corpus. This inciden-

---

[10] Emending to *havu*.

[11] Mark S. Smith, DJD 19:211–14.

[12] Carol A. Newsom, in J. VanderKam, consulting ed., *Qumran Cave 4.XVII: Parabiblical Texts, Part 3* (DJD 22; Oxford: Clarendon, 1996), 259.

tal usage has behind it the entire notion of the Jews as a people who entered into a covenant with God. Most probably it refers to Abraham's covenant, the covenant of circumcision. This interpretation is strengthened by the other references to this term in the Mishnah; *m. Ned.* 3:11, a beautiful lyrical passage extolling the importance of circumcision, says, "Great is circumcision, for thirteen covenants were made (lit. 'cut') for it." Here the Mishnah is referring to the occurrence of the word *berit* thirteen times in the passage in which Abraham is commanded regarding circumcision (Gen 17).

This term, *bene berit*, occurs in Qumran passages, also designating Israelites—male and female (1QM XVII, 8; 4Q284 [*Purification Liturgy*] 4 2).[13] If we are correct in our analysis of the tannaitic usage, then the Qumran term may also be taken as based on the place of circumcision in the formation of Jewish identity, a role well attested in a variety of Greek and Latin texts from Late Antiquity.[14]

The evidence of the Mishnah points in only one direction. In the legal context of this text, and in its ideological underpinnings, the covenant is that of Abraham, symbolized by circumcision. The basis of Jewish obligation and relationship with God stems from this covenant. The term *berit*, "covenant," denoted circumcision in this legal context, not only as a ritual performed at a specific time in the life of the male Jew, but as a covenantal sign borne at all times, eternally binding the Jewish people to their God.

The Tosefta, the earliest commentary and supplement to the Mishnah, shows evidence of a somewhat wider usage of this term. Nonetheless, the covenant of circumcision is still quite prominent. In *t. Ber.* (6)7:12–13 there is a description of the benedictions to be recited upon performing a circumcision.[15] Before the ceremony the father is to intone: "Blessed art thou, O LORD our God, King of the Universe, who has commanded us to initiate him (the eight-day old boy) into the covenant of Abraham our forefather." Those in attendance recite: "Just as he has been admitted to the covenant, thus may you admit him to observance of the Torah and to the marriage canopy." The benediction recited after the ritual refers to circumcision as "the sign of the holy covenant" and concludes: "Blessed

---

[13] Joseph M. Baumgarten, in Baumgarten et al., *Qumran Cave 4.XXV: Halakhic Texts* (DJD 35; Oxford: Clarendon, 1999), 127.

[14] Lawrence H. Schiffman, *Who Was a Jew?* (Hoboken, N.J.: Ktav, 1985), 84 n. 35.

[15] Cf. Lieberman ed., 1:36–37.

art thou, O LORD, who made (lit. 'cut') the covenant."[16] The expression *dam berit*, "the blood of the covenant," referring to the blood of the circumcision, appears twice in *t. Šabb.* 15(16):8–9.[17] This phrase continues to appear in all the later talmudic sources, often in quotations of this very text. Reference to those who perform epispasm as "effacing the covenant" occurs in *t. Sanh.* 12:9 where they are said to lose their portion in the world to come.[18]

Mekhilta de-Rabbi Ishmael Be-Šallaḥ 3 contains the view that the covenant of circumcision, the covenant applying day and night, referred to in Jer 33:25, sustains the existence of heaven and earth.[19] In other words, the text sees circumcision as the permanent sign of the Jew's connection to his or her Father in Heaven.

The importance of the commandment of circumcision is implicit in the amoraic ruling of *y. Ber.* 3d to the effect that one who omits the mention of this commandment from the second benediction of the Grace after Meals must repeat the Grace. The Grace recounted all the gifts that God had bestowed upon His people, and the covenant of circumcision which God had "sealed in our flesh" had to be included.

A beautiful *aggadah* in *b. Menaḥ* 53b pictures Abraham wandering in the Temple on the eve of its destruction. God finds him and asks him what he is doing there. He says that he has come regarding his children and begins to entreat God on their behalf. When God answers by recounting their transgressions, Abraham, close to desperation, says to God: "You should have remembered their covenant of circumcision and saved them on this account." God retorts that even this sign of His covenant they have removed. Nonetheless, He assures

---

[16] Lieberman, *Tosefta Ki-Feshuṭah*, 1:114–15.

[17] Lieberman ed., 2:70–72.

[18] The Mishnah, *'Avot* 3:11, lists several classes of individuals who have no portion in the world to come. This tradition is no doubt intended as a supplement to the more well known list in *m. Sanh.* 10:1. In any case, among these is listed, "he who effaces the covenant of Abraham our father, may peace be upon him." This clearly refers to the practice of epispasm, the removal of the sign of circumcision, known to have been practiced by some extremely assimilating Jews in the Greco-Roman period. The numerous uses in the Palestinian Talmud of *mefer berit*, to "efface the covenant," offer almost nothing which is not found in tannaitic sources. The only exception is the explicit identification in *y. Pe'ah* 16b and *y. Sanh.* 27c of such a person as the one who practices epispasm (*zeh she-hu' moshekh lo 'orlah*). Several passages in the Babylonian Talmud widen the meaning of *mefer berit* from that of effacing the physical sign of circumcision to neglecting the Sinaitic covenant. Therefore, it is necessary for the Babylonian Talmud to refer to *berit ba-basar* to designate circumcision (*b. Šebu.* 13a, *b. Yoma* 85b, *b. Ker.* 7a, *b. Sanh.* 99a).

[19] Horowitz-Rabin ed., 98.

Abraham that repentance will cause them eventually to be restored to their land and their Temple. The covenant is eternal. Israel's repentance will always be accepted, and the Land of Israel will be rebuilt.

While both the Qumran and rabbinic materials speak extensively about the covenant of Abraham, the emphases of these materials are completely different. For the Qumran and Second Temple texts, the covenant of Abraham is primarily tied up with the commitment of the Patriarchs to follow God's teachings. For the Rabbis, little else was symbolized by the Abrahamic covenant besides the centrality of circumcision.

III. COVENANT OF JACOB

Central to the *Temple Scroll* is a covenant of Jacob, which is mentioned at the end of the Sacrificial Festival Calendar source.[20] This passage, occupying virtually the whole of the preserved col. XXIX, is the conclusion, summing up the sacrifices, paralleling Num 29:39.[21] That text is expanded to refer not only to the various offerings but also to the Temple in which God makes His name dwell (all stated in the first person, with God as the speaker) and promises that the offerings of the Jewish people will be accepted by God Who will be their eternal God if they will be his people. The text then states that the Temple it describes will be the seat of God's presence until the day of blessing (so Yadin; Qimron: "creation")—the dawn of the eschaton—when God Himself will build a new one, "to establish it for myself for all times, according to the covenant which I have made with Jacob at Bethel" (XXIX, 10). This passage must have continued onto the top of col. XXX which is only minimally preserved.[22]

This notion of a covenant with Jacob at Bethel is based on the vision of Jacob's ladder, Gen 28:10–22 (cf. Lev 26:42).[23] The author

---

[20] See below, "Appendix: the Covenant of Jacob in the *Temple Scroll*," for more detailed treatment.

[21] See the restorations of Yigael Yadin, *The Temple Scroll* (3 vols.; Jerusalem: Israel Exploration Society, 1983), 2:130; Elisha Qimron, *The Temple Scroll: A Critical Edition with Extensive Reconstructions* (Beersheva: Ben-Gurion University of the Negev and Israel Exploration Society, 1996), 44, for 11QTª XXIX, 1–4. Cf. Michael O. Wise, "The Covenant of *Temple Scroll* XXIX, 3–10," *RevQ* 14 (1989): 49–60; and Hans A. Rapp, "Jakob in Bet-El: Gen 35,1–15 und die jüdische Literatur des 3. und 2. Jh. BCE" (Th.D. diss., Universitaren Hochschule Luzern, 1999), 87–118.

[22] Yadin, *Temple Scroll*, 2:130.

[23] Rapp clearly sees Gen 35 as the basis for this covenant. See "Jakob in Bet-El," 30–72.

of this section of the scroll understood Bethel, literally "House of God," to be the location of God's Temple in Jerusalem, for the text explicitly states in verses 17 and 22 that Jacob considered this place to be *Bet 'Elohim*, "the House of God." The covenant referred to in the *Temple Scroll*, therefore, is the establishment of the Temple Mount in Jerusalem as the permanent place of God's eternal Temple.[24] This promise was understood to have been made to Jacob at the time of his vision of the ladder.[25]

It is possible that this same covenant is alluded to in a sectarian manuscript, 5Q13 (*Sectarian Rule*) 2 6. As restored by Yadin, the passage reads, ". . .] To Jacob You made known [Your covenant] at Bethel."[26] The next lines (7–8) refer to the appointment of Levi to the priesthood, perhaps in accord with the passage in *Jubilees* to be discussed below.

The account of Gen 28:10–22 is repeated virtually verbatim in *Jub.* 27:19–27. But in *Jub.* 32 Jacob returns to Bethel (paralleling Gen 35 which appears at first glance to be a doublet of Gen 28), this time with Levi, to sacrifice again. Here Levi had a dream that he was appointed to the eternal priesthood, and they sacrificed in order to fulfil the vow of Gen 28:20–22. Jacob, after these offerings, wanted to build a permanent Temple there (v. 16), but God appeared and told him that it was not the correct place (v. 22). In other words, the covenant made with Jacob at Bethel in *Jubilees* (at his "second" visit) refers to the eternal priesthood of his son Levi, not to the location of the Temple itself.[27]

Rabbinic sources do not speak of a covenant made with Jacob. But they do speak of the experience of the vision of the ladder as referring to the establishment of the Jerusalem Temple. Effectively, two different views are expressed. One actually places the vision of "Bethel" on Mt. Moriah—the Temple Mount. The other approach

---

[24] Cf. also the derivation of this same obligation from different biblical passages in 4QFlorilegium 1–2 I. Cf. George J. Brooke, *Exegesis at Qumran: 4QFlorilegium in its Jewish Context* (JSOTSup 29; Sheffield: JSOT Press, 1985), 178–93; Daniel R. Schwartz, "The Three Temples of 4QFlorilegium," *RevQ* 10 (1979): 83–92; Michael O. Wise, "4QFlorilegium and the Temple of Man," *RevQ* 15 (1991): 103–32.

[25] For this entire section, cf. Yadin, *Temple Scroll*, 2:182–87.

[26] Yadin, *Temple Scroll*, 2:129; cf. M. Baillet, J. T. Milik, and R. de Vaux, *Les 'Petites Grottes' de Qumrân* (DJD 3; Oxford: Clarendon, 1962), 182–83; Lawrence H. Schiffman, "Sectarian Rule (5Q13)," in *The Dead Sea Scrolls: Hebrew, Aramaic, and Greek Texts with English Translations* (ed. J. H. Charlesworth; Tübingen: J. C. B. Mohr [Paul Siebeck], 1994), 1:134–35, and especially n. 5.

[27] Cf. Rapp, "Jakob in Bet-El," 211–59.

connects the Bethel vision with the Temple Mount by assuming that the ladder started in Bethel, extended such that its mid-point was over Jerusalem, and continued further to Haran in Assyria, the destination of Jacob.[28]

So, one can say that there is effectively no covenant with Jacob in the rabbinic corpus. Yet, for the Rabbis, the very same vision that lay at the core of the Jacob covenant of the *Temple Scroll* and *Jubilees* provided the patriarchal (or we might say pre-Israelite) basis for the same divine commitment to locate God's eternal Temple at Jerusalem.[29]

IV. THE COVENANT AT SINAI

Mention of the covenant of Sinai occurs in 1Q Divre Mosheh (1Q22, *Words of Moses*) which is essentially a covenant renewal and summary text.[30] The text is a speech supposedly given by Moses forty years after the Exodus, that is, in his last year. The people are to be assembled and told to remember the covenant of Sinai. The text relates, very much in a Deuteronomic manner, that they will sin and be punished. The Sabbath is referred to here as "the Sabbath of the covenant" (I, 8). The Sabbath and the covenant are closely associated also in 4QapocrJer C^c (4Q390) 1 8.[31] Singled out for observance after Israel crossed the Jordan are the laws of the Sabbatical year. This text appears to be some kind of a summary of the valedictory speech of Moses from Deuteronomy, rather than claiming to be an entirely different speech. But its main theme is the covenant of Sinai and the inevitable result of violation of its precepts.

---

[28] See *Gen. Rab.* 69:7 (Theodor-Albeck ed., 2:796).

[29] Some limited sense of a covenant with the sons of Jacob is found in rabbinic literature. In interpreting the priestly blessing, *Sifre Num.* 40 paraphrases, "God should preserve for you the covenant with your fathers" (Horowitz ed., 44). Indeed, the covenant was made even with the twelve sons of Jacob to the effect that their descendants would not be destroyed (*Sifra* [Weiss ed., 112c]). The very same passage asserts that the covenant includes the right of possession of the Land of Israel, an aspect of the Jacob covenant of 11QT XIX.

[30] D. Barthélemy and J. T. Milik, *Qumran Cave I* (DJD 1; Oxford: Clarendon, 1955), 91–97.

[31] D. Dimant, *Qumran Cave 4.XXI: Parabiblical Texts, Part 4: Pseudo-Prophetic Texts* (DJD 30; Oxford: Clarendon, 2001), 237–44. Cf. also the list of sins, including Sabbath violation, connected with breaking the covenant in 4Q390 2 I, 4–10 (DJD 30:244–49). Cf. Devorah Dimant, "New Light from Qumran on the Jewish Pseudepigrapha—4Q390," in *The Madrid Qumran Conference: Proceedings of the International Congress on the Dead Sea Scrolls, Madrid, 18–21 March 1991* (ed. J. Trebolle Barrera and L. Vegas Montaner; 2 vols.; STDJ 11; Leiden: Brill, 1992), 2:405–48.

Some sectarian texts use "covenant" to refer only to the Sinaitic covenant, as in the phrase *'am qeduše berit*, "a nation sanctified through the covenant" (1QM X, 10). Similar is the mention of the covenant with "our forefathers" (1QM XIII, 7) which is understood to remain in force for the descendants (cf. 1QM XIV, 4, 8–9, 9–10). This covenant is probably referred to in 1Q34[bis] 3 II, 6, "You renewed Your covenant with them in vision(s) of glory."[32] "Visions of glory" refers to the vision of God at Sinai, and it is most unlikely, therefore, that this passage refers to the renewal of the covenant at the time of the establishment of the sect. 4QpsEzek[a] (4Q385) 2 1 (= 4Q388 [psEzek[d]] 7 2–3) has God describing Himself as having rescued his people, apparently from Egyptian bondage, "to give them the covenant," that is, the Torah which He gave them at Sinai.[33]

Numerous passages in the Hodayot seem to use the term *berit* as equivalent to God's Torah and the covenant entered into at Sinai when it was given. The "laws of the covenant" (*ḥuqqe berit*) of CD V, 12 also refer simply to the laws of the Torah, although it is assumed that these laws existed already in the time of the Patriarchs. This Torah is to be observed even in the Babylonian exile, according to 4QapocrJerC[a] (4Q385a) 18 I, a–b 7–11.[34] Similar use of "covenant" parallel to "Torah" occurs in Barkhi Nafshi[c] (4Q436) 1 I, 4.[35]

The Jewish people seem to have been vouchsafed a "covenant of peace" (1QM XII, 3).[36] An appeal to God's covenant is made in 1QM XVIII, 7–8, reminiscent of biblical appeals to God's promises to Israel.

The covenant *par excellence* in rabbinic literature is certainly that of Sinai, where God and Israel were bound in an eternal relationship.[37] The expression *habberit* occurs in *t. Ḥal.* 1:6 as an oath formula in which a tanna swears by the Torah. Certainly, here *berit* is

---

[32] Barthélemy and Milik, DJD 1:154.

[33] Dimant, DJD 30:23–24, 83–84.

[34] Dimant, DJD 30:159–62.

[35] Moshe Weinfeld and David Seely, in J. VanderKam and M. Brady, consulting eds., *Qumran Cave 4.XX: Poetical and Liturgical Texts, Part 2* (DJD 29; Oxford: Clarendon, 1999), 297–301.

[36] Cf. 4Q491 (War Scroll) 11 II, 18; see M. Baillet, *Qumrân grotte 4.III (4Q482–4Q520)* (DJD 7; Oxford: Clarendon, 1982), 31–34.

[37] This paper will not discuss the chosen people motif in the scrolls which has been discussed in Lawrence H. Schiffman, "Non-Jews in the Dead Sea Scrolls," in *The Quest for Context and Meaning: Studies in Biblical Intertextuality in Honor of James A. Sanders* (ed. C. A. Evans and S. Talmon; Leiden: Brill: 1997), 153–71.

already a reference to the Sinaitic covenant, a usage which we will see appearing prominently in midrashic literature.

The picture of the concept of covenant which emerges from the Tosefta is considerably wider than that of the Mishnah. Here, in a somewhat more aggadic context, we find a series of covenants of eternal validity. The covenant of circumcision made with Abraham remains the basis of Jewish identity. To this is added the Sinaitic covenant. Also, we hear of an eternal covenant made with the Aaronide priesthood providing them with the priestly dues. These covenants guarantee the natural order of creation which will never again be reversed, the relationship of Israel to its God, the special role of the priesthood, and the obligation of Israel to live according to the Torah given at Sinai.

Mekhilta de-Rabbi Ishmael Bo' 5 contains a fascinating expansion on the phrase *mefer berit* which in the Mishnah and Tosefta meant "efface the covenant."[38] Here the expression is taken figuratively, in the sense of rejecting the Sinaitic covenant. This interpretation is accomplished through an exegesis of Deut 29:11 and 28:69. The net effect is that increasingly over time *berit* is being taken in ways going far beyond the Mishnah's more limited usage to denote circumcision. The Sinaitic covenant is gradually upstaging the Abrahamic.

Sifra Beḥuqotai parashah 2:3 draws a parallel between the notion of rejecting the covenant and rejecting God's sovereignty, *kofer ba'iqqar*.[39] Here the notion of covenant has been widened to the very existence of God Himself which is so bound up with the idea of a covenantal relationship with Israel. After all, the essence of Israel's acceptance of the covenant with God is the recognition of God's power and authority over the world.[40]

---

[38] Horowitz-Rabin ed., 15.

[39] Weiss ed., 111c.

[40] That the *berit* is an oath, *shevu'ah*, which the Israelites have taken upon themselves is clear from *Mekhilta de-Rabbi Ishmael Shirah* 9 (Horowitz-Rabin ed., 147; cf. *Be-Šallaḥ* 1, ibid., 76–77). *Mek. Yitro* 5 (ibid., 219) goes a long way toward clarifying the nature of the Sinaitic covenant. Based on an exegesis of Deut 29:28, we are told that God promised Israel that the covenant He would enter into with Israel would be composed of the publicly known commandments, but that the privately known commandments would be kept hidden and would not be presupposed by the covenant. By this He meant that Jews were to be held responsible for one another's actions only in regard to those which could be known. No Jew could be held responsible for the actions of another if they were done unbeknownst to him. This is an underlying concept of the rabbinic view of covenant. It is not simply that each Israelite at Sinai entered into a contract with the Deity; actually, the Jews banded together collectively to enter into this covenant to keep God's Torah. As

One who worships idols is seen as negating the Sinaitic covenant in *Sifre Numbers* 111.[41] The identity of the covenant with the Torah is explicitly stated, again indicating that this is the Sinaitic covenant, not the Abrahamic. Indeed, when *Sifre Numbers* 112 wants to refer to the reversal of circumcision, it has to use the term *berit baśar*, "the covenant of the flesh."[42] By this time the use of *berit* for the Sinaitic covenant had clearly become the most common.[43]

In *Sifra Beḥukotai pereq* 6:1, the word *berit* is used to refer to the covenant curses of Lev 26:14–46.[44] Here we see the notion of the tannaim that the entire Torah constituted the covenant made at Sinai, not just the Decalogue or some other portion of the Pentateuch.

Rabbi Yonatan states in *Mek. Yitro* 10 that just as a covenant was made regarding the Land of Israel, so was one made regarding chastisements.[45] The people of Israel were promised eternally the Land of Israel, yet the covenant included the provision that God would chastise Israel, but only temporarily and out of love. The covenant guarantees that the chastisements will be only temporary.[46] Even if Israel is temporarily expelled from its land, it will eventually return.

A thrice repeated passage in *y. Pe'ah* 2:6 (17a), *y. Meg.* 4:1 (74d) and *y. Ḥag.* 1:8 (76d) makes the point that when God entered into the Sinaitic covenant with Israel, He told them that He was only prepared to make the covenant with them if they agreed to observe both the oral Torah and the written Torah. To the Rabbis, the covenant was twofold. The validity of the written law was as interpreted in the oral law. Only the two together constituted the word of God.[47]

---

such, they form a covenantal community. It is because of this aspect of the covenant that they must be responsible for each other's actions. Nonetheless, the Israelites stipulated at the outset that such responsibility could not be undertaken regarding violations of the covenant which were performed in private.

[41] Horowitz ed., 116.

[42] Ibid., 121.

[43] That the salt of the sacrifices is to be paid for with funds contributed by the community is derived in *Sifra Lev. pereq* 12:6 (Weiss ed., 12c) from the use of the phrase "salt of the covenant" (Lev 2:13). The significance of this passage is that the word *berit* is taken automatically to indicate the communal nature of the obligation. After all, it flows from the covenantal community established at Sinai which collectively takes on the cultic obligations of the Levitical codes.

[44] Weiss ed., 112a.

[45] Horowitz-Rabin ed., 240.

[46] On chastisements and covenant, see *Sifre Deut.* 32 (Finkelstein ed., 57). We should note here the surprising paucity of material pertaining to the term *berit* in *Sifre Deuteronomy*.

[47] The Talmud, *b. Giṭ.* 60b, states in the name of the Palestinian amora Rabbi Yoḥanan that God entered into the Sinaitic covenant only for the sake of the oral law. This makes the point that it is the oral law, with its ability to adapt the writ-

The Babylonian and Palestinian Talmuds really add only one significant idea to our understanding of the covenant in rabbinic literature. They emphasize the dual Torah concept. This notion was becoming more and more prominent in amoraic Judaism, both in Babylonia and Palestine, and it is only natural that the Rabbis would have extended the concept of covenant to include the oral law explicitly. Both Torahs provide the basis for the eternal covenant of the Jewish people and God. Both were given at Sinai.

The Talmud (*b. Roš Haš.* 17b) quotes a statement attributed to the Babylonian amora Rav Judah regarding a covenant which provides that the Thirteen Attributes (Exod 34:6–7) cannot go unanswered when recited in prayer. Again, this use of the term *berit* is as a promise, not really a covenant. At the same time, this notion is linked with the Sinaitic covenant. The Thirteen Attributes are recited as part of the penitential prayers for forgiveness. God has promised Israel that their genuine repentance will indeed be accepted. Another figurative use of the term *berit* is the notion that a covenant is made with the lips as found in *b. Mo'ed Qaṭ.* 18a and *b. Sanh.* 102a. This implies that whatever comes out of one's mouth will be fulfilled, even if it is not intended. Similarly eternal is the covenant of kingship promised to David in *Commentary on Genesis A* (4Q252) V in accordance with this text's interpretation of Gen 49:10.[48]

Both sectarian and rabbinic texts place the Sinai covenant squarely at the center of Jewish commitment and the authority of the Torah. For Qumran texts, the Sinai covenant is the central referent of the term *berit*. For the Rabbis, the covenant ("*berit*") *par excellence* remains circumcision, and only in amoraic times does the Sinai covenant begin to rival circumcision as the essential and central covenant of God and Israel.

V. The Covenant with Levi and Aaron

Several Second Temple period texts refer to a covenant with Levi, which essentially establishes the permanent priesthood of the descendants of this son of Jacob. This theme is prominent in the book of *Jubilees*, where this covenant is repeated several times. As a result of

---

ten Torah to new and varied circumstances, which makes the covenantal relationship of Israel and God permanent. He has given them a law which is truly eternal, not a stagnant system unfit for the vicissitudes of life and time.

[48] Brooke, DJD 22:205–6.

the episode of Simeon and Levi and the people of Shechem (Gen 34), it is emphasized (*Jub.* 30:17–19). It is again confirmed at length as part of the blessing of Levi by Isaac (*Jub.* 31:13–17). At Bethel (on which see above) this blessing is again confirmed (32:1–3).[49]

This same notion is found in the *Aramaic Levi Document.*[50] According to CTLevi Bodl. a (= 4Q213b), apparently (in a lacuna) Isaac already designated Levi as priest and Jacob effected the actual appointment.[51] This status was also consummated at Bethel according to this text (Bodl. b). This text stresses the call to Levi (hence to the Aaronide priesthood) to maintain purity of behavior and family. Numerous laws of sacrifice, supposedly transmitted to Levi, then follow in the text. We can be assured that somewhere in the unpreserved portions of this text there is a mention of Aaron (his parents are mentioned) who was seen as a continuator of the priestly line of Levi as traced through Amram, whose name does appear in the text.

This priestly covenant is also echoed in the poem in 1QM XVII, 2–3 which refers to the eternal priestly covenant. The sons of Aaron as the maintainers of God's covenant, presumably of the priesthood, are mentioned in 4Q419 (*Instruction-like Composition A*) 1 1–8.[52] In *Rule of Benedictions* (1QSb) III, 22–30, there appears a blessing in honor of the Zadokite priesthood. This text asks God to renew "the covenant of [His] priest[hood]." This text indicates that the sectarians saw the priesthood as a covenant between God and specifically the Sons of Zadok, the only ones they (following the book of Ezekiel) regarded as legitimate priests.[53]

Rabbinic texts do not speak of a covenant with Levi, but rather mention extensively the covenant of Aaron, establishing the priesthood in his family. God's covenant with the descendants of Aaron to provide them the twenty-four priestly emoluments is the subject

---

[49] None of these passages is preserved in the Qumran manuscripts. Cf. on these passages Robert A. Kugler, *From Patriarch to Priest: The Levi-Priestly Tradition from Aramaic Levi to Testament of Levi* (SBLEJL 9; Atlanta: Scholars Press, 1996), 161–67; and Rapp, "Jakob in Bet-El," 207–59.

[50] Cf. Kugler, *From Patriarch to Priest,* 146–55; and Rapp, "Jakob in Bet-El," 119–41.

[51] Robert H. Charles, *The Greek Version of the Testaments of the Twelve Patriarchs* (Oxford: Clarendon, 1908), 245; Michael E. Stone and Jonas C. Greenfield, DJD 22:38–41. Cf. Kugler, *From Patriarch to Priest,* 77–93.

[52] Sarah Tanzer, in S. J. Pfann, J. VanderKam, and M. Brady, consulting eds., *Cryptic Texts; Miscellanea, Part 1: Qumran Cave 4.XXVI* (DJD 36; Oxford: Clarendon, 2000), 322–24.

[53] Lawrence H. Schiffman, *The Halakhah at Qumran* (SJLA 16; Leiden: Brill, 1975), 72–75.

of *t. Ḥal.* 2:7.[54] Behind this lies the wider concept that there is a covenant with the sons of Aaron bestowing upon them eternal priesthood. This passage speaks of the twenty-four priestly gifts as having been given to Aaron and his sons through a "covenant of salt" (*berit melaḥ*). The significance of the mention of salt is that it symbolizes the permanence of the covenant (cf. Num 18:19).[55]

That the priestly "covenant of salt," a biblical expression denoting a permanent covenant,[56] is to be eternal is stated in *Mek. de-Rabbi Ishmael, Pisḥa* 1[57] based on the citation of Num 18:19. Indeed, this covenant is singled out along with that of Sinai as being unconditional, as opposed to those pertaining to the Land of Israel, the Temple, and Davidic kingship (*Mek. de-Rabbi Ishmael 'Amaleq* 2).[58] While the Land of Israel, the Temple, and Davidic kingship can be taken away temporarily as a consequence of the transgressions of Israel, the Torah and the priestly status of the sons of Aaron can never be cancelled, not even temporarily.

Sifre Numbers 117 repeatedly mentions the covenant God made with Aaron that his sons would be required to eat the holiest of offerings in the Temple and that only male Aaronide priests who were ritually pure might eat of these sacrifices.[59] In *Sifr. Num.* 119 we hear of Aaron's joy at the covenant regarding the twenty-four priestly gifts. Aaron's covenant is greater than that of David.[60] Whereas David can only devolve his kingship on those of his descendants who are righteous, the Aaronide pedigree of priesthood can be passed on even to those who are not righteous. This difference results from the nature of the priestly office, which is representative of Israel and not dependent on the character of the individual priest. Further, we learn that God also entered into a covenant promising the Levites that they would serve before Him eternally.

---

[54] Cf. Lieberman, *Tosefta Ki-Feshuṭah*, 2:811–12.

[55] The *Temple Scroll* (11QTᵃ XX, 13–14 [restored] and 11QTᵇ IV, 24) mentions the requirement of salting all offerings, in accordance with Lev 2:13; cf. Num 18:19. The covenant of salt refers, according to most commentators, to the permanence of God's covenantal sacrificial requirements.

[56] Haim Beinart, "Melaḥ," *'Enṣiqlopedyah Miqra'it* (Jerusalem: Bialik Institute, 1962), 4:1055–56.

[57] Horowitz-Rabin ed., 2.

[58] Ibid., 201. Cf. *Mek. de-Rabbi Ishmael 'Amaleq* 2 (ibid., 200) on the covenant with Jonadab ben Rechab that was also unconditional. See also *Sifre Num.* 118 (Horowitz ed., 142) on Aaron's "covenant of salt."

[59] Horowitz ed., 134–36.

[60] Ibid., 143–45.

It is apparent that a fundamental difference exists between the priestly covenants of the Second Temple materials, including the scrolls, and the rabbinic view. The earlier sources create a preexisting priesthood, starting with Levi, in consonance with their attribution of later biblical—even post-biblical—practices to the patriarchal family. While some tendencies of this kind are part of the rabbinic approach they never gained prominence. So for the Rabbis, the priestly covenant was with the first priest, Aaron, and not with any of his ancestors.

VI. Covenant and the Qumran Sect

The use of the term "covenant" in reference to the sect itself is common, especially in the *Rule of the Community* (1QS). For example, in 1QS I, 8 *berit ḥesed* appears as a descriptor for the sectarian group. To "enter (*bw'*) [the covenant of Go]d" (1QS II, 26–27) was tantamount to joining the sect (cf. CD II, 2).[61] To reject the covenant of the sect is to "despise" (*m's*) it (cf. 4Q280 [Curses] 2 7 [restored]).[62] Those who attain the required state of purity are admitted to the covenant of the eternal community (*berit yaḥad 'olamim*; 1QS III, 11–12). God's covenant with the sect is eternal (1QS IV, 22; V, 5–6; cf. 1QSa I, 2–2, 25). Further, the leadership of the sectarians is described as "the Sons of Zadok, the priests who guard His covenant, and . . . the majority of the men of the community who hold fast to the covenant" (1QS V, 2–3, 21–22; cf. VI, 19). "A man from among the men of the community, the covenant of the community" can designate a sectarian (1QS VIII, 16–17).

The process in which the new sectarian swears allegiance when he begins the initiation process is termed, "entering the covenant," and requires that he swear to return to the Torah of Moses, as well as to the sectarian interpretations derived by the Sons of Zadok and the sectarian assembly (1QS V, 8–10; cf. V, 20; VI, 15; 1QSa I, 2–3). Those not in the sect will be punished with the covenant curses (1QS V, 10–13). They are described as outside of God's "covenant" (1QS V, 18–19) or as violators of the covenant (*marshi'e berit*, 1QM I, 2). This same phrase appears in 4Q387 (ApocrJer C^b) 3 6–8 which

---

[61] Saul Lieberman, *Texts and Studies* (New York: Ktav, 1974), 203.
[62] Bilhah Nitzan, DJD 29:5–7.

describes, in an *ex eventu* prophecy, Hasmonean rule and the war that would erupt "over the Torah and over the covenant," apparently an allusion to the sectarian struggles of the Hasmonean age.[63] Similar to the *marshi'e berit* are the *'arişe habberit* of *Pesher Psalms A* (4Q171 III, 12) who oppose the sect.[64] On the other hand, the sectarians are designated "[those] who observe (or maintain) the covenant, who turn aside from going [in the p]ath of the people" in 11QMelch (11Q13) II, 24.[65]

Apparently designating the sectarians are the expressions "the lot of his [co]venant" (1QM XVII, 6) and "sons of the covenant" (line 8). As noted above, rabbinic parallels indicate that the latter term often refers to the children of Israel and alludes to their observance of circumcision. In 1QSa I, 3, the eschatological *Rule of the Congregation*, we are told that the adherence of the sect to the covenant with God had atoned for the land. Had the sect not held fast to the correct interpretation of the law, the land would have been destroyed.[66]

As has been amply noted, the procedures for joining the Qumran sect are very similar to those for joining the *havurah* described in tannaitic sources.[67] Yet these groups are never termed a "covenant," and no connection to "covenant" is made. It is because the Qumran sectarians considered themselves as the true biblical Israel that they believed they were vouchsafed a special covenantal status as a group.[68] Because the Rabbis saw themselves as living in the post-biblical era, they saw their covenantal relationship as derivative from the Bible— but not from a direct, independent relationship with God. The Qumran sect, on the other hand, believed that it had an independent covenant with God.

---

[63] Dimant, DJD 30:191–94.

[64] Maurya P. Horgan, *Pesharim: Qumran Interpretations of Biblical Books* (CBQMS 8; Washington, D.C.: Catholic Biblical Association of America, 1979), translates "ruthless ones of the covenant." See her thorough discussion on p. 110.

[65] F. García Martínez, E. J. C. Tigchelaar, and A. S. van der Woude, *Qumran Cave 11.II: 11Q2–18, 11Q20–31* (DJD 23; Oxford: Clarendon, 1998), 226–33.

[66] Cf. Lawrence H. Schiffman, *The Eschatological Community of the Dead Sea Scrolls* (SBLMS 38; Atlanta: Scholars Press, 1989), 11–13.

[67] Lieberman, *Texts and Studies*, 200–207; Chaim Rabin, *Qumran Studies* (Scripta Judaica 2; London: Oxford University Press, 1957), 1–21.

[68] Shemaryahu Talmon, "The 'Desert Motif' in the Bible and in Qumran Literature," in *Biblical Motifs, Origins and Transformations* (ed. A. Altmann; Cambridge, Mass.: Harvard University Press, 1966), 55–63.

VII. Covenant Renewal Ceremony

A prominent part of the *Rule of the Community* (1QS I, 16–II, 25)[69] is devoted to the description of the annual covenant renewal and mustering ceremony of the sectarians at Qumran.[70] The ceremony consists of blessings uttered by the priests and curses recited by the Levites,[71] based on the model of the biblical covenant ceremony of Deuteronomy 27–28 (cf. 11:29), which took place at Mts. Gerizim and Ebal. But the sectarian covenant renewal ceremony is rife with sectarian theological concepts, such as the division of light and darkness and predestination, as well as the isolationist worldview of the sect. Those who "pass" through the covenant, i.e., who are mustered, recited a confession based on biblical models and similar to that which became the norm in later Jewish penitential ritual. They also respond "Amen" to the blessings and curses. The covenant renewal ceremony includes also a procession of priests, Levites, and the rest of the sectarians, organized according to the military organization of the desert period.

It appears from 1QSa I, 5 that it was expected that there would be a covenant renewal at the onset of the end of days.[72] This covenant renewal ceremony is based on the sect's peculiar concept of covenant, as described above. Accordingly, we cannot expect any rabbinic parallels to the covenant renewal ceremony performed annually by the sect. Again, this ceremony was based on the self-conception of the sect as biblical Israel and would have been totally irrelevant to the rabbinic concept of covenant—a permanent relationship of God and Israel seared in the flesh by circumcision and consummated with the giving of the Torah at Sinai.

---

[69] Cf. also 4Q256 II; see P. S. Alexander and G. Vermes, *Qumran Cave 4.XIX: 4QSerekh Ha-Yaḥad and Two Related Texts* (DJD 26; Oxford: Clarendon, 1998), 47–52.

[70] Cf. Jacob Licht, *Megillat ha-Serakhim mi-Megillot Midbar Yehudah* (Jerusalem: Bialik Institute, 1965), 63–65, 74–76; and Rachel Elior, *Miqdash u-Merkavah, Kohanim u-Malakhim, Hekhal ve-Hekhalot ba-Misṭiqah ha-Yehudit ha-Qedumah* (Jerusalem: Magnes, 2002), 142–61.

[71] Cf. also 4Q280 [*Curses*] edited by Nitzan, DJD 29:1–8; 4Q286 [Berakhot[a]] 7 II edited by Nitzan, in J. VanderKam and M. Brady, consulting eds., *Qumran Cave 4.VI: Poetical and Liturgical Texts, Part 1* (DJD 11; Oxford: Clarendon, 1998), 27–30.

[72] Schiffman, *Eschatological Community*, 13.

VIII. The Renewed Covenant

Much attention has been given to a passage in the *Zadokite Fragments* (CD VI, 19) which refers to the sectarians not simply as those who have entered the covenant, but also as having entered "the new (or better 'renewed') covenant,"[73] an allusion to Jer 31:30 which has resonated so deeply in the early Christian tradition (Luke 22:20; 1 Cor 11:25).[74] This same notion is paralleled in CD VIII, 21 = XIX, 33, and also in XX, 12.

That the sect saw itself as a collective "renewed covenant" is clear from *Pešer Habakkuk* (1QpHab) II, 2–10. There, the "treacherous ones" and the Man of the Lie are castigated because they did not believe in the renewed covenant, apparently the sect which had been proclaimed by the Teacher of Righteousness, as had been revealed to him by divinely inspired pesher exegesis of the biblical text. In rejecting the renewed covenant, apparently leaving the sect after initially being part of it, they profaned God's name. Early Christianity understood this passage in Jeremiah to refer to the replacement of God's covenant with the Jewish people by a "new covenant" with those who accepted the messiahship of Jesus. Needless to say, the Qumran view speaks of the renewal of God's ancient covenant with biblical Israel—with the sectarians who continue the role of ancient Israel—not of its replacement or displacement.

Sifra Beḥuqotai pereq 2:5 raises the notion of the "new covenant" of Jer 31:30–33.[75] As opposed to the previous agreement which Israel cancelled by violating the Torah, Israel will be faithful to the renewed covenant. To the Rabbis, this passage in Jeremiah referred not to a new covenant which would in some way replace the Torah, but to a renewal of commitment to the Torah of Sinai. It was to be not a new covenant, but a renewed covenant.[76]

---

[73] Deasley, *The Shape of Qumran Theology*, 140–50 deals with the renewed covenant.

[74] For a thorough discussion of this motif, see Jack R. Lundbom, "New Covenant," *ABD* 4:1088–94. Cf. Shemaryahu Talmon, "The Community of the Renewed Covenant: Between Judaism and Christianity," in *The Community of the Renewed Covenant: The Notre Dame Symposium on the Dead Sea Scrolls* (CJAS 10; ed. E. Ulrich and J. C. VanderKam; Notre Dame: University of Notre Dame Press, 1994), 12–15.

[75] Weiss ed., 111a.

[76] Cf. the detailed discussion of this and related issues in William D. Davies, *Torah in the Messianic Age and/or the Age to Come* (Philadelphia: Society for Biblical Literature, 1952), 50–83.

There is agreement between the sectarian texts and the Rabbis that the "new covenant" is in reality a "renewed covenant." At the same time, when we compare the sectarian and rabbinic views, there is a large discrepancy. For the Rabbis, the renewed covenant simply means a return by the entire Jewish people to the full observance of God's law which Israel had neglected. For the sectarians, the renewed covenant was the indication of their particular relation with God—what made them the true Israel and disqualified the rest of the Jewish people. In this respect, some affinity does exist between the Qumran "new covenant" and that of the early Christians.

IX. Conclusion

The results of our comparisons can be summed up in very simple terms. There is a large degree of incongruity between the concepts of covenant described in the sectarian and rabbinic corpora. While most of the basic elements are in some way shared, the differing ideological backgrounds and exegetical frameworks yielded basically disparate approaches to the details of the various covenants alluded to in our texts.

Despite these disagreements and the entirely different *Sitz-im-Leben* of each approach, all Jewish groups of Late Antiquity believed that Israel's covenant with God is an eternal covenant. It binds Israel to observe the commandments and to continue to live by the Torah. In return, God is to treasure Israel and to protect her. Israel is assured of the power of repentance. The sectarians and the Rabbis agreed heartily with the words of Deut 5:2–3: "The LORD our God made a covenant with us at Horeb. It was not with our fathers that the LORD made this covenant, but with us, the living, every one of us who is here today."

Appendix: The Covenant of Jacob in the *Temple Scroll*

One cannot discuss the specifics of the covenant of Jacob without some detailed knowledge of the location of this motif in the *Temple Scroll* and its particular role. The allusion to this covenant comes at the end of the source known as the "Sacrificial Festival Calendar" which occupies 11QT[a] XIII–XIX. This section represents a reworking of Num 28–29 in light of other parallel sacrificial commands found elsewhere in the Torah, especially in Lev 23, also a sacrificial festival cycle. It is generally accepted today that the Festival Calendar was available to the author/redactor of the complete scroll when he did his work early in the Hasmonean period. This section demonstrates the technique of midrashically harmonizing the disparate biblical texts relating to a specific topic and creating out of them a newly redacted whole. This new whole comes to an end in col. XXIX. After concluding his discussion of the Eighth Day of Solemn assembly (*Shemini Atseret*) (XXIX, 9–10), parallel to Num 29:35–38, the author of this section of the scroll turns to the summary section of Num 29:39–30:1 which was the conclusion of the Numbers Festival Calendar. Here the author mixes in language from the similar concluding passage from Lev 23:37–39.[77] At this point the scroll adds a section of original composition, either of the author of this source or the author/redactor of the scroll. In favor of the latter possibility is the presence of Deuteronomic name theology which pays so prominent a role throughout the *Temple Scroll* and may thus be attributed to the author/redactor of the complete scroll.

In this passage (lines 4–10) we are told that offerings should be made "according to the law of this ordinance" (*ke-torat hammišpat ha-zeh*) continuously, presumably on the festivals, besides the various freewill offerings and emoluments for priests and Levites, and that God promises to accept them. These rites are to continue in God's eternal dwelling place until the day of blessing (or [new] creation) when God will create a new Temple. Here we must note that the Temple of the *Temple Scroll* and its ritual law is therefore not eschatological but rather intended by the text to be the correct (that is, reformist) law for the present, pre-messianic period. The text then, in its preserved state, ends with the key words, "according to the covenant which I have made (lit. 'cut') with Jacob at Bethel."

The top (the zero lines) of the following column, col. XXX, may have contained further information on our topic. Yadin suggests that the text continued with details regarding the command to build the scroll's pre-messianic Temple. This section would have ended in line 3 with some text similar to ושמרתה כל אשר צוויתיכה ל[עשות, "and you shall be careful to do all which I have commanded you to do."[78]

---

[77] See the differing restorations of Yadin, *Temple Scroll*, 2:127 and Qimron, *Temple Scroll*, 44.

[78] Yadin, *Temple Scroll*, 2:130.

The entire missing conclusion would therefore have contained 15 lines (contra Wise, who suggests 12, the number of unpreserved lines at the top of the column).[79] Basing himself on the mention of the covenant of Jacob in Lev 26:42, Wise suggests that our text must have likewise mentioned all three forefathers. He accordingly restores, כברית אשר כרתי עם יעקב בבית אל ועם יצחק בגרר ועם אברהם בחרן "according to the covenant which I made with Jacob at Bethel and Isaac at Gerar and with Abraham at Haran."[80] In this reading, the covenant of 11QT XXIX is not to build the Temple, but rather a broad covenant with the Patriarchs that He would be present in the land and that they would worship and obey Him. The breaking of this wider covenant, in this view, would cause the punishment described in Leviticus. Wise goes on to suggest that this view was shared by the author of the *Zadokite Fragments*.

We have noted already that the *Jubilees* material evinced by Yadin is not really parallel. But the rabbinic parallels certainly lead us to recognize the close link between the Jacob-Bethel experience and the Jerusalem Temple. In fact, these parallels seem sufficiently clear to us to force rejection of Wise's reconstruction and maintenance of the basic idea of a Jacob covenant, partly similar and partly different from that of *Jubilees*.

---

[79] Wise, "The Covenant of *Temple Scroll*," 52.
[80] Ibid., 57.

OPEN AND CLOSED EYES IN THE ANIMAL APOCALYPSE (*1 ENOCH* 85–90)

James C. VanderKam

The Animal Apocalypse in *1 Enoch* 85–90, which appears to be one of the oldest apocalypses with a historical survey,[1] receives its name from the fact that almost all characters in it are represented as different kinds of animals and birds. Using the storyline of sacred history as his foundation, the author sets forth human interactions as if they were taking place between animals. A study of those images and their nuances (e.g., the nature and color of the animals) elucidates the message that the writer wished to express through his curious choice of symbols, although not all of the details have been explained satisfactorily. While the Animal Apocalypse belongs in the category of revelations with historical surveys, it is an unusual sort in that it uses images which do not receive explanations in the text.[2] No interpreting angel clarifies for Enoch the meaning of what he sees; all is considered clear enough without commentary because the familiar biblical text is so transparently reflected in most of the apocalypse.

While the animal imagery is the feature in *1 Enoch* 85–90 that first catches the eye, other types of beings also play important roles. So, for example, the symbol of the seventy shepherds, who appear to be angels and who rule and punish the flock Israel, dominates the text from the point at which it is introduced (89:59) until the

---

[1] Josef T. Milik (*The Books of Enoch: Aramaic Fragments of Qumrân Cave 4* [Oxford: Clarendon, 1976], 44) argues that the Animal Apocalypse dates from a time not long after 164 B.C.E. when the battle of Beth-Zur occurred, an event that is reflected in *1 En.* 90:13–15. Patrick Tiller discusses the various proposals at length and concludes that the apocalypse was written between 165 and 160 B.C.E. (*A Commentary on the Animal Apocalypse of* I Enoch [SBLEJL 4; Atlanta: Scholars Press, 1993], 61–79). George Nickelsburg (*1 Enoch 1: A Commentary on the Book of 1 Enoch, Chapters 1–36; 81–108* [Hermeneia; Minneapolis: Fortress, 2001], 360–61) comes to a similar conclusion and, like Tiller, discusses the complication raised by the duplication and possible updating evident in *1 En.* 90:9–18. Neither thinks the date for a revision would be later than 160 B.C.E.

judgment when the shepherds are among the preeminently evil ones
whose punishment is explicitly noted.

The image that is the subject of this essay is one that is not as
prominent as the animals/birds or the seventy shepherds but one
that still does occur often—the open and closed eyes of Israel.
Beginning at or near the Sinai pericope where the reader first meets
the expression (89:28),[3] the writer expresses the idea that God and
Israel are in a proper relationship by saying the sheep's (Israel's)
eyes were opened, and he articulates the notion that they are not
in a proper relationship by saying the sheep's eyes were closed or
blinded. The first part of this essay gathers from the Animal Apocalypse
the information about the figure of speech, while the second offers
a proposal regarding its origins by relating it to an etymology for
the name *Israel* that was widespread in antiquity: one who sees God.
The complete Animal Apocalypse is available in the Ethiopic version of *1 Enoch*, for a few passages the Aramaic fragments from
Qumran cave 4 preserve the text, and 89:42–49 is available in Greek
in Gr[Vat].

I. Sight and Blindness in the Animal Apocalypse

Since it is a dream vision (85:1), the text contains frequent references to seeing and sight. Enoch introduces the vision report to his
son Methuselah with the words "after this I saw another dream"

---

[2] John Collins ("The Jewish Apocalypses," *Semeia* 14 [1979]: 30–31) classifies the
Animal Apocalypse as a historical apocalypse with no otherworldly journey. As for
the lack of commentary, he writes: "There is no explicit interpretation although the
allegory clearly demands one" (31). Tiller, who, like Collins and others, calls the
Animal Apocalypse an allegory, says that "the referent of the surface story . . . is
the history of humanity as seen in the 'true' light of divine and angelic activity."
He adds that, "[a]lthough the allegory is not very subtle, it at least formally functions as a sort of riddle; only the wise who can make the proper inferences will be
able to understand the true meaning of history" (*Commentary*, 22). On the lack of
interpretation, see also Devorah Dimant, "History According to the Vision of the
Animals (Ethiopic Enoch 85–90)," מחקרי ירושלים במחשבת ישראל 2 (1982): 18–37,
esp. 22 [Hebrew].

[3] The appearance of the image at this point means that it occurs in the second
of the three ages distinguished in the apocalypse, the one that extends from after
the flood to the eschaton (see Dimant, "History According to the Vision of the
Animals," 23–25; Tiller, *Commentary*, 15–17; Nickelsburg, *1 Enoch 1*, 354–55).

(85:1; cf. v. 3),[4] and the author sprinkles other such notices throughout the text so that the reader is regularly reminded that the text
is an account of a visual experience (e.g. 85:4, 5, 7, 9; 86:1, 2, 3,
4; 87:1, 2, 4; 88:1, 3; 89:2, 3, 4, 5, 6, 7, 16, 19, 21, 27, etc.). The
sight/seeing of several characters in the narrative is also noted. So,
for example, the hyenas (= the Egyptians) had their eyes darkened
when the sheep (= the Israelites) left Egypt (89:21, 25, 26); and the
shepherds are also said to be blind (89:74).

The most interesting use of ocular language comes in connection
with the nation Israel. The first reference to the eyes of Israel is
found in *1 En.* 89:28. The verse is situated at the point where Israel
has departed from Egypt, crossed the sea, and entered the wilderness. The Ethiopic of 89:28 has Enoch say: "But the sheep departed
from that water, and they went out into a desert where there was
no water or grass, and they began to open their eyes and to see
[*wa-'axazu yekšetu 'a'yentihomu*[5] *wa-yer'ayu*]. And I saw <until> the owner
of the sheep pastured them, and he was giving them water and grass.
And that sheep [= Moses] <was> going and leading them."[6] 4QEn[e]
4 III, 15–19 preserves parts of this verse. It generally confirms the
Ethiopic wording and includes the following for the expression about
opened eyes: ועיניהון התפתח[ו] (line 17).[7] That is, the Aramaic appears
to lack an equivalent for "they began" and places the expression in
the passive voice. Israel did not open their own eyes; they were
opened for them or they simply opened.

The expression "their eyes were opened" and related ones, as well
as their opposites (e.g. their eyes were blinded), recur regularly in
the subsequent apocalyptic narrative. It is of some interest that as
soon as Moses ascends Mt. Sinai the text relates: "And after that I
saw the owner of the sheep who stood before them, and his appearance was great and awesome and powerful. And all of those sheep

---

[4] Quotations of the Animal Apocalypse, both the ancient versions and the English
translation, are from Tiller, *Commentary*, unless otherwise noted.

[5] The expression is, of course, influenced by scriptural language used in relation
to Israel. See, for example, Isa 42:7 (לפקח עינים עורות).

[6] On the passage see Tiller's textual notes (*Commentary*, 288).

[7] For the text, see Milik, *Books of Enoch*, 243 and pl. XXI, where the reading is
clear, with only the *ḥet* being damaged at the left edge of the fragment. Milik appropriately represents it with a supralinear circlet. See also Tiller, *Commentary*, 174.

saw him [*wa-kʷellomu zeku ʾabāgeʿ reʾyewwo*], and they were afraid of
him" (89:30).[8] In other words, at Sinai all Israel saw God. It does
not take long, however, for the event of the golden calf to transpire;
as we might expect, the author expresses the apostasy by saying that
Israel lacked vision: "And the sheep began to be darkened in their
eyes [*wa-ʾabāgeʿ ʾaxazu yeṣṣallalu ʾaʿyentihomu*] and to stray from the way
which he had shown them" (89:32; cf. v. 33 where a majority are
said to have had their eyes darkened/blinded [*za-ṣellul ʾaʿyentihomu*]).[9]
As Tiller notes, "[b]lindness is here equated with straying 'from the
way which he had shown them.' This 'way' is as clear a reference
to the law as we get in the *Animal Apocalypse*. It confirms the interpretation that sight and blindness correspond to obedience and disobedience to God's law (whether any particular understanding of
that law is intended by the author)."[10]

The eyes of the sheep gave the writer a convenient means for
expressing the alternating faithfulness and disobedience of Israel during the period of the judges. "And sometimes their eyes were opened,
and sometimes they were darkened [*wa-bo soba yetkaššat ʾaʿyentihomu
wa-bo soba yeṣṣallalu*], until another sheep arose. And it led them and
caused them all to return, and their eyes were opened [*wa-takašta
ʾaʿyentihomu*]" (89:41). Here again the meaning of the symbol is transparent. As the narrative reaches the time of Samuel and Saul we
encounter another use of the image (89:44), although here a textual
problem makes it uncertain whether Israel (so the Greek, which has

---

[8] Some letters and words from 89:30 have survived on 4QEn^d 2 II, 29–30 and
4QEn^e 4 III, 20–21, but the Aramaic equivalent of "all of those sheep saw him"
must be restored (see Milik, *Books of Enoch*, 223, 243).

[9] 4QEn^e 4 3 preserves some of v. 32, although the reading of the relevant verb
is most uncertain. Milik reads and restores (with *samekh* marked by a circlet): וע־נא
שריוא לאהסן[מיה (*Books of Enoch*, 204 and pl. XIV). If a form of סמי is to be read
(so too Tiller, *Commentary*, 176), the Ethiopic word translated as "darkened" by Tiller
might rather be rendered as "blinded." For this meaning of *ṣallala* and related forms,
see August Dillmann, *Lexicon Linguae Aethiopicae* (1865; repr., New York: Ungar, 1955),
1256 (with references to Isa 44:18; Job 16:10; Acts 22:11); Wolf Leslau, *Comparative
Dictionary of Geʿez (Classical Ethiopic)* (Wiesbaden: Harrassowitz, 1991), 555, who lists
the meaning "blind (an eye)" or in the passive "be blinded." Klaus Beyer (*Die
aramäischen Texte vom Toten Meer* [Göttingen: Vandenhoeck & Ruprecht, 1984], 245)
proposes לאהן[עורה for the Aramaic passage. In v. 33 the first two letters of the
verb survive on the fragment, but the remainder must be supplied (Milik: מתן[סמים;
ibid., at 4.5; Beyer: מעו]רין; ibid.).

[10] *Commentary*, 294, note to v. 32; cf. Dimant, "History According to the Vision
of the Animals," 25.

a plural [τὰ πρόβατα]) or just Samuel (so the Ethiopic, which has "that sheep" [*we'etu bag‛*]) is intended.[11]

The full-scale apostasy that occurred in the Northern Kingdom is the next sequence that calls forth the blindness image. Following Elijah's removal we read: "And afterwards I saw when they left the owner's house and his tower. They strayed from everything, and their eyes became dark [*wa-taṣallala 'aᶜyentihomu*]. And I saw that the owner of the sheep did much killing against them in their pastures until those sheep invited that killing and betrayed his place" (89:54).[12]

The period of the seventy shepherds which begins at 89:59 includes several references to Israel's sight or blindness. The first comes after the initial return from exile and the rebuilding of the temple: "And as regards all these things the sheep were blinded in their eyes [*'abāgeᶜ ṣellulān 'aᶜyentihomu*], and they were not seeing, and even their shepherds likewise. And they were handing them over even to their shepherds for destruction exceedingly, and they trampled the sheep with their feet and devoured them" (89:74).[13] The fate of the sheep deteriorated even further when a sundry host of birds attacked them and began "to dig out their eyes [*wa-yekreyu 'aᶜyentihomu*] and to devour their flesh" (90:2), thus precluding their ever seeing again short of a healing miracle.

Yet, only a few verses later the situation begins to improve—an improvement accompanied by a cluster of references to sight/blindness:

---

[11] Tiller (*Commentary*, 309) prefers the plural reading of the Greek. R. H. Charles, too, had opted for the Greek (*The Book of Enoch or 1 Enoch* [1912; repr., Jerusalem: Makor, 1973], 196), but François Martin (*Le livre d'Hénoch* [Documents pour l'étude de la Bible, Les apocryphes de l'Ancient Testament; Paris: Letouzey et Ané, 1906], 213) and Michael Knibb (*The Ethiopic Book of Enoch: A New Edition in the Light of the Aramaic Dead Sea Fragments* [2 vols.; Oxford: Clarendon, 1978], 2:207), the latter noting that both Ethiopic and Greek refer to Samuel in the next verse, prefer the Ethiopic singular. On 4QEn^d 2 III, 28–30 a few words from v. 44 can be read, but the part that would solve the problem is not among them; Milik does, though, argue for the singular (*Books of Enoch*, 225). From 89:44 on nothing of the Animal Apocalypse has survived in the Qumran fragments.

[12] Nickelsburg comments that this is the first passage since 89:32–35 (the golden calf episode) in which the notions of straying and blindness are coupled (*1 Enoch 1*, 385).

[13] Tiller (*Commentary*, 340) thinks the verse portrays the situation of the sheep as worse than it was before the exile: not only are they blind and without a proper place but they are also controlled by blind shepherds. Cf. Nickelsburg, *1 Enoch 1*, 395.

And behold lambs were born from those white sheep, and they began to open their eyes and to see [wa-ʾaxazu ʾaʿyentihomu yekšetu wa-yerʾayu] and to cry out to the sheep.[14] And they afflicted them, and they did not listen to their speech but were made very deaf, and their eyes were very much darkened [wa-taṣallala ʾaʿyentihomu fadfāda], and they prevailed. And I saw in the vision that the ravens flew upon those lambs and seized those lambs and crushed the sheep and devoured them. And I saw until horns came forth on those lambs, and the ravens were crushing their horns. And I saw until a big horn sprouted on one of those sheep, and their eyes were opened [wa-takašta ʾaʿyentihomu]. And it looked among them, and their eyes were opened [wa-tafatha[15] ʾaʿyentihomu], and it cried out to those sheep; and the rams saw it, and they all ran to it. (90:6–10)

The period in question seems to be the early years of Seleucid dominion down to the decrees of Antiochus IV and the rise of the Hasmoneans.[16]

Our image does not appear again until the apocalypse relates the various parts of the final judgment. In 1 En. 90:26, Enoch sees that the blind sheep [ʾabāgeʿ ṣellulān] are tossed into an abyss of fire and burned, while 90:35 says of all the sheep who were in the new house (see vv. 28–29): "the eyes of them all were opened [wa-ʾaʿyentihomu la-kʷellomu takašta], and they saw well [wa-yenēṣṣeru šannāya], and there was not one among them that did not see [wa-ʾaḥadu za-ʾi-yerēʾʾi ʾalbo ba-māʾkalomu]." The repeated expressions here offer the Animal Apocalypse's "definitive statement of the righteousness of surviving Jews and Gentiles."[17]

II. Origins of the Image

Scholars have assumed that the symbol of opened/closed eyes in the Animal Apocalypse should, given how the text follows the scriptural base, correspond to a word or expression in Exodus at the point

---

[14] See Nickelsburg (1 Enoch 1, 398) who calls attention to the similarity in wording between 90:6 and 89:28: "God grants a new revelation that parallels the revelation given in the wilderness after the exodus." For the movement depicted symbolically in these verses, see his excursus, "Traditions about a Religious Awakening in the Hellenistic Period" (398–400).

[15] Note the unexpected verb for "open"; in all other passages the Ethiopic version is consistent in using forms of kašata.

[16] Tiller, Commentary, 350–56.

[17] Tiller, Commentary, 382.

where it is first used. The period in question lies between the passage through the sea (89:21–27) and Moses' (= "that sheep") ascent of Mt. Sinai which is represented in 89:29. Commentators have made a number of suggestions regarding the possible biblical basis for the image. So, for example, François Martin pointed to Exod 14:31 where the idea of Israel's seeing in a religious sense is prominent. After the miracle at the sea, ". . . when Israel saw [וירא ישראל] the wondrous power which the LORD had wielded against the Egyptians, the people feared the LORD; they had faith in the LORD and His servant Moses."[18] On his view, Israel there began to open their eyes "pour reconnaître la puissance de Dieu."[19] Günter Reese has opted for the same base text.[20] The motif of Israel's seeing is indeed present here, and it is used in the immediate context where Israel is in proper relationship with the LORD; but the passage is located prior to the people's entry into the wilderness, whereas *1 En.* 89:28 uses the imagery of opened eyes at a point after the people have crossed the sea and begun their wilderness trek.[21]

Others[22] have maintained that the image was suggested by Exod 15:25b–26: "There He made for them a fixed rule, and there He put them to the test. He said, 'If you will heed the LORD your God diligently, doing what is upright in His sight, giving ear to His commandments and keeping all His laws, then I will not bring upon you any of the diseases that I brought upon the Egyptians, for I the

---

[18] Translations of the Hebrew Bible are from the JPS.

[19] *Le livre d'Hénoch*, 209. This view goes back to August Dillmann, *Das Buch Henoch uebersetzt und erklärt* (Leipzig: Vogel, 1853), 260 (where he also refers to Hos 2:15; Jer 2:2). Dillmann considered a curious interpretation of the open eyes expression in 89:28: "Man ist versucht, diess so zu verstehen, dass ihnen die Augen über diese unwirthbare Gegend aufgiengen und sie desshalb murrten und klagten Ex. 15, 23–K. 17" (260). However, he thought the subsequent uses of the expression required that one understand it differently also in v. 28: "Verblendete Augen bedeuten dort sittlich-religiöse Verfinsterung; sehende Augen werden denen zugeschrieben, die Gott und seinem Weg erkennen, an ihn glauben und ihn fürchten . . ." (260).

[20] Günter Reese, "Die Geschichte Israels in der Auffassung des frühen Judentums: Eine Untersuchung der Tiervision und der Zehnwochenapokalypse des äthiopischen Henochbuches, der Geschichtsdarstellung der Assumptio Mosis und der des 4Esrabuches" (Ph.D. diss., Ruprecht-Karl-Universität zu Heidelberg, 1967), 34.

[21] Perhaps because he senses this problem, Reese suggests that *1 En.* 89:28 be considered part of the story about crossing the sea, even as it leads into the wilderness section ("Die Geschichte," 34, 37 n. 77).

[22] See, for example, Tiller, *Commentary*, 292, where he notes that Carol Newsom, in an unpublished paper, also saw the inspiration for the image in this passage.

LORD am your Healer.'" For these scholars presumably it is the notion of obedience that is picked up in the apocalypse and symbolized as the opening of eyes. As Tiller puts it, "[t]he implication of seeing, then, seems to be possession of God's law and obedience to it. From this point on the ability of the sheep to see will represent Israel's obedience or disobedience to God."[23] Yet, this passage too precedes the entry into the wilderness and has virtually nothing to do with sight (only the LORD's eyes are mentioned [הישר בעיניו in v. 26]). If it is the base text, then one would have to argue that the motif of opened eyes was not suggested explicitly by the text of Exodus; only the theme of obedience was.

First Enoch 89:28 declares, directly after first mentioning the opened eyes, that "the owner of the sheep pastured them, and he was giving them water and grass." This may be an allusion to the contents of Exod 15–17 where the LORD gives the grumbling people first quail and manna and then water from the rock.[24] In these chapters there are a few references to seeing, with the one in 16:7 perhaps being a candidate for the scriptural trigger for the opened eyes imagery: "and in the morning you shall behold the Presence of the LORD [וראיתם את־כבוד יהוה]." Yet this passage, too, seems rather unlikely because the verb וראיתם is used in response to grumbling and refers to the food that will be rained down from the sky.

The chapters in Exodus having to do with the covenant made at Mt. Sinai contain several references to seeing. For example, at Exod 19:4–6 the LORD gives Moses a message for the people that combines the two names for the ancestor of the nation and speaks of the special covenant between them:

> Thus you shall say to the house of Jacob and declare to the children of Israel: "You have seen [ראיתם] what I did to the Egyptians, how I bore you on eagles' wings and brought you to me. Now then, if you will obey Me faithfully and keep My covenant, you shall be My treasured possession among all the peoples. Indeed, all the earth is Mine, but you shall be to Me a kingdom of priests and a holy nation." These are the words that you shall speak to the children of Israel.

Shortly thereafter, once the people have unanimously affirmed their obedience to the forthcoming divine commands, the LORD orders

---

[23] Tiller, *Commentary*, 292.
[24] See Nickelsburg, *1 Enoch 1*, 379–80.

Moses to say to them: "Let them be ready for the third day; for on the third day the LORD will come down, in the sight of all the people [לעיני כל־העם], on Mt. Sinai" (19:11). Ironically, the deity adds in 19:21 that the people were "not to break through to the LORD to gaze [לראות], lest many of them perish" (cf. 20:19; 33:20, 23). Later we learn that "Moses and Aaron, Nadab and Abihu, and seventy elders of Israel ascended; and they saw the God of Israel [ויראו] את אלהי ישראל" (24:9–10a; see v. 11 where they see God but the verb is ויחזו; v. 17 where his glory appears to Israel).

It may be, therefore, that one should search for the source of the opened eyes/seeing imagery, not in the chapters of Exodus preceding the Sinai pericope, but within it. This would be consistent with *1 En.* 89:28 which locates the Israelites in a desert after crossing the sea, with v. 29 mentioning Moses' ascent of the mountain. Yet, though some expressions in the chapters about the Sinai covenant probably contributed to the open eye imagery of the Animal Apocalypse, the thesis that will be defended here is that the image of sight/blindness to express Israel's relation to the deity also arose from a well-attested etymology of the name *Israel* as "one who sees God." As we have seen, both *Jacob* and *Israel* figure in Exod 19:3. The name *Israel* was first revealed to Jacob (Gen 32:29) and used for him alone, but it was later transferred to his descendants as a nation. That nation became the covenant people of God at Mt. Sinai. The idea is that Israel is truly Israel, the kind of people that it became at Sinai (Exod 19–24), when it sees God, that is, when it obeys him.[25] We should now turn to a consideration of Gen 32:29 where the name *Israel* is explained and then move to the evidence for the etymology in later literature and its relevance for the open eye imagery of the Animal Apocalypse.

Jacob, like his grandfather Abraham, received a new name after a defining episode in his life. The night before he was to meet his unpredictable brother Esau, Jacob wrestled with a being termed an

---

[25] Nickelsburg (*1 Enoch 1*, 380–81) supplies an excursus on "Blindness and Straying as Apostasy and the Opening of Israel's Eyes as Revelation," but in it he does not mention the etymology of *Israel* as a possible source for the expressions. He does note that the imagery "underscores the author's sharp distinction between right and wrong conduct and his belief that, for most of its history, the nation has violated God's revealed law, specifically with respect to cultic matters" (381).

אִישׁ (Gen 32:25), an individual who was not able to defeat the patriarch. After touching and injuring Jacob's thigh, he demanded to be
sent away, but Jacob refused to comply until he first blessed him.
Upon learning Jacob's name, the mysterious being said: "Your name
shall no longer be Jacob, but Israel, for you have striven [שָׂרִיתָ] with
beings divine [אֱלֹהִים] and human, and have prevailed" (Gen 32:29;
cf. 35:10). The passage supplies the word *Israel* with a compound
etymology: יִשְׂרָאֵל is playfully related to אִישׁ plus שָׂרָה plus (אֱלֹ)הִים.[26]
But Jacob, once his combatant had left, named the place of the bout
פְּנִיאֵל, explaining: כִּי רָאִיתִי אֱלֹהִים פָּנִים אֶל פָּנִים וַתִּנָּצֵל נַפְשִׁי.

Claus Westermann found similarities between the Peniel/Penuel
story and the strange account of the LORD's attack on Moses in Exod
4:24–26;[27] it also may be paralleled with an angel's appearance to
Samson's parents in Judg 13. But a more directly related text is Hos
12:4–5: וַיָּשַׂר אֶל־מַלְאָךְ וַיֻּכָל וַיָּשַׂר אֶת־אֱלֹהִים שָׂרָה וּבְאוֹנוֹ ("Grown to manhood, he strove with a divine being, He strove with an angel and
prevailed"). Here we have the individual with whom Jacob struggled identified more explicitly as an angel. The targums of Genesis
follow this approach. Naturally, the Aramaic translators were concerned to remove the possible anthropomorphism of Gen 32:29. So,
Tg. Ps.-J. Gen 32:29 reads: "because you have *gained superiority* over
the angels of the Lord and over men and you have prevailed *against
them.*"[28] In 32:25 the targumist renders "*an angel in the form of* a man
wrestled with him," while *Tg. Neof.* Gen 32:25 quite appropriately
names that angel who assumed human form *Sariel*. Much earlier evidence for a similar understanding can be found in Josephus who
refers to Jacob's adversary twice as a "phantom [φάντασμα]" and

---

[26] For surveys of etymological explanations offered by modern scholars, see Hans-
Jürgen Zobel, "יִשְׂרָאֵל," *TDOT* 6:399–401; John Skinner, *Genesis* (ICC; 2nd ed.;
Edinburgh: T & T Clark, 1930), 409–10 notes to v. 29.

[27] *Genesis 12–36* (Minneapolis: Augsburg, 1981), 517.

[28] The translation is from Michael Maher, *Targum Pseudo-Jonathan: Genesis* (The
Aramaic Bible 1B; Collegeville, Minn.: The Liturgical Press, 1992), 114. *Targum
Onqelos* avoids the potential anthropomorphism differently—by relating the verb שָׂרָה
in Gen 32:29 to the noun שַׂר: "for *you are a prince before the Lord*" (Bernard Grossfeld,
The Targum Onqelos to Genesis [The Aramaic Bible 6; Wilmington, Del.: Michael
Glazier, 1988], 116). As one might expect, the LXX translates more literally, rendering אֱלֹהִים in Gen 32:29 as θεοῦ, although it shows a different syntax at the end
of the verse by not using a conjunction before the equivalent of תוּכָל, yielding "and
with men you have been strong."

then identifies him as an angel, adding that Israel means "the opponent [ἀντιστάτην] of an angel of God" (*Ant.* 1.20, 2 [333]).[29]

The targumic treatments of Gen 32:29 already lead us far into the interpretive tradition around this intriguing verse.[30] Exegetes were concerned to identify Jacob's adversary for whom Genesis used different and suggestive designations (איש, אלהים). In the course of reflection on the problem, the information found in Gen 32:29 and in 32:31 (regarding Peniel) were conflated, yielding the explanation found in a number of sources that the word *Israel* means איש ראה אל. Oddly enough, our earliest evidence for this understanding is in Greek texts,[31] although the composite etymology is clearly Hebrew in origin.

Philo may provide the earliest Greek documentation for this meaning of *Israel*, a meaning that for him clearly implies high status and privilege. For example, in *Congr.* 51 he wrote: "Now to see the best, that is the truly existing, it is the lot of the best of races, Israel, for Israel means seeing God ['Ισραὴλ γὰρ ὁρῶν θεὸν ἑρμηνεύεται]."[32] The same explanation for the name occurs several times in the Alexandrian philosopher's works—some forty-nine in all.[33] He repeats it in connection with a number of biblical passages, including Exod 24:11 where Israel unanimously pledges to obey the entire covenantal law. In *Fug.* 208 he provides an interesting contrast in relation to the name Ishmael:

> thou shalt give birth with easy travail to a male offspring, Ishmael by name since thou shalt have been chastened by hearkening to the words of God; for "Ishmael" means "hearkening to God." Hearing takes the second place, yielding the first to sight, and sight is the portion of Israel, the son free-born and first-born; for "seeing God" is the translation of "Israel." It is possible to hear the false and take it for true,

---

[29] Thackeray, LCL. The references to the phantom are in §331.

[30] Our honoree has collected and discussed a very wide range of ancient passages that deal with the scene at the Jabbok and the name change. See James L. Kugel, *Traditions of the Bible: A Guide to the Bible As It Was At the Start of the Common Era* (Cambridge, Mass.: Harvard University Press, 1998), 384–89, 394–401.

[31] See the sources listed in Lester L. Grabbe, *Etymology in Early Jewish Interpretation: The Hebrew Names in Philo* (BJS 115; Atlanta: Scholars Press, 1988), 172–73.

[32] Colson, LCL.

[33] See the full enumeration of passages by Jonathan Z. Smith, "Prayer of Joseph" in *OTP* 2:703 n. 20, and especially the extended study of Ellen Birnbaum, *The Place of Judaism in Philo's Thought: Israel, Jews, and Proselytes* (BJS 290; Studia Philonica Monographs 2; Atlanta: Scholars Press, 1996), 61–127.

because hearing is deceptive, but sight, by which we discern what really is, is devoid of falseness.[34]

In the preface to *On the Embassy to Gaius*, Philo makes a similar point about the special relationship between God and his people with perhaps an allusion to Deut 32:6, 8–9.

> And yet the present time and the many important questions decided in it are strong enough to carry conviction even if some have come to disbelieve that the Deity takes thought for men, and particularly for the suppliants' race which the Father and King of the Universe and the Source of all things has taken for his portion. Now this race is called in the Hebrew tongue Israel, but, expressed in our tongue, the word is "he that sees God" and to see Him seems to me of all possessions, public or private, the most precious. (§§3–4)[35]

From the many uses of the etymology for Israel in the corpus, Ellen Birnbaum has concluded:

> By far, most of Philo's explicit references to "Israel" include the etymology either directly or indirectly. In addition, instead of using the term "Israel" itself, he frequently substitutes for it a variety of expressions, which in one way or another pertain to seeing or seeing God. Philo's predominant association with "Israel," then, whether the word occurs explicitly or not, depends upon his understanding of its etymology as ὁρῶν θεόν, one that sees God.[36]

Naturally, Philo relates the etymology for Israel to Gen 32:29 (e.g., *Ebr.* 82–83; *Migr.* 201; *Mut.* 81–88; *Praem.* 36–46; *Somn.* 1.129, 171), but he also employs it in connection with his exposition of passages from Exod 24, the covenant-making chapter. In *Conf.* 56 he quotes the Israelites (at the time of the war against Midian in Numbers 31): "'For we are the "race of the Chosen ones of that Israel" who sees God, "and there is none amongst us of discordant voice"'" (Ex. xxiv.11), that so the whole world, which is the instrument of the All, may be filled with the sweet melody of its undiscording harmonies."[37] Philo found a shared expression in Num 31:49 and Exod 24:11a and, as a consequence, read the two passages together. His text of

---

[34] Colson, LCL.
[35] Colson, LCL.
[36] *Place of Judaism*, 61. See her summary of the passages on 65–66 where she notes that he never includes a word for man or person in the etymology.
[37] Colson, LCL.

Exod 24:11a read: καὶ τῶν ἐπιλέκτων τοῦ Ἰσραηλ οὐ διεφώνησεν οὐδὲ εἶς, while Num 31:49 read: καὶ οὐ διαπεφώνηκεν ἀπ' αὐτῶν οὐδὲ εἶς.[38] The passages served for him as expressions of unity, of harmony and thus as apt characterizations of God's chosen people (see also *QE* 2.38, 39 on Exod 24:11b).

In his comments on Exod 24:12, which refers to God's inscribing the law on stone tablets for Moses, Philo associates the creation of the world with the giving of the law. Here he uses another of his formulations of the etymology of Israel—the contemplative race (ὁρατικὸν γένος):

> this world is a great city and is a legal one. And it is necessary for it to use the best law of the state. And it is fitting that it should have a worthy author of law and legislator, since among men He appointed the contemplative race in the same manner (as the Law) for the world. And rightly does He legislate for this race, also prescribing (its Law) as a law for the world, for the chosen race is a likeness of the world, and its Law (is a likeness of the laws) of the world. (*QE* 2.42)[39]

He makes the parallel with creation clearer in 2.46 where he explicates Exod 24:16b (the mountain was covered by a cloud for six days and Moses was summoned on the seventh): "The even number, six, He apportioned both to the creation of the world and to the election of the contemplative nation,[40] wishing to show first of all that He had created both the world and the nation elected for virtue. And in the second place, because He wishes the nation to be ordered and arranged in the same manner as the world . . ." (cf. his comments on the eighth day for circumcision in Gen 17:12 in *QG* 3.49).[41]

---

[38] The passages are cited from Alfred Rahlfs, *Septuaginta* (2 vols.; Stuttgart: Württembergische Bibelanstalt, 1935). The MT of both passages sounds quite different; in it they refer to people who survived, not people who were harmonious.

[39] Marcus, LCL; see §2.43 where "contemplative race" is again used.

[40] In this case a Greek fragment confirms the base text of the Armenian translation: τῇ τοῦ ὁρατικοῦ γένους ἐκλογῇ (Marcus, LCL 91 n. c). For the use of the expression in Philo's writings, see Birnbaum, *Place of Judaism*, 94–114, 125.

[41] Marcus, LCL. See Gerhard Delling, "The 'One Who Sees God' in Philo," in *Nourished With Peace: Studies in Hellenistic Judaism in Memory of Samuel Sandmel* (ed. F. Greenspahn, E. Hilgert, and B. Mack; Scholars Press Homage Series 9; Chico, Calif.: Scholars Press, 1984), 27–31. He comments: "In fact the epithet, 'the race able to see,' seems to have priority in those contexts which deal with the events of Moses' time" (31).

Israel is, then, the nation that sees, and that name is eloquent of the people's special relationship with God, a relationship that was established at Mt. Sinai where the law was given and the regular service of God was defined. "The gift of seeing God is bound up with the particular relationship to God that God accords the Jews, accords them as the company which worships him, the one God."[42]

It is not being claimed here that Philo uses his "seeing" etymologies for Israel only in connection with Sinai; that is not the case. The argument is rather that Philo (or his source[s]) has extended the explanation of Israel as "one who sees God" from the individual Jacob to the nation Israel and that he understands it as articulating the nation's special status before God, a status that comes to expression at Mt. Sinai.

If we apply such information to the image of opened eyes/seeing for Israel's proper relationship with God in the Animal Apocalypse of Enoch, we see that the author uses the expression beginning at or near Sinai in order to express the special event, the covenant, that took place there. Although the author of the apocalypse does not reproduce the story about Jacob's wrestling match at the Jabbok, he does, like Philo, transfer the etymology of Israel to the nation and uses it to define its unique status. Israel truly enfleshes the meaning of its revealed name—the one who sees God—when it obeys God, when it accepts his covenantal will disclosed at Sinai and obeys it. If this interpretation of the image of opened (and closed) eyes, of seeing (and blindness) is correct, another consequence follows. Although the earliest Hebrew attestation of the etymology of *Israel* as "one who sees God" is in the apparently late work *Seder Eliahu Rabba* 25 (a midrash on Hos 9:10),[43] if it lies behind the opened eye/seeing imagery of the Animal Apocalypse, then its use can now be traced back in an Aramaic source to the second century B.C.E.

---

[42] Delling, "The 'One Who Sees God' in Philo," 35 (where he refers to *Sacr.* 120).

[43] See the discussion of the date for this work in Hermann Strack and Günter Stemberger, *Introduction to the Talmud and Midrash* (Edinburgh: T&T Clark, 1991), 369–70.

BEFORE THE FALL: THE EARLIEST INTERPRETATIONS OF ADAM AND EVE

John J. Collins

James Kugel has contributed more than any other scholar of his generation to the retrieval of ancient biblical exegesis.[1] His massive research has established beyond dispute that exegetical concerns play a significant role in Jewish writings of the late Second Temple period, even where they are not the primary generating factor of the composition.[2] He has also shown the remarkable consistency with which the same interpretations appear in Jewish and Christian tradition. This is especially true in the case of pivotal texts such as the story of Adam and Eve. Consequently, as Kugel observes, modern readers have great difficulty in approaching such texts "without blinders." "Who nowadays, for example, does not automatically think of the story of Adam and Eve in the Garden of Eden as telling about some fundamental change that took place in the human condition, or what is commonly called the Fall of Man? Who does not think of the 'serpent' in the story as the devil, or paradise as the reward of the righteous after death?"[3] Yet, these assumptions go far beyond what is stated explicitly in the biblical text.[4] Kugel has shown brilliantly how the ancient interpreters arrived at the common understanding of the story. Only rarely, however, does he note that these interpretations were not always shared, and that some people read the text in ways that accord neither with traditional interpretations nor with modern critical understanding.[5] In this respect, the earliest interpretations of Genesis 2–3 are especially interesting, and it is remarkable that they have received little attention in recent studies of the ancient interpretation of Adam and Eve.[6]

---

[1] James L. Kugel, *The Bible As It Was* (Cambridge, Mass.: Harvard University Press, 1997); idem, *The Traditions of the Bible* (Cambridge, Mass.: Harvard University Press, 1998).

[2] See his nuanced remarks on *1 Enoch* in *Traditions*, 31.

[3] *Traditions*, 94.

[4] See the incisive study of James Barr, *The Garden of Eden and the Hope of Immortality* (London: SCM, 1992).

[5] See his comment on the exceptional position of Sir 17:1–2 (*Traditions*, 127).

[6] The wide-ranging study of Gary Anderson, *The Genesis of Perfection: Adam and*

I. EDEN TRADITIONS IN THE HEBREW BIBLE

The first thing to note about interpretations of the story of Adam and Eve is that they are entirely absent from the Hebrew Bible. However important the story later became, it does not serve as a point of reference for the later biblical writers. The absence of allusions to these chapters of Genesis is puzzling. They belong to the Yahwist (J) strand of the Pentateuch, which is generally regarded as the oldest, and has been dated by some critics as early as the tenth century B.C.E.[7] The lack of any references to the story in the remainder of the biblical corpus must cast some doubt on such an early dating.

There are references to "the garden of God" in Ezekiel chapters 28 and 32, but the prophet does not seem to have the Genesis story in mind. Ezekiel 32 compares the king of Assyria to a cedar of Lebanon and says that no tree in "the garden of God" could compare with him, and that all the trees of Eden envied him. Because he grows so tall, he becomes arrogant and is cut down. All we can infer from this allegory is that Eden was known as the name of the garden of God, which was conceived on the model of the gardens, or parks, of Mesopotamian kings. (The Greek word, *paradeisos*, is derived from the Persian *pardēs*, the name for the leisure park of the Persian king.)[8]

Ezekiel 28 is more intriguing. The context is a taunt-song to the King of Tyre. The passage reads as follows, in the translation of Moshe Greenberg:

> You were the sealer of proportion,
> full of wisdom and perfect in beauty!
> In Eden, the garden of God, you were,
> every precious stone your hedge . . .
> You were a great shielding cherub!
> And I set you

Eve in Jewish and Christian Imagination (Louisville: Westminster John Knox, 2001) does not deal at all with Ben Sira, *1 Enoch*, or the Dead Sea Scrolls. Neither does the study of J. T. A. G. M. van Ruiten, "The Creation of Man and Woman in Early Jewish Literature," in *The Creation of Man and Woman: Interpretations of the Biblical Narratives in Jewish and Christian Traditions* (ed. G. P. Luttikhuizen; Leiden: Brill, 2000), 34–62, which is focused on the issue of sexual differentiation in creation.

[7] See Richard Elliott Friedman, "Torah (Pentateuch)," *ABD* 6:605–22.

[8] James H. Charlesworth, "Paradise," *ABD* 5:154–5.

in the holy mountain of God you were;
amidst fire-stones you walked about.
Unblemished were you in your ways
from the day you were created,
until wrongdoing was found in you.
Because of your many dealings
your midst was filled with lawless gain, and you sinned.
So I desacralized [and barred] you from the mountain of God,
and I banished you, shielding cherub, from amidst fire-stones.[9]

Here we have reference to a story in which someone is driven out from Eden, the garden of God. There is no mention, however, of either a tree of life or a tree of the knowledge of good and evil. Neither is there a serpent or woman. The figure in question is expelled because of pride and is subsequently destroyed. It is not apparent, however, that his fall represents a turning point in the human condition. In Greenberg's translation, which follows the MT closely, the figure who is expelled is a cherub: *'att kᵉrûb*, "you were a cherub." On this reading, the story to which Ezekiel refers is not about the expulsion of a human being, but the fall of a demi-god, like the story of *Helal ben Shachar* in Isaiah 14.[10] The ancient versions (Greek and Syriac) read *'et kᵉrûb*, "with a cherub," assuming that the person addressed is not the cherub. Again in v. 16 the Greek reads "the cherub led you out." Either the Hebrew is corrupt in these verses,[11] or the Greek translators were influenced by the Genesis story, where the cherub functions as a guardian. In any case, the garden on the mountain of God,[12] with its fiery stones, is conceived in a way that is quite different from Genesis. We must assume that Ezekiel knew a myth about Eden that is different from the story of Adam and Eve.[13] This should hardly surprise us. The

[9] Ezek 28:12–17. Moshe Greenberg, *Ezekiel 21–37* (AB 22A; New York: Doubleday, 1997).

[10] For a recent discussion of Isaiah 14 see R. Mark Shipp, *Of Dead Kings and Dirges: Myth and Meaning in Isaiah 14:4b–21* (Atlanta: Society of Biblical Literature, 2002).

[11] This is the usual assumption. See Walther Zimmerli, *Ezekiel* (2 vols.; Hermeneia; Philadelphia: Fortress, 1983), 2:85–86.

[12] The temple mountain is often associated with Eden. See Jon D. Levenson, *The Theology of the Program of Restoration of Ezekiel 40–48* (Missoula, Mont.: Scholars Press, 1976), 25–36. But there is no allusion to the temple mountain in the Genesis story.

[13] *Pace* Greenberg (*Ezekiel 21–37*, 593), who finds here "known mythical motifs freshly combined in a unique structure." The "known mythical motifs" are supposedly a combination of the P and J accounts in Genesis, but key features of

material found in the Hebrew Bible can only be a fraction of the religious lore of ancient Israel. It will be important to keep that point in mind when we turn to the use of Eden traditions in *1 Enoch*.

II. Adam and Eve in Ben Sira

The earliest datable allusions to the story of Adam and Eve are found in the wisdom book of Ben Sira, which was composed in the first quarter of the second century B.C.E.[14] This is probably not the earliest reflection of Genesis 2–3; the Book of the Watchers in *1 Enoch* 1–36 is probably earlier, or the two may be roughly contemporary. Ben Sira has the advantage of reflecting fairly explicitly on the biblical text. His discussion provides a salutary reminder that what may seem obvious to a modern interpreter was not necessarily accepted in the ancient world.

Kugel has drawn attention to Sir 17:1–2:

> The Lord created Adam (or: a human being) out of the earth,
> and returned him to it again.
> He allotted them numbered days and time,
> and gave them authority over the things upon it.

As Kugel rightly notes, this passage is part of Ben Sira's recapitulation of the creation of the world. The passage appears to question one of the most widely held assumptions about Adam and Eve: that death was introduced as a punishment for their disobedience.[15] Just as the man was taken from the earth, so it would appear that he was destined to return to it, regardless of his obedience or disobedience. There is an apparent contradiction between this view of creation and Ben Sira's statement in Sir 25:24: "From a woman sin had its beginning, and because of her we all die." But the view that humanity was always meant to be mortal is found again in Sir 41:4, where we are told that death is "the LORD's decree for all flesh,"

Ezekiel's poem have no parallel in Genesis, while key features of the Genesis story have no parallel in Ezekiel.

[14] See John R. Levison, *Portraits of Adam in Early Judaism from Sirach to 2 Baruch* (Sheffield: JSOT Press, 1988).

[15] Kugel, *Traditions*, 127. On the discussion of this issue in rabbinic tradition see Ephraim E. Urbach, *The Sages: Their Concepts and Beliefs* (Jerusalem: Magnes, 1975), 421–36.

and not a punishment. It should be noted that Philo understood Genesis 2–3 to speak of the death of the soul, which "is practically the antithesis of the death which awaits us all."[16] The latter takes place "in the course of nature," whereas the "penalty-death" is the death of the soul which results from sin. Even the Wisdom of Solomon, which says emphatically that God did not make death and that it entered the world by the envy of the devil (Wis 1:13; 2:23–24), is most probably referring to spiritual death and taking mortality for granted.[17]

Sirach 25:24, then, is anomalous in the context of Ben Sira. The viewpoint it expresses becomes standard in later tradition. So, for example, the *Apocalypse of Moses*, a variant of the *Life of Adam and Eve*, has Adam accuse Eve of bringing destruction, in the form of death, over all the race. A similar sentiment is found in Pseudo-Philo (*L.A.B.* 13:10). In the New Testament, 1 Tim 2:13–14 declares that the woman, not Adam, was deceived and became a transgressor. In light of this tradition, most scholars assume that Ben Sira is referring to Eve in Sir 25:24. The reference has been questioned by Jack Levison.[18] There is a text from Qumran, the so-called "Wiles of the Wicked Woman" (4Q184), that says: "She is the beginning of all the ways of iniquity . . . for her ways are ways of death."[19] No one takes the Qumran text to refer to Eve. The biblical precedent for the passage is found in Proverbs 7, in the figure of the *'iššāh zārāh*, or "strange woman."[20] This figure stands in contrast to personified Wisdom in Proverbs 8, who says that "the LORD created me the

---

[16] Philo, *Leg.* 1.105–108. Other passages in Philo, which do not make this distinction explicitly, such as *QG* 1.45, 51, most probably assume it.

[17] Michael Kolarcik, *The Ambiguity of Death in the Book of Wisdom 1–6* (AnBib 127; Rome: Pontifical Biblical Institute, 1991), 180, and especially Karina Martin Hogan, "The Exegetical Background of the 'Ambiguity of Death' in the Wisdom of Solomon," *JSJ* 30 (1999): 1–24.

[18] John R. Levison, "Is Eve to Blame? A Contextual Analysis of Sirach 25:24," *CBQ* 47 (1985): 617–23.

[19] J. M. Allegro, with A. A. Anderson, *Qumrân Cave 4.I (4Q158–4Q186)* (DJD 5; Oxford: Clarendon, 1968), 82–85, with corrections by John Strugnell, "Notes en marge du volume V des 'Discoveries in the Judaean Desert of Jordan,'" *RevQ* 7 (1970): 263–68. See also Rick D. Moore, "Personification of the Seduction of Evil: The Wiles of the Wicked Woman," *RevQ* 10 (1981): 505–19.

[20] On the interpretation of this figure in the context of Proverbs see Christl Maier, *Die "fremde Frau" in Proverbien 1–9: eine exegetische und sozialgeschichtliche Studie* (Göttingen: Vandenhoeck & Ruprecht, 1997); Michael V. Fox, *Proverbs 1–9* (AB 18A; New York: Doubleday, 2000), 252–62.

beginning of his way" (Prov 8:22). The same word for beginning (*r'ēšît*) is used in Proverbs and in 4Q184, and it carries a sense of hierarchical as well as temporal primacy.

Ben Sira uses a different word, *t'hillāh*, which has a more strictly temporal sense. His statement comes near the end of a long diatribe against women that begins in 25:13: "Any wound, but not a wound of the heart! Any wickedness, but not the wickedness of a woman!" It is only one of several intemperate sayings of Ben Sira about the female sex.[21] Perhaps the most extreme is Sir 42:14: "Better is the wickedness of a man than a woman who does good; it is woman who brings shame and disgrace." In light of these sentiments, it is possible that Ben Sira was laying the blame for sin and death on woman in general rather than on Eve in particular. It must be admitted, however, that the coincidence with later traditions about Eve is remarkable. Ben Sira's thought is not especially consistent in any case, and we should hardly be surprised if he were inconsistent on the origin of death, but the statement in Sir 25:24 seems to arise from his distrust of women rather than from his exegesis of Genesis.

The origin of death is not, however, the only aspect of Ben Sira's rephrasing of Genesis that may surprise the modern interpreter. The passage in chapter 17 continues:

> He endowed them with strength like his own,
> and made them in his own image.
> He put the fear of them in all living beings,
> and gave them dominion over beasts and birds.
> Discretion and tongue and eyes,
> ears and a mind for thinking he gave them.
> He filled them with knowledge and understanding,
> and showed them good and evil. . . .
> He bestowed knowledge upon them
> and allotted to them the law of life.
> He established with them an eternal covenant
> and revealed to them his decrees. (Sir 17:3–12)

In this passage, Ben Sira makes no distinction between the two accounts of creation, in Genesis 1 (the image of God) and Genesis

---

[21] On Ben Sira's view of women see Warren C. Trenchard, *Ben Sira's View of Women* (Chico, Calif.: Scholars Press, 1982); Claudia Camp, "Understanding a Patriarchy: Women in Second Century Jerusalem through the Eyes of Ben Sira," in *"Women like This": New Perspectives on Jewish Women in the Greco-Roman World* (ed. A.-J. Levine; Atlanta: Scholars Press, 1991), 1–39.

2–3 (taken from the earth).[22] Moreover, he seems to collapse the time difference between Genesis and Deuteronomy.[23] God gives Adam his commandments right from the beginning. The latter point is even more clearly stated in Sir 15:14–17:

> It was he who created the human being (Adam) from the beginning
> and he left him in the power of his inclination.
> If you choose, you can keep the commandments,
> and to act faithfully is a matter of your own choice. . . .
> Before each person are life and death,
> and whichever one chooses will be given.

The last verse alludes to Deut 30:19. The situation of Adam was apparently no different from that of an Israelite in later times. He was in the power of his inclination (*yiṣrô*), or as later rabbis would have said, his two inclinations.[24] In this respect Adam is the paradigmatic human being rather than the first in a causal chain. Ben Sira acknowledges that people are swayed by their inclinations, but he vigorously affirms free will.[25] There is no place here for a theory of original sin.[26]

The most remarkable feature of Ben Sira's discussion of Genesis, however, is his blithe statement that God "filled them with knowledge and understanding and showed them good and evil." Genesis states rather explicitly that God forbade Adam and Eve to eat from the tree of the knowledge of good and evil, on pain of death. It is difficult to imagine how Ben Sira understood the biblical text. It should be noted, however, that several texts from Qumran also insist that God endowed Adam with wisdom and knowledge. The *Words of the Luminaries* (4Q504 fragment 8) says that when God fashioned

---

[22] The order is the reverse of Genesis. See L. Alonso Schökel, "The Vision of Man in Sirach 16:24–17:14," in *Israelite Wisdom: Theological and Literary Essays in Honor of Samuel Terrien* (ed. J. G. Gammie et al.; Missoula, Mont.: Scholars Press, 1978), 235–60.

[23] The expression "law of life" is derived from Deut 30:15–20.

[24] On the rabbinic view of the two inclinations see Urbach, *The Sages*, 471–83; G. H. Cohen Stuart, *The Struggle in Man between Good and Evil: An Inquiry into the Origin of the Rabbinic Concept of* Yeṣer Haraʿ (Kampen: Kok, 1984).

[25] The Hebrew text from the Cairo Geniza inserts "and he placed him in the power of his snatcher" in Sir 15:14c, apparently in reference to Satan. These words are not found in the versions and disrupt the poetic balance of the verse. They are universally rejected as secondary.

[26] See further Urbach, *The Sages*, 421; John J. Collins, *Jewish Wisdom in the Hellenistic Age* (OTL; Louisville: Westminster John Knox, 1997), 80–84.

Adam in the image of his glory he blew into his nostril the breath of life, and intelligence and knowledge.[27] Like Ben Sira, this text affirms that God gave Adam commandments ("you imposed on him not to turn away"), but evidently he was not prohibited from acquiring wisdom. Another fragmentary text, 4QMeditation on Creation (4Q303), mentions "the knowledge of good and evil" before the creation of Eve.[28] The most extensive wisdom text found at Qumran, 4QInstruction, says that God gave "the vision of Hagu" to a segment of humanity, "the people of spirit," but not to "the spirit of flesh," because it failed to distinguish between good and evil.[29] The knowledge of good and evil, it would appear, was not inherently off limits, but some people failed to master the distinction. Another fragment of the same work (4Q423) refers to "every fruit that is produced and every tree which is good, pleasing to give knowledge."[30] According to Genesis, every tree in the garden was pleasant to the sight and good for food, but only the forbidden tree of the knowledge of good and evil was said to confer wisdom. The Qumran text apparently understood Genesis to mean that all the trees were symbolic sources of wisdom and knowledge and does not mention any prohibition against eating from a tree of knowledge in the extant fragments. The passage seems to claim that the garden yields knowledge and wisdom to the good, but thorns and thistles to those who are unfaithful.[31]

Ben Sira, then, represents a line of interpretation of Genesis that took the story as paradigmatic of the human situation rather than

---

[27] Esther Chazon, "The Creation and Fall of Adam in the Dead Sea Scrolls," in *The Book of Genesis in Jewish and Oriental Christian Interpretation* (ed. J. Frishman and L. van Rompay; Leuven: Peeters, 1997), 15.

[28] Timothy H. Lim, "303. Meditation on Creation A," in J. A. Fitzmyer, consulting ed., *Qumran Cave 4. XV: Sapiential Texts, Part 1* (DJD 20; Oxford: Clarendon, 1997), 152–53.

[29] 4Q417 1 I, 116–18. For the text see John Strugnell and Daniel Harrington, in J. A. Fitzmyer, consulting ed., *Qumran Cave 4. XXIV: Sapiential Texts, Part 2* (DJD 34; Oxford: Clarendon, 1999), 151. On the interpretation of the passage see John J. Collins, "In the Likeness of the Holy Ones: The Creation of Humankind in a Wisdom Text from Qumran," in *The Provo International Conference on the Dead Sea Scrolls* (ed. D. W. Parry and E. Ulrich; Leiden: Brill, 1999), 609–18.

[30] See the edition of the text by Torleif Elgvin, DJD 34:507–8.

[31] See further John J. Collins, "Interpretations of the Creation of Humanity in the Dead Sea Scrolls," in *Biblical Interpretation at Qumran* (ed. M. Henze; Grand Rapids: Eerdmans, forthcoming).

as a narrative that explained its origin. Some wisdom teachers, at least, avoided the apparent implication of the text that the Lord had forbidden Adam and Eve to acquire wisdom. Rather, God had endowed his human creatures with wisdom, but some people fail to apply it properly. In this reading of Genesis, there is no Fall, in the sense of one fateful event that changed the circumstances of human life. Neither sin nor death can be attributed to the deed of Adam (or Eve). Death is simply the decree of God for all flesh, and sin is the responsibility of every human being.

III. THE BOOK OF THE WATCHERS (*1 ENOCH* 1–36)

Our brief consideration of Ben Sira can serve as a warning against taking traditional interpretations for granted when we consider the earliest interpreters of Adam and Eve. This warning is very pertinent when we turn to consider the work that probably gives us our earliest allusions to Genesis 2–3, the Book of the Watchers in *1 Enoch*.

The Book of the Watchers takes its name from the story of the Watchers, or Fallen Angels, in *1 Enoch* 6–11. This is the first narrative that we encounter in the Book of the Watchers. It is clearly extrapolated from the brief notice of the "sons of God" in Genesis 6.[32] It becomes apparent later in the book that the author is familiar with the story of Adam and Eve, but the prominence of the story of the Watchers has led many scholars to assume that this is the primary Enochic myth of the origin of evil.[33] The Watchers divulge knowledge that is not legitimate for human beings, and they facilitate the spread of violence by introducing weapons. They also beget giants, whose actions cause the whole earth to be filled with blood

---

[32] J. T. Milik, *The Books of Enoch: Aramaic Fragments from Qumran Cave 4* (Oxford: Clarendon, 1976), 31, famously argued that the story of the Watchers in *1 Enoch* 6–11 is older than Genesis 6, but his proposal has been almost universally rejected. See the comments of James C. VanderKam, "The Interpretation of Genesis in *1 Enoch*," in *The Bible at Qumran: Text, Shape, and Interpretation* (ed. P. W. Flint; Grand Rapids: Eerdmans, 2001), 133–34.

[33] So especially Paolo Sacchi, *Jewish Apocalyptic and its History* (JSPSup 20; Sheffield: Sheffield Academic, 1997), 32–87; Gabriele Boccaccini, "Jewish Apocalyptic Tradition: The Contribution of Italian Scholarship," in *Mysteries and Revelations: Apocalyptic Studies since the Uppsala Colloquium* (ed. J. J. Collins and J. H. Charlesworth; Sheffield: Sheffield Academic, 1991), 33–50.

and iniquity (9:9). This is the immediate reason for the Flood, to purge the earth. But the effects of the Watchers are not eliminated by the Flood. Evil spirits go forth from the bodies of the giants. These remain on earth, to lead astray and do various kinds of mischief (15:8–16:1). These demonic spirits would seem to be responsible for most of the evils that beset humanity from this time forward. They are not said to introduce death into the world, and neither are we told that the world was free from sin before the descent of the Watchers. But it does seem that the human condition takes a distinct turn for the worse because of the Watchers and their descendants.

A. *The tree of life on the mountain of God*

The Book of the Watchers makes no mention of Adam and Eve in its account of primeval history. It does, however, betray its awareness of the garden of Eden in two passages later in the book, in the course of Enoch's guided tour of the earth.[34]

Chapter 24 describes how Enoch sees seven glorious mountains, three to the east and three to the south, "whose stones were precious in beauty."[35] The seventh was in the middle, and it rose above the others like the seat of a throne. Fragrant trees encircled it, including "a tree such as I had never smelled, and among them was no other like it. It had a fragrance sweeter smelling than all spices. And its leaves and its blossom and the tree never wither. Its fruit is beautiful, like dates of the palm trees." The archangel Michael provides an explanation:

> This high mountain that you saw, whose peak is like the throne of God, is the seat where the Great Holy One, the Lord of glory, the King of eternity, will sit, when he descends to visit the earth in goodness. And (as for) this fragrant tree, no flesh has the right to touch it until the great judgment, in which there will be vengeance on all and a consummation forever. Then it will be given to the righteous and the pious, and its fruit will be as food for the chosen. And it will be transplanted to the holy place, by the house of God, the King of eternity. Then they will rejoice greatly and be glad, and they will enter

---

[34] The Book of the Watchers certainly grew in stages. It is my assumption, however, that it constitutes an editorial unity, and so we can ask about the relation between the Eden traditions and the Watcher traditions in the edited book.

[35] This passage is an elaboration of a shorter account in *1 En.* 18:6.

into the sanctuary. Its fragrances will be in their bones, and they will live a long life upon the earth, such as your fathers lived also in their days, and torments and plagues and suffering will not touch them. (*1 En.* 25:3–6)[36]

The tree in question is evidently the tree of life. Humanity does not have access to it now, but it will in the eschatological future. George Nickelsburg comments that "according to the present text, God has transplanted it from the original paradise in the east (see chap. 32) to the present inaccessible location, where it will remain until the universal judgment."[37] But the text does not say that it has been transplanted from the east. As we shall see, the garden in the east is also inaccessible to humanity. What the text does say is that it will be transplanted in the future, to the holy place, by the house of God. The implied geography is somewhat confusing. The seventh mountain in chapter 24 is to be the seat of the divine throne after the final judgment. But in chapter 26 Enoch proceeds to the center of the earth, where he sees a holy mountain, which is evidently Mount Zion. He does not mention the temple here, even as a future entity, but we should expect that "the house of God" is located here. It appears then that the text is saying that the tree of life will be transplanted from the mountain of God's throne to the temple mountain. There seem, in effect, to be two holy mountains associated with the presence of the LORD. The mountain of the LORD's throne, between the mountains to the south and those to the east, is most probably to be associated with Mt. Sinai, which is explicitly identified as the mountain where the LORD descends in *1 En.* 1:4.[38] Ultimately, however, the tree of life is established in the vicinity of Mt. Zion.

If this were the only allusion to Edenic motifs in the Book of the Watchers, we should scarcely infer that the author knew Genesis 2–3 at all. There is no mention here of Adam and Eve, or of the tree

[36] Trans. George W. E. Nickelsburg (*1 Enoch 1: A Commentary on the Book of 1 Enoch, Chapters 1–36; 81–108* [Hermeneia; Minneapolis: Fortress, 2001], 312).

[37] Nickelsburg, *1 Enoch 1*, 314.

[38] Compare *1 En.* 77:1, which says that the LORD descends in the south. See the discussion by Kelley Coblentz Bautch, *"No One Has Seen What I Have Seen": A Study of the Geography of 1 Enoch 17–19* (Leiden: Brill, 2003). Sinai is also the scene of the throne of God in Ezekiel the Tragedian. See Carl R. Holladay, *Fragments from Hellenistic Jewish Authors* (4 vols.; Atlanta: Scholars Press, 1989), 2:362–63. R. H. Charles, however, declares apodictically that "it is not Sinai" ("The Book of Enoch," *APOT* 2:204).

of the knowledge of good and evil. This passage recalls Ezekiel 28 rather than Genesis. In Ezekiel, we may recall, Eden was located "on the mountain of God" and was associated with precious stones. Whether the tree of life was transplanted from a garden in the east or not, its location in *1 Enoch* 24 reflects a separate tradition about Eden on the mountain of God, that is also attested in Ezekiel.[39] This location disassociates the tree of life from the story of Adam and Eve. The tree is important for the future of humanity rather than for its past.

B. *The tree of wisdom in the garden to the east*

The second passage with Edenic associations is in *1 Enoch* 32. Here we are told that Enoch journeyed far to the east, beyond the Red Sea. "I passed by the garden of righteousness, and I saw from afar trees more plentiful and larger than these trees, differing from those—very large and beautiful and magnificent—and the tree of wisdom, whose fruit the holy ones eat and learn great wisdom." The accompanying angel explains: "This is the tree of wisdom from which your father of old and your mother of old, who were before you, ate and learned wisdom. And their eyes were opened, and they knew that they were naked, and they were driven from the garden."[40]

In this case the allusion to the Genesis story is perfectly clear. But how is that story understood? We should begin by noting what Enoch does not say.[41] He does not say that this is the tree from which they were forbidden to eat, or that they incurred death because they ate from it. The tree itself is unambiguously good. Nickelsburg's reading, "whose fruit the holy ones ate," follows a disputed reading in the Greek.[42] The idea that the holy ones (angels) eat from the tree

---

[39] Martha Himmelfarb, *Ascent to Heaven in Jewish and Christian Apocalypses* (New York: Oxford, 1993), 73, argues that the Book of the Watchers is indebted to Ezekiel, especially to the vision of the new Jerusalem in Ezekiel 40–48.

[40] Trans. Nickelsburg, *1 Enoch 1*, 320.

[41] Compare the observation of Himmelfarb, *Ascent to Heaven*, 74.

[42] See Matthew Black, *The Book of Enoch or 1 Enoch: A New English Edition* (Leiden: Brill, 1985), 179, reading *hagioi*. The alternative reading is *hagiou*: "of whose holy fruit they eat." See also Randall Argall, *1 Enoch and Sirach: A Comparative Literary and Conceptual Analysis of the Themes of Revelation, Creation and Judgment* (Atlanta: Scholars Press, 1995), 33, who accepts the reading *hagiou* but argues that it should be emended to *hagioi*.

of knowledge is at best unusual. The Ethiopic text has no word for holy, but reads simply "from which they eat and know great wisdom."[43] The antecedent is indefinite. Black's slightly paraphrastic translation captures the sense: "of the fruit of which those who partake understand great wisdom."[44] On any reconstruction, the tree is a source of wisdom, and therefore good. Adam and Eve also acquired wisdom from it. The acquisition of wisdom was presumably a good thing. The gift of wisdom is promised to the righteous at the end of history (*1 En.* 5:8; 91:10, etc.). Since Adam and Eve are driven out from the garden, presumably they did something wrong. Perhaps they had been forbidden to eat from this tree as a test. Their expulsion, no doubt, constituted a change in the conditions of their life, but it is not necessarily tantamount to a "Fall" in the traditional sense of the word. It is not apparent that this is the reason why people die. For most of history, wisdom is inaccessible, except for exceptional revelation, such as Enoch receives.[45] Enoch never explains why this is so, but it is not clear that it should be understood as punishment for the putative sin of Adam. The whole episode of the garden is passed over briefly, in a way that suggests that it was not of great importance.

IV. The Origin of Death

Enoch never addresses the origin of death explicitly. There is some evidence, however, that the fleshly human nature was thought to be inherently mortal. In chapter 15, the LORD tells Enoch to speak to the Watchers and explain to them the nature of what they had done:

> You were holy ones and spirits, living forever.
> With the blood of women you have defiled yourselves,
> and with the blood of flesh you have begotten;
> And with the blood of men you have lusted,
> and you have done as they do—
> flesh and blood, who die and perish.

---

[43] Trans. Michael Knibb, *The Ethiopic Book of Enoch* (Oxford: Clarendon, 1978), 2:122. The Aramaic is too fragmentary to read at this point.

[44] Black, *The Book of Enoch*, 41.

[45] Compare the fragment of a myth in *1 Enoch* 42, which says that wisdom could not find a dwelling among the sons of men.

Therefore I gave them women,
that they might cast seed into them,
and thus beget children by them,
that nothing fail them upon the earth.
But you originally existed as spirits, living forever,
and not dying for all the generations of eternity.
Therefore I did not make women among you.
The spirits of heaven, in heaven is their dwelling. . . . (*1 En.* 15:4–7)[16]

According to this passage, women were created so that mortal men could attain a substitute for immortality by begetting children. If Adam were originally immortal, there would have been no reason to create Eve. It is unlikely, then, that death was introduced as a punishment for the sin of Adam. Rather, as we saw in Ben Sira, mortality seems to have been the divine plan for human beings from the beginning.

The Similitudes of Enoch, which are most plausibly dated to the early first century c.e., more than 200 years after the Book of the Watchers, express a different view on this subject. In *1 En.* 69:11, in the context of a catalogue of the fallen angels, we are told that "men were created no differently from the angels, that they might remain righteous and pure, and death which destroys everything would not have touched them, but through this knowledge of theirs they are being destroyed." This statement is difficult to reconcile with the passage in *1 Enoch* 16, which we have just cited, but it comes from a different author at a different time. In the context of *1 Enoch* 69, however, the knowledge that leads to death is not that which Adam and Eve derived from the tree in the garden. It is the wisdom revealed by one of the Watchers, Penemue, who "showed the sons of men the bitter and the sweet, and showed them all the secrets of their wisdom." This included the art of writing with pen and paper, through which many have gone astray! So while the Similitudes deny that humanity was inherently mortal, the change in the human condition is not attributed to the sin of Adam and Eve but to the revelation of the Watchers. In fact, Eve was led astray by another of the fallen angels, Gadreel.

---

[16] Trans. Nickelsburg, *1 Enoch 1*, 267.

V. ADAM AND EVE IN ENOCHIC PERSPECTIVE

The question remains why the authors of the Enoch tradition paid so little attention to the story of Adam and Eve, and attached so much importance to the story of the fallen angels. James VanderKam has suggested that these authors "perceived a deficiency in the text of Genesis." After the sin of Adam, the only infractions noted in the early chapters of Genesis are the murder of Abel by Cain and the boast of Lamech about killing a man (Gen 4:23). VanderKam suggests that

> a reader might be forgiven for wondering whether the flood was not something of an overreaction or that there must be something missing from the text when Genesis 6 claims that humanity's thoughts were evil continually and that the earth was thoroughly corrupt (vv. 5, 11–12). If such were the case, how did things get that way? Could eating the forbidden fruit in Eden cause such an epidemic of evil in ten generations, even if they were long ones?[47]

I wonder, however, whether the Book of the Watchers is so thoroughly exegetical in its origin. Rather than explaining the deficiencies of Genesis, the authors may have been trying to explain the rampant violence and sinfulness that they saw around them in the Hellenistic age. This wickedness seemed to them to require a supernatural origin.[48] The story of the sons of God in Genesis 6 suggested the kind of story that might give a satisfactory explanation. The story of Adam and Eve did not. (Satan had not yet acquired his status of Devil when the Book of the Watchers was written, nor had he yet been identified with the serpent in Genesis 2–3.) The Enochic authors were not alone in seeking a supernatural origin for human evil in this period.[49] But we should also note that this viewpoint did not go unchallenged within the Enoch tradition itself. It is directly challenged in the Epistle of Enoch: "I swear to you, you sinners, that as a mountain has not, and will not, become a slave, nor a hill a

---

[47] VanderKam, "The Interpretation of Genesis in *1 Enoch*," 139.

[48] Compare Sacchi, *Jewish Apocalyptic and Its History*, 72–87; Andreas Bedenbender, *Der Gott der Welt tritt auf den Sinai: Entstehung, Entwicklung und Funktionsweise der frühjüdischen Apokalyptik* (Berlin: Institut Kirche und Judentum, 2000), 192–200.

[49] See John J. Collins, "The Origin of Evil in Apocalyptic Literature and the Dead Sea Scrolls," in *Seers, Sibyls, and Sages in Hellenistic-Roman Judaism* (Leiden: Brill, 1997), 287–99.

woman's maid, so sin was not sent on the earth, but man of himself created it, and those who commit it will be subject to a great
curse" (*1 En.* 98:4).

Despite the fact that the Enochic writers were familiar with the
story of Genesis, they do not appear to have ascribed any great consequences to the putative sin of the first parents.[50] This can be seen
not only from the Book of the Watchers, but also from the apocalyptic overviews of history later in *1 Enoch*. The Animal Apocalypse
in *1 Enoch* 85 depicts Adam as a white bull and Eve as a heifer.
The allegory moves swiftly to the murder of Abel by Cain, but makes
no allusion to a sin of Adam and Eve, or to their expulsion from
the garden. The Apocalypse of Weeks, in *1 Enoch* 93, begins with
Enoch and does not mention Adam at all.

Later generations would give Adam his due and more. But however pervasive the traditional understanding of the Fall eventually
became it is salutary to bear in mind that in the beginning it was
not so. Not only does the traditional interpretation of Genesis 2–3
not represent "the Bible as it was" but it also does not correspond
to the earliest recorded understandings of the biblical text.

---

[50] Himmelfarb (*Ascent to Heaven*, 74) argues that the story of Eden presented
difficulties for the author of the Book of the Watchers, because of his preference
for a different explanation of the origin of sin, but that the story was too important to omit entirely. As we have seen, however, the Book of the Watchers is probably the earliest Jewish writing that refers to Adam and Eve at all, and so there is
no evidence that the story had yet acquired the importance it later enjoyed.

THE DEMOCRATIZATION OF KINGSHIP
IN WISDOM OF SOLOMON

JUDITH H. NEWMAN

In the post-exilic period, King Solomon was typically remembered for several attributes and accomplishments.[1] He was recalled as wise, and hence the inspired source of a portion of the biblical and extra-biblical corpus. He was recalled as heir to the divine dynastic promise to David, who was a wealthy king over an extensive empire. In this second connection, he was also recalled as the builder of the temple in Jerusalem. According to Israel's historians, both Solomon's acquisition of wisdom and his successful completion of the temple were marked by prayers (1 Kgs 3:6–9 // 1 Chr 1:7–10; 1 Kgs 8:23–53 // 1 Chr 6:14–42) and these prayers, too, are recalled.[2] Intriguing questions surround the use of pseudonymity in the Second Temple period.[3] This essay examines one aspect of the way in which

---

[1] My formulation of the questions raised in this essay and my method for answering them reveal a deep indebtedness to the honoree of this volume, whose creative scholarship and timely counsel have consistently provided inspired wisdom for my own research.

[2] The prayer most often mentioned in Second Temple literature is 1 Kings 8, the prayer at the dedication of the Temple. At least two lists of biblical prayers cite Solomon's dedicatory prayer as a particularly effective intercession. 4Ezra 7:106–10 recalls eight men who interceded on behalf of others; Abraham, Moses, Joshua, Samuel, David, Solomon "for those at the dedication" (1 Kings 8), Elijah, and Hezekiah. One of the Jewish prayers in the *Apos. Con.* 7.37:1–5 offers a longer list of thirty supplicants, though in the latter case, both of Solomon's prayers, at Gibeon in 1 Kings 3 and at Jerusalem in 1 Kings 8, are mentioned. 2 Macc 2:8–10 likens the efficacy of the prayer of Solomon at the dedication of the temple to the prayer of Moses at the tent of meeting in the wilderness.

[3] See, for example, David G. Meade, *Pseudonymity and Canon: An Investigation into the Relationship of Authorship and Authority in Jewish and Earliest Christian Tradition* (WUNT 39; Tübingen: Mohr Siebeck, 1986). See also the recent work of Hindy Najman who calls into question the notion of authorship implied by the term "pseudonymity" as anachronistic, asserting a more diffuse understanding of an authoritative text linked to a larger conception of discourse originating from a founding figure; *Seconding Sinai: the Development of Mosaic Discourse in Second Temple Judaism* (JSJSup 77; Leiden: Brill, 2003). Devorah Dimant ("Pseudonymity in the Wisdom of Solomon," in *La Septuaginta en la Investigacion Contemporanea* [V Congreso de la IOSCS; ed. M. Fernández Marcos; Madrid: Instituto Arias Montano, 1985], 243–55) has discussed

Solomon's pseudonymous authorship may be understood in the Wisdom of Solomon by seeking to answer one question: Why does Solomon's voice matter in this book? In other words, why was the book attributed to Solomon, rather than Ezra or Enoch or Esther? And though Solomon is the discernible pseudepigraphic author, why does he go unnamed? By looking closely at how the book has recast Solomon's prayer for wisdom in Wisdom 9, the rationale for the pseudonymous voice as a means for underscoring the book's major themes becomes apparent.

While many have discussed the distinctive religious ideas found in Wisdom of Solomon, such as the immanent *logos/Sophia* figure, the redemptive nature of suffering, and the preexistence and immortality of the soul, no one has considered how the ideas in the book may reflect the conceptualization of Jewish practice during the turn of the era when it was written. Yet it seems that Wisdom 9 offers a model for the function of prayer in the late Second Temple period. The ideal of piety is not concerned with the temple and its sacrificial offerings, but with a Jewish life lived at some geographical and cultural distance from that distinctive institution. Wisdom 9 forms a part of the larger rhetorical structure of the book which works to subvert, or, perhaps more accurately stated, to transform, the idea of Israelite kingship by retaining the power of scriptural ideas associated with it, but in a way only remotely related to kingship's historical manifestation in ancient Israel. The ideal for human governance no longer lies in the hope for restoration of the Davidic monarchy, but in a much more widespread diffusion of power. Elevation to the throne of monarch is as simple as offering a prayer for wisdom, available to all who are sincere in faith and righteous in their behav-

---

the issue of pseudonymity in connection with Wisdom of Solomon, though we differ greatly in approach to the question. Whereas she sees the role of Solomon as exemplar as essential to its pseudonymity, I see Solomon's effective "abdication" of his kingship as central to his pseudepigraphic function. She reads the references addressing kings literally to refer to human kings over the nations. And while she evaluates the reuse of scripture, she only sees significance in the reuse of scripture that would point to Solomonic authorship, that is, the use of Proverbs or those sections of Kings/Chronicles that relate to Solomon's reign. In short, the conclusions of this essay stand in stark contrast to her statement: "We may see, now, the particular significance of attributing the exhortation to Solomon: the fact that the admonition is delivered by someone who exemplifies its contents in his own life, furnishes further evidence of its truth; in other words, he personally practices the ideas that he advocates" ("Pseudonymity," 250).

ior. The kingdom that such monarchs inherit is immortality, a realm no longer invested solely in physical reality but in the nonmaterial world of the soul. Moreover, the gift of wisdom, which activates the inheritance, is available at human initiative.

The prayer in Wisdom 9 is a pivotal chapter in the book which reinforces the book's main points: that all human beings are worthy of the exalted status of monarchs with its attendant honors and responsibilities by virtue of their creaturehood; that wisdom is a gift from God obtainable by all human beings; and that just and right-eous behavior is a manifestation of wisdom that will result in immor-tality. The prayer also orients the reader toward the second half of the book which describes the guiding role of wisdom in the earliest scriptural history from Adam to Moses, an era prior to the estab-lishment of the monarchy. What is more, the prayer in Wisdom 9 offers a model for the function of prayer in this period, a develop-ment that occurs specifically in diaspora Judaism but that will ulti-mately influence the shape of Judaism and Christianity and their understandings of prayer as an indispensable and sufficient means for communing with God.

A notable feature of Wisdom of Solomon is the way in which the author, a master rhetorician, offers these views to readers through an imaginative reuse of scriptural language and imagery. A close examination of Solomon's prayer in Wisdom 9 reveals not only a creative reuse of scripture, but also the appropriation of certain inter-pretive trends that can be discerned in other contemporaneous Second Temple Jewish literature.[4] The author's language in the prayer also resonates with other parts of Wisdom to reveal a coherent rhetori-cal ambition. Pseudo-Solomon accomplished this rhetorical *tour de*

---

[4] On the use of scripture in Wisdom generally, consider William Horbury's astute comment, "One who comes to Wisdom from the scriptures, like Jerome, finds 'Greek eloquence' in vocabulary, rhetorical devices and patches of rhythmical prose. The Greek scent is heightened by the Hellenic themes of untimely death and ethical example which Wisdom shares with the epitaphs. Yet Wisdom eschews Greek metre, fails to echo Greek poets, and instead draws continually on the scriptures for read-ers who can understand. Not too much is conceded to the Greek literary tastes of Egyptian Jews" ("The Christian Use and the Jewish Origins of the Wisdom of Solomon," in *Wisdom in Ancient Israel* [ed. J. Day, R. Gordon, H. G. M. Williamson; Cambridge: Cambridge University Press, 1995], 182–96, here 194). Whereas close scholarly attention has been devoted to the use of scripture in the second half of Wisdom, particularly as it pertains to the Exodus account, no one has looked

force by using traditional scriptural interpretation interwoven with ideas from Hellenistic philosophy in a complex and original piece of Jewish wisdom literature. More specifically, one of his means for promoting "universal kingship" is to employ double meanings for biblical terms and scriptural concepts and to use the inherent tensions and contradictions in scripture against one another. The message of Wisdom is a distinctive product of Jewish Hellenism and reflects some themes that are shared by certain other texts of the period, for instance, *Baruch*, the *Psalms of Solomon*, and the somewhat later, so-called *Hellenistic Synagogal Prayers*, not to mention the author's near contemporaries Philo and Josephus. The prayer in Wisdom of Solomon 9 includes a number of distinct themes, none of which is present in the original prayer that Solomon offers in 1 Kings 3 or its later parallel in 2 Chronicles, but which reflect the interpretive development of scriptural wisdom traditions and are also evident in other Second Temple Jewish and Christian literature.

The first is that God created the world through wisdom and the divine word. The second theme is that the people of Israel are God's children and as God's creatures are endowed with the authority to rule and judge the world. The third is that the temple in Jerusalem was planned from the beginning of time, and wisdom was present with Solomon as he built the structure. These themes will be examined more closely in the treatment of the wording of the prayer.

---

specifically at the use of scripture in the prayer of Wisdom 9 and how it relates to the larger message of the book. Of recent note are P. T. van Rooden, "Die antike Elementarlehre und der Aufbau von SapSal 11–19," in *Tradition and Reinterpretation in Jewish and Early Christian Literature* (Leiden: Brill, 1986), 81–96; Peter Enns, *Exodus Retold: Ancient Exegesis of the Departure from Egypt in Wis 10:15–21 and 19:1–9* (HSM 57; Atlanta: Scholars Press, 1997); and Samuel Cheon, *The Exodus Story in the Wisdom of Solomon: A Study in Biblical Interpretation* (JSPSup 23; Sheffield: Sheffield University Press, 1998). Maurice Gilbert has treated the role of Solomon in Wisdom 7–9. He emphasizes the contrast made between the young Solomon in Wisdom 7–8 with the older Solomon who offers the prayer in Wisdom 9. Gilbert argues that Solomon is cast in the three central chapters of the book as a mature wise sage whose behavior can be universally adopted. In contrast to the present study, he considers Solomon's kingship as lacking relevance in the chapters he examines and he does not consider the interconnected rhetoric of the book as a whole ("La Figure de Salomon en Sg 7–9," in *Études sur le Judaïsme Hellénistique* [Paris: Cerf, 1984]), 225–49. Two insightful articles by Patrick W. Skehan identify borrowings from Isaiah and the Psalms in the book of Wisdom; however, he did not try to discern an overall pattern or strategy to the author's use of scripture; "Isaias and the Book of Wisdom," *CBQ* 2 (1940): 289–99 and "Borrowings from the Psalms in the Book of Wisdom," *CBQ* 10 (1948): 384–97.

Before turning to that task, a few comments are in order comparing the prayer in Wisdom more generally to its counterparts in the biblical historical narratives.

The contrast with Solomon's "prayer" in 1 Kgs 3:6–9, paralleled in 2 Chr 1:8–10, is deep and wide. The most obvious differences to note are in length and literary context. Solomon's prayer in the Deuteronomistic History is five verses long and comes in the larger context of a dream, though the Chronicler eliminates that narrative detail and portrays God talking to Solomon directly. Solomon explicitly invokes covenantal language by focusing on his father David, recognizing the great *chesed* (translated as *eleos*, or mercy, in the Greek) that God has shown in fulfilling his promise to David that his son would sit on the throne. Solomon then states that he is in the midst of the great people, whom God has chosen. Solomon then asks for a "listening heart," translated in the Greek literally as *kardian akouein*, in order to be able to distinguish between good and bad in judging the people. The Chronicler, perhaps through conflation of later Deuteronomistic accounts that extol Solomon's great wisdom, depicts Solomon asking explicitly for wisdom and understanding (2 Chr 1:10), *sophian kai sunesin*. The narrative role of the prayer in the Deuteronomistic History serves to underscore Solomon's worthiness as king of Israel by portraying him as recipient of the divine gift of wisdom. God's gift of wisdom to Solomon is immediately followed in the narrative by his movement to Jerusalem in 1 Kgs 3:15 where he offers sacrifices while standing before the ark. Then follows in 1 Kgs 3:16–28 Solomon's wise adjudication of the case of the two prostitutes vying over the same baby. The Chronicler, by contrast, places Solomon's prayer in a different narrative context, so that following a brief account of Solomon's wealth and commercial activity, the history continues with the account of Solomon's building of the Temple. The connection between Solomon's wisdom and the temple-building is also stated explicitly in Chronicles as evident in a blessing pronounced by King Hiram of Tyre. A comparison with the Deuteronomistic History again highlights the distinctive shaping of the Chronicler. The blessing in 1 Kgs 5:7 reads: "Blessed be the LORD today, who has given David a wise son to be over this great people." 2 Chronicles 2:12 offers an expanded version: "Blessed be the LORD God of Israel, who made heaven and earth, who has given King David a wise son, endowed with discretion and understanding, who will build a temple for the LORD, and a royal palace for himself."[5] The Chronicler seems clearly influenced by a theological perspective that stresses the centrality of the Temple to the people in the post-exilic period.[6] It is likely that the narrative placement in Chronicles with its emphasis on Solomon's wisdom being manifest in his construction of the temple influenced the author of Wisdom of Solomon.

In contrast to Solomon's rather brief petition in the Deuteronomistic History and Chronicles, the prayer in Wisdom of Solomon 9 stretches eighteen verses long. Pseudo-Solomon drew from sources other than the 1 Kings 3 or 2 Chronicles 1 version of Solomon's prayer for wisdom. The structure of Wisdom's prayer is more elaborate, with a formal invocation and a chiastic structure of three strophes.[7] Wisdom 9 does not stand in the middle of a narrative, but rather as the concluding segment to chapters 6–9, the second of the three major sections of the book. Wisdom 6–9 is written in the first person and includes a discourse on the nature of wisdom and a long autobiographical speech about Solomon's relationship to Woman Wisdom. At the outset of these four chapters, in Wis 6:1, the pseudonymous author addresses his audience, kings and judges, and calls upon them to listen to his instruction. As such, the chapters have features of traditional wisdom literature as well as elements of a testament. Yet one feature of the address is puzzling. The typical wisdom form is addressed to a sage's sons, a device found throughout the wisdom corpus, whereas the instruction in Wisdom is addressed to kings.[8]

---

[5] 1 Kings 5:7 includes a shorter version of the blessing: "Blessed be the LORD today, who has given to David a wise son to be over this great people."

[6] For more on the distinct perspective of the Chronicler, see Sara Japhet, *The Ideology of Chronicles and its Place in Biblical Thought* (BEATAJ 9; Frankfurt: Peter Lang, 1989).

[7] David Winston, *The Wisdom of Solomon* (AB 43; Garden City, N.Y.: Doubleday, 1979), 200; and Maurice Gilbert, "La Structure de la prière de Salomon (Sg 9)" *Bib* 51 (1970): 301–31. Gilbert makes a cogent argument for unity, finding in Wis 9:17 a negative conditional question in the third section of the prayer that balances the petitions for wisdom (Wis 9:4, 10) found in the first two sections; see "Structure," 326.

[8] Cf. Prov 4:1; 5:1; 7:24; 22:17; Sir 3:1; 23:7; 39:13. One exception to this general rule lies in Ps 2:10: "Now therefore, O kings, be wise; be warned, O rulers of the earth," although Psalm 2 is normally considered a royal psalm and not a wisdom psalm. As for issues related to classical influences on Wisdom's genre, James M. Reese points to a number of Greek rhetorical devices used by the author in chapters 6–9 as well, which reveal the author's erudition and point to a fine classical education; see his *Hellenistic Influence on the Book of Wisdom and Its Consequences* (AnBib 41; Rome: Pontifical Biblical Institute, 1970).

The rhetorical function of chapters 6–9 and the prayer that concludes these four chapters thus marks a departure from the traditional norm in biblical wisdom literature. The discourse is addressed to peers and not subordinates. Any earthly king with an ear to listen and a heart to discern can digest what Pseudo-Solomon is about to say. Another significant difference between the context of Solomon's prayer in Wisdom and the historical books is that there is no mention of prophetic mediation, or, for that matter, human mediation of any kind, in his obtaining and retaining the throne. Wisdom 7 purports to give an account of Solomon's youth but contains no mention of his adulthood and the human machinations that resulted in his succession to the throne. Nor is there any reference specifically to the theophanic appearance, whether through a dream as in Kings or through unmediated direct speech as in Chronicles, that spurred Solomon to make his request. According to Wisdom 9, Solomon obtains wisdom through his own initiative and not owing to any human or divine contact. A closer scrutiny of each of the prayer's strophes in turn will illuminate its nuances more completely.

> O God of my ancestors and Lord of mercy, who made all things by your word, and through your wisdom formed humanity to have dominion over your creatures you have made, and rule the world in loyalty and righteousness, and in uprightness of soul determine judgment, give me the wisdom that sits by your throne, and do not reject me from among your slaves. For I am your servant, the son of your slave girl, a human who is weak and short-lived, and inferior in comprehension of judgment and laws; for even one who is perfect among children of human beings will be considered as nothing without the wisdom that comes from you. (Wis 9:1–6)[9]

Solomon's prayer in Wisdom begins with an invocation to God that is six verses long. By contrast 1 Kings 3 has no formal invocation at the beginning of the prayer. In the Deuteronomistic History, Israel's God is only addressed directly in the second verse of the prayer. Wisdom 9 thus reflects the general trend toward longer and more elaborate invocations evident in Second Temple prayers. Yet the epithets are distinctive. The first address in Wisdom, "God of

---

[9] The Greek text used as the basis for my translation is Joseph Ziegler's critical edition in the Göttingen edition of the Septuagint, *Sapientia Salomonis* (Göttingen: Vandenhoeck & Ruprecht, 1962).

my ancestors," is precisely paralleled in scripture only in Dan 2:23.
"God of our ancestors" appears only in three other post-exilic texts:
1 Chr 12:17, 2 Chr 20:6, and Ezra 7:27, as well as Deut 26:7. The
much more frequent appellation, "God of Abraham, Isaac, and
Jacob/Israel" is eschewed in favor of the more general term, "ancestors."[10] The generic address is in keeping with the author's avoidance of proper names throughout the book. The second epithet,
"Lord of mercy," is unique to this prayer. The divine quality of
"mercy" here included in an address of God seems to originate from
the Greek translation of 1 Kgs 3:6, in which *eleous* normally translates the Hebrew *chesed*: "And Solomon said: 'You have dealt with
great mercy with your servant David my father.'" "Covenant loyalty" might be a more accurate English translation. So although the
divine attribute of mercy/covenant loyalty is called to the fore in
Wis 9:1 as a reminder of the dynastic promise made in 2 Samuel
7, there is no mention of Solomon's father by name, nor of Solomon
himself, also in keeping with the character of the book in which
famous biblical figures are left unnamed.

The use of scripture in the first part of the first verse of the prayer
is fairly transparent. The second half of the verse and verse two present a more complex appropriation of scripture. Solomon affirms
that God made all things "by your word, and through your wisdom
formed humankind." Creation by the preexistent divine word, the
logos, and wisdom is a well-known idea in Second Temple literature,
found in the Qumran corpus and Philo, as well as apocalyptic and
wisdom literature. A number of scholars have treated the topic in
general, and others specifically with reference to Wisdom of Solomon,
so such a discussion need not be repeated here, except to point out
that the idea is rooted in the exegetical problem posed by the appearance of the first person plural in Gen 1:26, "Let us make," and
interpretations of the creation found in such passages as Proverbs 8,
Psalms 33 and 104, and Job 28.[11] It may be that Wis 9:1 includes

---

[10] "*My* ancestors" is adopted here. The personal pronoun appears in several
Greek minuscule manuscripts. Given the absence of a definite article, the inclusion
of the personal pronoun seems likely to be original.

[11] Sirach 24 marks an important stage in the fusion of the concepts of wisdom
and *torah* in early Judaism; the prologue to John's gospel, which reflects the influence
of Hellenized Jewish thought, marks a similar landmark for Christianity. Compare
the discussions of James L. Kugel, *Traditions of the Bible: A Guide to the Bible as it Was*

this interpretive tradition in lieu of a theophany as occurs in 1 Kings 3 and 2 Chronicles 1. In a world that reflects the glory of an immanent presence of God, a *deus ex machina* is unnecessary.[12]

Let us take up in more detail Pseudo-Solomon's unique description in Wis 9:2–3 about the nature of human creaturehood. The prayer states that humans were created with a threefold vocation: to have dominion over the creatures, to rule in holiness and righteousness, and to pronounce judgment in uprightness of soul. This would seem to be an altered expansion of the divine mandate found in the creation story of Gen 1–2:4. How is this threefold mandate of humanity derived? The idea is rooted in certain biblical texts, as interpreted. It seems in particular to be drawing on the account of human creation in Genesis 1–2 and the view of humanity in Psalm 8. In the priestly creation account, the human vocation is different because it includes the command to procreate, "to be fruitful and multiply and fill the earth and subdue it and have dominion over living creatures" (Gen 1:28).[13] In Ps 8:5, the psalmist muses on the exalted place of humanity in the created order, as "little less than gods," or, as "less than angels," as the Septuagint translates '*elohim*. They are, in effect, royalty, crowned with glory and honor.[14] Humans are given dominion over the lower orders of creation: cattle, birds, fish, and insects, according to the psalm. Human vocation is then expanded and exalted further in the Wisdom of Solomon. The third dimension of the vocation in Wis 9:3 is "in uprightness of soul, to

---

at the Start of the Common Era (Cambridge, Mass.: Harvard University Press, 1998), 44–67; John J. Collins, *Jewish Wisdom in the Hellenistic Age* (OTL; Louisville: Westminster/John Knox: 1997), 196–209; and in reference to Wisdom of Solomon specifically: Winston, *Wisdom*, 200–201; and Moyna McGlynn, *Divine Judgement and Divine Benevolence in the Book of Wisdom* (WUNT 2.139; Tübingen: Mohr Siebeck, 2001).

[12] On the theological significance of this tendency in the wisdom tradition, see John C. Collins, "The Biblical Precedent for Natural Theology," *JAAR* 45 no. 1 Supp. B (1977): 177–92.

[13] In God's address to Noah after the flood, the Greek of Gen 9:1 repeats the wording of Gen 1:28 but includes the charge for humans to have dominion over the world. The MT contains only the command to *fill* the world.

[14] Compare also the citation of Ps 8:5 in application to Jesus in Heb 2:9 which connects the theme of royal messianism, the mortal condition and the implied hope (stated elsewhere in Hebrews) for life after death: "... but we do see Jesus, who for a little while was made lower than the angels, now crowned with glory and honor because of the suffering of death, so that by the grace of God he might taste death for everyone."

determine judgment." In ancient Israel and throughout the Near East, judging one's people righteously is the king's privilege and responsibility. This is enunciated in Psalm 72, for example, which carries the superscription "Of Solomon" and may well have influenced the phrasing of Wis 9:2. Psalm 72:1 reads: "For Solomon. 'O God, give your judgment to the king, and your righteousness to the king's son; that he may judge your people with righteousness, and your poor with judgment.'" On the other hand, judging the *nations*, that is, the world, is the prerogative of God, the divine king. In Wisdom's characterization of human creaturehood, they are not simply to have dominion over the world, but to render judgment in that sphere, a hefty responsibility and one normally associated with the divine monarch. God's creation of humanity vested with power to judge thus co-opts the power and prerogative of kings; indeed, it co-opts the prerogative supposedly given to King Solomon as articulated in the Deuteronomistic version of Solomon's prayer for wisdom, in which judging the people was a crucial part of his role as leader of the nation. Wisdom 9:3 thus provides the first instance in the prayer in which such subversion or transformation is articulated, yet it is in syncopation with the rhetoric of Wisdom of Solomon as a whole.

Before turning from Wisdom's depiction of humans as monarchs to the remainder of the strophe, a seeming digression is warranted. The change of route in fact points to the interconnected rhetoric in the book as a whole that undergirds the notion of the universalization of kingship. The discursus relates to a central theme of the book that is not stated explicitly in Wisdom 9, namely, that wisdom, which is made manifest in righteous behavior, bestows immortality.[15] A correlate to this idea is the middle-Platonic notion, articulated also in Philo, that posits a soul distinct from corporality.[16] The soul is poten-

---

[15] John Collins views the idea of the immortality of the soul articulated in Wisdom as counter to the Jewish wisdom tradition as a whole because it implies that death is not part of divinely ordered reality whereas Jewish wisdom relies on experiential knowledge as the basis for observation about life's workings; "The Root of Immortality: Death in the Context of Jewish Wisdom," *HTR* 71 (1978): 177–92. See, too, the more recent treatment of death in Wisdom and Philo by Karina Martin Hogan in which she looks specifically at the comparative interpretations of Genesis 1–4 in Wisdom and Philo: "The Exegetical Background of the 'Ambiguity of Death' in the Wisdom of Solomon," *JSJ* 30 (1999): 1–24.

[16] Wisdom seems not to draw on Philo's work directly, and the relationship between the two is not clear. See Chrysostome Larcher, *Études sur le livre de la Sagesse*

tially immortal. Such a notion of immortality marks a departure from the view that the eschaton will result in the physical resurrection of the bodies of righteous people. It seems that in Wisdom of Solomon, bodies no longer function meaningfully in the equation; souls alone suffice. Indeed, Wisdom of Solomon also points to the possibility of a spiritual death, distinct from corporal mortality, in a passage that articulates the voice of the wicked: "Thus we also, just born, had come to an end, and we had no sign of virtue to display, but were consumed in our wickedness" (Wis 5:13). And the converse is also stated in Wis 4:16: "The righteous who have died will condemn the ungodly who are living."

The book is framed in chapters 1–2 and 18–19 with a discussion of death, and inside the frame is the prescription for gaining freedom from mortality. At the outset of the book, readers are warned: "Do not invite death by the error of your life, or bring on destruction by the works of your hands; because God did not make death, and he does not delight in the death of the living" (Wis 1:12–13). The very purpose of God's creative work in making humans was so they might mirror the divine being in their immortality. So states Wis 2:23, drawing on creation language used in Gen 1:26–27: "For God created human beings for immortality; he made them as an image (eikona) of his own eternity." Human wickedness mars God's intent for the human creature and thus disrupts the plans of God. A grievous sin according to Pseudo-Solomon is thus worship of an image that does not reflect the glory of the eternal God nor the immortality of the human soul.[17]

Death and life take a different shape in the last two chapters, the culmination of the review of the role of wisdom in guiding the earliest scriptural history, which concludes with a reflection on the events at the Red Sea. Wisdom 18 describes a death scene, in which the all-powerful logos, looking strikingly like Sophia, not to mention Athena, leaps from the divine throne and acts as the divine warrior to inflict death and destruction on the Egyptians' firstborn. The tenor of

---

(Paris: Gabalda, 1969), 151–78; and Jean LaPorte, "Philo in the Tradition of Biblical Wisdom Literature," in *Aspects of Wisdom in Judaism and Early Christianity* (Notre Dame: Notre Dame University Press, 1975), 103–41.

[17] Cf. the idol polemic in which the image (eikon) is used, although here it is in reference to pagan images: Wis 13:13; 14:5, 17; 15:5.

Wisdom 18–19, like other passages of the book, is eschatological, for out of death comes a new creation and new life for the holy people of God.[18] Such renewal is stated explicitly in Wis 18:6: "For the whole creation in its nature was fashioned anew, complying with your commands, so that your children might be kept unharmed." The verse offers a restoration of divine purpose in creating human beings for immortality as stated in Wis 2:23. The important role of worship in the final chapters should not be overlooked. In Wis 18:9, the "holy children" offer sacrifice and, "with one accord," commit to the divine torah (*nomos*) and sing praises of old to God. So, too, in Wis 18:21–23 a "blameless man," that is, the priest Aaron, uses the tools of his holy office on behalf of the people to stave off the plague. He prays and makes incense offerings. Aaron's very word is of sufficient potency to combat the destruction of the plague.

The antidote to punishment by premature death is described in a number of places in the core chapters of Wisdom. Consider, for example, Wis 5:15–16: "But the righteous live forever, and their reward is with the LORD; the Most High takes care of them. Therefore they will receive a glorious crown and a beautiful diadem from the hand of the LORD, because with his right hand he will cover them, and with his arm he will shield them." Evident here is the connection between royal language and immortality that results from righteous behavior. Wis 5:16 contains a citation of Isa 62:3, though transformed by its placement in the book. Whereas in Isaiah, the prophet is describing personified Zion as the recipient of the crown and diadem, Wisdom removes the specificity of geographical location, ignores the female characterization of the city, but retains the tenor of the original passage. In Wisdom 5, the ones to be honored with a royal crown and diadem of immortality are those who live righteously.

A passage with a similar message, this time connected specifically with the acquisition of wisdom, appears in Wis 6:17–20. The form of the passage reflects a six-point syllogism, a common Greek rhetorical device, a *sorites*.[19] The content seems to be a reworked expansion of the biblical wisdom cliché, "the beginning of wisdom is the fear of the LORD." So, in effect, Israelite wisdom content, represented

---

[18] McGlynn, *Divine Judgement and Divine Benevolence*, 176–78.
[19] Winston, *Wisdom*, 154–55.

by King Solomon, and Greek form in the shapely Queen Sophia are betrothed with the promise of unique offspring:

> For the beginning of wisdom [literally, "of her"] is true passion for instruction,
> and concern for instruction is love of her
> and love of her is the obeying her laws (tērēsis nomōn)
> and attention to her laws confirms immortality
> and immortality draws one near to God;
> thus the passion for wisdom leads to a kingdom. (Wis 6:17–20)

In light of the other passages just reviewed, we must understand the royal reward mentioned in the "passion for wisdom which leads to a kingdom" as none other than the realm of immortality that is bestowed by righteousness.[20]

In contrast to the exalted view of creaturely humanity (Wis 9:2–3) with the promised reward of immortality for the royal righteous that is expounded throughout the book, the continuation of the prayer in Wis 9:5 contains Solomon's humble self-characterization. Though chosen by God as king, he is neither superhuman, nor god, but a mere slave and the son of a slave, a man with weak mental powers. The phrase "I am your servant, the son of your slave-girl" is in fact a direct citation from Ps 115:7 (MT 116:16).[21] Without divine aid through the gift of Wisdom, Solomon is a mere mortal. In the larger context of Wisdom of Solomon, Pseudo-Solomon thus seems to allude to a principal theme of death/immortality. Solomon's self-characterization also reinforces his earlier claim toward the beginning of the autobiographical section of the book, in Wis 7:1. In that verse, Solomon states that "I also am mortal, like everyone else, a descendant of the first-formed one of earth, and in the womb of a

---

[20] Such a reading is not apparent to all. So, for example, Joseph Reider refers to the last phrase of Wis 6:20, "the desire for wisdom leads to a kingdom," as "irrelevant" and "clearly a *non sequitur*" in *The Book of Wisdom* (New York: Harper & Brothers, 1957), 105. Winston comments: "The author thus turns in the next verse to his royal audience and draws the obvious conclusion that if they wish to retain their earthly sovereignty, they had better pursue wisdom" (*Wisdom*, 156).

[21] The context of the psalm itself may be significant, because in the psalm is a thanksgiving to God for sparing the psalmist from death. Psalm 115:8 reads: "For you have delivered my soul from death, my eyes from tears, my feet from stumbling." So, too, the neighboring verse, Ps 115:6 (MT 116:15), reads: "Precious in the sight of the LORD is the death of his saints."

mother I was sculpted in flesh." The word used for first-formed, *prōtoplastos*, appears again in 10:1 to refer to Adam, the first-formed human creature, who is the first to be protected by wisdom. Solomon is thus no more and no less than an *adam*. The prayer thus posits an egalitarian self-demotion by Solomon, yet the exalted status of human beings in the book makes for the equivalent of a "kingship of all righteous doers," Wisdom's analogue to the "priesthood of all believers."

> You have chosen me to be king of your people and to be judge of your sons and daughters. You commanded to build a temple on your holy mountain, and an altar in the city where you have pitched your tent, a copy of the holy tent that you prepared from the beginning. With you is wisdom, who knows your works and was present when you made the world; and understands what is pleasing in your eyes and what is right in your commandments. Send her forth from the holy heavens, and from the throne of your glory dispatch her, so that present with me she may labor, and that I may know what is pleasing to you. For she knows and understands all things, and she will guide me prudently in my actions and guard me with her glory. And (then) my works will be acceptable, and I will judge your people justly, and shall be worthy of the throne of my father. (Wis 9:7–12)

The prayer makes little reference to historical incidents in the life of Solomon.[22] While the second strophe mentions Solomon's temple-building, it is nonetheless not a central concern of this prayer. Aside from Wis 9:8, the temple is only mentioned in Wis 3:14 in connection with the reward of the eunuch, which itself alludes to Isa 56:3. Similarly, there is almost no mention of the sacrificial system and priesthood. Moreover, the temple in Jerusalem is understood in Platonic terms as a copy (*mimēma*) of the heavenly reality, the true temple above. The notion of a heavenly temple appears in

---

[22] Indeed, the author seems studiously to have ignored the Deuteronomistic History's rather mixed portrait of the third king of Israel as well as other Second Temple accounts of his reign. The book is something of a rehabilitation of Solomon, although burnishing Solomon's reputation is only a subsidiary aim, if that, of the book as a whole. A contrasting view of Solomon is offered in Sir 47:13–23, which states that Solomon was wise as a youth, author of meaningful proverbs and amasser of great wealth, with an international reputation. His later years were less rosy. Sirach and the Deuteronomistic History both point to his marriages with foreign women as the factor that led to his downfall. But in Wisdom of Solomon, Solomon holds a flame for only one woman, Sophia herself, the immanent *logos*, present with God at creation, and ongoing source of illumination for kinglike mortals.

a number of Second Temple books.[23] The book stands in sharp contrast to such works as the books of Judith and 1 Maccabees, in which the defilement of the temple by Antiochus Epiphanes IV was a major spur in their composition.[24] Temple worship and the high priesthood are likewise of great importance to Ben Sira, who concludes his review of famous ancestors in Sirach 44–50 with a lengthy discussion of high priest Simon ben Onias (Sirach 50). The use of the term, "holy tent" (*skēnē hagia*), nonetheless requires comment. The most obvious source for Pseudo-Solomon is Sir 24:10, in which the "holy tent" in Zion is mentioned. Its use in the hymn to wisdom in Sirach 24 offers a pointed contrast to Wisdom 9. In Sirach, Wisdom actually comes to pitch her tent (*kataskēnō*) in Jerusalem after the order of the divine command. Sirach presents Wisdom as limited to a fixed locale whether this be the temple in Jerusalem or the book of the Torah. The "holy tent" in Wisdom 9 only points to the heavenly reality. Sophia does not depart from the heavenly temple for a fixed or confined location, but remains a more diffuse part of the created order at God's bidding.

At the time and place in which Wisdom of Solomon is presumed to have been written, Alexandria in the late 1st century B.C.E. or the beginning of the 1st century C.E., the Jews possessed no king. Hope for an heir to the Davidic throne had passed into the realm of messianism in some circles, the Qumran community being one such group. Pseudo-Solomon has gone in another direction by applying the royal language of scripture figuratively. There is almost no discussion of dynastic kingship in Wisdom of Solomon. Indeed, "covenant," the term often used in connection with the divine promise to David's house, or God's relationship to the people established at Sinai, or the relationship between God and Abraham, Isaac, and Jacob, appears only once in Wis 1:16, but in reference to a covenant that the ungodly make with death as a result of their unrighteous

---

[23] It may be that the notion of the heavenly temple typically appears in Greco-Roman Jewish works that reflect either an estrangement from the Jerusalem temple or that were written in geographic distance from it: *1En.* 90:28ff.; *Jub.* 1:27–29; *4QFlor*; Tob 14:5; *Sib. Or.* 5.403, 414–44; 1Q32; 2Q24; 5Q15.

[24] On the centrality of the Jerusalem temple and the necessity of protecting its purity in the book of Judith, particularly as it is revealed in the book's central prayer, see Judith H. Newman, *Praying by the Book: the Scripturalization of Prayer in Second Temple Judaism* (EJL 14; Atlanta: Scholars Press, 1999), 117–54.

behavior. Neither Solomon nor David is mentioned by name in keeping with all unnamed parties in the book. Their identity is thus obscured. The one reference to dynastic kingship occurs in Wis 9:12, in which Pseudo-Solomon expresses the desire to be worthy of the throne of his father. But given the fact that God is also referred to as Father (Wis 14:13), and the Israelites are called God's children (Wis 12:19, 21; 16:10, 21, 26; 18:4; 19:6), certainly a double-entendre is here possible, the "throne of his father" being both that of David's dynastic kingship and the divine kingship itself.

Wisdom 9:8 nonetheless affirms God's choice of Solomon as king, but one must ask what kind of kingship is envisioned because at the same time, in its first two strophes, the prayer makes affirmations that suggest all human beings were created to function as monarchs. The wording of 9:8 is also important to this construction because it describes Solomon's subjects as God's "sons and daughters." There are two distinct aspects to the idea of the universality of kingship, or the "every man is king" concept. Wisdom's affirmation of universal kingship depends on the selective fusion of two distinct biblical views: the election of all Israel, seen most clearly in one strain of the Sinai covenant traditions, and the election of the Davidic royal house. The first is that of familial language which views the Israelites as the divine children or "sons" of God. The second dimension is that kingship is bestowed on a mortal by God, seen most clearly in the Zion theology and election of David described in 2 Samuel 7 and echoed in the royal psalms. The divine adoption language in both cases signals an intimate relationship between God and humanity. Many biblical passages make the claim not only that the Israelites are God's children, but that Israel is God's firstborn, that is, the one with the rights to inheritance and the one that must be offered up to God. Perhaps the most prominent articulation of the idea lies in Exod 4:22–23, in which Moses is instructed by God to tell Pharoah: "Thus says YHWH; Israel is my firstborn son. I said to you, 'Let my son go that he may worship me.' But you refused to let him go; now I will kill your firstborn son.'"[25] The language characterizing

---

[25] As Jon D. Levenson has argued, the notion that Israel is God's firstborn must be considered in relation to the demand that all firstborn, whether that of women or animals, were considered God's rightful due sacrifice, hence the command in Exod 34:19–20 which requires that a substitionary offering be made if the firstborn is not offered in sacrifice to God; see his *The Death and Resurrection of the Beloved Son* (New Haven, Conn.: Yale University Press, 1993), especially 36–52.

the relationship between God and Israel as one of father and firstborn continues into the Second Temple period and is developed in different directions, as James Kugel has detailed.[26] The idea is present in the *Psalms of Solomon*, for example, which are roughly contemporaneous with Wisdom of Solomon, though are thought to be of Palestinian origin.[27] *Pss. Sol.* 13:9, in the context of a psalm on the theme of the contrasting punishment of the righteous and wicked, states: "For he will admonish the righteous as a beloved son and his discipline is as for a firstborn." Though not stated explicitly by name in this particular psalm because of its wisdom tenor, another psalm in the collection, *Pss. Sol.* 18:3–4, makes the connection explicit: "Your compassionate judgments are over the whole world, and your love is for the descendants of Abraham, an Israelite. Your discipline for us is as for a firstborn son, an only child."

Yet the prayer of Solomon in Wisdom 9, indeed, the book as a whole, has shed the notion of Israel as the firstborn. Wisdom 9:7 suggests simply that Solomon has been chosen to be judge over "your sons and daughters."[28] The only mention of the firstborn occurs in reference to the death of the Egyptians' firstborn (Wis 18:13) which caused them to realize that the people were "God's son." Is this because Solomon himself was not the firstborn of his father David? Perhaps, but it seems more likely that the concept of a firstborn that must be sacrificed to God has been replaced in Wisdom with the election of Israel, conceived in terms akin to the royal election of David. The universality of kingship is thus manifest in the use of royal language both in connection with the creation of human beings and with the election of Israel as "God's son."

> For what human can know the purpose of God? Or who can discern what the LORD wills? For the reasoning of mortals is fearful, and our plans are risky; for a perishable body weighs down the soul, and an

---

[26] James L. Kugel, "4Q369 'Prayer of Enosh' and Ancient Biblical Interpretation," *DSD* 5 (1998): 119–48.

[27] See the discussion of provenance by R. B. Wright, "Psalms of Solomon," in *Old Testament Pseudepigrapha* (ed. J. H. Charlesworth; Garden City, N.Y.: Doubleday, 1985), 2:640–41.

[28] The notion of a "holy people," by contrast, has currency in Wisdom. The phrase is used twice in Wisdom (10:15, 17), and "holy children," once (Wis 18:9). The phrase is common to Deuteronomy (Deut 7:6; 14:2, 21; 28:9) and Trito-Isaiah (62:12; 63:18) and simply the familial language that does not need to specify birth order. Cf. also 2 Macc 16:24 and 3 Macc 2:6.

earthy tent burdens thoughtful reason. And we can scarcely imagine what is on earth, and what is at hand we discover with labor; but who has searched out what is in the heavens? Who has learned your purposes, unless you have given wisdom and sent your holy spirit from on high? And thus the paths of those on earth were straightened, and humanity was taught what pleases you, and was saved by wisdom. (Wis 9:13–18)

The final strophe of the prayer contains a series of cosmic questions that raise the issue of the frailty of humankind without the possession of the spirit of wisdom. The questions can be understood to be an expansion of the final rhetorical question in Solomon's prayer of 1 Kgs 3:9 which is concerned only with the king's capacity to rule the Israelites: "for who can govern this your great people?" Pseudo-Solomon's questions reflect a wisdom genre and such rhetorical questions as found in Job 38.[29] Wisdom 9:17 indeed provides an answer to the rhetorical questions that God poses to Job. Yet the ordering of the questions is distinctive. As Maurice Gilbert has pointed out, the argumentation of the prayer in effect descends to its apogee in Wis 9:15, in which humans without divine help are described as weighted down by an "earthy tent" only to ascend again to the height of heavens.[30] Human beings will remain only witless and misguided creatures without the wisdom that comes from the holy spirit of God. Wisdom 9:18 offers a conclusion to the prayer and a smooth transition to the second half of the book.[31] The final verse points to additional instruction that will be offered, derived not from Solomon's own wealth of experience but from the experience of the elect "holy people" themselves.

The book's historical review in Wisdom 10–18 ends, significantly, not with the establishment of kingship, which one might expect given the pseudonymous voice of the Davidide Solomon in the book, but only with the crossing of the Red Sea. The review of Israelite his-

---

[29] Cf. also Prov 30:2–4; Isa 40:13–14; Sir 1:1–10; *1 En.* 93:11–14.

[30] Gilbert, "Structure," 310–11.

[31] In point of fact, from a formal perspective, it has been argued that the prayer continues through the end of the book, because passages phrased in second address to God continue throughout the last half of the book. For a discussion of the structure of the book which includes a review of various positions, see James M. Reese, "Plan and Structure in the Book of Wisdom," *CBQ* 27 (1965): 391–99. In any case, a clear break occurs with the inauguration of the discussion of the role of wisdom in Israel's early history.

tory in Wisdom 10–19 stretches only from Adam to Moses. The Exodus event and the crossing of the Red Sea are cast by Pseudo-Solomon as a new creation. Through God's, and by extension, the spirit of Wisdom's, action through the Exodus and crossing the Red Sea, Israel as a nation has become the new, pre-expulsion humanity, the new Adam. Similarly, we might say that Solomon's prayer in Wisdom 9, seen in the larger context of chapters 6–9 and, indeed, the first five chapters as well, points to the crowning of new kings and queens, the righteous of Israel who faithfully praise God's work in their salvation. The degree to which these two categories overlap, and whether in Pseudo-Solomon's view one can be righteous outside of Jewish observance, are topics for another paper, but let it be said that a tension remains in the book between the particularism reflected in the election of Israel as a "holy people" adopted by God and the universalism seen in the possibility that anyone can gain wisdom and thus attain immortality.

In conclusion, the prayer in Wisdom 9 adopts the language of kingship only ultimately to undermine its original historical sense in the ancient Near East and Greco-Roman world by affirming all human creatures as regents. The prayer, and the book as a whole, also answers an implicit question in an age during which there was a Jewish diaspora spread throughout the Mediterranean basin and beyond, in which there was no independent Jewish nation. What would become of God's promise to the Davidic house? When would a Judahite monarch rise to rule over Israel as a whole? The answer is simply: there is no need for one king, because all righteous Jews are monarchs by virtue of their creaturehood. Wisdom is not the sole possession of kings; and indeed, sovereignty is not the sole prerogative of kings. Rather, the book affirms the democratization of kingship: "Everyman" can be a king, to the degree that it is possible for all to gain wisdom.

There is further irony in the fact that the temple builder, Solomon, provides a means of access to God outside the sacred precincts. Whereas Solomon's prayer of dedication in 1 Kings 8 would use the temple in Jerusalem as the fulcrum for access to God by having all prayers turned toward Jerusalem during their petitions, the retrieval and reworking of Solomon's prayer in 1 Kings 3 offers a new conceptualization of prayer. Wisdom is available to those who live righteously by doing the will of God and the means for acquiring wisdom is through prayer. The grounds for such an affirmation lay squarely in scripture, but scripture as interpreted. The Hebrew Bible offers more than one paradigm for the use of royal language and imagery. There are tensions between the two. Is Israel, the people as a whole, the adopted children of God, the son who will be heir to the kingship, or is a Davidide of the house of Judah to be so designated? Pseudo-Solomon provides an answer by speaking in a forked tongue, in words with hidden, or double, meanings. Let the wise parse the mystery. Solomon's legacy, if we accept Wisdom of Solomon's view, is to bequeath the crown not to his own son but to all God's children. These kings and queens of the earth have been crowned and their inherited realm will encompass immortality if they follow the divine will enlightened by the path of Sophia herself. In offering a prayer of praise and petition, Solomon models the most important vehicle for discerning the will of God and obtaining the spirit of Wisdom: communicating with God not through sacrificial offering in the temple but through praise and petition.[32] The medium of Solomon's prayer is thus, in part, its message. Though Solomon, with the help of wisdom, was builder of the temple, he makes clear through the medium of his prayer that the act of prayer, like kingship itself, is universally available to those who exhibit covenant loyalty and righteousness.

---

[32] The patterns of Jewish ritual practice in the Second Temple era, particularly as they relate to prayer practices, remain a murky subject. Diaspora Judaism and Palestinian Judaism undoubtedly developed in different ways, and Palestinian Judaism itself reflected a variegated pattern of understanding the significance of Temple, cult, and prayer, perhaps in part depending on the degree of assimilation to Greco-Roman culture, but clearly for other issues as well. The Qumran community in particular may offer a significant example of a Jewish group that conceived of its participation in liturgical worship as an experience that in effect brought them to the heavenly temple in which they participated in the heavenly worship of God. See most recently Crispin H. T. Fletcher-Lewis's book, in which he vigorously argues for a divine anthropology, *All the Glory of Adam: Liturgical Anthropology in the Dead Sea Scrolls* (STDJ 42; Leiden: Brill, 2002).

PART THREE

THE INTERPRETIVE LIFE OF BIBLICAL TEXTS
FROM EARLY JUDAISM TO THE PRESENT

TWO POWERS IN HEAVEN;
OR, THE MAKING OF A HERESY

Daniel Boyarin

> If you come to a fork in the road, take it.
>
> Lawrence Peter Berra
> (with gratitude to Vincent P. Bynack)

Among his many achievements, James Kugel has also done very important work in the field of establishing connections between rabbinic and other Judaisms in the early period, notably in his classic, *In Potiphar's House*.[1] I hope therefore to be honoring his career and person with this contribution.

Scholarship on the *Memra*, particularly in the twentieth-century, has tended to recapitulate the rabbinic repudiation of Logos theology rather than interrogate it. A not-atypical scholarly comment on the Rabbis and the *Memra* reads: "Students of Rabbinic Judaism were convinced from the outset that the theory represented by views [of the *Memra* as a Logos-like intermediary] was incorrect, and that the *Memra* could not be an hypostasis within the Godhead: the fundamental monotheism of mainstream Rabbinic Judaism could tolerate no such *deuteros theos*."[2] This argument, as I have shown elsewhere,[3] is incoherent and circular because it is the "fundamental monotheism" of the Rabbis that is the discursive project both of their texts and our scholarship. The conviction of "students of rabbinic Judaism" is a parade example of begging the question. The formulation is accordingly instructive heuristically precisely because the problematic should be to see how "the fundamental mainstream

---

[1] James L. Kugel, *In Potiphar's House: the Interpretive Life of Biblical Texts* (San Francisco: Harper & Row, 1990).

[2] Robert Hayward, *Divine Name and Presence: The Memra* (Oxford Centre for Postgraduate Hebrew Studies; Totowa, N.J.: Allanheld, 1981), 4.

[3] Daniel Boyarin, "The Gospel of the *Memra*: Jewish Binitarianism and the Crucifixion of the Logos," *HTR* 94 (2001): 243–84.

of rabbinic Judaism" emerged, struggled with others, and finally
became hegemonic.

The position that I occupy here is quite different in some respects
from that of the pioneering work of Alan Segal. Segal writes, "A
few have even suggested that there was no concept of orthodoxy in
rabbinic Judaism. Part of the importance of these reports about 'two
powers in heaven' is that they show us that the rabbis, in common
with their brethren in the diaspora, were concerned about the theological and orthodox center of Judaism when other sectarian groups
of their day seemed willing to compromise Judaism's integrity."[4]
While I am in total sympathy with Segal's critique of those who see
rabbinism as a doctrine-free orthopraxy, from my point of view, the
orthodoxy that the Rabbis were concerned about was an orthodoxy
that they were making by *constructing* "Two Powers in Heaven" as
heresy, at just about the same time that bishops were declaring the
belief in "One Power in Heaven"—"Monarchianism"—a leading
heresy of Christianity.[5] The Rabbis, by defining elements from within
their own religious heritage as not Jewish, were, in effect, producing
Christianity, just as Christian heresiologists were defining traditional
elements of their own religious heritage as not Christian and thereby
producing Judaism. The Christian heresiologists, as was their wont,
were more explicit about naming the "heresy" as Judaism, while the
Rabbis, as theirs, were more circumspect. Neither was "protecting
the integrity of the theological and orthodox center" of their respective religions,[6] but rather constructing them through discursive analogue of the psychic process known as splitting, wherein unwanted
parts of the psyche are projected "out there," producing a sense of
good self and bad other:

> In so far as the objects which are presented to [the ego] are sources
> of pleasure, it takes them into itself, 'introjects' them . . .; and, on the

---

[4] Alan F. Segal, *Two Powers in Heaven: Early Rabbinic Reports About Christianity and Gnosticism* (SJLA 25; Leiden: Brill, 1977), x.

[5] Thus the question posed by Segal: "A most significant question is whether or not such ideas were ever current within rabbinic Judaism" (Segal, *Powers*, 69) begs the question. Rabbinic Judaism, in my view, is precisely the religion that is made by expelling "such ideas" by crossing them and their traditionalist believers with a border of orthodoxy. On Monarchianism, see also Ronald Heine, "The Christology of Callistus," *JTS* 49 (1998): 56–91.

[6] Segal is capable, of course, of seeing the matter in a much more critical and nuanced light also: "Preliminary indications are, therefore, that many parts of the

other hand, it expels whatever within itself becomes a cause of unplea-
sure (. . . the mechanism of projection). . . . For the pleasure-ego the
external world is divided into a part that is pleasurable, which is incorporated into itself, and a remainder that is extraneous to it. It has
[also] separated off a part of its own self, which it projects into the
external world.[7]

I am suggesting that this is a useful analogy for understanding how
Christianity and Judaism each produced their respective other by
disavowing parts of themselves.

Pointing to a conceptual difficulty raised by Segal's otherwise excellent book will help make clearer the difference and the stakes involved
between our approaches to the same materials and questions. Segal
summarizes his results on his first page: "It became clear that 'two
powers in heaven' was a very early category of heresy, earlier than
Jesus, if Philo is a trustworthy witness, and one of the basic categories by which the rabbis perceived the new phenomenon of Christianity. It was one of the central issues over which the two religions
separated."[8]

The conceptual problem should be clear. Particularly insofar as
the very category of heresy in Judaism did not exist in the first century or indeed before the rabbinic formation,[9] a point that Segal
himself makes elsewhere,[10] "Two Powers in Heaven" could not have
been an early category of heresy but could only have been one of
the options for Jewish belief at the time. If, then, the Rabbis named
this as a heresy, which they did, and made it a sort of touchstone
for splitting between their "orthodox" Judaism and the *minut* of
Christians (and others), this cannot be formulated as one of the issues

---

Jewish community in various places and periods used the tradition which the rabbis claim is an heretical conception of the deity" (*Powers*, 43). Yet he is still willing
to speak of a "theological and orthodox center of Judaism," which these "many
parts of the Jewish community" seem "willing to compromise."

[7] Sigmund Freud, "Instincts and Their Vicissitudes," in *The Standard Edition of
the Complete Psychological Works of Sigmund Freud* (ed. and trans. J. Strachey; 24 vols.;
1915; repr. London: Hogarth, 1957), 14:136.

[8] Segal, *Powers*, ix.

[9] As I have argued in Daniel Boyarin, "A Tale of Two Synods: Nicaea, Yavneh
and the Making of Orthodox Judaism," *Exemplaria* 12 (2000): 21–62. Cf. also the
complications that Segal makes for himself on *Powers*, 215, because he has not completely clarified these two issues (the existence of "Two Powers" theology and the
appearance of the notion of heresy) separately.

[10] Segal, *Powers*, 5–6.

over which the two religions separated but as the means through which a border was inscribed. That is, through the naming of "Two Powers" as heresy and the deeding (avidly colluded in by some Christians) of that doctrine to Christianity, an ancient Jewish doctrine was marked as a heresy, and the two "religions" were produced as different.[11] I would thus rewrite Segal's sentence in my own terms in the following way: There is significant evidence (uncovered in large part by Segal) that in the first century many—perhaps most—Jews held a binitarian doctrine of God.[12] This Jewish doctrine was named *minut* by the Rabbis as an important part of the project of constructing Jewish orthodoxy as separate from Christianity.[13]

---

[11] This position is comparable to the general view of Lawrence H. Schiffman, "At the Crossroads: Tannaitic Perspectives on the Jewish-Christian Schism," in *Aspects of Judaism in the Greco-Roman Period: Jewish and Christian Self-Definition* (ed. E. P. Sanders, A. I. Baumgarten, and A. Mendelson; Philadelphia: Fortress, 1981), 2:115–56, 338–52. Schiffman sees a transition from "sectarianism" to "consensus" in the rabbinic period and even remarks that certain views that had been accepted among Jews were now defined as *minut* and thus left to the Christians. He even considers the rise of Christianity a main cause for this development within Judaism. My disagreements with Schiffman would be two: First of all, he would locate this development a century earlier than I would, and secondly, for his "consensus" I would substitute orthodoxy.

[12] Segal, *Powers*, 43.

[13] At the same time that I am (gratefully) building on the vital work that Segal performed in his book, I must comment that Segal consistently confounds his own project and mislays, as it were, his own best insights. He writes: "It is not possible to decide exactly when rabbinic opposition to such doctrines started. For one thing, it is nearly impossible to be sure of the wording of rabbinic traditions before 200 C.E much less before 70 C.E., when the rabbis became the leaders of the Jewish community [sic!]. Most rabbinic traditions, at least as we have them, were written subsequently. So we cannot blithely assume that the rabbinic reports date from the Second Commonwealth" (*Powers*, 43). So far so good, but then he continues, "However, with Philo's evidence, we have reason to suppose their antiquity." Segal has begun asking about the dating of the rabbinic opposition to the doctrine and seems to have tried to supply an answer by citing Philo, but Philo, of course, is only evidence for the *existence* of the doctrine and not for rabbinic opposition to it; in fact he himself (Philo) holds a version of the "heresy," as stated explicitly by Segal (*Powers*, 50). This ambiguity as to the question at hand pervades Segal's discussion and frequently weakens his answers considerably. A clearer distinction between the search for the doctrine and the search for its expulsion as "heretical" would have served Segal's inquiry well. There is, I submit, no pre-Christian (or even first-century) evidence for the latter. This distinction should also serve (negatively) the enterprise of the search for the so-called Jewish origins of Gnosticism. See the otherwise compelling Menahem Kister, "'Let Us Make a Man'—Observations on the Dynamics of Monotheism," in *Issues in Talmudic Research: Conference Commemorating the Fifth Anniversary of the Passing of Ephraim E. Urbach, 2 December 1996* (Jerusalem: Israel Academy of Sciences, 2001 [Hebrew]), 53, who also seems to hold that there is some essentialist entity called "Jewish Monotheism," which various doctrines can

Just as for Christian orthodoxy, the arch-heresy for the Rabbis also involved, not surprisingly, a "flaw" in the doctrine of God:[14] "Two Powers in Heaven"—"binitarianism"—of which one major manifestation was traditional Jewish Logos theology.[15] I would suggest that this issue of the doctrine of God is one archaeological site where making the distinction between the (metaphorically) excavated Synagogue and the House of Study[16] or between rabbinic and other forms of Jewish piety in the rabbinic period becomes crucial.[17] Alejandro Díez Macho has observed that it is no mere coincidence that the more rabbinized of the Targums (Targums *Onkelos* and *Pseudo-Jonathan*) and rabbinic literature itself suppress the use of the term *Memra* quite observably. Indeed, in rabbinic literature, it has disappeared entirely,[18] and in the more rabbinized Targums, it appears much less frequently, suggesting a struggle between the forms of piety that were current in the Synagogues and those that were centered in the Houses of Study of the Rabbis. This strongly implies that Logos theology was a living current within non-Christian Judaic circles from before the Christian era until well into late antiquity, when the Palestinian Targums were produced.[19] We must avoid the serious

---

threaten or endanger, rather than seeing that very entity itself as a constructed and contested field as I suggest we must.

[14] See the near-classic Richard P. C. Hanson, *The Search for the Christian Doctrine of God: The Arian Controversy 318–381 A.D.* (Edinburgh: T&T Clark, 1988).

[15] Boyarin, "Jewish Binitarianism."

[16] Thus, for instance, it has often been remarked that nearly all of the late ancient Synagogues excavated in Palestine significantly contradict rabbinic prescriptions for the building of such edifices.

[17] Cf. Galit Hasan-Rokem, "Narratives in Dialogue: A Folk Literary Perspective on Interreligious Contacts in the Holy Land in Rabbinic Literature of Late Antiquity," in *Sharing the Sacred: Religious Contacts and Conflicts in the Holy Land First–Fifteenth Centuries C.E.* (ed. G. Stroumsa and A. Kofsky; Jerusalem: Yad Ben Zvi, 1998), 109–29, esp. 128, who somewhat underplays this dimension in my opinion. For other instances of disparity between the "Judaism" of the Rabbis and that of the Synagogue in late antique Palestine, see William Horbury, "Suffering and Messianism in Yose Ben Yose," in *Suffering and Martyrdom in the New Testament: Studies Presented to G. M. Styler* (ed. W. Horbury and B. McNeil; Cambridge: Cambridge University Press, 1980), 143–82.

[18] See, however, Hans Bietenhard, "Logos Theologie im Rabbinat. Ein Beitrage zur Lehre vom Worte Gottes im rabbinischen Schrifttum," *ANRW* II, 19.2:580–618.

[19] Note how different this formulation is from the traditional scholarly one whereby John's Logos was influenced by the Targum's *Memra*. See, e.g., Martin McNamara, "Logos of the Fourth Gospel and *Memra* of the Palestinian Targum," *ExpTim* 79 (1968): 115–17.

methodological error of regarding all non-rabbinic religious expression by Jews during the rabbinic period as somehow not quite legitimate or of marginalizing it by naming it as syncretistic or uninformed, thus simply reproducing the rabbinic ideology, rather than subjecting it to historical criticism.[20] In other words, the consensus of scholars of rabbinic Judaism referred to by Robert Hayward simply replicates the consensus of the Rabbis themselves, whereas the current scholarly task is to read this latter consensus against its grain, in order to see what it is that it mystified in order to construct its hegemony.[21]

Extant rabbinic texts demonstrate that the Rabbis, too, knew of Logos theology, but that they constructed their own "orthodoxy" by excommunicating the Jewish Logos from within their midst. As Hayward put it, "The Logos is an intermediary, and Abelson rightly remarks that the Rabbis repudiate all intermediaries."[22] This repudiated or disowned entity, however, was a part of themselves.[23]

"We must think of heresy not so much as something that attacked the church from without, as of something that grew up within it,"

---

[20] An error committed as well by the otherwise very astute Darrell D. Hannah, *Michael and Christ: Michael Traditions and Angel Christology in Early Christianity* (WUNT 2.109; Tübingen: Mohr Siebeck, 1999), 109–10.

[21] See also Naomi Janowitz, "Rabbis and Their Opponents: The Construction of the 'Min' in Rabbinic Anecdotes," *JECS* 6 (1998): 449–62; Christine E. Hayes, "Displaced Self-Perceptions: The Deployment of *Mînîm* and Romans in *B. Sanhedrin* 90b–91a," in *Religious and Ethnic Communities in Later Roman Palestine* (ed. H. Lapin; Potomac, Md.: University Press of Maryland, 1998), 249–89.

[22] Hayward, *Divine Name and Presence*, 4.

[23] Compare the very helpful discussion of J. Rebecca Lyman of Christian heresiology:

> I am suggesting that problems of assimilation and authority were already present in the form of universal Christianity taught by Justin, which could lead to the polemical invention of "Gnosticism" as philosophical and superstitious at once, whatever may have actually been taught by Valentinus or Ptolemy. Irenaeus's concern with identifying valid sacraments, lasting conversions, and legitimate successions reveals the instability of the inherited discourse of Justin, and the necessity of establishing the correct *diadoche* and belief within the baptized community itself. If we restore a primary teaching identity to Irenaeus as a leader, the controversial rhetoric of his text reflects a continuing debate over identity and authority by competitive intellectuals within the community rather than a defensive protection against outsiders. ("The Politics of Passing: Justin Martyr's Conversion as a Problem of 'Hellenization,'" in *Conversion in Late Antiquity and the Early Middle Ages* [ed. A. Grafton and K. Mills; Rochester, N.Y.: University of Rochester Press, forthcoming])

writes C. K. Barrett, paraphrasing Bartsch,[24] and the same goes, *mutatis mutandis*, for the House of Study. Having shown the likelihood that Logos theology is an ancient heritage of the Jews, we can begin to imagine a complex process of splitting (the psychoanalytic term is chosen advisedly) that ultimately gave rise to Judaism and Christianity. Christianity and Judaism became constructed in part through the rabbinic repudiation of all intermediaries, that is, its alienation of that native son, the Logos, and at the same time through the orthodox Christian nomination of this very repudiation when enacted by Christians as heresy and as "Judaizing." Theorist Homi Bhabha has given a perfect description of this psycho-cultural process:

> Produced through the strategy of disavowal, the *reference* of discrimination [heretics, DB] is always to a process of splitting as the condition of subjection: a discrimination between the mother culture and its bastards, the self and its doubles, where the trace of what is disavowed is not repressed but repeated as something *different*—a mutation, a hybrid [a *minut*, a Jewish-Christianity, DB]. It is such a partial and double force that . . . disturbs the visibility of the colonial presence and makes the recognition of its authority problematic. To be authoritative, its rules of recognition must reflect consensual knowledge or opinion; to be powerful, these rules of recognition must be reached in order to represent the exorbitant objects of discrimination that lie beyond its purview.[25]

One could hardly hope for a more precise description of the heresiological process in general, or of the specific instance of the production of that bastard, "Two Powers in Heaven," as that which is not so much repressed but disavowed, produced as a mutation, a hybrid, a "Jewish Christianity."[26]

The Rabbis, I suggest, were engaged in a strenuous project of divesting "Judaism" of Logos theology and thus were absorbed in the same search for a doctrine of God that animated Christians, as well.[27] Rather than the heresy of "Two Powers in Heaven" being

---

[24] C. K. Barrett, "Jews and Judaizers in the Epistles of Ignatius," in *Jews, Greeks and Christians: Religious Cultures in Late Antiquity. Essays in Honor of W. D. Davies* (Leiden: Brill, 1976), 220–44, here 223.

[25] Homi K. Bhabha, *The Location of Culture* (London: Routledge, 1994), 111.

[26] Even to the point of helping us understand the insistence on "consensual orthodoxy."

[27] As Winston points out, even this divestiture was not total, since there are occasional midrashic texts that do refer to a hypostasized Divine Speech (the דבור),

interpreted, then, as an outside intruder into the world of "ortho-dox" Judaism, I suggest that the construction of this "heresy" in rab-binic texts represents the border making and self-definition that ultimately produced orthodox rabbinism.

Rabbinic discourse about "Two Powers in Heaven" is not a rab-binic "report" of essential differences between Christianity (or "Gnos-ticism") and Judaism, but rather a rabbinic production of that which marks the defining limits of what the Rabbis take to be Judaism via the abjection of one traditional element in Jewish religiosity, a production almost identical, as we shall see, to the Christian here-siological naming of "One Power in Heaven" (Monarchianism) as "Judaism," when, in fact, it was, of course, an internal and once-acceptable version of Christian theology.[28] I am suggesting that for the Rabbis, the discourse of heresiology, that is the collection of laws and narratives about *minut* and especially about the "heresy" of "Two Powers in Heaven," is not *about* Christianity but may, in part, be a response *to* Christianity. Thus when we examine particular instances of such discourse, we need not expect to find notions particular to Christianity but rather a general formation of a space between self and other produced by marking certain differences within and differences between. "Jewish-Christian" heresies function in the same way for Christian identity-formation. As Jonathan Z. Smith has written:

> From heresy to deviation to degeneration to syncretism, the notion of the different which claims to be the same, or, projected internally, the disguised difference within has produced a rich vocabulary of denial and estrangement. For in each case, a theory of difference, when applied to the proximate "other," is but another way of phrasing a theory of the "self."[29]

---

specifically the ten Words that we know of as the ten commandments; David Winston, *Logos and Mystical Theology in Philo of Alexandria* (Cincinnati: Hebrew Union College Press, 1985), 16.

[28] Bhabha, *Location of Culture*, 44–45 provides elegant theoretical analysis of the mechanics of such specular differentiating and identification, without, however, being able to see such processes as mutual (quite). See also discussion in Virginia Burrus, *The Sex Lives of Saints* (Divinations: Reading Late Ancient Religions; Philadelphia: University of Pennsylvania Press, forthcoming), chapter 3; and especially Willis Johnson, "Textual Sources for the study of Jewish Currency Crimes in 13th-century England," *British Numismatic Journal* 66 (1996): 21–32.

[29] Jonathan Z. Smith, "Differential Equations: On Constructing the 'Other,'" (lec-ture; Tempe, Arizona, 1992), 14, Pamphlet.

"Two Powers in Heaven" is such a "disguised difference within."

Karen King has observed that "the attempt at domination in naming one's opponents (as heretics, for example) has a reciprocal effect on the namer as well."[30] Taking up this observation, I am hoping to show how crucial elements of rabbinic Judaism were formed in the attempt at "othering" these *minim*. Once again, to adopt a formulation of King's, "Constructing a heretical other simultaneously and reciprocally constructed an orthodox self."[31] Another way of saying this would be to suggest that while there were genuine differences between nascent "Judaism" and "nascent" Christianity, they were not necessarily precisely where the discourse of *minut* would place them, but this discourse, itself, helped to shape and make the difference between the "two religions" in the place that we still, to this day, take it to be, such as, for instance, in the acceptance or rejection of the "Logos" and "Logos theology." Put one final way, I am partially reversing Alain Le Boulluec's claim (made, to be sure, with respect to Christianity) that strategies initially developed in conflict with Jews and Greeks were adapted by Christians in their fight against internal differences,[32] suggesting, rather, that the tools that the Rabbis developed in their own struggles for power and identity ended up (in the same process) in marking difference between Judaism (rabbinic) and Christianity.

I. "Two Powers in Heaven" as Jewish Theology

The notion of a second and independent divine agent can be found already in the Bible itself, as has been emphasized by earlier scholars. Darrell Hannah makes the point that the Exodus angel . . .

> becomes to some extent an expression of the divine absence in that he is a substitute for Yahweh (Ex. 33:1–3). As a replacement for the divine presence, it would appear that the angel of the Exodus is beginning to have a quasi-individual existence. Significantly, unlike מלאך יהוה [the angel of the LORD] in the patriarchal narratives, the Exodus angel

---

[30] Karen L. King, *What is Gnosticism?* (Cambridge, Mass.: Belknap Press of Harvard University Press, 2003).

[31] Ibid.

[32] Alain Le Boulluec, *La notion d'hérésie dans la littérature grecque IIe–IIIe siècles* (Paris: Études Augustiniennes, 1985), 16; King, *Making Heresy*, chapter 2.

is spoken of by God in the third person (23:20–21, 32:34 and 33:2–3).
So the Exodus angel seems to betray a certain development in the
מלאך יהוה concept, away from an extension or manifestation of the
divine presence and toward an individual existence.[33]

Hannah makes the significant double observation that in the earlier
strata of biblical writing, the patriarchal narratives and the Exodus,
there is frequent confusion, if not conflation, between the Angel of
H' and H' himself, and that this particular hypostasization seems to
disappear during the period of the monarchy, to be replaced by a
host of angels who are fully separate beings and clearly subordinate
to God.[34] This ambiguity in the early biblical narratives, particularly
when they are read together—as one phenomenon—with the later
texts and ideas, was to fuel much interpretative controversy and angst
in the early years of Judaeo-Christianity, for many of these very passages served as the origin and prooftext for Logos theology, as manifested in Justin Martyr's *Dialogue* on nearly every page. What is
important in this context, however, is not so much the implication
of the biblical passages themselves, but the strenuous energy that
rabbinic literature mobilized in order to *deny* these implications, an
expenditure of energy that indicates the attractiveness of the *deuteros
theos* idea among Jews.

An elegant example of this energy can be found in the following
early rabbinic midrash:

> "H' smote every first-born in the land of Egypt" [Exod 12:29]: I might
> have understood by means of an angel or by means of an agent, there-
> fore Scripture teaches: "And I have smitten all of the first-born" [Exod
> 12:12]; not by means of an angel and not by means of an agent. (*Mek.,
> Pisḥa* 13)[35]

Precisely the sort of ambiguity that would lead to the theological
ambivalence and the production of notions of a fully divine angel is
thoroughly repulsed by the rabbinic midrash. It has frequently been
theorized that when the midrash writes "I might have understood,"
another, "sectarian," interpretation is being raised in order to discredit it. This, in any case, would be a fine example for that the-

---

[33] Hannah, *Michael and Christ*, 21.
[34] Ibid., 22.
[35] S. Horovitz and Israel Abraham Rabin, eds., *Mechilta d'Rabbi Ismael* (ed. S. Horovitz; Jerusalem: Wahrmann Books, 1970), 43; compare also p. 33.

ory. Ancient Jews and Christian writers like Justin would certainly
have seen in this combination of verses evidence for their various
versions of Logos theology, and it is these findings that the Rabbis
dispute here vigorously.[36] However, there is more, for there are
ancient variants of the text that explicitly add to "not by means of
an angel, and not by means of an agent"—"not by means of the
Logos [לא על ידי הדיבר]."[37]

---

[36] Judah Goldin, "Not by Means of an Angel and not by Means of a Messenger,"
in *Religions in Antiquity: Essays in Memory of Erwin Ramsdell Goodenough* (ed. J. Neusner;
Leiden: Brill, 1968), 412–24.

[37] See Arthur Marmorstein, *The Old Rabbinic Doctrine of God* (London: Oxford
University Press, 1937), 57: "Israel was delivered neither by the Logos, nor angels,
but by God Himself." This version of the text was originally published from more
than one Geniza fragment by Israel Abrahams, "Some Egyptian Fragments of the
Passover Haggada," *JQR* o.s. 10 (1898): 41–51, who understood these readings as
"repeated references to the Memra or Logos" (41). The Targum reads here, "And
I will pass in my *Memra* [var. I will be revealed in my *Memra*] through the land of
Egypt this night *of the Passover*, and I will kill all the first-born in the land of Egypt"
(*Targum Neofiti 1: Exodus* [trans. M. McNamara; notes by R. Hayward; The Aramaic
Bible; Edinburgh: T&T Clark, 1994], 47–48). In my opinion, it is very difficult to
see this as a mere *façon de parler*. According to the Wisdom of Solomon 18, this
plague was carried out precisely by the Logos. See, *The Wisdom of Solomon* (AB 43;
trans. and commentary by D. Winston; Garden City, N.Y.: Doubleday, 1979), 313,
and see also his fascinating notes (with which I partially disagree for reasons that
will be obvious), 317–19; and Joseph Reider, *The Book of Wisdom: An English Translation
with Introduction and Commentary* (Dropsie College Edition: Jewish Apocryphal Literature;
New York: Harper & Brothers, 1957), 210–11, with whom my disagreement is even
sharper. Similarly, for Melito, it was Christ who executed the plague; see Melito
of Sardis, *On Pascha and Fragments* (OECT; ed. S. G. Hall; Oxford: Oxford University
Press, 1979), line 657. For the view which I maintain, see Shlomo Pines, "'From
Darkness to Light': Parallels to *Haggada* Texts in Hellenistic Literature," in *Studies
in Literature Presented to Simon Halkin* (ed. E. Fleischer; Jerusalem: Magnes, 1973
[Hebrew]), 176–79. Aside from every other argument, if the *Memra* of the Targum
was "purely a phenomenon of translation, not a figment of speculation," as George
Foot Moore maintained (*Judaism in the First Centuries of the Christian Era* [New York:
Schocken, 1971], 1:419), and if the Logos of Wisdom "is in reality God himself in
one of his aspects," and, therefore, "our author's position is almost identical with
that of the rabbis" (Winston, *Wisdom*, 319), then why all the rabbinic textual energy
expended in denying that God had any agent in the execution of the plague (even
if we grant, with Winston, that "not by means of the Logos" is a Byzantine innovation in the text)? Pines, it should be emphasized, was also one of the first to see
that "influences" could run from Christian texts, such as Melito, to rabbinic texts,
an important line of research continued in Israel Jacob Yuval, "Easter and Passover
as Early Jewish-Christian Dialogue," in *Passover and Easter: Origin and History to Modern
Times* (Two Liturgical Traditions 5; ed. P. F. Bradshaw and L. A. Hoffman; Notre
Dame: University of Notre Dame Press, 1999), 127–60. See also Menahem Kasher,
Hagadah Shel Pesah: Lel Shimurim (Jerusalem: Bet Torah Shelemah, 1982), 42 and
now Israel Jacob Yuval, *Two Nations in Your Womb: Perceptions of Jews and Christians*
(Tel-Aviv: Alma, 2000 [Hebrew]), 95–97. Yuval quite brilliantly argues that certain

One very rich example for my purposes here has been treated by Hayward, but I interpret the text differently. The text is from the fourth-century midrash, the *Mekhilta d'Rabbi Ishma'el*, to Exod 20:2:

> I am the LORD your God [Exod 20:2]: Why was it said? For this reason. At the sea He appeared to them as a mighty hero doing battle, as it is said: "The LORD is a man of war." At Sinai he appeared to them as an old man full of mercy. It is said: "And they saw the God of Israel" (Ex 24:10), etc. And of the time after they had been redeemed what does it say? "And the like of the very heaven for clearness" (ibid.). Again it says: "I beheld till thrones were placed, and one that was ancient of days did sit" (Dan 7:9). And it also says: "A fiery stream issued," etc. (v. 10).[38] Scripture, therefore, would not let the nations of the world[39] have an excuse for saying that there are two Powers, but declares: "The LORD is a man of war, the LORD is His name." He, it is, who was in Egypt and He who was at the sea. It is He who was in the past and He who will be in the future. It is He who is in this world and He who will be in the world to come, as it is said, "See now that I, even I, am He," etc. (Deut 32:39). And it also says: "Who hath wrought and done it? He that called the generations from the beginning. I, the LORD, who am the first, and with the last am the same" (Isa 41:4).[40]

---

features of the Haggada for Passover, namely the total absence of Moses, can be best explained as tacit polemic against "Christian" notions of mediation.

[38] Segal understands the citation of verse 10 as an attempt to answer the claim of the heretics because it says that "A fiery stream issued from *Him*," implying only one divine figure, and writes that, "the argument of the rabbis is not completely convincing for the text may only be referring to one of the two figures at this point" (*Powers*, 40 n. 9). Segal misconstrues the text, however. According to midrashic form the citation "and it also says" must be a continuation of the problem and not the answer. The "etc." refers then to the following verses in which it seems clear that two divine figures are envisioned, and this citation is, then, indeed part of the problem (and not an unconvincing solution, *pace* Segal). The solution comes with the citation of Exod 20:2, which is precisely what the midrashic form would lead us to expect.

[39] Segal remarks that the text has "identified the people who believe in 'two powers in heaven' as gentiles" (*Powers*, 41) and then later is somewhat nonplussed, remarking, "they must have been gentiles well-versed in Jewish tradition to have offered such a dangerous and sophisticated interpretation of Dan 7.9f" (*Powers*, 55). Well, Gentiles who are so well-versed and who would make such a dangerous and sophisticated interpretation, precisely of Daniel 7, are called Christians! What he misses is that "nations of the world" in the *Mekhilta* usually refers to Christians, "the Church from the *ethne*," to be sure, although he does allow for this as a possibility (*Powers*, 56–57). It is precisely with reference to that group that the *Mekhilta* frequently insists on referring to God as "He who spoke and the world was," which I have interpreted as an attack on the *Memra*, as an insistence that there is none; only the "Father" spoke and the world was.

[40] Horovitz and Rabin, *Mechilta*, 220–21. Cf. the following parallel text:

It is the passage from Daniel that is alluded to, *but not cited*, in the anti-"heretical" discourse, the "Son of Man" passage so pivotal for the development of early Christology, that is the real point of contention here and the reason for the citation of Exod 20:2. There

---

H' is a man of war; H' is his name [Exod 15:3]: Why was it said? For this reason. At the sea He appeared to them as a mighty hero doing battle, as it is said: "The LORD is a man of war." At Sinai he appeared to them as an old man full of mercy. It is said: "And they saw the God of Israel" (Ex 24:10), etc. And of the time after they had been redeemed what does it say? "And the like of the very heaven for clearness" (ibid.). Again it says: "I beheld till thrones were placed, and one that was ancient of days did sit" (Dan. 7.9). And it also says: "A fiery stream issued," etc. (v. 10). Scripture, therefore, would not let the nations of the world have an excuse for saying that there are two Powers, but declares: "The LORD is a man of war, the LORD is His name." He, it is, who was in Egypt and He who was at the sea. It is He who was in the past and He who will be in the future. It is He who is in this world and He who will be in the world to come, as it is said, "See now that I, even I, am He," etc. (Deut 32:39). And it also says: "Who hath wrought and done it? He that called the generations from the beginning. I, the LORD, who am the first, and with the last am the same" (Isa 41:4).

From: *Mekilta DeRabbi Ishmael* (ed. and trans. J. Z. Lauterbach; 1934; repr., Philadephia: Jewish Publishing Society, 1961), 2:31–32; Horovitz and Rabin, *Mechilta*, 129–30. For extensive discussion of this and parallel passages, see Segal, *Powers*, 33–57. I will refer to this analysis as relevant for my particular focus on the text and the questions involved.

Reading this parallel text, Hayward argues that the purpose of this text is to say that "the fact that the divine Name YHWH is found twice in one verse of Scripture is not to be taken as a point of departure for the heretical proposition that there are two Lords." Hayward, however, misunderstands how midrash "works." The verse that is cited at the opening of the midrash is not the verse that causes the problem but the verse that will provide a solution to the problem. The point of the midrash is to demonstrate the *necessity* for the verse cited in the lemma by showing that without it, there would be some error or difficulty. The text cited in my main text demonstrates in any case that the so-called repetition of the name is not the difficulty here. Indeed, Exod 15:3, "The LORD is a Man of War; The LORD is His name," is taken by the Rabbis to mean that the two appearances of God, as youth and elder, are two modalities of the same person—dynamic Modalism—and not two persons, thus refuting the "heretics." Hayward is in good company here. So too Segal, *Powers*, 36. I believe that the same false interpretation is proffered by Segal to *Sifre Deuteronomy* 379, where the text cites the verse, "So now that I, even I, am He," as a *refutation* to heretics, while Segal sees it as the heretical provocation (*Powers*, 86). The verse asserts the identicality of God with himself, making it an effective refutation of binitarianism rather than a support for it. Even less plausible is Segal's remark with regard to another passage that it, too, "uses the repetition in scripture as an occasion to discuss 'two powers in heaven'" (*Powers*, 90). The alleged "repetition" here is simply the use of the conjunctive "and" which Rabbi Aqiva used for all sorts of *drashot* on many themes and has absolutely nothing to do with "Two Powers." Cf. also Elliot R. Wolfson, *Through a Speculum That Shines: Vision and Imagination in Medieval Jewish Literature* (Princeton: Princeton University Press, 1994), 32–35.

are two descriptions of God as revealed in the Torah, one at the splitting of the Red Sea and one at the revelation of the ten commandments at Sinai. In the first, God is explicitly described as a warrior, that is, as a young man, as it were, while at the latter, as the Rabbis read it, God is described as an elder, full of wisdom and mercy. The problem is the doubling of descriptions of God as *senex* (judge) and *puer* (man of war) and the correlation of those two descriptions with the divine figures of Ancient of Days and Son of Man from Daniel, which together might easily lead one to think that there are Two Powers in Heaven, indeed that God has two persons, a Father-person and a Son-person. These were, of course, crucial loci for Christological interpretations. The citation of God's Name in Exod 20:2, at the beginning of those same ten commandments, thus answers possible heretical implications of those verses by insisting on the unity of H' in both instances. The text portentously *avoids* citing the Daniel verses most difficult for rabbinic Judaism, 7:13–14: "I saw in the vision of the night, and behold with the clouds of the Heaven there came one like a Son of Man and came to the Ancient of Days and stood before him and brought him close, and to him was given rulership and the glory and the kingdom, and all nations, peoples, and languages will worship him. His rulership is eternal which will not pass, and his kingship will not be destroyed."[41] The tacit contention with the Logos theology of the Targum appears especially strong when we remember that in targumic texts, we can find the Son of Man identified as the Messiah.[42] Furthermore, in a talmudic passage to be discussed below (*b. Ḥag.* 14a), Rabbi Aqiva himself is represented as identifying the "Son of Man" with the heavenly David, and thus with the Messiah, before being "encouraged" by his fellows to abandon this "heretical" view. This would suggest the possibility that there were non-Christian Jews who would have identified the Messiah himself (necessarily incarnate) as the Son of Man.

Hayward believes that this midrash represents an assertion of *Memra* theology and concludes, therefore, that "this midrash presents *Memra-*

---

[41] For another instance in which, also in a polemical context, the Rabbis avoid citing the really difficult part of Daniel 7, see Segal, *Powers*, 132.

[42] Sigmund Mowinckel, *He That Cometh: The Messiah Concept in the Old Testament and Later Judaism* (trans. G. W. Anderson; Oxford: Basil Blackwell, 1956), 357. See also Moshe Idel, *Messianic Mystics* (New Haven: Yale University Press, 1998), 89.

Theology in Rabbinic terms, and is a means of proving nothing less than the unity of God, the *very opposite* of the use to which the Gnostics or Christians are supposed to have put it."[13] However, there is no reference whatsoever to the *Memra* in this or any other rabbinic text, so it seems entirely unjustified to see here a presentation of *Memra* theology. Indeed it is much more plausible to see here a polemic against a *Memra* theology that would indeed project in rabbinic terms any doctrine of the *Memra* as "Two Powers in Heaven" and thus *minut*.

Segal has suggested independently that "in view of the importance of the name of God in this midrash it is not unlikely that the midrash is relying on the mysterious name of God which was revealed to Moses at the burning bush. 'I am that I am' is being interpreted with past and future implications of the Hebrew verb forms and is being understood to be an eternal pledge to remain with Israel."[14] We have seen, however, that this revelation and its mysterious name are indeed a central locus for deriving the *Memra*, and our text makes no mention whatever of that hypostasis, suggesting that rather than *Memra* theology being elaborated here, it is being silently refuted, along with, perhaps, its more radical form: Logos (Son of Man) Christology. In a slightly later, but still classically rabbinic, parallel to these texts (cited as well by Segal), we find, "And thus Daniel says: 'I beheld till thrones were placed, and one that was ancient of days did sit.' Rabbi Ḥiyya bar Abba taught: Should a whoreson say to you, 'They are two gods,' reply to him, I am the one of the sea; I am the one of Sinai!"[15] This seems quite plausibly an allusion to Christians who would read the Daniel passage as referring to one like a Son of Man (the warrior at the Sea; the Son) and an Ancient

---

[13] Hayward, *Divine Name and Presence*, 31.

[14] Segal, *Powers*, 37. Segal prefers to analyze the shorter version of the *Mekhilta DeRashbi*. However, it is almost certain that this text is dependent on the earlier *Mekhilta d'Rabbi Ishma'el* and frequently misunderstands his sources, as held with respect to this passage by Jacob Z. Lauterbach, "Some Clarifications on the Mekhilta," in *Sefer Klausner Maasaf le-Mada: Ule-Sifrut Yafah Mugash le-Prof. Josef Klausner le-Yobel Ha-Shishim* (ed. N. H. Torczyner et al.; Tel-Aviv: Hozaat Va ad-Hayobel, 1937 [Hebrew]), 181–88; and strongly demonstrated recently in general by Menahem Kahana, *Two Mekhiltot on the Amalek Portion: The Originality of the Version of the Mekhilta De'Rabbi Ishma'el with Respect to the Mekhilta of Rabbi Shim on Ben Yohay* (Jerusalem: Hotsa'at sefarim a. sh. Y. L. Magnes, ha-Universitah ha-'Ivrit, Keren ha-Rav David Mosheh ve-'Amalyah Rozen, 1999 [Hebrew]).

[15] *Pesiq. Rab.* 21 100b.

of Days (the judge at Sinai; the Father), not least owing to the pejorative reference to the interlocutor as "whoreson," a charge that
since Celsus at least had been known as a Jewish calumny against
Jesus.[46] Jewish/Christian binitarianism is being answered, therefore,
by rabbinic Modalism; or rather, Jewish/Christian Modalism is being
constructed as Jewish, Jewish/Christian binitarianism as *minut*.[47]

Interestingly enough, Justin's construction of Trypho and his teachers as the opponents of Logos theology can be seen as precisely part
of the same cultural "conspiracy." That is, both the Rabbis and
Justin agree that the distinction between orthodoxy and heresy, or
between Judaism and Christianity (and vice-versa), is marked by the
signifier of the Logos. The rabbinic text could almost be the answer
of a very articulate and learned Trypho against the Logos theology
of Justin or the Christology of the Fourth Gospel.[48] The whole point
of this text is to combat the "heresy" that there are two Gods, two
Powers in Heaven, God and his Logos or Son (of Man), by offering
what is a Modalist solution: the seeming appearance of two persons
is only a manifestation of different aspects of the same person. That
which Hayward took to be the problem of the Midrash, the dual
appearance of the name H' in the verse, is precisely the solution:
both appearances are the same God, the same hypostasis. As in the
Christian Modalist "heresy," the Rabbis believe in "one identical
Godhead Which could be designated indifferently Father [Old Man]
or Son [Mighty Hero]; the terms did not stand for real distinctions,
but were mere names applicable at different times."[49]

---

[46] As argued, correctly in my view, by R. Travers Herford, *Christianity in Talmud
& Midrash* (1903; repr., New York: KTAV, 1978), 304, as well as by Jacob Z.
Lauterbach, *Rabbinic Essays* (New York: KTAV, 1973), 549. Oddly, Segal claims
both that a "gnostic impulse" was the cause of the redaction of this text (*Powers*,
54) and then later, "'two powers' refers to Christians and not extreme gnostics"
(*Powers*, 58), on the basis of the same passage. I obviously agree with the latter point
and not the former. See too Wolfson, *Through a Speculum*, 39–40.

[47] For at least a hint that Modalism is the dominant rabbinic doctrine of God,
see Elliot R. Wolfson, "Judaism and Incarnation: The Imaginal Body of God," in
Christianity in Jewish Terms (Radical Traditions; ed. T. S. Frymer-Kensky; Boulder,
Colo.: Westview, 2000), 239–54, esp. 241.

[48] I am accordingly in great sympathy with the line of argument taken by Díez
Macho in general and particularly in A. Díez Macho, "El Logos y el Espíritu
Santo," *Atlántida* 1 (1963): 381–96, esp. 392.

[49] J. N. D. Kelly, *Early Christian Doctrines* (rev. ed.; New York: Harper & Row,
1978), 120.

It now becomes clear why midrashim of this period, especially in covert or overt polemic against Christianity, designate God fairly routinely as "The One Who Spoke and the World Was." This is a name for God that resists *Memra* or Logos interpretations of Genesis 1, and, therefore, a designation for God that serves to displace *Memra* theology, naming it implicitly as the "heresy" of "Two Powers."[50] Although Hayward is absolutely correct in his assertion that "the identity of those who taught that there were two *ršwywt* [powers] in heaven is uncertain: favourite candidates have included Gnostics and Judaeo-Christians,"[51] for this particular text, there really is little doubt to whom the reference is. The text tells us who its opponents are: "The Nations of the World," which in this midrash (and other works of this period, the late third century) refers to Christians and in particular Gentile Christians.[52] However, insofar as we have seen that *Memra*/Logos theology is not a Gentile product, or even a specifically Christian product in its origins, this rabbinic text represents the movement of repudiation of which I have been speaking. That which is a difference *within* Judaism is projected onto an external other, not only Christian, but Gentile Christian, referred to as the "Nations of the World" to distance it from Israel, to render its binary opposition to Israel even more unequivocal, a virtual given.

As in Christian heresiology, the difference within has been renominated a contamination from without. As in Christian heresiology, where *disbelief* in "Two Powers in Heaven," so-called Sabellianism, Modalism, or Monarchianism ("One Power in Heaven"), is named— accurately—"Judaism,"[53] to produce a binary opposition between the inside and the outside of Christianity and to disavow the threatening

---

[50] This was surely not the most common or general designation for the deity in rabbinic texts. Thus, for instance, the slightly earlier Mishna usually refers to God as "Heaven." This shift in the midrashic literature of the latter half of the third century seems to me significant, therefore, particularly as it comes in texts that can be otherwise arguably read as anti-Christian propaganda.

[51] Hayward, *Divine Name and Presence*, 31.

[52] Daniel Boyarin, *Dying for God: Martyrdom and the Making of Christianity and Judaism* (The Lancaster/Yarnton Lectures in Judaism and Other Religions for 1998; Stanford: Stanford University Press, 1999), 113. For this identification, see also Yuval, *Nations*, 91 n. 111.

[53] Note that according to Hippolytus, Noetus (the most important of the early modalists) used the same verses to argue against the Second Person that the Rabbis used against Two Powers heretics; Segal, *Powers*, 229.

difference within (the Modalists "argued that the Power issuing from
the Godhead was distinct only verbally or in name"),[54] here in the
rabbinic text the *belief* in "Two Powers in Heaven" is being excom-
municated from within Judaism and named (albeit slightly, but *only*
slightly obliquely) as "Christianity." "Modalism" is, of course, rabbinic Jewish orthodoxy: All doubleness and all difference within God
suggested by the Bible are to be understood, according to the Rabbis,
as only aspects of the one God.

In other "Judaisms" (including some later versions of rabbinic
Judaism), this was not the case. Daniel Abrams has recently named
this a virtually perennial issue in Jewish conceptions of God:

> One of the central aspects of Jewish theology, and Jewish mysticism
> in particular, is the conception of the nature of God's being and the
> appearance of the divine before humanity. No one view has domi-
> nated the spectrum of Jewish interpretations, since the biblical text is
> the only common frame for the wide variety of speculations. At issue
> is whether the one God depicted in the Hebrew Bible is manifest to
> humans directly or through the agency of a divine, semidivine, or cre-
> ated power.[55]

Elliot Wolfson, in a typically brilliant reconstruction, has shown that
in rabbinic and extra-rabbinic traditions of Jewish late antiquity
(including texts of the Gnosis falsely so-called), Jacob himself, the
Father of Israel, is recognized as precisely a second divine figure.[56]
If prior to the rabbinic intervention a Jew could believe comfortably
in the Logos or Wisdom or Metatron[57] or Yaho'el or the supernal

---

[54] Kelly, *Doctrines*, 119–20. For a fine succinct discussion of Modalism, see Kelly,
Doctrines, 119–23.

[55] Daniel Abrams, "The Boundaries of Divine Ontology: The Inclusion and
Exclusion of Metatron in the Godhead," *HTR* 87 (1994): 291–321, here 291.

[56] Elliot R. Wolfson, "The Image of Jacob Engraved Upon the Throne: Further
Reflection on the Esoteric Doctrine of the German Pietists," in *Along the Path: Studies
in Kabbalistic Myth, Symbolism, and Hermeneutics* (Albany, N.Y.: State University of New
York Press, 1995), 4–7 and throughout. See especially his statement: "In the earliest sources the motif of the icon of Jacob engraved on the throne may have been
related to the hypostatization of the Logos" (18).

[57] In this context fit as well Enoch traditions. As Abrams has again phrased the
point well: "Moshe Idel has drawn our attention to texts that understand Enoch
to be the angelic figure of Metatron and yet others where Metatron is identified
with God, bridging all the gaps between humanity and God" ("Metatron," 292–93;
citing Moshe Idel, "Enoch is Metatron," *Imm* 24/25 [1990]: 220–40). See also
Gedaliahu Stroumsa, "Form(s) of God: Some Notes on Metatron and Christ," *HTR*
76 (1983): 269–88.

Jacob as a hypostasized virtual second God,[58] once the denial of such beliefs had been named "Judaism" by Christians in order to set themselves off theologically from Jews, the countermove for rabbinic Jews resisting Christianity was an obvious one. "Two Powers in Heaven" became the primary heresy for the Rabbis, and Modalism, the Christian heresy par excellence, became the only "orthodox" theology allowed to Jews. We could, moreover, almost as easily describe the developments in the opposite direction, namely that Christianity insisted on separate persons and rejected modalism as a response to the rabbinic insistence that binitarianism was equal to ditheism. In this context, it is important to remind ourselves that Justin himself and other "orthodox" theologians of the second century were constantly defending themselves against charges from other Christians that their theology was ditheistic.[59] The same process of splitting between Christian and Christian, with one group being marked as not-Christian and thus Jews, can thus be seen at work.

---

[58] Idel, *Messianic Mystics*, 85–94. Almost unbelievably we learn there of a medieval Jewish mystic who writes, "'Enoch is Metatron' . . . and the first name out of the seventy names of Metatron is Yaho'el whose secret is Ben [Son!]" (85). As Idel remarks compellingly, it is impossible to imagine that in the Christian Middle Ages an orthodox Jewish thinker would have produced such a "dangerously" Christian-sounding text, and therefore we must almost perforce be dealing with a mythologoumenon from the time when Judaism and Christianity were not yet distinct theological entities, when it was still possible for the second God to be referred to as the "Son" by "Jewish" writers. It is not the Logos that distinguishes "Judaism" from "Christianity." See also Nathaniel Deutsch, *The Gnostic Imagination: Gnosticism, Mandaeism, and Merkabah Mysticism* (Brill's Series in Jewish Studies; Leiden: Brill, 1995), 98; and Gedaliahu Stroumsa, *Savoir et salut* (Paris: Cerf, 1992), 58–59. As Idel perspicaciously puts the possibilities: "How early such a text is difficult to calculate. Whether this text reflects a pre-Christian Jewish concept of the angelic son who possesses or constitutes the divine name is also hard to ascertain. If late, the Christian, or Jewish-Christian, nature of such a Hebrew text cannot be doubted" (*Messianic Mystics*, 87). But in any case, stunningly, it cannot be doubted that it remained in the end part and parcel of a non-Christian "Jewish" traditional mythologoumenon/theologoumenon. The reader, interested in early Christology, who reads these pages of Idel's work will be, I think, illuminated. Another important example of the same phenomenon, of distinctly christological motifs preserved in early medieval Kabbalistic texts, is exposed in Elliot R. Wolfson, "The Tree That is All: Jewish-Christian Roots of a Kabbalistic Symbol in Sefer Ha-Bahir," in *Along the Path*, 63–88. Also, Wolfson, "Judaism and Incarnation," 244–46 is very important.

[59] See Hippolytus, *Haer.* 9.7 (*ANF* 5:130):

And having even venom imbedded in his heart, and forming no correct opinion on any subject, and yet withal being ashamed to speak the truth, this Callistus, not only on account of his publicly saying in the way of reproach to us, "Ye are Ditheists," but also on account of his being frequently accused

Over and over again, in contexts within which the Targum has the activity of the *Memra*, the rabbinic midrash has the designation of God as "He who spake and the world was," thus constituting a most impressive body of important evidence for the tacit, but nonetheless vigorous, repudiation of *Memra* theology on the part of the Rabbis. At Exod 4:31, the *Targum Neofiti* reads:[60] "And Israel saw the mighty hand which the LORD performed on the Egyptians, and the people were afraid from before the Lord and believed in the name of the *Memra* of the LORD, and the prophecy of Moses his servant," while the same midrash that I have cited above, the *Mekhilta*, comments:

> *And they believed in the Lord and in his servant Moses.* If you say that they believed in Moses, is it not implied by *Kal vaḥomer* that they believed in God? But this is to teach you that having faith in the shepherd of Israel is the same as having faith in Him who spoke and the world came into being. . . . Great indeed is faith before *Him who spoke and the world came into being.* (*Bešallaḥ* 6)[61]

In other words, once more, precisely in a context in which the targumic tradition refers to the *Memra* as a hypostasis, a person of the

---

by Sabellius, as one that had transgressed his first faith, devised some such heresy as the following. Callistus alleges that the Logos Himself is Son, and that Himself is Father; and that though denominated by a different title, yet that in reality He is one indivisible spirit. And he maintains that the Father is not one person and the Son another, but that they are one and the same; and that all things are full of the Divine Spirit, both those above and those below. And he affirms that the Spirit, which became incarnate in the virgin, is not different from the Father, but one and the same. And he adds, that this is what has been declared by the Saviour: "Believest thou not that I am in the Father, and the Father in me?" For that which is seen, which is man, he considers to be the Son; whereas the Spirit, which was contained in the Son, to be the Father. "For," says (Callistus), "I will not profess belief in two Gods, Father and Son, but in one. For the Father, who subsisted in the Son Himself, after He had taken unto Himself our flesh, raised it to the nature of Deity, by bringing it into union with Himself, and made it one; so that Father and Son must be styled one God, and that this Person being one, cannot be two."

[60] Hayward, *Divine Name and Presence*, 82. Hayward himself wishes to learn from here a point directly opposite to mine. For Hayward the designation of God as "He who spake and the world was" is "intimately bound up with the Targumic *Memra*" (87), a point with which I certainly agree, seeing it, however, in direct contrast to Hayward, as the denial of the *Memra*, and not as its assertion. It is not the *Memra*, the Logos, the Word, that does these activities, say the Rabbis, but God himself, the God who spoke and the world was, without any intermediary hypostasized Word.

[61] Lauterbach, *Mekilta DeRabbi Ishmael*, 1:252.

Godhead, the rabbinic midrash insists on referring to YHWH as the one who spoke and the world was. Do not follow those Jewish traditions that understand Genesis 1 as describing a creative Word, a *Memra*, a Logos, separate from God, say the Rabbis implicitly, as is their wont, but rather understand that God (I was almost tempted to write "the Father") is the only creator, and his word is no more separate from him than any speech from its speaker. In an astonishing convergence, however, Nicene orthodoxy also effectively "crucifies the Logos." While not ceasing to speak of the Logos, in the move to a trinitarian theology within which the entire trinity is both self-contained and fully transcendent, Athanasius and his fellows insist that God alone, without a mediator, without an angel, without a Logos, is the creator. Logos theology is, ultimately, as thoroughly rejected within Nicene Christianity as within orthodox rabbinism.[62]

II. THE APOSTASY OF RABBI AKIVA

The heresiological energy that was being expended within rabbinic circles to produce the heresy of "Two Powers in Heaven"—that is, to externalize, Christianize, the internal theologoumena of a second or assistant God—helps us understand some rabbinic texts that are otherwise mysterious.[63] One of the most evocative and revealing of these texts involves the heresy of Rabbi Aqiva in a discussion about the "Son of Man" passage from Daniel:

> One verse reads: "His throne is sparks of fire" (Dan 7:9) and another [part of the] verse reads, "until thrones were set up and the Ancient of Days sat" (7:9). This is no difficulty: One was for him and one was for David. As we learn in a *baraita*: One for him and one for David; these are the words of Rabbi Aqiva. Rabbi Yose the Galilean said to him: Aqiva! Until when will you make the *Shekhina* profane?! Rather. One was for judging and one was for mercy. Did he accept it from him, or did he not? Come and hear! One for judging and one for mercy, these are the words of Rabbi Aqiva. (*b. Ḥag.* 14a)

As we see from this passage, the second-century Rabbi Aqiva is portrayed as interpreting these verses in a way that certainly would seem

---

[62] Virginia Burrus, *"Begotten, not made": Conceiving Manhood in Late Antiquity* (Figurae; Stanford: Stanford University Press, 2000).

[63] Segal, *Powers*, 47–49.

consistent with "Two Powers in Heaven." The crux is his identification of David, the Messiah, as the "Son of Man" who sits at God's right hand,[64] thus suggesting not only a divine figure but one who is incarnate in a human being as well[65]—"I am [the Messiah] and you shall see 'the son of man' sitting on the right hand of power and coming in the clouds of heaven" (Mark 14:62). Hence, his objector's taunt: "Until when will you make the Divine Presence profane"?![66] Rabbi Aqiva is seemingly also projecting a divine-human, Son of Man, who will be the Messiah. His contemporary R. Yose the Galilean (perhaps a more assiduous reader of the Gospels) strenuously objects to Rabbi Aqiva's "dangerous" interpretation and gives the verse a "Modalist" interpretation. Of course, the Talmud itself must record that Rabbi Aqiva changed his mind in order for him to remain "orthodox." "Two Powers in Heaven" is thus not foreign even at the very heart of the rabbinic enterprise. Even a figure like Rabbi Aqiva has to be educated as to the heretical nature of his position.[67]

It is not too much to suggest, I think, that the pressure against "Rabbi Aqiva's" position was generated by the hardening of Logos theology and its variants into Christology as that was beginning to take place in the second century. "Orthodox" Jewish versions of this theological option must then be "corrected"—not incidentally with many of the techniques which Christians in the post-Nicene era were to use in order to produce the "Fathers" as speaking with one theological voice.[68] Segal also writes, "By the third century . . . the rabbis seem to be fully aware of the kinds of claims that could be made

---

[64] As it is almost impossible not to hear echoes of Ps 110:1 here or of the story of *Aḥer* who sees Metatron sitting at God's right hand and writing the merits of Israel. But if this seems over-reading, I can let go of it and the point still stands if a bit less elegantly.

[65] Segal, *Powers*, 47.

[66] Segal writes that "both apocalyptic Jews and Christians can be shown to combine the angelic or divine interpretations of the passage with their messianic candidate" (*Powers*, 49). *Pace* Segal, the doctrine of God's two attributes is not used here as a remedy to Messianism per se but as a remedy to binitarianism.

[67] Moreover, as pointed out by Segal, "nor was R. Akiva alone in the rabbinic movement in identifying the figure in heaven as the messiah" (*Powers*, 48).

[68] E.g., "the coercive inscription of consensuality by which an authoritative patristic body of literature is continually reconstituted as such—not least via lengthy catenae of citations meant to demonstrate widespread ancient unanimity on a given point" (Burrus, *Begotten*, 16); see also Patrick T. R. Gray, "'The Select Fathers':

about a 'son of man' or Metatron or any other principal angel. So they reject the idea of divine intermediaries totally."[69] I would agree with Segal but argue that there is important evidence that they did not do so entirely successfully. In the late-ancient mystical text known as "The Visions of Ezekiel," a secondary divine figure, Metatron, is posited on the grounds of Dan 7:9f. This is the same figure who in other texts of that genre is called "The Youth," נער, i.e., that figure known by other Jews (e.g., the Fourth Evangelist) as the "Son of Man"![70] Putting together the different bits and pieces that other scholars have constructed into a new mosaic, I would suggest that we have a very important clue here to follow. From the text in Daniel it would seem clear that there are two divine figures pictured, one who is ancient and another one who is young. "Son of Man" here in its paradigmatic contrast with the Ancient of Days should be read as youth, young man (as it is even in the rabbinic texts that deny that it represents a second person). The usage is similar to "sons of doves" meaning young of the dove as in Num 6:10. It should be noted that the figure of the "Youth" appears as well (at least once) in texts accepted into the rabbinic canon itself, such as *Num. Rab.* 12:12, and explicitly denoted there as Metatron.[71] We end up with

---

Canonizing the Patristic Past," *StPatr* 23 (1989): 21–36; Mark Vessey, "The Forging of Orthodoxy in Latin Christian Literature: A Case Study," *JECS* 4 (1996): 495–513; Éric Rebillard, "A New Style of Argument in Christian Polemic: Augustine and the Use of Patristic Citations," *JECS* 8 (2000): 559–78. My point is not, of course, that rabbinic culture was less "coercive" in its "consensuality," just that different textual strategies were mobilized to secure that consent.

[69] Segal, *Powers*, 71.

[70] Ibid., 67. See Nathaniel Deutsch, *Guardians of the Gate: Angelic Vice Regency in Late Antiquity* (Brill's Series in Jewish Studies; Leiden: Brill, 1999), 45–46, from whose discussion it would seem that Metatron is paradoxically the Ancient of Days here (and not the Son of Man), a development that I am at a loss to understand, nor am I convinced that it is a necessary one in the context. The rabbinic texts that Deutsch adduces to indicate identification of the Youth (Son of Man) and the Ancient of Days seem to me less than relevant since they are primarily evidence, on my view, precisely for rabbinic Modalism, in contrast and in opposition to the distinction of persons in the other texts. I thus thoroughly disagree with Deutsch's conflation of the rabbinic virtual polemic against binitarianism with binitarianism itself. Somewhat polemically myself, I daresay that more sustained reading of these texts together with early Christian traditions would reveal much that is left obscure in most scholarly treatments of them (as well, perhaps, as obscuring some matters that are revealed in contemporary scholarship).

[71] *Contra* Segal, *Powers*, 67, who claims that the name נער is never used in this sense in rabbinic literature (unless I have misread him).

a clear indication of a second divine person, called the Youth (Son of Man), about whom it can be discussed whether he is *homoousios*, *homoiousios*, *homoion*, or *anomoion* with the first person. When he is called or calls himself the "Son of Man," this is a citation of the Daniel text. He is called the "Youth," i.e., the "Son of Man," in contrast to the "Ancient of Days."[72] These traditions all understand accordingly that two divine figures are portrayed in Daniel 7, whom we might be tempted to call the Father and the Son. Evidence for this concatenation of Enoch, Metatron, and the Son of Man can be adduced from *1 Enoch* 71, in which Enoch is explicitly addressed as the Son of Man, and Enoch is, of course, Metatron before his apotheosis.[73] Non-rabbinic and even anti-rabbinic ideas (that is, ideas that the Rabbis themselves mark as heretical) appear more than occasionally in the heart of rabbinic literature.[74] It is not, then, as Segal would have it, that "other groups beside Christians were making 'dangerous' interpretations of that verse [Dan 7:9]," as that this commonplace of theological, mystical hermeneutics had become dangerous to the Rabbis and had to be expelled from its original home. For Segal, the "enemy" is still outside, external, marginal to the rabbinic community and religious world: "Identifying the specific group about whom the rabbis were concerned in this passage can not be successful."[75] He still worries that "determining the identity of the group of heretics in question remains a serious problem,"[76] as if there *were* a real group of external heretics to whom the texts refer, while from my point of view, the Rabbis are implicitly saying: We have met the heretics and they are us, expelling the Two-Powers heresy from within themselves. Although he uses the point to slightly different purpose, I would endorse the formulation of Nathaniel Deutsch who writes with respect to the same texts that Segal treats and which I

---

[72] Although Scholem famously interpreted "youth" in these contexts as "servant," there is little warrant for this interpretation; David J. Halperin, "A Sexual Image in Hekhalot Rabbati and Its Implications," *Jerusalem Studies in Jewish Thought* 6 (1987): 117–32, esp. 125.

[73] See on this also Deutsch, *Guardians*, 32. For Metatron as Enoch, see Idel, "Enoch."

[74] Cf. "The line between rabbinic and Hekhalot literature is sometimes difficult to discern" (Deutsch, *Guardians*, 49).

[75] Segal, *Powers*, 71.

[76] Ibid., 55.

read here: "The reification of boundaries, therefore, rather than their crossing, is the goal of these passages."[77]

I would read the famous narrative of Elisha ben Abuya's apostasy, in the sequel to the story of Rabbi Aqiva—where, upon seeing a vision of the glorious being named Metatron sitting at the right hand of God, he concluded that there are "Two Powers in Heaven" and became a heretic—as a further oblique recognition and allegorical representation of the fact that this heresy was once comfortably *within* "Judaism" and has only lately become *Aḥer*, "Other"—*Aḥer* being, of course, the pejorative nickname for this once "kosher" Rabbi after his turn to "heresy." A brief look at this text will help make this point. According to the Talmud:

> Our Rabbis have taught: Four went into the *Pardes*, and who are they? Ben 'Azzai and Ben Zoma, *Aḥer*, and Rabbi Aqiva.... *Aḥer* chopped down the shoots. Rabbi Aqiva came out safely....
>
> '*Aḥer* chopped down the shoots': Of him the verse says, "Do not let your mouth cause your flesh to sin" [Qoh 5:5]. What does this mean? He saw that Metatron had been given permission to sit and write the good deeds of Israel. He said, but it is taught that on high there will be no sitting, no competition, no . . ., and no tiredness! Perhaps, G-d forbid, there are two powers! They took Metatron out and whipped him with sixty whips of fire. They said to him: "What is the reason that when you saw him, you did not get up before him?" He was given permission to erase the good deeds of *Aḥer*. A voice came out from heaven and said: Return O backsliding ones [Jer 3:14, 22]—except for *Aḥer*. He said, "Since that man has been driven out of that world, let him go out and enjoy himself in this world!" He went out to evil culture. He went and found a prostitute and solicited her. She said, "But aren't you Elisha ben Abuya!?" He went and uprooted a radish on the Sabbath and gave it to her. She said, "He is an other [*Aḥer*]." (*b. Ḥag.* 15a)

This is a remarkable story that, as can well be imagined, has excited much scholarly attention. Yehuda Liebes emphasizes correctly that it is impossible to see this as a narrative of a real Elisha who joined a heretical sect.[78] Segal nicely observes that "in its present context

---

[77] Deutsch, *Guardians*, 48. Deutsch is referring to the ontological boundaries between divine and human that the texts reify, while I, to the social boundaries between orthodox and heretical. It can be seen that the two reifications are homologous.

[78] Yehuda Liebes, *The Sin of Elisha: Four Who Entered* Pardes *and the Nature of Talmudic Mysticism* (Jerusalem: Academon, 1990 [Hebrew]), 12.

[the story] is an etiology of heresy. It explains how certain people, who had special Metatron traditions, risk the heretical designation of 'two powers in heaven.'"[79] This can be pushed a bit further. The structural comparison with Christian etiologies of heresy and here-siarchs suggests that, like those, *Aher* represents older theological tra-ditions which have been anathematized as heresy by the authors of the story. Almost certainly underlying *Aher*/Elisha's vision of Metatron is the same passage in Daniel that "misled" Rabbi Aqiva, taking the "One like a Son of Man" as a separate person. The latter's error was hermeneutical/theological, the former's is visionary/theological, but the error is essentially precisely the same, the assumption that the second throne is for a second divine figure. Whether called Metatron or David, the second divine figure is the Son of Man.[80] Locating this "heretical" interpretation right at the heart of the rab-binic academy and indeed among some of its leading figures strongly suggests that these views had been current in the very Jewish circles from which the Rabbis emerged and were eventually anathematized by them and driven out. Metatron is punished by being scourged with sixty *pulse* of fire. As we learn from *b. B. Mesi'a* 47a, this prac-tice (whatever it quite means in terms of *realia*) represents a partic-ularly dire form of anathema or even excommunication. The dual inscription of excommunication in the narrative, that of Metatron on the one hand and of his "devotee" on the other, suggests strongly to me that it is the belief in this figure as second divine principle that is being anathematized (although somehow the Rabbis seem unable to completely dispense with him—he was just too popular it would seem).

A further parallel is instructive. In an amazing passage in *b. Yoma* 77a, which I cannot discuss here at length, the archangel Gabriel is

---

[79] Segal, *Powers*, 62.

[80] According to this reading, it is the "sitting" that is the crux of the matter, as it invokes the Daniel 7 passage as interpreted, e.g., in Mark, with the "Son of Man" sitting at the right hand of God, the source of Rabbi Aqiva's "error" as well (see above). This passage deserves a longer treatment than I can give it here, particu-larly in the light of questionable interpretations of the textual evidence that have been offered recently (see Deutsch, *Guardians*, 48–77). Since these interpretations rely on variant readings within the Ashkenazi manuscript tradition as relating to different stages of redaction within the rabbinic period, they rest on a very weak reed, but fuller demonstration of this point as well as reinterpretation will have to wait for another context.

taken out to be scourged with the sixty *pulse*, because he acted independently of the divine will, another seeming case of "Two Powers in Heaven." Note that in that story, as opposed to the *Aḥer* one, the *possibility* of the high angel acting independently is comprehended. It is almost as if not only the heresy of Two Powers but also the Second Power itself is being suppressed in these accounts. The statement that Rabbi Aqiva came out safely (lit. "in peace"), while *Aḥer* died in infamy, would, on this possible but by no means proven interpretation, then represent a Rabbi Aqiva who turned away from "heresy" to orthodoxy and an Elisha who remained adamant in the old views.

The two others who entered *Pardes* [the Garden, Paradise] with Rabbi Aqiva and *Aḥer* in search of enlightenment were Ben Zoma and Ben ʿAzzai. Of one we are told that he died and of the other that he became insane. Is it accidental that we read then in *Genesis Rabbah* the following astounding text: "Rabbi Levi said: There are among the expounders [דרושות], those who expound, for instance Ben Zoma and Ben ʿAzzai, that the voice of the Holy, Blessed One became Metatron on the water, as it is written, 'The voice of God is on the water' [Ps 29:3]."[81] This extraordinary passage "remembers," as it were, that such central rabbinic figures, whose halakhic opinions are authoritatively cited in the classic rabbinic literature, were, like Rabbi Aqiva himself, champions of a distinct Logos theology which had to be somehow warded off via the legendary narrative of their bad end. Only Rabbi Aqiva repented of his former views, and therefore, we are told, only he of the four "entered in peace and left in peace" (*b. Ḥag.* 14b). All four of the relevant Rabbis made statements indicating that they had believed in a *deuteros theos*. The *Pardes* is not, therefore, on this reading, so much the site of mystical experience, or of philosophical speculation, but the trace of the ancient Logos theology. It seems hardly irrelevant that it is on this very page of the Talmud that we are told that "the world was created with ten Words," which became afterwards the main prooftext for the mystical doctrine of the hypostases (ספירות).[82]

---

[81] *Gen. Rab.* 5.

[82] Daniel Abrams, *"The Book of Illumination" of R. Jacob Ben Jacob HaKohen: A Synoptic Edition from Various Manuscripts* (New York: New York University, 1993 [Hebrew]), 70. For another recent discussion of the *"Aḥer"* material, see Abrams, "Metatron,"

Segal claims that: "Rabbinic theology could withstand, and may even have encouraged, the mythic or dramatic depiction of God's attributes in various forms, including at times a *logos*-like manifestation, depicted as an angelic being such as Metatron" and, moreover, that "those who adopt a more literal view of the rabbis' view of divine unity may find any hint of plurality to be heretical. Here, however, I argue that the rabbis objected only to an opposition or competition of wills."[83] To claim this, however, is to assume that there is no opposition or competition of wills *among the Rabbis*. There are places indeed where *some* Rabbis' "theology could withstand, and may even have encouraged, the mythic or dramatic depiction of God's attributes in various forms, including at times a *logos*-like manifestation," but this view was vigorously disputed and finally ousted by other Rabbis, at least in its more obvious forms. This perspective obviates the need to draw a distinction between two different versions of "Two Powers" theology, one acceptable and one unacceptable.[84] Our story of Rabbi Aqiva's "heresy" certainly does not suggest a "Gnostic" version of "Two Powers" in opposition to the other, but rather a very "Christian"-appearing version in which the second power is precisely the "Son of Man" doing his Father's will by inscribing Israel's virtues.[85] This story of Rabbi Aqiva and his fel-

---

293–98. Dunn, in contrast, still speaks of "the emergence of the 'two powers heresy,'" in James D. G. Dunn, *The Partings of the Ways Between Christianity and Judaism and Their Significance for the Character of Christianity* (London: SCM Press, 1991), 219, which, of course, I would regard rather as the rabbinic projection and abjection of the Two Powers heresy. This is doubly surprising, in that Dunn's view of the history of Judaism is nuanced enough to contain a statement like, "the period between 70 and 100 saw the first proponents of rabbinic Judaism taking a deliberate step to mark themselves off from other claimants to the broad heritage of pre-70 Judaism" (Dunn, *Partings*, 221), a formulation with which I would completely agree in spite of dating this development quite a bit later than Dunn does, given the methodology—which Dunn himself insists on elsewhere—of dating material in rabbinic texts as roughly pertaining to the time of attestation and not the time of which the text speaks. This difference in dating is, of course, highly significant, because insofar as Dunn allows himself to credit certain developments, such as the introduction of the "curse of the heretics," to the "historical Yavneh" and to see these as representing a growing early consensus in Judaism, he will predate "partings of the ways" far earlier than I would.

[83] Segal, *Powers*, 298.
[84] Cf. Segal, *Powers*, 5–6.
[85] Cf. Dunn, *Partings*, 218–19; and a small library of prior literature.

lows constitutes, on this reading, a highly compressed synecdoche of
the process of the repudiation of Logos theology.[86]

Further evidence for the notion that Logos theology was a once-
accepted but now rejected theologoumenon within rabbinic circles
is constituted by remnants (almost revenants) of that very theology
within the texts. A very rich example has been discussed by Azzan
Yadin.[87] The text in question is to be found in the *y. Sukkah* 1:1
[51,d] (with a parallel in the same text at *y. Šabb.* 1:2 [2,d]):[88]

> Rabbi Abbahu teaches in the name of Rabbi Shim'on ben Laqish:
> "There I will meet you and I will speak to you from above the cover
> of the Ark from between the two cherubim" (Ex 25:22). And it is writ-
> ten, "You have seen that I spoke to you from the heavens" (Ex 20:19).
> Just as the verse cited there refers to a different domain [*reshut*], so
> the verse here refers to a different domain [*reshut*].

As Yadin points out, the term *reshut* (the same term as that used for
"Two Powers"), which I have translated here "domain," is ambiguous in reference. Sometimes it can mean a legal domain, in the sense
of a territory controlled by a particular instance of ownership or
authority. The Palestinian Talmud emphasizes this meaning in using
this verse to prove that when God spoke from above the cover of
the Ark, this demonstrates that the Ark constitutes a separate domain
of control within the Temple precincts. However, as Yadin emphasizes, this usage of the midrash within the halakhic context of the
Talmud is very forced and artificial: "The significance of this rather

---

[86] Compare the similar conclusion, expressed in different theoretical terms, of
Segal himself:

> Since the tradition comes to us only in a later text, we must be prepared to
> accept the probability that the alternate interpretation of Dan 7:9f.—namely,
> that the two thrones were for mercy and justice—was a later addition, ascrib-
> ing the 'orthodox' interpretation to a great rabbinic leader, whom time had
> proven wrong. Thus, the messianic controversy over Dan 7:13 is probably
> from R. Akiba's time; the mercy-justice revision is probably from his students."
> (*Powers*, 49)

Once again, and with the risk of introducing tedium, the way that my formulation
would be different would be precisely by shifting "time had proven wrong" to something like, the rabbinic production of orthodoxy was being enacted through this
story of Rabbi Aqiva's error and his reproof and repentance.

[87] Azzan Yadin, "'Two Verses Contradict and a Third Resolves': The Theological
Dimension of Rabbi Ishmael's 'Shnei Ketuvim'," *JSQ* (2003): forthcoming.

[88] I have used Yadin's translation but modified it here and there.

forced series of arguments is that the *derashah* was not generated by
the previously established height of the Ark. Instead, the Palestinian
Talmud is making a concerted effort to contextualize Resh Laqish's
[third-century] *derashah* in a halakhic context (the height of ten *tefaḥ*
marks the end of one *reshut* and the beginning of another) not provided by the *derashah* itself."[89] This argument to the effect that the
present use of the *derashah* is not and cannot be its "original" meaning and, indeed, that concerted effort is being made to neutralize
the original meanings suggests to Yadin that the midrash originally
was making use of another sense of *reshut*, the sense in which it is
used in the context of discussion of the "heresy" of "Two Powers
[*reshuyot*] in Heaven," reconciling the two verses (one that indicates
that God spoke from the heaven and one that He came down, as
it were, to speak below) by suggesting that the Speaker who spoke
below is not the speaker who spoke above. To represent this well-
known sense of *reshut*, Yadin cites the following evocative text:

> "See, then, that I, I am He" (Deut 32:39): This is the refutation to
> those who say that there is no *reshut* (i.e., atheists who claim that there
> is no power in heaven). He who says that there are two powers in
> heaven is refuted by saying it has already been written, "There is no
> God beside Me" (Deut 32:39). (*Sifre Deut.* 329)[90]

Yadin concludes his discussion by referring to this instance in the
Palestinian Talmud as "an acceptable, legal understanding camouflag-
ing a no-longer acceptable theological position."[91] Thus, the theology
of "Two Powers in Heaven" (a High God and an intermediary for
creation, revelation, and redemption, as we still find in the *Memra*
theology of the Targums) was once, at least, an acceptable theological
current within the circles from which the Rabbis and their theolo-
gies grew, but was offered up, as it were, in the dual production of
rabbinic Judaism as Judaism and patristic Christianity as Christianity.

---

[89] Yadin, "Two Verses."
[90] *Sifre on Deuteronomy* (ed. L. Finkelstein; 1939; repr., New York: The Jewish
Theological Seminary of America, 1969), 379.
[91] Yadin, "Two Verses."

III. Justin's Jewish Heresiology

As one very telling piece of evidence for the idea that there was a virtual "conspiracy" between the Rabbis and the Christian discourse of orthodoxy, I would adduce the apparent fact it is in Justin Martyr that we find for the first time *hairesis* in the sense of "heresy" attributed to Jewish usage as well. In the *Dialogue*, Justin addresses the Jew Trypho in attempting to convince him of the existence of the Logos:

> I will again relate words spoken by Moses, from which we can recognize without any question that He conversed with one different in number from Himself and possessed of reason. Now these are the words: *And God said: Behold, Adam has become as one of Us, to know good and evil.* Therefore by saying *as one of Us* He has indicated also number in those that were present together, two at least. *For I cannot consider that assertion true which is affirmed by what you call an heretical party among you, and cannot be proved by the teachers of that heresy* [Οὐ γὰρ ὅπερ ἡ παρ' ὑμῖν λεγομένη αἵρεσις δογματίζει φαίην ἂν ἐγὼ ἀληθὲς εἶναι, ἢ οἱ ἐκείνης διδάσκαλοι ἀποδεῖξαι δύνανται], that He was speaking to angels, or that the human body was the work of angels. (*Dial.* 62.2)[92]

Justin quotes Gen 3:22 to prevent the Jewish teachers' "distortion" of Gen 1:26, "let us make," since in the later verse it is impossible to interpret that God is speaking to the elements or to himself. In order, however, to demonstrate that his interpretation whether God is speaking to the Logos is the only possible one, Justin has to discard another possible reading that some Jewish teachers, those whom Trypho himself would refer to as an *hairesis*, have offered but cannot prove: that God was speaking to angels.

The text is extremely difficult, and the Williams translation does not seem exact, but nevertheless periphrastically captures the sense of the passage. A more precise translation, although still difficult, would be: "For I cannot consider that assertion true which is affirmed by what you call an *hairesis* among you, or that the teachers of it are able to demonstrate."[93] "It" in the second clause can only refer

---

[92] *Justin Martyr: The Dialogue with Trypho* (Translations of Christian Literature; ed. and trans. A. L. Williams; London: SPCK, 1930), 129; *Dialogus Cum Tryphone* (Patristische Texte und Studien 47; ed. M. Marcovich; Berlin: de Gruyter, 1997), 176–77, emphasis added.

[93] I am grateful for Erich Gruen's and Chava Boyarin's help with construing this

to *hairesis*, so Williams's translation is essentially correct, although somewhat smoothed out. Justin cannot consider the assertion true, nor can he consider that the teachers of the *hairesis* can prove it. There are two reasons for reading *hairesis* here as "heresy." First, this is consistent with the usage otherwise well attested in Justin with respect to Christian dissident groups, and therefore seems to be what Justin means by the term in general; and second, the phrase "what you call" implies strongly a pejorative usage.

This interpretation is consistent with the view that a major transition took place within Judaism from a sectarian structure to one of orthodoxy and heresy and that it presumably took place between the time of Acts and that of Justin.[94] As Marcel Simon comments:

> When this passage, written in the middle of the second century, is compared with the passage in Acts, it seems that the term *hairesis* has undergone in Judaism an evolution identical to, and parallel with, the one it underwent in Christianity. This is no doubt due to the triumph of Pharisaism which, after the catastrophe of 70 c.e., established precise norms of orthodoxy unknown in Israel before that time. Pharisaism had been one heresy among many; now it is identified with authentic Judaism and the term *hairesis,* now given a pejorative sense, designates anything that deviates from the Pharisaic way.[95]

There is a noteworthy (if somewhat later) rabbinic parallel to this passage, which, to my knowledge, has not been noted in the literature.[96] According to Justin, those whom the "Jews" denominate a

---

passage, although neither are responsible for my interpretation of it. Cf. the old translation in the *ANF* edition: "For I would not say that the dogma of that heresy which is said to be among you is true, or that the teachers of it can prove that [God] spoke to angels, or that the human frame was the workmanship of angels" (Justin Martyr, *Dial.* 62 [*ANF* 1:228]). David Runia for his part translates: "For personally I do not think the explanation is true which the so-called sect among you declares, nor are the teachers of that sect able to prove that he spoke to angels or that the human body is the creation of angels" (David T. Runia, "'Where, Tell Me, is the Jew?': Basil, Philo and Isidore of Pelusium," *VC* 46 [1992]: 178).

[94] For Luke-Acts, see Hubert Cancik, "The History of Culture, Religion, and Institutions in Ancient Historiography: Philological Observations Concerning Luke's History," *JBL* 116 (1997): 673–95, esp. 677, 688.

[95] Marcel Simon, "From Greek Hairesis to Christian Heresy," in *Early Christian Literature and the Classical Intellectual Tradition: in Honorem R. M. Grant* (ThH 53; ed. W. R. Schoedel and R. L. Wilken; Paris: Beauchesne, 1979), 101–16, here 106.

[96] Jarl Fossum, "Gen 1,26 and 2,7 in Judaism, Samaritanism, and Gnosticism," *JSJ* 16 (1989): 202–39. That is, apparently even not in the very recent Kister, "'Let Us.'"

heresy interpret God as speaking here to the angels.[97] In the *Mekhilta d'Rabbi Ishma'el,* a late third-century or early fourth-century midrash, we find recorded the following dialogue:

> Papos [mss. Papias] expounded: 'Behold, Adam has become as one of Us,' *like one of the serving angels.* Rabbi Aqiva said: Shut up, Papos! Papos said to him, and how will you interpret 'Behold, Adam has become as one of Us'? [Aqiva answered] Rather the Holy, Blessed One gave before him two ways: one of life and one of death, and he chose the way of death.[98]

Although much about this text and its context remains obscure, it is clear that a marginal, even heretical figure, Papos, is being ascribed here a view very close to that which Justin is claiming for the *hairesis* among the Jews.[99] Rabbi Aqiva's response—"Shut up"—is a representation of the intensity of the response that the alleged Papos's

---

[97] Cf. Simon, "Hairesis," 106; Le Boulluec, *La notion,* 78 who both consider Justin's *"hairesis"* here as unidentifiable. Furthermore, Runia writes, "If Justin's evidence is taken seriously, at least one branch [of *minim*] represents a Gnosticizing group within Judaism, whose negative attitude to material creation encourages them to introduce angels into the interpretation of the creation account" ("Where is the Jew," 179). Given the interpretation of this verse in *Genesis Rabbah,* cited by Runia himself, this conclusion is hard to maintain. I detect no phantom Gnostics here. See also Ephraim E. Urbach, *The Sages: Their Concepts and Beliefs* (trans. I. Abrahams; Jerusalem: Magnes, 1975), 203–8, who cites the Justin passage but seems not to have seen the relevance of the *Mekhilta* to it.

[98] Lauterbach, *Mekilta DeRabbi Ishmael,* 1:248.

[99] See Menahem Kahana, "The Critical Editions of *Mekhilta De-Rabbi Ishmael* in the Light of the Genizah Fragments," *Tarbiz* 55 (1985): 499–515 [Hebrew], who shows that ancient manuscripts preserve traditions from which it appears that Papos/Papias maintained "gnosticizing" views, a not irrelevant point for our comparison here with Justin. (See, however, Kister, "'Let Us,'" 34.) Note that it is precisely with reference to Gen 3:22 that the "heretical" view is attributed in both Justin and the *Mekhilta,* while the interpretation that Gen 1:26, "Let us make man," is addressed to angels can be found in the "orthodox" rabbinic voice of *Gen. Rab.* 8, as pointed out in Runia, "Where is the Jew." On the Justin passage, see now Kister, "'Let Us,'" 42–43, as well. Kister observes there that the rabbinic formulation that "God took counsel with the angels" constitutes a mitigation of the Logos-theological view (as expressed by Justin) that God actually had a partner in the creation of Adam. Note that this "solution" was unavailable for Gen 3:22, explaining, perhaps, why here Papos's view was considered heresy, even though it is seemingly closely related to the "orthodox" statement of *Genesis Rabbah.* Particularly impressive is Kister's brilliant suggestion that the speaker in *Genesis Rabbah* who says that "God spoke to his heart" intends to understand God's hypostasized Wisdom, or Logos (Kister, "'Let Us,'" 45–46). For reasons that should be obvious, I would not agree, however, to Kister's strong nexus between Justin and Plato's *Timaeus.* Kister himself supplies a better explanation, namely that the Jewish Logos/Sophia doctrine grew up in Second-Temple theology as a way of deflecting polytheistic

interpretation aroused and thus of its apparent heterodox nature. Justin thus does seem to have here accurate information about a Jewish sectarian interpretation of the verse and asserts that the "Jews" refer to it as *hairesis*, presumably in Hebrew *minut*. The *Mekhilta* text, therefore, provides evidence—albeit somewhat ex post facto—for the authenticity of Justin's information and its richness of detail. At least, we might see here a sort of *terminus post quem* for this contestation in Rabbi Aqiva's second century, very close to the time that Justin was beginning to confront his Gnostics as well.[100]

For Simon, it is obvious that when Justin refers to "your teachers" here the Pharisees are the object, while the *hairesis* in question "designates anything that deviates from the Pharisaic way."[101] There is, however, another important wrinkle that Simon has seemingly overlooked, for in another passage in Justin, "Pharisees" are named as one of the heresies, and not as "authentic Judaism":[102]

> For I made it clear to you that those who are Christians in name, but in reality are godless and impious heretics, teach in all respects what is blasphemous and godless and foolish. . . . For even if you yourselves have ever met with some so-called Christians, who yet do not acknowledge this, but even dare to blaspheme the God of Abraham, and the God of Isaac, and the God of Jacob, who say too that there is no resurrection of the dead, but that their souls ascend to heaven at the very moment of their death—do not suppose that they are Christians, any more than if one examined the matter rightly he would acknowledge as Jews those who are Sadducees,[103] or similar sects of

---

understandings and out of the reading of Genesis with Proverbs 8 ("'Let Us,'" 53). On this point, see also M. J. Edwards, "Justin's Logos and the Word of God," *JECS* 3 (1995): 261–80; and Virginia Burrus, "Creatio ex Libidine, or the Secret of God's Desire: Rereading Ancient Logos," to appear in *Other Testaments*, eds. Yvonne Sherwood and Kevin Hart (Sheffield: Sheffield University Press, 2003). Cf. *b. Sanh.* 38b, where "heretical" interpretation of Gen 1:26 as implying two creators is "refuted."

[100] In other words, I am saying that this text can certainly not be dated before Rabbi Aqiva and possibly could be later. Assuming a dating, then, sometime between the mid-second century (or a bit earlier) and the late third is reasonable. Looking for discursive developments from about the middle of that period, we would land somewhere in the late second century, roughly the time of Justin.

[101] Simon, "Hairesis," 106.

[102] Even in Marcel Simon, *Jewish Sects at the Time of Jesus* (Minneapolis: Fortress, 1967), 85–107, where he discusses the entire Justinian catalogue of Jewish heresies, Simon ignores Justin's mention of the Pharisees, so set is he on his notion that orthodox Judaism at this time is consubstantial with Pharisaism.

[103] Who also deny the resurrection of the dead and are, therefore, singled out. See Le Boulluec, *La notion*, 71–72.

Genistae, and Meristae, and Galileans, and Hellelians,[104] and Pharisees and Baptists[105] (pray, do not be vexed with me as I say all I think), but (would say) that though called Jews and children of Abraham, and acknowledging God with their lips, as God Himself has cried aloud, yet their heart is far from Him. (*Dial.* 80.3–4)[106]

It is highly significant for understanding this passage that the Rabbis themselves, as Shaye Cohen has emphasized, never understand themselves as Pharisees, thus explaining how for them, too, "Pharisee" could be a designation of a sect or even heresy: "The tannaim refused to see themselves as Pharisees."[107] Indeed, as we shall see below, in the Tosefta, a rabbinic text of approximately a century after Justin,

---

[104] Following the conjecture, Ἑλληλιανςῶν (accepted in *Dialogus Cum Tryphone*, 209), which gives "Hellelians" and not "Hellenians" as Williams has it. To this, compare the text from the Tosefta which refers to the Shammaites and the Hillelites as having divided the Torah into two Torahs (*t. Soṭah* 14:9). See also for discussion Daniel Gershonson and Giles Quispel, "'Meristae,'" *VC* 12 (1958): 19–26; Matthew Black, "The Patristic Accounts of Jewish Sectarianism," *BJRL* 41 (1959): 285–303; Simon, *Sects*, 74–85; Leslie W. Barnard, *Justin Martyr: His Life and Thought* (London: Cambridge University Press, 1967), 49–52.

[105] I would take "Genistae and Meristae" as a Greek *calque* on the Tosefta's *minnim weparošim*, i.e. as those who separate themselves. For μερισμός as a term of art in (proto)heresiology, see Ignatius's *Phld.* 2:1 (William R. Schoedel, *Ignatius of Antioch: A Commentary on the Letters of Ignatius of Antioch* [Hermeneia; trans. and ed. W. R. Schoedel; Philadelphia: Fortress, 1985], 197). Cf. Gershonson and Quispel, "'Meristae.'" The Galileans are to be plausibly identified with the *minim glilim* [Galilean heretics] of the Mishna *Yadayim*, a reading only found in manuscripts of the Mishna, as observed by Yaakov Sussmann, "The History of *Halakha* and the Dead Sea Scrolls—Preliminary Observations on *Miqṣat Maʿase Ha-Torah* (4QMMT)" [Hebrew], *Tarbiz* 59 (1990): 11–76, 51, who does not connect them with Justin's notice here. These Baptists are almost surely the "morning baptizers" mentioned as heretics in *t. Yad.* 2:20 (*Tosephta: Based on the Erfurt and Vienna Codices, "Supplement" to the Tosephta* [ed. M. S. Zuckermandel with S. Lieberman; Jerusalem: Bamberger & Wahrmann, 1937 (Hebrew)], 684). The net result is that Justin seems to have had very good knowledge of Jewish heresiology, indeed, even of some of its obscure corners which increases my confidence in his knowledge of matters Jewish and even rabbinic in his time.

[106] Williams, *Dialogue*, 169–71; *Dialogus Cum Tryphone*, 208–9. For the crucial (Platonic) distinction between being called a Jew and being one, see Shaye J. D. Cohen, *The Beginnings of Jewishness: Boundaries, Varieties, Uncertainties* (Hellenistic Culture and Society 31; Berkeley: University of California Press, 1998), 60–61. See on this passage Le Boulluec, who considers that "La représentation hérésiologique a cependant besoin de déformer la conception juive des divers courants religieux pour attendre son efficacité entière" (*La notion*, 71). In my view, this is less of a deformation than Le Boulluec would have it.

[107] Shaye J. D. Cohen, "The Significance of Yavneh: Pharisees, Rabbis, and the End of Jewish Sectarianism," *HUCA* 55 (1984): 27–53, here 29.

"Pharisee" is associated with *min*, as precisely heretics to be anathematized. Those whom we (and other Jewish texts, such as those by
Josephus and Acts) called Pharisees, were, for the Rabbis, simply
Rabbis. Cohen has captured the import of this passage when he
writes: "This rabbinic ideology is reflected in Justin's discussion of
the Jewish sects: there are Jews, i.e., the 'orthodox,' and there are
sects, among them the Pharisees, who scarcely deserve the name
Jew."[108] Indeed Justin testifies that the name "Jew" would be denied
to any of these sectarians, including Pharisees. Let me clarify this
point once more. It is not that the Rabbis would deny the legitimacy of "historical" Pharisees such as Rabban Gamaliel. Nothing
could be more implausible than that. It is rather—I suggest, following Cohen—that they would not use the name "Pharisees" for
their legitimated ancestors.

Matthew Black, followed by L. W. Barnard, explained away the
references to Sadducees and Pharisees as heresies in Justin by virtual sleight of hand,[109] analogous to the attempts to emend the Tosefta
and remove the curse against the Pharisees there as well.[110] Such a
notion that both Sadducees and Pharisees were sects, and therefore "heretics," could very well have been characteristic of a second-
century Judaism moving toward a notion of "orthodoxy" in which
all *named* sects are *ipso facto* heresies. There are Jews, and there are
minim (= "kinds"), a usage that can perhaps be compared with that
of Athanasius, for example, for whom there are "Christians" and
there are "Arians."[111] Even more appositely, one might quote Justin
himself:

---

[108] Cohen, "Yavneh," 49.

[109] Black, "Patristic"; and Barnard, *Justin Martyr*, 50–52.

[110] See also Le Boulluec: "La suggestion de M. Black . . . . est tout à fair fantai-
siste" (*La notion*, 72).

[111] Earlier, Justin's explanation of the origins of the philosophers' *haireseis* bears
some relation to this topos:

> But the reason why [philosophy] has become a hydra of many heads I should
> like to explain. It happened that they who first handled philosophy, and for
> this reason became famous, were followed by men who made no investigation
> after truth, but were only amazed at their patience and self-restraint and their
> unfamiliar diction, and supposed that whatever each learned from his own
> teacher was true. And then they, when they had handed on to their succes-
> sors all such things, and other like them, were themselves called by the name
> borne by the originator of the teaching. (*Dial.* 2.2; Williams, *Dialogue*, 4)

And there shall be schisms and heresies . . . many false christs and many false apostles shall arrive, and shall deceive many of the faithful, . . . but these are called by us after the name of the men from whom each false doctrine and opinion had its origin. . . . Some are called Marcionites, some Valentinians, some Basilideans, and some Saturnalians and some others by other names. (*Dial.* 35.6)

"We," of course, are called "Christians." Assuming the same topos, the Rabbis, therefore, as Catholic Israel, could hardly recognize a named sect, the Pharisees, as their predecessors, whatever the historical "reality."[112] The Rabbis are just "Israel." This interpretation is consistent with the other rabbinic evidence, as well as with the hypothetical etymology of the term *min* offered here.

By naming the traditional Logos or *Memra* doctrine of God a heresy, indeed, *the* heresy, "Two Powers in Heaven," the rabbinic theology expels it from the midst of Judaism, hailing that heresy at least implicitly as "Christianity," at the same time that in a virtual cultural "conspiracy" the emerging Christian orthodoxy embraces the Logos theology and names its repudiation "Judaism." We have seen this historical, socio-cultural process being virtually enacted within Justin's *Dialogue*. Without ascribing a literal value to the term "conspiracy" here, I would, nevertheless, point to the striking cooperation of the two discursive forces. The orthodox rabbinic solution to

---

The implication of this statement is, of course, that there is "philosophy" and there are the *haireseis* (although the term is not used here) named after the divergent originators of each school. See also the same topos vis-à-vis Christian heresies:

> And they say that they are Christians. . . . And some of them are called Marcionites, and some Valentinians, and some Basilidians, and some Satornalians, and others by other names, each being named from the originator of the opinion, just as also each of those who think they are philosophers, as I said already in the beginning [of my discourse], thinks it right to bear the name of the father of that system. (*Dial.* 35.6; Williams, *Dialogue*, 70)

Of course, from the point of view of the Rabbis, the name "Christian" would be just such an "other name."

See also *Cod. theod.* 16.5.6: "The contamination of the Photinian pestilence, the poison of the Arian sacrilege, the crime of the Eunomian perfidy, and the sectarian monstrosities, *abominable because of the ill-omened names of their authors*, shall be abolished even from the hearing of men" (Clyde Pharr, *The Theodosian Code and Novels, and the Sirmondian Constitutions: a Translation with Commentary, Glossary, and Bibliography* [Princeton: Princeton University Press, 1952], 451, emphasis added).

[112] Cf. also on these points Stephen Craft Goranson, "The Joseph of Tiberias Episode in Epiphanius: Studies in Jewish and Christian Relations," (Ph.D. diss., Duke University, 1990), 80.

the problem of verses that seem to imply any doubleness in God is
to read them modalistically: one refers to God's aspect, or quality,
of mercy and the other to God's aspect of justice. In precise sym-
metry, Christian orthodoxy of the second century regarded Modalism
as a heresy, a heresy that could easily be named "Monarchianism,"
"One Power in Heaven," expelling the once "orthodox" Sabellius
(and even Pope Callistus),[113] as the Rabbis had done in their stories
with Elisha. J. N. D. Kelly makes the point that already in Justin's
day, other Christians were accusing him of ditheism because he
argued that the Logos is "something numerically other" (*Dial.* 128.3).[114]
By constructing his opponent in the *Dialogue* as a "Jew," then, Justin
is also engaged in splitting, taking a part of his own self, so to speak,
and projecting it outward as Judaism. The notion of conspiracy
should be clear by now; Justin and the Rabbis, ostensibly bitter opponents, in a strong sense fondly desire the same consummation. At
the same time that the Jew was being hailed by the Christian heresiologists,[115] via their calling Monarchianism and Modalism "Judaism,"
the Rabbis were constructing their own orthodoxy by naming the
believer in "Two Powers in Heaven," the "Christian," as their heretic-
in-chief and thus in some sense calling Christianity into existence as
a separate social entity. Once more, the heresiologists got that right,
just as the Rabbis who identified "Two Powers in Heaven" with the
Christianity that they were expelling from within got that right.[116]
Judaism is Monarchianism; Monarchianism is Judaism, and the Rabbis
by identifying "Two Powers in Heaven" as the arch-heresy thus participated in the discursive work of the making of Christian orthodoxy, while the Christian heresiologists who insisted that one *must*
assert the existence of separate "persons" in order to be an orthodox Christian—in order, that is, not to be a Jew—similarly participated in the discursive work of the making of orthodox rabbinic
Judaism.

The function of the denomination "Two Powers in Heaven" for
rabbinic ecclesiology is thus formally and structurally equivalent to
Ioudaïzein (Judaizing) within Christian writing of the time. Just as the

---

[113] Heine, "Callistus."

[114] Kelly, *Doctrines*, 83–132.

[115] Virginia Burrus, "Hailing Zenobia: Anti-Judaism, Trinitarianism, and John Henry
Newman," *Culture and Religion* 3:2 (2002) 163–177.

[116] See also *b. Sanh.* 38a.

latter is a term of approbation and exclusion of Christians from the community because they hold ideas from within Christianity that have become anathema to certain teachers and leaders, those figures who are named as possessing the heretical notion of "Two Powers in Heaven" are Jews holding one traditional Jewish theological position who are now declared anathema in the new regime of the Rabbis. Thus, this "heresy" is the exact structural parallel for the Rabbis of Sabellianism within Christian discourse at the same time, an aspect of Judaeo-Christian religious imagination that threatens the being constructed differentiation between the emerging twin religions—the twin orthodoxies struggling to emerge from Rebecca's womb, to use Alan Segal's elegant conceit.[117]

It is this supersession of the Logos by Writing that arguably gives birth to rabbinic Judaism and its characteristic forms of textuality. I would thus reverse Melito's famous παλαιὸς μὲν ὁ νόμος, καινὸς δὲ ὁ λόγος ("Of old there was the Nomos, the Law, now there is the Logos"), claiming for the Rabbis that formerly there was the Logos, but now God's Word can be found, literally, only in the black marks on the white parchment of the *Nomos*.[118] This theological stance, which finally only after much struggle came to characterize the

---

[117] Alan F. Segal, *Rebecca's Children: Judaism and Christianity in the Roman World* (Cambridge, Mass.: Harvard University Press, 1986).

[118] In a fascinating study, Glenn Chesnut has shown that the Logos and the Nomos were, in some important Hellenistic philosophies, alternate names for the *same* principle of divine order present in the soul of the ruler-savior (Glenn F. Chesnut, "The Ruler and the Logos in Neopythagorean, Middle Platonic, and Late Stoic Political Philosophy," *ANRW* II, 16.2:1310–32, esp. 1312–13). For the king as "Living Nomos," see Chesnut, "Ruler and the Logos," 1317; and Frances Dvornik, *Early Christian and Byzantine Political Philosophy* (2 vols.; Locust Valley, N.Y.: J. J. Augustin, 1966), 1:245–48. And for the king as "Living Logos," in parallel with Nomos, see Chesnut, "Ruler and the Logos," 1323, referring to Plutarch, *Princ. iner.* 780c. I disagree somewhat, however, with Chesnut's interpretation of this passage. The text reads:

Τίς οὖν ἄρξει τοῦ ἄρχοντος; ὁ
  νόμος ὁ πάντων βασιλεὺς
  θνατῶν τε καὶ ἀθανάτων,
ὡς ἔφη Πίνδαρος, οὐκ ἐν βιβλίοις ἔξω γεγραμμένος οὐδέ τισι ξύλοις, ἀλλ' ἔμψυχος
ὢν ἐν αὐτῷ λόγος.

Who, then, shall rule the ruler? The
  Law, the king of all,
  Both mortals and immortals,
as Pindar says—not law written outside him in books or on wooden tablets or the like, but reason endowed with life within him. . . . (Fowler, LCL)

rabbinic doctrine of God, carried in its wake profound shifts within rabbinic textuality, even between the earlier Palestinian and the later Babylonian Talmuds, shifts that were ultimately to serve as the very difference between Christianity and Judaism.

It is actually clear from this passage that Plutarch is *not* speaking of the King as a Living Nomos or as a Living Logos but rather as the lifeless Logos being endowed with life by dwelling within a human being. The comparison with Paul's comments in 1 Corinthians about the Law written on tablets and the Law written on the heart seems more apposite here than notions of Incarnation or other christological intimations.

ITERATED QUOTATION FORMULAE IN TALMUDIC NARRATIVE AND EXEGESIS

Bernard Septimus

When two characters converse in talmudic narrative, a new quotation formula generally signals a change of speaker. Suppose, for example, that A and B are conversing: A's words are introduced by the formula, "A said" (or an analogous formula); then, once A has had his say and B begins, his words are introduced by the formula, "B said" (or an analogous formula). Occasionally, however, we have the following anomaly: there is no change of speaker; A is still speaking; his interlocutor remains B; yet his speech is punctuated by a second quotation formula, "A said."[1]

As far as I can tell, this phenomenon has not been discussed in the scholarly literature. My aim here is to call attention to it and to explore its significance. Although I can discuss only a small and somewhat random sample, the reader, once alerted, will find iterated quotation formulae cropping up frequently in talmudic sources, often revealing interesting nuances, and occasionally helpful in resolving interpretive and textual problems.[2]

A parallel phenomenon *has* been noted in biblical narrative and sporadically discussed. Though generally recognized as a genuine element of ancient Hebrew style, there has been uncertainty and vagueness about its function. Consideration of the analogous talmudic phenomenon may provide helpful comparative perspective. I hope,

---

[1] Iterated quotation formulae were the subject of several delightful conversations with my old friend and colleague James Kugel, soon after we first met in New Haven in the late 1970s. I offer this essay to him in friendship, admiration, and gratitude.

[2] The phenomenon is found throughout classical rabbinic literature— talmudic and midrashic, halakhic and aggadic, Palestinian and Babylonian. I refer to this whole corpus as "talmudic." Translation and commentary in this essay are attentive to the topic at hand and do not pretend to precision and comprehensiveness in other regards. Texts are cited from the standard published editions; textual problems and manuscript variants are discussed only when relevant to the topic at hand. Talmudic manuscripts are cited according to the transcription in the Talmud Text Databank of the Saul Lieberman Institute.

therefore, that this study, though focused primarily on talmudic materials, will interest biblical scholars as well. I have tried, throughout, to correlate talmudic and biblical examples in the hope that the reader will find them mutually illuminating.

The literary function of iterated quotation formulae in biblical narrative has been variously described: sharpening the reader's attention, introducing a new theme, introducing a new aspect to the argument, distinguishing different elements within a speech in a manner analogous to punctuation and paragraphs, etc.[3] There are indeed instances in which viewing a repeated quotation formula as a form of punctuation can be helpful,[4] but there is often a more satisfactory explanation.

On this explanation, the second quotation formula retains something of its usual function: introducing new speech. So if A and B are conversing, a repeated, "And A said," indicates that A has momentarily paused and is now taking up his speech again.[5] Not all

---

[3] A literary function for iterated quotation formulae is recognized (in at least some instances) by Charles Conroy, *Absalom, Absalom!* (Rome: Biblical Institute Press, 1978), 130; Georg Fischer, *Ja-hwe unser Gott: Sprache, Aufbau und Erzähltechnik in der Berufung des Mose (Ex 3–4)* (OBO 91; Göttingen: Vandenhoeck & Ruprecht, 1989), 40–45; R. W. L. Moberly, *The Old Testament of the Old Testament* (OBT; Minneapolis: Fortress, 1992), 18. The explanations cited in the text are culled from these sources. The view of Hermann Gunkel (*Genesis* [trans. M. Biddle; Macon, Ga.: Mercer University Press, 1997], xxxvi, 208) that iterated quotation formulae *violate* a rule of Hebrew style, and must therefore indicate a composite text, seems not to have current support. I am grateful to my colleagues Jon Levenson and Peter Machinist for providing initial bibliographical orientation in an area far from my usual field.

A wholly different approach to iterated quotation formulae is proposed by Umberto Cassuto, *A Commentary on the Book of Exodus* (Jerusalem, 1983), p. 38, who suggests that the first formula introduces the words actually spoken, while the second introduces the elucidation of their inner meaning. The same idea, but in reverse (the first formula introduces the inner thought, while the second introduces the words actually spoken) is cited in the name of an eleventh-century scholar, R. Ḥananel b. Ḥushiel, to explain the iterated quotation formulae in Gen. 15:2–3 (by an author writing at the turn of the thirteenth century); see *Perush Rabbeinu Ḥananel ʿal ha-Torah*, ed. C. D. Chavel (Jerusalem, 1972), p. 7. (My thanks to Richard Steiner for alerting me to this passage.) This interesting theory does not, in my opinion, have sufficient textual support.

[4] See, e.g., the discussion below of Rebecca's twofold response to Eliezer in Gen 24:23–25.

[5] See, e.g., Meir Shiloah, "Va-Yomer . . . Va-Yomer," in *Sefer Korngreen* (ed. A. Weiser et al.; Tel-Aviv: ha-Ḥevrah le-Ḥeqer ha-Miqra be-Yisraʾel, 1964), 251–57; Neḥama Leibowitz, *Studies in Bereshit* (4th ed.; trans. A. Newman; Jerusalem: World Zionist Organization, Dept. for Torah Education and Culture in the Diaspora, 1981), 447 and 450 n. 7; idem, *Studies in Shemot* (trans. A. Newman; 2 vols.; Jerusalem: World Zionist Organization, Dept. for Torah Education and Culture in the Diaspora, 1993), 2:563 and 592 n. 10. The influence of this approach has perhaps been slowed

the readings that have been proposed on this explanation are convincing.[6] Nor is it clear that this approach can explain all of the iterated quotation formulae in the Bible. But it can, in my judgment, explain many, and perhaps most, of them and add significant nuance to our understanding of the conversations in which they occur.

The other explanations, by focusing exclusively on the content of A's speech, lose sight of A's interlocutor. But noticing a pause in A's speech often tells us something about B as well. For often, A appears to pause because it is B's turn to speak; A waits for B's response; but, for one reason or another, B fails to respond (or responds with silence); A then resumes his speech, a resumption signaled by the second quotation formula, "And A (or he/she) said."[7] Consideration of the parallel talmudic phenomenon will, I think, clarify and reinforce this line of interpretation.

* * *

by its emergence in traditionalist circles, on the periphery of the academic guild and in Hebrew. Some of Shiloah's more persuasive readings are made accessible in English in Shimon Bar-Efrat, *Narrative Art in the Bible* (Sheffield: Almond, 1989), 43–45. Recent scholarship that is aware of Shiloah or Bar-Efrat includes: Moberly, *Old Testament*; Samuel Meier, *Speaking of Speaking: Marking Direct Discourse in the Hebrew Bible* (Leiden: Brill, 1992), 73–81; Cynthia Miller, *The Representation of Speech in Biblical Hebrew Narrative* (Atlanta: Scholars Press, 1996), 239–43. In fact, Leibowitz, whose studies were appearing in the fifties in pamphlet form, seems to have preceded Shiloah. Thus her reading of the iterated quotation formulae in Num 32:2–5 (utilized below) in her *Studies in Bamidbar* (Jerusalem: World Zionist Organization, Dept. for Torah Education and Culture in the Diaspora, 1980), 380f., appeared in *'Iyyunim be-Farashat ha-Shavua: Sidrah Rishonah* (Jerusalem: World Zionist Organization, Dept. for Torah Education and Culture in the Diaspora, 1958), 38, several years before Shiloah's paper; cf. Shiloah, "Va-Yomer," 252. Leibowitz's remarks are also the more consistent and cogent, though she did not, like Shiloah, undertake a comprehensive review of the sources.

[6] See, e.g., Meier, *Speaking of Speaking*, and the notes below. In fact, Shiloah is at his weakest when he fails to make adequate use of the insight that iterated quotation formulae can indicate a pause. Most of those readings are wisely ignored in Bar-Efrat, *Narrative Art in the Bible*.

[7] I am aware that silence is (even) harder to interpret than speech. But if iterated quotation formulae do, in fact, indicate significant silence, that is what the texts demand of us.

A very different approach is applied by the twelfth-century Byzantine exegete Tobias ben Eliezer (*Leqah Tov* [ed. S. Buber; Jerusalem: Eshcol; repr., n.d.], 1:112a) to the iterated quotation formulae in Gen 47:3–7. He recognizes that the second quotation formula indicates that the first speaker is resuming "out of turn." However, he posits not a long pause, because the interlocutor fails to respond, but a shortened interval, because the first speaker resumes early, before his interlocutor can deliver an unwelcome response! I have not found this (intentionally?) humorous explanation elsewhere.

Let me first illustrate with two biblical examples. Consider 1 Sam 17:34–37. Saul has just declined David's offer to engage Goliath in single combat because of his youth and inexperience. David persists (iterated quotation formulae are underlined):

ויאמר דוד אל שאול רעה היה עבדך לאביו בצאן ובא הארי ואת הדוב ונשא שה מהעדר: ויצאתי אחריו והכתיו והצלתי מפיו ויקם עלי והחזקתי בזקנו והכתיו והמיתיו: גם את הארי גם הדוב הכה עבדך והיה הפלשתי הערל הזה כאחד מהם כי חרף מערכת אלהים חיים: ויאמר דוד יהוה אשר הצלני מיד הארי ומיד הדב הוא יצילני מיד הפלשתי הזה ויאמר שאול אל דוד לך ויהוה יהיה עמך.

And David said to Saul, "Your servant has been a shepherd for his father's flock. When a lion or a bear came and carried off a lamb of the herd, I would go out after it, strike it, and rescue it from its mouth. If it rose against me, I would take hold of its beard, strike it, and kill it. Your servant has killed both lion and bear, and this uncircumcised Philistine will be like one of them; for he has reviled the armies of the living God." And David said, "The Lord who delivered me from the hand of the lion and the bear will deliver me from the hand of this Philistine." And Saul said to David, "Go, and the Lord be with you!"

David argues his ability to defeat Goliath from his success against wild animals. Saul, unconvinced, remains silent. So David picks up the conversation, adding that God has granted him these victories and will do so against Goliath as well. This argument tips the balance, as indicated by Saul's response, "Go, and the Lord be with you!"[8] The second quotation formula marks the resumption of David's speech, after Saul's pregnant silence.

Or, consider Gen 20:9–11. Abimelech, warned by God that the woman he has taken is, in fact, Abraham's wife, is outraged:

ויקרא אבימלך לאברהם ויאמר לו מה עשית לנו ומה חטאתי לך כי הבאת עלי ועל ממלכתי חטאה גדלה מעשים אשר לא יעשו עשית עמדי: ויאמר אבימלך אל אברהם מה ראית כי עשית את הדבר הזה: ויאמר אברהם כי אמרתי רק אין יראת אלהים במקום הזה והרגוני על דבר אשתי.

And Abimelech called Abraham and said to him, "What have you done to us, and how have I offended you, that you have brought on

---

[8] Shiloah's explanation of this passage ("Va-Yomer," 264) seems to adopt Cassuto's approach (*Commentary on the Book of Exodus*) and is, to my mind, unsatisfactory.

me and on my kingdom great sin? You have done deeds to me that ought not to be done." <u>And Abimelech said to Abraham</u>, "What did you see, that you did this thing?" And Abraham said, "Because I thought, surely there is no fear of God in this place, and they will kill me on account of my wife."

Abimelech confronts Abraham with his fabrication and demands an explanation. Abraham is thrown off balance and reduced to silence. But Abimelech will not relent: he resumes the conversation, pressing Abraham for an explanation. By then Abraham has regained his balance and delivers his sardonic repartee.[9] The iterated quotation formulae capture Abraham's painful moment of silence.

* * *

[9] Shiloah's explanation of this passage ("Va-Yomer," 258) is also, in my opinion, unsatisfactory. The interpretation of these passages by Robert Alter, building on Bar-Efrat, is far better; see his *Genesis: Translation and Commentary* (New York: W. W. Norton, 1996), 94; *The David Story: a Translation with Commentary of 1 and 2 Samuel* (New York: W. W. Norton, 1999), 107. The attempt to remedy the perceived awkwardness of an iterated quotation formula by rendering, "And A also (further, moreover) said," though now widespread, is not helpful. For a fine rendition of the twice-repeated quotation formula in Exod 33:17–23, see James Kugel, *The God of Old* (New York: Free Press, 2003), 131.

It would be interesting to explore parallels in other ancient Near Eastern literatures (cf. Fischer, *Ja-hwe unser Gott*; Meier, *Speaking of Speaking*), a task well beyond my ken. My colleague, Paul-Alain Beaulieu, informs me that the passage from *The Epic of Gilgamesh* cited by Fischer is, in fact, one of three in which Gilgamesh addresses different characters (Siduri the barmaid, Ur-Shanabi the boatman, and Ut-napishti the sage) with precisely the same speech mourning Enkidu (in response to the very same question). In each case, the iterated quotation formula then introduces a shorter speech, requesting something particular from that character. See *The Epic of Gilgamesh* (trans. A. George; London/New York: Penguin, 1999), 77f. (X, 46 and X, 72), 80f. (X, 112 and X, 149), 84f. (X, 219 and X, 249). Although the narrator could be indicating that, in each case, Gilgamesh's first speech was met with silence, he may simply be separating what he sees as two different components of Gilgamesh's speech: the first, a recurring "module," the second, a particularized request. But Prof. Beaulieu calls my attention to another passage that is more suggestive. In tablet III of the *Epic* (ibid., 24–26), the goddess Ninsun entreats the god Shamash, beginning at III, 45. Then at III, 100, immediately after her first entreaty, we have a second introduction ("Again . . . Ninsun made her request before Shamash. . . ."). Perhaps Ninsun has paused for Shamash's reply (which, as a goddess, she expects). When he fails to respond to her first plea, she begins again with a second plea. Unlike most of the biblical and talmudic instances, the iteration is underscored by the term "again." But this too is not without parallel; see below, n. 42, on Exod 3:15.

We turn now to some talmudic texts in some ways reminiscent of
Abraham's awkward moment with Abimelech. The following pas-
sage opens the well-known account of the deposition of the *nasi,*
Rabban Gamliel:

מעשה בתלמיד אחד שבא לפני רבי יהושע, אמר לו: תפלת ערבית רשות או
חובה? אמר ליה: רשות. בא לפני רבן נמליאל, אמר ליה: תפלת ערבית רשות
או חובה? אמר לו: חובה. אמר לו: והלא רבי יהושע אמר לי רשות! אמר ליה:
המתן עד שיכנסו בעלי תריסין לבית המדרש. כשנכנסו בעלי תריסין, עמד
השואל ושאל: תפלת ערבית רשות או חובה? אמר לו רבן נמליאל: חובה.
אמר להם רבן נמליאל לחכמים: כלום יש אדם שחולק בדבר זה? אמר ליה
רבי יהושע: לאו. <u>אמר ליה</u>: והלא משמך אמרו לי רשות! <u>אמר ליה</u>: יהושע,
עמוד על רנליך ויעידו בך! עמד רבי יהושע על רנליו ואמר: אלמלא אני חי
והוא מת - יכול החי להכחיש את המח ,ועכשיו שאני חי והוא חי - היאך יכול
החי להכחיש את החי? היה רבן נמליאל יושב ודורש, ורבי יהושע עומד על
רנליו . . . .

Once, a student came to R. Joshua and said to him: "Is the evening
prayer optional or mandatory?" He said to him: "Optional." He came
to Rabban Gamliel and said to him: "Is the evening prayer optional
or mandatory?" He said to him: "Mandatory." He said to him: "But
R. Joshua told me 'optional.'" He said to him: "Wait till the [acade-
mic] warriors[10] enter the study-house." When the warriors had entered,
the questioner rose and asked: "Is the evening prayer optional or
mandatory?" Rabban Gamliel said to him: "Mandatory." Rabban
Gamliel said to the Sages: "Is there anyone who disagrees on this
point?"[11] Rabbi Joshua said to him: "No." He said to him: "But you
were quoted to me as saying, 'Optional'!" He said to him: "Joshua,
stand up, so testimony can be given against you." R. Joshua stood up
and said: "If I were alive and [the questioner], dead, the living could
contradict the dead. Now that I am alive and he is alive, how can
the living contradict the living?" Rabban Gamliel sat expounding, while
R. Joshua remained standing. . . ."[12]

---

[10] Literally, "shield-bearers."

[11] The quotation formula that introduces this question should not be seen as iterated, since the addressee has changed. The particle כלום, with which this question
begins, often introduces a rhetorical question expecting the answer "no" and may
serve as Rabban Gamliel's cue to "the warriors" that he will brook no battle on
this issue. Perhaps it should be translated: "Can anyone [possibly] disagree on this
point?!"

[12] *b. Ber.* 27b.

Like Abraham, R. Joshua is caught lying, thrown off balance, and reduced to silence. His mute discomfiture is evoked by the second quotation formula, which introduces Rabban Gamliel's order to him to stand and face the testimony against him. But unlike Abraham, R. Joshua cannot rebound, and his humiliation ends only in the story's sequel when the study-house revolts.

The movement from silent discomfiture to recovery of wit is, however, captured in the following parable (designed to explain Hosea's charge [12:4] that "in the womb," Jacob "took hold of his brother's heel"):

לאשה אלמנה שהיתה קובלת על בנה לדיין, כיון דחמאה דיינא דהוא דאין
בנור ובזפת בדינין ומנלבין, אמרה אין אנא מודע ליה לדיינא סורחנין דברי
קטיל ליה כיון דאחסל אמר לה איינוי בריך, אמר לה מה סרה עליך הדין
בריך, אמרה ליה מרי כד הוה במעיי הוה בעט בי, אמר לה לאו דינא הוא.

[This may be compared] to a widow bringing charges against her son to a judge. When she observed that the judge was punishing [the condemned] by fire, pitch, torture, and whips she said [to herself]: "If I tell the judge my son's offence, he'll kill him." When [the judge] had finished [the previous cases], he said to her, "Is this your son?" He said to her: "How has this son of yours wronged you?" She said to him, "My lord, when he was in my belly, he used to kick me." He said to her: "That's no case." [13]

The widow, seeing the judge's severity, realizes what awaits her son and is frightened out of her wits. To the judge's initial question ("Is this your son?"), she responds with silence, afraid to proceed, but unsure of what to say. So the judge presses on: "How has this son of yours wronged you?" By now, the woman has recovered her wits and responds with a "charge" so trivial, even a hanging judge is sure to dismiss. [14]

* * *

---

[13] *Song Rab.* 6:2 (S. Dunski ed., 138f.).

[14] Interestingly, the iterated quotation formula is absent in the otherwise close parallel in *Lev. Rab.* 27:6 (M. Margulies ed., 635f.). Cf. also below, n. 19. On this passage, see Saul Lieberman, "Roman Legal Institutions in Early Rabbinics and the Acta Martyrum," *JQR* 35 (1944): 1–57, esp. 15f.

Silence of a different sort is evoked in Ruth 2:20. When Ruth tells
her mother-in-law the name of the generous man in whose field she
has collected grain, this information educes a grateful exclamation:

ותאמר נעמי לכלתה ברוך הוא ליהוה אשר לא עזב חסדו את החיים ואת
המתים ותאמר לה נעמי קרוב לנו האיש מגאלנו הוא.

And Naomi said to her daughter-in-law, "Blessed be he of the LORD,
who has not abandoned his kindness to the living and to the dead!"
And Naomi said to her, "The man is a relative of ours, one of our
redeemers."

Ruth is not in a position to understand why the name (Boaz) should
have elicited Naomi's joyful praise of God. So she reacts with puzzled silence. Naomi, noticing her puzzlement and realizing the need
to clarify, picks up her speech and supplies the missing context.[15]

Something similar happens in Gen 15:2–3. God has told Abram
that his reward will be very great. This evokes a pained cry:

ויאמר אברם אדני יהוה מה תתן לי ואנכי הולך ערירי ובן משק ביתי הוא
דמשק אליעזר? ויאמר אברם הן לי לא נתתה זרע והנה בן ביתי יורש אתי.

And Abram said, "LORD God, what will you give me seeing that I am
going childless, and the steward of my house is Eliezer of Damascus?"
And Abram said, "Behold, to me you have given no seed, and so my
domestic will be my heir."

Abraham's initial exclamation seems like a non sequitur, its second
clause lacking logical connection to the first. God remains silent, giving Abraham a chance to regain his composure and reformulate his
complaint, this time making clear the connection between his child-
lessness and his steward Eliezer.[16]

This pattern finds interesting talmudic parallels. Consider, for example, the following passage:

מעשה בר' יוסי בן דורמסקית שהלך להקביל פני ר' אליעזר בלודו, אמר לו מה חדוש
היה בבהמ"ד היום? א"ל נמנו ונמרו עמון ומואב מעשרין מעשר עני בשביעית. . . .
בכה ר' אליעזר ואמר סוד ה' ליראיו ובריתו להודיעם. אמרלו לך אמור להם אל

---

[15] It is not entirely clear to me how Shiloah understands this passage; see "Va-
Yomer," 262, and the rubric under which it is classified on p. 257.
[16] Shiloah ("Va-Yomer," 237) and Bar-Efrat (Narrative Art in the Bible, 43) explain
the silence differently. Some current translations strain to avoid Abram's initial non
sequitur, ill-advisedly, on my reading.

תחושו למניינכם, כך מקובלני מרבן יוחנן בן זכאי ששמע מרבו ורבו מרבו הלכתא
למשה מסיני, עמון ומואב מעשרין מעשר עני בשביעית.

Once R. Yose of Damascus went to pay respects to R. Eliezer in
Lydda. [R. Eliezer] said to him: "What novelty emerged today in the
study-house?" He said to him: "It was concluded by vote that [crops
grown in the lands of] Amon and Moav are subject to the poor-tithe
in the Sabbatical year." . . . Rabbi Eliezer wept and said: "God's counsel belongs to those who fear Him, and He instructs them in His
covenant"[17] (Ps 25:14). He said to him: "Tell them, 'Do not be appre-
hensive about your vote, I have it on tradition from Rabban Yoḥanan
ben Zakkai, who heard from his teacher, and the latter from *his* teacher,
as a legal tradition going back to Moses at Sinai [that crops grown
in the lands of] Amon and Moav are subject to the poor-tithe in the
Sabbatical year.' "[18]

R. Yose reacts to R. Eliezer's tearful citation of Ps 25:14 with puzzled silence: what can Ps 25:14 have to do with the day's decision
on the poor-tithe? R. Eliezer regains his composure, sees his interlocutor's puzzlement and picks up the conversation, this time making sense of his emotional citation: Providence has guided the sages
in their deliberations to a conclusion known to be true by R. Eliezer
on tradition.[19]

Another cryptic comment greeted by puzzled silence, which then
prompts the speaker to explain his remark, is found in the following parable. A slave, purchased on the understanding that he is of
a bad disposition, is beaten by his master when that disposition
becomes manifest:

התחיל העבד צווח ביא מעביר עלי. א״ל אדוניו סרחת כל הסרחון הזה ואתה
צווח ביא העברת לי? אמר העבד באמת ביא העברת עלי. א״ל מרי היאך
לקחת אותי בעבד טוב או בעבד רע? א״ל בעבד רע. אמר לו בעבד רע אתה
לקחתני ותבקשני עבד טוב?

<hr />

[17] "Covenant" (ברית) is apparently equated here with Torah, as in *Mekhilta, Pisḥa*,
no. 5 (S. Horowitz and I. A. Rabin ed., 15); *b. Šabb.* 33a.

[18] *b. Ḥag.* 3b. Recent editions corrupt אליעזר to אלעזר.

[19] R. Eliezer's tearful ascription of providential guidance to his erstwhile colleagues becomes especially poignant if we take this account to assume familiarity
with the traditions about R. Eliezer's appeal to divine vindication in controversy
with those same colleagues and his subsequent banishment for rejecting their authority; see *y. Mo'ed Qaṭ.* 3:1, 81c–d; *b. B. Meṣi'a* 59a–b; and Maimonides, *Perush ha-
Mishnah, Yadayim* 2:3 (ed. Y. Kafiḥ; 7 vols.; Jerusalem: Mosad ha-Rav Kuk, 1963–1967),
7:716.

The slave began to cry out: "Injustice, injustice, he wrongs me!" His master said: "You've done all this wrong and *you* cry out, 'Injustice, you wrong me!'?" <u>The slave said</u>: "Injustice, indeed, you have wronged me." <u>He said to him</u>: "Master, how did you buy me, as a good or a bad slave?" He said to him: "As a bad slave." He said to him: "You bought me as a bad slave and you expect me to be a good slave?!"[20]

The master protests that the slave's charge of injustice makes no sense. The slave simply reasserts the truth of his charge, without explanation. The master responds with puzzled silence. So the slave picks up the conversation and helps him understand. Here again the moment of silent puzzlement is captured by use of an iterated quotation formula.[21]

*   *   *

The use of an iterated quotation formula need not indicate a pregnant silence. Consider, for example, the response of Rebecca to Eliezer's question in Gen 24:23–25:

ויאמר בת מי את הגידי נא לי היש בית אביך מקום לנו ללין: <u>ותאמר</u>
<u>אליו</u> בת בתואל אנכי בן מלכה אשר ילדה לנחור: <u>ותאמר אליו</u> גם תבן גם
מספוא רב עמנו גם מקום ללון.

And he said to her: "Whose daughter are you, tell me please, is there room in your father's house for us to spend the night?" <u>And she said to him</u>: "I am the daughter of Bethuel, son of Milcah, whom she bore to Naḥor." <u>And she said to him</u>: "We have plenty of straw and fodder, and room to spend the night."

The versions of this story in *m. Yad.* 4:3 and in *t. Yad.* 2:16 (M. S. Zuckermandel ed., 683) do not have the second quotation formula but a single continuous statement by R. Eliezer. The iterated quotation formula in our *beraita* may be a later literary flourish. On the interesting history of this *beraita*, see Shamma Friedman, *Talmud 'Arukh, Pereq Ha-Sokher et ha-Ummanin* (2 vols.; New York: Jewish Theological Seminary of America, 1996), 8f.

[20] *Exod. Rab.* 43:8.

[21] There is a very impressive use of iterated quotation formulae to evoke a complex silence, that reflects both puzzlement (of the sort discussed in this section) and the incipient panic of someone whose deception is about to unravel (cf. the previous section), in the story of the Aramean caught infiltrating the paschal meal in *b. Pesaḥ.* 3b.

In this instance, the two quotation formulae may simply be a narrative device used to separate Rebecca's responses to what were, in fact, two discrete questions. But such cases can also be assimilated to a more general pause-principle: Asked two questions, Rebecca answers the first, pauses a bit, then answers the second.[22]

There is, perhaps, an intimation of the latter understanding in a rabbinic source. Mishnah 'Avot 5:7 lists among the qualities of the wise: "addressing first things, first, and last things, last." 'Avot de-Rabbi Natan illustrates this quality by:

רבקה בת בתואל [שנאמר ויאמר בת מי את הגידי נא לי היש בית אביך
מקום לנו ללין. ותאמר אליו בת בתואל אנכי וגו׳] ותאמר אליו גם תבן גם
מספוא [רב עמנו גם מקום ללון].

... Rebecca daughter of Bethuel. [For it is said, "And he said to her: 'Whose daughter are you, tell me please, is there room in your father's house for us to spend the night?' And she said to him: 'I am the daughter of Bethuel, etc.']. And she said to him: 'We have plenty of straw and fodder [and room to spend the night].'"[23]

The proof is primarily from sequence: Rebecca answers Eliezer's questions in the order they were asked. But there is an additional nuance: to have a true first and last, you need demarcation. The old servant breathlessly runs one question into the next without demarcation, while young Rebecca responds with learned decorum, pausing between her answers and taking each question separately.[24]

Whatever the explanation, we can see iterated quotation formulae of a similar sort in the following story:

שאל רבי עקיבא את רבי נחוניא הגדול: במה הארכת ימים? אתו
נווי וקא מחו ליה. סליק יתיב ארישא דדיקלא, אמר ליה: רבי, אם נאמר כבש
למה נאמר אחד? - אמר להו צורבא מדרבנן הוא, שבקוהו. אמר ליה: אחד -
מיוחד שבעדרו. אמר לו: מימי לא קבלתי מתנות, ולא עמדתי על מדותי,
וותרן בממוני הייתי.

---

[22] The latter view is taken by Shiloah ("Va-Yomer," 257); Miller thinks that no actual pause is implied (*Representation of Speech*, 241).

[23] 'Avot R. Nat. B 40 (S. Schechter ed., 112). See also Rashi to Gen 24:24.

[24] It would seem that the unreconstructed manuscript reading cited only the second quotation formula and a few subsequent words. The additional, bracketed material represents Schechter's conjectural completion. It may, however, be precisely the second quotation formula that the original means to stress.

> R. 'Aqiva asked R. Neḥunya the Great: "Whereby have you attained to old age?" The servants[25] came and began beating him. [So] he climbed up and stationed himself atop a date-palm and said to him: "Master, if it is said [in Num 28:4] *keves* [a lamb], why [must] it [also] say *'eḥad* [one]?" [i.e., the word *'eḥad* in the phrase, *'et ha-keves 'eḥad*, seems redundant]. He said to [the servants]: "He's a young scholar, let him be." <u>He said to him</u>, "[what Scripture means by] *'eḥad* is the prime of its flock." <u>He said to him</u>: "I never accepted gifts, never took tit for tat, and was liberal with my money."[26]

We are dealing here with a young R. 'Aqiva, who has not yet established his reputation (and can still scurry up a tree). He hopes to hear of the ethical qualities that have earned an aged scholar his long life. But his question is mistaken for coarse insolence, the rough equivalent of, "Why are you still around, old man?" So he is set upon by the scholar's servants. Rabbi 'Aqiva makes a quick vertical escape and, from the safety of his perch, puts a nice academic question to the old man, thus establishing his scholarly credentials. So R. Neḥunya calls his servants off and answers both questions.

Again, the iterated quotation formulae could simply be a conventional device adopted by the narrator to separate the responses to two discrete questions. Notice, however, that unlike Rebecca, R. Neḥunya does *not* answer "first things first." He is quick to take up R. 'Aqiva's scholastic challenge, the second question. We may then envision a short, slightly awkward silence before R. Neḥunya accedes to answering the initially offensive query.

* * *

An interesting instance of iterated quotation formulae is found in Num 32:1–7:

ומקנה רב היה לבני ראובן ולבני גד עצום מאד ויראו את ארץ יעזר ואת ארץ
גלעד והנה המקום מקום מקנה: <u>ויבאו בני גד ובני ראובן ויאמרו אל משה ואל</u>
<u>אלעזר הכהן ואל נשיאי העדה לאמר</u>: עטרות ודיבן ויעזר ונמרה וחשבון
ואלעלה ושבם ונבו ובען: הארץ אשר הכה יהוה לפני עדת ישראל ארץ מקנה
הוא ולעבדיך מקנה: <u>ויאמרו</u> אם מצאנו חן בעיניך יתן את הארץ הזאת לעבדיך

---

[25] See Nathan ben Jehiel, *Aruch Completum* (ed. A. Kohut; 9 vols.; 1878–1937; repr., Jerusalem: Makor, 1970), 2:256f.

[26] *b. Meg.* 28a.

לאחזה אל תעברנו את הירדן: ויאמר משה לבני גד ולבני ראובן האחיכם יבאו
למלחמה ואתם תשבו פה: ולמה תנואון את לב בני ישראל . . . .

Now the children of Reuben and the children of Gad had an exceedingly large number of livestock. They saw the land of Jazer and the
land of Gilead, and behold it was a place for livestock. And the children of Gad and the children of Reuben came and spoke to Moses
and to Eleazar the priest and to the leaders of the congregation, saying: "Ataroth, Dibon, Jazer, Nimrah, Heshbon, Elealeh, Sebam, Nebo,
and Beon, the land which the LORD conquered before the congregation of Israel is a land for livestock, and your servants have livestock."
And they said, "If we have found favor in your sight, let this land be
given to your servants as a possession; do not take us across the Jordan."
And Moses said to the children of Gad and to the children of Reuben:
"Shall your brothers go to war while you sit here? Why do you discourage the children of Israel . . .?"

The Reubenites and Gadites anticipate that Moses may find their
scheme to opt out of Canaan disagreeable. So instead of making a
request, they try to elicit an offer: they tell Moses, "This place is
perfect for livestock, and we have lots of livestock," hoping he will
reply, "Well, in that case, why not settle right here?" Moses understands precisely what they are up to but refuses to play along: he
responds with stony silence. The Reubenites and Gadites, not to be
deterred, are forced to make their request explicit. And once they
do, they elicit Moses' angry excoriation.[27]

This pattern (iterated quotation formulae, in the context of a hint
ignored that then forces explicitness) may be helpful in deciphering
the opening to a talmudic story,[28] designed to illustrate the ideal of
judicial impartiality:

אושפיזכניה דרב אתא לקמיה לדינא אמר לו: לאו אושפיזכני את? - אמר
לו: אין. אמר ליה: דינא אית לי. - אמר ליה: פסילנא לך לדינא . . . .

I translate first following Rashi:

Rav's host (ushpizkhan) came before him to have a case adjudicated.
He said to him: "Weren't you my guest (ushpizkhan)?" He said to him:

---

[27] This reading follows Leibowitz, *Studies in Bamidbar*.
[28] *b. Sanh.* 7b–8a.

"Yes." He said to him: "I have a case for adjudication." He said to
him: "I am disqualified to act as your judge. . . ."

On Rashi's interpretation, the meaning of *ushpizkhan* changes from
host, in the first sentence, to guest, in the second. But the meaning
guest is not, as far as I can tell, attested elsewhere.[29] Rashi is operating with the natural assumption that consecutive quotation formulae introduce the words of different speakers and is ready to
tolerate some lexical awkwardness to preserve such a sequence.[30]

If, however, we assume that *ushpizkhan* maintains its usual meaning (= host), the passage is using iterated quotation formulae:

> Rav's host (*ushpizkhan*) came before him to have a case adjudicated.
> He said to him: "Weren't you my host (*ushpizkhan*)?" He said to him:
> "Yes." He said to him: "I have a case for adjudication." He said to
> him: "I am disqualified to act as your judge. . . ."[31]

On this reading, Rav, seeing someone who has given him hospitality bring him a case, first tries subtlety. Rav asks him, "Weren't you
my host?" and, eliciting an affirmative reply, remains silent, hoping
his host will realize that this makes it inappropriate for Rav to serve
as his judge. But the host refuses (or is too obtuse) to take the hint,
resumes the conversation, and insists on enunciating his request: "I
have a case for adjudication." So Rav has to turn explicit: "I am
disqualified to act as your judge."

The manuscripts preserve some instructive attempts to deal with
these problematic quotation formulae surgically. Two simply omit
the second quotation formula, yielding a combined statement: "He
said to him, 'Yes, I have a case for adjudication.'"[32] In another, the

---

[29] See, e.g., Marcus Jastrow, *A Dictionary of the Targumim, the Talmud Babli and
Yerushalmi, and the Midrashic Literature* (New York: Judaica Press, 1996), 36a; Kohut,
Aruch Completum, 1:322a; and (for the definition that best fits the context) the note
of Bernhard Geiger, op. cit., 9:71a.

[30] Perhaps Rashi's reading was unconsciously reinforced by the French *hôte* (from
the oblique forms of Latin *hospes*) which can mean both "guest" and "host."

[31] This translation follows from the commentary of R. Adin Steinsaltz, ed., *Talmud
Bavli: Masekhet Sanhedrin* (2 vols.; Jerusalem: Ha-Makhon ha-Yisre'eli le-firsumim
Talmudiyim, 1974–1975), 1:33, which does not, however, address the iterated quo-
tation formulae.

[32] *Yad ha-Rav Herzog*, Florence II I 9–7. For a curious parallel, note the removal
of the second quotation formula from the conversation of David and Saul, discussed
above, in the Septuagint; see Samuel R. Driver, *Notes on the Hebrew Text and Topography
of the Books of Samuel* (Oxford: Clarendon, 1912), ad loc.

emendation is more radical: "Rav's host (*ushpizkhan*) came before him for the adjudication of a case. He said to him: 'I have a case for adjudication.' He said to him: 'I am disqualified to act as your judge.' "[33]

The iterated quotation formula is, in this case, the *lectio difficilior* because it defies the natural expectation that a second introduction is indicating a shift in speaker. That expectation can inspire emendation or interpretative efforts in its behalf. This sort of passage can be especially tricky because the subject of "said" is not defined in either of the quotation formulae, leaving one confused as to who said what to whom.

* * *

It is not surprising, then, that not all iterated quotation formulae have survived the transmission process. Consider the following conversation between plaintiff and defendant over contested land:

ההוא דאמר ליה לחבריה: מאי בעית בהאי ארעא? אמר ליה: מפלניא
זבינתה דאמר לי דזבנה מינך. אמר ליה: את לאו קא מודית דהאי ארעא
דידי היא, ואת לא זבינתה מינאי? זיל לאו בעל דברים דידי את.

Someone said to his fellow: "What are you doing on this land?" He said: "I bought it from So-and-So, who told me he bought it from you." He said to him: "Do you not concede that this land [was] mine, and that you did not buy it from me? Go! Your case is not with me."[34]

The thirteenth-century Catalan talmudist, R. Jonah Gerondi, cites a variant reading of the plaintiff's last words:

I have found . . . a Spanish version that reads: "He said to him: 'Do you not concede that this land [was] mine, and that you did not buy it from me?' He said to him: 'If so, your case is not with me.' "[35]

---

[33] Munich 95.

[34] *b. B. Bat.* 30a–b.

[35] For another case of iterated quotation formulae in the context of court litigation, see R. Ḥisda's conversation with the hapless brother of the tough Mari bar Isaq in *b. B. Meṣiʿa* 39b.

R. Jonah continues:

> Since we read "He said," twice [in this version], it would seem that
> [the plaintiff] first asked him, "Do you not concede [etc.]" and then,
> *seeing that he remained silent* or conceded, said to him, "Your case is not
> with me."[36]

R. Jonah is the earliest author I have found to say explicitly that
an iterated quotation formula can indicate a significant silence.

It is not surprising that the manuscripts show instability on this
passage. One, Munich 95, preserves the iterated quotation formulae
cited by R. Jonah. Others, like the standard printed texts, remove
the second formula, thus collapsing the plaintiff's two last statements
into one.[37] Still others insert an intervening concession on the part
of the defendant ("He said to him: 'Yes.'").[38] Again, the iterated
quotation formula must be viewed as the *lectio difficilior*, which defied
the expectation that a second quotation formula signals a shift in
speaker. So the problem was solved either by removing the second
introduction or by adding an intervening speaker.

Although R. Jonah embraces the reading that preserves the iterated quotation formula, and takes it to indicate that the defendant
responded to the plaintiff's first statement with silence, he also mentions a second possibility: that the iterated quotation formula indicates an ellipsis, with the reader expected to reconstruct an intervening
response (in this case, the defendant's concession).[39] This approach
too, i.e., the view that an iterated quotation formula can indicate
an ellipsis, which requires that we reconstruct a missing response,
can be seen in more imaginative form in midrashic exegesis.

---

[36] *'Aliyyot de-Rabeinu Yonah, Bava Batra* (ed. M. Hershler; Jerusalem: Mekhon ha-
Talmud ha-Yisre'eli ha-Shalem, 1966), 1:130 (bottom) (Pardes ed., 54b). (Emphasis
is, of course, added.)

ולא ומצאתי סיוע בנסחא ספרדית ספרדית דנרסינן בה. ולא קא מודית דארעא דידי היא ואת לאו
מנאי זבנתיה א״ל א״כ לאו בעל דברים דידי את. מדנרסי א״ל תרי זימני
משמע כי מתחילה שאלו ולא קא מודית ואח״כ שראה ששתק או שהודה לו
א״ל לאו בעל דברים דידי את.

I am grateful to my son Yehuda for bringing this important passage to my
attention.

[37] Hamburg 165; Escorial G-I-3; Florence II I 9–7; Paris 1337.

[38] Oxford Opp. 249 (369); Vatican 115.

[39] This possibility may have seemed especially plausible for this passage because
the second speech begins אם כן, which suggests a conclusion drawn from something
that has just been said.

* * *

Consider, for example, the iterated quotation formula of Exod 3:13–14:

ויאמר משה אל האלהים הנה אנכי בא אל בני ישראל ואמרתי להם אלהי
אבותיכם שלחני אליכם ואמרו לי־מה שמו מה אמר אלהם: <u>ויאמר אלהים אל</u>
<u>משה</u> אהיה אשר אהיה <u>ויאמר</u> כה תאמר לבני ישראל אהיה שלחני אליכם.

And Moses said to God, "Behold, when I come to the children of
Israel and say to them, 'The God of your fathers has sent me to you,'
and they say to me, 'What is His name?' what shall I say unto them?"
<u>And God said to Moses</u>, "'*Ehyeh asher 'Ehyeh*." <u>And He said</u>, "Thus
shall you say to the children of Israel, '*Ehyeh* sent me unto you.'"

This cryptic passage is given the following interpretation:

אהיה אשר אהיה. אמר לו הקדוש ברוך הוא למשה: לך אמור להם לישראל:
אני הייתי עמכם בשעבוד זה ואני אהיה עמכם בשעבוד מלכיות. אמר לפניו:
רבונו של עולם! דיה לצרה בשעתה. אמר לו הקדוש ברוך הוא: לך אמור
להם אהיה שלחני אליכם.

'*Ehyeh 'asher 'Ehyeh* (Exod 3:14) [understood: "I am as I shall be"]. The
Holy One (blessed be He) said to [Moses]: "Go tell Israel, 'I have
been with you during this subjugation and *will* be with you in [your]
subjugation to the [future] empires.'" [Moses] said to Him: "Master
of the Universe, one tribulation at a time!"[10] [So] the Holy One (blessed
be He) said to him: "Go tell them, '*Ehyeh* [understood to mean, "I
am (with you)"] has sent me to you' (ibid.)."[11]

Here the iterated quotation formula (which has no obvious plain-
sense interpretation) is taken to signal an ellipsis, which is then filled
in with some imagination and humor.[12] It is possible, however, that
Moses' objection is offered not as a reconstructed ellipsis, but as the
import of his silence (which the iterated quotation formula is taken
to indicate).

---

[10] More literally, "It suffices [to confront] a tribulation in its time."

[11] *b. Ber.* 9b.

[12] Of course, much ink has been spilled on this difficult biblical passage, most
of it in vain. While not pretending to have plumbed its depths, I will nevertheless
venture a (more prosaic) conjecture on the significance of its iterated quotation formulae: Moses has asked God for His name. God's response, "I am that I am,"
does not sound like a name. It sounds more like a sentence asserting God's unknowa-
bility. So Moses is silent, perhaps confused as to whether God is deflecting his
request. God's second speech then clarifies: the abbreviated form, '*Ehyeh*, can, in

We can see this sort of gloss on a pregnant silence in the following talmudic conversation:

בשעת פטירתו אמר לו: [רבי], ברכני! אמר לו: יהי רצון שתגיע לחצי ימי. -
ולכולהו לא? אמר לו: הבאים אחריך בהמה ירעו?

When [R. Judah the Prince] was taking leave of [the aged R. Joshua ben Qorḥah], he said to him: "My master, bless me." He said to him: "May it be [God's] will that you live to be half my age." *And not all of it?* He said to him: "And [what of] your successors, shall they graze livestock?"[43]

The passage is Hebrew, but the italicized question, "And not all of it?" is Aramaic—a telltale sign of a later insertion.[44] We can therefore conjecture the following original:

בשעת פטירתו אמר לו: [רבי], ברכני! אמר לו: יהי רצון שתגיע לחצי ימי. אמר
לו: הבאים אחריך בהמה ירעו?

When [R. Judah the Prince] was taking leave of [the aged R. Joshua ben Qorḥah] he said to him: "My master, bless me." <u>He said to him:</u> "May it be [God's] will that you live to half my age." <u>He said to him:</u> "And [what of] your successors, shall they graze livestock?"

The iterated quotation formula, in the original, evokes R. Judah the Prince's stunned silence on hearing R. Joshua's odd "blessing." So R. Joshua, who undoubtedly intended to puzzle, picks up the conversation and provides the young hereditary patriarch with acerbic

---

fact, serve as God's name. At this point, with God still speaking, we have yet another quotation formula (Exod 3:15): "<u>Again God said to Moses,</u> 'Thus you shall say to the children of Israel, "The LORD [*YHVH*], God of your fathers, the God of Abraham, the God of Isaac, and the God of Jacob, has sent me to you."' This is My name forever, and this is My designation unto all generations." This time the quotation formula uncharacteristically includes "again" (*'od*), perhaps because it is a second iteration. It may reflect a second puzzled silence: *'Ehyeh* ("I am") still sounds like God referring to Himself. It seems inappropriate for use by others in referring to God! So God revises a bit more, switching to a third person form that Israel can use in referring to Him. (He also makes clear that it is the name of the God of the patriarchs.) So, while God may have momentarily referred to Himself as *'Ehyeh*, the Tetragrammaton will be the name used by Israel "forever" and "unto all generations." See Rashbam, ad loc.

[43] *b. Meg.* 28a.

[44] See, e.g., Shamma Friedman, "A Critical Study of *Yevamot X* with a Methodological Introduction," in *Texts and Studies: Analecta Judaica* (ed. H. Z. Dimitrovsky; 2 vols.; New York: Jewish Theological Seminary of America, 1977, 1990), 1:275–441, esp. 296, 301f. [Hebrew].

commentary: If you live too long, how will your aristocratic sons occupy themselves while you linger—with shepherding?!

The Aramaic insertion can be viewed as an attempt to fill in an ellipsis, supplying the missing words spoken by R. Judah on hearing R. Joshua's "blessing." But the words "And not all of it?" are not introduced by a quotation formula in any of the versions I have seen.[45] So they are perhaps better viewed as an editorial clarification, inserted into the original story, designed to spell out the significance of the surprised prince's silence.

* * *

Something similar occurs in a midrashic reading of God's first revelation to Moses. In Exod 3:4–6, as Moses approaches the burning bush, we read:

וירא יהוה כי סר לראות ויקרא אליו אלהים מתוך הסנה ויאמר משה משה
ויאמר הנני: <u>ויאמר</u> אל תקרב הלם של של נעליך מעל רגליך כי המקום אשר
אתה עומד עליו אדמת קדש הוא: <u>ויאמר</u> אנכי אלהי אביך אלהי אברהם
אלהי יצחק ואלהי יעקב ויסתר משה פניו כי ירא מהביט אל האלהים.

When the LORD saw that he had turned aside to see, God called to him out of the bush and said, "Moses, Moses!" And he said, "Here I am." <u>And He said</u>, "Do not come near; take your shoes off your feet, for the place on which you are standing is holy ground." <u>And He said</u>, "I am the God of your father, the God of Abraham, the God of Isaac, and the God of Jacob." And Moses hid his face, for he was afraid to look upon God.

Why the iterated quotation formulae? One current explanation sees them indicating a pause, in which God gives Moses time to remove his sandals before continuing his speech.[46] But there is another possible

---

[45] Oxford Opp. Add. fol. 23 (366); Munich 95; Columbia 141X893–T; Pisaro ed., 1516. The Aramaic insertion is garbled in Vatican 134. However, British Museum Harl. 5508 (400) omits "he said" before R. Joshua's clarification; this reading could reflect an understanding of the Aramaic insertion as reflecting R. Judah's spoken words.

[46] Shiloah, "Va-Yomer," 254; Leibowitz, *Studies in Shemot*, 51; Bar-Efrat, *Narrative Art in the Bible*, 44; see also Amos Ḥakham, *Sefer Shemot* (2 vols.; Jerusalem: Mosad ha-Rav Kuk, 1991), 1:42. The first three authors apply this sort of explanation more convincingly to Gen 15:5. See also below on Gen 19:9.

reading (preferable, in my opinion): Moses hears a mysterious voice call him and responds, "Here I am." The voice then commands: "Do not come near; take your shoes off your feet," etc. Moses is silent, surprised, and puzzled: Who is addressing these orders to him?[47] So God picks up the conversation and identifies Himself: "I am the God of your father, the God of Abraham, the God of Isaac, and the God of Jacob."[48] Only then, when he realizes before whom he stands, does Moses hide his face, for fear of looking upon God.[49]

The view that Moses initially failed to recognize his interlocutor as God assumes more imaginative form in midrashic exegesis:

> [God] revealed Himself to him in the voice of Amram, his father, so he would not be afraid. Moses then rejoiced, saying, "Amram my father is alive." The Holy One (blessed be He) then said to him: "You said I am your father, but I am, in fact, the *God* of your father." Then, "Moses hid his face, etc."[50]

When this midrashic passage has Moses say, "Amram my father is alive," the reference is apparently to what he was saying inwardly, while standing alone in puzzled silence. But other versions seem to be reconstructing an ellipsis: "Moses said, 'Amram, my father!'"[51] In either case, the motivating crux is the iterated quotation formula.

* * *

We turn now to a more detailed consideration of a midrashic passage that appears to be based on scriptural use of iterated quota-

---

[47] In Gen 46:2–3, Jacob responds to a similar call ("Jacob, Jacob!") identically ("Here I am"). He too does so before his interlocutor has identified Himself. But in that case there is no cause for a puzzled pause because God identifies Himself immediately—before delivering the substance of His message.

[48] Cf. 1 Sam 3:1–10, where the theme of the prophetic novice who does not, initially, recognize the voice addressing him as God's is spelled out explicitly.

[49] Compare the way in which Saul's response to David's second argument in 1 Sam 17:7 (discussed above) calls attention to its new element, which now leads him to see things differently.

[50] *Midrash Tanḥuma, Shemot,* no. 16 (S. Buber ed., 2:5a–b). The midrashic springboard here is the puzzling "God of your father" (as opposed to "God of your fathers"); see R. Baḥya ben Asher, *Be'ur 'al ha-Torah* (ed. C. B. Chavel; 3 vols.; Jerusalem: Mosad ha-Rav Kuk, 1966–1968), 2:26, who also notes the similarity to the story of Samuel's first prophecy.

[51] *Yalquṭ Shim'oni, Shemot,* no. 168/171 (D. Hyman and Y. Shiloni ed., 1:50). Cf. *Exod. Rab.* 3 (A. Shinan ed., 119f.).

tion formulae. This well-known passage tells how Moses came to
"stand in the breach" and save Israel when they had sinned with
the golden calf:

וידבר יי' אל משה לך רד, מאי לך רד? אמר רבי אלעזר, אמר לו הקדוש ברוך
הוא למשה: משה, רד מגדולתך! כלום נתתי לך גדולה אלא בשביל ישראל,
ועכשיו ישראל חטאו - אתה למה לי? מיד תשש כחו של משה ולא היה לו
כח לדבר. וכיון שאמר: הרף ממני ואשמידם, אמר משה: דבר זה תלוי בי - מיד
עמד ונתחזק בתפלה ובקש רחמים. משל, למלך שכעס על בנו והיה מכהו מכה
גדולה, והיה אוהבו יושב לפניו ומתירא לומר לו דבר. אמר המלך: אלמלא
אוהבי זה שיושב לפני הרנתיך! אמר: דבר זה תלוי בי - מיד עמד והצילו.

"And the LORD said to Moses, 'Go, get down'" (Exod 32:7). What is
[the sense of], "Go, get down"? Said Rabbi El'azar: "The Holy One
(blessed be He) said to Moses, 'Moses, get down from your greatness!
Did I grant you greatness on any account but Israel? Now Israel has
sinned, what use are you to me?' Straightaway Moses' strength ebbed
and he was rendered speechless. But when [God] said, 'Let me be
that I may destroy them,' (Deut 9:14), Moses said [to himself], 'This
thing depends on me.' Straightaway, he fortified himself in prayer and
begged mercy [for them]. This may be compared to a king who became
angry with his son and was beating him badly. The king's friend was
sitting before him, afraid to say anything to him. The king said [to
his son]: 'Were it not for this friend of mine, sitting before me, I would
kill you.' [The king's friend] said [to himself]: 'This thing depends on
me.' Straightaway, he rose up and rescued him."[52]

The exegesis is, by midrashic standards, straightforward. Moses has
been told only to "get down," not what to do once he gets there.
So R. El'azar takes "Go, get down" to be the core of the message:
Moses' elevation (atop a mountain, or, traditionally, in Heaven) symbolizes his spiritual rank. God's order, "Go, get down," which seems
harsh and abrupt in tone, is taken to be a demotion, not just a
directive to get down and address the crisis at hand. The explanatory clause that follows, "for your people have acted corruptly"
(though not explicitly cited), is understood as God's explanation for
the demotion: "Did I grant you greatness on any account but Israel?
Now Israel has sinned, what use are you to me?"[53] On the other
hand, God's request, "Let me be that I may destroy them," signals

---

[52] *b. Ber.* 32a.
[53] See, e.g., *Exod. Rab.* 42:2. As noted by Yiṣḥaq Heinemann, this interpretation

to a stunned Moses that the people's fate nevertheless remains in his hands.

The detail relevant to our subject is Moses' reaction to this demotion: "Straightaway Moses' strength ebbed, and he was rendered speechless." For, it apparently derives from an iterated quotation formula.

Exodus 32:7–11 reads as follows:

וידבר יהוה אל משה לך רד כי שחת עמך העלית מארץ מצרים: סרו מהר
מן הדרך אשר צויתם עשו להם עגל מסכה וישתחוו לו ויזבחו לו ויאמרו אלה
אלהיך ישראל אשר העלוך מארץ מצרים: ויאמר יהוה אל משה ראיתי את
העם הזה והנה עם קשה ערף הוא: ועתה הניחה לי ויחר אפי בהם ואכלם
ואעשה אותך לגוי גדול: ויחל משה את פני יהוה אלהיו ויאמר למה יהוה יחרה
אפך בעמך . . .?

And the LORD said to Moses, "Go, get down; for your people whom you brought up from the land of Egypt have acted corruptly. They have turned away quickly from the way I commanded them, making for themselves a molten calf, worshiping it, sacrificing to it, and saying, 'These are your gods, O Israel, who have brought you up out of the land of Egypt!'" And the LORD said to Moses, "I have seen this people, and behold, it is a stiffnecked people. Let Me alone, then, that My wrath may burn hot against them, and I may consume them; and I will make of you a great nation." And Moses implored the LORD his God and said, "LORD, why does Your wrath burn hot against Your people . . .?"

God's initial speech is introduced by the formula, "And the LORD said to Moses." The formula is then repeated though God is still the speaker. This indicates that after God's initial speech, He paused; it was Moses' turn to reply. But Moses had been reduced to silence by God's words: once told, "Now Israel has sinned, what use are you to Me?" what is there left to say?[54] So God (who wants Moses

---

of לך רד should be seen in the context of a broader aggadic tendency to interpret spatial/locational terms symbolically (*Darkei ha-Aggadah* [Jerusalem: Magnes, 1970], 120f.).

[54] On the plain sense, Moses' silence reflects the fact that he is stunned to hear of his people's descent into idolatry and by the rough language with which God delivers the news. See, e.g., Ḥakham, *Sefer Shemot*, 2:293; Leibowitz, *Studies in Shemot*, 2:563. The explanation of Shiloaḥ ("Va-Yomer," 258) is not adequate.

to come to Israel's defense) picks up the conversation again, hinting broadly that the "matter depends upon" him.[55]

It is striking that this very device also appears in the parallel passage in Deut 9:12–14!

ויאמר יהוה אלי קום רד מהר מזה כי שחת עמך אשר הוצאת ממצרים סרו
מהר מן הדרך אשר צויתם עשו להם מסכה: ויאמר יהוה אלי לאמר ראיתי את
העם הזה והנה עם קשה ערף הוא: הרף ממני ואשמידם ואמחה את שמם מתחת
השמים ואעשה אותך לגוי עצום ורב ממנו.

And the LORD said to me, "Get up, go down quickly from here, for your people whom you have brought out of Egypt have acted corruptly. They have turned away quickly from the way I commanded them, and have made a molten idol for themselves." And the LORD said this to me: "I have seen this people, and it is indeed a stiff-necked people. Let me be that I may destroy them and blot out their name from under heaven. And I will make of you a nation, stronger and more numerous than they."

It is these iterated quotation formulae that stand behind the conclusion that, "Moses' strength ebbed and he was rendered speechless."[56] But an intriguing problem remains: in our talmudic passage לך רד (from Exod 32:7) strikes Moses dumb, but הרף ממני (from Deut 9:14) spurs him to action—Why the sudden jump from Exodus to Deuteronomy? Why not stay within a single passage and cite ועתה הניחה לי (from Exod 32:10) as spurring Moses to action?[57]

---

[55] Naḥmanides' *Commentary on the Torah* extends this theme to Num 17:10 (where we do not, however, have an iterated quotation formula).

[56] Some allusion to scriptural support may be suggested by the word *miyyad* (straightaway), which often indicates a return from midrashic elaboration to some element in the biblical text itself; see *Midrash Bereshit Rabba* (ed. Ch. Albeck and J. Theodor; 3 vols.; 1965; repr., Jerusalem: Shalem Books, 1996), 3:30 (*Mavo'*). But I would not press this point.

That our text derives Moses' silence from the iterated quotation formula is noted by Leibowitz, *Studies in Shemot*, 2:563. It is interesting, however, that what is, for us, the critical point (that Moses was "unable to speak") is not spelled out in all the manuscript versions. Thus Florence II I 9–7 and Paris 671 say only that "Moses' strength ebbed" and do not say explicitly, "he was rendered speechless"!

[57] The problem is not the citation of הרף ממני *per se*. It seems quite interchangeable with הניחה לי and is in fact mentioned in *Sifre Devarim, Va-Etḥanan*, no. 27 (L. Finkelstein ed., 2:41f.) as providing Moses with "an opening" to pray for Israel. The problem is rather the unexpected leap from the Exodus account to the Deuteronomy account in a single passage.

The answer may lie in the sequel:

ועתה הניחה לי ויחר אפי בהם ואכלם ואעשה אותך לגוי גדול וגו' – אמר
רבי אבהו: אלמלא מקרא כתוב אי אפשר לאומרו מלמד, שתפסו משה
להקדוש ברוך הוא כאדם שהוא תופס את חבירו בבגדו, ואמר לפניו: רבונו
של עולם, אין אני מניחך עד שתמחול ותסלח להם.

"And now let me alone that I may become angry with them and
destroy them. And I will make of you a great nation, etc." (Exod.
32:10). Said Rabbi Abbahu: "Were it not inscribed in Scripture, it
would be impossible to say: This teaches [us] that Moses took hold of
the Holy One (blessed be He) like a person who takes hold of his fellow by his garment and said to Him: 'Master of the Universe, I am
not letting go of you till you pardon and forgive them.'"[58]

Here, ועתה הניחה לי, precisely the phrase from Exodus we expected
in the previous section, is used to derive the opposite picture: far
from being paralyzed, Moses is stirred to action so assertive as to
strain theological decorum![59] On this reading, we may imagine the
following: God tells Moses לך רד, etc. and breaks for Moses to comply. Moses does not. Instead, he "takes hold of God" and demands
that He forgive Israel. So God says: הניחה לי. This is, of course, a
far more imaginative reading of the iterated quotation formula than
the first. But the pattern it assumes (A orders B to act and pauses
for compliance; B silently refuses to comply; A responds to this
refusal) is not without biblical parallel.

Consider Lot, confronted by the men of Sodom, refusing to yield
up his guests to them (Gen 19:9):

ויאמרו גש הלאה ויאמרו האחד בא לגור וישפט שפוט עתה נרע לך מהם
ויפצרו באיש בלוט מאד ויגשו לשבר הדלת.

---

[58] b. Ber. 32a.

[59] See Moshe Halbertal, "Ilmalei Miqra Katuv Iy Efshar le-Omero," Tarbiz 68
(1998): 39–59, esp. 54. As noted by Halbertal, the formula, "Were it not inscribed
in Scripture, it would be impossible to say," is used to justify bold, anthropomorphic dicta that appear to transgress the appropriate relationship between man and
God. But one sometimes detects a touch of humor as well. For, the original audience of these aggadot must have been amused by the claim that these bold teachings are written black on white in familiar verses, when they would not have dreamed
of finding them there. Indeed, in our case the reading used by R. Abbahu is declared
self-evidently ludicrous in the passage from Exod. Rab. 42:9, cited below.

They said: "Step aside." <u>And they said</u>, "This fellow came to sojourn and wants to play the judge! Now we will deal worse with you than with them." Then they pressed hard against the man Lot and approached to break down the door.

The Sodomites order Lot to step aside and wait a moment for him to comply. Lot silently stands his ground. Infuriated, they resume their speech with sarcasm and threat.

Our talmudic passage, in its present state, may, therefore, represent a reconciliation of two originally conflicting traditions about Moses' reaction to לך רד. A purer form of the first tradition is preserved in the following passage:

... ועתה הניחה לי ויחר אפי בהם ואכלם, וכי משה היה תופש בהקב״ה
שהוא אומר הניחה לי אלא למה״ד למלך שכעס על בנו והכניסו לקיטון
ומחיל לבקש להכותו והיה המלך מצעק מן הקיטון הניחה לי שאכנו, והיה פדנוג
עומד בחוץ אמר הפדנוג המלך ובנו לפנים בקיטון למה הוא אומר הניחה
לי אלא מפני שהמלך מבקש שאלך ואפיסנו על בנו, לכך הוא מצעק הניחה לי,
כך אמר הקב״ה למשה ועתה הניחה לי אמר משה מפני שהקב״ה רוצה שאפיס
על ישראל, לפיכך הוא אומר ועתה הניחה לי, מיד התחיל לבקש עליהם רחמים
הוי ויחל משה את פני ה' אלהיו.

"... Now let me alone that I may become angry with them and destroy them" (Exod 32:10). *But was Moses holding on to God, that he should say, "Let me alone"?* This may rather be compared to a king who became angry with his son, brought him into the bed-chamber, and wanted to strike him. The king was shouting from the bed-chamber, "Let me strike him!" as the [son's] pedagogue stood outside. The pedagogue said [to himself]: "The king and his son are [alone] in the bed-chamber; why then does he say, 'Let me alone'? Only because the king wants me to go and propitiate him regarding his son does he shout, 'Let me alone.'" Similarly, [when] the Holy One (blessed be He) said to Moses, "And now let me alone," Moses said, "It is because the Holy One (blessed be He) wants me to go and propitiate for Israel that he says, "Let me alone." Straightaway he began to seek mercy for them, and thus: "Moses besought the LORD his God" (Exod. 32:11).[60]

Here, the notion that ועתה הניחה לי implies that Moses "took hold of" God is dismissed as patently absurd![61] Though the element of

---

[60] *Exod. Rab.* 42:9.

[61] The same rhetorical question is found in *Sifre Devarim, Va-Ethanan*, no. 27 (Finkelstein, 2:41f.) with regard to הרף ממני: "Now was Moses really holding on to the Holy One?!"

Moses' paralysis is not stressed here, he is clearly seen as unable to speak until given an opening. The parable is clearly a variation on R. El'azar's. And the words that spur Moses to action are ועתה הניחה לי (from Exodus), just as expected.

Our talmudic passage may represent an attempt to reconcile and join the two traditions: Moses was indeed paralyzed by God's demotion. The signal, by which God spurred him to action, was הרף ממני ("Let me alone") from Deut 9:14. But once mobilized, Moses' defense of Israel was fierce. God then asked him to let go with ועתה הניחה לי from Exod 32:10, tempting him with his own great nation.[62]

Abraham ibn Ezra, the prototypical *pashṭan*, cites ועתה הניחה לי and הרף ממני as a manifest example of Scripture saying the same thing in different words.[63] Some of the rabbinic sources seem to share this view. But midrashic method postulates Scripture's verbal economy, presumes differences to be significant, and allows for the construction of a narrative sequence from the details of disparate passages. It thus opens the door for a composite reading that differentiates between slightly different details in parallel passages.[64]

The originator of our composite narrative may have been the "editor" of the larger aggadic unit to which it belongs.[65] We may imagine that he had before him two conflicting readings: that of R. El'azar, which, in its original form, traced a path from לך רד directly to ועתה הניחה לי (seen as encouragement to a dumb-struck Moses) and the conflicting reading of ועתה הניחה לי of R. Abbahu (who sees it as temptation to an aggressive Moses to abandon his defense). The editor then reconciled and merged these two accounts by changing the initial ועתה הניחה לי to הרף ממני—thus establishing a composite narrative.

---

[62] Cf. R. Samuel Edels, *Hiddushei Aggadot Maharsha, ad loc.* (standard editions of the Talmud). The sequel in the Talmud turns quite naturally, at this point, to Moses' explanation for declining God's offer of a great nation that will replace Israel.

[63] Abraham ibn Ezra, *Yesod Mora*, 1:7 in *Yalquṭ Ibn Ezra* (ed. I. Levine; New York: Israel Matz Hebrew Classics and I. Edward Kiev Library Foundation, 1985), 379.

[64] An interesting example is the differentiation of לך רד (in Exodus) from קום רד מהר מזה (in Deuteronomy) in *Exod. Rab.* 41:7; cf. *Deut. Rab.* 3:11.

[65] On the incorporation of pre-existing (Palestinian and Babylonian) aggadic units in the Babylonian Talmud, see S. Friedman, "La-Aggadah ha-Historit ba-Talmud ha-Bavli" in *Saul Lieberman Memorial Volume* (New York: Jewish Theological Seminary of America, 1993), 119–64 (with bibliography). On this particular unit, see Abraham Weiss, *'Al ha-Yeṣirah ha-Sifrutit shel ha-Amoraim* (New York: Yeshiva University Press, 1961), 251–56, who terms it a מסכת הפילה.

This question, in part, turns on a textual issue; for there is a manuscript tradition that has R. El'azar (not R. Abbahu) as the author of the second tradition as well.[66] On this reading it is R. El'azar himself who distinguished the Exodus and Deuteronomy accounts, creating a single narrative, which takes Moses from stunned immobility to unrelenting intercession.

There is, in any case, evidence for a tradition that took Moses' response to the order לך רד to have been assertive from the start. Happily, its formulation uses an iterated quotation formula of its own, this time featuring God as the silent party:

לך רד בזעף... אותה שעה ראה משה למלאכי השרת שהם עומדים ומבקשים
לצאת ולחבל כל ישראל. אמר משה אם מניח אני את ישראל וארד אין
להם תקומה לעולם, איני זז מכאן עד שאבקש עליהם רחמים. מיד התחיל
מלמד עליהם סניגוריא, אמר להקב״ה יש לי זכות ללמד עליהם. אמר לו
רבון העולם הזכר להם כשבקשת ליתן תורה לבני עשו ולא קבלוה וישראל
קבלוה... אמר הקב״ה עברו... אמר לו הזכר להם כשהלכתי בשליחותך
למצרים ואמרתי להם שמך, מיד האמינו.

"Go, get down" [was said] angrily.... Moses then noticed the ministering angels seeking to go out and injure all Israel. Moses said [to himself]: "If I abandon Israel and go down, their fall will be irreversible; I won't budge from here, without seeking mercy for them." Straightaway, he began to advocate in their behalf. He said to the Holy One (blessed be He): "I have arguments in their defense." He said to Him: "Master of the Universe, remember in their behalf that when you sought to give the Torah to the sons of Esau and they declined, Israel accepted...." The Holy One (blessed be He) said: "They violated...." He said to him: "Remember, in their behalf, that when I went on your mission to Egypt and told them your name, they immediately believed...."[67]

---

[66] The reading of the Vilna edition, "R. Abbahu," is found also in Florence II I 9–7 and the Soncino edition of 1484. On the other hand, Paris 671 and Munich 95 read "R. El'azar." Oxford Opp. Add. fol. 23 (366) has no name, which suggests that it continues the previous material cited in the name of R. El'azar; see further Raphael Rabbinovicz, *Diqduqe Soferim, Berakhot* (Munich: H. Roesl, E. Huber, 1867), ad loc. (1:85 n. 100). The formula אלמלא מקרא כתוב אי אפשר לאומרו is often linked with R. Abbahu elsewhere in the Babylonian Talmud; see Halbertal, "Ilmalei Miqra Katuv," 39 n. 2. The reading "R. El'azar" accords with the pattern of the larger aggadic unit, which is structured around a sequence of R. El'azar traditions; see Weiss, *'Al ha-Yeṣirah*, 253 and n. 17.

[67] *Exod. Rab.* 42:1.

Moses ordered by God, לֵךְ רֵד, fears that if he complies without
praying for Israel, they are doomed. His first words to God, "I have
arguments in their defense," seeks His sufferance to stay and speak.
But it is met with stony silence. Moses, not to be deterred, launches
into his defense anyway and succeeds in drawing God into debate.
(This pattern—A speaks; B reacts with stony silence; A, persisting,
resumes his speech—is precisely the one we saw above in Num
32:1–7.) In short, Moses' immediate reaction to לֵךְ רֵד was to disobey and mount a vigorous defense, precisely what we have posited
as the second tradition, in its pure form.

                              *   *   *

Midrashic interpretation of iterated quotation formulae seems not to
argue explicitly from the iteration, or even identify it.[68] It rather
assumes that one knows how this pattern is supposed to work. That
was a reasonable assumption since, as we have seen, iterated quotation formulae were very much part of the repertoire of contemporary literary devices. They may well have worked in conjunction
with a reading (or oral-recitation) tradition that paused a bit before
the second quotation formula, thus helping to evoke the pause that
the narrative wants to represent. This tradition gradually died out
in the post-talmudic period: it is not used in original writing and is
sometimes misunderstood in the talmudic manuscript tradition. Its
demise may have resulted from the decline of orality and the ascen-
dancy of a reading culture.[69]

---

[68] What *is* sometimes identified and said to require explanation, is a doubling in
the language of a quotation formula without *any* intervening speech; see, e.g., *Lev.
Rab.* 26:8 (M. Margulies ed., 608–11).

[69] We hear of an oral tradition of Talmud study that preserves nuances of recitation not captured in writing still alive in the Babylonian academies of the Geonim.
Thus, R. Aaron Sarjado (mid-tenth century) reports that his entire college has it
on tradition that a certain clause is recited with the inflection of a rhetorical question; see *Oṣar ha-Ge'onim, Yevamot* (ed. B. M. Lewin; 13 vols.; 1928–1944; repr.,
Jerusalem: H. Vagshal, 1984), no. 170, p. 71, cited in Robert Brody's summary of
his very important research on this subject in *The Geonim of Babylonia and the Shaping
of Medieval Jewish Culture* (New Haven: Yale University Press, 1998), 156–61. For
further discussion and bibliography on the role of oral vs. written transmission of the
classical rabbinic sources, see Yaakov Elman, "Orality and the Transmission of Tosefta
Pisḥa in Talmudic Literature," in *Introducing Tosefta: Textual, Intratextual, and Intertextual
Studies* (ed. H. Fox and T. Meacham; Hoboken, N.J.: KTAV, 1999), 123–80.

MOSES AND THE COMMANDMENTS:
CAN HERMENEUTICS, HISTORY, AND RHETORIC BE DISENTANGLED?

Steven D. Fraade

I. The Book of Moses

What precisely was the nature and extent of Moses' intermediary role in the transmission of the divine commandments to Israel at Mt. Sinai and thereafter, and in the creation of the written record (Torah) of that communication? This question has perplexed biblical interpreters from Scripture's very origins until the present.[1] The account of the revelation at Mt. Sinai is famously ambiguous as to which commandments were directly communicated to the Israelites by God, and which only via Moses at God's instruction, either then or subsequently in the Tent of Meeting.[2] From the perspective of

---

[1] I have dealt previously with rabbinic understandings of revelation, including its mediated nature, in the following publications: *From Tradition to Commentary: Torah and Its Interpretation in the Midrash Sifre to Deuteronomy* (Albany: State University of New York Press, 1991), 25–68; "Rabbinic Views on the Practice of Targum, and Multilingualism in the Jewish Galilee of the Third-Sixth Centuries," in *The Galilee in Late Antiquity* (ed. L. I. Levine; New York: The Jewish Theological Seminary of America, 1992), 253–86; "'The Kisses of His Mouth': Intimacy and Intermediacy as Performative Aspects of a Midrash Commentary," in *Textual Reasonings: Jewish Philosophy and Text Study at the End of the Twentieth Century* (ed. P. Ochs and N. Levene; London: SCM, 2002), 52–56.

[2] For example, does the change from first to third person speech with respect to God after Exod 20:6 (that is, following the second commandment by Jewish reckoning) denote a change in the speaker from God to Moses? What is the relation of what was communicated to Moses during his first forty-day sojourn on Mt. Sinai (Exod 24:3–18; before the incident of the Golden Calf) to that which was communicated to him during his second forty-day sojourn on Mt. Sinai (34:27–28; after the Golden Calf)? The Book of Deuteronomy assumes that only the Decalogue was delivered to the people at Sinai, the rest having been conveyed to Moses at Sinai but not delivered by him to the people until they reached the land of Moab and prepared to enter the promised land. See Deut 5:19, 28; 6:1; 10:4. This is in contrast to Exod 24:3–8; 35:1, 4; Lev 7:38; 25:1; 26:46; 27:34. According to the Book of Numbers (26:3; 33:50; 35:1; 36:13) the instructions for a census, dividing the land, conquest of the land, and designation of the Levitical cities of refuge were not communicated until the covenant at Moab. For continuing revelation after Sinai,

biblical tradition, to what extent was Moses' intermediary role required from the beginning by the impossibility of an ongoing direct encounter between God and ordinary humans, or only as a concession to the people's fear of engaging the divine presence directly?[3] To what extent did Moses record the divine commandments immediately, as if by divine dictation, or only subsequently from his memory and/or in his own words?[4] To what extent is the book that comes to be called the Torah (Pentateuch) the direct product of the divine revelation at Mt. Sinai or the cumulative record of Moses' ongoing intermediary activity up to (or even beyond) his death?[5] Put differently, when biblical writers refer to Moses' having commanded the people, is that simply shorthand for God's having commanded the people through Moses?[6] Or, when later the biblical writers speak of the Torah as the "Torah of Moses," or the "Book of Moses," or the "Book of the Torah of Moses," in what sense is he assumed to have been its "author," and if he is not, what degree of editorial and/or transmissional credit is he being given?[7] In sum, was Moses' media-

---

as interpreted in rabbinic literature, the following is still useful for its collection of sources: Bernard J. Bamberger, "Revelations of Torah after Sinai," *HUCA* 16 (1941): 97–113.

[3] See Exod 3:6; 19:21; 20:15–18 (18–21); 33:18–20; Deut 5:5, 20–24.

[4] As the "author" of the Temple Scroll is well aware (and seeks to rectify), the Book of Deuteronomy is particularly problematic in this regard, since it presents itself narratively as Moses' own retelling of what previously transpired and was previously divinely commanded (in the preceding three books of the Pentateuch), even where Deuteronomic commandments are previously absent or different. Hence, the Temple Scroll's transformation of Moses' third person references to God's commandments into God's own first person commanding voice can be understood as a way of asserting that Moses spoke the word of God. See Moshe Weinfeld, "God versus Moses in the Temple Scroll," *RevQ* 15 (1991): 175–80. See below, n. 27.

[5] What does it mean (Deut 31:24) that Moses wrote "the words of this Torah on a scroll to their very end" if the last eight verses of Deuteronomy follow his death? The problem of the "authorship" of these final eight verses of Torah following Moses' death is acknowledged by *Sifre Deut.* 357 (Finkelstein ed., 427–28); *b. B. Meṣ'ia* 15a (*baraita*); *b. Menaḥ.* 30a (*baraita*); where several solutions are proposed. Cf. Philo, *Mos.* 2.291. Note also the talmudic discussion (*b. Giṭ.* 60a, with Rashi) of whether Moses wrote the Torah "scroll by scroll" in chronological progression, or all at once shortly before his death.

[6] For the former, see Exod 16:24; Lev 9:5, 21; and especially Deut 33:4: "Moses commanded us [the] Torah." Similarly, Josh 1:13; 8:31, 33, 35; 11:12; 22:2, 5; 2 Kgs 18:12; 21:8; 1 Chr 6:34; 15:15; 2 Chr 8:13. The expression "I [Moses] have commanded (מצוה)" appears some thirty-seven times in the Book of Deuteronomy, whereas it is used only once in Deuteronomy with God as the third person subject (26:16), and once in the Tetrateuch with God as the first person subject (Exod 34:11). For God's commanding "through Moses" (ביד משה) see Exod 35:29; Lev 8:36; Num 4:49; 15:23; 27:23; 36:13; Josh 14:2; 21:2, 8; Neh 9:14.

tive role in the transmission of the commandments to the people a purely passive, conductive one, or did he have a more active, transformative role in the process of translating the commandments from divine source to human targets? These are questions that are not simply answered by the scriptural text itself, opaque and multivalent as it is, and therefore of necessity demand the efforts of scriptural

---

[7] For the first, see Josh 8:32; 1 Kgs 2:3; 2 Kgs 23:25; Mal 3:22; Dan 9:11, 13; Ezra 3:2; 7:6; 2 Chr 23:18; 30:16; for the second, see Ezra 6:18; Neh 13:1; 2 Chr 25:4; 35:12; for the third, see Josh 8:31; 23:6; 2 Kgs 14:6; Neh 8:1. These expressions presumably arise under the influence of the Book of Deuteronomy. It is in the Book of Deuteronomy that the word "Torah" first refers to something more than the discrete "torah" or teaching on a specific subject or of a specific group, presumably now to the Book of Deuteronomy (or some antecedent) as a whole. See Deut 1:5; 4:8, 44; 17:18, 19; 27:3, 8, 26; 28:58, 61; 29:20, 28; 30:10; 31:9, 11, 12, 24, 26; 32:46; 33:4. Of these, the following stress the written nature of the Torah in a book (scroll): Deut 17:18; 28:58, 61; 29:20; 30:10; 31:9, 24, 26. On the developing nature of the conception of Torah within the Hebrew Bible see: Mordechai Cogan, "On the Borderline between Biblical Criticism and Hebrew Linguistics: The Emergence of the Term ספר משה," in *Tehillah le-Moshe: Biblical and Judaic Studies in Honor of Moshe Greenberg* (ed. M. Cogan, B. L. Eichler, and J. H. Tigay; Winona Lake, Ind.: Eisenbrauns, 1997), 37*–43* [Hebrew]; Michael Fishbane, "תורה" in אנציקלופדיה מקראית (Jerusalem: Bialik Institute, 1982), 8:469–83; Moshe Greenberg, "Three Conceptions of the Torah in Hebrew Scriptures," in *Die Hebräische Bibel und ihre zweifache Nachgeschichte: Festschrift für Rolf Rendtorff zum 65. Geburstag* (ed. E. Blum et al.; Neukirchen-Vluyn: Neukirchener, 1990), 365–78; repr. in *Studies in the Bible and Jewish Thought* (Philadelphia: Jewish Publication Society, 1995), 11–24; James L. Kugel, "Rise of Scripture," in J. L. Kugel and R. A. Greer, *Early Biblical Interpretation* (Philadelphia: Westminster, 1986), 13–26; Barnabas Lindars, "Torah in Deuteronomy," in *Words and Meanings* (ed. P. Ackroyd and B. Lindars; Cambridge: Cambridge University Press, 1968), 117–36; Hindy Najman, "Torah of Moses: Reading Interpretation and Authority," in "Authoritative Writing and Interpretation: A Study in the History of Scripture" (Ph.D. diss., Harvard University, 1998), 75–118; Jacob Neusner, "From Scroll to Symbol: The Meaning of the Word Torah," in *Formative Judaism: Religious, Historical, and Literary Studies: Third Series: Torah, Pharisees, and Rabbis* (Chico, Calif.: Scholars Press, 1983), 35–57. Note the brilliant way in which Philo of Alexandria cuts through these questions by unambiguously positing Moses as the writer of the Pentateuch, after having had his purified soul "engraved," like the tablets of the Ten Commandments, by the divine logos at Sinai. For an excellent account of Philo in this regard, see David Dawson, *Allegorical Readers and Cultural Revision in Ancient Alexandria* (Berkeley: University of California Press, 1992), 110–12. See also below, n. 43. Most recently, see Najman, "The Divine Moses and His Natural Law: Philo on Authority and Interpretation," in "Authoritative Writing," 179–231. In the Dead Sea Scrolls: for the "Torah of Moses," see 1QS V, 8; VIII, 22; CD XV, 2–9, 12; XVI, 2, 5; 4Q266 (4QDᵃ) 11 6; for "commanded by the hand of Moses," see 1QS VIII, 15; 1QM X, 6; 1QH XVII, 12; 4Q504 (4QDibHamᵃ) V, 14; for "by the hand of Moses and the prophets," see 1QS I, 3; CD V, 21; for the "Book of Moses," see 4Q174 (4QFlor) 1 I, 2; 4QMMT C 10, 17, 21; 4Q247 1 verso; for "Moses said," see CD V, 8; VIII, 14 (= XIX, 26). For the New Testament, see below, n. 45.

interpretation, already inner-biblically, but more ambitiously post-biblically. As we shall see, the nature of Moses' intermediary role was of significance to post-biblical interpreters not just for their under-standing of Scripture, but also for their self-understanding as scrip-tural interpreters.

II. THE MEKILTAS

Although the question of Moses' intermediary role in revelation comes up frequently, albeit often only implicitly, in post-biblical literature of Second Temple and early rabbinic times,[8] I wish to focus here on a parallel pair of early midrashic texts that comment on one locus of this larger question and which have not received the atten-tion they deserve, in part because they have been previously mis-understood and mistranslated. The passages, from the two Mekiltas, comment on Exod 19:9a in a section describing Moses' shuttle diplo-macy in preparing the people for the revelation: "And the LORD said to Moses, 'I will come to you in a thick cloud, in order that the people may hear when I speak with you and so trust you ever after'" (NJPS). This verse appears immediately after Moses conveys to the people "all that the LORD had commanded him" (19:7), the people unanimously respond, "All that the LORD has spoken we will do!" (19:8a), and Moses relays the people's words back to God (19:8b). Exod 19:9b would appear to reiterate 19:8b: "Then Moses reported the people's words to the LORD." Thus, it might be midrashically assumed that Exod 19:9a refers to yet another communication, not explicitly quoted in the biblical text as we have it, supplementary to the preceding exchange, that results in the people's trust in Moses for ever after.[9] What specifically did God say to Moses in the peo-ple's hearing that would elicit not only their assent but their con-tinuous confidence in a human intermediary?

---

[8] For Philo and the Temple Scroll, see above, nn. 4, 5, 7. Similarly worth con-sidering in this context is the Book of *Jubilees*, in which it is emphasized that Moses, while on Mt. Sinai, writes what is dictated to him by an angelic intermediary from heavenly tablets. See Hindy Najman, "Interpretation as Primordial Writing: Jubilees and its Authority Conferring Strategies," *JSJ* 30 (1999): 379–410. For aspects of this issue in other early rabbinic texts, see my earlier publications cited in n. 1.

[9] Similarly, the *Mekilta* to Exod 19:9b presents multiple other views of what this "missing" communication might have been. Of course, modern critical Bible schol-

Mekilta of R. Ishmael Baḥodesh 2 (henceforth, MRI):[10]

"In order that the people may hear when I speak with you": R. Judah [bar Ilai] says: From whence can you say that the Holy One, blessed be he, said to Moses, "Behold, I will say something to you, and you will challenge me (מחזירני), and I will accede (מודה) to you, in order that Israel will say, 'Great is Moses, for God acceded to him'?" As it is said, "And also trust in you for ever."[11] Rabbi [Judah the Patriarch]

---

arship, not sharing these midrashic assumptions, must interpret the seeming disjunctiveness of Exod 19:9 in literary terms, whether compositional or redactional. Thus, Nahum Sarna explains 19b as follows: "This phrase refers not to the immediate antecedent but to the quote in verse 8. It is an instance of resumptive repetition, a literary device in which the text, following a digression, reconnects with an earlier text" (*Exodus* [JPS Torah Commentary; Philadelphia: Jewish Publication Society, 1991], 105). Similarly, U. Cassuto, *A Commentary on the Book of Exodus* (Jerusalem: Magnes, 1982), 157–58 [Hebrew]. For more on such repetitive resumption (or *Wiederaufnahme*, as it is commonly termed) in biblical narrative, see Bernard M. Levinson, *Deuteronomy and the Hermeneutics of Legal Innovation* (Oxford: Oxford University Press, 1997), 17–20; Shemaryahu Talmon, "The Presentation of Synchroneity and Simultaneity in Biblical Narrative," in *Studies in Hebrew Narrative Art Throughout the Ages* (ed. J. Heinemann and S. Werses; ScrHier 27; Jerusalem: Magnes, 1978), 9–26. On the literary structure of the Sinaitic narrative more generally, see Baruch J. Schwartz, "The Priestly Account of the Theophany and Lawgiving at Sinai," in *Texts, Temples, and Traditions: A Tribute to Menahem Haran* (ed. M. V. Fox et al.; Winona Lake, Ind.: Eisenbrauns, 1996), 103–34; Benjamin D. Sommer, "Revelation at Sinai in the Hebrew Bible and in Jewish Theology," *JR* 79 (1999): 422–51; Arie Toeg, *Lawgiving at Sinai: The Course of Development of the Traditions Bearing on the Lawgiving at Sinai within the Pentateuch, with a Special Emphasis on the Emergence of the Literary Complex in Exodus xix–xxiv* (Jerusalem: Magnes, 1977 [Hebrew]).

[10] Lauterbach ed., 2:207–8; Horovitz-Rabin ed., 210. Except where noted, manuscript variations are inconsequential to the meaning. The translation that follows is my own.

[11] This prooftext, but not "from whence can you say," is absent in the best textual witnesses, MSS Oxford, Munich, Vatican 299, and the first printing (Constantinople, 1515), but included in modern critical editions, which rely here on the late *Midrash Ḥakhamim. Yal. Shim'oni* omits "as it is said" but has the prooftext. The parallel in MRSBY (below) has neither "from whence can you say" nor the prooftext. A later reiteration of R. Judah's statement in MRI (see below, n. 21), has "from whence can you say," but no prooftext according to all the witnesses, including a Cairo Geniza fragment (MS St. Petersburg Antonin 957). Thus, on text-critical grounds, it is most likely that the prooftext was not original to the Mekilta. The question "from whence can you say" without a concluding prooftext is anomalous. Perhaps the text once read "from here" (מכאן, but written as מכן), which could easily have been mistaken by a scribe for "from whence" (מנין), which subsequently required the addition of a prooftext. Alternatively, and I think preferably, the following interpretation attributed to Rabbi [Judah the Patriarch] (through the citation of Exod 19:20) may not be original to our text, but an insertion made at a later stage of editing. For this possibility, evidenced elsewhere, see Menahem Kahana, "'Marginal Annotations' of the School of Rabbi in the Halachic Midrashim" in *Studies in the Bible and Talmud: Papers Delivered at the Departmental Symposia in Honour of*

says: We need not make Moses great, if, in order to do so, we cause the Holy One, blessed be he, to reverse himself and his word (שחזר ובדברו בו).[12] Rather, this teaches that God said to Moses, "Behold, I will call to you from the top of the mountain and you will ascend," as it is said, "And the LORD called Moses to the top of the Mountain and Moses went up" (Exod 19:20). "And also trust in you forever": Also in you, also in the prophets who will in the future arise after you.

Mekilta of R. Shimᶜon bar Yoḥai 19:9 (henceforth, MRSBY):[13]

"In order that the people may hear when I speak with you": Rabbi Judah [bar Ilai] says: The Holy One, blessed be he, said to Moses, "Behold I will say something to you and you will challenge me (משיבני), and behold I will retract (חוזר) and accede (מודה) to your words." Rabbi [Judah the Patriarch] says: It was not because of the honor of Moses that God acceded to his words, rather this is what he said to him: "The commandments which I gave to you at Marah, behold I will again teach (חוזר ושונה) them to you here [at Sinai]." It does not say, "which the LORD commanded," but, "which the LORD commanded him" (Exod 19:7). This teaches that one who hears from your [Moses'] mouth is as one who hears from the mouth of the Holy One, and not [just] from your mouth, but from the mouth of elders who in the future will come after you and from the mouth of the prophets. Therefore it is said, "And also trust in you for ever."

---

the Sixtieth Anniversary of the Institute of Jewish Studies (ed. S. Japhet; Jerusalem: Hebrew University, Institute of Jewish Studies, 1987), 69–86 [Hebrew]. If so, then in the original version of the text, the subsequent citation of Exod 19:9b would have been the direct answer to "from whence can you say," before being commented upon itself. Its not being preceded by "as it is said" is not a problem since this word is often absent in the best witnesses to tannaitic midrashim. The version in MRSBY (below) and the later attestations of MRI would be based on the later editing of MRI but would have smoothed out the text by either removing "from whence can you say" (MRSBY) or adding a prooftext before Rabbi's statement (later attestations of MRI). Notwithstanding this possibility, I treat Rabbi's statement as part of MRI and MRSBY (except MRSBY Exod 9:23, where it is lacking) as it appears in all of our extant witnesses.

[12] This is the reading in MS Oxford and the first printing (Constantinople, 1515), adopted by Lauterbach. Horovitz-Rabin has שחזר בו בדבורו, which is the reading in *Yal. Shimᶜoni*. MS Munich, has שחזר בו ובדבריו. In any case, the meaning is the same: God changed his mind and retracted his previous words.

[13] Epstein-Melamed ed., 140. The translation that follows is my own. On the relation between MRI and MRSBY, especially with regard to their narrative exegeses, see Menahem I. Kahana, *The Two Mekhiltot on the Amalek Portion: The Originality of the Version of the Mekhilta d'Rabbi Ishmaᶜel with Respect to the Mekhilta of Rabbi Shimᶜon ben Yoḥay* (Jerusalem: Magnes, 1999), 15–32 [Hebrew]. Kahana demonstrates the overall dependency of MRSBY on MRI.

Although there are significant differences of wording and substance between these two texts, in both, the interpretation of R. Judah bar Ilai (ca. 150 c.e.) is stunning. According to him, God stages a rabbinic-style halakhic dispute with Moses in the hearing of the whole people, in which Moses challenges God's articulation (whether outrightly refuting or simply correcting is not clear), whereupon God retracts and accepts instead Moses' alternative formulation.[14] Others have rendered Rabbi Judah b. Ilai's interpretation more weakly, but the wording of R. Judah b. Ilai's representation of the dialogue in MRSBY (הריני חוזר ומודה לדבריך), and the force of R. Judah the Patriarch's objection in both texts and his wording according to MRI (שחזר בו ובדברו), make the stronger reading inevitable: in response to Moses' objection, God immediately retracts his original formulation and accepts Moses' alternative.[15] All of this is done in Israel's hearing so that they will, *in the future and for all time* (לעולם), have confidence in Moses as the divinely authorized transmitter of the

---

[14] For the verb חזר (especially חזר ב-) denoting a sage's retracting of his halakhic opinion in favor of another, see, for example *m. Hor.* 1:2: הורו בית דין וידעו שטעו וחזרו בהן: "If a court gave a decision, which they [later] realized was wrong, and they retracted. . . ." See also *m. 'Ed.* 1:12, 13, 14; 5:6, 7. The force of the *hiphʿil* of חזר in this context would be, literally, to cause to retract, or, as I have translated, to challenge. Similarly, the use of *hiphʿil* form מודה to denote acceding to another's halakhic opinion is common in rabbinic legal disputes. See, for example, *m. 'Ed.* 2:6, 8; 3:9; 4:2, 6; 5:1, 4. For this understanding of MRI, see the commentary *Merkevet Hammishneh* (R. Moses David Ashkenazi; Lvov, 1895) *ad loc.*, who relates R. Judah b. Ilai's interpretation to the view of R. Jose in *b. Šabb.* 87a, that Moses added on his own an extra day to the two days commanded by God for the men to separate from their wives in preparation for the revelation at Sinai (on which see below, n. 31). Whatever the imagined content of their exchange, my point is that the language employed by the *Mekilta* is intended to represent a halakhic dispute and not simply a one-time disagreement over what needed to be done in preparation for the revelation. This is further supported by the interpretation of Exod 19:7 in MRSBY as referring to commandments in general, which may be read as a continuation of R. Judah b. Ilai's interpretation after R. Judah the Patriarch's interruption (see above, n. 11). For the broader motif of the praiseworthiness of God's acceding to human objections, see MRI *Baḥodesh* 9 (Lauterbach ed., 2:271; Horovitz-Rabin ed., 237); *Sifre Deut.* 176 (Finkelstein ed., 221); *Sifre Num.* 134 (Horovitz ed., 177–78); *Midr. Tanna'im* Deut. 18:17 (Hoffmann ed., 111); *'Abot R. Nat.* A37, B40 (Schechter ed., 112).

[15] Compare Lauterbach's translation of MRI (2:207–8), "I will be saying something and you shall answer Me, and I will then agree with you"; and a recent translation of MRSBY as cited in S. Y. Agnon's *'Atem Re'item*: "I will say something to you, you will answer Me, then I will acknowledge your answer" (*Present at Sinai: The Giving of the Law. Commentaries selected by S. Y. Agnon* [trans. M. Swirsky; Philadelphia: Jewish Publication Society, 1994], 125). These make it sound as though

commandments, not simply as unthinking stenographer, but, as it were, as contributor to revelation, with advance divine approval. In exegetical terms, R. Judah b. Ilai understands Exod 19:9a to mean that what was communicated between God and Moses in the public hearing must have had an effect on the people's trust that would transcend the present moment.

In both Mekiltas, R. Judah b. Ilai's interpretation is too audacious for R. Judah the Patriarch (ca. 200 C.E.), who according to MRI objects to building up Moses at God's expense.[16] However, the two texts attribute entirely different alternative interpretations to R. Judah the Patriarch and yet another one elsewhere in MRI (see below). According to MRI, Rabbi Judah the Patriarch understands Exod 19:9 to refer to the people's hearing of God's calling Moses to ascend the mountain. They thereby will know that when Moses disappears into the cloud at the top of the mountain he will be in direct communication with God, even though they will not be able to witness it directly.[17] According to MRSBY, Rabbi Judah the Patriarch argues that what the people hear is God's repeating to Moses of the presinaitic commandments previously issued at Marah, but which now need to be repeated in the presence of all the people in order to be formally included in the Sinaitic covenant.[18]

Both MRI and MRSBY end by interpreting Exod 19:9b to refer not only to the people's trust in Moses, but also to their trust in his successor prophets (MRI) or elders and prophets (MRSBY). This is based on the interpretation of the unnecessary Hebrew word בם

God is testing Moses for his correct understanding of what God had previously said, rather than Moses' questioning of the correctness of God's previous words. See previous note. Louis Ginzberg, in condensing and paraphrasing MRSBY, leaves R. Judah b. Ilai's interpretation out entirely and gives R. Judah the Patriarch's (unattributed) interpretation alone (not as a rebuttal): "God hereupon said to Moses: 'I will come to thee in a thick cloud and repeat to thee the commandments that I gave thee on Marah, so that what thou tellest them may seem as important as what they hear from Me. But not only in thee shall they have faith, but also in the prophets and sages that will come after thee'" (*Legends of the Jews* [trans. P. Radin and H. Szold; 7 vols.; Philadelphia: Jewish Publication Society, 1968], 3:87).

[16] For the possibility of R. Judah the Patriarch's statement being an insertion here, see above, n. 11.

[17] *Midrash Leqaḥ Tob* (Buber ed., 64b) and *Midrash Sekel Tob* (Buber ed., 340) give this interpretation alone, unattributed, for Exod 19:9.

[18] For the giving of commandments to Israel at Marah, see also the view attributed to Rabbi (Judah the Patriarch) in MRI *Baḥodeš* 3 (Lauterbacked ed., 2:211; Horovitz-Rabin ed., 211). See also *b. Sanh.* 56b (*baraita*); Ginzberg, *Legends*, 3:39–40, 47; 6:15 (n. 83), 18–19 (n. 129).

("also") as a term of inclusion (*ribbui*).[19] MRSBY derives this as well from the preceding words of Exod 19:7, where the pronominal suffix of "commanded him" (צוהו) is, strictly speaking, redundant. Rather, it comes to specify that Moses communicates to the elders (and they to the people) what was commanded to him directly by God. The elders and prophets stand in relation to Moses as Moses stands in relation to God, and those who receive commandments from the elders and prophets should regard them *as if* received from the mouth of God. The order of elders and prophets in MRSBY is reminiscent of their identical order in the "chain of tradition" of *m. 'Abot* 1:1, and is thereby suggestive of the full line of Mosaic descendents in that chain down to and including the rabbinic sages of the Mekiltas' textual community.[20]

Both MRI and MRSBY cite R. Judah b. Ilai's interpretation again in their commentaries to Exod 19:23, but in MRI with yet another contrary interpretation attributed to R. Judah the Patriarch.[21] In Exod 19:21, God tells Moses to go down to warn the people not to break through to the mountain. But in 19:23, Moses reminds God that he had previously warned the people not to approach the mountain, in accord with God's previous instruction to him in 19:12, therefore making God's latest instruction unnecessary. MRI interprets 19:23 so as to have Moses say, "I have already warned them

---

[19] The word לעלם ("forever") might also have suggested Moses' successors. The explicit repetition of the word גם in MRI makes clear that it is the primary basis of the inclusive interpretation.

[20] According to *m. 'Abot*, second temple and rabbinic links in that chain both transmit and contribute to the words of Torah they receive. Compare *Sifre Deut.* 41 to Deut 11:13 (Finkelstein ed., 86), where biblical elders are similarly authorizing antecedents to rabbinic sages, treated by me in *From Tradition to Commentary*, 79–83, 234–36 nn. 33–47; as well as the partial parallel in *t. Soṭah* 7:9–12. On the association of biblical elders with rabbinic sages, see *From Tradition to Commentary*, 75–79, 233–34 nn. 27–31. Note that MRI *Baḥodesh* 2 (Lauterbach ed., 2:206; Horovitz-Rabin ed., 209) interprets Exod 19:7 ("and Moses came and summoned the elders of the people") to mean: "This teaches that Moses shared his glory (status) with the elders." *Tgs. Geniza, Fragment, Neofiti* and *Samaritan* to Exod 19:7 all have "sages" (חכמים) for "elders."

[21] MRI *Baḥodesh* 4 (Lauterbach ed., 2:226; Horovitz-Rabin ed., 217–18); MRSBY 19:23 (Epstein-Melamed ed., 145). However, note that in MRI MS Oxford, "another interpretation" (abbreviated, ד״א) appears in place of "Rabbi says." However, this may simply be a scribal error for "Rabbi says" (abbreviated, ר״א), as is evidenced elsewhere. See Kahana, "'Marginal Annotations,'" 81. Note that MS Vatican 299 and a Cairo Geniza fragment (St. Petersburg Antonin 957) have ר׳ אומ׳.

and set boundaries for them." To this God responds abruptly, "Go, descend" (19:24), which MRI interprets as, "You have spoken well," meaning that Moses was right in telling God that there was no need to warn the people again. We are next told that this is the sort of exchange to which R. Judah b. Ilai referred previously. It is clear from this that MRI understands R. Judah b. Ilai's interpretation to refer, as I previously argued, to Moses' challenging of God's instruction and to God's acceding to Moses' objection.[22]

Once again, according to MRI, R. Judah the Patriarch objects to R. Judah b. Ilai's elevating of Moses at God's expense, arguing instead that it was necessary for God to repeat his warning: "One should warn a person at the time of instruction and warn him at the time of execution." MRSBY omits here any mention of R. Judah the Patriarch's objection to R. Judah b. Ilai's interpretation. Thus, in three places R. Judah the Patriarch denies the possibility of a dispute, even if staged, between God and Moses in the context of Sinaitic revelation and interprets the biblical grounds for such a dispute in ways that affirm Moses' role as passive recipient and transmitter of God's words/commandments.

Did Moses as prophetic lawgiver play an intellectually active and independent role in the transmission of the commandments or was he rather a passive transmitter to Israel of the divine commandments communicated to him? The Mekiltas never resolve the differences of interpretation between the two R. Judahs, setting them, rather, alongside one another without favoring outrightly either (with the exception of MRSBY to Exod 19:23). R. Judah b. Ilai's interpretation has the advantage of remaining constant and generalizable, whereas R. Judah the Patriarch's objections and three alternative interpretations are tailored to each scriptural application. Nevertheless, the views of the two R. Judahs remain in dialectical suspension within our present texts.[23] The scene of Moses and God engaged in dis-

---

[22] See above, nn. 14, 15. For the same understanding, see the commentary *Zayit Ra'anan* to *Yal. Shim'oni Yitro* 285 (n. 49).

[23] Compare David Weiss Halivni's sketching of maximalist and nonmaximalist rabbinic views of how much of Torah was directly revealed at Sinai: *Peshat & Derash: Plain and Applied Meaning in Rabbinic Exegesis* (New York: Oxford University Press, 1991), 112–19. If my suggestion (see above, n. 11) that R. Judah the Patriarch's view is an editorial insertion to the *Mekilta* is correct, then this dialectical suspension would be the product of a secondary level of editorial construction.

pute is mirrored in, and thereby lends authority to, the narrative frame of the interpretive dispute between the two R. Judahs, two of the most distinguished successors in the revelatory chain of tradition extending back through the prophets and elders to Moses. However, there is one crucial difference: whereas, according to R. Judah b. Ilai, God quickly retracts and accedes to Moses' correction, according to the final framers of the Mekiltas, the rabbinic dispute remains open-ended.

III. Related Tannaitic Texts

R. Judah the Patriarch would presumably not have been the only early sage to take issue with the strong interpretation of R. Judah b. Ilai. In fact, it runs counter to a frequent theme in early rabbinic texts, which asserts the faithful and absolute accuracy with which Moses transmitted and recorded God's commands. For example, elsewhere in the *Mekilta*'s commentary to the giving of the Torah at Sinai it makes this very point:

> "Thus (כה) shall you say" (Exod 19:3): "Thus," in the holy language; "thus," in this order; "thus," in this manner; "thus," that you should not subtract and not add.[24]
> "These are the words" (Exod 19:6): That you should not subtract and not add. "That you shall speak to the children of Israel": In this order . . . "All these words" (19:7): The first, first and the last, last.[25]

Similarly, in commenting on Exod 19:15, where Moses instructs the people (men) to separate from the women in preparation for the theophany, an instruction which is not explicitly given to him by God, the *Mekilta* raises the possibility that perhaps Moses added to God's command. As MRSBY rhetorically asks, "Is it possible that

---

[24] MRI *Baḥodesh* 2 (Lauterbach ed., 2:201; Horovitz-Rabin ed., 206, with note for parallels). The same is found, in even more detail, in MRSBY ad loc. (Epstein-Melamed ed., 138). That the Torah is not to be altered by addition or subtraction derives from Deut 4:2; 13:1 (12:32 LXX). Josephus frequently denies having done so (although he does plenty of both): *Ant.* 1.17; 2.234; 4.196–198; 10.218; 20.261; cf. *Ant.* 9.242; 12.109; 14.2–3; *C. Ap.* 1.42. For discussion of this topos, see *Flavius Josephus: Translation and Commentary. Volume 3: Judean Antiquities 1–4* (trans. and commentary by L. Feldman; ed. S. Mason; Leiden: Brill, 2000), 7–8. Compare Philo, *Spec.* 4.143; *Let. Aris.* 311.
[25] MRI *Baḥodesh* 2 (Lauterbach ed., 2:206; Horovitz-Rabin ed., 209). Similarly, in even more detail, in MRSBY ad loc. (Epstein-Melamed ed., 139, 140).

Moses said this on his own (מפי עצמו)?" Rather, according to both
Mekiltas, Moses correctly inferred from God's words, "Let them be
ready for the third day" (19:11), that separation from wives is intended.
Moses added nothing that could not have been inferred from God's
own words.[26] The tannaitic midrashim, especially to Deuteronomy,
frequently attribute to Moses the following assurance to the people:
"I do not say this to you of my own (מעצמי), but from the mouth
of the Holy One I say this to you."[27]

This possibility, that Moses might have altered or added to the
commandments in transmitting them to the people, is strikingly raised
and rejected in two other tannaitic midrashim:

> "And I besought the LORD at that time, saying" (Deut 3:23): . . . Moses
> said to the Holy One, blessed be he: "Master of the universe, let any
> transgression that I have committed be recorded against me, so that
> people will not say, 'Moses seems to have falsified (זייף) the Torah,'
> or 'said something that had not been [divinely] commanded.'"[28]
>
> "For he has spurned the word of the LORD" (Num 15:31): . . . One
> who says, "All of the Torah I accept as binding except for this thing/
> commandment," is what is meant by "for he has spurned the word
> of the LORD." One who says, "All of the torah is from the mouth of
> the Holy One, but this thing/commandment Moses said on his own
> (מפי עצמו)," is what is meant by "for he has spurned the word of the
> LORD."[29]

---

[26] MRI *Baḥodesh* 3 (Lauterbach ed., 2:216–17; Horovitz-Rabin ed., 213–14);
MRSBY 19:15 (Epstein-Melamed ed., 142). Note as well *Sifre Num.* 103 (Horovitz
ed., 101), where Moses' own separation from his wife is said to have been at God's
express command, whereas in later sources this is said to have been at Moses' own
(commendable) initiative. Cf. *Tg. Ps.-Jon.* Num 12:8; Rashi Num 12:8. Cf. below,
n. 32.

[27] *Sifra Shemini pereq* 1:8 (Weiss ed., 47a); *Sifre Deut.* 5, 9, 19, 25 (Finkelstein ed.,
13, 16, 31, 35); *Midr. Tanna'im* Deut 1:6; 1:9; 1:20; 1:29 (Hoffmann ed., 5, 6, 11,
12). This is particularly apt for the Book of Deuteronomy since it might appear to
contain Moses' own commandments to the people. See Finkelstein ed., 13, note ad
loc. See above, n. 4.

[28] *Sifre Deut.* 26 (Finkelstein ed., 36). For treatment of this passage in its larger
textual context, see my article, "Sifre Deuteronomy 26 (ad Deut 3:23): How Conscious
the Composition?" *HUCA* 54 (1983): 245–301. Note the parallel in the *Mekilta to
Deuteronomy* (ed. M. Kahana, *Tarbiz* 54 [1985]: 518).

[29] *Sifre Num.* 112 (Horovitz ed., 121). A similar *baraita* is given in *b. Sanh.* 99a,
but extends the argument to one who says all of the Torah is from heaven, except
for particular rules derived from Scripture by rabbinic hermeneutical rules. For
other rabbinic texts that show an awareness of critiques of Moses' trustworthiness,
see *Sifre Deut.* 5, 102 (Finkelstein ed., 13, 161); *b. Ḥul.* 60b. See also Josephus, *C.
Ap.* 2.25, 145, 161–162, with remarks of Louis H. Feldman, *Jew and Gentile in the
Ancient World* (Princeton: Princeton University Press, 1993), 142.

While these two passages strongly deny and condemn the view that Moses either falsified or fabricated commandments on his own, it would appear they do so in polemical recognition of those who made such claims. Who such people might have been, and how the previously examined tradition of R. Judah b. Ilai might have related to them, is a subject to which I will return in due course.

IV. Moses Takes the Halakhic Lead (with God's Approval)

Later rabbinic texts specify and celebrate specific acts or rules initiated by Moses on his own, but to which God immediately agrees. These begin with a *baraita* appearing twice in the Babylonian Talmud: "It is taught: Moses did three things of his own mind (מדעתו) and the Holy One, blessed be he, agreed with him: He added a day of his own mind, he separated from his wife, and he broke the tablets."[30] The *gemara* next explains Moses' own exegetical reasoning for each of the things he did, usually by applying a hermeneutical rule of logic to one or more scriptural verses of divine command in order to derive a new understanding. Space only allows me here to summarize each of these, without going into the various exegetical arguments:

(1) In Exod 19:10 God tells Moses to have the people purify themselves "today and tomorrow" in preparation for the theophany, while in 19:15 Moses "adds a day," telling them to "be ready for the third day," to which God accedes in 19:11, therefore not allowing his *shekhinah* to descend to their midst until after three days.[31]

(2) Although the Israelites were told to return to conjugal relations after completion of the revelation (Deut 5:27), Moses applies an *a fortiori* argument to himself, whereby he concludes that he must continue to remain separate from his wife ever hence, to which God accedes (Deut 5:28).[32]

---

[30] I translate from *b. Šabb.* 87a. Similarly in *b. Yebam.* 62a, but with differences in wording and order. Note in particular the latter's: והסכים דעתו לדעה המקום, "and his mind agreed with the mind of God."

[31] See *b. Šabb.* 87a (*baraita*); *b. Yebam.* 62a (*baraita*); *'Abot R. Nat.* A2, B2; *Pirqe R. El.* 41; פסיקתא חדתא לחג השבועות (in Jellinek, *Bet ha-Midrash*, 6:41).

[32] See *b. Šabb.* 87a (*baraita*); *b. Yebam.* 62a (*baraita*); *Exod. Rab.* 19:3 (but note

(3) Upon witnessing Israel's apostasy with the Golden Calf, Moses applies another *a fortiori* argument that leads him to break the first set of tablets with the Ten Commandments, even though not told to do so by God. But God approves of his act after the fact (Exod 34:1).[33]

Later midrashic collections add other Mosaic initiatives to this list, variously grouping them:

(4) Moses applies hermeneutical logic to conclude that he should not enter the Tent of Meeting until called upon to do so by God, to which God agrees (Lev 1:1).[34]

(5) Following the Golden Calf incident, Moses convinces God to address Israel as "I am the LORD your (pl.) God," instead of "I am the LORD your (sing.) God" as in the Decalogue (Exod 20:2), so that they would know that he was addressing all of them and not just Moses. Here (as in other such cases), God says to Moses: "You have taught me" (למדתני).[35]

(6) Whereas God, in listing his attributes of mercy, holds children culpable for the sins of their parents (Exod 34:7), Moses convinces God that this is unfair, causing him to revoke his own words and to establish Moses' in their place (Deut 24:16; 2 Kgs 14:6).[36]

(7) Although God commanded Moses to conquer Sihon the Amorite straight away (Deut 2:24–25), Moses instead sent messengers with an offer of peace (Deut 2:26; Num 21:21–22), contrary to God's instructions. However, Moses was able to convince God that seeking peace was a primordial value consistent with the

---

contrary views that God commanded him to do so; cf. above, n. 26); *'Abot R. Nat.* A2 (with contrary views), B2; *Pirqe R. El.* 46 (according to God's command). On Moses' abstinence from sexual relations with his wife, see also *Sifre Num.* 99 (Horovitz ed., 98). For further textual discussion, see Menahem Kister, *Studies in Avot de-Rabbi Nathan: Text, Redaction and Interpretation* (Jerusalem: Hebrew University, Department of Talmud; Yad Izhak Ben-Zvi, Institute for Research of Eretz Israel, 1998), 183.

[33] See *b. Šabb.* 87a (*baraita*); *b. Yebam.* 62a (*baraita*); *Exod. Rab.* 19:3; 46:3; *Deut. Rab.* 5:13; *'Abot R. Nat.* A2 (with contrary view that God commanded), B2; *Tanḥ. Shofetim* 19.

[34] *'Abot R. Nat.* A2, B2; *Exod. Rab.* 19:3; 46:3; but cf. *Sifra Achare Mot parashah* 1:6 (Weiss ed., 80a), according to which Moses is not limited from access to the Tent of Meeting.

[35] See *Num. Rab.* 19:33.

[36] See *Num. Rab.* 19:33; *Tanḥ. Shofetim* 19.

teachings of the Torah, causing God to institute Moses' practice as the law for all wars (Deut 20:10).[37]

All of these Mosaic innovations are generated by a seeming gap or
inconsistency in the biblical text. They all have Moses applying rabbinic hermeneutical rules and reasoning to scriptural/divine words
so as to determine his action independently (מדעתו, מעצמו) of, or
even in contradiction to, a previously articulated divine command.
In each case, Moses convinces God of the correctness of his action,
in some cases leading to new or changed divine imperatives. However, it should be noted that in some of the later texts, we hear
minority rabbinic counter-voices arguing that what might appear as
Moses' independent action or ruling is already implicit in God's command; that is, what might appear to be a Mosaic innovation is in
actuality not.

V. Korah's Rebellion

In contrast to the preceding traditions, other midrashim emphasize
that Korah's chief complaint against Moses, for which he was killed,
was that Moses had instituted commandments on his own, without
divine authorization. This is occasioned by the ambiguous scriptural
expression "And Korah took" (Num 16:1) as an expression of Korah's
rebellion,[38] immediately following God's command to Moses to instruct
the Israelites to make fringes on the corners of their garments, each
with a blue cord (15:37–38). In response to Korah and his followers, Moses states that if the rebels die an unusual death, "by this
you shall know that it was the LORD who sent me to do all these
things; that they are not of my own devising (מלבי)," but if not, "it
was not the LORD who sent me" (16:28–29).

---

[37] See *Num. Rab.* 19:33; *Deut. Rab.* 5:13 (Lieberman ed., 29–30); *Tanḥ. Ḥuqqat*
22 (Buber ed.); *Tanḥ. Devarim* supp. 10 (Buber ed.); *Tanḥ. Ḥuqqat* 51 (Buber ed.);
Tanḥ. Tzav 5 (Buber ed.). For an excellent analysis, see Adiel Schremer,
"הפרשנות העוקרת והעקירה המפורשת (פירוש רדיקלי לי׳אדם־הברית׳ של דוד הרטמן)"
in *Renewing Jewish Commitment: The Work and Thought of David Hartman* (ed. A. Sagi
and Z. Zohar; 2 vols.; Tel-Aviv: Hakibbutz Hameuchad & The Shalom Hartman
Institute, 2001), 2:759–63.
[38] Expressed in all of the targumim *ad loc.*, including *Tg. Onqelos, ad loc.* ואתפליג
קרה.

From these verses, rabbinic midrashim weave a rich set of narratives of how Korah (in some versions at his wife's urging) challenges Moses' commandment of the fringes, arguing the illogic of the commandment, that it was Moses' own invention, that Moses was not a prophet, and that the Torah was not from heaven. Thus, whereas the central theme of the biblical narrative is Korah's jealousy of Moses' and Aaron's holy, supreme position among the people, the midrashic tradition turns Korah into a heretical *epikorsi* (Epicurean) who challenges Moses' prophetic status and the divine origins of the commandments communicated and recorded by him. As one midrashic tradition has Korah say to Moses: "You were not commanded regarding these matters, but you invented them of your own design (מלבך)."[39] Or, "From his heart and of himself (מלבו ומעצמו) Moses said all of these things/commandments."[40] According to another version of the midrash, Korah and his band said:

> When the Ten Commandments were given to us, each and every one of us was nursed from Mt. Sinai, but we were only given the Ten Commandments, and we did not hear there about [laws of] *ḥallah*, nor of priestly offerings, nor of tithes, nor of fringes. Rather, you said these on your own (מעצמך) in order to give authority to yourself and honor to Aaron your brother.[11]

---

[39] *Num. Rab.* 18:3; *Tanḥ. Korah* 2; *Tanḥ. Korah* 4 (Buber ed.). These interpretations clearly play on מלבי of Num 16:28, taking the ambiguous "these things" to refer not simply to Moses' actions as commander in chief in the present crisis, but more broadly to his central role in the communication of the divine commandments.

[10] *Num. Rab.* 18:12; *Tanḥ. Korah* 22 (Buber ed.).

[11] *Yal. Shim'oni Korah* 752 (*Yelammedenu*). For other sources not mentioned in the preceding notes, see: *Tg. Ps.-J., Frg. Tg.* Num 16:1, 28; *y. Sanh.* 10(17):1 (27d–28a); *b. Sanh.* 110a; *Tanḥ. Korah* 5 (Buber ed.); *Tanḥ. Korah* supp. 1, 2 (Buber ed.); *'Ag. Esth.* 28a (Buber ed.); *Midr. Prov.* 11; *Midr. Haggadol* Num 16:1; *Leqaḥ Tob* Num 16:1; *Chron. Jerahmeel* 55:5 (trans. Gaster, 161). For a fuller treatment of rabbinic interpretations of Korah's rebellion, see Moshe Beer, "Korah's Revolt—Its Motives in the Aggadah," in *Studies in Aggadah, Targum and Jewish Liturgy in Memory of Joseph Heinemann* (ed. J. J. Petuchowski and E. Fleischer; Jerusalem: Magnes, 1981), 9*–33* [Hebrew]. These rabbinic understandings of Korah's rebellion find no direct mention in tannaitic midrashim. However, Philo already interprets the biblical episode as a challenge to the divine origins of the commandments, specifically that "there were spiteful rumours that he [Moses] had falsely invented the oracles" (*Mos.* 2.176–177 [Colson, LCL], 278; *Praem.* 78); and Pseudo-Philo (*L.A.B.* 16:1) has Korah rebel because of the burden of the command of the fringes. Cf. *L.A.B.* 25:13, where "the forsaken of the tribe of Benjamin" say: "We desired at this time to examine the book of the law, whether God had plainly written that which was therein, or whether Moses had taught it of himself." See Frederick J. Murphy, "Korah's

It is striking that these midrashic traditions employ much the same language (e.g. מלבו, מדעתו, מעצמו) in attributing to Korah the heresy of denying Moses' intermediary, divinely authorized role in the transmission of the commandments as do other midrashic traditions, in the same collections, in celebrating Moses' halakhic innovations and their winning of divine approval and adoption. The dialectical tension between the juxtaposed views of R. Judah b. Ilai and R. Judah the Patriarch in the texts of the Mekiltas with which we began continue through a long history of midrashic tradition, even as many new halakhic examples and narrative elaborations are added: Moses as a passive transmitter and recorder of divine commandments vs. Moses as an active participant and contestant in the process by which the commandments came to be and to become authoritative. One (late) midrashic text best sums up this ambivalence as follows:

> "And the LORD said to Moses: Write for yourself (כתב לך) these commandments": . . . Another explanation of "Write for yourself": The ministering angels began to say before the Holy One, blessed be he, "Have you given permission to Moses to write whatever he wants, so he may say to Israel, 'I gave you the Torah; it is I who wrote it and gave it to you'?" The Holy One, blessed be he, said to them, "Perish the thought, that Moses would do such a thing, and *even were he to do so*, he is to be trusted, as it is said, 'Not so my servant Moses; he is trusted throughout my household' (Num 12:7)."[42]

In short, Moses and, I will further argue, his human (rabbinic) successors are divinely authorized and trusted *both* to transmit and to transform received tradition.

Rebellion in Pseudo-Philo 16," in *Of Scribes and Scrolls: Studies on the Hebrew Bible, Intertestamental Judaism, and Christian Origins* (ed. H. W. Attridge, J. J. Collins, and T. H. Tobin; New York: University Press of America, 1990), 111–20. On the rebellion of Korah, see further Ginzberg, *Legends*, 6:100–102 n. 566.

[42] *Exod. Rab.* 47:9. The Soncino translation seriously mistranslates the last phrase before the prooftext as, "and in whatever he does he can be fully trusted." The Hebrew is: חס ושלום שמשה עושה את הדבר הזה ואפילו עושה נאמן הוא. That is, even if Moses were to take full credit for having written the Torah and given it to Israel, what he has written in the Torah is still reliable as divine revelation. For this understanding, see the commentaries of RaDaL (R. David Luria) and MaHaRZU (R. Ze'ev Wolf b. Israel Issar Einhorn) *ad loc.*: even if Moses writes something on his own, he does so prophetically in harmony with God's intent. See also A. Schremer, "הפרשנות העוקרת והעקירה המפורשת," 763 n. 51, who similarly sees here an attempt to ground rabbinic legal authority.

VI. THREE EXPLANATORY STRATEGIES

How are we to understand this deeply ambivalent record of rabbinic understandings of Moses' intermediary role in the communication of divine commandments to Israel? I shall heuristically posit
three vectors, which for purposes of simplification I shall refer to as
scriptural hermeneutic, historical polemic, and *performative rhetoric*.

As I sketched at the outset, the need to define Moses' mediative
role in revelation is abundantly supplied by the Hebrew Bible itself,
i.e., in the differing perspectives of the latter four books of the
Pentateuch, one from the other, as to what was communicated by
God to Moses and by Moses to the people, when and where, and
in the developing understandings of "Torah" as a written record of
revelation in the subsequent books of the Bible. Since others have
dealt with these matters extensively, I need not draw them out here.[43]
But for the rabbis, such macro issues are not what most immediately and rhetorically prompt midrashic responses so much as the
need to fill apparent gaps and resolve seeming redundancies, ambiguities, and inconsistencies at the micro level of the scriptural text
(even while the macro issues remain in broader interpretive play).
As we have repeatedly seen, both in the narrative account of the
revelation at Sinai and in the particular formulations of laws and
practices, this is the level at which scriptural difficulties generate, formally at least, the wealth of rabbinic interpretations that we have
surveyed. Of course, it is not the scriptural barbs alone that are
responsible for the generation of the midrashic solutions (otherwise
we should have seen many more such responses in pre-rabbinic,
Second Temple Jewish writings), but rather the meeting of discrete
scriptural stimuli and distinctive rabbinic "reading" practices, predicated as the latter are on rabbinic assumptions regarding the inter-
pretability of the divine words of Scripture. But while local textual
challenges and rabbinic exegetical practices are *necessary* for the generation of these rabbinic responses, they are not *sufficient* for understanding them in their dialectical plenitude nor in their historical
context. Scriptural exegesis is not a linear, mechanical process whose
course can be simply reversed back from midrashic interpretation to

---

[43] See above, n. 7.

its scriptural origins as if anesthetized from historical, social, and cultural intrusions along the way.

Can we identify parties, whether intramural or extramural, toward whom the midrashic arguments we have surveyed might have been polemically targeted, even if indirectly? For example, several midrashic texts that we examined, both early and late, presuppose the existence of a "heretical" claim that not all of the Torah was "from heaven" and that some of the commandments were Moses' own invention. This view is clearly evidenced in early Christian writings, already suggested in the New Testament. In Mark 10:2–9 Jesus argues that while Moses commanded/permitted divorce with a "certificate of dismissal," this had not been God's original intent when he joined together male and female at creation. It was only in response to the people's stubbornness that Moses "made this rule for you. . . . Therefore what *God* has joined together, *man* must not separate." In other words, the law of divorce could be understood to be Moses' own invention and not necessarily indicative of the divine will, and hence only a temporally-bound concession to human weakness.[44] Similarly, in Mark 7:1–13 Jesus argues against the Pharisees' "ancestral tradition" (*paradosis tōn presbyterōn*, literally, "teaching of the elders") on the grounds that the Pharisees give priority to such "ancestral tradition" over the Ten Commandments. "In this way by your tradition, handed down among you, you make God's word null and void."[45]

The fact that it is one of the Ten Commandments that is singled out for contrast with the "ancestral tradition" as an example of divine commandment versus humanly devised and transmitted tradition is telling. According to one mishnaic tradition, the Ten Commandments

---

[44] Note that in the parallel in Matt 19:3–9, Jesus argues this in response to a challenge from the Pharisees.

[45] In the parallel in Matt 15:1–9, the contrast is drawn even more sharply: "For God said . . . But you say. . . ." Of course, the contrast in these passages is not between Moses' word and God's word, but between the Pharisaic ancestral human tradition and the divine commands as communicated by Moses. Thus, where Mark (7:10) has "Moses said," Matthew (15:4) has "God said." Similarly, Mark 12:26 has "have you not read in the Book of Moses," whereas Matt 22:31 has "have you not read what was said to you by God." For New Testament passages that assume Moses' "authorship" of the "law" in a positive sense, see Luke 16:29, 31; John 1:17, 45; 5:46–47; 7:19, 22, 23. Compare Josephus's portrayal of the Sadducees' rejection of the Pharisaic extra-scriptural "ancestral tradition," for which the Pharisees claim divine approval: *Ant.* 13.297; 17.41.

had formerly been read daily as part of the liturgy in the second temple, and according to its talmudic elaboration, that practice was abolished so as not to strengthen the view of heretics (*minnim*), who would argue that "these alone were given to Moses at Sinai."[46] Whatever the historicity of this account, it testifies at least to the rhetorical possibility of claiming a unique *revelatory* status for the Decalogue. Whoever such *minnim* may have been, we know that there were early Christians who differentiated between the status of the Ten Commandments as divinely revealed and permanent and that of other commandments in the "Old Testament" as having been humanly devised and temporary. This view is most sharply expressed by a second-century Valentinian Christian teacher named Ptolemy (fl. 136–180, possibly in Rome) in his *Epistle to Flora*, which divides the laws of the Old Testament according to their authorship, and thereby, authority:

> Now, first you must learn that, as a whole, the law contained in the Pentateuch of Moses was not established by a single author, I mean not by god alone: rather, there are certain of its commandments that were established by human beings as well. Indeed, our savior's words teach us that the Pentateuch divides into three parts. For one division belongs to god himself and his legislations; while <another division> belongs to Moses—indeed, Moses ordained certain of the commandments not as god himself ordained through him, rather based upon his own thoughts about the matter; and yet a third division belongs to the elders of the people, <who> likewise in the beginning must have inserted certain of their own commandments. (33.4.1–2)[47]

---

[46] See *m. Tamid* 5:1; *y. Ber.* 1:8 (3c); *b. Ber.* 11b–12a. For a classic discussion, see Ephraim E. Urbach, "The Role of the Ten Commandments in Jewish Worship," in *The Ten Commandments in History and Tradition* (ed. B.-Z. Segal; Jerusalem: Magnes, 1990), 161–89; repr. in *Collected Writings in Jewish Studies* (ed. R. Brody and M. D. Herr; Jerusalem: Magnes, 1999), 289–317. For a more critical analysis, see Reuven Kimelman, "The Shema' and Its Rhetoric: The Case for the Shema' Being More than Creation, Revelation, and Redemption," *Journal of Jewish Thought and Philosophy* 2 (1992): 111–56, esp. 155–56; idem, "The Shema' Liturgy: From Covenant Ceremony to Coronation," in *Kenishta: Studies in the Synagogue World* (ed. J. Tabory; Ramat-Gan: Bar-Ilan University Press, 2001), 68–80.

[47] Translation is from Bentley Layton, *The Gnostic Scriptures* (New York: Doubleday, 1987), 309. The word "elders" translates the Greek *presbyteroi*. As Layton notes *ad loc.*: "Or 'presbyters.' Ptolemy refers here to the elders who were with Moses 'in the beginning.'" For the critical Greek text, see Gilles Quispel, ed., *Ptolémée, Lettre à Flora: Analyse, texte critique, traduction, commentaire et index grec* (2nd ed.; SC 24; Paris: Cerf, 1966), 54–57. For a discussion of Jewish hellenistic (and Jewish-Christian) antecedents to Ptolemy's division of the commandments, particularly in the writings of Philo, see Francis T. Fallon, "The Law in Philo and Ptolemy: A Note on the Letter to Flora," *VC* 30 (1976): 45–51.

The divine laws of the Pentateuch are themselves divided into three categories: The Ten Commandments alone are "pure legislation not interwoven with evil, which alone is properly called law, and which the savior did not come to abolish but to fulfill" (33.5.1); while other laws are either "interwoven with injustice" (the *lex talionis*), and abolished by "the savior as being incongruous with his own nature" (ibid.), or are "symbolic," that is, "allegorical" (ritual laws), whose "referent" the "savior changed . . . from the perceptible, visible level to the spiritual, invisible one" (33.5.2). For our purposes it is important to stress Ptolemy's assertion that the laws devised by Moses and the elders are contrary to the law of God (and rejected as such by Jesus).[48]

Given the near contemporaneity of Ptolemy and R. Judah b. Ilai (ca. 130–160 c.e.), and the degree to which their arguments would appear to mirror one another, it is tempting to imagine the latter responding to the former (or at least his ideas) in exegetical dispute: What if Moses altered or added to the directly revealed divine commands? He did so as a divinely pre-authorized agent of revelation, as did the elders who succeeded him! But there are problems with positing a Christian (or gnostic Christian) context for the origins of the midrashic traditions that we have examined. The most significant is chronological: the traditions we have examined, while reaching full bloom in late midrashic sources, are already well evidenced in tannaitic midrashic collections (generally thought to have been redacted in the mid- to late third century, but containing earlier materials).[49] Scholars who wish to demonstrate the direct influence of Christianity in the formation of distinctive aspects of rabbinic Judaism are on stronger grounds if those aspects only emerge when Christianity has

---

[48] For a similar, but somewhat later and less radical, early Christian formulation, see *Didascalia Apostolorum Syriacae* chap. 26 (trans. Vööbus [CSCO 408], 223–48), which differentiates between the Law, comprising the Ten Commandments and the Judgments (the *mishpatim* of Exod 21–23), which was given prior to the incident of the Golden Calf and is indissoluble, and the more burdensome "second legislation," the rest of the laws (especially dietary and sacrificial), which were given by God in anger after the Golden Calf and from which Christians are freed through baptism. According to some rabbinic traditions, Israel received the commandments directly from God before the Golden Calf incident, but only through mediation thereafter. See my "'The Kisses of His Mouth.'"

[49] On the dating of the *Mekilta*, see most recently Menahem Kahana, "The Critical Edition of *Mekhilta de-Rabbi Ishmael* in the Light of the Geniza Fragments," *Tarbiz* 55 (1986): 515–20 [Hebrew].

already ascended to imperial power after the Christianization of the
Roman Empire (mid-fourth century on).[50] Whether nascent Christianity already had such an influential presence in relation to rabbinic
Judaism in mid-second century to mid-third century Galilee is difficult
to tell, but certainly less likely. It is more likely that later Christian
writings give expression to ideas that might have earlier circulated
within Jewish society, or on its fringes. Furthermore, the very questions with which the early rabbinic traditions that we have examined deal—to what extent are laws divinely revealed, divinely inspired,
or the product of the human mind—were longstanding subjects of
interest among Greek Jewish writers, ancient pagan philosophers,
and pagan writers on Jews and Judaism, among whom Moses as the
Jewish "Lawgiver" was both acclaimed and debunked.[51]

Before being forced to choose between hermeneutical or historicist positivisms (as the choice is too often posed), we need to consider a third possibility: that these traditions are not so much about
the biblical past or contemporary extramural polemics as internal
rabbinic self-understandings of the privileged human role of the sage
in the performative enactment of Torah law and legal discourse as
part of a continual process of revelation from Sinai to the present
and beyond. This is suggested by the interpretation (apparently shared
by the two R. Judahs) of Exod 19:9, that whatever the content of
the dialogue between God and Moses, it was staged in the hearing
of all of Israel so that they would trust not only in Moses but in
the elders and prophets who would succeed him thenceforth and

---

[50] For this line of argument, see most recently Daniel Boyarin, *Dying for God:
Martyrdom and the Making of Christianity and Judaism* (Stanford: Stanford University
Press, 1999); Seth Schwartz, *Imperialism and Jewish Society, 200 B.C.E. to 640 C.E.*
(Princeton: Princeton University Press, 2001).

[51] See John J. Gager, *Moses in Greco-Roman Paganism* (Nashville: Abingdon, 1972),
25–112; Menahem Stern, *Greek and Latin Authors on Jews and Judaism* (3 vols.; Jerusalem:
Israel Academy of Sciences and Humanities, 1976), 1:32, in note to Hecataeus of
Abdera 6: "Among the Greeks there was much discussion regarding the origin of
the laws, i.e., whether they were divinely inspired or only products of the human
mind." For Ptolemy's possible (at least partial) dependence on Hellenistic Jewish
antecedents, see Fallon, "The Law in Philo and Ptolemy." For evidence from
Josephus, see above, n. 29. For antecedents in Pseudo-Philo (usually dated to early
first century C.E.), see above, n. 41. For Moses as lawgiver in a wide range of Jewish
and non-Jewish sources, see Wayne Meeks, *The Prophet-King: Moses Traditions and the
Johannine Christology* (NovTSup 14; Leiden: Brill, 1967), 107, 112–13, 130, 132–33,
171–72.

forever. In this context, it is R. Judah b. Ilai's interpretation (and similar, later rabbinic interpretations of specific Mosaic legal innovations) that is the more radical and in need of explanation: not so much that Moses reliably recorded and transmitted God's words, but that God acceded to Moses' rational arguments and legal innovations as a model for all times thenceforth. Students of rabbinic literature can easily bring to mind other texts in which similarly radical (yet also ambivalent) divine authorizations of rabbinic legal initiative are exegetically grounded in the words of Scripture and, in some cases, traced back to the biblical elders, even while narratively framed in the context of intramural rabbinic disputes.[52] Such texts are not simply etiological, in the sense of tracing claims of rabbinic interpretive authority back to Sinai. Rather, in dialogically drawing their own readers/students into such interpretive debate they are rhetorically performative and transformative in the here-and-now of their textual communities.

By now it should be clear that the three alternatives that I have set out here are really not alternatives at all but are deeply interconnected to, and inclusive of, one another.[53] If hermeneutics is an interpretive shuttle between a scriptural text and a scriptural community situated in a different historical and cultural setting, then hermeneutics cannot exist apart from having one foot planted in that setting. Likewise, if the most proximate historical context of any text is its own community of "readers," and if a text responds to and is shaped by extramural historical circumstances only via its dialogical engagement with, and transformation of, its intramural textual

---

[52] Examples that come to my mind, focusing on earlier rabbinic sources, are as follows: *Sifre Deut.* 154 (Finkelstein ed., 207, with note ad loc.), on Deut 17:11, concerning the (rabbinic) high court: "Even if they show you that right is left and left is right, obey them" (cf. *Song Rab.* 1:2[18]); *m. Roš Haš.* 2:9 (cf. *Sifra 'Emor* parashah 9:9, 10), interpreting Lev 23:4 to mean, "whether at their proper time or not at their proper time, I [God] have no other festivals than these," as set by the human (rabbinic) courts, extending the authority of the elders of Moses' time thenceforth; the much celebrated story of R. Eliezer and the "Oven of Aknai" in *b. B. Meṣʿia* 59b (*baraita*): "It is not in heaven. . . . After the majority must one incline." See also above, n. 20.

[53] For a more extensive discussion of these three "facings," see my *From Tradition to Commentary*, 13–18; as well as Richard S. Sarason, "Interpreting Rabbinic Biblical Interpretation: The Problem of Midrash, Again," in *Hesed Ve-Emet: Studies in Honor of Ernest S. Frerichs* (ed. J. Magness and S. Gitin; Atlanta: Scholars Press, 1998), 132–54, including discussion of other recent scholarship.

community, then the connection between that text and its historical context must run through its hermeneutical and rhetorical engagement with that community of readers, or in our case, students.

To conclude, in the words of Qohelet (4:12): החוט המשלש לא במהרה ינתק ("A threefold cord is not readily broken"). Rather than seeking in vain to isolate these three strands, we need to attend to the dynamic of their interplay.[54]

[54] An earlier version of this paper benefited from the critical responses of Richard Sarason and Derek Krueger at a session of the History and Literature of Early Rabbinic Judaism Section, Society of Biblical Literature Annual Meeting, November 25, 2002. Friends and colleagues contributed in ways large and small to its progress, especially when they criticized my interpretations: Rachel Anisfeld, Beth Berkowitz, Adela Yarbro Collins, Alon Goshen-Gottstein, Christine Hayes, Menahem Kahana, Ranon Katzoff, Bernard Levinson, Chaim Milikowsky, Adiel Schremer, and Aharon Shemesh.

THE *ALPHABET OF BEN SIRA* AND THE EARLY HISTORY OF PARODY IN JEWISH LITERATURE

David Stern

Parody may be the last virgin territory in the study of classical Hebrew literature, one of the few realms in Jewish literary tradition as yet unsullied by scholarly hands. The only monograph on the subject to this day remains Israel Davidson's 1907 doctoral dissertation, "Parody in Jewish Literature," and though the book is not without value, it hardly begins to scratch the surface of the subject. For one thing, its treatment of parody begins only with the twelfth century when, Davidson claims, "we first meet with parody in Jewish literature."[1] As we now know, this is not true. Parody in Jewish literature can be documented much earlier, possibly as early as the Rabbinic period, and certainly in the Geonic, as I hope to show in this article. Yet even in post-twelfth-century Jewish literary tradition, there have been few serious studies devoted to the topic. RAMBI, the database for scholarly publications in Jewish Studies, lists a grand total of 24 publications for "parody." Of these, eight are in the Bible (e.g. Jonah, Song of Songs); another eight in twentieth-century Jewish letters, mainly the usual suspects (e.g. Freud, Malamud, Agnon); and the remainder a hodge-podge of different topics. Only one publication is explicitly on a medieval Hebrew text and none is in post-biblical or Rabbinic Hebrew writing.

In this article I would like to help fill this deplorable hole in Jewish Studies by exploring one famously problematic text, the *Alphabet of Ben Sira*, which, as I intend to show, contains some of our earliest examples of clear-cut literary parody in classical Jewish literature; in the course of discussing the *Alphabet*, I also hope to suggest a few other candidates for the genre. I feel especially fortunate to be able to offer this small contribution to knowledge as a way of honoring my good friend and colleague, James Kugel. Jim, as we all know,

---

[1] Israel Davidson, "Parody in Jewish Literature" (Ph.D. diss., Columbia University, 1907), 3.

has probably done more than anyone else in our generation to further our understanding of Second Temple literature (including texts
like the Book of Ben Sira) and of the literary "afterlife" of biblical
and early postbiblical texts, namely, the later careers of their interpretations, elaborations, and extrapolations (as found in books like
the *Alphabet of Ben Sira*). On top of that, Jim is one of the few truly
witty scholars in Jewish Studies with a genuine appreciation of the
comic and the outrageous, and with a real feel for the scandalous
underbelly of classical Jewish tradition. For all these reasons, I can't
think of a more appropriate place than this volume in Jim's honor
to publish an article on the *Alphabet*, arguably, our earliest example
of Jewish scatology.

By literary parody, I mean specifically a literary work that "imitates the serious materials and manner of a particular literary work,
or the characteristic style of a particular author, or the stylistic and
other features of a serious literary form, and applies them to a lowly
or comically inappropriate subject."[2] As I will use the term in this
paper, I mean to distinguish this type of literary parody from a
merely "comic" or "humorous" story, on the one hand, and from
the highly stereotyped and moralistic narrative discourse that characterizes most other Rabbinic writing, on the other. As distinct from
these types, a literary parody requires the parodic work to be an
imitation of another recognizable and known literary work or genre
(whether transmitted in writing or orally), and it requires the parodic work to be a travesty of the work or genre parodied, that is, a
deliberately inappropriate and intentionally outrageous comic imita-

---

[2] Meyer H. Abrams, *A Glossary of Literary Terms* (5th ed.; New York: Holt Rhinehart
& Winston, 1988), 18. Clearly, the definition of literary terms is hardly absolute,
and their use essentially heuristic. It is, however, helpful to have a working definition
if only to differentiate the subject of this paper—what I call "literary parody"—
from merely humorous or satirical works. Abrams's definition of literary parody is
largely identical with "burlesque" which he defines

> as "an incongruous imitation"; that is, it imitates the matter or manner of a
> serious literary work or of a literary genre, but makes the imitation amusing
> by a ridiculous disparity between its form and style and its subject matter. The
> burlesque may be written for the sheer fun of it; usually, however, it is a form
> of *satire*. The butt of the satiric ridicule may be the particular work or gen-
> eral type that is being imitated, or (often) both of these together. (17)

Other terms associated with both parody and burlesque are "lampoon," "travesty,"
"mock-epic," or "mock-heroic." As we shall see, most of these terms could be
applied with justice to the *Alphabet of Ben Sira*.

tion—a presentation, for example, in which content and style not only clash but violate the very rules of generic decorum.

We do not know where the parodic tradition in classical Jewish literature actually begins. Like most things in classical Judaism and its culture, the roots of parody surely lie in the Bible,[3] but in the case of parody, the route from the biblical to the classical Jewish period is an obscure one. For different reasons, it is difficult to speak about parody in classical Rabbinic literature. This is not because the rabbis were humorless or because parody as a genre was considered too sacrilegious to be tolerated or preserved. Rather, the main difficulty we face in identifying literary parody in classical Jewish literature is methodological: on the one hand, parody is inherently a *literary* genre while so much of Rabbinic literature was composed and transmitted *orally*; on the other, what does remain of the earlier oral discourse in the written texts is often both so stereotyped and so fragmentary that it is difficult to identify the background against which the parody is projected.[4] The great Russian literary theorist and still one of the most perceptive writers on parody, Mikhail Bakhtin, once wrote that "in world literature there are probably many works whose

---

[3] For parody in the Bible, see Gale A. Yee, "The Anatomy of Biblical Parody: the Dirge Form in 2 Samuel 1 and Isaiah 14," *CBQ* 50 (1988): 565–86; Athalya Brenner, "'Come back, come back, the Shulammite' (Song of Songs 7:1–10): A Parody of the 'Wasf' Genre," in *On Humour and the Comic in the Hebrew Bible* (ed. Y. T. Radday and A. Brenner; Sheffield: Sheffield Academic, 1990), 251–75. Judges 5:28–30, from Deborah's victory song, is sometimes cited as well as a parody of the lament-form.

[4] On parody in Rabbinic literature, see Davidson's comments ("Parody in Jewish Literature," 1–2). For a good example of the problems in identifying whether or not a passage is parodic, see *Lev. Rab.* 12, an entire chapter devoted almost exclusively to the prohibition addressed to priests in Lev 10:9, "Drink no wine or other intoxicants [. . . when you enter the Tent of Meeting]"; as any reader of the chapter recognizes, the midrash tends to lurch, somewhat like the drunk father in 12:1, back and forth between praise and blame of wine (and drinking), without being able to make up its mind whether it is good or bad. In the final passage, the midrash cites the aggadot about Solomon who, it claims, never drank wine all seven years he was building the Temple until the night he completed the building when he married the daughter of Pharoah, overdrank, and then overslept, with the keys of the Temple under his pillow, thereby making it impossible for the Temple service to begin until his mother, Bathsheba, came into his bedroom and harangued him for oversleeping! As a further example of a possibly parodic passage, my colleague Yaakov Elbaum has called to my attention *Midr. Tehillim* 1:15 with Korah's complaint against Moses and Aaron. One should also mention here the examples cited by Saul Lieberman in *Midreshei Teiman* (2nd ed.; Jerusalem, Wahrmann, 1970), 26–32, which I discuss at length later in this essay.

parodic nature has not even been suspected."[5] This is especially true
of Rabbinic literature. Even so, one assumes that the rabbis, if they
did not actually *write* parodies, certainly engaged in the *activity* of
parody. The occasion in the Rabbinic calendar most appropriate for
such indulgences was, of course, Purim, and there are, in fact, sections of some midrashim on the Book of Esther, like *Midrash Abba
Gurion*, which contain identifiably parodic sections.[6] *Amat Di Itstalvu*,
the Aramaic lament-parody purportedly recited by Zeresh over
Haman, recently published by Yosef Yahalom and Michael Sokoloff,
is still another example of the types of parody that would have been
traditionally associated with Purim. These surviving texts are undoubtedly only a fraction of what once existed.[7]

As thin and fragmentary as this material may be, it is nonetheless the background against which texts like the *Alphabet of Ben Sira*
should be viewed. This text is one of the truly exceptional—that is
to say, both unusual and problematic—works in all classical Hebrew
literature. Since the beginning of its modern study, scholars have
been both scandalized and intrigued by its outrageousness. The seventeenth-century Christian Hebraist, Giulio Bartolocci, called it a book
full of "words of vanity and lies."[8] Jacob Reifmann, one of the first
modern Jewish scholars to deal with the text, wrote in 1873 that the
work is "full of nonsense and folly . . . and even abomination and
disgust," and "warranted being burned even on a Yom Kippur that
happened to coincide with the Sabbath."[9] Happily, it was not, and
thanks to the magisterial edition produced by Eli Yassif (already some
twenty years ago), it is now possible to resolve some of the difficulties

[5] Mikhail M. Bakhtin, *The Dialogic Imagination* (ed. M. Holquist; trans. C. Emerson
and M. Holquist; Austin: University of Texas Press, 1981), 374.

[6] For the text of *Midrash Abba Gurion*, see *Sifrei De-aggadeta ʿal Megillat Esther* (ed.
S. Buber; 1886; repr., Jerusalem: Vagshall: 1989), 1–57, and Buber's brief introductory notes; for parodic sections, see the beginning of chapters 1 and 5. See also
Zvi M. Rabinovitz, *Ginze Midrash* (Tel Aviv: Tel Aviv University Press, 1976), 161–71,
and Rabinovitz's comments ad loc. Interestingly, the manuscript he publishes there
is written in a tenth-century Oriental (Babylonian or Iraqi) script, a fact that at
least shows that such parodic texts circulated in those general environs.

[7] Poem 32 in Yosef Yahalom and Michael Sokoloff, *Shirat Bnei Maʿarava* (Jerusalem:
Israel Academy of Sciences, 1999), 196–201.

[8] Giulio Bartolocci, *Bibliotheca Magna Rabbinica* (5 vols.; Rome: Sacrae Congregationis
de Propaganda Fide, 1675–1694), 1:683–89; cited in Eli Yassif, *Sipurei Ben Sira Biyemei
Habeinayim* (Jerusalem: Magnes, 1984), 130 n. 3.

[9] Jacob Reifmann, *Ha-karmel* (Vilna, 1873), 2:124–38.

that the text posed to these earlier scholars.[10] My own remarks on the text that follow are deeply indebted to Yassif's extraordinarily thorough and comprehensive study, including both its critical text and introductory monograph. My sole original (I hope) contribution is a somewhat different interpretation of the "facts" that Yassif has so carefully assembled. Let me begin with a brief introduction to the work, summing up Yassif's discoveries and conclusions in the process, then follow with my own interpretation of the work's literary character as a literary parody and its significance.

Yassif has convincingly dated the work, or works, known collectively by the title of the *Alphabet of Ben Sira*, to 8th–10th century Iraq, the period known in Jewish historiography as the Geonic, after its spiritual leaders, the Geonim, the heads of the great post-classical Babylonian *yeshivot*.[11] As Yassif shows, the *Alphabet* is less a single or discrete literary document than a tradition of different texts and stories collected together through association with the character of one Ben Sira. This character takes his name, of course, from the ancient 3rd–2nd century B.C.E. sage, Yeshua Ben Sira, the author of the Second Temple-era wisdom book, the Book of Ben Sira [a.k.a. Sirach or Ecclesiasticus, "the little Ecclesiastes"] which has been preserved in a Greek translation among the Apocrypha and whose original Hebrew text was famously discovered by Solomon Schechter in the Cairo Geniza.[12]

Aside from his name, however, the *Alphabet*'s Ben Sira has little in common with his austere predecessor. Far from being a venerable moralist and sage, the *Alphabet*'s Ben Sira is the ultimate *yanuka*, a brash and impudent, praeternaturally precocious *Wunderkind* who, as the first part of the text tells us, was conceived by the daughter of the prophet Jeremiah from her father's semen (which had been left floating in the waters of the bathhouse after the prophet had been forced to masturbate publicly by the wicked members of the tribe of Ephraim!), and who emerged from his mother's womb with full-grown teeth and eloquent speech. In addition to (1) this initial section of the work which recounts the story of the birth of Ben

---

[10] Yassif, *Sipurei Ben Sira*.

[11] Yassif, *Sipurei Ben Sira*, 19–29.

[12] On Ben Sira, see *Sefer Ben Sira Hashelem* (ed. M. Z. Segal; Jerusalem: Mossad Bialik, 1953).

Sira, the traditions associated with the *Wunderkind* include (2) an account of Ben Sira's "education" in which he first learns the alphabet from a hapless *melamed*, an elderly elementary school teacher of reading and writing; (3) an account of Ben Sira the precocious *Wunderkind* in the court of Nebuchadnezzar including a series of twenty-two tasks and questions which the Babylonian king poses to the boy (including such questions as, Why do dogs hate cats? Why were mosquitoes, wasps, and spiders created? and, Why does the donkey urinate in the urine of another donkey and smell its own excrement?); (4) a second alphabet sequence, this one illustrated by alphabetically-listed proverbs in Aramaic followed by moralistic homilies and exemplary stories illustrating the proverbs; and finally, (5) a series of "additional" questions posed by Nebuchadnezzar to Ben Sira. In addition, as Yassif notes, much of sections 1 and 2 exist in two versions or recensions that are sufficiently different as to be considered separate and independent works.[13]

What the textual evidence suggests, then, is that the works known as the *Alphabet of Ben Sira* constitute a tradition of many different types of works that are united only by their all being connected to the legendary character of the *Wunderkind* Ben Sira, and that even the various texts we possess are themselves composites of separate traditions. Aside from having a common hero/protagonist, the contents of these texts and their traditions are highly varied and span numerous literary genres. These range from the quasi-scatological contents of the initial story of Ben Sira's birth to the many folkloric animal stories and the various pseudo-heroic burlesques detailing Ben Sira's exploits (like the story of how he shaved the hare's head or the famous episode relating how he cured Nebuchadnezzar's daughter of her bad case of farts) contained in the sections detailing Nebuchadnezzar's questions. All these traditions and their genres share, however, the feature of being, as it were, *uncanonical*. That is to say, they fall on the margins of the high, serious, and canonical

---

[13] See Yassif, *Sipurei Ben Sira*, 7–12. So far as I understand Yassif, the question nonetheless remains whether the two versions are actually different texts or recensions. Yassif notes that Version A is preserved in Ashkenazic manuscripts of a northern French provenance; Version B is preserved in manuscripts in Italian hands (and of a somewhat later date than the French Ashkenazic MSS.) Nonetheless, Yassif believes that Version B (Italy) is probably closer to what the "original" text of the *Alphabet* looked like—if there ever was an "original" text.

literature of Rabbinic tradition, specifically the Talmudim and the classical midrashic collections. Within the confines of this article, it is of course impossible to deal with the full variety of texts found in the *Alphabet*; the reader should consult Yassif's splendid edition and his notes particularly in reference to the more folkloric passages and tales. Here I will limit myself to the first two sections of the *Alphabet*, passages which, I hope to show, directly relate to the genre of literary parody.

The first passage—the story of Ben Sira's conception and birth, to which I have already referred—is probably the single most infamous passage in the *Alphabet of Ben Sira*. Despite its length, I will cite the entire text; the translation is based on Version 2 in Yassif's text (although I will add parenthetically a few lines from Version 1).[14]

> "Who does great things without limit and wonders without number" (Job 9:10). If it is said, "Who does great things without limit," why does [Scripture] say, "and wonders without number"? How did the sages explain, "Who does great things"—this refers to all the creatures in the world (*yetzirot*) [who were created or born in normal fashion]. "And wonders without number" refers to the three persons who were born without their mothers having slept with a man. And these were Rav Zeira, Rav Pappa, and Ben Sira.

> About Rav Zeira and Rav Pappa, it is said that in their entire lives they never engaged in trivial conversation; that they never slept in the house of study, neither regular sleep nor even a nap; that no one ever arrived at the house of study before them; that no one ever found them sitting in silence, but they were always occupied in study. They never gave a bad name to their fellows; they never failed to perform the sanctification of the Sabbath day; they never honored themselves by disgracing their fellows. They never went to bed cursing their colleagues, and they never looked into the face of a wicked person, so as to fulfill what is said, "I will endow those who love me with substance; I will fill their treasuries" (Prov 8:21). And how did their mothers give birth to them without having [intercourse with] a male? It is said that they went to the bathhouse, Jewish semen[15] entered their vaginas, and they conceived and gave birth.

---

[14] I have also utilized the English translation by Norman Bronznick that Mark Jay Mirsky and I revised and published in *Rabbinic Fantasies* (Philadelphia: Jewish Publication Society, 1990; repr., New Haven: Yale University Press, 1998), 169–202, which was done (alas) before Yassif's edition was available.

[15] Hebrew: *eren sid havi*, which is *zera yehudi*, "Jewish seed," spelled backwards. Cf. Yassif, *Sipurei Ben Sira*, 198 n. 6 and his reference to Shraga Abramson's article on the subject.

And Ben Sira—how did his mother become pregnant? It is said about her that she was the daughter of Jeremiah. For once Jeremiah the prophet went to the bathhouse, and he saw that everyone there was masturbating. His initial impulse was to flee, but the people would not leave him; they were all from the tribe of Ephraim during the reign of Zedekiah, and that entire generation—the generation of Zedekiah at that time—was wicked; that is why it is written about them, "And they did evil in the eyes of God" (2 Kgs 24:19). They immediately grabbed him and said, "On account of what you have seen, you will now go [and tell others]! You do the same right now!"[16] He said to them, "I beg you! Leave me, and I swear to you I won't ever tell anyone." They replied, "Did not Zedekiah see Nebuchadnezzar eating a hare and he swore that he would never tell a person? Yet as soon as he left him, he broke his oath! And you'll do the same! If you join us now, fine. And if not, we'll do to you what they did in Sodom!" Jeremiah immediately did so [and masturbated] though only out of great fear. [Version 1 adds: When he left, he cursed his days, as it said, "Cursed be the day on which I was born" (Jer 20:14).][17] Later he fasted on its account ninety-one fast days, and the Holy One, blessed be He, preserved his semen until Jeremiah's daughter came [to the bathhouse] and the seed entered her womb, and she conceived.

Seven months later, a son was born, and he was born with teeth and with speech. But once [Jeremiah's daughter] bore [the boy], she became ashamed that people would now say, The child is a bastard!

Immediately, the child opened his mouth and said, "Mommy, mommy! Why are you ashamed? The son of Sira am I, the son of Sira!" His mother said to him, "My child, who is this Sira—is he a gentile or a Jew?" Ben Sira responded, "Mother, Sira is Jeremiah, and he is my father. And why is he called Sira? Because he is the *sar*, the ruling officer, over the officers [of the gentile nations], and he is destined to make all of them and their kings drink the cup of punishment. Don't be surprised at this. Just add up the numerical equivalents of the letters in the name Jeremiah, which come to 271, and those in the name Sira, which also add up to 271 [thus proving that Jeremiah is the same as Sira]!" His mother said to him, "But if this is true, you should have said, 'I'm the son of Jeremiah.'" Ben Sira replied, "I wanted to say that, but it was too shameful to suggest that Jeremiah had sex

---

[16] The text here seems to be corrupt. Version A reads, "Jeremiah began to reprove them until they stopped him and said, 'Why are you reproving us? You won't leave until you act like us.'"

[17] It is unclear whether, in the *Alphabet's* narrative, the "I" in the Jeremiah verse refers to Jeremiah or to Ben Sira; see the use of the verse in *Pesiqta Rabbati* to be discussed shortly in this article.

with his daughter!" His mother said, "My child, is it not written, 'That which has been is that which shall be' (Qoh 1:9)? But who has ever seen a daughter giving birth by her father?" Ben Sira replied, "My mother, 'There is nothing new under the sun' (Qoh 1:9). For the daughters of Lot became pregnant through their father, and just as Lot was a perfectly righteous man so was my father perfectly righteous. . . ." [Ben Sira then proceeds to point out all the similarities between Lot and Jeremiah, after which:] His mother said to him, "My son, the only thing that astonishes me is how you know how to say all these things." Ben Sira responded, "Mother, don't be astonished! For my father Jeremiah did the same. When his mother was about to give birth, the child opened his mouth from out of his mother's womb and said, 'I won't come out until you tell me my name.' [Ben Sira then goes on to list all the equivalences between himself and his father Jeremiah, the last of which is:] Just as Jeremiah composed a book arranged in alphabetic acrostics [namely, the book of Lamentations, each of whose first three chapters have their verses arranged alphabetically], and there were things in it so difficult that people wished to destroy it, so too I will compose a book in alphabetic acrostics, and there will be things in it so difficult that people will wish to destroy it. And in the future I will be revealed to them. So don't be amazed!"

More than any other passage in the *Alphabet*, this story has aroused the attention—and the ire—of numerous scholars. To be sure, as Yassif points out, in itself the story of an extraordinary birth amid supernatural circumstances is not out of the ordinary for heroes and other legendary figures. In ancient literature it is commonplace for miracles to attend the births of heroic figures; consider the birth-stories of Moses, Jesus, Darius, Mohammed—the list goes on and on.[18] Even so, the story of Ben Sira's conception, with its account of the near-sodomizing of the solemn prophet Jeremiah by the Ephraimites, then the divinely-ordained preservation of the prophet's semen in the bathhouse water, the subsequent impregnation of his daughter, and finally the birth of the young *Wunderkind* who emerges out of the womb brashly proclaiming his paternity—this birth-narrative is literally over-the-top, unparalleled in its improbability and effrontery by any other birth-narrative. Not surprisingly, the story has elicited numerous responses from scholars though virtually no one has acknowledged the outrageous humor of the original. Early on scholars like

---

[18] Yassif, *Sipurei Ben Sira*, 32.

Reifmann proposed that the story was the creation of "forgers"—
that is to say, Karaites—who invented it in order to mock Rabbinic
tradition.[19] Israel Levi proposed in an article in 1891 that the story's
motifs were borrowed from early Persian myths about the birth of
Zarathustra; as Levi pointed out, both Syrian Christian and some
early Moslem traditions assert that Jeremiah was in fact Zarathustra's
teacher.[20] Somewhat more obviously, Adolph Jellinek, in his introduction to his text of the work in *Beit Hamidrash*, pointed out the
parallels between the story of Ben Sira's birth and that of Jesus and
argued that the *Alphabet*'s narrative was in fact composed as a satire
or parody of Jesus' "immaculate" conception and virgin birth.[21]

As more recent scholars like Joseph Dan have pointed out, however, these various theories of the text's origins all fail to account
for the fact that the text satirizes biblical figures like Jeremiah and
Lot as much as Ben Sira or any other unnamed figure from later
Rabbinic tradition; further, if the text were a polemic against either
Karaism, Christianity, or Islam, one would expect to find in it some
kind of defense of Rabbinic Judaism, which it utterly lacks. According
to Dan, the real target of the text's polemics is religious hypocrisy,
which he sees as being the butt and moral of many of the text's
constituent tales. Yet this "explanation" for the text is also not satisfactory; for one thing, it is far from clear how exactly hypocrisy
explains the details of Ben Sira's extraordinary birth nor, as Dan
himself acknowledges, do we know from which Jewish group or sect
a text like Ben Sira with its polemic against (Rabbinic?) hypocrisy
would have emerged.[22] Yassif, in turn, has argued that the story of
Ben Sira, from his birth on, is meant to be taken entirely seriously
as an attempt on the part of its author(s) to create a Jewish mythic
hero on the model of other mythic heroes found in national epics.
Yassif correctly warns us against applying an anachronistic reading
that would impose upon the text modern assumptions about what
an ancient or early medieval Jew could take seriously; instead, he

---

[19] Reifmann, *Ha-karmel*, 133. See as well Abraham Epstein, *Mikadmoniyot Hayehudim*
(Vienna: n.p., 1887), 119ff.
[20] Israel Levi, "La nativité de Ben Sira," *REJ* 23 (1891): 197–205.
[21] Adolph Jellinek, *Beit Hamidrash* (6 vols.; 1873; repr. Jerusalem: Wahrmann,
1967), 2.6:xi–xiii.
[22] Joseph Dan, *Hasippur Ha'ivri Biyemei Habeinayim* (Jerusalem: Keter, 1974), 74–76.

argues that the story should be taken more or less at face value, as a work of pure literary art.[23]

The difficulty with Yassif's approach to the passage is that it overlooks the manifestly *low* voice that is evident in both the work's vulgarity and its comedy. To paraphrase Oscar Wilde, one need have a sense of humor made of stone not to be entertained by Ben Sira's antics. To be sure, the identification of a parody is always a tricky matter. As Wayne Booth has remarked, "the contrasts between an original [work of literature] and a really skillful parody [of it] can be so slight that efforts to explain them can seem even less adequate to the true subtleties than explanations of other ironies."[24] Parody inevitably involves an ironic compact between the author and the reader whereby the reader is expected to recognize the signals pointing to the "original" text (or genre, if a specific literary work is not involved) being parodied—the "victim," in Booth's felicitous terminology. The irony inherent in parody consists of the reader's recognition of precisely that distance between the "victim" text and the parody text, the clash between the "victim's" decorous combination of style and content with the parody's undecorous combination. This ironic element is also what distinguishes a parody from a mere travesty or a satire.

In the case of our Ben Sira narrative, the "victim" is both classical midrash generally and a specific midrashic text with whose traditions we may also assume a reader of the *Alphabet* to have been familiar. Thus, to any reader acquainted with midrash, the interpretive conventions and exegetical language of the *Alphabet* passage would have been, and will be, immediately recognizable. The opening interpretation of Job 1:10 has countless parallels in classical midrash which frequently play on the seeming redundancy of parallelistic verses in biblical poetry: see, for one example, *Lev. Rab.* 1:1 *ad* Ps 103:20. So too the *gematriah* (arithmological analogy) between the letters in the name Jeremiah and those in Ben Sira is typically midrashic. The passage in praise of Rav Zeira and Rav Pappa imitates many passages of Rabbinic hagiography (although the final citation of Prov 8:21 as a "fulfillment-prooftext" seems to be nonsensical,

---

[23] Yassif, *Sipurei Ben Sira*, 38–39.
[24] Wayne Booth, *A Rhetoric of Irony* (Chicago: University of Chicago Press, 1974), 72.

thrown in purely for affect).[25] Similarly, the repartee between Ben Sira and his mother, wherein the mother begins Qoh 1:9 and the boy retorts with the verse's conclusion, also imitates many midrashic stories, most famously the story of R. Joshua ben Hananiah and the Jewish slave-boy in Rome recorded in *Lam. Rab.* 4:1.

Yet beyond all these easily identifiable conventions of classical midrash, the *Alphabet* passage also parodies a specific midrashic text— a famous passage in chapter 26 of *Pesiqta Rabbati*, a collection of homilies that was probably edited in fifth or sixth century Palestine though it contains much older material as well.[26] This text is indeed identified by Yassif, who acknowledges its presence behind the Ben Sira birth-narrative though he treats it purely as a putative source for some of the latter's details.[27]

In fact, its role behind the Ben Sira passage is far more crucial than being merely a source for some details. Knowledge of the *Pesiqta Rabbati* passage and of its context is indispensable for appreciating the humor of the *Alphabet*'s story.

A few words about that context are therefore necessary. *Pesiqta Rabbati*, chapter 26, is an unusual homily in that it does not begin with an explicit citation of the initial verse of the weekly Torah reading or, as would be the case here, the first verse of the week's *haftorah* (the reading from the Prophets that follows the Torah reading in the synagogue). Even so, it is clear that the *haftorah* reading that is the subject of the homily is Jer 1:1, and that the Sabbath for which this homily was composed is the first of the three special Sabbaths preceding the ninth of Av, the fast day in the Jewish calendar that commemorates the destruction of the Temple. Along with the month

---

[25] For Rabbinic parallels, see Yassif's notes (*Sipurei Ben Sira*, 197–98).

[26] Rivka Ulmer, *Pesiqta Rabbati* (Atlanta; Scholars Press, 1997), 1:xiii. See as well, Hermann L. Strack and Günter Stemberger, *Introduction to the Talmud and Midrash* (trans. M. Bockmuehl; Minneapolis: Fortress, 1996), 299–302. Chapter 26 is considered by some scholars to have originally been a separate work, but the specific questions of dating, etc., do not affect our argument here. Unfortunately, the second volume of Ulmer's critical edition containing chapter 26 has not yet appeared. My translation and references are all based on the edition of Meir Friedmann [Meir Ish-Shalom], *Midrash Pesikta Rabbati* (1880; repr., Tel Aviv: n.p., 1963), 129b–130a. I have also consulted the translation of William G. Braude, *Pesikta Rabbati: Discourses for Feasts, Fasts, and Special Sabbaths* (New Haven: Yale University Press, 1968), 525–27. The passage is also cited in slightly different form in *Yalkut Shimeoni, Jeremiah*, par. 262—indicating, if nothing else, that the passage enjoyed wide circulation.

[27] Yassif, *Sipurei Ben Sira*, 33–34.

of Ellul and the High Holy days, these three weeks are among the most solemn—literally mournful—periods in the Jewish ritual calendar.

Pesiqta Rabbati's homily on Jer 1:1 for the first Sabbath in this period is appropriately grave and serious in tone, and especially so when it describes the singularity of the prophet Jeremiah, Judaism's prophet of doom *par excellence*. Following a short introduction, the chapter begins with an exegetical enumeration (a common midrashic literary form that typically begins with a statement enumerating the number of instances of a given phenomenon, followed by prooftexts for each instance). In this case, the reader will immediately recognize *Pesiqta Rabbati*'s enumeration as the "victim" text of Ben Sira's opening enumeration of three persons who were born without their mothers having slept with their father. Without translating the passage in its entirety, let me cite the relevant passages and summarize the rest:

> [Jeremiah] was one of four men who were known as *yitsurim* (creatures who were directly created by God). [The passage then goes on to name the other three—Adam, Jacob, and Isaiah—and cites a prooftext for each figure.] And the fourth was Jeremiah to whom God said, "Before I created you (*etsarkha*) in the womb, I knew you" (Jer 1:5). These are the ones about whom the word *yetsirah* (creature) is employed.

The passage then continues:

> [When he came out of the womb, Jeremiah] cried a great cry as though [he were already] a full-grown youth, and exclaimed, "My bowels! my bowels! I writhe in pain! The chambers of my heart are in agony! My limbs are all trembling. Destruction upon destruction! I am the one who will destroy the entire world!" And how do we know that Jeremiah spoke thus? Because it is written, "Oh, my suffering, my suffering! How I writhe! Oh, the walls of my heart! My heart moans within me, I cannot be silent . . ." (Jer 4:19).

> Jeremiah opened his mouth and reprimanded his mother, "My mother, my mother! Is it not true that you did not conceive me in the manner of other women, and that you did not give birth to me in the way of other women who give birth? Perhaps your ways were like the ways of unfaithful women? Perhaps you cast your eye upon another man? As one who has been unfaithful to her husband, why have you not drunk the bitter waters?[28] You are brazen!" And how do we know

---

[28] See Num 5:11.

that Jeremiah spoke thus? Because it is written, "You had the fore-
head [i.e. brazenness] of a woman of the street" (Jer 3:3).

Once his mother heard these things, she said, "What makes this one
speak thus? Surely not on account of sins [that I have committed]!"

He opened his mouth and said to her, "Not about you, my mother,
do I speak thus. Not about you, my mother, do I prophesy. But to
Zion and Jerusalem do I speak. For she adorns her daughters and
clothes them with scarlet and crowns them with gold. But the spoil-
ers are coming and will despoil them, 'And you, who are doomed to
ruin, what do you accomplish by wearing crimson, by decking yourself in jewels of gold, by enlarging your eyes with kohl?'" (Jer 4:30).

The chapter then goes on to describe how God designated Jeremiah
to deliver the message of doom to the nation of Israel first of all
nations, after which it concludes:

When Jeremiah heard this command, he opened his mouth and cursed
the day of his birth, as it is written, "Accursed be the day that I was
born!" (Jer 20:14).

The reader familiar with this passage in *Pesiqta Rabbati* will easily
hear its numerous echoes as travestied in the birth-narrative of Ben
Sira. These begin with the use of the word *yetsirah* in the opening
enumeration that is echoed in the *Alphabet*'s playful exegesis of Job
9:10 to relate to all the *yetsirot* (creatures) in the world who are born
normally, on the one hand, and those who were created (*notsru*) without their mothers having slept with their father. The mode of Ben
Sira's emergence from his mother's womb—full-grown, with teeth,
and talking—clearly imitates Jeremiah's emergence from his mother's
womb, with the difference of course that Jeremiah emerges in character, that is, mournfully—mourning his fate and mourning the message of doom that he is doomed to prophesy to Israel. And Ben
Sira also emerges in character, that is, with the unabashed *sprez-
zatura* of a young *Wunderkind*, shamelessly boasting of his incestuous
paternity. So, too, the story of Ben Sira's conception—the entire
bathhouse tale which explains how his grandfather became his father—
would seem to travesty Jeremiah's remonstration of his mother for
having committed adultery (since the identity of his father seems to
be clearly unknown, even to Jeremiah), though again with the difference
that Jeremiah immediately clarifies the fact that he is speaking only
of his allegorical "mother"—Israel—not his biological parent. Ben
Sira, in contrast, comes out of the womb boasting of his parentage,

telling his mother to be proud of it and not embarrassed, and as "proof" of the legitimacy of his pedigree, he cites Lot as an analogously righteous figure who also had children through incestuous relations with his daughters; as many scholars have noted, Lot is far from the typical example of a righteous figure in Rabbinic lore. And so, as well, at the passage's conclusion, Ben Sira draws an equally outrageous, mocking analogy between his father and himself, citing the fact that both of them will or have composed compositions with alphabetic acrostics—the one, the Book of Lamentations, certainly the saddest book in all Scripture; the other, Ben Sira's own *Alphabet*, doubtless the least solemn composition in classical Jewish literature.

To be sure, not every detail in Ben Sira's travesty derives from the *Pesiqta Rabbati* passage. The notion of a woman becoming pregnant through seed preserved (miraculously or not) in bathhouse waters is drawn from a famous Talmudic passage in *b. Hagigah* 14b–15a. This passage was first pointed out (and dismissed) by Levi, and it is again cited by Yassif who takes it more seriously as a putative source for the narrative; however, he does not look at the passage within its Talmudic context and thus seems to miss the point.[29] Within its Talmudic context, the line about a virgin becoming pregnant through semen left in the waters of a bathhouse is cited within the context of a passage that follows the famous story about the Four Who Entered Pardes, one of whom, Ben Zoma, we are told, "looked and became demented." Following that story the Talmud records two questions which were said to have been asked of Ben Zoma. The first of these is, Is it permissible to castrate a dog?[30] The second is, Can a virgin who has become pregnant be married to a High Priest (who must marry a virgin)? The Talmud then naturally asks how a virgin can become pregnant, and offers two possible scenarios: The first of these is proposed by the Babylonian sage Samuel who boasts that he was so skillful a lover that he was able to penetrate virgins without breaking their hymens(!), but the Talmud dismisses this

---

[29] Yassif, *Sipurei Ben Sira*, 37–38.

[30] It is forbidden to mutilate any animal in such a way that the mutilation would make the animal unfit to be sacrificed in the Temple. A dog, however, cannot be sacrificed under any circumstance, nor can it be exchanged for a sacrifice. The question therefore arises whether or not the general prohibition against mutilation attaches to a dog; canine-lovers will be relieved to know that the Talmud decides that, regardless of a dog's sacrificial status, it is forbidden to castrate it.

possibility as very unlikely and instead provides an alternative scenario, namely that the virgin became pregnant through seed preserved in bath-water.

Given this context for the statement, it is not disrespectful to suggest that the notion of becoming pregnant through seed preserved
in bath-water should be taken, even by a serious student of the
Talmud, with a grain of salt, as it were.[31] The very fact that the
question instigating the scenario is asked of a *demented* sage should
minimally indicate to the reader that we are close to entering a
world of demented questions. At the least, a pregnant virgin is a
case of Talmudic hyperbole—an *extremely* hypothetical case—and not
far from being a kind of Rabbinic joke. And the *Alphabet of Ben Sira*
merely turns that joke into the premise of a comic narrative.

In short, I am suggesting that the entire passage in the *Alphabet*
is a literary parody of the homily about Jeremiah in *Pesiqta Rabbati*
and a pastiche of references to other passages like the gemara in *b.
Hagigah* as worked into the parodic narrative. Let me emphasize that
these other texts—both *Pesiqta Rabbati* and the *b. Hagigah* passage—
are not mere literary footnotes to the *Alphabet*; they are the indispensable "victim" texts to the parodic text of Ben Sira's conception
and birth—passages and traditions that the *Alphabet*'s author expected
his reader to know and to recognize. He also expected the reader
to recognize the grotesque (and funny) disparity between the somber
Pesiqta Rabbati homily and the low, vulgar style of the *Alphabet*—the
parodic irony, in other words. Nor does the *Alphabet*'s irony end here.
An even more profound irony lies behind the text though it is never
explicitly mentioned. This is the irony inherent in the reader's knowledge that Ben Sira, the very unexemplary grandson of Jeremiah, the
exemplary prophet of doom, will shortly end up in the court of
Nebuchadnezzar—Jeremiah's foe, the agent of the Temple's Destruction—but acting as the latter's Daniel-like interpreter/counselor and
performing such feats of wonder as curing Nebuchadnezzar's daughter of a bad case of farting. To be sure, the Destruction of the
Temple is never so much as hinted at in the *Alphabet*, but its gloomy

---

[31] Not, of course, that it ever necessarily was. But, then, see the Taz ad Shulkhan
Arukh, *Yoreah De'ah* 195:7, who cites our story in the *Alphabet of Ben Sira* as a putative authority for the halakhic permissibility of artificially inseminating a woman
with her father's semen.

presence hovers behind the text, shrouding the entire parody in the gallows humor of Jewish history.[32]

To be sure, the *Alphabet*'s King Nebuchadnezzar is more like Ahasuerus than either the arch-villain of later Rabbinic aggadah or even the maddened-by-arrogance king of Dan 4:30 who "ate grass like cattle, and his body was drenched with the dew of heaven until his hair grew like eagle's [feathers] and his nails like [the talons of] birds." But it is safe to assume that none of these ironies would have been lost upon the text's original or its intended audience, for whom this narrative—and here we come to the question of its function— would have doubtless been experienced as truly entertaining. And who, conceivably, would have been entertained by a literary parody of this sort? Only a reader who (as I have argued) would have been able to recognize the parodic references to the traditions like those preserved in *Pesiqta Rabbati* and *b. Hagigah*. And who could such a reader have been? Only a *talmid hakham*, namely, a scholar or a student of the scholars who filled the courts of the Geonic *yeshivot* in Babylonia during the ninth and tenth centuries.

Before we explore this last suggestion more fully, let us consider the second text from the *Alphabet* that also possesses clear parodic elements. This second text immediately follows the story of Ben Sira's birth. When Ben Sira is a year old, we are told, he goes to the synagogue where he finds a teacher of children (*melamed tinokot*) "who has seven daughters," and he commands him to teach him. The teacher refuses, telling the child he is too young to be taught, and citing as his authority *m. Avot* 5:21, which states that a child should begin to study Bible only at the age of five. To this Ben Sira retorts by quoting verbatim the saying of R. Tarfon in *m. Avot* 2:15, "The day is short but the work is great, the workers are lazy and the reward is great," and berating the teacher for not being willing to teach him. The teacher, in turn, reproves Ben Sira for violating the Rabbinic prohibition against teaching the law in the presence of one's teacher—a prohibition the rabbis took so seriously that they made its violation a capital offense—to which Ben Sira, ever the smart-ass, responds by telling the teacher that as yet he has taught him nothing, and so he cannot be considered his teacher. At this point, the *melamed* capitulates and the lesson begins.

---

[32] Cf. James L. Kugel, "Two Introductions to Midrash," in *Midrash and Literature* (ed. G. H. Hartman and S. Budick; New Haven: Yale University Press, 1986), 80.

The lesson is a lesson in the alphabet—the *aleph-bet*—and it follows a pedagogical method that is attested in the Talmud (*b. Shabbat*
104a) wherein the alphabet is taught by associating each letter with
a maxim or proverb whose initial word begins with that letter in
the alphabet; this pedagogical method is also attested in Roman
sources.[33] Thus, the teacher says to Ben Sira, "*Aleph*," and Ben Sira
responds with the saying, "*A*bstain from worrying in your heart (*al
titein deagah belibekha*), for worry has killed many men who were mighty
(*gibborim*)." The teacher then says, "*Bet*," and the child responds, "By
a beautiful woman's countenance many have been destroyed, and
numerous are all her slain ones." And so on.

In the *Alphabet of Ben Sira*, however, the lesson does not stop with
the alphabet. Each maxim that the child Ben Sira quotes in turn
elicits a confession from the elderly teacher. Thus, in response to
Ben Sira's maxim about abstaining from worry (as quoted above),
we are told that the teacher immediately "was thrown into a panic,
and said, 'I don't have a worry in the world—except for the fact
that my wife is ugly.'" In response to the maxims for the letters *bet*
and *gimmel*, we learn that the elderly man wishes to divorce his wife
"on account of an especially beautiful widow who lives in my courtyard." In response to *dalet, heh* and *zayin*, the teacher reveals that
the woman flaunts herself before him every day; that she practiced
witchcraft against her first husband; and that he would already have
married her if he did not fear that she would bear him more daughters. And as the lessons continue, the maxims themselves become

---

[33] See Judah Goldin, "Several Sidelights of a Torah Education in Tannaite and
Early Amoraic Times," in *Ex Orbe Religionum: Studia Geo Widengren Oblata* (Leiden:
Brill, 1972), 176–91, esp. 184 on students learning aphorisms and on learning how
to finish a verse that someone else has begun. For Greco-Roman parallels, see
Stanley Bonner, *Education in Ancient Rome* (Berkeley/Los Angeles: University of
California Press, 1977), 172–73, on the use of *sententiae* and *gnomai*—moral maxims
usually in short sentences—as the subject matter for learning to read and write.
On 173–74, Bonner discusses the Bouriant papyrus of Menander which has an
entire series of such lines written out in alphabetical order according to the initial
letter in the line. Yassif also cites the story about the king and his wife whom he
orders to be executed from the Arabic collection *Kalilah and Dimnah*, chapter XI, as
a source for the use of a similar structure in a tale (*Sipurei Ben Sira*, 22–23); in the
Kalilah and Dimnah tale, the king's counselor makes the king remember his love
for his wife by citing alphabetic maxims to him. The English translation that I consulted (*Kalilah and Dimnah* [trans. T. B. Irving; Newark, Del.: Juan de la Cuesta,
1980]) retells the story in chapter VII.B (133–47), but the translation does not follow an alphabetic series.

increasingly misogynistic, bewailing the misfortune of a father of daughters (let alone seven daughters!). A daughter, Ben Sira tells us, is only a source of worry—"when she is a child, he fears that she will be molested; when she is a girl, that she will be promiscuous; when she is a young woman, that she will not marry; and when she is old, that she will practice witchcraft." And so, we are told, Ben Sira "traded words with [the teacher] until he had completed all twenty-two 'chapters' in the alphabet."

As Yassif and others have noted, this entire passage is a work of considerable literary craft. The alphabet lesson is joined with the elderly *melamed*'s confession in such a way as to reverse the roles of teacher and student. Each letter that the *melamed* teaches Ben Sira evokes a maxim from the student that in turn draws out of the teacher one more confession that he seems incapable of *not* making to his disciple. And each confession in turn confirms the hapless fate to which the teacher seems doomed of being victimized by females— his ugly wife, the beautiful but sorceress widow, his seven daughters. And all this is accomplished, as Yassif has noted, with great literary skill.

In constructing this narrative, its author has drawn, in turn, upon at least three literary traditions and texts (in addition to *b. Shabbat* 104a, mentioned earlier). In the first place, he has drawn upon a widespread tradition that one scholar has recently called, "The Wise Child's Alphabet," in which a child-prophet, in the course of learning the alphabet, teaches his teacher the true meaning of the letters; the tradition is attested in stories about the Buddha, Jesus, the Shi'ite Fifth Imam, the Sikh Guru Nanak, the Bab of the Bahai and, of course, Ben Sira.[34]

Second, the passage reflects a widespread tradition of derisive tales told about teachers of children that is especially well-attested in Near Eastern literature, both Jewish and Arabic. The Jewish sources have been collected by Saul Lieberman as they have been preserved particularly in Yemenite midrashim.[35] The texts abound in insults about elementary teachers, both calling them "the weakest-minded of the weak-minded" (*kal hakalim*) and condemning them as teachers of false

---

[34] Steven M. Wasserstrom, *Between Muslim and Jew: The Problem of Symbiosis Under Early Islam* (Princeton: Princeton University Press, 1995), 167–69.
[35] Lieberman, *Midreshei Teiman*, 26–31.

teachings; the person who pays them honor, one midrash states, is doomed to hell (*yoreish geihinom le'atsmo*).[36] The Arabic sources, in turn, have been described by Ignaz Goldziher who cites one typical epigram, "It is sufficient indication of a man's inferiority—be he never so eminent—to say that he is a teacher of children."[37] Other texts abound in stories about lecherous schoolteachers. As Lieberman notes, the Jewish texts may well reflect the prejudices of the Arabic sources.

Third and finally, the *Alphabet*'s narrative directly derives from an actual literary text—to use Wayne Booth's terminology once again, a "victim" text, namely, *b. Sanh.* 100b. Again, I am far from being the first to call attention to the relevance of this text, but where others have seen it at best as a source from which the *Alphabet* drew its material, I would like to argue that it is in fact the very target of the *Alphabet*'s parody. The gemara under discussion is a commentary upon the Mishnaic dictum attributed to Rabbi Akiba: "Even one who reads 'Outside Books' (*sefarim hahitzoniyim*) has no place in the world-to-come" (*m. Sanh.* 10:1). In response to the question, "What are 'Outside Books'?" the Talmud records two opinions: first, a Tannaitic tradition that interprets the phrase to refer to Zadokite documents (*sefer tzedukim*) (whatever those may have been); and then, in the name of R. Joseph, a fourth-century Babylonian sage, the Book of Ben Sira. The Talmudic passage continues with the following discussion: Abayye asks, "Why is it forbidden to read from the book of Ben Sira?" and then goes on to quote a verse from Ben Sira—"Do not strip the skin of a fish even from its ear, lest you spoil it"—and to show that in fact the Torah states the same idea expressed in the "forbidden" book (whether the latter's verse is understood literally or figuratively). Following this exchange, the Talmud

---

[36] *Pirkei Derekh Eretz* 1 (= *Seder Eliyahu Zutta* 16), in *Nispahim LeSeder Eliyahu Zutta*, (ed. M. Friedmann [Meir Ish-Shalom]; Wien: Achiasaf, 1902), 5 and n. 21; repr., in *Seder Eliyahu Rabbah VeSeder Eliyahu Zutta (Tanna DeBei Eliyahu)* (ed. M. Friedmann [Meir Ish-Shalom]; Jerusalem: Wahrmann, 1969). Also cited and discussed in Lieberman, *Midreshei Teiman*, 28.

[37] Ignaz Goldziher, "Education (Muslim)," *ERE* 5:201–2 (the epigram quoted is on 201). See also Ulrich Marzolph, "The Qoran and Jocular Literature," *Arabica* 47 (2000): 478–87; and Franz Rosenthal, *Humor in Early Islam* (Philadelphia: University of Pennsylvania Press, 1956). I wish to thank my colleagues Everett Rowson, Roger Allen, and David Hollenberg for referring me to these sources and for enlightening me in general about the tradition of *Majun* (profligacy, libertinism) with its profane, quasi-blasphemous parodies of *hadith*.

(or Abbaye) goes on to quote several more verses from Ben Sira and to show, again, that either the Bible or the rabbis themselves expressed the same sentiments. The passage concludes with the anonymous editor of the Talmud citing a verse—"A thin-bearded man is very wise; a thick-bearded one is a fool"—that has no biblical or Rabbinic parallel and thus may be said to be the reason why the Book of Ben Sira may not be read. Following this apparent conclusion, however, R. Joseph is cited as making an exception to his own prohibition, and as saying that it is permissible to expound the "profitable verses" (*milei ma'alyata*) in Ben Sira; he then proceeds to list a whole series of such "profitable verses."

Yassif, through an exhaustive inspection of the manuscripts, has shown that the original text of the *Alphabet* contained only the initial eleven maxims with which Ben Sira responds to the first twelve letters in the alphabet (*aleph* through *lamed*; there does not appear to have been an original maxim for the letter *vav*); only a later editor filled in verses for the remaining letters (which lack, however, a corresponding confession from the *melamed*, thus re-confirming Yassif's conclusion that only the first eleven maxims are authentic).[38] As it happens, ten of these eleven maxims are verses drawn from the Talmudic passage in *b. Sanhedrin* as examples of either profitable or unprofitable verses from the Book of Ben Sira.[39] The author of the *Alphabet* extracted these ten verses from the *b. Sanhedrin* passage, arranged them in alphabetic order, and then inserted them into his narrative of Ben Sira's lesson in the alphabet—and, in the process, used each verse as a building block for his secondary narrative built out of the *melamed*'s confession.

To this extent, then, the *b. Sanhedrin* passage obviously served as a "source" for the *Alphabet*; as Moshe Z. Segal showed nearly half a century ago, it is nearly certain that the *Alphabet*'s author's knowledge of the Book of Ben Sira was not first-hand but derived from

---

[38] Yassif, *Sipurei Ben Sira*, 39–44.

[39] There are two exceptions to this rule: First, the maxim for the letter *dalet* is not in the *b. Sanhedrin* passage (although the maxim's misogynistic idea certainly is); and second, the maxim for the letter *zayin*, which uses part of the verse cited by the Talmud's editor as a reason not to read Ben Sira ("A thin-bearded man is very wise; a thick-bearded one is a fool"), modifies the Talmudic version so as to make it less offensive; according to Yassif these changes were made deliberately by the author of the *Alphabet* so as not to violate the apparent Talmudic consensus that these verses are unworthy to be read (*Sipurei Ben Sira*, 43).

citations and quotations in Rabbinic (and perhaps early post-Rabbinic) literature.[40] But the indispensability of the *b. Sanhedrin* text for appreciating the *Alphabet* goes beyond this borrowing of verses. The *Alphabet*'s lesson plays upon the very meaning of the Talmudic passage. The latter is a discussion of the canonicity of the Book of Ben Sira—or more accurately, its non-canonicity; indeed, the *b. Sanhedrin* passage is perhaps the *locus classicus* for the rabbis' ambivalence towards Ben Sira, a topic discussed extensively in modern scholarship.[41]

In the *Alphabet*, that very ambivalence is thematized. Ben Sira, the *Wunderkind*, quotes the verses back to his teacher, seemingly as authoritative, "canonical" maxims to illustrate the letters of the alphabet. But the actual literary function of these verses in the narrative is to serve as "bait" for the elderly teacher; the misogynistic warnings immediately become inducements to make the elderly *melamed* confess to his hapless yearnings. By turning the verses into "bait," the narrative registers its ambivalence about their canonical status. Yes, the text seems to be saying, the verses from Ben Sira (never, to be sure, identified as such in the *Alphabet*) are authoritative, but their authority seems to work best for a lecherous old *melamed* with an ugly wife, seven daughters, and a bad case of the hots for a beautiful young widow across the courtyard who is probably a witch. Is this the same canonical authority that the Talmudic rabbis were disputing?

In contrast to the *Alphabet*'s use of the *Pesiqta Rabbati* homily, which it imitated in the form of a burlesque, the *Alphabet* transforms *b. Sanhedrin*'s lofty discussion of canonicity into a low-style lesson—or counter-lesson—in which the student instructs the teacher in the perils of women. What purpose does such a parodic displacement serve? Part of the answer may lie in the tradition mocking teachers of children that, as we have already noted, is one of the subtexts behind

---

[40] Segal, *Ben Sirah Hashalem*, 44.

[41] For discussion and other sources, see Segal, *Ben Sirah Hashalem*, 36–46; and Sid Z. Leiman, *The Canonization of Hebrew Scripture: The Talmudic and Midrashic Evidence* (Hamden, Conn.: Archon, 1976), 92–101. While the question of the rabbis' attitude towards the book lies beyond the scope of this article, it should be noted that Akiba's phrase *hakorei bisfarim hahitsoniyim* probably refers not to the mere "reading" of these books but to their "liturgical recitation" in the synagogue service in the same manner as the Pentateuch or other books of the Hebrew Bible were liturgically recited. On this, see Menachem Haran, *Haasuppah Hamikrait* (Jerusalem: Mossad Bialik and Magnes, 1996), 124–36.

the *Alphabet*'s narrative. In his discussion of the Yemenite sources for this tradition, Lieberman suggests that these nasty attacks on schoolteachers—teachers of elementary reading and writing, and particularly of Bible (which was the first subject to be taught to children)—were motivated by animus against Karaism; even though these schoolteachers were in most cases Rabbinites, they were suspected by the rabbis of teaching Bible in such a way as to support Karaite readings.[42] This may be true, but it is equally possible that what motivated Rabbinic sages to make scurrilous attacks on schoolteachers may have had less to do with fighting heresy than with expressing the rabbis' concerns about their own status and particularly their fear of being seen as mere schoolteachers—a profession whose status among the rabbis seems to have been one of some ambiguity, and thus a source of serious anxiety.[43]

This anxiety seems to go back quite early and is already evident in the Babylonian Talmud. A fascinating passage in *b. Baba Mezi'a* 97a records an exchange between the fourth-century sage Raba and his students in the course of which Raba quotes a law concerning "a teacher of children (*makrei dardekei*), a gardener, a butcher, a cupper, and a town scribe," to which Raba's students respond, equating him with a teacher of children, "O Master, you are in our service!" The passage continues: "This enraged him (*akpeid*)!" following which Raba, accusing the students of trying to rob him, angrily insists that he is not their employee, not a hired worker like a teacher of children. In an important, as yet unpublished article, Barry Wimpfheimer has called attention to this passage and highlighted the unusual emotional register in the verb *akpeid* ("this enraged him").[44] Why is Raba so enraged? Because his students equate him with a teacher of children. Raba's anger seems to stem precisely from an anxiety over being mistaken in such a way—not an unreasonable anxiety given the fact that the difference between a mere elementary teacher and a Rabbinic sage may not have seemed so

---

[42] Lieberman, *Midreshei Teiman*, 30–31.

[43] See Ish-Shalom's lengthy footnote cited above in which he collects numerous statements from Rabbinic literature that both praise and condemn schoolteachers (*Seder Eliyahu Rabbah VeSeder Eliyahu Zutta*).

[44] I want to thank Barry Wimpfheimer for bringing this passage to my attention, and for sharing with me his article, "Anger, Shame, and the Literariness of Legal Narrative in the Talmud."

enormous to some people. As the writer Samuel Roth once remarked, "It should be possible for a man to remain a Jew without developing a serious case of high blood pressure."[45]

The *Alphabet* works out this same anxiety about Rabbinic identity in its own fashion. Ben Sira, *Wunderrabbi*—after all, he knows everything he needs to be taught even before he's taught it!—both appropriates the Talmudic passage and its verses and uses the latter to upstage the *melamed* and to prove to the reader who is the real teacher in this lesson. Once again, the question we need to ask ourselves is: Who would have been so concerned with presenting such a narrative? Who would have wished to mock schoolteachers in such a nasty way so as to confirm and bolster their own senses of identity? The answer, once again, points to the rabbis themselves—that is to say, to Ben Sira's contemporary rabbis, the Geonim and their students in the Babylonian *yeshivot* that dominated Jewish intellectual life in the period between the eighth and the ninth centuries.

Alas, our knowledge of the Geonic period—and, more generally, of the early post-Rabbinic, pre-medieval period—particularly in Babylonia and its Near Eastern environs, is far more limited than for many other periods in Jewish history, but it has grown enormously in the last two decades. In the case of the Babylonian Talmud itself, scholars have increasingly come to recognize the formative, indeed creative role of the anonymous sages who edited the Talmud both as halakhists and as story-tellers, and of their successors.[46] So, too, our knowledge of the Geonic *yeshivot* and of the rich and sometimes turbulent intellectual life of the Geonic period in its many facets has been considerably enriched by the work of recent scholars.[47] The picture of that world as it is beginning to emerge is of a rich and complex society—far more culturally open than was previously thought on both the popular and more intellectual levels, intensely dominated by the Geonic *yeshivot* and their overriding inter-

---

[45] Samuel Roth, *Jews Must Live* (New York: Golden Hind, 1934), 13.

[46] Given the scope of the scholarship, it is impossible to give adequate bibliographical references here. The names most frequently associated with our new appreciation of the anonymous editors of the Talmud are David Weiss-Halivni and Shamma Friedman. For the Stammaim as storytellers, see Jeffrey Rubinstein's recent work, *Talmudic Stories: Narrative Art, Composition, and Culture* (Baltimore: Johns Hopkins University Press, 1999) and his bibliography there.

[47] For the best overview of the many developments in the field, see Robert Brody, *The Geonim of Babylonia and the Shaping of Medieval Jewish Culture* (New Haven: Yale University Press, 1998).

est in the study of Talmud and Jewish legal tradition, and yet not closed to a willingness to engage in heretofore uncontemplated intellectual and literary pursuits. While the Geonic period has often been characterized in the past as a largely homogeneous, somewhat dictatorial culture, concerned mainly with establishing the absolute hegemony of Babylonian spiritual leadership throughout the Jewish world, it now seems that Jewish culture in the Geonic period was both more open to outside influence and more heterogeneous in its internal composition. It maintained, as Brody has written, "an ongoing intellectual discourse."[48]

In the more belletristic or poetic sphere, our knowledge of Geonic culture is even more limited both because of the reticence of our sources and because of their limited genres and number. Most surviving literature from the period is halakhic, while our most significant non-halakhic corpus of material is that of *piyyut*, liturgical poetry. But if *piyyut* is to be its index, the Geonic contribution to literary culture was far from insignificant. As scholars have only begun to recognize, the classical tradition of *piyyut* was massively, even radically, reshaped in the Geonic period, particularly in Babylonia where the opposition to Palestinian *piyyut* had originally been most vehement.[49] Yet Babylonian sages like Saadiah and Hai Gaon reshaped the classical genres and vastly expanded the scope of Hebrew poetry, writing compositions that were never intended for the synagogue liturgy including (in Hai's case) some of the first Hebrew secular poetry and some of the earliest uses of quantitative meters based on the model of Arabic poetry.

My point in offering this brief sketch of Geonic culture is simply to suggest that the composition of a learned parodic work like the *Alphabet* would not have been out of place in Geonic Babylonia. Quite the opposite: it seems very much a product of that world and its culture. As I have already argued, the parodic nature of both passages discussed in this article presupposes a deep familiarity with Rabbinic literature and its conventions—the kind of deep familiarity that would have been possessed only by a student of the Talmud of the sort that populated the Babylonian *yeshivot*. So, too, the anxieties

---

[48] Ibid., 334.

[49] On *piyyut* in the Geonic period, see Ezra Fleischer, *Shirat Hakodesh Ha‛ivrit Biyemei Habeinayim* (Jerusalem: Keter, 1975), 289–329; Brody, *Geonim of Babylonia*, 323–32.

behind those works are the anxieties of scholars. As we know, parodies do not merely entertain; they can also do double-duty—by
subverting cultural norms, and by reinforcing them. The *Alphabet of
Ben Sira* does both: it mocks the somber sanctity of Rabbinic hagiography as found in *Pesiqta Rabbati*'s portrait of Jeremiah by creating
a kind of anti-hagiography for Ben Sira's conception and birth; at
the same time, it reinforces Rabbinic self-identity by mocking the
melamed in the *Alphabet*-lesson.

To be sure, it is very important that scholars be careful not to
read ancient texts anachronistically and read into them the conventions and predispositions of one's own, later age. In the case of parody, this is an especially challenging task if only because the very
identification of a literary work as a parody is always an extremely
subtle matter—a matter of literary discrimination—and we have,
alas, no external evidence or proof that the *Alphabet* should be a
parody. On the other hand, we know—if only because they were a
little bit like ourselves—that the inhabitants of the Babylonian *yeshivot*,
those ever-serious and grave Talmudists, must have done something
in their spare time, must have had some form of entertainment. No
less authoritative a figure than Maimonides tells us that even a
philosopher engaged in difficult and weighty matters must have some
outlet for relaxation, and as a prooftext he quotes an Aramaic saying, "The Rabbis, when they tired of their studying (*garsayhu*), used
to speak among themselves words of amusement (*milei devedihuta*)."[50]
The source for this prooftext has never been identified, nor do we
know to which specific rabbis Maimonides was referring, but is it
too remote to imagine that they may have been Maimonides's own
Babylonian predecessors, the Geonim? Yes, scholars must always
beware the trap of anachronism, but what greater anachronism can
there be than to assume that the ancient rabbis lacked a sense of
humor, or a gift for parody less literary or sharp than our own?

---

[50] Rabbi Moshe ben Maimon (Rambam), "Shemoneh Perakim-Hakdamah Lemasek-
het Avot," chap. 5, in Rabbeinu Mosheh ben Maimon, *Hakdamot Lefeirush Hamishnah*
(ed. M. D. Rabinovits; Jerusalem: Mosad Harav Kuk, 1961), 189. I want to thank
Yaakov Elbaum for referring me to this passage; on its background and later literary echoes, see Yaakov Elbaum, *Lehavin Divrei Hakhamim* (Jerusalem: Mosad Bialik,
2000), 84 n. 28. The phrase *milei devedihuta* is found twice in the Babylonian Talmud,
in a story about the sage Raba who would preface his lessons with such "words of
amusement" (*b. Shabb.* 30b; *b. Pesah.* 117a), but Maimonides's statement about
Rabbinic entertainment is unattested elsewhere.

DOES RASHI'S TORAH COMMENTARY RESPOND TO CHRISTIANITY? A COMPARISON OF RASHI WITH RASHBAM AND BEKHOR SHOR

SHAYE J. D. COHEN

In numerous learned and elegant essays, James Kugel has demonstrated how Jewish exegesis of the Bible was provoked by the Bible itself. Ancient Jewish exegetes, and their medieval continuators, attempted to solve difficulties, clarify ambiguities, and fill in gaps that were—and are—evident to any attentive reader of the sacred text. But, of course, as our honoree knows well, exegesis can also be stimulated by factors external to the biblical text. This brief essay is devoted to the impact of one such factor, namely Christianity, on the biblical exegesis of Rashi and his school.

I. ANTI-CHRISTIAN EXEGESIS IN THE COMMENTARIES OF RASHI, RASHBAM, AND BEKHOR SHOR

Rashi (acronym for R. Shelomo [Solomon] b. Isaac, 1040–1105) was perhaps the most important and influential sage produced by the Jewish communities of medieval Christian Europe. His commentaries on the Bible and the Talmud have shaped the interpretation of those canonical documents from that day to this. His sons-in-law, grandsons, and their successors in northern France over the next generations followed his lead in writing commentaries and glosses on the Bible and Talmud. A common theme in these biblical commentaries is the relationship of *peshat*, the "plain" or "simple" meaning of a given biblical verse, to *derash*, its "homiletical," or "expounded" or "derived," meaning, especially the interpretation given to the verse in the Talmud and classic Midrash. In his commentary on the Torah, Rashi constantly balances *peshat* and *derash*. Two important successors who wrote commentaries on the Torah were Rashbam (acronym for R. Shmuel [Samuel] b. Meir, ca. 1080–ca. 1160), Rashi's grandson, and Bekhor Shor (cognomen of R. Joseph b. Isaac of Orleans, flourished in the third quarter of the twelfth century), a disciple of

Rashbam's younger brother R. Jacob Tam (ca. 1100–1171).[1] Rashbam was a brilliant exponent of *peshat*, arguing that his grandfather Rashi had not gone far enough in its pursuit. In one passage Rashbam even claims that Rashi conceded to him that "if he only had the time, he would have written new [revised] commentaries, based on the insights into the plain meaning of Scripture that are newly thought of day by day."[2] Bekhor Shor is a more complicated case; he too was a partisan of *peshat*, often following the interpretations of Rashbam, but he was also capable of flights of exegetical fantasy that seem to have been motivated by nothing more than a desire for originality and novelty. Here then are three Torah commentaries written in northern France by adherents of a single school over the course of a century or so: Rashi, Rashbam, and Bekhor Shor.[3]

Many scholars have noted the anti-Christian animus of the biblical exegesis of Rashi's school, even if there is some disagreement on its significance. Some scholars have argued that the polemic against Christianity was a central and defining element of the exegesis; in this view, the Christian appropriation of the "Old Testament" and the increasingly aggressive anti-Judaism of the Church impelled Rashi and his successors to search for the "plain meaning" of Scripture. In contrast other scholars have argued that the need for anti-Christian polemic was but one of many stimuli to the emergence of Jewish Bible exegesis in northern France in the eleventh and twelfth centuries. But all scholars seem to agree that Rashi, like Rashbam and

---

[1] Bibliographical note: I cite Rashi, Rashbam, and Bekhor Shor on Genesis from *Mikra'ot Gedolot Haketer* (ed. M. Cohen; 2 vols.; Ramat Gan: Bar Ilan University, 1997). I have also consulted *Torat Hayyim Hamishah Humshe Torah* (7 vols.; Jerusalem: Mosad ha-Rav Kuk, 5747/1987), which includes Rashi and Rashbam, but not Bekhor Shor; the edition of Rashi by H. D. Chavel (Jerusalem: Mosad ha-Rav Kuk, 5743/1983); *The Pentateuch with Rashi Hashalem* (3 vols. on Genesis; Jerusalem: Ariel United Israel Institutes, 1986); the edition of Rashbam by David Rosin (5642/1882; repr., Tel Aviv: Sifriyati, 5725/1965); and the edition of Bekhor Shor by Yehoshafat Nevo (Jerusalem, Mosad ha-Rav Kuk, 5754/1994). All translations in this essay are mine unless otherwise noted.

This paper has benefited much from the comments and suggestions of my friends Rabbi Reuven Cohn, Professor Martin Lockshin (York University), and Professor Ivan Marcus (Yale University), to whom I am most grateful.

[2] Rashbam on Gen 37:2 in *Rabbi Samuel ben Meir's Commentary on Genesis: An Annotated Translation* (trans. M. Lockshin; Lewiston, N.Y.: Edwin Mellen, 1989), 241–42.

[3] Rashbam and Bekhor Shor wrote commentaries on other biblical books too, but most of them are lost.

Bekhor Shor, used his commentaries on the Bible to defend Judaism and attack Christianity.[4]

In this brief essay I would like to propose a small but significant modification to the scholarly consensus. My thesis is that Rashi in his Torah commentary paid no attention to Christianity and its truth claims, in contrast with Rashbam and Bekhor Shor who did. In their Torah commentaries Rashbam explicitly rejects christological exegesis of Scripture, and Bekhor Shor explicitly rejects not only christological exegesis but also some of the core tenets of Christianity such as the Trinity and the Virgin Birth. These explicit and unambiguous passages allow us to see the anti-Christian intent of many additional passages that otherwise lack any signs of polemic. Rashi's Torah commentary, however, contains not a single explicit and unambiguous attack on Christian truth claims and Christian exegesis. In the absence of explicit polemic there is no methodological basis for positing the existence of implicit polemic. Rashi's Torah commentary is not a response to Christianity.

---

[4] The bibliography is enormous; I note the following. In general: E. I. J. Rosenthal, "Anti-Christian Polemic in Medieval Bible Commentaries," *JJS* 11 (1960): 115–35; Marianne Awerbuch, *Christlich-jüdische Begegnung im Zeitalter der Frühscholastik* (Munich: C. Kaiser, 1980); Avraham Grossman, "The Jewish-Christian Polemic and Jewish Bible Exegesis in Twelfth Century France," *Zion* 51 (1986): 29–60 [Hebrew]; Sarah Kamin, *Jews and Christians Interpret the Bible* (Jerusalem: Magnes, 1991) [Hebrew]. I have not yet seen *With Reverence to the Word: Medieval Scriptural Exegesis in Judaism, Christianity and Islam* (ed. J. D. McAuliffe, B. D. Walfish, and J. W. Goering; New York: Oxford University Press, 2002).

On anti-Christian polemic in Rashi: Samuel Poznanski, *Mavo al Hakhme Tzorfat Meforshe ha Miqra, Kommentar zu Ezechiel . . . von Eliezer aus Beaugency . . . mit einer Abhandlung uber die nordfranzösischen Bibelexegeten* (Warsaw: Verein Mekize Nirdamim, 1913), xx [Hebrew]; Yitzhaq Baer, "Rashi and the Historical Reality of his Time," *Tarbiz* 20 (1950): 320–32 [Hebrew]; repr. in *Sefer Rashi published at the 850th anniversary of the death of R. Solomon Yitzhaqi* (ed. Y. L. Hakohen Maimon; Jerusalem: Mosad ha-Rav Kuk, 5716/1956), 489–502; E. I. J. Rosenthal, "Anti-Christian Polemic," 124–26; Samuel Krauss, *The Jewish-Christian Controversy from the Earliest Times to 1789 I: History* (ed. W. Horbury; TSAJ 56; Tübingen: Mohr-Siebeck, 1995), 82–84; Judah Rosenthal, "Anti-Christian Polemic in Rashi on the Tanakh," in *Rashi: His Teachings and Personality* (ed. S. Federbush; New York: World Jewish Congress/Jewish Agency, 1958), 45–59 [Hebrew]; repr. in *Mehqarim u Meqorot* (2 vols.; Jerusalem: R. Mass, 1967), 1:101–16; Awerbuch, *Begegnung*, 101–30; Esra Shereshevsky, *Rashi the Man and his World* (New York: Sepher-Hermon Press, 1982), 119–32; Elazar Touitou, "Rashi's Commentary on Genesis 1–6 in the Context of the Judeo-Christian Controversy," *HUCA* 61 (1990): 159–83; Avraham Grossman, *The Early Sages of France* (Jerusalem: Magnes, 1995), 142–46, 205–7, 477–79 [Hebrew].

On anti-Christian polemic in Rashbam: Poznanski, *Mavo*, xlvii–xlix; E. I. J. Rosenthal, "Anti-Christian Polemic," 126 n. 29; Krauss-Horbury, *Controversy*, 84;

II. Rashi and Rashbam on Gen 49:10

A three-way comparison of Rashi, Rashbam, and Bekhor Shor on
Gen 49:10 will make this point clear. (I discuss Rashi and Rashbam
in this section, Bekhor Shor in the next section.) Genesis 49:10, perhaps the most famous Christian prooftext in the Torah, reads as follows: *The scepter shall not depart from Judah, Nor the staff from between his
feet; Until Shiloh comes* [or: *until he comes to Shiloh*], *And the homage of peoples be his.* Here is Rashi:[5]

> *The scepter shall not depart from Judah*: from David onwards. These are
> the exilarchs in Babylonia who rule the people with a scepter, because
> they are appointed by the kingdom.
> *Nor the staff* disciples[6] *from between his feet*: these are the patriarchs of
> the land of Israel.
> *Until Shiloh comes*: the king messiah, because kingship is his (under-
> standing the word *Shiloh* as *shelo*, "his"); and thus did Onqelos inter-
> pret it. A midrashic interpretation: (the word *Shiloh* should be understood
> as) *shay lo*, "tribute to him," as it says (Ps 76:12), *they shall bring tribute*
> (in Hebrew, *shay*) *to the awesome one*.

This exegesis can be understood as a response to the Christian read-
ing of Scripture. Jews and Christians agree that the mysterious word
Shiloh is the Messiah, but disagree, of course, on the identity of that
Messiah. Christian exegetes from antiquity through the Middle Ages

---

Awerbuch, *Begegnung*, 143–53; Elazar Touitou, "Peshat and Apologetics in the
Rashbam's Commentary on the Biblical Stories of Moses," *Tarbiz* 51 (1982): 227–38
[Hebrew]; idem, "The Exegetical Method of Rashbam against the Background of
the Historical Reality of His Time," in *Studies in Rabbinic Literature Bible and Jewish
History dedicated to Prof. E. Z. Melamed* (ed. Y. D. Gilat et al.; Ramat Gan: Bar Ilan
University Press, 1982), 48–74 [Hebrew]; Grossman, *Early Sages*, 479–80. Elazar
Touitou, *Exegesis in Perpetual Motion: Studies in the Pentateuchal Commentary of R. Samuel
b. Meir* (Ramat Gan: Bar Ilan University Press, 2003 [Hebrew]) reached me after
the completion of this essay.
  On anti-Christian polemic in Bekhor Shor: Poznanski, *Mavo*, lxix; E. I. J. Rosenthal,
"Anti-Christian Polemic," 127 n. 31; Krauss-Horbury, *Controversy*, 85; Awerbuch,
Begegnung, 153–63; Nevo, introduction to his edition of Bekhor Shor, 9–10; Grossman,
Early Sages, 493–95.
  [5] In translating rabbinic texts I place in parentheses material that is implicit in
the original or material that any reader schooled in rabbinic lore would instantly
know; brackets indicate my additions to the text.
  [6] I have rearranged the text to make it clear that "disciples" is a gloss on *staff*.
Perhaps *talmidim* should be translated here "teachers" rather than "disciples." The
Guadalajara 1476 edition of Rashi's commentary (see *Rashi Hashalem*, 3:311) omits
talmidim and indeed the text is smoother without it.

uniformly understood *Shiloh* to refer to Jesus, so that the verse is a prophecy that Jesus will be the last king of the house of David. "When Jesus came the kingdom of Judah ceased."[7] The absence of Jewish national sovereignty, specifically Davidic kingship, after the time of Jesus is proof of the truth of Christianity. Rashi contends that the verse has yet to be fulfilled because *Shiloh*, the Messiah, has not yet come. The continued existence of Davidic royalty, exilarchs in Babylonia and patriarchs (*nesi'im*) in the land of Israel, disproves the Christian exegesis and Christian truth claims. Rashi's exegesis, it has been suggested, is a response to Christianity.[8]

This approach to Rashi on this verse, however, is neither demonstrable nor necessary; Rashi's exegesis may have nothing to do with Christianity. Rashi in his usual way is paraphrasing a piece of rabbinic exegesis that appears in slightly different forms in the Talmud and Midrash. In the talmudic version the point is that the exilarchs, the Davidic leaders of the Jewish community of Babylonia, who are called *scepter*, outrank the patriarchs, the Davidic leaders of the Jewish community of the land of Israel, who are called *staff*. No anti-Christian polemic here.[9] Had Rashi intended his comment to serve as a response to Christian exegesis, surely he would have updated his talmudic source to make it reflect the realia of his own time, for without such updating this reading of Scripture is not an effective response.[10] In the Talmudic period the exilarchs of Babylonia were indeed powerful figures who ruled the people with a scepter, but in Rashi's time they were but pale shadows of what they once had been.[11] In the

---

[7] This is the summary of the Christian argument in *Sefer Nizzahon* sec. 28; see David Berger, *The Jewish-Christian Debate in the High Middle Ages: A Critical Edition of Nizzahon Vetus* (Philadelphia: Jewish Publication Society, 1979), 60, along with the note on 249. (*Sefer Nizzahon* was written in Germany about 1300). For an exhaustive survey of Christian exegesis of Gen 49:10, see Adolf Posnanski, *Schiloh: Ein Beitrag zur Geschichte der Messiaslehre* (Leipzig: Hinrichs, 1904), 288–449; for a survey of some ancient Jewish exegesis of the verse see James Kugel, *Traditions of the Bible* (Cambridge, Mass.: Harvard University Press, 1998), 469–74.

[8] See, for example, J. Rosenthal, "Anti-Christian Polemic," 52 (= *Mehqarim*, 1:111).

[9] *B. Sanh.* 5a and *b. Hor.* 11b; *Gen. Rab.* 97 (Theodor-Albeck ed., 1219); Posnanski, *Schiloh*, 33–34 and 117.

[10] For a good example of such updating, see R. Aaron ben Gerson Abulrabi (fl. ca. 1400) in Posnanski, *Schiloh*, 161–62 and xxviii–xxix n. 66.

[11] Avraham Grossman, *The Babylonian Exilarchate in the Gaonic Period* (Jerusalem: Shazar Center, 1984), 11–12 [Hebrew]. I am grateful to my colleague Bernard Septimus for this reference.

Talmudic period the princes or patriarchs of the land of Israel were indeed "disciples" of the sages, but the office ceased in the fifth century C.E.; in Rashi's time the office did not exist. It is possible, of course, that Rashi was ill-informed about these matters and believed that even in his own time the Babylonian exilarchate still exerted great power and the Israelian patriarchate still existed, but surely it is simpler to assume that in his comment on Gen 49:10 Rashi is living in talmudic time, not his own. That is, he is not interested in shaping an exegesis that will be "useful" or "relevant" for his Jewish contemporaries in northern France in the eleventh century; his goal, rather, is to see the Torah as part of classical rabbinic literature, and classical rabbinic literature as part of the Torah.[12] If so, he does not have Christian exegesis in view.

Contrast Rashbam:[13]

> *The scepter shall not depart from Judah*: The kingship that was granted to him—namely, that all twelve of his brothers shall bow low to him (v. 8)—that greatness of his shall not cease, *nor the staff from between his feet*, nor shall power cease from his progeny, *until he* Judah *comes to Shiloh*— in other words until a Judaean king, Rehoboam the son of Solomon, comes to Shiloh, which is near Shechem, to renew the monarchy. However, then the ten tribes will desert him and proclaim Jeroboam king, leaving only Judah and Benjamin for Rehoboam the son of Solomon. *And his is the assemblage of nations*: The assemblage of nations that were subordinated by his father Solomon . . . gathered together there to proclaim Rehoboam king, as it is written, *Rehoboam went to Shechem, for all Israel had come to Shechem to acclaim him king* (1 Kgs 12:1 and 2 Chr 10:1). Shechem is near Shiloh. . . .
>
> This interpretation is a refutation of [or: response to] the heretics.[14] *Shiloh* that is written here is just the name of a city. For there are no vernacular words in the Bible. Nor is *shelo*, "his," written here, as some Hebrews claim, nor *shaliah*, "messenger," as the Christians say.

---

[12] Cf. Moshe Greenberg, "Parshane Tzorfat [The Commentators of Northern France]," in *Encyclopaedia Biblica* (9 vols.; Jerusalem: Mosad Bialik, 1982), 8:694 [Hebrew]: "[in Rashi's conception] the Bible and rabbinic literature are one world, and it is permissible to draw from the latter, which is far more extensive, to illuminate the former." My thanks to Ivan Marcus for this reference.

[13] Rashbam on Gen 49:10 (Lockshin trans., 359–63, slightly modified).

[14] The phrase is *teshuvah la minim*, which can be understood either as "refutation of the heretics" or "response to the heretics," as is well noted by J. Rosenthal, *Mehqarim*, 1:368, and by Elazar Touitou, "On the Meaning of the Concept *teshuvat ha minim* in the Writings of our French Sages," *Sinai* 99,3–4 (5746/1986 nos. 603–604): 144–48 [Hebrew].

Jacob made explicit the true greatness of Judah, which was from David to Rehoboam, but did not wish to make explicit the diminution of that greatness; however, from the phraseology of the verse you may infer that from Shiloh onwards the greatness was diminished.

According to Rashbam this verse has nothing to do with messianic kings, either past (as the Christians would have it) or future (as Rashi says). Rather, it is entirely historical. Jacob prophesied that the royal power would not depart from the tribe of Judah until a Judaean king would go to Shiloh. This prophecy was fulfilled when Rehoboam son of Solomon went to Shechem, which is near Shiloh, to be installed as king. Shortly thereafter the northern tribes broke away from the southern, the kingdom of Ephraim was established, and the greatness of Judah was diminished. At that moment the scepter did indeed depart from Judah. "This interpretation is a refutation of [or: response to] the heretics (*minim*)," namely Christians.

Rashbam specifically rejects three versions of the messianic exegesis that is shared by Jews and Christians. First, "there are no vernacular words (*la'az*) in the Bible." David Rosin, the editor of the standard critical edition of Rashbam, conjectures that Rashbam is rejecting an explanation advanced by some unknown contemporary (Jewish? Christian?) that interpreted *Shiloh* as the French word *salut*, "salvation." Second, "nor is *shelo*, 'his,' written here, as some Hebrews claim"; this of course is the explanation advanced by Rashi (following the Targumim).[15] Third, "nor [is] *shaliah*, 'messenger,' [written here] as the Christians say." Rashbam here rejects the interpretation of the Vulgate, which takes *Shiloh* to mean *qui mittendus est*, "he who is to be sent." The messianic exegesis of Gen 49:10 in all its manifestations is wrong, says Rashbam.

This passage exemplifies three aspects of Rashbam's anti-Christian polemic in his Torah commentary: he explicitly rejects Christian interpretation of Scripture; in order to subvert Christian "messianic" exegesis he advocates "historical" exegesis; and when refuting Christian truth claims he refers to the Christians as *minim*, "heretics." All of these features recur in Bekhor Shor; none of them appears in the Torah commentary of Rashi. Let us look at each of these in turn.

---

[15] I do not know why Rashbam uses the locution "Hebrews" (*Ivrim*) here, which would seem to translate the standard Christian term *Hebraei*. As far as I know nowhere else does Rashbam use *Ivrim* in this sense.

III. Explicit and Implicit Anti-Christian Polemic

Rashbam cites and rejects the Christian interpretation of Gen 49:10. Similarly, in his comment on Exod 20:13 he cites and rejects the rendering of the Vulgate.[16] These two passages, each of which refers to Christians as *minim*, make it likely that the *minim* who appear elsewhere on the pages of Rashbam's Torah commentary are also Christians.[17] Additional passages, too, appear to be anti-Christian in spite of the absence of any reference to "Christians" or "heretics."[18]

Bekhor Shor attacks Christian exegesis and Christian truth claims far more often than Rashbam. He refers to Christians as "heretics" (*minim*), "gentiles" (*goyim*), "errant ones" (*to'im*),[19] and "nations" (*umot*); he explicitly and unambiguously attacks the Christian allegorization of the laws of the Torah, the veneration of images, the doctrines of the Trinity and the Virgin Birth, and the ritual of the Eucharist.[20] Additional passages also appear to be anti-Christian despite absence of any explicit reference to Christians.[21] Among these is Bekhor Shor's commentary on Gen 49:10:

> *The scepter shall not depart from Judah*: (Jacob) meant to explain to him (Judah) when the kingdom would be his, and said to him, "Do not think that you will be in poverty until the time of your kingdom arrives,

---

[16] Thus leading some scholars to suggest that Rashbam knew Latin. There is no sign whatsoever that Rashi knew Latin.

[17] In response to *minim* Rashbam offers rational explanations of biblical laws (Lev 11:3, 34; 19:19; Deut 22:6)—is it possible that Rashbam is combating Jewish "rationalist" heretics here?—and apologetic explanations of the actions of the Israelites (Exod 3:22; see Grossman, *Early Sages*, 491–92).

[18] With Deut 22:6, cf. Exod 23:19; with Exod 3:22, cf. Exod 11:2 and 12:36. See Elazar Touitou, "The Method in Rashbam's Commentary on the Halakhic Parts of the Torah," *Milet: Everyman's University Studies in Jewish History and Culture* 2 (Tel Aviv, 1985): 275–88, here 278–80 [Hebrew].

[19] This is also a common pejorative designation for the Crusaders.

[20] Polemic against the Christian allegorization of the laws of the Torah: Num 12:8 (a passage that also includes polemic against "some of our people," that is, Jews; cf. Lev 17:13 and Deut 6:9). Polemic against the Christian veneration of images: Exod 20:4; 33:25. Polemic against the doctrine of the Trinity: Gen 1:26; 3:22; 19:1; Deut 6:6. Polemic against the doctrine of the Virgin Birth: Gen 24:2. Poznanski (*Mavo*, lxix), followed by Krauss-Horbury (*Controversy*, 85), assembles all of these passages. Polemic against the ritual of the Eucharist: Exod 32:20.

[21] Poznanski (*Mavo*, lxix), followed by Krauss-Horbury (*Controversy*, 85), lists Gen 18:3 (cf. Gen 19:1) and Exod 31:18 as implicit anti-Christian polemic. In my forthcoming *Why aren't Jewish Women Circumcised?* I hope to demonstrate that Bekhor Shor's comment on Gen 17:11 is also directed against Christianity.

because *the scepter* and governance *shall not depart from* you. They (your brothers) will always esteem you a great one, and stick and strap will (always) be in your hand."

(Nor) the staff (from between his feet): He will write and legislate decrees that are incumbent on others. In other words: *until Shiloh comes* you will be a magistrate and a ruler, but once *Shiloh comes* you will be a king. Once the day of Shiloh came, (meaning) that it was destroyed, then the kingdom of the house of David flourished, as it is written in the book of Psalms (78:60–68), *He forsook the tabernacle of Shiloh . . . he rejected the tent of Joseph . . . he chose David his servant, and Jerusalem which he desired.*[22] This verse implies that (the rise of) the kingdom of the house of David depends on the arrival of the day of Shiloh (that is, its destruction). Jacob forecast to him that then he would be king, and until the destruction of Shiloh he would not be in a low state but would (carry) a stick and staff.

When *Shiloh comes* (that is, when Shiloh is destroyed, then) *the homage of peoples will be his:* then all Israel will congregate to him in order to make him king. . . .

Like Rashbam, Bekhor Shor adopts a "historical" exegesis of the verse, but unlike Rashbam, who understood *scepter* and *staff* as signs of royal authority, Bekhor Shor understands them to be signs of non-royal authority.[23] For Rashbam this verse predicts when royal power will depart from Judah; for Bekhor Shor the verse predicts when royal power will come to Judah. The key is the phrase *until Shiloh comes/until he comes to Shiloh.* For Rashbam this meant that Judean royal power will endure until Rehoboam comes to Shiloh, that is, Shechem. Bekhor Shor, perhaps to avoid the obvious problem confronting Rashbam, namely that Shiloh is not Shechem, rather ingeniously understands *until Shiloh comes* to mean "until Shiloh is destroyed."[24] The destruction of Shiloh marks the ascent of the house of David. Until that point, Jacob says, non-royal authority will be his; after that point, Jacob implies, royal authority will be his.

Unlike Rashbam, Bekhor Shor does not mention here either Christianity or Christian exegesis. Nevertheless, we may be sure that Bekhor Shor intended his exegesis to be a response to, or a refutation of, the Christian reading of Gen 49:10 because Bekhor Shor

---

[22] Bekhor Shor's citation is not accurate; we may assume that he is citing from memory.

[23] Whether *scepter* and *staff* necessarily imply royal authority was much debated; see Berger, *Jewish-Christian Debate*, 251.

[24] So too Ibn Ezra.

elsewhere explicitly and unambiguously attacks Christian exegesis.[25] Rashi's case is different: in the absence of any explicit and unambiguous polemic against Christian exegesis anywhere in his Torah commentary, we have no basis on which to attribute such intent to his commentary here. Explicit polemic allows us to see the implicit; in Rashi there is no explicit polemic.

IV. HISTORICAL EXEGESIS VERSUS MESSIANIC EXEGESIS

Rashbam and Bekhor Shor, on Gen 49:10, adopt a "historical" exegesis to counter Christian "messianic" exegesis. The Christians think that the verse refers to their messiah, but in reality, say Rashbam and Bekhor Shor, it does not refer to any messiah, either theirs or ours. It refers to figures and events from the history of biblical Israel. Rashbam and Bekhor Shor know full well that the midrash had understood the verse to refer to the messiah, but for the sake of anti-Christian polemic they were prepared to reject rabbinic exegesis.

Rashi adopted this strategy in his commentary on the Psalms. On *Why do nations assemble . . . against the Lord and his anointed* (Ps 2:1), Rashi writes as follows:[26]

> Our rabbis interpreted the subject of the chapter as a reference to king Messiah. However, according to its basic meaning and for a refutation of [or: response to] the heretics it is correct to interpret it as a reference to David himself in consonance with what is stated in the Bible, *The Philistines heard that Israel had anointed David as king over them* (2 Sam 5:17), *the Philistines gathered their troops* (1 Sam 28:4) and they fell into his hand. It is concerning them that David asked here, *Why do nations assemble?*

Compare Rashi's comment on *The king rejoices in your strength* (Ps 21:2):[27]

> Our rabbis interpreted it as a reference to king Messiah, but it is correct to interpret it as a reference to David himself as a refutation of [or: response to] the heretics who find in it support for their erroneous beliefs.

---

[25] In addition, Bekhor Shor here, as so often, is trying to improve upon what Rashbam had said. Rashbam here is overtly anti-Christian, and we may safely assume that Bekhor Shor is, too.

[26] Rashi on Ps 2:1 in *Rashi's Commentary on Psalms 1–89* (trans. M. Gruber; South Florida Studies in the History of Judaism 161; Atlanta: Scholars Press, 1998), 52.

[27] Rashi on Ps 21:1 (*Rashi's Commentary*, 123; Gruber trans.).

In these two passages there can be no question: the heretics (*minim*) whom Rashi is refuting are Christians.[28] Anti-Christian polemic is prominent throughout Rashi's commentary on Psalms, and historical exegesis is one of his techniques.[29]

The contrast between Rashi on the Psalms and Rashi on the Torah is striking. The anti-Christian polemic in the Psalms commentary is unmistakable and unambiguous; not so the Torah commentary, where, if it be found at all, it is mistakable and ambiguous. In their commentaries on Gen 49:10 Rashbam and Bekhor Shor apply the technique that Rashi promoted in his commentary on Psalms: in order to rebut Christian messianic exegesis they adopt a historical exegesis, even if that means rejecting the exegesis of the rabbis of the Talmud and Midrash. Rashi himself, however, in his commentary on Gen 49:10, was content to follow the messianic exegesis of the ancient rabbis.

V. CHRISTIANS AND OTHER HERETICS

The word *minim* is the talmudic appellation for "heretics."[30] When Rashbam and Bekhor Shor use the word, they mean Christians. Rashi in his commentary on Psalms similarly uses *minim* to mean Christians, as we have seen, and this usage may well be found in his commentary on other books of the Prophets and Writings.[31] The usage in the Torah commentary, however, is different. In his Torah commentary Rashi refers to *minim* in only three passages. Of these, one almost definitely refers to Christians, one almost definitely does not, and one definitely is ambiguous. Let us look at these passages in turn.

---

[28] So much so that Gruber even translates *minim* "Christians." See Gruber, *Rashi's Commentary*, 54–55 n. 6.

[29] Anti-Christian polemic in the commentary on Psalms: Gruber, *Rashi's Commentary*, 10. Historical exegesis: Gruber, *Rashi's Commentary*, 394 n. 19 on Ps 84:10; Schereschevsky, *Rashi*, 123–24, regarding Psalms 40 and 80. Rashi uses the same technique elsewhere, too: E. I. J. Rosenthal, "Anti-Christian Polemic," 124–26; Awerbuch, *Begegnung*, 109; Grossman, *Early Sages*, 479.

[30] Which individuals or groups the Talmud had in mind with this designation is a much-debated question that does not concern us here.

[31] J. Rosenthal, "Anti-Christian Polemic." A study of Rashi's use of *umot*, "nations," and *umot ha'olam*, "nations of the world," is a desideratum.

Here is Rashi's comment on Deut 32:21, *They incensed me with no-gods, Vexed me with their futilities; I'll incense them with a no-folk, Vex them with a nation of fools*:

> *With a no-folk*: with a nation that has no reputation,[32] as it says, *Behold the land of the Chaldeans, This is a nation that should never have been*[33] (Isa 23:13), [and] concerning Esau it says, *You are most despised* (Obad 2).
>
> *A nation of fools* (in Hebrew, *naval*): These are the heretics, as it says, *The foolish one* (in Hebrew, *naval*) *says in his heart "There is no God"* (Ps 14:1).

Deuteronomy 32 sets forth the paradigm of Jewish history: Israel is chosen by God, becomes overconfident and arrogant, goes astray by worshiping other gods, and is punished by God for her disobedience. Rashi understands v. 21 to refer to the destruction of the first and second temples in Jerusalem, the first at the hands of the Chaldeans (= Babylonians), and the second at the hands of Esau (= Rome). Both the Babylonians and the Romans are nations-that-are-not-nations; each is a *no-folk*. The Babylonians, says Isaiah, should never have been, and the Romans, says Obadiah, are despicable. These are the agents by which God punishes Israel. Who then is *a nation of fools* by which God also punishes Israel? "These are the heretics (*minim*)," Rashi says, basing his interpretation on Ps 14:1 which shows that a *foolish one* is one who denies God, in other words, a heretic.

The heretics who vex Israel—surely Rashi means Christians.[34] Rabbinic exegetes and historians did not distinguish between pagan Rome and Christian Rome; both alike were Esau, and both alike were chosen by God to subjugate Israel.[35] As one of the signs of the end time, the Mishnah says, "the kingdom will be given over to heresy." Rashi explains, "The kingdom that rules most of the world shall become heretical and drawn after his error [perhaps a mis-

---

[32] Lit. "name."

[33] I am translating the verse as Rashi understood it; see his commentary on Isa 23:13.

[34] Whether Rashi's source, too, meant Christians is a separate question; see *b. Yebam.* 63b (the Vulgate text reads "these are the Sadducees" but all manuscripts and testimonia read "these are the *minim*") and *Sifrei Deuteronomy* 320 (Finkelstein ed., 367).

[35] Gerson D. Cohen, "Esau as Symbol," in *Studies in the Variety of Rabbinic Cultures* (Philadelphia: Jewish Publication Society, 1991), 243–69, esp. 249.

print for "drawn after the error of Jesus"]; his disciples were called heretics (*minim*)."[36] Until they are delivered by the messiah, Jews must endure the dominion of a "heretical" kingdom, that is, Christendom.

I conclude that in his comment on Deut 32:21 Rashi refers to Christians and dubs them *minim*. Note, however, what this passage does not do: it does not dispute Christian truth claims or Christian exegesis of Scripture. Instead Rashi simply alludes to a fact that every medieval Jew knew all too well, namely, that God has given the Jews into the hands of the Christians. Christianity is not the subject of this—or, so I am arguing, of any other—passage of the Torah commentary.

In contrast, in his comment on Gen 6:6 Rashi also refers to *minim* but in all likelihood does not have Christians in mind. The verse reads, *And the Lord regretted that he had made humanity*[37] *on the earth, and his heart was saddened.* Rashi comments:

> *And the Lord regretted*: (Do not translate *vayinnahem* "regretted"; rather it should be translated "he was consoled.") God took consolation in the fact that he had created him (Adam, that is, humanity) among the terrestrial creatures, for had he been among the supernal creatures he would have incited them to rebel. (This is the interpretation of) *Genesis Rabbah*.[38]
>
> *And humanity was saddened* in God's *heart*: God intended to make him (humanity) sad. This is the interpretation of *Onqelos*.
>
> Another interpretation:
>
> *And the Lord regretted*: God's intention changed from mercy to justice. God (now) considered what to do with the humanity that he had made on earth. Likewise wherever in Scripture the expression *nihum* is used, it means "having second thoughts about what to do. . . ." [Rashi here cites several examples]. In all these verses the verb *n-h-m* denotes a change of mind.
>
> *And his heart was saddened*: God mourned the death of the work of his hands; (the verb was *saddened* means "mourned") just as in the verse (2 Sam 19:3), *the king was saddened by* (that is, mourned the death of) *his son.*
>
> And this I have written in order to refute [or: respond to] the heretics.

[36] *M. Sotah* end, *b. Sotah* 49b. Rashi's comment appears in the margin of the Vilna edition; perhaps *ta'ut shelo* is a misprint for *te'ut yeshu*. See Rosenthal, "Anti-Christian Polemic," 48 (= *Mehqarim*, 1:105).

[37] Lit. "the Adam," and so throughout.

[38] *Gen. Rab.* 27:4 (Theodor-Albeck ed., 258).

A gentile once asked R. Joshua b. Qorha. He said to him, "Do you not believe that the Holy One, blessed be He, foresees the future?" "Yes," he replied. "But it is written and *his heart was saddened*." R. Joshua said to him, "Have you ever had a son born to you?" "Yes." "And what did you do (when he was born)?" "I rejoiced, and made everyone else rejoice." R. Joshua then said, "And did you not know that your son is destined to die?" The gentile replied, "At a time of rejoicing—let there be rejoicing; at a time of mourning—let there be mourning." R. Joshua said, "Thus too is the way of the Holy One, blessed be He." Even though it is revealed before him that they were destined to sin and die, he did not refrain from creating them, for the sake of the righteous who would later emerge from them.

This passage, which is too long and too rich to be fully unpacked here, has three sections: the first interpretation of the verse; the second interpretation of the verse; and a story featuring a conversation between a gentile and R. Joshua b. Qorha.

One thousand years before Rashi, Philo of Alexandria devoted an essay to the difficulties raised by Gen 6:6. In fact, one does not need to be a philosopher to be troubled by this verse: How can God regret something he has done, and how can God become sad? Is God capable of emotions? Or, in philosophical language, is God mutable?[39] These questions are at the core of Rashi's exegesis. According to Rashi's first interpretation of the verse, God did not regret; rather God took consolation in the fact that he had made Adam a terrestrial creature. God was not saddened; rather God caused humanity to be saddened at the prospect of destruction by the flood. The subject of the verb "was saddened" is not God but humanity. This reading of the verse allows God to be immutable and unmoved. According to Rashi's second interpretation, God indeed did regret; he changed his mind. By applying the attribute of justice rather than the attribute of mercy, God decided to wipe out humanity and mourned the impending death of the work of his hands. In this reading God is mutable and moved. The story about the gentile and R. Joshua revolves around a slightly different but closely related question: Does God know the future? If he does— and of course all pious Jews believe that he does—what can the verse mean when it says that God's *heart was saddened*? Did not God know from the beginning of creation that human sin would neces-

---

[39] Philo, *Quod Deus sit immutabilis.*

sitate the flood? R. Joshua's answer is that divine lamentation does not necessarily indicate the absence of divine foreknowledge. Just as we celebrate the birth of a baby, even though we know that this new human will eventually die, so too the Holy One, blessed be he, laments the impending death of the humans that he had created, even though he knew all along that this would be their fate.[40]

Between the second interpretation and the story Rashi adds the arresting comment, "And this I have written in order to refute [or: respond to] the heretics (minim)." Since Rashi often writes in the first person singular in his Torah commentary,[41] there is nothing particularly unusual about this sentence even if it is not precisely paralleled elsewhere. The sentence raises two problems: who are these minim, and what is the antecedent of the word "this"? The answer to the former question depends on the answer to the latter, so I begin with the latter. To what does "this" refer? The first interpretation? The second interpretation? The story? If I could, I would choose the first interpretation, which keeps God philosophically respectable by keeping him immutable and unmoved. Heretics argued that Gen 6:6 illustrates the philosophical crudity and un-Godlike characteristics of the biblical God, and Rashi is responding to them.[42] Alas, this reading, which makes so much sense, is impossible; I do not see how the word "this" can refer back to the first interpretation when it is sandwiched between the second interpretation and the story about the gentile and R. Joshua. The second interpretation and the story are closely connected: in *Genesis Rabbah* they form a single block of material, and both interpret the phrase *was saddened* to mean that God mourned.[43] Therefore Rashi's "this" must refer to the second interpretation and the story together. The heretic to

---

[40] As the commentators on Rashi observe, the parable does not really work; human mortality is a given for humans, a fact over which we have no control, while God certainly is in control of the fate that is meted out to humans. The commentators also debate how the last line of the story, which Rashi has added to his source (*Genesis Rabbah*), is to be combined with the story: does Rashi intend the line to be a continuation of the reply of R. Joshua? Or, as I have punctuated it above, is it meant to be a comment of Rashi on the story? I cannot pursue these questions here.

[41] See the list of such passages in Chavel's edition of Rashi, 630.

[42] Judah Rosenthal, *Hiwi al-Balkhi: A Comparative Study* (Philadelphia: Dropsie College, 1949), 11.

[43] *Gen. Rab.* 27:4 (Theodor-Albeck ed., 258–59).

whom Rashi is responding must have been arguing, like the gentile
in the story, that God's sadness proves that God did not know the
future. In response, Rashi says that God did not really feel sad; he
mourned, and he mourned that which he knew all along would happen. Rashi thus protects the notion of divine omniscience from the
attack of heretics, but apparently neither he nor his heretical interlocutor is perturbed by the regret, hence mutability, of God.

I am not sure that I have explained this Rashi correctly, but one
point at least seems clear: the heretics (minim) whom Rashi is addressing are not Christians.[44] There is no sign or hint of Christianity anywhere in this passage, or, for that matter, in the story drawn from
Genesis Rabbah. Bekhor Shor devotes his commentary on Gen 6:6 to
a long discussion of divine regret and divine mutability; here too
there is no sign or hint that Christianity is the target, and this in the
work of a man who, as we have seen, was neither discreet nor cautious in his anti-Christian polemics.[45] I conclude that the *minim*
addressed by Rashi are not Christians.[46]

About two hundred years after Rashi, this verse figured in Jewish-
Christian polemic. In the middle of the thirteenth century (ca. 1260)
in northern France, R. Joseph b. Nathan Official compiled his *Book
of Joseph the Zealot*, a veritable encyclopedia of anti-Christian polemic.
He systematically reviews the exegesis of those verses of the Hebrew
Bible that Christians had adduced in support of their faith; needless
to say, the Christian exegesis is always found wanting. On Gen 6:6
he writes that the Christians have argued that this verse, along with
others, proves divine mutability: God changes his mind. This is
entirely consistent with the idea, say the Christians, that God has
withdrawn his Old Testament and replaced it with a new one.[47] This

---

[44] Poznanski, *Mavo*, xx n. 3. Even Touitou seems to concede this point, albeit
tacitly; he once mentions Rashi's reference to *minim* in Genesis 6:6 ("Rashi's Commentary on Genesis," 170), but fails to discuss it anywhere in his article.

[45] Alas, Rashbam's commentary on Gen 6:6, as on most of the early chapters
of Genesis, is lost.

[46] If not Christians, then who? I do not know. Perhaps Rashi was addressing
some free-thinking Jews of his time and place (cf. nn. 17 and 20 above); perhaps
he was addressing in the abstract all heretics, of whatever time and place, who
might adduce Gen 6:6 as support for their heretical ideas. Poznanski, *Mavo*, lxix
n. 2, is puzzled by the identity of the Jewish heretics denounced by Bekhor Shor.

[47] *Sepher Joseph Hamekane* (ed. J. Rosenthal; Jerusalem: Mekize Nirdamim, 1970),
37–38 sec. 11.

remarkable argument turns a philosophical liability into a theological asset. Divine mutability is invoked as evidence of Christian truth! I cannot imagine this argument being advanced by Christian schoolmen, who of course believed that God is immutable and that the substitution of the Old Testament by the New was part of the divine plan from the beginning of creation.[48] Perhaps this was a "popular" anti-Jewish argument, advanced by Jewish apostates to Christianity. In any event, R. Joseph responds that God is not mutable and that those biblical verses that seem to suggest that he is are simply examples of "the Torah speaking in common language." R. Joseph then adduces Rashi's first interpretation to show that Gen 6:6 does not, in fact, support the notion of divine mutability. Rashi had thought that his *second* interpretation was a response to *minim*, but R. Joseph realizes that the *first* one is useful in order to rebut Christian claims. The *minim* addressed by Rashi are not Christians.

Rashi's third reference to *minim* is ambiguous. Genesis 1:26 has God say, *Let us make Adam in our image, after our likeness*—why the plural? In his first comment on this verse Rashi argues that God is giving an object lesson in humility, since he made a point of consulting his inferiors, the angelic members of his heavenly court, before creating Adam. He continues in the same vein:

> *Let us make Adam.* Even though they (the angels) did not assist him in the creation of Adam, and there is an opportunity for the heretics to LORD it (over us), (nevertheless) Scripture did not refrain from (using the plural, thus) teaching proper conduct and the measure of humility. (The lesson we are to learn is) that the great should consult and take advice from the small. If it had written, "I shall make Adam," we would not have learned that he spoke with his court, but (we would have concluded that he spoke only) with himself. The refutation of [or: response to] the heretics is written in the next verse, *And God created Adam* (Gen 1:27) (which is) written (in the singular and) not in the plural.

God alone created Adam, as the singular verb in Gen 1:27 makes clear. However, God consulted the angels of his heavenly court before

---

[48] Divine immutability: Thomas Aquinas, *Summa Theologiae* I.9, "On the Unchangeableness of God," in *Basic Writings of St. Thomas Aquinas* (ed. A. C. Pegis; 2 vols.; New York: Random House, 1945), 1:70–73. The replacement of the Old Law by the New Law was purposeful (and therefore not a symptom of God's change of plan): Thomas Aquinas, *Summa Theologiae* II.1.98.6 (*Basic Writings*, 2:815–16) and II.1.106.3 (*Basic Writings*, 2:952–54).

creating Adam, hence the plural of v. 26. Why did he consult them?
In order to teach us proper conduct and the importance of humility: those who are great and powerful should consult their inferiors
and should make a point of consulting their inferiors. This vital lesson would have been lost had Scripture written, "I shall make Adam."
This lesson is so important that Scripture even used the plural in
v. 26, knowing full well that the heretics (*minim*) might use it to
support their baseless claim that God did not act alone when creating Adam. Heretics use this verse "to LORD it (over us),"[49] as if
Scripture supports their heresy; but the lesson in proper conduct out-
weighs the threat from the heretics. Thus Rashi.

Rashi, in his usual way, is paraphrasing a talmudic-midrashic
source.[50] That text is directed against heretics (*minim*) who believe in
"two powers in heaven," that is, in the plurality of Gods. These
heretics are not (necessarily) Christians; they are just as likely to be
Jews who, like Philo, accept a developed Logos theology or who
assign too high a role to angelic intermediaries.[51] As in his commentary on Gen 49:10, perhaps here too Rashi is living in talmudic time. Certainly there is no sign in Rashi's text that his *minim* are
Christians or that the heretical theology that they espouse is the doctrine of the Trinity. (Contrast Bekhor Shor, who explicitly polemi-
cizes here against the doctrine of the Trinity.)[52] Even without the
presence of Christianity or Christian exegesis, the plural verb and
pronouns of Gen 1:26 demand explanation.[53] When Jews became
active in anti-Christian polemic they of course used Rashi's explanation to help rebut the christological reading of the verse,[54] but this
fact does not demonstrate that Rashi himself intended his exegesis
to serve as a response to Christianity. The *minim* addressed by Rashi
in his commentary on Gen 1:26 may be Christians but are not necessarily Christians. The text is ambiguous. If we believe that Rashi's

---

[49] I translate *lirdot* as Rashi understood it; see Rashi on *b. Yoma* 40b.
[50] *Gen. Rab.* 8:8–9 (Theodor-Albeck ed., 61–63); *b. Sanh.* 38b.
[51] Alan F. Segal, *Two Powers in Heaven* (SJLA 25; Leiden: Brill, 1977), 121–34.
[52] Rashbam here basically follows Rashi (God took counsel with the angels of his heavenly court). Christian exegetes knew—and rejected—this exegesis but did not associate it with Jews; see Thomas Aquinas, *Summa Theologiae* I.91.4 (*Basic Writings*, 1:877), behind whom ultimately stands Augustine, *Civ.* 16.6.
[53] See, for example, Kugel, *Traditions of the Bible*, 51–52 and 79–80.
[54] *Yosef HaMekane* (Rosenthal ed., 31 sec. 3).

Torah commentary is a response to Christianity, no doubt we will identify these *minim* with Christians and adduce this passage as further proof that Rashi indeed is engaged in anti-Christian polemic. If, as I have been arguing here, we believe that Rashi's Torah commentary is not a response to Christianity, we will not identify these *minim* with Christians, and we will adduce this passage as further proof that Rashi is living in talmudic time.[55]

In sum, in only three passages of his Torah commentary does Rashi refer to *minim*. Of these, one refers to Christians, but that passage does not address Christianity, Christian exegesis, or Christian truth claims. One passage is inspired directly by *Genesis Rabbah* and clearly does not address Christianity. The third passage, also inspired by *Genesis Rabbah*, may be a response to the Christian reading of Gen 1:26, but is not necessarily so. This record cannot be squared with the view that Rashi conceived of his Torah commentary as a response to Christianity. If he had, his responses to *minim* would have been more pointed and more frequent, and the Christian identity of his opponents would have been more evident.

VI. Conclusions

In a recent study of "Rashi's Commentary on Genesis 1–6 in the Context of the Judeo-Christian Controversy," Elazar Touitou, a distinguished and learned interpreter of the exegesis of Rashi's school, argues that in the course of his Torah commentary Rashi "presented a Jewish position in the Jewish-Christian debate."[56] That is, Rashi was aware of Christian teachings and Christian exegesis of Scripture, and, although refraining from overt engagement with Christianity, carefully and deliberately presented interpretations that would be "potentially useful for anti-Christian polemic."[57] For example, Touitou argues that, in order to rebut the Christian doctrines of Original Sin and the Fall, Rashi chose to emphasize that Adam and Eve had sex and became parents while still in the Garden of Eden.[58] Touitou,

---

[55] Poznanski, *Mavo*, xx n. 3, thinks these *minim* are not Christians.

[56] Touitou, "Rashi's Commentary on Genesis," 183.

[57] Ibid., 170.

[58] This is by far the most convincing of the six conjectures advanced by Touitou, but here again the explanation is not necessary. Rashi is following *Genesis Rabbah*

following the consensus of modern scholarship, sees Rashi as an ardent but tacit defender of the faith throughout his biblical commentaries. In this article I am arguing that the scholarly consensus may well be wrong, at least with regard to Rashi's commentary on the Torah.

That Rashi's commentary on the Torah presents a "Jewish" reading of Scripture hardly needs to be said. That it was exploited by later Jewish apologists and polemicists in their struggle with Christianity also hardly needs to be said. But neither of these self-evident truths proves that the rebuttal of Christianity was on Rashi's agenda when writing his Torah commentary. The *Bavli*, the *Yerushalmi*, and the classical midrashim were also exploited by later writers and thinkers on the prowl for anti-Christian arguments, but no one[59] will suggest that the *Bavli*, the *Yerushalmi*, and the classic midrashim were written for the purpose of rebutting Christianity. Intent and self-consciousness are at the core of the problem before us: did Rashi intend his commentary on the Torah to respond to Christian exegesis? Did Rashi self-consciously shape his exegesis of the Torah so as to rebut Christian truth claims?

(and other sources), which was responding to various clues and problems in the text of Genesis; the ancient exegetes were not necessarily responding to Christianity, and there can be no certainty that Rashi was either. For an excellent discussion see Gary Anderson, "Celibacy or Consummation in the Garden? Reflections on Early Jewish and Christian Interpretations of the Garden of Eden," *HTR* 82 (1989): 121–48, esp. 139: "The rabbinic position cannot be a reaction to a Christian position . . . the rabbinic idea of sexual relations before the fall [is] found in *Jubilees.*" Touitou, like others before him, also conjectures that Rashi's comment on Gen 1:1, which defends the claims of the Jews to the land of Israel, is a response to the first crusade of 1096, or perhaps better, a response to the idea of a Christian crusade to reclaim the holy land—hence written long before 1096 ("Rashi's Commentary on Genesis," 171). This conjecture, too, is possible but unnecessary. If Rashi were responding to the Christian (and Muslim) claims to the land of Israel, he should have rewritten his midrashic source to emphasize the superiority of the Jewish claim to those of the "nations." But Rashi does not do this. Instead he defends the Israelites/Jews from the charge that they are "brigands" (on the grounds that they seized the land from the Canaanites) and says nothing about the subsequent claims of other peoples. This midrashic motif is pre-Christian; see not only *Tanḥ. Gen.* 4a (Buber ed.) and *Gen. Rab.* 1:2 (Theodor-Albeck ed., 4–5), which are Rashi's sources, but also *b. Sanh.* 91a, with the excellent discussion of Hans (Yohanan) Lewy, *Olamot Nifgashim: Studies in Jewish Hellenism* (Jerusalem: Bialik Institute, 1969), 60–78 [Hebrew]; German original in *MGWJ* 77 (1933): 84–99 and 172–80.

[59] More accurately: hardly anyone. Some scholars have suggested that *Genesis Rabbah* and *Song of Songs Rabbah* were redacted with Christianity in view.

In the absence of any explicit evidence that would support a positive answer to these questions, the scholarly consensus relies on "what must have been." Surely Rashi "must have" known what the Christians were saying, and surely when writing his commentary on the Torah, the most important books of the Jewish canon, he "must have" had Christian exegesis and truth claims in view.[60] This argument is a logical "vicious circle" that is impossible to break: we assume that Rashi's Torah commentary contains anti-Christian polemic; since the polemic is not obvious to the naked eye, we assume that it must be covert, implicit, disguised; having revealed and decoded the polemic, we pronounce our initial assumption correct. But what if our initial assumption is not correct? What if we assume that Rashi's Torah commentary does not contain anti-Christian polemic? In this case, there is no hidden polemic to discover. Indeed, the absence of explicit polemic betokens the absence of implicit polemic as well. The unambiguous and unmistakable anti-Christian polemic of Rashi on Psalms, and the explicit anti-Christian polemic of Rashbam and Bekhor Shor on the Torah, show what anti-Christian exegesis looks like. Anti-Christian exegesis is not to be found in Rashi's Torah commentary.

Upholders of the scholarly consensus, who argue that Rashi's Torah commentary is a studied if implicit response to Christian exegesis, will no doubt seek to buttress their position by appealing to the cultural connection between the Jews and Christians of northern France and the Rhineland. Scholarship of previous generations tended to emphasize the cultural isolation of Ashkenazic Jewry, in contrast with the fruitful symbiosis that characterized Jewish life in "golden age" Spain, but more recent work tends to emphasize the cultural connectedness of Ashkenazic Judaism as well. The cultural trends in Christian society in the eleventh and twelfth centuries produced analogous trends in Jewish society as well.[61] Therefore it is perfectly

---

[60] Kamin (*Jews and Christians*, 32) and Krauss-Horbury (*Controversy*, 83) are forthright on this point. Baer is one long exercise in "what must have been" ("Rashi and the Historical Reality of his Time"); against Baer see the strictures of Grossman, *Early Sages*, 161.

[61] See, e.g., Touitou, "Exegetical Method"; Ivan Marcus, *Rituals of Childhood: Jewish Acculturation in Medieval Europe* (New Haven: Yale University Press, 1996); Yisrael Yuval, "*Two Nations in your Womb*" (Tel Aviv: Am Oved, 2000) [Hebrew]; Ivan Marcus, "A Jewish-Christian Symbiosis: The Culture of Early Ashkenaz," in *Cultures of the Jews* (ed. D. Biale; New York: Schocken, 2002), 449–516.

reasonable to assume that Rashi "must have" known what the Christians were saying and doing, and "must have" intended to respond to them.

I am not advocating a return to the "isolationist" scholarship of yesteryear; Ashkenazic Judaism must be studied within the context of its time and place. I do not dispute the assumption that Rashi must have known what Christians were saying and doing. I am simply disputing the assumption that Rashi's knowledge of Christianity was a formative factor in his composition of his Torah commentary. Of course Rashi must have known Christianity, but did he feel a need to respond to it? We can just as easily assume the negative as the positive. In writing his Torah commentary, Rashi was not following a model; his work is completely unprecedented in the history of Judaism. What assumptions can we bring to the interpretation of such an innovative work? I do not know, but I do know that a convincing argument needs evidence, and evidence for Rashi's concern with Christianity in his Torah commentary is absent. Surely the burden of proof is upon those who would have us believe that Rashi's Torah commentary is a response to Christianity; they have no proof.

Why then does Rashi care about Christian exegesis in his commentary on Psalms? Why the contrast between Rashi on the Torah and Rashi on the Psalms?[62] I am not sure of the answer, but I can see two possible solutions, each entailing its own problems and difficulties. First possible solution: perhaps Rashi privileged the Torah over the rest of the Bible. Perhaps he conceived of the Torah as the Jewish book par excellence, so much so that in his mind Christian exegesis could be ignored. No Christian argument concerning the Torah needed to be taken seriously. The rest of the Tanakh, however, was a different matter altogether, for here, especially in Isaiah and Psalms, Christians claimed to find the outlines of their faith, and the Jewish exegetical tradition was much thinner than for the Torah. In his commentaries on these books Rashi turned polemicist. This suggestion awaits full discussion; without a substantive

---

[62] The contrast between Rashi on Psalms and Rashi on the Torah exists even if my thesis is incorrect. I need to explain why Rashi on the Torah paid no attention to Christianity while Rashi on Psalms polemicized against it. Upholders of the consensus need to explain why Rashi on the Torah polemicized against Christianity discreetly and implicitly while Rashi on Psalms did so unambiguously and unmistakably.

grounding in Rashi's text it seems to suffer from the same logical circularity against which I have been arguing in this paper.

Second possible solution: perhaps the events of 1096 marked a change in Rashi's attitude towards Christianity. In that year the first crusade caused great destruction and loss of life in many of the Jewish communities of the Rhineland, and Ashkenazic Jews in general began to perceive themselves as a persecuted lot, a people of holy martyrs and sacrificial victims. Perhaps in this environment Rashi developed hostility towards Christianity, an attitude that manifested itself in his commentaries on Psalms and other books of the Prophets and Writings. This explanation might work if we knew the chronology of Rashi's commentaries, and if we could be sure that 1096 marked a change in Rashi's worldview. As to the former point, Poznanski makes the reasonable assumption that Rashi began with the commentary on the Torah and then proceeded to the other biblical books, more or less in order.[63] If so, we may safely assume that the Torah commentary was substantially complete—aside from revisions and additions[64]—long before 1096. May we assume that all of the anti-Christian passages in Rashi's commentaries, including the commentary on Psalms, were written or added after 1096? This assumption is certainly possible, but depends on the fact that 1096 was a pivotal year for Rashi—was it? Abraham Berliner, the editor of the first modern edition of Rashi's Torah commentary, a great scholar, and an expert in all of Rashi's oeuvre, could find only one passage in all of Rashi's commentaries that alluded to the events of 1096. Later scholars, of course, using a looser set of criteria, perhaps, found many additional passages.[65] The repercussions of the

---

[63] Poznanski, *Mavo*, xiv.

[64] Rashbam's comment cited above at n. 2 implies that Rashi did not revise his Torah commentary; on additions and revisions see Grossman, *Early Sages*, 210–12.

[65] According to Abraham Berliner, the comment on Isa 53:9 is "the only place" in which Rashi refers to the events of 1096; see his, "The Origins of the Interpretations of Rashi," in *Sefer Rashi*, 129–64, esp. 155 [Hebrew] (trans. of *Beiträge zur Geschichte der Raschi-Commentare* [Berlin: E. Rosenstein, 1903]). Other scholars see traces of 1096 in many other passages as well, all of them from the Prophets and Writings. See, e.g., Bernard Weinryb, "Rashi against the background of his Epoch," in *Rashi Anniversary Volume* (Texts and Studies 1; ed. H. L. Ginsberg; New York: American Academy for Jewish Research, 1941), 39–46, esp. 40 n. 7, and Baer, "Rashi and the Historical Reality of his Time," 495–501 (followed by Awerbuch).

events of 1096, and the extent of anti-Christian polemic, in Rashi's commentaries on the Prophets and the Writings—these questions merit renewed investigation.

In any case, however it is explained, there is a disparity between Rashi on the Torah and Rashi on the Psalms. Rashi on the Psalms, like Rashbam and Bekhor Shor on the Torah, refutes Christian exegesis and Christian truth claims, but Rashi on the Torah does not. Does Rashi's Torah commentary respond to Christianity? In the absence of any evidence that it did, the answer must be that it did not.

RASHI AND IBN EZRA ON THE *HITPAEL: PESHAT* IN THE MEDIEVAL DISPUTES OF HEBREW GRAMMAR

Isaiah Teshima

In the 11th and the 12th centuries, Jewish exegetes known as *pashtanim* began to seek the literal meaning of the biblical text.[1] The greatest of these exegetes were Rashi and Ibn Ezra, each devoted to establishing the *peshat* of the Bible, the plain or literal meaning.[2] However, their quest for this literal meaning yielded very different understandings of the Bible. While an explanation of the differences can be approached from many angles, I would like to focus on aspect in Hebrew grammar as a factor which inspired different interpretations of the literal meaning of the text.

Scholars believe that the scientific study of the Hebrew language began in the 10th century with Saadiah Gaon, reaching its apotheosis in Spain as early as the middle of the 11th century.[3] In particular,

---

[1] There is extensive literature on the history of Jewish exegesis. In particular, I recommend the following: Menahem Haran, "Midrashic and Literal Exegesis and the Critical Method in Biblical Research," in *Studies in Bible* (ed. S. Japhet; ScrHier 31; Jerusalem: Magnes, 1986), 45–56; Isaac L. Seeligmann, "Voraussetzungen der Midraschexegese," in *Congress Volume: Copenhagen 1953* (VTSup 1; Leiden: Brill, 1953), 150–81; Uriel Simon, "The Spanish School of Biblical Interpretation," in *Moreshet Sepharad: The Sepharadi Legacy* (ed. H. Beinart; 2 vols.; Jerusalem: Magnes, 1992), 1:115–239.

[2] The definition of the idea "peshat" is not self-evident. The difficulties are argued by Sarah Kamin with an overview of the debates of modern time such as between Abraham Geiger and Zacharias Frankel; see her *Rashi's Exegetical Categorization: in Respect to the Distinction between Peshat and Derash* (Jerusalem: Hebrew University Press, 1986), 11–22 [Hebrew].

[3] The origin of Hebrew grammar is an interesting question. Profiat Duran (15th cent.) considers Judah b. Hayyuj and Abdul Walid ibn Janah to be the first Hebrew grammarians. See *Maase Efod* (ed. J. Friendländer; Vienna: J. Holzwarth, 1865), 16. Whereas, Richard Simon and Hartwig Hirschfeld regard Saadiah to be the first Jewish grammarian. See Richard Simon, *A Critical History of the Old Testament* (3 vols.; London: Walter Davis, 1682), 1:192–93; Hartwig Hirschfeld, *Literary History of Hebrew Grammarians and Lexicographers* (London: Oxford University Press, 1926), 11. But, the present state of Hebrew scholarship tends to consider the origin even before Saadiah. See Angel Sáenz-Badillos, "Hebrew Philology in Sefarad: The State of the Question," in *Hebrew Scholarship and the Medieval World* (ed. N. de Lange; Cambridge: Cambridge University Press, 2001), 38–59.

Hebrew grammar became the foundation of *peshat* for Abraham Ibn
Ezra, a Bible scholar and Hebrew grammarian born in Spain in the
last half of the 11th century. He believed that his scientific knowledge of Hebrew would determine a literal reading of the text.[4]
Therefore, his grammarian's approach to *peshat* was in a way the
precursor to the biblical studies of today in which historical Hebrew
grammar is a cornerstone for critical understanding of the Bible.

Although "Hebrew grammar" obviously constitutes the basis for
the literal meaning of the text, I must wonder at the same time
whether Hebrew grammar of the Bible was understood uniformly
by Jewish exegetes in those days. What if different ideas of Hebrew
grammar were competing with one another for *peshat*? I think that
this may be the case regarding Rashi (Solomon b. Isaac: 1040–1105)
and Abraham Ibn Ezra (1089–1164) and their respective reading of
the *Hitpael* stem (*binyan*) in the Bible.[5]

I. THE *HITPAEL* PROBLEM

Indeed, the grammar of Hebrew as we know it today is only a theory of how the language works. Earlier exegetes understood Hebrew
grammar differently, sometimes differing in basic explanations. One
of these disputes concerned the Hebrew system of verbs, namely,
how many stems (*binyanim*) actually existed within the system. We
learn about the dispute through *Mikne Abram* written by Abraham
de Balmes, the 15th century grammarian. The book was published
in the 16th century and was closely studied by Spinoza in his attempt
to explain Hebrew grammar.[6]

---

[4] In the introduction to his Torah commentary, Ibn Ezra reviews various exegetical approaches to the text of the Torah. For him, Hebrew grammar is the best
means with which to interpret *peshat* in the narrative sections, whereas in the legal
portions Ibn Ezra chooses to follow the Oral Torah as a key to meanings.

[5] Saadiah seems not to have had an idea of classifying the Hebrew verbs into
stems (*binyanim*) as we do. His concern was the semantic functions of verbs. See
Aharon Dotan, *The Dawn of Hebrew Linguistics: The Book of Elegance of the Languages of
the Hebrews by Saadiah Gaon* (2 vols.; Jerusalem: World Union of Jewish Studies, 1997),
1:146ff.; see also Bruce K. Waltke and Michael O'Connor, *An Introduction to Biblical
Hebrew Syntax* (Winona Lake, Ind.: Eisenbrauns, 1990), 343–61.

[6] See Isaiah Teshima, "Spinoza and the Medieval Dispute on Hebrew Grammar
among Jewish Scholars: Towards the Critical Edition of *Compendium Grammatices
Linguae Hebraeae*," *Bulletin of the Society for Near Eastern Studies in Japan* 41 (1998): 110–24

Today, however, we understand the verbal system to consist of the seven *binyanim* which can be ordered symmetrically like a seven-branched menorah; *Qal* corresponds to *Nifal*, *Piel* to *Pual*, *Hifil* to *Hofal*, whereas *Hitpael* is placed in the center between the two sets.

The problem of the *Hitpael* is its ambiguous place in this frame-work. Generally speaking, *Qal*, *Piel*, *Hifil* are the active voice stems, which can be both transitive and intransitive; these stems can take the direct object marker and produce sentences like נָתַתִּי אֶת־הָאָרֶץ הַזֹּאת "I gave this land" (Gen 15:18). On the other hand, *Nifal*, *Pual*, *Hofal* are the passive voice stems, which cannot be principally tran-sitive. These stems cannot take the direct object marker, so that syn-tactically their sentences confine themselves to the combination of subject and verb like לָנוּ נִתְּנָה הָאָרֶץ לְמוֹרָשָׁה "To us the land was given for inheritance" (Ezek 33:24). They tolerate no transitive object.[7]

The *Hitpael* is an exception to this neat scheme. The majority of occurrences of the *Hitpael* does not take the direct object, so that the *Hitpael* appears to be a part of the passive voice group. At the same time, there exist several cases of the *Hitpael* which are accom-panied by the direct object marker (אֵת). In those cases, the *Hitpael* appears to be a normal transitive verbal stem, like *Piel* or *Hifil*, that is capable of taking a direct object preceded by the marker (אֵת) when it is definite. The *Hitpael* can thus take on the function of either of the two kinds of verbal stems described above.

The ambiguity of the *Hitpael* inevitably raises a semantic question, namely, how to distinguish the semantic function of the *binyan Hitpael* from the rest of the stems. For instance, if one designates the *Hitpael* to be of the passive voice, then what is the difference between the *Nifal* of אִם־נִשְׁמְרוּ הַנְּעָרִים אַךְ מֵאִשָּׁה (1 Sam 21:5) and the *Hitpael* of וָאֶשְׁתַּמֵּר מֵעֲוֹנִי (Ps 18:24)?[8] In these instances, *Nifal* and *Hitpael* occur

---

[Japanese]. Cf. Philippe Cassuto, *Spinoza Hébraïsant: L'hébreu dans le "Tractatus theo-logico-politicus" et le "Compendium grammatices linguae hebraeae"* (Leuven: Peeters, 1999), 4–16.

[7] Note the instances of the *Nifal* (Exod 12:8 and 21:28) which take the direct object marker. See Waltke and O'Connor, *Introduction to Biblical Hebrew Syntax*, 382. I agree with their argument which views the case not as transitive use but as some-thing else, like that of ergativity. Another opinion is expressed in Paul Joüon and Takamitsu Muraoka, *A Grammar of Biblical Hebrew* (2 vols.; Rome: Pontifical Biblical Institute, 1991), 2:461–62. Cf. Emil Kautzsch and Arthur E. Cowley, *Gesenius' Hebrew Grammar* (Oxford: Clarendon, 1910), 387–88.

[8] Compare the RSV renderings of 1 Sam 21:5, "Of a truth women have been kept from us," and Ps 18:24, "I kept myself from guilt." The difference between

with the same preposition and in the same root. Readers must wonder if these verbs should have the same meaning, or if not, how their meanings might be different. Alternatively, if the *Hitpael* is supposed to imply an intransitive-stative sense, then what is the difference between the *Qal* of תֵּן לְחָכָם וְיֶחְכַּם־עוֹד (Prov 9:9) and the *Hitpael* of וְאַל־תִּתְחַכַּם יוֹתֵר (Qoh 7:16)?[9] If one assumes that the *Hitpael* is an active-transitive verb, then there would be no difference between the *Qal* of וַיִּפְשַׁט גַּם־הוּא בְּגָדָיו (1 Sam 19:24) and the *Hitpael* of וַיִּתְפַּשֵּׁט יְהוֹנָתָן אֶת־הַמְּעִיל אֲשֶׁר עָלָיו (1 Sam 18:4).[10]

In today's Hebrew grammar, therefore, we are accustomed to distinguishing the *Hitpael* from the others by considering the *binyan Hitpael* to be the reflexive or middle stem, which expresses the action the subject does for oneself.[11] But, do these proposed differences of the *Hitpael* work exegetically in these verses? The answer is far from clear.

---

the two is slight, since David's statement (1 Sam 21:5) implies that the action was not forced by others but initiated by David and his followers themselves during the expedition. Profiat Duran already noted the problem of ambiguity; see *Maase Efod*, 54.

[9] In the RSV, Prov 9:9, "He will be still wiser," and Qoh 7:16, "Be not righteous [wise] overmuch," are indistinguishable in understanding the verbs as stative, while the JPS renders Prov 9:9, "He will grow wiser," and Qoh 7:16, "Don't act the wise man to excess," to distinguish the basic meanings of the verbs.

[10] Compare the RSV renderings between 1 Sam 19:24, "And he too stripped off his clothes," and 1 Sam 18:4, "And Jonathan stripped himself of the robe that was upon him." There seems to be little meaningful differences between these translations as far as the intransitiveness of their actions is concerned.

[11] See Carl Buck, *Comparative Grammar of Greek and Latin* (Chicago: University of Chicago Press, 1933), 237. Buck points out the ambiguities of morphology and semantics in Latin and Greek verbs, e.g., those between passive and deponent in Latin and between passive and middle in Greek, which are not always distinguishable from one another but up to their given context. That is to say, while German can show its reflexiveness through syntax and pronoun (e.g., *Er setzt sich auf die Bank*), Greek and Latin do not always indicate their reflexiveness in that way. But the middle voice of Greek is indicated by the morphological forms which can be the passive voice in some cases. The problem emerges if the readers are perplexed about a certain verb which can be read as middle or passive or active. The answer depends upon the reader's interpretation of the text and his or her understanding of the semantic/philosophical distinction between the notions of "reflexiveness" and "transitiveness" and "intransitiveness." I believe this also is the case for the *Hitpael* in Hebrew, as I will demonstrate in the present discussion.

II. The *Hitpael* as Intransitive

The notion of "reflexive or middle" is a convenient remedy for the syntactical and semantic ambiguity of the *Hitpael*. But we should remember that this idea has a history, arising in the Qimḥi school of the 12th century (especially, Joseph Qimḥi).[12] Before then the *Hitpael* could be construed in different ways. Consider a comment in *Sefer-Rikma* of Ibn Janaḥ in the 11th century:

דע כי מן ההתפעל מה שיתעבר—ורובו לא יתעבר—כאשר נאמר: ויתפרקו
כל העם את נזמי הזהב אשר באזניהם, כי נזמי הזהב פעול בויתפרקו, ונאמר:
והתנחלתם אותם לבניכם וזולת זה הרבה.

Know that the majority of *hitpael* are intransitive. But the transitive cases exist such that וַיִּתְפָּרְקוּ כָּל הָעָם אֶת־נִזְמֵי אֲשֶׁר הַזָּהָב בְּאָזְנֵיהֶם (Exod 32:3), because נִזְמֵי הַזָּהָב is the direct object of וַיִּתְפָּרְקוּ. And we will say so about וְהִתְנַחַלְתֶּם אֹתָם לִבְנֵיכֶם (Lev 25:46). And besides them, many more.[13]

This reflects the position of the Spanish school on the *Hitpael*, which admits both intransitive and transitive roles for the *binyan Hitpael*. Thus, Exod 32:3 may be understood as, "the people took away the golden earrings which were in their ears and brought them to Aaron," while construing Lev 25:46 as, "And you may take them as an inheritance for your children after you." Modern translations of the Bible agree with this approach.[14] Rashi, however, understood all these verses as intransitive. Consider the following interpretation of Exod 32:3 by Rashi:

ויתפרקו: לשון פריקת משא, כשנטלום מאזניהם נמצאו הם מפורקים מנזמיהם,
דישקריי״ר בלעז. את נזמי, כמו: מנזמי, כמו: כצאתי את העיר, מן העיר.

---

[12] See Wilhelm Bacher, *Sepher Zikkaron* (Berlin: M'kize Nirdamim, 1888), 37:
ואין בבנין זה (התפעל) פעול כי הפועל הוא הפעול ואין בבנין שהקדמנו לא פועל
ולא פעול כי הנפעל אינו פועל אחרים והוא עצמו הפעול על כן אין לו פועל ולא פעולה . . . ובבנין
פעולה . . . ובבנין התפעל יש לו פועל והוא מתפעל אך אין שם פעול כי הוא עצמו המתפעל
[13] See Michael Wilensky, *Sefer ha-Rikmah* (Jerusalem: The Academy of the Hebrew Language, 1964), 14:191.
[14] The JPS translates Exod 32:3, "And all the people took off the gold rings that were in their ears." The RSV's rendering is, "So all the people took off the rings of gold which were in their ears." As for Lev 25:46, the JPS's rendering is, "You may keep them as a possession for your children after you." The RSV translates, "And ye shall make them an inheritance for your children after you." Both translations understand the verb to take the direct object.

ויתפרקו: this means stripping of the object. (That is to say,) when they had taken them out from their ears, they were found in the state of being stripped out from their ears. In the foreign language, it means "discrete." את נזמי: it is like "from the ears." That is like כצאתי את העיר, "as I went out from the city (Exod 9:29)." את העיר means מן העיר "from the city."[15]

Key to understanding Rashi's interpretation is his construal of the object marker (את). The word which is normally taken to indicate the direct object is interpreted by Rashi to be like the preposition "from" (מן), as he cites the same use of the word in Exod 9:29. By that effect, he can read the *Hitpael* in Exod 32:3 as an intransitive verb, understanding the meaning thus: "And the people were found in the state of being stripped off from the golden earrings."

He repeats this in his interpretation of Lev 25:46. Rashi explicitly denied the possibility of such a transitive meaning as found in the *Hifil* stem.

> והתנחלתם אתם לבניכם, הזיקו בהם לנחלה לצורך בניהם אחריכם. ולא יתכן
> לפרש: הנחילום לבניכם, שאם כן היה לו לכתוב והנחלתם אותם לבניכם,
> והתנחלתם כמו והתחזקתם.

והתנחלתם אתם לבניכם: cling yourselves to them [the strangers] as regards the inheritance for the need of your children after you. It is not possible to interpret it like "Inherit them for your children." If so, it should be written as, והנחלתם אותם לבניכם. והתנחלתם is like והתחזקתם.

Here, Rashi clearly supposes that the *Hitpael* stem of the root (נחל) should be distinguished from its *Hifil* stem. His differentiation is clear-cut; *Hifil* invests the root with a transitive meaning, so that והנחלתם אותם means "you should inherit them (the strangers)." On the contrary, the *Hitpael* stem gives the root an intransitive sense, accord-

---

[15] Every quote from Rashi's commentary is based upon the Mosad Ha-Rav Kuk edition, תורת החיים. I make my own decision with regard to punctuation when minor differences are noted between Abraham Berliner and the Mosad Ha-Rav Kuk edition. About the textual problems of Rashi's commentary, see Yesha'yahu Zanah, "לבקרת הטכסט של פירוש רש״י על התורה," *HUCA* 15 (1940): 37–56. The oral nature of Rashi's commentary is attested by the medieval Latin-Hebrew manuscripts which show that their accompanied Hebrew vocalizations were not from an existing vocalized exemplar of Rashi's commentary but oral instructions of Jewish teachers of those days. See Judith Olszowy-Schlanger, "The Knowledge and Practice of Hebrew Grammar among Christian Scholars in Pre-Expulsion England: The Evidence of 'Bilingual' Hebrew-Latin Manuscripts," in *Hebrew Scholarship and the Medieval World*, 107–28, esp. 126–27.

ing to which והתנחלתם אתם should mean "you should cling yourselves to them (the strangers)."[16]

Ibn Ezra approaches the *Hitpael* differently and draws a parallel
to our view (Lev 25:46) with that of Num 34:10. He simply says,
"והתנחלתם (Lev 25:46) is from the *Hitpael* stem, parallel to והתאויתם לכם
(Num 34:10)."[17] The intention of Ibn Ezra in this comment can be
gathered from his interpretation of Num 33:54:

> והתנחלתם כמו והתאויתם. והפעול הארץ. וטעם להזכיר לרב תרבו לדבק
> אחריו ואם לא תורישו.

וְהִתְנַחַלְתֶּם: it (Num 33:54) is like וְהִתְאַוִּיתֶם (Num 34:10). The Land
[הָאָרֶץ] is the direct object. The accent serves to remind (us) of the
part (which begins with) לָרַב תַּרְבּוּ, "To a large one you shall give a
large inheritance," that is bound to the following part (of Num 33:55),
וְאִם־לֹא תוֹרִישׁוּ, "But if you do not drive out."

This comment is significant as it shows that Ibn Ezra considers the
Hitpael stem (והתנחלתם) as the transitive verb which accompanies the
direct object "The Land (אֶת הָאָרֶץ)." In the light of this we can conclude that Ibn Ezra clearly sees the verb in Num 34:10 (והתאויתם)
as transitive. (He considers the word לִנְבֹּל as its direct object, understanding the verse as, "You shall mark out the boundary.") From
there, he returns to Lev 25:46 and its *Hitpael*, which Ibn Ezra understands as transitive.[18]

Interestingly, in contrast with Rashi, who insists on the distinction
of the *Hifil* and the *Hitpael*, Ibn Ezra considers two possibilities regarding the verb of Num 34:10, thus,

> ואלף והתאויתם תחת ויו והתוית תו, ואם הם שני בנינים והתאויתם כמו עד
> תאות גבעות עולם.

---

[16] Rashi's interpretation considers a context in which the Israelites sell themselves
to the strangers. The context would be contradictory if Lev 25:46 is understood to
be a command whereby the Israelites possess strangers as an inheritance. On the
usage of החזיק, התחזק by Rashi, see Isaac Avinery, *Heichal Rashi* (2 vols.; Jerusalem:
Mosad Ha-Rav Kuk, 1979), 1:439 [Hebrew].

[17] והתנחלתם, מבנין התפעל. וכמוהו והתאויתם לכם: the Hebrew text is from the
Mosad Ha-Rav Kuk edition prepared by A. Wizer. See Menachem Cohen, *Mikra'ot
Gedolot 'Haketer': Be'reshit 1–2* (Ramat-Gan: Bar Ilan University Press, 1997), 7–14
of introduction. Note his assessments of the state of textual criticism to Rashi's and
Ibn Ezra's commentaries.

[18] Another reading of Ibn Ezra is proposed by Luba R. Charlap, whose claim
is that Ibn Ezra, in opposition to Hayyuj and Ibn Janah, regards the *Hitpael* as
intransitive; see Charlap, *Rabbi Abraham Ibn-Ezra's Linguistic System: Tradition and
Innovation* (Beersheva: Ben-Gurion University of the Negev Press, 1999), 149 [Hebrew].

Alef of וְהִתְאַוִּיתֶם is replaced for *waw* of וְהִתְוִיתָ תָו (Ezek 9:4). But if they are two stems, וְהִתְאַוִּיתֶם is like עַד תַּאֲוַת נִבְעֹת עוֹלָם (Gen 49:26).

The comment, "If they are two stems," derives from his uncertainty over the stem of התאויתם. If the verb is *Hitpael*, the root should be *alef-waw-he*. Therefore, he resorts to the word (תאות) of Gen 49:26 which attests to the root.[19] At the same time, by that "if," Ibn Ezra alludes to the opposite case that they (the verbs of Num 34:10 and Ezek 9:4) are one stem, that is to say, that the verb התאויתם is some-how the same *Hifil* stem as found in Ezek 9:4 (וְהִתְוִיתָ תָו) whose root is *taw-waw-he*.[20] This is why Ibn Ezra mentioned *alef* standing for *waw*, not for *taw*. Ibn Ezra seems to suggest in this case, after all, that התאויתם is a kind of spelling variation of the *hifil* verb (התוית).[21] Otherwise he should have said *alef* standing for *taw* in order to main-tain the *Hitpael* stem for the root (*taw-waw-he*) as of Ezek 9:4.

In short, there is no difference between the *Hifil* and *Hitpael* stems for Ibn Ezra; they are interchangeable as shown by his substitution of one for the other in Num 34:10. This is to be expected as he was a scholar from the Spanish school.

III. Rashi and Onkelos

In contrast, Rashi insists that every *Hitpael* verb be intransitive. This attitude is consistent in his Torah commentary, where he is ready to disagree even with *Onkelos*, which he otherwise respects as a source for the understanding of *peshat*.[22]

---

[19] Likewise, Ibn Janaḥ (R. Jona) thinks of the root אוה for the *Hitpael* of Num 34:10. See Wilhelm Bacher, *Sepher Haschoraschim* (Berlin: M'kize Nirdamim, 1896), 16. Ibn Ezra simply follows the opinion of Ibn Janaḥ as a possibility.

[20] Rashi interprets the verb of Num 34:10 with respect to תתאו in 34:7 which means to "go around," saying: והתאויתם לשון הסיבה ונטיה כמו תתאו. Again, his read-ing is consistent with his view of the *Hitpael* as intransitive. See Rashi at Num 34:10.

[21] Ibn Ezra sometimes regards *alef* as an empty letter which carries no sound. See his comment on Ps 58:8 (e.g., ימאסו = ימסו). Also note his comment on Gen 37:25 in which Ibn Ezra argues for the exchange of *alef* and *waw* (e.g., נכות = נכאת) for the reason that *waw* and *alef* are the letters void of sounds. These two com-ments assist the view that התאויתם is a spelling variation of התויתם for Ibn Ezra; see Ibn Ezra on Isa 2:6 and see Ezra Z. Melamed, *Bible Commentators* (2 vols.; Jerusalem: Magnes, 1978), 2:645 [Hebrew]. Also see Nahum Sarna, "Abraham Ibn Ezra as an Exegete," in *Rabbi Abraham Ibn Ezra: Studies in the Writings of a Twelfth-Century Jewish Polymath* (ed. I. Twersky and J. M. Harris; Cambridge, Mass.: Harvard University Press, 1993), 1–27.

[22] See Melammed, *Bible Commentators*, 1:378–98. When the word has two possi-

Here are two examples. Exodus 10:2 reads:

וּלְמַעַן תְּסַפֵּר בְּאָזְנֵי בִנְךָ וּבֶן־בִּנְךָ אֵת אֲשֶׁר הִתְעַלַּלְתִּי בְּמִצְרַיִם

. . . and that you may tell in the ears of your son and your son's son what I have done in Egypt.

The phrase אשר התעללתי is translated by *Onkelos* as ית נסין דעבדית
במצרים, "the miracles which I did in Egypt." *Onkelos* gives it a transitive meaning but Rashi differs, commenting:

התעללתי: שחקתי. כמו: כי התעללת בי. הלא כאשר התעלל בהם. האמור כמו
במצרים ואינו לשון פועל ומעללים שאם כן היה לו לכתוב עוללתי.
לי. אשר עולל לי. ועולל למו כאשר עולל

הִתְעַלַּלְתִּי: that means "I laughed." It is like in Num 22:29, "Because
you have made sport of me (כִּי הִתְעַלַּלְתְּ בִּי)," or as in 1 Sam 6:6,
"When he had made sport of him (כַּאֲשֶׁר הִתְעַלֵּל בָּהֶם)." It is said of
Egypt (or Egyptians), and it is neither a transitive verb or מַעֲלִים
(which means "deeds"). If it were so, he had to write עוֹלַלְתִּי. That is
like Lam 1:22, "and do unto them, as thou hast done unto me (וְעוֹלֵל
כַּאֲשֶׁר עוֹלַלְתָּ לִי)," or Lam 1:12, "which is done unto me (אֲשֶׁר
עוֹלַל לִי)."

According to Rashi, the biblical writer would have used the *Piel* stem
instead of the *Hitpael* had he wished to indicate the transitive sense.
Again, Rashi is trying to protect the semantic uniqueness of the
Hitpael stem as opposed to the *Piel* and interprets the verse: "and
that you may tell in the ears of your son and your son's son about
the Egyptians whom I have laughed at in Egypt." In this regard,
Ibn Ezra posits the opposite:

ודברה תורה כלשון בני אדם לומר התעללתי כאדם. משנה התולדות להנקם
מאחר.

The Torah speaks in the human language (expression): God is speaking like a man, saying "I did viciously (הִתְעַלַּלְתִּי)." He altered nature in order to exact revenge upon someone.

Ibn Ezra's interpretation basically follows that of *Onkelos* by using
the phrase which refers to the plagues God wrought on the Egyptians

---

ble meanings, Rashi uses *Onkelos* for clarification. For instance, see Gen 34:31: את
can be the preposition "with" as well as the object marker. Rashi, along with *Onkelos*,
interprets the word to be an object marker.

(vermin and boils).[23] Ibn Ezra's understanding of this verse is consistent with the view we outlined above; he allows the verb to have
a transitive meaning. Again, Ibn Ezra and Rashi disagree on the
function of the *Hitpael*. While Rashi denies that the stem *Hitpael* is
transitive, examining the meaningful differences between them, Ibn
Ezra allows no difference between the two stems *Hitpael* and *Piel*
when the *Hitpael* is used as transitive.

Our last instance is found in Gen 37:18:

וַיִּרְאוּ אֹתוֹ מֵרָחֹק וּבְטֶרֶם יִקְרַב אֲלֵיהֶם וַיִּתְנַכְּלוּ אֹתוֹ לַהֲמִיתוֹ.

> They saw him afar off, and before he came near to them they con-
> spired against him to kill him.

The phrase וַיִּתְנַכְּלוּ אֹתוֹ לַהֲמִיתוֹ is understood by *Onkelos* as "they
thought of murdering him (וחשיבו עלוהי למקטליה)." The same understanding is found in Ibn Ezra, "They conspired a bad thought
(חשבו מחשבה רעה). It is like וְאָרוּר נוֹכֵל (But cursed be the deceiver)."[24]

What is common to both Ibn Ezra and *Onkelos* is their taking the
subject of וַיִּתְנַכְּלוּ as Joseph's brothers who hated their younger brother.
Therefore, the *Hitpael* וַיִּתְנַכְּלוּ needs to be transitive, as it parallels the
Qal נוֹכֵל (Mal 1:14), and should be related to the action taken by
the brothers against Joseph.

In contrast, Rashi understands the verb to mean that the deceit-
ful emotion and the evil intention reached full against Joseph:

ויתנכלו: נתמלאו נכלים וערמומיות. אותו כמו אתו עמו כלומר אליו.

> וַיִּתְנַכְּלוּ: evil thoughts and hatred reached full against him. אוֹתוֹ is like
> אִתּוֹ, which means "with him," namely "against him."

By contrast, Rashi understands the subject of the verb not as Joseph's
brothers but rather the hatred they felt, thus making the *Hitpael*

---

[23] See Exod 10:2 in his shorter commentary on the Torah התעללתי: על דרך
דבור בן אדם בעבור הנגעים. הם הכנים והשחין. Today's understanding following Ibn
Ezra does not consider it unusual to have את before אשר. See Jouön and Muraoka,
Grammar of Biblical Hebrew, 2:590–91.

[24] Note that Ibn Ezra compares *Hitpael* with *Qal*, thus: ויתנכלו חשבו מחשבה רעה.
וכן ואָרוּר נוכל. However, the spelling of the *Qal* participle with *waw* is common in
later Hebrew. See Frank M. Cross and David N. Freedman, *Early Hebrew Orthography*
(New Haven: Yale University Press, 1952), 69. The ultimate question remains, with
regard to the development of Hebrew spelling, whether the word should be understood as a *Qal* participle or as something else.

intransitive. In line with this, Rashi suggests that the אֹתוֹ should be read as אִתּוֹ, not as an object marker but as a preposition ("with him" or "against him"). For him, the verse means that the brothers' emotions against Joseph reached their peak. Rashi thus discounts Joseph's brothers as the subject of the verb and Joseph as its direct object and so removes the necessity to read the *Hitpael* in this verb as transitive. All this is in contrast to Ibn Ezra who identifies the *Hitpael* (וַיִּתְנַכְּלוּ) with the transitive *Qal* (נוכל) verb.

IV. The Ambiguity of Hebrew Grammar

Both Rashi and Ibn Ezra understood their interpretations as *peshat*, and yet they construed their *peshat* differently. In this essay we have learned that one reason they read the text so differently is that they were operating with different theories about Hebrew grammar.

My argument ends here but raises some questions to which I have no answers. It is nevertheless important that they be raised for the sake of their significance for the history of biblical interpretation. First, what made Rashi so certain of his understanding of the *Hitpael?* Where did Rashi's knowledge of Hebrew grammar originate? It is usually assumed that Rashi did not know Arabic whereas the Spanish school did. Was this the source of differences?[25]

Ultimately, the Qimhi school, which laid a basis for the modern understanding of the *Hitpael* as reflexive, was promulgated by Christian Hebraists in the 16th to 17th centuries.[26] But, given the context of the development of Hebrew grammar, Qimhi's idea appears to be an elegant synthesis to the contradiction between the views represented by Rashi and Ibn Ezra, respectively.[27] Do we accept the idea

---

[25] See Joüon and Muraoka, *Grammar of Biblical Hebrew*, 1:157. Ibn Janah noted a parallel between the Arabic *tafa''ala* and the Hebrew *Hitpael*. It seems to me that the Spanish school of Hebrew grammar looks at the Hebrew *Hitpael* based upon the fact that the Arabic verb can be active and passive.

[26] See Moshe Goshen-Gottstein, "Foundations of Biblical Philology in the Seventeenth Century: Christian and Jewish Dimensions," in *Jewish Thought in the Seventeenth Century* (ed. I. Twersky and B. Septimus; Cambridge, Mass.: Harvard University Press, 1987), 77–94. The Qimhi school of Hebrew grammar became popular among the Christian Hebraists due to the efforts of Elijah Levita. See also Edward Breuer, *The Limits of Enlightenment: Jews, Germans, and the Eighteenth-Century Study of Scripture* (Cambridge, Mass.: Harvard University Press, 1996), 77–107.

[27] Ibn Ezra, *Sefer Tsahot* (ספר צחות,מבואר באר היטיב מאת נבריאל הירש ליפמאן),

of the *Hitpael* as reflexive because it is a convenient resolution to the conflict or because it is correct? If the latter is true, how can we account for the views of Ibn Ezra and Rashi historically? What is the origin of their views? What is clear is that Hebrew grammar did not exist *a priori*; it emerged in its complexity in the pursuit of *peshat*. Hebrew grammar is an outcome of interpretation as much as the other way around.[28]

65–66. Ibn Ezra interprets Gen 22:18 (וְהִתְבָּרְכוּ) as different from the meaning of the *Nifal* of Gen 12:3, saying כי והתברכו הוא יתברך בו ויתכן שלא והתברכו'] יהיה ואינו כן ונברכו כן is to mean 'one will bless oneself.' Therefore, there is a possibility that the blessing may not extend into the future. But it is not the same."] Ibn Ezra seems to recognize the reflexiveness in the meaning of Gen 22:18, thereby distinguishing the promise of the blessing given in Gen 22:18 from that given in Gen 12:3, which intends to say that all the families of the earth will be blessed by Abraham. Interestingly, this interpretation agrees with that of David Qimḥi. See David Qimḥi on Gen 22:18 and 12:3. The fact may indicate that the idea of the *Hitpael* as reflexive had been known to Ibn Ezra. But Ibn Ezra did not adopt it systematically. See Abraham Berliner, *Beiträge zur hebräischen Grammatik im Talmud und Midrasch* (Berlin: M. Driesner, 1878/1879), 51–53. He notes Ibn Janaḥ and Jefet b. Ali who consider reflexiveness in *Nifal* rather than *Hitpael*.

[28] This paper is based on the following papers delivered in Hebrew and Japanese: see Isaiah Teshima, "הבה נתחכמה לו פן ירבה: התמודדותו הלשונית של רש״י על תפקידי המלה הבה", *Beit Mikra* 132 (1992): 29–40; and "Rashi's Understanding of *Hitpael*: A Medieval Conflict between Biblical Interpretation and Hebrew Grammar," *Bulletin of the Society for Near Eastern Studies in Japan* 43 (2000): 70–83. I thank Dr. Steven Weitzman and Ms. Eva Lazarus for valuable comments and stylistic improvements of the paper.

PARADISE LOST AND TRADITIONAL EXEGESIS

LAWRENCE F. RHU

Milton, in his prose tracts, emphatically rejects traditional exegesis. In "Of Prelaticall Episcopacy," for example, he calls the Bible "the only Book left to us of divine authority" and asserts its "all-sufficiency."[1] In his polemical pamphlets against divorce, even though Milton expresses some sense of continuity with "orthodoxicall" or "common Expositers," he still decries the limitations of such "quotationists and commonplacers." Moreover, he distinguishes his own interpretations as mediators of "the truth" and his personal manner of interpretation as a purveyor of "divine insight."[2] Milton seems ever ready to state the extreme opposition between Scripture and tradition. As he phrases it in the chapter "Of Holy Scripture" in *De Doctrina Christiana*: "Human traditions, written or unwritten, are expressly forbidden."[3] Although Milton's authorship of this treatise has lately been questioned, it was an accepted fact for well over a century and a half since its discovery in 1823, and this conviction about "human traditions" sounds a genuinely Miltonic note. In *Paradise Lost* (*PL*), for example, the archangel Michael voices a comparable claim in denouncing those who succeed the Apostles and

> the truth
> With superstitions and traditions taint,
> Left only in those written records pure,
> Though not but by the Spirit understood. (*PL* 12.511–514)[4]

"The Spirit," of course, strikes traditionalists as a dangerously mercurial criterion for interpretation, if not merely a cover for wanton indulgence of subjective opinion. At best, claiming the Spirit's exclusive

---

[1] *Complete Prose Works of John Milton* (ed. D. Wolfe et al.; 8 vols.; New Haven: Yale University Press, 1953–1982). All references to Milton's prose are to this edition. Here, *Complete Prose Works* 1:695.

[2] *Complete Prose Works* 2:230, 598.

[3] *Complete Prose Works* 6:591.

[4] All citations of Milton's poetry come from Merritt Y. Hughes, *John Milton: The Complete Poems and Major Prose* (New York: Odyssey, 1957).

authority for biblical exegesis sounds like a naïve effort to abstract oneself from the irrepressible entailments of tradition that will mark virtually any reading or recounting of Scripture.[5]

In the "Afterword" to his compendious anthology, *Traditions of the Bible*, James Kugel suggests that the end result of modern biblical scholarship, in its programmatic disregard for traditional exegesis, has been to discover that the Bible is not biblical enough. Moreover, this approach to biblical study has been animated by a distinctly confessional bias, the Protestant movement, whose spirit of polemical hostility toward tradition pervades Milton's writings. Yet the very process by which the habits of mind characteristic of early exegesis have been systematically broken by modern biblical scholars (whose disregard for tradition ultimately derives from something very much like Milton's scorn for it) has also left us with an utterly human document shorn of the mystery and relevance that once animated the Bible's claims upon communities of faith.[6] In compiling patterns of interpretation that constitute the early exegesis of the Pentateuch, one of Kugel's basic assertions bears particular relevance to Milton's effort to "justify the ways of God to men" (*PL* 1.26). Kugel argues that, among the Bible's earliest interpreters, expansive retellings of biblical stories serve exegetical purposes. In *The Legends of the Jews*, what Louis Ginzberg called "legends" were actually interpretations that directly respond to textual problems.[7] They seek to explain puzzles and answer questions that regularly challenged readers of the Hebrew Scriptures.

In theorizing about the heroic tradition that Milton sought to inherit and transform, Torquato Tasso enunciated a Counter-Reformation version of this insight. He urged poets to eschew biblical subjects for Christian heroic poetry because stories from Scripture often serve as

---

[5] See Alasdair MacIntyre, "Epistemological Crises, Dramatic Narrative, and the Philosophy of Science," *The Monist* 60 (1977): 54–74, esp. 59–60. Protestant crises of authority over biblical interpretation bear striking resemblances to MacIntyre's account of Descartes's epistemological crisis in their comparable efforts to escape the entailments of tradition.

[6] James L. Kugel, *Traditions of the Bible: A Guide to the Bible As It Was at the Start of the Common Era* (Cambridge, Mass.: Harvard University Press, 1998), 889–98. See also idem, "The Bible in the University" in *The Hebrew Bible and Its Interpreters* (ed. W. H. Propp, B. Halpern, and D. N. Freedman; Winona Lake, Ind.: Eisenbrauns, 1990), 143–65.

[7] Kugel, *Traditions*, 24–29, 46.

the basis of sacred doctrine. Retelling these stories thus limits a poet's imaginative options because it could shake the foundations of such belief systems. Therefore, it should be avoided.

> The epic poet, thus, must take his theme from the history of a religion held true by us. But either such histories are so sacred and venerable that it is impiety to change them (the establishment of our faith being based upon them), or they are not so holy as to contain an article of faith within them, and thus do allow some things to be added, some removed, and others changed without the sin of impudence or irreligion. The epic poet will not dare reach his hand toward histories of the first kind; rather, he will leave them, in their pure and simple truth, for the pious, because invention here is not permitted.[8]

Milton willingly accepted precisely such a narrative challenge as Tasso felt obliged to forego. Milton's memory of his visit with Tasso's friend and biographer, Giovanni Battista Manso, epitomizes the contrasting temperaments of the Counter-Reformation Italian and the English Protestant in this regard. On Milton's departure from Naples, Manso "apologized for not having shown [Milton] more civility, which he said he had been restrained from doing, because [Milton] had spoken with so little reserve on matters of religion."[9] Milton's willingness in his poems to recount biblical stories upon which are founded articles of faith indicates the very lack of reserve in such matters that influenced Manso to limit the hospitality he showed to Milton in Naples.

Paradise Lost qualifies, as a whole and in many of its parts, as an expansive retelling of biblical narrative, of "sacred and venerable histories" which serve as the basis for tenets of faith. Regina Schwartz has persuasively demonstrated how the exigencies of narration compromise Milton's theology in *Paradise Lost*, where storytelling requires primal conflict that doctrine does not underwrite.[10] However, the contradiction that narrative demands force upon Milton's fundamental conviction in the "all-sufficiency" of Scripture remains in need of detailed exploration. In the light of such scrutiny, moreover,

---

[8] Torquato Tasso, "Discourses on the Art of Poetry" in Lawrence F. Rhu, *The Genesis of Tasso's Narrative Theory: English Translations of the Early Poetics and a Comparative Study of Their Significance* (Detroit: Wayne State University Press, 1993), 99–153, 105.
[9] *Complete Prose Works* 4:618.
[10] Regina Schwartz, *Remembering and Repeating: Biblical Creation in Paradise Lost* (Cambridge/New York: Cambridge University Press, 1988), 8–10.

Milton's emphatic rejection of tradition becomes a highly questionable claim, especially when we appreciate the exegetical dimension
of early retellings of stories from the Bible such as James Kugel has
recently elaborated with remarkable acumen.

I. MILTON, ARIOSTO, AND ENOCH

As a daunting precursor for both Tasso and Milton, Ariosto rarely
engaged Christian themes with sustained seriousness, and explicitly
biblical subjects hardly appear in his work at all. However, when
they do, his manner of addressing them could prove disquieting to
successors whose religious culture entailed sober consideration of such
matters. In *Paradise Lost*, the first explicit reference to *Orlando Furioso*
(*OF*) could hardly be more conspicuous. The initial sentence of
Milton's poem concludes with a line that virtually translates the claim
that Ariosto promptly made in his exordium to distinguish his poem
from Boiardo's *Orlando Innamorato*: "Things unattempted yet in prose
or rhyme" (*PL* 1.16). Thus, Milton literally cites Ariosto's *cosa non
detta in prosa mai nè in rima* (something never said in prose nor in
rhyme, *OF* 1.2.2) in order to claim that his poem's subject matter
is without precedent.[11] Quotation seems an odd way to go about
being original, to strike a bold note of innovation in an established
tradition; but it also points to the complexity of the connection
between Ariosto and Milton.

As I have argued elswhere, the predominant genre of Ariosto's
poem, romance, becomes effectively demonized by its clear association with Satan and the false religion of Roman Catholicism in
Paradise Lost.[12] Romances, moreover, are twice-told tales that openly
acknowledge their origins in some previous account of the events
they retell. Ariosto's ostensible source of this kind is Turpin, and it
is a running joke in his poem to invoke Turpin's authority precisely
at points in the story where credibility is out of the question. The

---

[11] Ludovico Ariosto, *Orlando Furioso* (ed. L. Caretti; Turin: Einaudi, 1971). All
citations of *Orlando Furioso* come from this edition.

[12] See Lawrence F. Rhu, "Romancing the Pope: Tasso's Narrative Theory and
Milton's Demonization of a Genre" in *"All in All": Unity, Diversity, and the Miltonic
Perspective* (Selinsgrove, Pa.: Susquehanna University Press, 1999), 128–37.

preposterousness of such a notion is intended to offer amusement.

Milton's poem stands in this relation to the Bible, only seriously so; it is his reliance upon Scripture that allows him to claim an unimpeachable source of truth. So long as he hearkens aright to this version of things, Milton can trump rival accounts as fables and dreams unworthy of belief. Indeed, you might say that if Scripture serves as the gold standard for truth in *Paradise Lost, Orlando Furioso* serves as a sort of lead standard. Just as its genre becomes for Milton the apt form for the adventures of the Prince of Lies, the poem itself is emphatically associated with falsehood in the Limbo of Vanities/ Paradise of Fools. In transit to the new-made earth, Satan lights upon the future location of this domain. He touches down

> upon the firm opacous globe
> Of this round world, whose first convex divides
> The luminous inferior orbs, enclosed
> From Chaos and the inroad of darkness old. (*PL* 3.418–421)

This landing offers Milton the chance to censure, as mere fantasy, the lunar locale of Ariosto's valley of lost things. By this emulous relocation, Milton announces that he is putting Ariosto's fictions in their true place, "[n]ot in the neighboring moon, as some have dreamed" (*PL* 3.459).

No moment in *Orlando Furioso* better illustrates the disturbing precedent of Ariosto's approach to biblical matters than Astolfo's visit with St. John the Evangelist on the moon. The moral that St. John draws from the allegory of the poets that he and Astolfo witness is notoriously irreverent. Initially, St. John explains that reputations for heroism and virtue, such as those enjoyed by Aeneas and Penelope, depend not upon their deeds but upon their image as it is manufactured by poets. Ostensibly historical accounts reflect the cash flow from patron to poet, not the course of events as they actually transpired. Such an assertion, of course, ironically insinuates a threatening appeal for Estense patronage while it reveals the thoroughly conditional nature of supposedly free-standing truths. However, St. John ultimately legitimates this unsettling claim and brings this moral to bear by referring to his own experience as a writer. As the author of the Fourth Gospel, St. John claims firsthand knowledge of how such arrangements work. Ariosto thus represents the Bible as a thoroughly human document subject to the same constraints as courtly literature in his own time and place.

St. John first meets Astolfo in the terrestrial paradise. He attributes his residence there to the generosity of his patron, Jesus Christ, whose reputation evidently owes much to this evangelist's propaganda on his behalf. In Milton's epic such a benefaction would be impossible because Paradise itself gets washed down the great river into the Persian Gulf and becomes "an Island salt and bare, The haunt of Seals and Orcs, and Sea-mews' clang" (*PL* 11.834–835). Thus, Milton grounds the lore of Paradise in a down-to-earth explanation of its post-lapsarian fortunes and anticipates its spiritualization into a place in the heart, "a paradise within" (*PL* 12.587). Of course, Milton is gesturing emphatically beyond a merely geological or geographical explanation about shifting land formations upon the surface of the earth. Michael's explicit didacticism draws the moral of this event for Adam in the clearest terms imaginable:

> To Teach thee that God attributes to place
> No sanctity, if none be thither brought
> By men who there frequent, or therein dwell. (*PL* 12.836–838)

Still, it is notable that Milton includes this account of Eden's future location in his poem. Empirical demonstrability was becoming a criterion of truth that one could ignore only at some hazard. The sort of doubts Thomas Hobbes raised in challenging the attribution of the Pentateuch to Moses' authorship exemplifies this phenomenon. Hobbes observed, for example, that "to say Moses spake of his own sepulcher" was, as he put it, "a strange interpretation" of Deut 32:6.[13] How could Moses write an account of the post-mortem fortunes of his own remains? Even though Milton continued to assert the pseudepigraphical tradition of Moses' authorship of the Pentateuch, he was not immune to the interrogative mood that such skepticism about biblical authority greatly enhanced.

Milton's specification of Eden's locale after the flood perhaps bespeaks a mode of writing—a proto-realism, if you will—that seeks to dispel such skepticism. If so, it is nonetheless seasoned with poetic fiction, and the mention of "Orcs" can serve as a cue to the presence of such elements. *Orlando Furioso*, like classical mythology, exemplifies idle dreams of the sort that Milton felt obliged to put decisively in their place on numerous occasions in *Paradise Lost*. Both

---

[13] Thomas Hobbes, *Leviathan* (Harmondsworth, Eng.: Penguin, 1961), 417, §3.33.

Orlando and Ruggiero, the major male protagonists of Ariosto's poem, encounter and defeat the orc on the isle of Ebuda. Perhaps this is not such a contemptible fiction as placing the Paradise of Fools/Limbo of Vanities on the moon, and thus it does not require the poet's direct scorn and dismissal. Rather, Milton discredits such a fabulous monster by association with Satan; and by calling it "that Sea-beast/Leviathan" (*PL* 1.200–201), he manages to discredit Hobbes in the process. We first encounter Satan in the guise of a sort of whale that can easily be mistaken for an island and lead hapless mariners to fix their anchors "in his scaly rind" (*PL* 1.206). Such a mistake in *Orlando Furioso* leads Astolfo to the false paradise of Alcina's island, which Ariosto describes in terms clearly evocative of the myth of Eden and the Fall of Man:

> Caschiamo tutti insieme in uno errore.
>
> We all fell together into error. (*OF* 6.37.5)
>
> Queste, con molte offerte e con buon viso
> Ruggier fecero entrar nel paradiso.
>
> With smiles and charms, these women welcomed Ruggiero into paradise. (*OF* 6.72.7–8)

In *Of Reformation*, when he refers to the episode of Astolfo's encounter with St. John, Milton misremembers the site of their initial meeting. "*Ariosto of Ferrara*," Milton avers, "following the scope of his Poem in a difficult knot how to restore *Orlando* his chiefe hero to his lost senses, brings *Astolfo* the English knight up into the moone, where S. *John*, as he feignes, met him."[14] Actually, the two meet earlier, in the terrestrial paradise, whither the hippogriff has carried Astolfo and whence the chariot of fire in which Elijah was rapt aloft will carry them both to the moon. However, Ariosto, with characteristic matter-of-factness, represents this vehicle as a sort of interplanetary taxi that routinely makes such flights through the heavens.

> un carro apparecchiòsi, ch'era ad uso
> d'andar scorrendo per quei cieli intorni:
> quel già ne le montagne di Giudea
> da' mortali occhi Elia levato avea.
>
> A chariot was made ready which customarily travelled about those skies. Once it had lifted Elijah from mortal sight in the mountains of Judea. (*OF* 34.68)

---

[14] *Complete Prose Works* 1:559–60.

In fact, we have heard a bit earlier of Elijah, because together with the patriarch Enoch, that great prophet kept St. John company when he first arrived in the terrestrial paradise.

> Quivi fu assunto, e trovò compagnia,
> che prima Enoch, il patriarca, v'era,
> eravi insieme il gran profeta Elia,
> che non han vista ancor l'ultima sera.

> He (St. John) was taken here and found company, for the patriarch Enoch was here before him, and the great prophet Elijah was also here: they had not yet seen their final evening. (*OF* 34.59)

Indeed, this particular threesome shares a reputation for immortality that made it something of a reflex to locate them in the earthly paradise after the gate had been shut to the rest of humanity. Enoch best exemplifies the work of tradition in creating such a reputation because the book of Genesis itself says so little about him.

Genesis 5, which begins by identifying itself as "the book of the generations of Adam," dedicates four brief verses to Enoch during his turn in this genealogical sequence that accounts for the descendants of Adam from Seth to Noah. In a "scene" that runs over seventy lines (*PL* 11.638–710), Milton dedicates seventeen of them specifically to Enoch (11.665–670 and 700–710), and he draws upon terse references to Enoch in two New Testament books (Heb 11:5 and Jude 14–15), as well as the four Enoch verses in Genesis (5:21–24). Given how little genuinely "biblical" material he has to work with, and how scattered these slight sources are, the skill of Milton's narrative synthesis in fashioning the figure of Enoch in *Paradise Lost* deserves full acknowledgment.

Moreover, his borrowing from the Letter of Jude, like Gen 5's labeling of itself as "the book of the generations of Adam," indicates how synthetic a composite each of these biblical texts is, as well. A distinct transition from the Yahwist, or J source, to the Priestly tradent marks the passage from the end of Gen 4 to the beginning of chapter 5. The relevant verses from the letter of Jude consist mainly in a citation from *1 Enoch*, which Jude explicitly identifies as prophecy. Such a claim can serve, in turn, to justify Milton's assertion that Enoch "[uttered] odious truth, that God would come To judge them with his saints" (*PL* 11.704–705).

It is worth noting, however, that Luther challenged the presence of this epistle in the biblical canon, as he also sought to exclude that

of James.[15] The foundations of truth in Scripture were thus radically
unsettled when "those written records pure" themselves became
increasingly subject to such challenges by the very believers whose
faith relied heavily upon the authority of the biblical canon. Just as
Milton's effort to "justify the ways of God to man" itself opens the
question of whether or not they are justifiable, so challenges to the
canonicity of one text or another cast suspicion more broadly and
broach the questionability of all canonical texts. Their authority
becomes more evidently a matter of deliberation and judgment, and
the fallibility of these human faculties should be especially apparent
to those who habitually appeal to the higher authority of divine
sanction.

About Enoch this passage from *Paradise Lost* continues:

> him the most high
> Rapt in a balmy cloud with winged steeds
> Did, as thou saw'st, receive, to walk with God
> High in salvation and the climes of bliss,
> Exempt from death. (*PL* 11.705–709)

In glossing this continuation of Enoch's story, Fowler, as usual, is
helpful: "The cloud with winged steeds is puzzling," he acknowledges, "though it may simply be based on the description of Elijah's
translation." Then, Fowler adds parenthetically, "Enoch and Elijah
were often associated."[16] Thus, Fowler's tentative claim for the basis
of Milton's narrative process appeals to the traditional association of
Enoch and Elijah, both of whom were reputed to have escaped
death. Enoch's immortality depends on reading a particular clause
of Gen 5:24—"for God had taken (or transferred) him"—to mean
that he had either ascended into heaven or entered the earthly paradise. Elijah's immortality depends not only on the account of his
ascent into heaven in 2 Kgs 2:11 during the reign of Ahaziah but
also on the subsequent receipt of an apparently post-mortem letter
from Elijah by Jehoram, Ahaziah's successor, in 2 Chr 21:12.
Milton's mortalism[17] will not allow these ascents to be merely

---

[15] "Preface to the Epistles of St. James and St. Jude" in *Martin Luther: Selections
from His Writings* (ed. J. Dillenberger; Garden City, N.Y.: Anchor, 1961), 35–37.
[16] Alastair Fowler, ed., *Milton: Paradise Lost* (New York: Longman, 1971), 599.
[17] In his clearest enunciation of this belief, Milton uses the same phrase, "exempt
from death" (*Complete Prose Works* 6:407), which appears in the Enoch episode in
PL 11.709.

metempsychosis, just as his disbelief in an earthly paradise after the fall eliminates its availability as a penultimate reward for immortal tenants such as we find in Ariosto. Thus, Milton faces a concrete problem of celestial navigation in the case of Enoch, and Elijah's chariot seems the only authorized version of how to get there from here intact, body and soul. Still, Fowler admits he is not sure that is what is happening in these lines.

Where, then, does one walk with God, as Enoch is supposed to have done? On earth, it seems, in Enoch's case, at least for a good long while. For it is written that Enoch did so for 300 years after the birth of Methuselah (Gen 5:22). As Kugel has noted, this account led interpreters to see Enoch as a repentant sinner during these three centuries, whose mention itself signals Enoch's change of heart. Moreover, it was his penitence that made him worthy of God's favor.[18] After "God had taken him" (Gen 5:24), however, reclamation of the moon from Ariosto's mistaken placement of the debris of human folly upon it enabled Milton to suggest that

> Those argent fields more likely habitants,
> Translated Saints, or middle Spirits hold
> Betwixt th'Angelical and Human kind. (*PL* 3.460–462)

Perhaps Enoch would encounter Elijah and St. John the Evangelist there, rather than in the earthly paradise, where Ariosto locates the meeting of these three. Fowler acknowledges this probability with regard to Enoch and Elijah; but only sixty lines later, when Satan descries the stairway to heaven, we hear of those who arrived there "[r]apt in a Chariot drawn by fiery Steeds" (*PL* 3.521). This description, as we have seen, applies in significant part to Enoch in *Paradise Lost* (11.706) and to Elijah in 2 Kgs 2:11. Without tradition, Scripture seems incomplete in Enoch's case. But with it, or rather, *them*—traditions—the expanded narrative raises questions as much as it resolves them.

In the Geneva Bible of 1560, whose title page famously advertises "most profitable annotations upon all the hard places," the gloss at Gen 5:24 offers this warning: "to inquire where [Enoch] became is mere curiosity."[19] Such a caveat may persuade some to suspend

---

[18] Kugel, *Traditions*, 178–79.
[19] *The Geneva Bible: A facsimile of the 1560 edition* (Madison, Wis.: University of Wisconsin Press, 1969).

judgment in the manner of Pyrrhonian skepticism. Raphael famously
makes such a recommendation to the pre-lapsarian Adam with regard
to his inquiries about different world systems at the beginning of
book 8 (*PL* 8.70–75). However, there are numerous places in *Paradise
Lost* where the exigencies of Milton's narrative and the limits of
strictly biblical sources become especially clear, and the stakes on
such occasions can often be far higher than either Pyrrhonian *epoché*
or a cursory dismissal of such questions (which suspension of judgment sometimes serves to cover) will ever recognize. To claim the
Spirit's guidance as a decisive alternative at such a crossroads is perhaps an obligatory move for the individual reader, but to imagine
that spirit is somehow pure and untainted by the influence of tradition seems wishful thinking.

II. Cain and Abel

For example, following the Elijah connection can lead us to Adam's
vision of Abel's sacrifice for which, according to Gen 4:4, the Lord
had regard or respect. As Milton puts it:

> His Off'ring soon propitious Fire from Heav'n
> Consum'd with nimble glance, and grateful steam;
> The other's not, for his was not sincere. (*PL* 4.441–443)

A likely source for this turn in Milton's story occurs in the account
of Elijah's contest with the prophets of Baal on Mt. Carmel, where
we read, in 1 Kgs 18:38, how "the fire of the Lord fell, and consumed the burnt sacrifice." However, such a claim requires me to
acknowledge some prematurity in my assertion about "the limits of
strictly biblical sources." Obviously the favor shown Elijah's sacrifice
is a "biblical source," and one only needs to believe that the Bible
speaks with one voice—God's—to realize that Milton's conviction in
the "all-sufficiency" of Scripture and his expansive retelling of the
story of Cain and Abel undergo no particular strain in this representation of the signs that God received Abel's sacrifice with favor.

However, even in these three lines another claim surfaces whose
strictly biblical foundation is tenuous, if not non-existent. Where does
it say, in Gen 4 or elsewhere in the Bible, that Cain's sacrifice was
"not sincere," as Milton puts it in *PL* 11.443? The fire that descends
upon Elijah's altar distinguishes him from the prophets of Baal as a
spokesperson of the true God, Yahweh. Likewise, the fire that consumes

Abel's offering in Adam's Miltonic vision makes a major difference or, rather, reveals one previously undisclosed. For Milton, this manifestation of spiritual differences between Cain and Abel is so crucial that he pads the Genesis story with a decisive contrast between the supposed inward dispositions of the two brothers: Cain's alleged insincerity is opposed to the presumed "meekness" of Abel (*PL* 11.437). Moreover, Milton adds a similarity to their sacrifices that enables him to further this contrast between the otherwise scarcely distinguishable temperaments of these biblical figures.

Although the Bible tells us that Abel offered the Lord "the firstlings of his flock," it does not say, as Milton does in *PL* 11.435, that Cain offered the "First Fruits." Rather, as Kugel demonstrates, in its quest for some distinction between the two offerings, traditional exegesis has sometimes fixed upon Gen 4:3's description of Cain's having made his offering "in process of time" as a sign of some delay or tardiness in his observance that would clarify God's mysterious response.[20] Milton, however, credits each brother with apparent timeliness, which would be an external and merely formal accommodation of a law, had one yet been established. Although he further credits Abel with the performance of "all due Rites" (*PL* 11.440), he attributes to Cain a crucial failing of another kind, one far more central to Milton's theology of rational liberty. The "First Fruits" that Cain lays on the altar are "unculled, as came to hand" (*PL* 11.436) whereas "the Firstlings of [Abel's] flocks" are characterized as "[c]hoicest and best" (*PL* 11.437–438).

When Cain offers "First Fruits," described as "uncull'd," his negligence bespeaks the moral challenge that Milton characterizes in *Areopagitica* by summoning the image of "those confused seeds which were imposed on Psyche as an incessant labor to *cull* out and sort asunder" (emphasis added). Moreover, he finds in that myth an analogue for "the doom Adam fell into,"[21] which is, of course, the doom that his descendents inherit from him. When Abel offers the "choicest" among "the Firstlings of his Flock," he is exercising the faculty of reason which God gave him and which Milton also claims that God gave Adam. As Milton puts it (also in *Areopagitica*), God gave

---

[20] Kugel, *Traditions*, 150.
[21] *Complete Prose Works* 2:514.

Adam "freedom to choose, for reason is but choosing; he had been else a mere artificial Adam, such an Adam as he is in the motions."[22]

Although there is no apparent textual warrant for such a claim, Milton's Cain is represented as negligent in the exercise of choice, which is the hallmark of Christian liberty to Milton. The absence of "Fire from heaven" signals Cain's failure in this regard. Thus, Milton is *producing* biblical theology from a passage of Scripture, which, it seems, is not "biblical" enough for his purposes. Therefore, he supplements it, relying on passages from elsewhere in the Bible and upon exegetical tradition and upon inspiration or, perhaps, personal inclination.

This sort of response is a long-standing habit of mind in approaching Scripture. Hebrews 11, Milton's foremost model from the Christian Bible for the whole series of episodes that Michael expounds to Adam, epitomizes this way of reading that supplements narrative passages with interpretive glosses or telling details. That catalogue of exemplary heroes of faith features Abel as such an illustrious figure: "By faith Abel offered to God a more acceptable sacrifice than Cain, through which he received approval as righteous, God bearing witness by accepting his gifts" (Heb 11:4). The author of this epistle has grafted a theology upon Gen 4 that derives in particular from Abraham's interaction with God in Gen 15:6, where it is written that Abraham "believed the LORD; and he counted it to him as righteousness."

But this sort of conviction, construed as it was by Martin Luther— that faith counts as righteousness—leads directly to a central dispute in Reformation theology about the relation between faith and works. More important in our present context, however, is the way in which Luther's theological convictions, which obviously derive from the Bible, could lead him to question the contents of that authoritative text when theological discrepancies became apparent in it. The exception that Luther took to the Epistle of James focused upon its divergence from the central message that he discerned elsewhere in the Bible. This theological difference prompted him to speculate upon the legitimacy of that epistle's origins and of its inclusion in the canon of biblical texts. Luther's argument for such a demotion in the authority of a particular text corresponds to Milton's impulse to

---

[22] *Complete Prose Works* 2:527.

rewrite it in such a way that its meaning becomes unmistakable. Each response is governed by the drive to establish clear and unimpeachable meanings. But, either way, the instability of the biblical foundation of such meanings becomes apparent in the process.

The murder scene that Adam witnesses transpires in nineteen lines (*PL* 11.429–447). It includes details about both participants' moral character, about the nature and reception of their sacrifices, and about the murder weapon, all of which severely strain the limits of biblical evidence for these representations. Securely to police the boundary between Scripture and tradition in this passage requires more than a spirit single-mindedly determined to establish such a boundary. With considerable urgency, Milton has staked important claims upon the existence of such a clear division; but that does not guarantee their validity. It merely indicates that there is a lot at stake in this premise. Indeed, we might fairly speak here of an epistemology of moods and a quest for certainty that would link Milton and Descartes and, for that matter, Tasso in a drive toward unexceptionable criteria upon which to ground their otherwise profoundly unsettled beliefs.

III. The *Protoevangelium*

In his effort to "justify the ways of God to men," Milton courageously acknowledges the possibility that they were not justifiable. At the pitch of his tragic ordeal Adam directly confronts this challenge:

> Ah, why should all mankind
> For one man's fault thus guiltless be condemn'd,
> If guiltless? (*PL* 10.822–824)

To answer this question Adam interprets the words of judgment passed upon him and his wife and the serpent in the aftermath of their transgression. The characteristically personal intensity of Protestant exegesis only increases when the interpreter is in the middle of a tragic agon, such as Adam and Eve are undergoing after their commission of "the mortal Sin/Original" (*PL* 9.1003–1004). Initially, Adam's doubts about God's word mount as he suffers through this ordeal in a process that ultimately culminates in the breakthrough of understanding Gen 3:15 as the so-called *protoevangelium*. Adam's traumatic puzzlement occasions further questions that reveal how cryptic Scripture is, how in need of a supplement to fill out its meaning.

> Why comes not Death,
> Said he, with one thrice acceptable stroke
> To end me? Shall Truth fail to keep her word? (*PL* 10.854–856)

Inasmuch as Truth resides in God's word—or, as Milton puts it on behalf of Adam's post-biblical descendants, "those written records pure" (*PL* 12.513)—Adam reasonably expects the punishment promised when God explained the rules of residence in Eden. As He warns Adam about the forbidden fruit in Gen 2:17: "in the day that thou eatest thereof thou shalt surely die," though we later learn that Adam dies at the age of 930 in Gen 5:3–4. Tradition solves this problem by reference to Ps 90:4, where we hear that "a thousand years in [God's] sight are but as yesterday when it is past, and as a watch in the night." Second Peter 3:8 reprises this thought in these terms: "one day is with the Lord as a thousand years, and a thousand years as one day." Although neither of these passages makes reference to Adam's problematic longevity, both were available to explain it with a solution that clearly demonstrates the sufficiency of Scripture.

In *Paradise Lost* Adam at first construes Eve's and his "long day's dying" as a sign of divine sadism, "a slow-pac'd evil . . . to augment our pain" (10.964–965). Adam's interpretive breakthrough begins when it dawns upon him that the serpent whose head Eve's seed shall bruise may well be their "grand Foe, Satan" (10.1033–1034), and the prospect of such apposite revenge helps soften Adam's heart toward God. Of course, this intuition is demonstrably true if you have read the previous book of *Paradise Lost*, though it is not so if you rely merely on the Genesis account of Adam and Eve, which nowhere mentions Satan. However, the Miltonic Adam's accurate inkling about Satan's serpentine disguise leads him to revise his judgment about Truth's failure "to keep her word": "wee expected/ Immediate dissolution, which we thought/Was meant by Death that day" (10.1048–1050).

Though the nature of death remains a haunting mystery for Adam anxiously to contemplate, remorse and contrition now guide the regenerate pair through their traumatic ordeal toward a further reversal of fortunes. The change of note from pastoral happiness to tragedy that characterizes the narrative action in books 9 and 10 gradually changes to happiness once more, though happiness of an utterly different order. That change transpires as Adam learns the meaning of the biblical story from Genesis 4 through the book of Revelation, a spiritual exercise in Christian exegesis that reconciles him to the fall. But it is his intuition of the *protoevangelium* that has prepared him for such a change.

Milton published two tragedies during the Restoration, if we count books 9 and 10 of *Paradise Lost* (where Milton prominently announces his change of note to tragic) along with *Samson Agonistes*. Suffering is the true mode of action in *Samson Agonistes*, as Milton acknowledges in his prefatory poetics, where he significantly transforms his epigraph from Aristotle. Pity and terror are raised and purged in an audience not by the imitation of an action but, in Milton's words, "by reading or seeing those *passions* well imitated" (emphasis added).[23] But the evolution of these passions toward what Dr. Johnson called the play's "just and regular catastrophe" remains a challenging interpretive puzzle famously expressed by his critique of the "poetical architecture" of *Samson Agonistes*. "[T]he poem has a beginning and an end," Johnson observes, "but it must be allowed to want a middle."[24] In contrast, the problem of a missing middle does not arise in books 9 and 10 of *Paradise Lost* because the ordeal of exegesis fills that place in the story. Indeed, Adam's exegetical ordeal *becomes* the developing action of the tragedy. But such an expressive option remains unavailable in a drama about a categorically "Old Testament" hero like Samson. While Adam is exempt from the confines of that category, Samson is consigned to ignorance of the Christian message that prophetic interpretation reveals to the progenitor of our race.

In characterizing this interpretive breakthrough and the early modern context in which it could carry such critically decisive weight, C. A. Patrides speaks of the "frantic search for 'origins' [in which] Protestant apologists did not hesitate to hark back as far as the first of men." Indeed, for such believers, Patrides demonstrates, "Adam's recognition of the Savior made him not merely a Christian but, more precisely, the first Protestant."[25] Although this strikes me as a

---

[23] Hughes, *John Milton*, 549.

[24] *The Rambler* (16 July 1751) quoted in *Milton: Comus and Samson Agonistes: A Casebook* (ed. J. Lovelock; London: Macmillan, 1975), 158, 162–63.

[25] C. A. Patrides "The 'Protoevangelium' in Renaissance Theology and *Paradise Lost*," *Studies in English Literature* 3 (1963): 19–30, here 28–29.

curious notion (and I doubt I am alone in that impression), the mood in which it might carry conviction seems quite recognizable, if not wholly familiar. What Patrides calls "a frantic search for 'origins'" rhymes fully with the infinite regress that classical skepticism exposes in the search for a criterion by which to measure truth claims. It also resonates clearly with the melodramatic extremes to which Descartes pursues doubt before he secures a foundation whence he can work his way back to confidence even in his own existence.

Work such as James Kugel's compendious compilation, *Traditions of the Bible*, can help us to put this particular state of mind in historical perspective because it takes as a point of departure the Protestant impetus that has driven so much of modern biblical scholarship. This impetus can be traced back to the early modern period and the dismissal of tradition even in the midst of the immense erudition that Protestant scholars applied in sifting through customary readings of Scripture to reclaim those that served their immediate purposes. Indeed, Milton can help us see that what was occurring was as much a contest within or over a particular tradition, despite the demonization of tradition per se that his own polemical formulations sometimes expressed.

IV. Enoch, Noah, and Abraham

The Reformation crisis over biblical authority figures centrally among the phenomena routinely cited as signs, or indeed causes, of skepticism's emergence in early modern Europe.[26] The lack of stable criteria for interpretation of Scripture threatens the validity of normative claims made by invoking biblical prooftexts. This instability helps open the abyss that Descartes later tries to sound with hyperbolic doubt. Descartes resolves this crisis by discovering an indubitable proposition: his skeptical thought can entertain doubt about the existence of virtually everything except his own existence as the entertainer of such radical and comprehensive doubts. Unlike the Pyrrhonist or proponent of mitigated skepticism, such as Montaigne,

---

[26] Richard H. Popkin, *The History of Scepticism: From Erasmus to Spinoza* (Berkeley: University of California Press, 1979), esp. 1–17. Charles Larmore, "Scepticism," in *The Cambridge History of Seventeenth-Century Philosophy* (ed. D. Garber and M. Ayers; 2 vols.; Cambridge: Cambridge University Press, 1998), 2:1145–92.

the fallibility of human understanding does not lead the Cartesian to acknowledge the limitations of human intelligence as a prelude to humble acceptance of human traditions and the wisdom of time-tested custom. The sixteenth-century Protestant faced a similar dilemma, a need for certainty in a world whose traditional authorities were under radical assault; and Scripture was taken as an unquestionable authority to satisfy that need. Scripture, however, requires interpretation, and the institutions that presided over that process and conferred validity upon it were precisely what Protestants summoned Scripture to challenge. Thus, the magisterium of the Church of Rome could not sanction Protestant interpretation of Holy Writ, nor indeed could any merely human authority. That was the Spirit's role, but those who surrender to the Spirit's rule can easily seem both as hyperbolic and as egocentric as the Cartesian in their resolution of the skeptic's dilemma. Where does the self leave off and the Spirit begin?

In discussing Milton's mortalism, William Kerrigan demonstrates not only the importance of Enoch in relation to that doctrine but also the subjective pressures that shaped Milton's ostensibly biblical religion in this regard. "Milton," Kerrigan bluntly states in conclusion, "bent his religion into conformity with himself."[27] How could he not, we may wonder, given the rejection of tradition to which he subscribes and the inevitably indefinite, or simply mysterious, boundary between Spirit and self in Protestant interpretation of the Bible? But the boundary between tradition and Spirit, or self, seems equally blurry, although a work like James Kugel's *Traditions of the Bible* can help make that boundary clearer. We have already noted the oddness of Milton's claim to originality via citation from Ariosto. However, there is a difference in Milton's quotation via translation that warrants attention: "Thing*s* unattempted yet in prose or rhyme" (*PL* 1.16, emphasis added). The "thing" that makes *Orlando Furioso* new is Orlando's madness, just as his *inamoramento* conferred originality upon Boiardo's account of that hero's adventures. But Milton seems to be claiming more than a single innovation. What then is new about Milton's poem?

---

[27] William Kerrigan "The Heretical Milton: From Assumption to Mortalism," *English Literary Renaissance* 5 (1975): 125–66, here 166.

The poet's most obvious assertion of originality occurs in the proem to book 9 when he emphatically specifies the new kind of heroism that he will sing. His poem will rescue "the better fortitude/Of Patience and Heroic Martyrdom" (*PL* 9.31–32) from previous silence in poems such as his. First, however, he must tell the tragic story of the fall, and according to this poet, tragedy deserves the name heroic as much as those exploits recounted by Homer and Virgil. Then, Michael's subsequent relation, via vision and narration in books 11 and 12, will introduce unprecedented material into heroic song. The solitary courage of such figures as Enoch, Noah, and Abraham, as they appear in *Paradise Lost*, notably distinguishes them not only from the likes of Achilles, Odysseus, and Aeneas, but also from unnamed myriads of chivalrous knights. The classic and medieval heroes of epic and romance pale by comparison with these prophetic witnesses to truth who face down multitudes of violent, depraved, and idolatrous antagonists.

We have some evidence that the narrator of *Paradise Lost* viewed himself in such terms, as beleaguered and isolated but still outspoken:

> More safe I sing with mortal voice, unchang'd
> To hoarse or mute, though fall'n on evil days,
> On evil days though fall'n, and evil tongues;
> In darkness, and with dangers compass round,
> And solitude. (*PL* 7.24–27)

As *persona non grata* under the restored Stuart monarch, Milton, the notorious defender of regicide, clearly fit such a description while he was completing *Paradise Lost*. It was by no means guaranteed that he would be spared from capital punishment after the Restoration. But Milton also represented himself as the target of plotting Jesuits during his stay in Rome almost three decades earlier; and we have already cited his recollection of Tasso's patron, Manso, who "apologized for not having shown [Milton] more civility, which he said he had been restrained from doing, because [Milton] had spoken with so little reserve on matters of religion."[28]

Besides intrepid outspokenness, however, patience is a keynote of the distinctively new heroism that Milton celebrates in his epic, and its connection with Milton's self-image as a prophetic poet requires

---

[28] *Complete Prose Works* 4:1, 618; see Barabara K. Lewalski, *The Life of John Milton: A Critical Biography* (Oxford: Blackwell, 2000), 98–99.

special emphasis. Milton's moral theology stresses freedom of the will so centrally, and the gendered values of his convictions decry "effeminate slackness" (*PL* 11.634) and praise autonomy and discipline so memorably, that patience for Milton is likeliest to seem the stiff upper lip of unyielding stoic resistance. But Milton's poetic process, as he represents it in *Paradise Lost*, emphasizes receptivity and surrender to divine inspiration. Spontaneity and ease, the very opposite of unrelenting determination, characterize the disposition in which the poet receives his

> . . . Celestial Patroness, who deigns
> Her nightly visitation unimplor'd,
> And dictates to me slumb'ring, or inspires
> Easy my unpremeditated Verse. (*PL* 9.21–24)

The "patience" of such an attitude entails letting go of the will's preemptive impulses; it is, as the etymology of the word itself suggests, the "suffering" of submission to forces beyond one's conscious control. Miltonic heroism in the sequence of exemplars from Enoch to Noah to Abraham involves bearing witness to truths that hostile communities refuse to acknowledge, but such prophetic speech is conferred upon the speaker who passively yields to its summons. It is not simply conceived by him on his own.

The mystery of the source of such inspiration should not be underestimated, but Milton certainly thought that, properly understood, the Bible itself was such a source. As a Protestant polemicist, however, he was eager to distinguish between Holy Writ *per se* and the "human traditions" that had attached themselves to it and represented to Milton the corrupt Church of Rome and all other such "papistical" alternatives. Of course, Milton was deeply learned in biblical traditions, and the project he undertook is inconceivable without the resources of those exegetical motifs expressed in the earliest retellings of Scripture, which themselves so often rely upon other places in the Bible that they arguably stay within bounds of Protestant purism in these matters.

If we return to the figure of Enoch, as Milton presents him, we can find, in what might seem the most trivial details, the influence of received interpretations conflated with distinctly Miltonic constructions. The drama of Enoch's ascent occurs as the sequel to Milton's expansive account of the catastrophic marriages between the sons of God and the daughters of men. It is set in a context allusively reminiscent of Homer's description of the shield of Achilles, though the divisions between peace and war, between civil and military action in that episode from book 18 of the *Iliad* collapse in Milton as violence erupts in the council meeting when

> Of middle age one rising, eminent
> In wise deport, spake much of Right and Wrong,
> Of Justice, of Religion, Truth and Peace,
> And Judgment from above. (*PL* 11.665–668)

This is Enoch, whose proper name the poem never mentions; and the telling words here are deceptively simple, easily overlooked, and, compared with a chariot of fire, utterly undramatic: "one," "wise," and "middle age" signal either a distinctively Miltonic concern or some biblical traditions at work. This "one" will become compellingly isolated in his exceptional worthiness: "The only righteous in a world perverse" (*PL* 11.701), a recurrent distinction of this series of exemplars, each of whom Michael singles out against a background of pervasive violence, depravity, and idol-worship. But Enoch's age and his wisdom suggest traditional aspects of this personage as early exegetes imaginatively developed them from the slightest of textual cues. That Enoch "walked with God" indicated his special worthiness, but that he did so "after the birth of Methuselah" prompted a particular widespread response that Kugel identifies as the tradition of "Enoch the Penitent." In other words, Enoch's career divides neatly in two for early exegetes, a story with a before and after that explains why Enoch became favored with divine companionship: he underwent a significant change of heart. Such a development makes Enoch's stage of life important, and Milton duly notes it. Similarly, the immortality that Enoch traditionally enjoyed made him available as a messenger from beyond this world, and the attribution of authorship to him became an attractive possibility. His exemption from death and his translation made him privy to the ways of heaven, which he supposedly communicated through pseudepigraphical writings like *1 Enoch*. He became "Enoch the Scribe," observes Kugel, adding that "any Jewish scribe of late antiquity was almost by definition a sage." Milton employs this tradition in describing Enoch as "eminent/In wise deport" (*PL* 11.665–666).[29]

Milton may find in the Epistle of Jude a citation from *1 Enoch* that affiliates this patriarch with the denunciation of the ungodly,

---

[29] Kugel, *Traditions*, 178–79 and 177.

but he himself must single Enoch out for that specific role as a solitary individual in his poem. In the case of Noah, who is twice identified as a moral exception "in his generation," the Genesis story obligingly performs this service for Milton. That he is deemed "righteous" and "blameless" or "perfect" in the context of such a notoriously wicked age raised what seems an inevitable question for early interpreters: compared to what or to whom? But the specter of relativism does *not* haunt this figure in *Paradise Lost*, where absolute differences prevail in Milton's procession of solitary heroes. In a world where "all turn degenerate, all deprav'd," Noah emerges as

> One Man except, the only Son of light
> In a dark Age, against example good. (*PL* 11.406, 408–409)

Noah's exceptionality in the biblical story thus corresponds to Milton's emphasis upon the singularly upright individual and underwrites the pattern of one against all that Enoch first illustrates in Milton's sequence of heroic patriarchs. Indeed, the anonymous way in which that first hero is presented helps to establish the possibility of recurrence inherent in the very idea of a pattern.

But another question about Noah obviously vexed ancient interpreters, and, like many such questions, it becomes evident through an exegetical motif that pervades retellings of his story. Why did God single out Noah to be spared? What did he do that was so special that he earned for himself and his family what amounts to a unique reprieve among humans alive at the time of the flood? Without any explicit scriptural warrant, with only a series of inferences, early exegetes concluded that Noah must have warned people about the flood. Prompted by what we might call the *in*sufficiency of Scripture and its clear need of a supplement, "[t]his tradition of Noah the preacher helped to explain why God saved him. Noah had gone about trying to get others to repent—certainly this was one good deed to his credit. Perhaps this was why Scripture calls him 'righteous.'"[30] The merest glimpse of this motif appears in 2 Pet 2:5, where Noah is called "a herald of righteousness." Moreover, an obscure verse in 1 Peter obliquely links Noah with Christ, who "preached to the spirits in prison, who formerly did not obey, when God's patience waited in the days of Noah" (3:19–20). Perhaps such

---

[30] Kugel, *Traditions*, 186.

phrases from the Epistles of Peter inspired Milton to represent Noah
in this manner:

> At length a Reverend Sire among them came,
> And of their doings great dislike declar'd,
> And testifi'd against thir ways; hee oft
> Frequented thir Assemblies, whereso met,
> Triumphs or Festivals, and to them preach'd
> Conversion and Repentance, as to Souls
> In Prison under Judgments imminent:
> But all in vain: which when he saw, he ceas'd
> Contending, and remov'd his Tents far off . . .
> . . . hee of thir wicked ways
> Shall them admonish, and before them set
> The paths of righteousness, how much more safe,
> And full of peace, denouncing wrath to come
> On thir impenitence; and shall return
> Of them derided, but of God observ'd
> The one just man alive. (*PL* 11.719–727, 712–718)

This portrait may derive solely from New Testament traces of Noah's
career as a preacher. Still, rather than being prompted by such slen-
der scriptural cues as the Epistles of Peter offer, it seems likelier that
the boundaries between Scripture and tradition, or between Spirit
and tradition, were simply more permeable than Protestant polemic
could comfortably acknowledge. The inspired poet yielded to the
guidance of extrabiblical knowledge that the ideologue felt constrained
to disown.

Kugel lists an array of texts that attest to the tradition of Noah
the preacher, and their very number serves as an index of the widespread currency of Noah in this guise. Flavius Josephus's *Antiquities*,
which Milton certainly knew, is among them; but the point is not
to trace one's way back to a single, unique source. Rather, Kugel's
compilations seek to illustrate what, in another context, W. H. Auden
called "a whole climate of opinion."[31] Like weather systems, traditions do not automatically comply with our changing sense of priorities. They affect us despite our best intentions to shed them, for
they are what make us intelligible both to ourselves and to others.
Milton's occasionally extreme opposition between Scripture and

---

[31] W. H. Auden, "In Memory of Sigmund Freud," in *Collected Shorter Poems 1927–
1957* (London: Faber & Faber, 1966), 166–70, here 168.

tradition seems of a piece with the Protestant rallying cry of "Sola scriptura!" Ironically, however, even when we can find some slight biblical warrant for largely extrabiblical traditions that Milton employs, we are conceiving of the poet in terms that characterize the ways early interpreters read the Bible in the process of developing the traditions associated with it.

Their conviction that the Bible spoke with one voice, for example, induced them to rely upon places in Scripture quite remote from the passage in need of immediate explanation. As we have seen, puzzlement over the apparent contradiction of God's clear declaration in Gen 2:17 about the immediately fatal consequences of eating the forbidden fruit led early exegetes to Psalm 90 for a resolution to this dilemma. Puzzlement over this Genesis verse inspires Milton to sustain a profound *contemplatio mortis* over the last three books of his poem, a mode of reflection introduced earlier by Adam's poignant expression of innocent uncertainty: "whate'er Death is/Some dreadful thing no doubt" (*PL* 4.424–425).

Likewise, in the case of Abraham, questions as to why God singled him out as the recipient of exceptional favor seemed unanswerable without recourse to Josh 24:2, where it is possible to infer a difference between Abraham and others in his family and in Ur of Chaldea: "*they* served other gods" (emphasis added), but *not* Abraham or, at least, not for long. Traditions that derived from reading these passages together clearly stand behind Milton's representation of Abraham, although their biblical premise alone appears in the poem. Moreover, we can hear a medley of explicitly scriptural echoes, mainly from Gen 12 and 15, in this excerpt from *Paradise Lost*:

> Him on this side Euphrates yet residing,
> Bred up in Idol-worship; O that men
> (Canst thou believe?) should be so stupid grown,
> While yet the Patriarch liv'd, who scap'd the Flood,
> As to forsake the living God, and fall
> To worship thir own work in Wood and Stone
> For Gods! yet him God the most High voutsafes
> To call by Vision from his Fathers house,
> His kindred and false Gods, into a Land
> Which he will show him, and from him will raise
> A mighty Nation, and upon him show'r
> His benediction so, that in his Seed
> All Nations shall be blest; he straight obeys
> Not knowing to what Land, yet firm believes:

I see him, but thou canst not, with what Faith
He leaves his Gods, his Friends, and native Soil
Ur of Chaldæa, passing now the Ford
To Haran, after him a cumbrous Train
Of Herds and Flocks, and numerous servitude;
Not wand'ring poor, but trusting all his wealth
With God, who call'd him, in a land unknown. (*PL* 12.114–134)

A dense network of allusions to Genesis helps to produce, via a sort
of biblical "thick description," the figure who emerges as "faithful
Abraham" in line 152.[32] As Kugel demonstrates, this image of
Abraham is a corollary of his image as Abraham the Tested, a picture that surfaces most dramatically via the binding of Isaac in
Genesis 22, when "God *tested* Abraham." Further, it inspired a view
of Abraham's entire life as "one long series of divinely instituted
challenges." Ezra, for example, sums up Abraham's life in words
that include God's "[finding] his heart to be faithful" (Neh 9:7–8)
before he made the covenant with him in Genesis 15.[33] The first of
these tests in the biblical narrative would be the divine summons
from Ur at the start of Abraham's story, which, for Milton (following Josh 24:2), also calls Abraham from "false Gods," despite his
early indoctrination in "Idol-worship" (*PL* 12.115, 122). The alacrity
with which Abraham answered that sudden call demonstrates his
unquestioning faith, for which he became duly renowned. For those
who inevitably wondered why God would choose Abraham for so
great a blessing, the traditions of Abraham's resistance to Chaldaean
idolatry (or his reclamation from it) silently fill in the background,
although Milton eschews specific mention of them.

Thus, you might say (with a Protestant sigh of relief) that Milton's
biblicism in this passage is "tradition-free." Indeed, the Abraham we
have here corresponds both to the Pauline version of this patriarch
in Rom 4 and Gal 3 and to his representation in Heb 11. But it is
remarkable how much of the *biblical* story of Abraham is eclipsed in
the process of creating this theologically acceptable rendition. The
drama of Abraham's family life and the trials of exile—Sarah, Hagar,

---

[32] Line 121 merges the phrase "from [his] father's house" in Gen 12:1 with
"vision" in 15:1; "a mighty Nation" in line 124 comes from Gen 12:2. Lines 126–127
blend elements from Gen 12:2–3 and 15:6. Ur of Chaldaea in line 130 appears in
Gen 11:31 and 15:7, and lines 135–138 depend upon Gen 12:6–7.
[33] Kugel, *Traditions*, 308–11 and 296–97.

Ishmael, Isaac, Lot, and the Pharaoh—all disappear in this specially edited version of "faithful Abraham." A significant majority of the biblical seems to vanish in the "Bible-based" religion produced in this passage, which, despite Milton's contempt for tradition, requires reading in the manner of an early exegete to establish the premise of Abraham's flight from idolatry.

Milton wanted to write a poem that would be not only exemplary but also doctrinal to a nation, and while the poet emphatically voices his disapproval of idolatry, he is obliged to represent it abstractly and moralistically. As Joseph Addison famously remarked of this book, "in some places the author has been so attentive to his divinity that he has neglected his poetry."[34] The poet's impatient outburst of exasperation over human stupidity illustrates how reductive polemical intolerance can become. Unfortunately, he does not take his own parenthetical question to heart, for it opens up the possibility of an answer. Providing one, however, would require empathy rather than dismissal, and the accusation of idolatry categorically preempts any effort of further understanding. Milton's acquaintance with both Philo and Josephus could have supplied him with anthropological explanations on this topic, but, secure in the truth as he ostensibly was, Milton felt no need to look further. Were his question sincere, rather than merely rhetorical, it would reveal the insufficiency of Scripture, for it is virtually a prelude to the sorts of stories that such puzzlement occasioned among early exegetes.

It is more than an amusing irony that Milton read the Bible so much in the manner of the early interpreters who created the traditional Bible. For them the Bible only becomes intelligible through an awareness of those "common expositions" that Milton sometimes decried. Yet Kugel's inventory of four assumptions that underlie ancient exegesis all apply to Milton's interpretive practice, though I have had occasion to stress only one of them: the perfection of Scripture and the consequent links of agreement and supplementation between otherwise discrete and remote passages, like Gen 2:17 and Ps 90:4 or Gen 12:1–3 and Josh 24:2.[35] In the case of Abraham, however, Milton's moralism is another quality he shares with ancient

---

[34] Joseph Addison, *Addison's Criticisms on* Paradise Lost (ed. A. S. Cook; New York: Phaeton, 1968), 148.

[35] Kugel, *Traditions*, 14–19, esp. 17.

exegetes. Edifying purposes prompted them to transform ambiguous, if not unflattering, specifics into clear alternatives of good and evil, as in such cases as those of Cain and Abel or Jacob and Esau. Likewise, Milton, who feels inhibited from employing traditional stories of Chaldaean idolatry, creates a decisive contrast between Nimrod and Abraham as opposed founders: one of the elect nation, the other of tyranny.

Gary Anderson's *The Genesis of Perfection* is the only book I know that both takes inspiration from Kugel's work and discusses *Paradise Lost* in some detail.[36] It is an excellent book, but Anderson treats Milton almost as though he were one of the ancient exegetes. Their readings of Scripture complement and explain Milton's poem as though there never were a Renaissance and a Reformation, as though the application of historical philology to sacred texts either did not create disturbingly different approaches to reading the Bible or Milton was somehow immune to such disturbances. However, the urgency of Milton's biblicism belies such an impression, especially in its polemically Protestant mode. In *Paradise Lost* this urgency becomes apparent on occasions where the insufficiency of Scripture creates incertitude that cannot be avoided. Where *was* it that the heavenly muse first inspired Moses? Oreb or Sinai (*PL* 1.7)? Where *did* those skins come from to cover the nakedness of Adam and Eve? Did the beasts simply shed them, or were they slain and then skinned (*PL* 10.216–217)? What trumpet *would* they blow in heaven to "call to synod all the Blest"? The one we'll hear at Judgment Day? Perhaps (*PL* 11.67–76). Why *did* the animals enter the ark in "sevens, and pairs" (*PL* 11.735)?

These may seem nitpicking details or "mere curiosity," as questions about Enoch's extraterrestrial abode seemed to the Geneva commentator. But the need for certainty varies not only from temperament to temperament but from age to age. In Milton's time such questions were increasingly unavoidable. As we have seen, Thomas Hobbes had memorably raised some of them. Moreover, in doing so, Hobbes is the inheritor of developments that derive from sixteenth-century humanism, which, as Kugel insists, occasions a decisive shift in approaches to biblical study and ultimately produces modern hostility to the traditions of the Bible.[37]

---

[36] Gary Anderson, *The Genesis of Perfection: Adam and Eve in Jewish and Christian Imagination* (Louisville: Westminster John Knox, 2001).
[37] Kugel, "The Bible in the University," 143–65.

Of Hobbes it is fair to say that in politics he was Milton's mighty opposite, a defender of absolutism against the republicanism of Milton and other foes of the Stuart monarchy. In the study of the Bible, however, Hobbes was Milton's worst nightmare. Neither the sacredness of the text nor the guidance of the Spirit constrained Hobbes's inquiries, and Hobbes was only symptomatic of what was to come. Milton stood on a faultline in the development of attitudes toward reading the Bible, and the anxieties generated by such a precarious position prompted him, like Descartes, to hyperbole. Today's claims of the Bible's "inerrancy" articulate a similarly untenable extreme which Milton, the traditionalist *malgré lui*, foreshadows in his polemical mode. Indeed, the genre of the polemic may itself force such false alternatives as Scripture or tradition upon its practitioners. In Milton's case, the particular intensities of both his historical moment and his kind of writing should be put in perspective to appreciate both his deep kinship with the makers of "the Bible as it was" and his profound debt to the traditions that, consciously or unconsciously, we inherit from them.

A NAZI NEW TESTAMENT PROFESSOR READS HIS BIBLE: THE STRANGE CASE OF GERHARD KITTEL

Wayne A. Meeks

James Kugel has shown us that "the Bible that was" for generations of Jews and Christians was "the interpreted Bible"—that the traditions of interpretation in each community of readers were simply and unselfconsciously assumed to be what the text *said*.[1] Kugel himself is so humane and gentle, and many of the examples of early interpretations he cites are so innocent and, to tell the truth, such fun, that we might imagine the interpreted Bible to be harmless, however unfashionable today. Unfortunately, evidence continues to abound that sacred texts in the hands of their most devoted readers have great power not only to comfort and to inspire but, sometimes, to wreak terrible harm. For Protestant Christians, the most painful example in recent history is the support by some leading German biblical scholars for the Nazi anti-Jewish program. Among those careers complicit in the Shoah, none raises more troubling questions than that of Gerhard Kittel, Professor of New Testament in the Protestant Theological Faculty of the University of Tübingen, and no other continues to have so much influence. His monumental project, the *Theological Dictionary of the New Testament* (*TDNT*), translated into English in the 1960s, stands on the shelves not only of every theological seminary's library, but also of the personal libraries of many pastors and priests.[2] Very few of the users of that work are aware of the paradoxes in Kittel's career or of the fundamentally anti-Jewish structure of *TDNT* itself. Hence it may be worthwhile to

---

[1] This is the burden of James L. Kugel, *Traditions of the Bible: A Guide to the Bible as It Was at the Start of the Common Era* (Cambridge, Mass.: Harvard University Press, 1998), e.g., the Preface, xviii–ix; and its shorter predecessor, James L. Kugel, *The Bible as It Was* (Cambridge, Mass.: Harvard University Press, 1997).

[2] Gerhard Kittel, Otto Bauernfeind, and Gerhard Friedrich, *Theological Dictionary of the New Testament* (ed. and trans. G. W. Bromiley; Grand Rapids: Eerdmans, 1964–1976). The first volume of the German edition began to appear in 1932. Kittel edited the first four volumes. After he was removed from the editorship in 1945, Gerhard Friedrich took over the general editorship for volumes 5–10.

revisit Kittel's sad and perplexing story, even though it has been told several times in recent years, for his biographers have not emphasized sufficiently the interpretive strategies that were central to Kittel's own understanding of the world.[3] Those strategies were not unique to Kittel, nor did they vanish from modern biblical interpretation with his death.[4]

I. KITTEL PARADOXES

Gerhard Kittel was born in 1888, son of the Old Testament scholar Rudolf Kittel. The younger Kittel early determined on an academic career and rose rapidly in the university system. By 1913 he was a *Privatdozent* at Kiel, then in Leipzig four years later. In 1921, at age

---

[3] An exception is Leonore Siegele-Wenschkewitz, *Neutestamentliche Wissenschaft vor der Judenfrage: Gerhard Kittels theologische Arbeit im Wandel deutscher Geschichte* (Theologische Existenz Heute 208; Munich: Chr. Kaiser, 1980), who points out that Kittel "wants to obtain his answer to the Jewish Question directly from the Bible, from precise exegetical results" [er will seine Antwort auf die Judenfrage unmittelbar aus der Bibel, aus dem exakten exegetischen Befund gewinnen] (99), and gives important examples of Kittel's theological exegesis. (All translations of ancient and modern authors in this essay are mine unless otherwise indicated.) For more general accounts of Kittel's career, see Max Weinreich, *Hitler's Professors: The Part of Scholarship in Germany's Crimes Against the Jewish People* (New York: Yiddish Scientific Institute—YIVO, 1946), 40–43; Martin Rese, "Antisemitismus und Neutestamentliche Forschung: Anmerkungen zu dem Thema 'Gerhard Kittel und die Judenfrage,'" *EvT* 39 (1979): 557–70; Robert P. Ericksen, *Theologians Under Hitler: Gerhard Kittel, Paul Althaus, and Emanuel Hirsch* (New Haven: Yale University Press, 1985), 28–78. I have drawn extensively from these accounts in my sketch of Kittel's career. I have not been able to obtain J. S. Vos, *Politiek en exegese: Gerhard Kittels beeld van het jodendom* (Verkenning en Bezinning; Kampen: Kok, 1983). For the historical context, out of the vast and growing literature, the following have been especially helpful: Werner Jochmann, *Gesellschaftskrise und Judenfeindschaft in Deutschland 1870–1945* (Hamburger Beiträge zur Sozial- und Zeitgeschichte; Hamburg: Christians, 1988); *"Beseitigung des jüdischen Einflusses—": Antisemitische Forschung, Eliten und Karrieren im Nationalsozialismus* (ed. Fritz Bauer Institut; Frankfurt/NewYork: Campus, 1999); *Betrayal: German Churches and the Holocaust* (ed. R. P. Ericksen and S. Heschel; Minneapolis: Fortress, 1999); and Shelley Baranowski, *The Confessing Church, Conservative Elites, and the Nazi State* (Texts and Studies in Religion; Lewiston, N.Y.: Edwin Mellen, 1986). On the silence in most American scholarship about the flaws in *TDNT* itself, see Alan Rosen, "'Familiarly known as Kittel': The Moral Politics of the *Theological Dictionary of the New Testament*," in *Tainted Greatness: Antisemitism and Cultural Heroes* (ed. N. A. Harrowitz; Philadelphia: Temple University Press, 1994), 37–50.

[4] I am grateful to Judith Colton, Dale Martin, Matin Rese, and Margaret Mitchell for reading this essay in draft, making precise and helpful suggestions, and asking just the right questions. For any unclarities that remain, responsibility rests with me (and perhaps the late Professor Kittel).

33, he became a full professor at Greifswald, and in 1926 he moved to the distinguished chair at Tübingen. His early career coincided with the tumultuous period during and just after World War I. From the beginning he devoted himself to the study of the Jewish roots of early Christianity. The intellectual freedom of the Weimar Republic, including the vigorous Jewish scholarship in the era of the *Wissenschaft des Judentums*, produced a climate in which Kittel flourished. He called for collaboration between Jewish scholars of rabbinic tradition and scholars of early Christianity, and he embodied this ideal in his own work. His book *Die Probleme des palästinischen Spätjudentums und das Urchristentum*, published in 1926, was dedicated to the memory of the rabbi and scholar Israel I. Kahan, with whom Kittel had had a long working relationship.[5] When Kittel was inaugurated that same year as Professor at Tübingen, he was widely recognized as one the world's two or three leading Christian authorities on Judaism at the time of Christianity's beginnings. He was particularly sympathetic to the early rabbinic movement, emphasizing the closeness of its values to those of Jesus and calling attention to "the depth and religious seriousness" of the rabbinic texts.[6]

Yet Kittel's career ended in May 1945 when he was arrested, on the charge of war crimes, by the French representatives of the Allied Military Government of defeated Germany. There was reason for the charges. Kittel had publicly joined the Nazi party in May 1933, only five months after Hitler came to power. In the same year he gave the keynote address at the fiftieth-anniversary celebration in Tübingen of the founding of the fraternity he had joined in his student days, the *Verein deutscher Studenten*. The fraternity had been antisemitic from its foundation.[7] Kittel's topic: "The Jewish Question."

---

[5] Gerhard Kittel, *Die Probleme des palästinischen Spätjudentums und das Urchristentum* (BWANT 3.1; Stuttgart: W. Kohlhammer, 1926).

[6] G. Kittel, *Probleme*, 17.

[7] So Siegele-Wenschkewitz who describes the club as "anti-Semitic, anti-Catholic, monarchist, and after 1918 Nazi" (*Neutestamentliche Wissenschaft*, 79). For the content of the speech, see below. On the formation of the German student fraternities and their role in the propagation of antisemitism, see Werner Jochmann, "Die Ausbreitung des Antisemitismus in Deutschland 1914–1923," in *Gesellschaftskrise und Judenfeindschaft in Deutschland 1870–1945* (Hamburg: Hans Christians, 1988), 146–49; and Paul Lawrence Rose, *Revolutionary Antisemitism in Germany from Kant to Wagner* (Princeton: Princeton University Press, 1990), 125, 244; on their part in creation of the German "national myth" in the age of Bismarck, Hans-Ulrich Wehler, "Der deutsche Nationalismus bis 1871," in *Scheidewege der deutschen Geschichte: Von der Reformation bis zur Wende, 1517–1989* (Munich: C. H. Beck, 1995), 125–26.

In the speech, which was published and sold in thousands of copies, Kittel enthusiastically endorsed the Nazi program for removing Jews from all parts of Germany's professional, governmental, and educational life.[8] Kittel was a charter member and active participant in the Nazi thinktank, *Reichsinstitut für Geschichte des neuen Deutschlands*, founded by Walter Frank. Moreover, he was also active in another institute directly organized by Goebbels's *Propagandaministerium* and called *Antijüdische Aktion*.[9]

Kittel himself apparently saw no contradiction in these positions. He continued to regard himself as a moderate, opposing the extremes of the Nazi party and of the German Christian movement, and sympathetic toward individual Jews. Indeed, he urged Christians to act as "Good Samaritans" to help Jews who would undoubtedly suffer under the program he advocated, and in his war crimes defense he was able to introduce affidavits of Jewish individuals who were grateful for his help in enabling them to escape the Final Solution.[10] He sent a copy of his 1933 speech to Martin Buber and was surprised and hurt that Buber found it outrageous.[11] When the Swiss theologian Karl Barth sarcastically noted in a letter to Kittel that the

---

[8] Kittel was clearly aware that, even at this early date, there were some among his fellow enthusiasts in the NSDAP who were discussing the possibility of an extermination campaign ("eine gewaltsame Ausrottung des Judentums"). He himself scoffs at the idea: if neither the Spanish Inquisition nor the Russian pogroms could accomplish the elimination of the Jews, how could such a plan be taken seriously? Kittel thought the whole idea so "absurd" that there was no reason even to offer reasons for the "schlechthinige Unchristlichkeit einer solchen 'Lösung'" (Gerhard Kittel, *Die Judenfrage* [2nd ed.; Stuttgart: W. Kohlhammer, 1933], 14). Apparently he underestimated the confidence of some of his fellow Nazis in technology and superior German organizing ability.

[9] Kittel joined several other professors at Tübingen and elsewhere in formally withdrawing from the German Christian organization in November 1933, after a speaker at the Sports Palace rally in Berlin denounced such "Jewish remnants" in Christianity as the Old Testament, the Apostle Paul, and the symbol of the cross, as well as "the mental gymnastics" of theology (James A. Zabel, *Nazism and the Pastors: A Study of the Ideas of Three Deutsche Christen Groups* [AARDS 14; Missoula, Mont.: Scholars Press, 1976], 33–34 and 47 n. 43; Doris L. Bergen, *Twisted Cross: The German Christian Movement in the Third Reich* [Chapel Hill, N.C.: University of North Carolina Press, 1996], 17–18, 173–74). Nevertheless, he continued to be active in support of the Nazi program, even as the Party became more and more contemptuous of its would-be Christian allies. On Kittel's publications on behalf of the Nazi cause, see Ericksen, *Theologians Under Hitler*, 54–68, as well as Zabel, 41–42.

[10] G. Kittel, *Die Judenfrage*, 67–69; see further Siegele-Wenschkewitz, *Neutestamentliche Wissenschaft*, 26–27, 117 n. 116.

[11] G. Kittel, "Antwort an Martin Buber," in *Die Judenfrage*, 87–100; in the first

speech made Kittel's pretense of taking a mediating position absurd, Kittel retorted that he stood by everything he had said. He simply was following the New Testament.[12] In a document he drafted for his defense in the 1945 trial, he retracted nothing. He had only been "mistaken" about Hitler. But his position on *Judentum*, he said, was simply that of an exegete and theologian. The central question, he asserted, was "Whether it counts as a crime in the world of Christian culture, if a Christian theologian takes a stand on the Jewish Question that is based on and normed by the directives and teachings of Jesus Christ and the Apostles and on the position of the ancient church."[13]

What reading of the New Testament yielded those "directives and teachings of Jesus Christ" that led Gerhard Kittel into a position that seems to us now so tragically self-contradictory? How did that reading justify in his eyes policies that seem on their face diametrically opposed to his earlier insistence on the Jewishness of early Christianity and the need for Christian and Jewish scholars to work "hand in hand"? We are tempted to dismiss his theological assertions as a rationalizing cloak for naked opportunism—in the Weimar Republic he was a liberal; weeks after its demise he was a Nazi.[14] That would be too easy a judgment, for it would deflect our attention from the culture of interpretation that made Kittel's paradoxical positions seem to him coherent. "The Bible that was" for Kittel was constructed on the one hand by a specifically modern historicist project, on the other by an ancient and widely shared theological conception of history.

---

edition he had expressed the hope that Buber would see that the forced end of "assimilation" of Jews into German culture would encourage their "return to biblical religion" (74). Buber's open letter was published in *TBl* 12 (1933): 148–50. See also Siegele-Wenschkewitz, 105–8.

[12] Karl Barth and Gerhard Kittel, *Ein theologischer Briefwechsel* (Stuttgart: W. Kohlhammer, 1934), 23, 25.

[13] Quoted by Siegele-Wenschkewitz, *Neutestamentliche Wissenschaft*, 116, from "Drei Erklärungen von Professor D. theol. Gerhard Kittel," undated, probably May or June 1945, now in the possession of his son Dr. Eberhard Kittel. For a more detailed account of Kittel's self-defense, see Ericksen, *Theologians Under Hitler*, 31–45.

[14] That is Ericksen's assessment (*Theologians under Hitler*, 74), though oddly he then says, "I believe Kittel's stance under Hitler was sincere" (75).

II. The Interpreter as Historian

Kittel saw himself as a historian of religions at a time when that phrase pointed to a quite specific direction in German scholarship. In his inaugural address as Professor of New Testament at Tübingen, 28 October 1926, he defined the business of New Testament scholarship as "the historical comprehension of the world of the New Testament."[15] The first step toward understanding Kittel's way of reading the Bible is to examine the way he construed *history*. Some fundamental elements of that construction are clear in several lectures and essays written before 1933; others become plain only when we examine his later work, especially his program for *TDNT*.

A. *Kittel and the History of Religions*

When Gerhard Kittel began teaching, the greatest excitement and controversy in Protestant biblical scholarship in Germany was being provoked by the publications of a group who called themselves "the History of Religions School." Originating at the University of Göttingen in the 1880s, this movement insisted on "a sharp distinction between religion and theology, relinquishing the biblical canon as the sole source for knowledge [of biblical religion], and seeing early Christian literature as embedded in the sphere of the common religious life of antiquity."[16] The separation of theology from religion would be problematic for Kittel—but that was also true of some others more closely identified with the program of the History of Religions School, like Kittel's famous contemporary, Rudolf Bultmann.[17] The second

---

[15] Gerhard Kittel, *Urchristentum, Spätjudentum, Hellenismus: akademische Antrittsvorlesung gehalten am 28. Oktober 1926* (Stuttgart: W. Kohlhammer, 1926), 2.

[16] Gerd Lüdemann and Martin Schröder, *Die religionsgeschichtliche Schule in Göttingen: eine Dokumentation* (Göttingen: Vandenhoeck & Ruprecht, 1987), 7. This little book provides a good introduction to the School, with facsimiles of original documents and photographs of the principals. See further Otto Eissfeldt, "Religionsgeschichtliche Schule," *RGG* 4: cols. 1898–1905; Hans-Joachim Kraus, *Geschichte der historisch-kritischen Erforschung des Alten Testaments* (3rd exp. ed.; Neukirchen-Vluyn: Neukirchener, 1982), 327–40; and Werner Georg Kümmel, *Das Neue Testament: Geschichte der Erforschung seiner Probleme* (Orbis Academicus; Munich: Karl Alber, 1958), 261–414.

[17] The problematic of "theology" and "religion" was starkly laid out in a programmatic essay by William Wrede, one of the inner circle of the *Religionsgeschichtler*; see the translation with helpful discussion of its context and afterlife in Robert Morgan, William Wrede, and Adolf Schlatter, *The Nature of New Testament Theology:*

and third of these guidelines, on the other hand, Kittel could endorse enthusiastically.

Kittel shared with the History of Religions School a confidence in the power of scientific historiography to produce a normative picture of religion. To a significant extent, he, like his father, shared also the evolutionary conception of religious history that characterized Protestant modernism at the beginning of the twentieth century. However, he disagreed strongly with the Göttingen group and their allies on three important matters. First, while they located the dominant influences that shaped early Christianity in the world of "Hellenistic" culture, Kittel insisted that "From the very beginning [the new Christian religion] is just what the pagan world for a very long time saw in it—a Jewish sect." The new religion might wear the clothing of Hellenism, but its fundamental categories are Jewish.[18] Second, Kittel disagreed sharply with the way leading representatives of the History of Religions School described "Late Judaism" and its influence on early Christianity. Third, while the *Religionsgeschichtler* regarded early Christianity as "a syncretistic phenomenon," Kittel would undertake to show that it had been protected—precisely by its Jewish matrix—from succumbing to the syncretism that otherwise pervaded the Greco-Roman world.

From the beginning of his career, Gerhard Kittel focused his research on ancient Judaism as the context for historical understanding of Christian beginnings. As a young *Privatdozent* in Kiel in 1914, in an essay in a series intended for the educated layperson ("zur Aufklärung der Gebildeten"), Kittel already showed his extensive knowledge of the rabbinic literature and of secondary discussions of it as well as his clear understanding of methodological issues. By the time he moved to Tübingen a dozen years later, he was a master of the materials and a sophisticated historian, as he demonstrated in the important, programmatic book he published in 1926, "Problems of Palestinian Late Judaism and Primitive Christianity." In it he insisted that because the religious history of "Late Judaism"

The Contribution of William Wrede and Adolf Schlatter (SBT, 2nd Ser.; Naperville, Ill.: A. R. Allenson, 1973). See also Rudolf Bultmann, *Theology of the New Testament* (trans. K. Grobel; 2 vols.; New York: Scribner, 1951), 2:237–51.

[18] G. Kittel, *Urchristentum, Spätjudentum*, 14–15.

remained to be written, so also the religious history of primitive Christianity could not yet be written.[19] This statement of his theme makes it clear that he was writing in conscious opposition to the dominant point of view in the History of Religions School, although he does not name the school as such. He accepted the prevailing cultural map of early Christianity's environment, in which "Judaism" and "Hellenism" were separate and antithetical realms of culture, "two worlds," but for him it was "beyond any discussion that the foundational phase [of early Christianity] was in Palestinian Judaism."[20] In his inaugural lecture at the University of Tübingen later the same year, Kittel emphasized this point more clearly and briefly. Primitive Christianity was uniquely "a religion of two cultures," but its native realm was Judaism. Kittel paid tribute to both his predecessors in the Tübingen chair, Adolf Schlatter, who had emphasized the Palestinian Jewish roots of Christianity, and Wilhelm Heitmüller, who had been one of the leading lights of the History of Religions movement. Such a "division of labor" might be necessary as a practical matter, said Kittel, but the temptation to view the Hellenistic and the Jewish perspectives on Christianity as interpretive alternatives must be resisted. Both were necessary. Nevertheless, he made it clear where he thought the emphasis must be put, for the roles of Hellenism and of Judaism in the formation of early Christianity were structurally asymmetrical.[21]

In the 1926 publication, Kittel also systematically distinguished his way of understanding Judaism from that of the Göttingen school, especially as represented by the widely-read handbook published by

---

[19] G. Kittel, *Probleme*, 71. There is no simple English translation of the German *Ur-*; I have reluctantly resorted to the conventional "primitive," though it carries connotations not present in the German.

[20] Ibid., 2. On the peculiar fixation on the dichotomy between "Hellenism" and "Late Judaism" in modern New Testament scholarship, see Wayne A. Meeks, "Judaism, Hellenism, and the Birth of Christianity," in *Paul Beyond the Judaism/Hellenism Divide* (ed. T. Engberg-Pedersen; Louisville: Westminster John Knox, 2001), 17–28.

[21] G. Kittel, *Urchristentum, Spätjudentum*, 4–15. Wilhelm Heitmüller had lived less than two years after he took up the professorship in Tübingen in 1924 (over considerable resistance from conservative church leaders in Württemberg). His research had sought out Hellenistic religious sources for the sacraments and beliefs of early Christianity; see, e.g., his essay, "Zum Problem Paulus und Jesus," *ZNW* 13 (1912): 320–37. Schlatter had had a long and very influential career in the university. Kittel had placed him in his earlier book along with Dalman and Billerbeck among the German scholars whose interest in ancient Judaism was closely tied to their support for the evangelical mission to the Jews (G. Kittel, *Probleme*, 29).

Wilhelm Bousset and reissued in a new edition by Hugo Gressmann shortly before Kittel's arrival in Tübingen.[22] Bousset-Gressmann distinguished "scribalism," assumed to be represented in the rabbinic corpus, from "popular piety," which they believed could be discerned in the so-called Apocrypha and Pseudepigrapha of the Old Testament. This popular religion, they thought, had been significantly influenced by the "oriental" (especially Persian) religious patterns that produced, among other things, the apocalypticism that was so prominent in the New Testament. It was the popular, syncretistic form of Judaism— not the scribal, "official" Judaism that would eventually produce the Talmuds—that the Göttingen comparativists took to be the matrix of "primitive Christianity." Kittel rejected this construction and the disdain for the principal rabbinic sources that Bousset-Gressmann shared with the older, dogmatic handbook on ancient Judaism, by Ferdinand Weber, which theirs had largely replaced.[23] On the other side, Kittel sharply criticized the reasons Bousset gave for ignoring the rabbinic literature. Though it was true, against Weber and conservative Jewish scholars, that the rabbinic sources were all later than the first century, and the danger of anachronism must be guarded against case by case, nevertheless these sources were *traditional literature* and could be used, with all due caution, to discover the "fundamental character of religion and piety" in earlier periods. The distinction between folk piety and scribalism contained a partial truth, said Kittel, but he pointed out that there were many echoes of popular religion in the Talmuds. Above all, he agreed with the American scholar George Foot Moore that apocalypticism was only a by-form (*Nebentypus*) of Judaism. The decisive reason for neglect of the rabbinic sources by Christian scholars, he declared, was ignorance reinforced by the difficulty of acquiring the necessary linguistic and historical expertise. For this, it would be necessary for Jewish and

---

[22] Wilhelm Bousset, *Die Religion des Judentums im späthellenistischen Zeitalter* (ed. H. Gressmann; 3rd rev. ed.; HNT 21; Tübingen: Mohr, 1926).

[23] Ferdinand Wilhelm Weber, *Jüdische Theologie auf Grund des Talmud und verwandter Schriften* (ed. F. Delitzsch and G. Schnedermann; 2nd ed.; Leipzig: Dörffling & Franke, 1897). The first edition of Weber's book (1880) had borne the title, "Das System der altsynagogalen palästinischen Theologie." "System," observed Kittel, was the fateful word here, for it signaled Weber's lack of a sense of history and his forcing of Talmudic diversity into the straitjacket of Lutheran dogmatics (G. Kittel, *Probleme*, 25–26).

Christian scholars to work "hand in hand," as Kittel himself was
doing with several Jewish scholars.[24] Though Kittel placed decisive
emphasis on the rabbinic sources, he also emphasized the variety of
forms of Judaism not only in the Diaspora but even in first-century
Palestine. In this respect as well his views in the Weimar period
seem now quite ahead of his time, especially when compared with
the Bousset-Gressmann description of Judaism in antiquity.

The interests that led Kittel to focus on pre-rabbinic and rabbinic
religion were more than historical. There were also strong theological concerns—better said, his construction of history was thoroughly
theological—that impelled him to dispute one of the most central
and controversial contentions of the History of Religions School, that
"early Christianity was a syncretistic phenomenon." Kittel cites this
famous declaration by one of the leaders of the Göttingen school,
Hermann Gunkel, and undertakes to refute it in the lectures he was
invited to give at the University of Uppsala in 1931.[25] The first lecture, "Hellenistic Syncretism," presents an apt summary of the main
themes of the History of Religions School's work, with nicely chosen illustrations from iconography. These themes are: the characteristic mixing of motifs from diverse origins in the age of Hellenism,
a tendency toward one or another kind of monotheism, and a growing individualism. The reader is struck by the extraordinary balance

---

[24] G. Kittel, *Probleme*, 5–19; quotations from 11 and 19. It is not surprising that
Gressmann responded with a sharp attack—quite personal in tone—on Kittel's book,
which Kittel answered, equally sharply, in an appendix to the printed edition of
his inaugural address (G. Kittel, *Urchristentum, Spätjudentum*, 29–32). Kittel admired
G. F. Moore's work and agreed with his privileging of the sources of "normative"
or "catholic" or "normal" Judaism against such enthusiasts for apocalypticism as
Bousset and the English scholar R. H. Charles. He also joined Moore in rejecting
the apologetic and polemical stances of many Christian writers on Judaism (ibid.,
25, 28; cf. George Foot Moore, "Christian Writers on Judaism," *HTR* 14 [1921]:
197–254; the first volume of Moore's *magnum opus, Judaism in the First Centuries of the
Christian Era: The Age of the Tannaim* [3 vols.; Cambridge, Mass.: Harvard University
Press, 1927–1930] would appear a year later. See also the remarks of J. S. Vos,
"Antijudaismus/Antisemitismus im Theologischen Wörterbuch zum Neuen Testament," *NedTT* 38 [1984]: 89–90).
[25] Gerhard Kittel, *Die Religionsgeschichte und das Urchristentum* (Gütersloh: C. Bertelsmann,
1931), 150, citing Hermann Gunkel, *Zum religionsgeschichtlichen Verständnis des Neuen
Testaments* (3rd ed.; FRLANT 1; Göttingen: Vandenhoeck & Ruprecht, 1930); Kittel
cited page 95 of the first edition from 1903. Cf. the discussion by Kittel's contemporary and opponent, Rudolf Bultmann, *Primitive Christianity in Its Contemporary
Setting* (trans. R. H. Fuller; New York: Meridian, 1956), 175–79.

and careful judgment of Kittel's presentation, by his ability to break through stereotypes by means of his attention to primary texts, but also by the degree to which his interpretive schema is nevertheless finally determined by a distinctive theological *Grundkonzeption.*

The second lecture, "The Religion of Judaism in the Age of Primitive Christianity," takes up many of the themes Kittel had developed in his earlier writings, but now under the viewpoint of Judaism's interaction with the Hellenistic syncretism around it. Kittel takes as full account as one could imagine for his day (the surprising synagogues at Dura Europos and at Sardis, for example, not to mention the Dead Sea Scrolls, had not yet been revealed) of both the variety of Judaisms, popular as well as learned, in the Roman era, and of the manifold engagement of Jews with Hellenistic syncretism—mainly outside Palestine, but even to some extent, he grants, within. He uses, again, iconographic and archaeological evidence to illustrate the influences Judaism experienced. "It becomes clear," he acknowledges, "that in fact there can be no talk of Judaism's being excluded from the movements of the syncretistic age." Nevertheless, his conclusion is that *real* Judaism "did not become a syncretistic religion." Against the pressures of mixed culture stood "Old Testament religion"—the religion of historical revelation, of Law, of the Word. It was the role of Pharisaism, the synagogue, and the rabbis to preserve this "orthodoxy." "Here is the answer [to the question], why Judaism did not dissolve into syncretism. It is at the same time the answer, why its religion did not perish, when Jerusalem and the Temple went up in flames."[26]

In the final two lectures, it remains for Kittel to show two things about early Christianity: (1) from its Jewish roots it, too, gained the power to remain "an unsyncretistic religion" (despite the profound mixing of Jewish and Greek elements that he freely admits is found throughout the New Testament—apparently he chooses to regard these as mere "forms" into which a different "content" is poured), and (2) that Christianity "fulfilled" this true Judaism, i.e., the Old Testament orthodox religion of the Word and of History, and therefore superseded it. In his penultimate lecture, "The Religious Concepts and Forms of Expression of the Primitive Christian Religion," Kittel employs the semantic arguments that would become the backbone

---

[26] G. Kittel, *Religionsgeschichte,* 66, 78.

of *TDNT.* He argues that such common Greek words as δόξα ("fame, opinion, glory"), ἀλήθεια ("truth"), and κόσμος ("world") are invested with new "content" by the Septuagint's use of them to translate Hebrew concepts.[27] I shall return to this odd but remarkably influential linguistic notion further below. Here it is important to note two further dimensions of Kittel's focus on early Palestinian Judaism for the historical elucidation of Christian origins. First, he not only aims to show that its Jewish matrix protected primitive Christianity from syncretism—which is to say, it kept Christianity religiously "pure," a key metaphor in Kittel's later writings—but at the same time he wants to demonstrate Christianity's historical continuity with "Old Testament religion." Second, it becomes clear that the continuity with ancient Israel that Kittel imagines is supersessionist. Judaism has played out its role in God's plan—except for one final scene, as we shall see; the church has now replaced it. In short, Kittel's construction of the history of religions is inseparable from his theological conception of *Heilsgeschichte,* the history of salvation.

B. *History as salvation history*

Perhaps the most significant literary invention of the early Christian communities was a way of reading the Bible that made the story of Israel the central chapter of a larger narrative, the story of all humankind and of God's plan to redeem his rebellious creatures and to restore a spoiled creation. Perhaps it would be better to speak of a family of ways of reading, for those Christians who saw their own story reflected in Israel's adopted several different interpretive strategies, ranging from the "types" that Paul found in the accounts of Adam and of Israel's adventures in the Wilderness, through the prophecy-fulfillment schemes in all the canonical Gospels, to the imaginative allegories of the Alexandrian theologians. These strategies enabled the new communities—or at least those groups of them that would eventually emerge as the dominant representatives of catholic Christianity—to assert the antiquity of their faith and the unity of a single Bible, even as they added their own writings to that Bible, eventually producing two "Testaments."[28] Some Christians,

---

[27] Ibid., 82–92.
[28] The story of the emergence of the Christian canon and of the narrative shape it imposed on the scriptures it adopted from Israel has often been told. For a brief

however, did not accept this emerging consensus. The strongest attack on the story of biblical continuity came from the second-century figure Marcion and his followers, who declared the God of Israel and the Old Testament to be altogether different from the God who had appeared in the guise of Jesus Christ. The scriptures Christians should accept (which Marcion provided in a critically expurgated edition) had only an antithetical relationship to the scriptures of Israel.

The ghost of Marcion reappeared often in the history of western Christianity, but nowhere was he conjured more deliberately than in certain circles of liberal German Protestantism at the turn of the twentieth century. Adolf von Harnack, the famous Berlin church historian, labored for years to reconstruct Marcion's teaching and the text of his New Testament. In the introduction to the resulting monograph, he made it clear that he aimed not only at understanding but also at rehabilitating Marcion: "It is a joy to occupy oneself with a deeply religious man of intellectual purity, who rejects all syncretism, allegory, and sophistry." Though Harnack reacted defensively to the attacks some theologians launched against the first edition of his Marcion book, he did not yield on his conviction that some of Marcion's teachings "remain of importance for all time."[29] Harnack consciously compared Marcion with Luther and argued that Luther's reformation should be completed by removing the Old Testament altogether from the canon of Christian scripture.[30] After 1933, the extreme wing of the German Christians would campaign to do just

---

summary, focusing on the key role of Irenaeus in articulating the catholic viewpoint in the second century, see Wayne A. Meeks, *The Moral World of the First Christians* (LEC; Philadelphia: Westminster, 1986), 154–60.

[29] Adolf von Harnack, *Marcion: das Evangelium vom fremden Gott; Neue Studien zu Marcion* (2nd ed. 1924; repr., Darmstadt: Wissenschaftliche Buchgesellschaft, 1960), 21; *Neue Studien zu Marcion* (originally published separately in 1923), 25.

[30] In the final chapter of the Marcion book, Harnack drew out lessons for the church of his time. His principal thesis was: "To jettison the Old Testament in the second century was a mistake, which the Great Church rightly rejected; to retain it in the 16th century was a fate that the Reformation was not yet able to escape; but after the 19th century to preserve it as a canonical document in Protestantism is the result of a religious and ecclesiastical paralysis" (Harnack, *Marcion*, 217). For help in understanding Harnack's position and his social and cultural setting I am endebted to Bart D. Ehrman, who kindly provided me with a copy of his unpublished paper, "Adolf von Harnack's *Marcion* in Socio-Historical Context" (paper presented at the annual meeting of the SBL, Orlando, Fla., November 1998).

that, though with hardly a nod in the direction of history or of
Harnack's arguments, for his politics would have been in most respects
anathema to them.[31]

For Gerhard Kittel, the rejection of the Old Testament both by
the liberal theologians like Harnack and by the radical German
Christians was abhorrent. Indeed, it was Kittel's resistance to the
latter that led him to think of himself as a "moderate" among the
pro-Nazi theologians. The story of God's plan of salvation, which
Christian readers from Paul to Augustine had elaborated into a plot-
structure embracing their entire Bible, was fundamental to Kittel's
own religious convictions, and "Old Testament religion" was a vital
part of it. Indeed that Old Testament religion, Kittel insisted, was
the heart of "true Judaism," and he saw the program of forced dis-
assimilation of the Jews, which he advocated in his 1933 fraternity
speech, as a means of helping the Jews "to convert to the sources
of the Jewish religion—not to modern philosophical notions, but to
the living God, whom Moses and the prophets and the Psalms
proclaim."[32]

In Gerhard Kittel's version of salvation history, "Late Judaism"
had helped early Christianity to incorporate Old Testament religion
as its own. That religion was at the same time the inner meaning
of the (separate and unequal) "true Judaism" to which Kittel thought
real Jews ought to aspire. It had very specific contours, for it was
the religion that Rudolf Kittel, Gerhard's father, had described as
the culmination of the long evolution from roots in ancient Canaan,
Mesopotamia, and Egypt to the "ethical monotheism" invented by
ancient Israel's religious geniuses, above all Moses and the classical
prophets.[33] The elder Kittel, now remembered chiefly as the principal editor of the Bible Societies' edition of the Hebrew Bible, enthusiastically applied the methods of the History of Religions School to
"the history of the people of Israel," producing a multi-volumed book
with that title which ran to six editions.[34] Exhibiting a remarkably

---

[31] See Bergen, *Twisted Cross*, 143–54.
[32] G. Kittel, *Die Judenfrage*, 73.
[33] Siegele-Wenschkewitz, *Neutestamentliche Wissenschaft*, 60 n. 39 et passim, rightly
calls attention to the importance of the elder Kittel's work for the son.
[34] Rudolf Kittel, *Geschichte des Volkes Israel* (3 vols.; Gotha: Klotz [vol. 3; Stuttgart:
Kohlhammer], 1923–1929). The first edition, under the title *Die Geschichte der Hebräer*,
appeared in 1888; the new title was given the second, "completely reworked" edition in 1909.

wide-ranging curiosity, he showed rather less concern about the role of syncretism in Israel's story than did his son. Late in his life he even published a small book on "The Hellenistic Mysteries [a focal interest of the History of Religions School] and the Old Testament."[35] He also published a popular book on "The Religion of the People of Israel," based on lectures he gave at the University of Uppsala just a decade before his son lectured on the same platform.[36] Two features of his work seem in retrospect particularly noteworthy. One is the importance of the word *Volk* in the titles of the works just mentioned. The other is the belief in "progressive revelation" that both Kittels shared with liberals like Harnack. The romantic notion of peoplehood (*Volkstum*), defined by "blood and race," was at the center of German nationalist ideology. It is both poignant and, in view of the later exploitation of the notion in the Nazi program, ironic to read the elder Kittel's remarks in the preface to his Uppsala lectures, written with the aftermath of the Treaty of Versailles very much in mind:

> It will not escape the notice of anyone who follows carefully the author's exposition that it lingers with particular sympathy over that point where a people, utterly broken and robbed of all power, found means to recover and to start life afresh solely because of their faith in themselves [sic] and in their future. May this little book find readers who are prepared to be instructed by the lessons of history![37]

Kittel *fils* would, in a strange way, take up this romantic identification with the Jews as a *Volk* even as he undertook to view the recent history of Germany in the language of the history of ancient Israel as his father had described it.[38] Progressive revelation, on the other hand, was the overarching category that permitted Gerhard Kittel and other German Christians to see in Hitler and the Nazi revolution one of "the lessons of history," indeed "a work of God."[39]

---

[35] Rudolf Kittel, *Die hellenistische Mysterienreligion und das Alte Testament* (BWAT 32; Stuttgart: W. Kohlhammer, 1924).

[36] Rudolf Kittel, *Die Religion des Volkes Israel* (Leipzig: Quelle & Meyer, 1921). An English version appeared a few years later: Rudolf Kittel, *The Religion of the People of Israel* (London: G. Allen & Unwin, 1925).

[37] R. Kittel, *Religion*, 7–8. This is a hidden cross-reference to a very similar statement with which Kittel sums up his chapter on the Babylonian exile of Israel, except there he at least refers to "faith in itself *and in its God*" (170, italics added).

[38] See further Siegele-Wenschkewitz, *Neutestamentliche Wissenschaft*, 83–90.

[39] Barth and Kittel, *Briefwechsel*, 10; his letter of 15 June 1934 replying to Karl

C. *The* Unheilsgeschichte *of the Jews*

Despite Gerhard Kittel's early and enduring enthusiasm for the study
of rabbinic literature, the important role he attributed to the scribes,
Pharisees, and rabbis in preserving "Old Testament religion" against
Hellenistic syncretism, and the central place that the story of ancient
Israel occupied in his theology of salvation, there was also a strong
undercurrent of negative stereotypes that surfaced repeatedly in his
writings about Judaism from the beginning of his career. In his popular book of 1914, in which he pointed out many parallels between
rabbinic dicta and the teachings of Jesus, nevertheless the characteristics of the rabbis are "conservatism," "traditionalism," "deathly
legal studies and scholasticism," over against Jesus' "lively work for
the Kingdom of God"—illustrated by sayings often nearly identical.
Jesus' pure religious concerns are contrasted with "pragmatic life
skills" (*praktische Lebensvernunft*) and "the bondage of traditionalism
and the ceremonial apparatus," which the occasional "noble spirit"
among the rabbis might break, but which still characterize the whole
of the rabbinic corpus.[40] Such negative clichés are muted in his 1926
book and through most of his inaugural lecture at Tübingen that
year. Only near the end of the lecture certain themes appear, like
the characterization of Judaism as an anxious "ethical performance
religion" (*Leistungsreligion*) contrasted with Christianity as a uniquely
self-confident religion of forgiven sinners, which echo traditional
Augustinian-Lutheran apologetics and which would flower into something much uglier after 1933.[41]

In this lecture, and in the Uppsala lectures five years later, it
becomes clear that something deeper is at work than the popular
antisemitic prejudices that Gerhard Kittel, like most of the intellec-
tuals of his time, had imbibed from his student days.[42] There is a

---

Barth's protest of 12 June that the German Christians had "made of this 'historical moment' a second source of revelation and a second object of revelation and
set it up as a willfully constructed and cast idol in the church" (ibid., 7).

[40] Gerhard Kittel, *Jesus und die Rabbinen* (ed. F. Kropatscheck; Biblische Zeit- und
Streitfragen zur Aufklärung der Gebildeten 9.7; Berlin: Edwin Runge, 1914), 7–15.

[41] G. Kittel, *Urchristentum, Spätjudentum*, 19–27; Kittel here follows a schema set
out by Karl Holl, the Luther scholar, in a lecture delivered not long before Holl's
death, in *Urchristentum und Religionsgeschichte* (Gutersloh: C. Bertelsmann, 1925).

[42] On the centrality of the universities in the antisemitic campaigns of which so
many members of the German intelligentsia became willing agents around the turn
of the twentieth century, see W. Jochmann, "Die Ausbreitung des Antisemitismus

very special way of reading the story of the Old and New Testaments so that the "salvation history" in which the Jews had been the primary human characters became for them, upon their rejection of Jesus as their Messiah, *Unheilsgeschichte*—an untranslatable term that refers in this context not to ultimate condemnation, but to the suspension of God's saving activity for the Jews *until the end of the ages, viz. the "Second Coming" of the Christ.* The roots of this way of reading reach back deep into the struggles of the early Christian communities to understand and sustain themselves by appeal to the scriptures they shared with other Jewish movements. It was Augustine of Hippo who gave it the grand design that would dominate Western Christian thought through the Middle Ages, and at the heart of Augustine's design was his interpretation of Paul's Letter to the Romans, particularly chapters 9–11, which themselves contain Paul's "strong misreading" (as Harold Bloom might say) of certain passages in Deuteronomy, Isaiah, and the Psalms.[43] This grand rhetorical climax of Paul's longest and, in the West, most influential letter reaches its acme in his warning to his audience, constructed as Gentiles who have been granted faith through Jesus' faithfulness and thus been "grafted" onto the tree of Israel, not to lord it over the Jews. "Has God rejected his people? Certainly not" (Rom 11:1). "Have [the Jews] stumbled so as to fall? Certainly not" (v. 11). The Gentile believers must recognize "this mystery, lest you be too smart for yourselves, that a hardening has come in part to Israel until the fullness of the Gentiles enter and thus all Israel will be saved" (vv. 25–26). Augustine understood this to mean that the "fall" of the Jews, in failing to believe in Jesus, was "not in vain, since it profited the Gentiles by salvation," nor was the result of their fall only

---

in Deutschland 1914–1923," 99–170; and idem, "Antisemitismus im Deutschen Kaiserreich 1871–1914," in *Gesellschaftkrise und Judenfeindschaft in Deutschland 1870–1945* (Hamburg: Hans Christians, 1988), 30–98, esp. 60.

[43] For example, *Civ.* 18.46–48; 20.30; early indications of Augustine's exegesis: *Propositions from the Epistle to the Romans* 59–70. A useful summary of Augustine's exegesis of Romans 9–11, particularly in the *Propositions* and in the *Unfinished Commentary on Romans*, contrasted with Thomas's later, more positive reading, may be found in Steven Chrysostom Boguslawski, "Aquinas' Commentary on Romans 9–11," (Ph.D. diss., Yale University, 1999), 108–29 (a revised version of this dissertation is forthcoming from Paulist Press). More fully, Bernhard Blumenkranz, *Die Judenpredigt Augustins: Ein Beitrag zur Geschichte der jüdisch-christlichen Beziehungen in den ersten Jahrhunderten* (Basler Beiträge zur Geschichtswissenschaft 25; Basel: Helbing & Lichtenhahn, 1946), who provides a bibliography of earlier scholarship on pages 4–6.

punishment.[44] The "scattering" of the Jews also served the divine purpose that the prophecies in their scriptures should be known throughout the world and serve as "testimony" concerning the Christ.[45] At the end of the age, they (or some of them) were destined to convert:

> And at or in connection with [the final] judgment the following events shall come to pass, as we have learned: Elias the Tishbite shall come; *the Jews shall believe*; Antichrist shall persecute; Christ shall judge; the dead shall rise; the good and the wicked shall be separated; the world shall be burned and renewed.[46]

The Augustinian outline of salvation history became more brittle in some medieval versions, and the role of the Jews in the cosmic drama more negative, particularly in the age of the Crusades. From time to time popes and other ecclesiastical leaders intervened to restrain acts of aggression against the Jewish communities. These admonitions frequently revert to the Augustinian scheme. For example, Pope Alexander II writes to the bishops of Spain, ca. 1060:

> We are pleased by the report which we have heard concerning you, that you have protected the Jews living among you, lest they be slain by those who set out to war against the Saracens in Spain. These warriors, moved surely by foolish ignorance and strongly by blind cupidity, wished to bring about the slaughter of those whom divine charity has perhaps predestined for salvation. In the same manner Saint Gregory also admonished those [who] agitated for annihilating them, indicating that it is impious to wish to annihilate those who are protected by the mercy of God, so that, with homeland and liberty lost, in everlasting penitence, damned by the guilt of their ancestors for spilling the blood of the Savior, they live dispersed throughout the various areas of the world.[47]

Thus chapters 9–10 of Romans are understood to declare God's *curse* on the Jews, transforming their *Heilsgeschichte* into *Unheilsgeschichte*.

---

[44] *Propositions* 70, from *Augustine on Romans: Propositions from the Epistle to the Romans, Unfinished Commentary on the Epistle to the Romans* (trans. P. F. Landes; Texts and Translations 23: Early Christian Literature Series 6; Chico, Calif.: Scholars Press, 1982), 41.

[45] *Civ.* 18.46.

[46] *Civ.* 20.30, from *The City of God* (trans. M. Dods; The Modern Library; New York: Random House, 1950), 762, italics added.

[47] Translated in *Church, State, and Jew in the Middle Ages* (ed. R. Chazan; New York: Behrman House, 1980), 99–100.

The promises enunciated in Rom 11, then, are taken to be eschatological and interpreted as the *conversion* of the Jews at the end of time. In the interim they wander the world, accursed and hated, but under divine protection, like Cain. Luther and his followers notoriously continued and exaggerated this tradition.[48] This reading of Rom 9–10 placed it under the control of other passages of the New Testament that could be taken with considerably less distortion as anti-Jewish and, in the context of modern European racial constructs, antisemitic. The narrative line of the Acts of the Apostles depicts repeated refusals of the Jewish communities in various cities to accept the "message of salvation," despite conversions of large numbers of individual Jews, until the conclusion of the story with Paul's solemn declaration that now, "This salvation of God is sent to the Gentiles; *they* will listen" (Acts 28:28). The Gospel of Matthew has Jesus declare to the Jewish leaders, "The kingdom of God is taken away from you and given to a nation that yields its fruits" (Matt 21:43). The Gospel of John depicts Jesus declaring that the father of his Jewish opponents is not Abraham but Cain's father, the devil (John 8:44). It is ironic that precisely those chapters of Romans in which revisionist Christian exegetes, since the Holocaust, have found the strongest counterweight to those harsh passages and to anti-Jewish readings of Paul were at the center of the Augustinian-Lutheran version of the history of salvation. The role of the Jews in that version was at best tragic.[49]

---

[48] The notion of Jewish *Unheilsgeschichte* is personified in the peculiar myth of "the eternal Jew" (known elsewhere in Europe as "the wandering Jew"). A pamphlet published in 1602 reported that the Lutheran bishop Paul von Eitzen, a student of Luther (at just the time when Luther was writing his fiery tract, "Concerning the Jews and their Lies") had seen a wretched figure in a Hamburg church, who identified himself as "Ahasverus." For having scoffed at Jesus on the way to Calvary, Ahasverus said, he had been condemned to wander the earth, having no home and not permitted to die until Christ's Second Coming. R. Edelmann has argued that this transformation of the varied medieval legends about a figure (Johannes Buttadaeus, Cartaphilus, etc.) forbidden to die until Christ returned, was a piece of deliberate propaganda against Sephardic refugees settling in Hamburg in the second half of the sixteenth century (R. Edelmann, "Ahasuerus, the Wandering Jew: Origin and Background," in *The Wandering Jew: Essays in the Interpretation of a Christian Legend* [ed. G. Hasan-Rokem and A. Dundes; Bloomington, Ind.: Indiana University Press, 1986], 1–10). In the early eighteenth century a work by one J. Schudt first explicitly identifies Ahasverus with the entire Jewish people. See Rose, *Revolutionary Antisemitism*, 23–43. The literature on the "Wandering Jew" legend is vast; for a selected bibliography see Hasan-Rokem and Dundes, *Wandering Jew*, 272–78.

[49] The most influential pioneer in the revisionist reading of Romans was Krister

It is not surprising that this ancient schema of salvation history at crucial moments controlled Gerhard Kittel's reading of scripture, even as he wrestled intelligently and vigorously with the implications of the modernist history of religions. In his 1933 lecture to the Union of German Students, as we have seen, he defines "true Judaism," in distinction from Orthodoxy, Liberalism, and Zionism, as Old Testament biblical theology, more or less identical with that outlined by his father. He imagines, with perhaps some strained justification, that such a "return to biblical religion" would have resonance with the aims of Martin Buber and Hans Joachim Schoeps (a Jewish scholar who would write important works on early Christianity). That conceit shows his blindness to the decisive point: Kittel has subsumed the prophetic religion of Israel, which often speaks of God's punishment of Israel's apostasy, entirely under the traditional Christian perspective, that the final apostasy is the crucifixion of the Messiah Jesus and that all subsequent history of Israel is *Unheilsgeschichte*, under God's curse. The "pious Jew" (*frommer Jude*) then is the one who accepts that condemnation to homelessness, statelessness, wandering, and suffering in the world as God's judgment, awaiting the eschatological redemption of his people—that is, one who completely adopts the standard Lutheran way of reading Rom 9–11 as the last word about his own identity in relation to God.[50]

Kittel's 1933 lecture reveals one further permutation of the Augustinian-Lutheran narrative of salvation history, for he introduces into the story the *völkisch* ideal of racial purity. "Genuine, pious Judaism itself has at all times held fast to the clear recognition of what a curse assimilation is." This was the theme that Kittel found in "the Old Testament prophets," viz. "that mixing with the other peoples was Israel's worst sin."[51] Pure Israel and the pure German *Volk* are thus for Kittel mirror images. And where was this "genuine, pious Judaism" to be found? In the postexilic program of Ezra as Kittel described it.

Stendahl; see the essays collected in his *Paul Among Jews and Gentiles and Other Essays* (Philadelphia: Fortress, 1976). Many others have followed; for an overview see Robert Jewett, "The Law and the Coexistence of Jews and Gentiles in Romans," *Int* 39 (1985): 341–56.

[50] G. Kittel, *Die Judenfrage*, 40–45, 73 (biblical theology), 74 (Buber), 125 n. 69 (Schoeps), 75. See also n. 11 above.

[51] G. Kittel, *Die Judenfrage*, 38.

In an odd sort of way Ezra, the very father of "Late Judaism" so often tarred with the brush of "legalism" and "particularism" in German scholarship, is a hero for Kittel. This becomes clearest— and most bizarre—in a lecture Kittel gave at the University of Berlin in 1939 (published under the aegis of Walter Frank's National Institute for the History of the New Germany), entitled "The Historical Presuppositions of Jewish Race-mixing." Ezra's program of separating Israel from the nations, especially by ending mixed marriages, Kittel thought, was motivated by the clear vision of a pure *Volk*. His accomplishments were undone in the age of Hellenism. First the existence of the Diaspora, from the Exile on, brought "world Judaism"—that bugaboo of antisemites—onto the world stage. Then the invention of *proselytizing* compounded the issue, not only by mixing alien races into the Jewish stock, but also by *implying* the "world domination" that German antisemites so hysterically feared. Kittel, by creating the myth of an ideal, racially pure *Judaism*, corrupted first by ancient assimilation in the Diaspora and now, most disastrously, by emancipation, was thus able to perform another feat of mental gymnastics. This enabled him to imagine that people like Buber and Schoeps ought to welcome his support for the Nazi program of forcing the Jews, as he puts it in this lecture, "for the last time into the closet."[52]

The basic schema on which Kittel elaborates here was not original to him. Indeed, once again, its essentials had been spelled out by his father in his "History of the People of Israel," who had described the work of Ezra and the scribes after him as one of preservation, a holding operation for the coming Messiah, who would recover the prophetic conception of God.[53] However, there is a new

---

[52] Gerhard Kittel, *Die historischen Voraussetzungen der jüdischen Rassenmischung* (Schriften des Reichsinstituts für Geschichte des neuen Deutschlands; Hamburg: Hanseatische Verlagsanstalt, 1939).

[53] R. Kittel: "The task which the prophets had set themselves of raising Israel's national religion to a world religion was stopped in mid-course, was indeed shipwrecked" by the Exile and the (necessary) form of reconstruction under Ezra and after (*Religion*, 195). "Jesus going back behind Judaism took over the prophetic conception of God" (ibid., 224); here is Gerhard Kittel's schema for *TDNT in nuce*. (Rudolf Kittel was active in the planning of the latter project; shortly before his death he selected the OT scholars to write the sections on "the more important Old Testament terms" for *TDNT*; see the Preface to vol. 1 [ET, viii].) So "the Law came at the right moment between Jesus and the prophets" (*Religion*, 194). "In the

dimension in Gerhard Kittel's adaptation of the old story. "Purity" as a metaphor for orthodoxy had a long history in both Christian and Jewish discourse, and we have seen how important it was for Kittel to deny that earliest Christianity had been syncretistic. The introduction of the category of *race* gives the concept a new force. Reaching for a scientific definition of race, he appeals to the German anthropologist Hans F. K. Gunther and to the Nazi racial specialist Eugen Fischer (whose fantasies about the racial composition of ancient Israel Kittel himself later recognizes as absurd). However, it is the metaphor of *blood* that really controls Kittel's language of race. For a man who devoted most of his career to the study of language, Kittel shows a remarkable obtuseness to metaphoricity. He writes, as do his Nazi colleagues, as if "mixing of blood" were a physical description of genetic inheritance.[54] We see later, in his work on *TDNT*, that this is not the only instance of Kittel's fatal naiveté about semantics.

III. Sacred Lexicography

Kittel began work in 1928 on the publication that was to be his lasting monument, and the first stout volume of the *Theologisches Wörterbuch zum Neuen Testament* appeared in 1933. Three more would follow during the years of the Third Reich; the remainder were completed under other hands after Kittel's arrest in 1945.[55] We have already had occasion to notice Kittel's claim, in his Uppsala lectures, that when a text is translated into another language, the *words* used in the host language (Greek) thereafter are charged with new meaning derived from the translated concepts (Hebrew and Aramaic).[56] That semantic principle was one of the axioms on which the plan

---

grand total of the great development of religion in the field with which we are concerned post-exilic Judaism takes the place of the Middle Ages. Just as the service of the Middle Ages to Christian thought in the years between the ancient and the modern world lies in the link that is made possible for us with Paul and Jesus, so the service of legal Judaism to the Israelite-Christian religion lies in the link made possible with the achievements of the prophets" (ibid., 195).

[54] E.g., G. Kittel, *Judenfrage*, 22–25; idem, *Rassenmischung*, 43–45 et passim.

[55] "The final volume," 9, appeared under the general editorship of Gerhard Friedrich in 1973; later an index volume was added (the English version has a different index volume prepared especially for it).

[56] See above, section II.A.

of *TDNT* was founded, making possible the organization of "biblical theology" into individual *word*-studies—which Kittel dubbed "sacred lexicography."

That was the title Kittel gave to a series of two lectures he gave at the University of Cambridge in October 1937, in which he set forth the goals and methods of the forthcoming *Dictionary*. The project had originally been conceived as a new edition of a venerable reference work, Hermann Cremer's *Biblical-Theological Lexicon of New Testament Greek*, which had first appeared in 1866.[57] Cremer's belief that the peculiarities of New Testament Greek amounted to a new dialect, however, had proven to be untenable, and Kittel, aware that his "sacred lexicography" sounded very much like Cremer's method, attempted in his first Cambridge lecture to distance himself somewhat from it. He is careful to insist on the continuation of ordinary usage in the New Testament; Cremer's search for coinage of new words that would demonstrate a peculiar New Testament dialect was in vain, with one or two insignificant exceptions. The creativeness of the first Christians was manifested, rather, in putting new content into old words, and that did not keep the Christians from continuing to use the words also in the ordinary senses. For example, ἐξουσία ("power, authority") and ἄρχοντες ("governors, rulers") have their ordinary, political reference in Rom 13, not, as in Ephesians, pointing to demonic powers.[58] Kittel recognized that the Christians did not speak in some technical language: "The primitive Christian writer sought in no way to schematise his words."[59] Yet he still asserted that words could be "absorbed by the exclusiveness of their new content." The words of the New Testament "are bound up inextricably with a definite historical fact to which they bear witness."[60]

> New Testament words are thus essentially like a mirror; they reflect the fact of Christ, and this they do not in any broken or indirect way,

---

[57] Hermann Cremer, *Hermann Cremers Biblisch-theologisches Wörterbuch des neutestamentlichen Griechisch* (ed. J. Kögel; 11th ed.; Stuttgart: F. A. Perthes, 1923). See Kittel's Preface to the first volume of *TDNT*.

[58] Kittel made this point (rightly) against his theological and political opponent Karl Barth in Gerhard Kittel, *Christus und Imperator: Das Urteil der ersten Christenheit über den Staat* (Stuttgart: W. Kohlhammer, 1939), 48–54.

[59] Gerhard Kittel, *Lexicographia Sacra: Two Lectures on the Making of the Theologisches Wörterbuch zum Neuen Testament* ("Theology" Occasional Papers; London: SPCK, 1938), 10–14.

[60] G. Kittel, *Lexicographia Sacra*, 12, 7.

but in actual reality and in genuine truth. . . . For the words and sentences in which the message is framed are formed by men who are imbued with the fact of Christ. . . . Thus it inevitably happens that a stream of life pours forth from the fact of Christ's Incarnation and Resurrection and passes through those whose lives have, under the influence of that fact, been renewed, and flows right into the words and sentences of the New Testament message. In such a sense we may rightly claim that the New Testament presents a new language and a new manner of speech.[61]

Moreover, "Nothing reveals more clearly the important influence that this linguistic development had upon early Christianity than prepositions. . . ." For example, "In the New Testament phrase διὰ Χριστοῦ ['through Christ'] quite a new interpretation has been *bestowed upon the preposition.*"[62]

There is at work here some fundamental confusion about the way language works. James Barr has analyzed that confusion with all necessary clarity, so I do not need to dwell on it. It is evident, as Barr points out, that Kittel had not departed at all from the idealist theory of language on which Cremer's project had been based, nor from the romantic mode of interpretation that both had inherited from Schleiermacher.[63] Barr accuses Kittel and his associates of fuzzy thinking about linguistic matters. They failed to distinguish between words and concepts, often using *Begriff* where they really meant "word." They confused the function of words with the functions of larger syntactic units, and thus managed to read into specific words freights of meaning that are really drawn from large interpretive schemas created by certain modern theological systems. There is no place in Kittel's understanding of language for its social dimensions, so that the relation between words and external events or realities becomes a kind of magic. Many of the articles in *TDNT* suffer from the errors that Barr calls "illegitimate identity transfer" and "illegitimate totality transfer." The former takes an instance in which a word is used to refer to some object or event and assumes that the word will always *mean* that object or event. For example, ἀγάπη

---

[61] Ibid., 7.

[62] Ibid., 10–11, my italics.

[63] James Barr, *The Semantics of Biblical Language* (Oxford: Oxford University Press, 1961), chap. 8, "Some Principles of Kittel's Theological Dictionary" (on Cremer-Kögel, 238–46; on the Schleiermacher tradition, 257–60).

("love") may be used in a New Testament passage to refer to the love of God manifested in Christ; then every occurrence of ἀγάπη in the New Testament is taken to contain that love concept. "Illegitimate totality transfer" makes a composite theological doctrine from many uses of a term in the New Testament and attributes that composite to each instance. Most of the contributors also share the fallacy that Barr deplored in much of the modern "biblical theology movement," the assumption of a fundamental difference in mentality between Semitic and Greek consciousness, so that the claim is often made that Greek words take on a Hebrew content, either in the Septuagint or in the New Testament.[64]

What remains to be done here is to show how Kittel and his collaborators in the *TDNT* project put this confused theory of language to work, controlling an immense collection of lexicographical evidence, to support the Augustinian-Lutheran tradition of salvation history described above and particularly the negative role of the Jews in that theologically and politically constructed history. In his second Cambridge lecture Kittel stated the controlling principle rather vividly: "Now there are cases in which the New Testament and Old Testament language and ideas, though identical, have yet been disconnected as a result of transformations that took place in words in later Hellenistic or Palestinian Judaism. We often find that in such cases the New Testament goes right back through the Jewish depraved form to the Old Testament origin of the word."[65]

Here and elsewhere in the lectures, the ideological framework that comprises the heart of the *lexicographia sacra*, the history of biblical language as Kittel himself conceived it, is candidly presented. Putting these remarks into the context of what we have seen from Kittel's previous work, the framework can be outlined as follows:

(1) The religion and theology of Israel reaches its supreme expression in the great prophets of the eighth century and following.

(2) From the end of the Babylonian exile and particularly in the assimilationist era of Hellenism, the era of "Late Judaism," Israel falls into a state of decadence. Though the Pharisees and then the rabbis are able to ward off the surrounding syncretism, they

---

[64] Barr, *Semantics*, 210–13, 217–18 et passim.

[65] G. Kittel, *Lexicographia Sacra*, 24.

do so at a high cost. Judaism becomes a legalistic, anxious religion, turned in on itself, jealously protecting its own prerogatives as God's elect, but surrendering the eschatological, universalist
hope of the great prophets.

(3) Through Jesus and the Apostles the prophetic content of the
words is rediscovered and now expressed most fully and truly.

(4) Those changes are to be found embedded, as it were, in the
individual words of the Bible, so that by studying the history of
the words one can lay bare the theological development.

As editor of *TDNT*, Kittel constructed an outline that, with variations, can be seen in each of the major entries. First comes a general
survey of usage of the word in classical and hellenistic Greek, then
the use of the corresponding Hebrew word(s) in the Old Testament,
next post-Exilic developments, particularly usage by the Septuagint
translators and hellenistic Jewish writers, the concept in Rabbinic
Judaism, and finally the New Testament usage.

Commonly Kittel divided the sections among different specialists—
for the entry on "word" (λέγω, λόγος, etc.), for example, Kittel himself wrote the portion on "Word and Speech in the New Testament,"
but gave the other divisions to five other contributors.[66] Kittel by no
means limited his recruits to those who shared his theological and
political opinions. The very important entry on "truth" (ἀλήθεια) in
the first volume, for example, is shared between Kittel and one of
his strongest opponents, Rudolf Bultmann, as well as the Old Testament
scholar Gottfried Quell.[67] It is also evident that Kittel did not impose

---

[66] Kittel, Bauernfeind, and Friedrich, *TDNT* 4:100–36. For convenience I cite
the English edition, in Bromiley's translation, throughout.

[67] *TDNT* 1:232–51. Kittel proudly reports his early consultation with Bultmann,
"whose theological position is to all appearances so very different from mine," in
his Cambridge lectures (*Lexicographia Sacra*, 5). On the range of political positions of
the contributors to *TDNT*, see Vos, "Antijudaismus," 90–91. Vos profiles the contributors who were involved in the *Reichsinstitut für Geschichte des Neuen Deutschlands*
(Kittel, K. G. Kuhn; 91–94); those active in the *Institut zur Erforschung des jüdischen
Einflusses auf das deutsche kirchliche Leben* (Walter Grundmann, Georg Bertram, Hugo
Odeberg, Carl Schneider, Herbert Preisker, Gerhard Delling; 95–102); those who
were German Christians, but less passionately antisemitic (Ethelbert Stauffer, Hermann
Wolfgang Beyer; 102–3); those with "divided hearts" (Hermann Strathmann—an
opponent of national socialism but enthusiastic about early German conquests in
the war and anti-Jewish in his articles; Karl-Heinrich Rengstorf—who vacillated;
103–7); and opponents of *völkische Theologie* (Bultmann, Gottlob Schrenk, Friedrich
Büchsel—all of whom nevertheless show clear signs of theological or exegetical anti-
judaism; 107–9).

his ideological framework on the contributors, nor was the schematic outline rigidly applied. In his own entry on "word" there is, surprisingly, no section at all on Rabbinic Judaism. It is also true that statements of explicitly racist antisemitism are hardly to be found in *TDNT*, as J. S. Vos of Amsterdam has pointed out after a careful analysis of the first four volumes. Vos also observes that, in the twenty-six articles or parts of articles that Kittel himself contributed, there is "by and large . . . no onesidedly negative picture of Judaism."[68]

Nevertheless, that grand scheme that Kittel had described in his Divinity School lectures at Cambridge, in which the history of biblical language embodied the Augustinian-Lutheran history of God's plan of salvation, pervades almost every article. Vos uses measured language and is careful to be fair to Kittel; his exposé is thus all the more damning, for he discovers a pervasive tendency in *TDNT* articles, even those written by opponents of "*völkisch* theology," to parody "Jewish legalism," the "religion of retribution," the supposed lack in Judaism of faith in God's future salvation, and especially the tendency to see in Judaism a decadent retreat from the heights of prophetic religion, to be restored only in Jesus.[69] All this belongs to the structure of the grand design—the same construct that, as we have seen, led Kittel to embrace the Nazi program for removal of Jews from German public life. It comes through in one of Kittel's own short essays, that on ἀββᾶ ("father"): "In any case there can be no doubt that the use of the word in the community is linked with

---

[68] Vos, "Antijudaismus/Antisemitismus," 93. Vos distinguishes three "different forms of antijudaism": theological antijudaism, exegetical antijudaism, and antisemitism (89–90), though he admits that the three forms "are not always clearly distinguishable" (90). Kittel himself, in his less scholarly publications, did not hesitate to speak of "a genuine antisemitism of the people," for which he undertook to provide a theological basis, deploring the "mob antisemitism" that was the natural result of failure of the intelligentsia on that score (*Judenfrage*, 34–35). Birgit Gregor, "Zum protestantischen Antisemitismus: Evangelische Kirchen und Theologen in der Zeit des Nationalsozialismus," in "*Beseitigung des jüdischesn Einflusses—*," 171–200, warns that the common distinction between "religious anti-Judaism" and "racist antisemitism" is misleading and "trivializes" the deep roots of the latter in the former (174–77). Cf. Rose, who argues further that the sharp divide made often between racial antisemitism after 1860 and the much older anti-Jewish sentiment in Germany and elsewhere in Europe is misleading, for ". . . racist thinking was predicated on the notion of 'national character' that is central to the evolution of modern antisemitism" (*Revolutionary Antisemitism*, 15).

[69] Vos, "Antijudaismus/Antisemitismus," 91–109. Most chilling, Vos finds the same tendencies in the post-war volumes (110).

Jesus' term for God and thus denotes an appropriation of the relationship proclaimed and lived out by Him. Jewish usage shows how this Father-child relationship to God far surpasses any possibilities of intimacy assumed in Judaism, introducing indeed something which is wholly new."[70]

The scheme is more egregious in many other articles, by contributors of varying theological and political stripes. A few examples may suffice to illustrate its pervasiveness.

Hermann Strathmann is one of those contributors to *TDNT* whom Vos describes as being "of divided heart." Though he had once opposed National Socialism (in 1931), he greeted early German victories in the war as the result of "divine leading," and he wrote some articles that contained vehemently anti-Jewish elements.[71] He wrote five of the six parts of the article λαός ("people," *Volk*; Rudolf Meyer wrote the section on "People and Peoples in Rabbinic Literature"). At the conclusion of his survey of Septuagint usage he says, "Prophetic preaching with all its profundity and force brought to full expression the unique relation between God and Israel which is implied in Israel's designation as the λαὸς θεοῦ ["people of God"] and in the resultant and increasing exclusiveness with which עם = λαός is applied to Israel alone." Then he adds,

> As compared with this prophetic attitude, the tendency of later writings to speak self-evidently of Israel as the ἅγιοι ["holy ones"] (1 Esdr. 8:57; 2 Esdr. 8:28), or as the λαὸς ὅσιος ["hallowed people"] [etc.] . . . represents a certain regression which forms a transition to Pharisaic Judaism with its stubborn insistence on a position of privilege granted once and for all to the people. This is a transition to the spiritual outlook and conduct against which the protest of John the Baptist was directed.[72]

The article on "love" (ἀγαπάω, ἀγάπη, ἀγαπητός) is by Ethelbert Stauffer, who was active in the German Christian movement, but

---

[70] *TDNT* 1:6. Kittel had laid out this argument for Jesus' unique use of "Father" earlier, in his lectures at Uppsala (*Religionsgeschichte*, 93–94) and in the Cambridge lectures (*Lexicographia Sacra*, 15–16). This dubious claim was first suggested by Gustaf Dalman in *Die Worte Jesu mit Berücksichtigung des nachkanonischen jüdischen Schrifttums und der aramäischen Sprache erörtert* (Leipzig: J. C. Hinrichs, 1930), 157–58; after World War II it was given still wider currency by Joachim Jeremias in *Abba: Studien zur neutestamentlichen Theologie und Zeitgeschichte* (Göttingen: Vandenhoeck & Ruprecht, 1966), 15–67.

[71] Vos, "Antijudaismus/Antisemitismus," 103–5.

[72] *TDNT* 4:37.

less univocally racist than many of his associates.[73] The *Dictionary* article conveys some of his ambivalence or confusion. After several pages demonstrating the importance of divinely initiated, other-regarding love in all varieties of Judaism, climaxing in a note on *4 Ezra* that reveals "the clear recognition that God cannot order the world aright without love," Stauffer then concludes: "This insight could not establish itself in its full scope without shaking the foundations of the Jewish view of God, the world and life. It did not do so. The lofty sayings about love remain isolated. The underlying basis of Judaistic theology is still righteousness—in spite of everything. Jesus alone broke free from the old foundations and ventured a radically new structure."[74]

As our final example, consider an article published in volume 6, long after National Socialism had been defeated and Kittel forced to relinquish the editorship—indeed, eleven years after his death. The important article on "faith" (πιστεύω, πίστις, κτλ.) was written by Kittel's theological and political opposite, Rudolf Bultmann, together with the Tübingen Old Testament scholar Artur Weiser. Bultmann had been much closer to the History of Religions School than Kittel and shared the tendency of that school to emphasize the Hellenistic antecedents of Christianity more than the Jewish. Kittel, we have seen, parted company with the History of Religions school precisely on that point. Bultmann had been engaged in the "dialectical theology" identified with Karl Barth, later modified by his adoption of the existentialist philosophy of Martin Heidegger. Kittel's theology was a blend of Lutheran orthodoxy and the old liberalism. Though Bultmann was heavily dependent on his Marburg colleague Heidegger, he shared nothing of Heidegger's attraction to National Socialism. His disdain for the Nazis and his support for the Confessing Church in its opposition to the German Christians were public, though not so vociferous that he was not able to retain his position at the University of Marburg throughout the war. On the question that rent the churches in 1933, whether converts or descendents of converts from Judaism who had been ordained should be removed from their ecclesiastical offices—under the legislation that forbade government positions to non-Aryans—Bultmann stood resolutely against

---

[73] Vos, "Antijudaismus/Antisemitismus," 102–3.
[74] *TDNT* 1:44.

the antisemitic measure, while Kittel published a pamphlet supporting it.[75] Accordingly, one is surprised to find in Bultmann's article
on faith a characterization of Judaism that is not so different from
Kittel's.

Bultmann wrote most of the article, including the section on "The
Concept of Faith in Judaism." That section culminates with a paragraph on "The Difference from the Old Testament." It is heavily
laden with Bultmann's own existentialist language, but the denigration of Judaism as a religion of "works righteousness" and relega-
tion of its place in salvation history to that of a barren place-holder
between the prophets and Jesus is as clear as in anything Kittel
wrote:

> History [in post-Exilic Judaism] is arrested, and there is no true rela-
> tion to it. The significance of past history is restricted to the fact that
> it gives the Jew the sense of being a member of the chosen people.
> The present can no longer continue history and its tradition in a liv-
> ing way. It simply mediates canonized tradition. The codex of Scripture,
> now given as a timeless present, is adapted and interpreted by theo-
> logical-juridical study. Faith loses the character of present decision in
> the historical situation, and "thus represents itself as something objec-
> tive and static, as the form of consciousness which results when the
> doctrine of scripture enters into it." [The quotation is from Adolf
> Schlatter.]

> Belief in retribution is also belief in merits. Believing obedience to the
> Law leads to obedience to the letter and to the reckoning of fulfilled
> commands as merits.... The righteous man does not need grace....
> [He] stands on his own merits. As faith is set alongside works, it is
> certainly perceived that there is an obedience of faith which is not
> replaced by the righteousness of works but which involves submission
> to the divine will as a whole. This insight is robbed of its character,
> however, by the understanding of faith itself as a merit.[76]

Bultmann was very critical of the way the concept of the history of
salvation was being used in the "biblical theology" movement after
World War II.[77] He was wary of any interpretation of history as a

---

[75] Rudolf Bultmann, "Der Arier-Paragraph im Raume der Kirche," *TBl* 12 (1933):
cols. 359–70; Gerhard Kittel, *Kirche und Judenchristen* (Stuttgart: W. Kohlhammer,
1933); idem, *Die Judenfrage*, 101–13. See also Vos, "Antijudaismus/Antisemitismus,"
107–8.

[76] *TDNT* 6:201. I have modified Bromiley's translation.

[77] See, for example, his sharp critique of Oscar Cullmann's theology of history
in "Heilsgeschichte und Geschichte," *TLZ* 73 (1948): 569–66; ET: "History of

grand design. For him what was important was the "historicity" (*Geschichtlichkeit*) of human existence, the confrontation of every individual with each moment's "historical situation" in which faith was an ever new "present decision." Yet in this article he construes the Old Testament as a treasury of true theological concepts, whose content is perverted by later Judaism, then renewed and perfected in the New Testament. That is the Kittel schema in a nutshell, and it is operative in a writer who was scarcely subject to direct influence by Kittel. Obviously Gerhard Kittel and the theologians who, like him, gave public support to the National Socialist regime were not the only people who read the Bible in this way. For vast numbers of theologians and ordinary Christians—by no means only in Germany and by no means only in the past—"the Bible that was" was a Bible whose very plot structure pivoted on the failure of the Jews to achieve their true destiny, with the result that their subsequent history was *Unheilsgeschichte*.

What made the difference between the vast number of European Christians who read more or less that same anti-Jewish Bible and those—a much smaller number but still far more numerous than Christian apologists have often pretended in the years since the Shoah—who became active in the attempt to remove all Jews from the Christian world? What made the difference, to put it crudely, between a Bultmann and a Kittel? Apart from the social and political and psychological factors that I have ignored here, we have seen two or three dimensions of Kittel's interpretive program that deserve to be remembered as a warning to all interpreters. First, he was naively oblivious to the ideological dimensions of the history he constructed. Second, his obsession with religious *purity* was open to perversion by the newly invented science of *race*. Third, and perhaps most important of all, he made a fatal distinction between personal morality and social policy. That division, which no doubt has some connection with the Lutheran tradition of the "two realms" of the world and the gospel, manifests itself in a series of bizarre contradictions. Kittel the scholar honors and works closely with individual Jews; Kittel the Party member urges the removal of all Jews from academic and professional life. Recognizing that this "solution" to

---

Salvation and History," in Rudolf Bultmann, *Existence and Faith* (ed. and trans. S. M. Ogden; New York: World Publishing and Meridian, 1960), 226–40.

the "Jewish question" would result in great suffering—but never publicly acknowledging the existence of the extermination camps—he
urges kindness toward individuals, and indeed acts himself to help
a few Jewish persons to escape. Warm appreciation of the rabbinic
tradition stands alongside cold repetition of the stereotypes of "legalism," "particularism," "scholasticism."

Gerhard Kittel's story is perhaps extreme in its paradoxes, but it
is not unique. "The Bible that was" for him is still the Bible that is
for a great many Christians. The mystery is that reading the same
Bible sometimes nourishes moral intuitions that in times of crisis are
capable of resisting the seductions of power and rationalizations of
vengeance, capable even of shattering the traditions themselves that
have become the ideologies of power. Only those who face squarely
the devastation wrought by beliefs grounded and excused by those
well-known ways of reading can also seek to discover, among the
complex layers deposited by generations of diverse interpretations,
the healing and the joy that those glorious and malleable stories of
which Jim Kugel has repeatedly reminded us can still evoke.

THE HERMENEUTICAL SIGNIFICANCE OF
EMMANUEL LEVINAS'S TALMUDIC READINGS

GERALD L. BRUNS

> The Torah is given in the Light of a face.
>
> —Levinas, "The Temptation of Temptation"

Let me introduce Emmanuel Levinas (1905/6) by citing the first paragraph of his autobiographical sketch, "Signature":

> The Hebrew Bible from childhood years in Lithuania, Pushkin and Tolstoy, the Russian Revolution of 1917 experienced at eleven years of age in the Ukraine. From 1923 on, the University of Strasbourg. . . . Friendship with Maurice Blanchot and, through the teachers who were adolescents at the time of the Dreyfus Affair, a vision, dazzling for a newcomer, of a people who equal humanity and of a nation to which one can attach oneself by spirit and heart as much as by roots. A stay in 1928–29 in Freiburg, and an apprenticeship in phenomenology begun a year earlier with Jean Hering. The Sorbonne, Léon Brunschvicg. The philosophical avant-garde at the Saturday soirées of Gabriel Marcel. The intellectual, anti-intellectualist refinement of Jean Wahl and his generous friendship, regained after a long captivity in Germany; regular conferences since 1947 at the Collège Philosophique which Wahl founded and inspired. Director of the one-hundred-year-old *École Normale Israélite Orientale*, training teachers of French for the schools of the *Alliance Israélite Universelle du Bassin Méditerranéen*. Daily communication with Dr Henri Nerson, frequent visits to M. Chouchani, the prestigious—and merciless—teacher of exegesis and of Talmud. Annual conferences, since 1957, on Talmudic texts at colloquia of the French Jewish Intellectuals. Thesis for the Doctor of Letters degree in 1961. Professorship at the University of Poitiers, from 1967 on at the University of Paris-Nanterre, and since 1973 at the Sorbonne. This disparate inventory is a biography.[1]

---

[1] Emmanuel Levinas, *Difficult Freedom: Essays on Judaism* (trans. S. Hand; Baltimore: Johns Hopkins University Press, 1990), 291.

I. The Levinasian Reversal

Emmanuel Levinas was one of the most important European philosophers of the twentieth century. It was he who, in the 1930s, introduced the work of Edmund Husserl and Martin Heidegger into French intellectual culture, thereby inaugurating a French phenomenological tradition that continues to flourish today (and not only in France). Moreover, quite independently of Sartre, and even before him, Levinas brought phenomenology down to earth by giving us rich descriptions of non-intentional states of consciousness—fatigue, indolence, horror, insomnia—in which "the subjectivity of the subject" is, as he liked to say, turned "inside-out," exposed to the world that intentionality or cognitive action otherwise tries to reduce and control from a safe distance.[2] This reversal of subjectivity defines the basic structure of Levinas's thought, including his talmudic lectures, and it also describes his relation to philosophical tradition. Traditional moral philosophy tries to characterize ethical reality in terms of rules, principles, theories of the right and the good, just and rational communities, and so on, where to be moral—to be justified—is to act in accord with these things, assuming them to be somehow in place. Here the goal of ethics is good conscience, or (as in John Rawls) acting without self-reproach. As Foucault has shown, Western ethics, including Christian ethics, can be summarized by the phrase, *epimeleia heautou*, "care of the self."[3] By contrast, Levinasian ethics—as developed in *Totality and Infinity* (1961) and *Otherwise than Being or Beyond Essence* (1974)—is an ethics of alterity or of responsibility for others in which we are constituted as human beings by the claims that others have on us.[4] These claims impinge on us in advance of whatever obligations we might freely enter into after careful deliberation. Our responsibility for others is anarchic in the sense of being on the hither side of commands or principles, older than any law. Prior to every principle or rule of reason, which is to say prior to cognition,

---

[2] *Existence and Existents* (trans. A. Lingis; Dordrecht: Kluwer Academic Publishers, 1978), 61.

[3] Michel Foucault, *The Care of the Self* (vol. 3 of *The History of Sexuality*; trans. R. Hurley; New York: Vintage Books, 1988), esp. 29–68.

[4] *Totality and Infinity: An Essay on Exteriority* (trans. A. Lingis; Pittsburgh: Duquesne University Press, 1969); *Otherwise than Being or Beyond Essence* (trans. A. Lingis; The Hague: Martinus Nijhoff, 1981).

intentionality, and freedom as autonomy or self-possession, I am answerable to and for the other (*Autrui*)—indeed, even more absolutely, I am "responsible for the universe."[5] As Levinas says, "[This] is a *responsibility that is justified by no prior commitment*";[6] it is "a responsibility that precedes freedom."[7] It cannot be mitigated by an appeal to conditions, whether logical or *sittlich*. "Thou shalt not kill" is certainly a universal principle, but the principle would not even arise if I did not already exist in a face-to-face relation with others in which I find myself responsible to the other and for the other's life, unable to carry out the act that is otherwise in my power. For the other is not in my power. My encounter with the other calls into question my sovereignty as a disengaged punctual ego exercising rational control over myself and my world. It is a prophetic encounter that summons me out of my place of insulation and comfort and exposes me to the suffering of the world for which I am, against every canon of reasonableness, responsible. The good of the other depends on me despite myself. Here one faces, indeed experiences, the inexorability of bad conscience.[8] As Levinas makes clear in his talmudic readings, the ethical relation in this sense is biblical rather than philosophical in its deep structure and essential force; it is Jewish rather than Greek, the product of an anarchic calling like the one that summoned Abraham out of the comfort of his sheikdom.[9] The burden of both Levinas's philosophical writings and his commentaries on Talumudic texts is to translate this biblical calling, this

---

[5] *In the Time of Nations* (trans. M. B. Smith; Bloomington, Ind.: Indiana University Press, 1994), 126.

[6] *Otherwise than Being*, 102.

[7] *Beyond the Verse: Talmudic Readings and Lectures* (trans. G. Mole; Bloomington, Ind.: Indiana University Press, 1994), 107.

[8] Levinas writes:

I wonder whether there has ever been a discourse in the world that was not apologetic, whether the *logos* itself is not apology, whether our first awareness of our existence is not an awareness of rights, whether it is not from the beginning an awareness of responsibilities, whether, rather than comfortably entering into the world as if into our home, without excusing ourselves, we are not, from the beginning, accused. I think it is a little like that that one tries to be Jewish, that it is like that that one merits being called a human being. (*Nine Talmudic Readings* [trans. A. Aronowicz; Bloomington, Ind.: Indiana University Press, 1990], 82)

[9] See especially, "The Temptation of Temptation" [1964], *Nine Talmudic Readings*, 32–42.

anarchic election, into the language of the Greeks, or what Levinas calls the "modern language" of concepts and reasons.[10] The basic idea is to translate Talmud into philosophy.

II. HERMENEIA

The purpose of my paper is to give an account of the hermeneutical significance of this translation of Talmud into Levinasian philosophy. What do I mean by "hermeneutical significance"? Hermeneutics, of course, is concerned with the understanding and interpretation of texts. More generally philosophical hermeneutics is concerned reflectively with the question of what it is to understand anything at all, whether a poem, a law, a human action, another person, an alien culture, or oneself. What are the conditions, historical as well as logical, in which this event takes place? Historically hermeneutics is older than philosophy. It is concerned with the flights of birds and changes in the weather. But even older—prior to the grammatical division of speech into words and meanings—*hermeneia* is a word for saying, the movement of venturing into the world, uncovering oneself by speaking. When one speaks one does not simply say one thing about another or interpret this as that; one also journeys outside oneself in a movement toward the one to whom one speaks. This is what expression means. One comes out of hiding. This movement, as we shall see, is the keystone of Levinasian ethics; it articulates, as Levinas puts it, a "sense" (*sens*) that is deeper than the "meaning" (*signification*) of words.[11] It is summarized in Levinas's statement that "The essence of discourse is prayer,"[12] where prayer is not a statement but a movement of oneself for another, one-for-the-other, a desire for the other that is a generosity rather than an appetite.[13] One point I will want to make about Levinas's talmudic readings is that they have this hermeneutical structure of saying as a gratuitous movement toward another person. In the Torah, he

---

[10] See "The Translation of the Scripture" [1984], *In the Time of Nations*, 33–54.

[11] *Collected Philosophical Papers* (trans. A. Lingis; The Hague: Martinus Nijhoff, 1987), 93–100.

[12] *Entre nous: Essais sur le penser-à-l'autre* (Paris: Éditions Grasset & Fasquelle, 1991), 7.

[13] *Collected Philosophical Papers*, 94.

says, "there is a propensity for the outside."[14] The purpose of Levinas's commentaries is not so much to enter into the talmudic texts as if they were ancient caves; the idea is rather to disseminate what the texts teach by making these teachings available in another's language. For Levinas this means recontextualizing the Talmud in the language of universals. In "Toward the Other," he says, "My effort always consists in extricating from this theological language [of Talmud] meanings addressing themselves to reason."[15] So in his commentaries Levinas thinks of himself as belonging to the history of Philo and Maimonides, which is to say the history of allegory, where allegory means reading traditional texts in such a way as to make them commensurable with prevailing rules of reason. This is also the history of the Jewish community in Lithuania into which Levinas was born in 1905, where the Talmud was studied within the framework of an Enlightenment Judaism concerned to demystify and demythologize Torah in order to turn its face toward modern Europe.[16] This turning of the Talmud toward modernity—toward European Enlightenment, with its ideas of rationality and individual freedom— is the upshot of Levinasian hermeneutics: "It is," he says, "a way for us Jews to claim our modernity alongside our antiquity older than all antiquity: the possibility and necessity of being able to express—or trying to express—the Torah in Greek."[17] "Greek" here is a covering term, a universalism in direct contrast to the historicity of Jewish particularism. In "The Bible and the Greeks" Levinas says:

> Greek is a term I use to designate, above and beyond the vocabulary, grammar and wisdom with which it originated in Hellas, the manner in which the universality of the West is expressed, or tries to express itself—rising above the local particularism of the quaint, traditional, poetic, or religious. It is a language without prejudice, a way of speaking that bites reality without leaving any marks—capable, in attempting to articulate the truth, of obliterating any traces left by itself—capable of unsaying and resaying. It is a language that is once a metalanguage, careful and able to protect what is said from the structures of language itself, which might lay claim to being the very categories of meaning.[18]

---

[14] *In the Time of Nations*, 2.
[15] *Nine Talmudic Readings*, 14.
[16] See Levinas's discussion of this tradition of "intellectual Judaism" in "Judaism and Kenosis" [1985], *In the Time of Nations*, 119–21.
[17] *In the Time of Nations*, 51.
[18] Ibid., 134–35.

In short, Greek is the Enlightenment ideal of a philosophical language, a language without materiality and without a history, a transparent language whose signs are never in excess of their significations, a language in which philosophy can at last free itself from relativism and contingency. Of course, as Levinas's lifelong friend, Maurice Blanchot, never tired of telling him, there is no such language, and even if there were, it would still have to take the form of writing (*l'écriture*).[19] But however that might be, Levinas's hermeneutical project is to provide a language, or at all events a place, in which the talmudic sea can flow into intellectual worlds outside of Judaism.

III. A HERMENEUTICS OF THE ENIGMA

Let me approach this project by trying to clarify the thesis that "The essence of discourse is prayer." This expression appears in a relatively early essay from 1951, "Is Ontology Fundamental?" in which Levinas first articulates his conception of the originary character of the ethical relation by opposing it explicitly to the tradition of philosophical hermeneutics and, in particular, to Martin Heidegger's idea that our fundamental relation to the world and to others in it—our being-in-the-world—is a relation of understanding (*verstehen*), where understanding is conceived as a practical involvement with the things around us in our everyday environment, in contrast to various theoretical attitudes that we might have reason to adopt, including the propositional attitude in which we lift things out of their contexts and objectify them according to the rule of identity. As Hans-Georg Gadamer says: Understanding is more being than consciousness.[20]

---

[19] See Maurice Blanchot:
How can philosophy be talked about, opened up, and presented, without, by that very token, using a particular language, contradicting itself, mortgaging its own possibility? Must not the philosopher be a writer, and thus forgo philosophy, even while pointing out the philosophy implicit in the writing? Or, just as well, to pretend to teach it, to master it—that is, this venture of a nonmastered, oral speech, all the while demeaning himself from time to time by *writing* books? ("Our Clandestine Companion," in *Face to Face with Levinas* [ed. R. Cohen; Albany, N.Y.: SUNY Press, 1986], 45)

[20] Hans-Georg Gadamer writes:
The "understanding" that Heidegger described as the basic dynamic of *Dasein* is not an "act" of subjectivity, but a mode of being. By proceeding from the

Basically Heidegger's "hermeneutics of facticity," as he calls it, is just the application of the philologist's hermeneutical circle to our everyday lifeworld: things make sense to us because they belong to the horizon within which we exist. They have a place alongside of us within the whole. Understanding in this sense is just the familiarity of things. We know what hammers and nails are doing in our world: they are not sensations but entities and meanings. To make sense of something strange, something from the outside, is to find a place for it—to integrate it into our scheme of things. Understanding is just this primordial grasp of the total ontological background against which everything stands out in its intelligibility. Meaning, in short, means belonging to a context.

Levinas's philosophy begins by contesting this ontological primacy of *verstehen* as contextualization. There is a relation which is prior to understanding as well as irreducible to it, and that is my relation to another person.[21] This relation is a relation of language, where language, however, is not a logical system for framing representations but a solicitation, an appeal, an address, a vocative, which is (says Levinas) "an event of language [that] can no longer be situated at the level of understanding" because here I encounter the other as singular and irreducible to any context, outside the relationship between universal and particular, outside every form of mediation, a transcendent singularity that does not stand out against any background.[22] In his essay, "Is Ontology Fundamental?" Levinas gives this relation to the other a remarkable characterization. He writes:

> This bond with the other which is not reducible to the representation of the other, but to his invocation, and in which invocation is not preceded by an understanding, I call *religion*. The essence of discourse is prayer. What distinguishes thought directed toward a thing from a

---

special case of the understanding of tradition, I have myself shown that understanding is always an event. The issue here is not simply that a nonobjectifying consciousness always accompanies the process of understanding, but rather that understanding is not suitably conceived at all as a consciousness of something. ("The Philosophical Foundations of the Twentieth Century," in *Philosophical Hermeneutics* [trans. D. E. Linge; Berkeley and Los Angeles: University of California Press, 1976], 125)

[21] *Entre nous*, 4.

[22] Ibid., 6. See *Totality and Infinity*, 202–9; and "Language and Proximity, *Collected Philosophical Papers*, 115–20.

bond with a person is that in the latter case a vocative is uttered: what is named is at the same time what is called.[23]

This is a religion, Levinas says, that is without mysticism and without theology[24]—although not without God, but evidently a God who cannot be comprehended or even approached by any theology ("the voice of God," Levinas will say in one of his talmudic commentaries, "is a human voice, inspiration and prophecy in the speech of men").[25] To put it philosophically, the infinity of the other person, his or her transcendence with respect to every context, horizon, or totality that gives meaning to things, is continuous with the infinity of the absolute other whom Descartes identifies as God, namely the thought I cannot think, that which is absolutely outside my grasp as a cognitive agent.[26] It is this transcendence of the other that determines my humanity as something different from the self-assertion of rationality and conceptual control.

Moreover, this relation to the other is religious in the sense that, in contrast to understanding and, in particular, to conceptual representation, it is an absolutely non-violent relation. Levinas does not hesitate to describe understanding as an aggressive action in which I take possession of whatever stands out in the openness of being.[27] For example, the German word for concept, *Begriff*, is rooted etymologically in the hand's power of grasping whatever is within reach ("The metaphor," Levinas says in "Ethics as First Philosophy," "should be taken literally"; knowledge is "the embodiment of seizure.").[28] The thesis of Western philosophy is: Whatever is, is mine. And as in Hobbes or in Hegel I can approach the other in this conceptualizing and possessive spirit. But (says Levinas) "my meeting with the other person consists in the fact that, despite the extent of my domination over him and his submission, I do not possess him. He does not enter entirely into the opening of being in which I already stand as in the field of my freedom."[29] I can certainly kill him.

---

[23] *Entre nous*, 7.
[24] Ibid., 8.
[25] *Nine Talmudic Readings*, 73.
[26] See "God and Philosophy," *Collected Philosophical Papers*, 159–61.
[27] *Entre nous*, 9.
[28] *The Levinas Reader* (ed. S. Hand; Oxford: Basil Blackwell, 1989), 76.
[29] *Entre nous*, 9.

I can kill the way I hunt, or cut down trees, or slaughter animals—
but then I have grasped the other in the opening of being in general,
as an element of the world in which I stand. I have [merely] seen
him on the horizon I have not looked straight at him. I have not
looked him in the face.... To be in relation with the other face-to-
face—is to be unable to kill.[30]

This seems counter-intuitive until one understands that for Levinas
the face is not an empirical visage that I can apprehend from an
impersonal standpoint. From an impersonal standpoint I can only
see Heidegger's *das Man*, the one of many in a faceless crowd. The
face is not just a visage but an event in which I find myself in proximity with another person—more exactly, under the claim of another
person. In this event I am no longer comprehensible as a cognitive
subject but am obligated to occupy the world differently. As Levinas
says in *Totality and Infinity*, "the face resists possession, resists my powers. In its epiphany, in expression, the sensible, still graspable, turns
into total resistance to the grasp."[31] This resistance is what the transcendence of the other, his or her infinity with respect to the totality of things, means:

This infinity, stronger than murder, already resists us in his face, is
his face, is the primordial expression, is the first word: "you shall not
commit murder." The infinite paralyses power by its infinite resistance
to murder, which, firm and insurmountable, gleams in the face of the
Other, in the total nudity of defenceless eyes, in the nudity of the
absolute openness of the Transcendent.[32]

It is important to stress that the transcendence of the other is neither mystical nor otherworldly but immediately intelligible: it signifies
of itself and not through the mediation of categories and distinctions.[33] In two essays, "Meaning and Sense" (1964) and "Enigma

---

[30] Ibid., 9–10.
[31] *Totality and Infinity*, 197.
[32] Ibid., 199.
[33] See *Totality and Infinity*:
The ethical relation, the face to face, also cuts across every relation one could
call mystical, where events other than that of the presentation of the original
being come to overwhelm or sublimate the pure sincerity of this presentation,
where intoxicating equivocations come to enrich the primordial univocity of
expression, where discourse becomes incantation as prayer becomes rite and
liturgy, where the interlocutors find themselves playing a role in a drama that

and Phenomenon" (1965), Levinas conceptualizes this intelligibility in expressly hermeneutical terms. It is true, he says, that the other person is intelligible the way anything is: "Another is present in a cultural whole and is illuminated by this whole, as a text by its context. . . . The understanding of the other is thus a hermeneutics and an exegesis."[34] However, "the epiphany of the other involves a signifyingness of its own independent of this meaning received from the world. The other comes to us not only out of the context, but also without mediation; he signifies by himself."[35] This primordial signifying is not made of words; it is contained entirely in the enigma of the face. The face is not a phenomenon. It is not a mask or an image. It does not present itself as a silhouette whose essence can be marked out against the horizon; it is outside my horizon. Instead of appearing, "the face speaks,"[36] and its speaking is a disturbance of presence, an interruption of being and "the rational enchainment of its significations. . . . [Its] message is untranslatable into objective language, undefendable by coherent speech, null compared with the public order of disclosed and triumphant significations of nature and history."[37] An enigma is not a riddle that interpretation might overcome:

> what in an enigma has signifyingness [*signifiance*, as against *signification*, or meaning] does not take refuge in a sphere that is present in its own way and awaits a concept capable of finding and grasping it there. The signifyingness of an enigma comes from an irreversible and irrecuperable past which it has *perhaps* not left since it has already been absent from the very terms in which it was signaled ('perhaps' is the modality of an enigma irreducible to the modalities of being and certainty).[38]

---

has begun outside of them. Here resides the rational character of the ethical relation and of language. No fear, no trembling could alter the straightforwardness of this relationship, which preserves the discontinuity of relationship, resists fusion, and where the response does not evade the question. To poetic activity—where influences arise unbeknown to us out of this nonetheless conscious activity, to envelop it and beguile it as a rhythm . . .—is opposed the language that at each instant dispels the charm of rhythm and prevents the initiative from becoming a role. Discourse is rupture and commencement, breaking of rhythm which enraptures and transports the interlocutors—prose. (202–3)

[34] *Collected Philosophical Papers*, 95.
[35] Ibid.
[36] *Totality and Infinity*, 66.
[37] *Collected Philosophical Papers*, 70.
[38] Ibid., 71.

Here is a hermeneutics beyond the understanding of being and beings. More accurately, it is a hermeneutics on the hither side (*en deçà*) of being, a hermeneutics of the enigma that is older than being.

IV. TALMUDIC HERMENEUTICS

However, if the face is an enigma, resistant to interpretation, the Torah is not. It is important to understand that Levinasian hermeneutics is not simply continuous with his ethical theory. Levinas is emphatic that the other cannot be approached in an exegetical spirit, but for him exegesis is, if one may say so, the condition of Revelation, the modality of its existence. Without exegesis, there is no Torah, nor, as it happens, is there any possibility of being human. But exegesis in what sense? For Levinas, exegesis is Talmud, and also the commentaries on Talmud, and also the commentaries on the commentaries, with no end in sight. Revelation is not *vergangung*, not over and done with. Prophecy has not fallen silent. It is ongoing and open-ended, contemporary with the history of Judaism, which is to say Holy History itself, in which there is no "end of history." As Levinas understands it, his own commentaries are not just ancillary readings of ancient texts but a *participation* in a continuous *scriptural* tradition that draws its authority from the epiphany at Sinai and which, moreover, flows through history from the bottom up, not from the top down, meaning that every single person who studies Talmud—that is, every person for whom the close study of Talmud is a form of life—is internal to the event of Sinai, is a continuation, a renewal, an extension of Revelation into the future: each person who studies Talmud is, in effect, responsible for Revelation, indispensable to its life, so that if there is one person who leaves Talmud unstudied, that much of Scripture remains undisclosed—that much is lost. In other words, the interpreter is internal to the Scriptures, not a supplement but the thing itself. Hence, as Levinas likes to say, Revelation *is* the human. Here is how Levinas expresses it in "Revelation in the Jewish Tradition" (1977):

> The reader, in his own fashion, is a scribe. This provides us with a first indication of what we might call the "status" of the Revelation: its word coming from elsewhere, from outside, and simultaneously dwelling in the person who receives it. More than just a listener, is not the human being the unique "terrain" in which exteriority [transcendence] can appear? Is not the personal—that is, the unique "of

itself [*de soi*]"—necessary to the breach and the revelation taking place
from the outside? Is the human as a break in substantial identity not,
"of itself," the possibility for a message coming from the outside . . .
to take on the unique figure that cannot be reduced to the contingency of a "subjective impression"? The revelation as calling to the
unique within me is the significance particular to the signifying of
Revelation. It is as if the multiplicity of persons—is not this the very
meaning of the personal?—were the condition for the plenitude of
"absolute truth"; as if every person, through his uniqueness, were the
guarantee of the revelation of a unique aspect of truth, and some of
its points would never have been revealed if some people had been
absent from mankind. This is not to say that truth is acquired anony-
mously in History, and that it finds "supporters" in it! On the contrary, it is to suggest that the totality of the true is constituted from
the contribution of multiple people: the uniqueness of each act of listening carries the secret of the text; the voice of the Revelation, as
inflected, precisely, by each person's ear, would be necessary to the
"Whole" of the truth: the multiplicity of irreducible people is necessary to the dimensions of meaning; the multiple meanings are multiple people. We can thus see the whole impact of the reference made
by the Revelation to exegesis, to the freedom of this exegesis, the participation of the person listening to the Word making itself heard, but
also the possibility for the Word to travel down the ages to announce
the same truth in different times.[39]

This important passage contains many of the basic principles of
Levinas's talmudic hermeneutics. A number of points are worth
emphasizing. The study of Talmud as Levinas understands it is personal and intimate, a mode of listening to the text—although it is
not therefore a private or isolated event, since "a right reading of
the Torah should include the necessity of teaching,"[40] that is, the
production of commentaries, lectures, or readings—readings which
have the structure of prayer, a movement out of oneself toward others. But study is not a scholasticism. For Levinas it is liturgy:[41] study
is observance—"equal in religious value to the actual carrying out"
of the commandments;[42] it is, not to put too fine a point on it, being
Jewish.

This emphasis on the personal—on the unique human individual
as the modality of scriptural existence—explains Levinas's disregard,

---

[39] *Beyond the Verse*, 133–34.
[40] *In the Time of Nations*, 66.
[41] Ibid., 120.
[42] *Beyond the Verse*, 141.

even dismissal, of historical criticism or of any attempt to historicize the Scriptures according to the procedures of modern philological hermeneutics. Schleiermacher gave the modern theory when he said that the task of hermeneutics is to understand the text first as well as and then even better than its author. This means reconstructing through historical research the time and place of the text's composition and reading it with the eyes of its first audience. And what is more it means recovering the original and originating intention, re-experiencing, as Dilthey would later say, the historical "lived experience" (*Erlebnis*) of which the text is the expression. Levinas is closer to Hans-Georg Gadamer's hermeneutics than to traditional historicism (for Gadamer, "understanding always involves something like applying the text to be understood to the interpreter's present situation").[43] For Levinas as for Gadamer what is important is how the text speaks to the present and, indeed, to the future. The task of hermeneutics is not simply the reconstruction of original meanings but the *actualization* of the text within the life and circumstances (and, indeed, within the temporality and community) of the one who interprets. (*Aktualität* is perhaps the key term in Gadamer's hermeneutics.) Levinas writes: "The Torah not only reproduces what was taught yesterday, it is read according to tomorrow; it does not stop at the representation of what yesterday and today goes by the name of the present."[44] The Torah is not only meaningful in itself. As Levinas says: "The Scriptures are not a history book. . . . [They] confer a meaning upon events: they do not ask for a meaning from them."[45] That is, the Scriptures open onto the present and the future rather than (just) the past.[46]

From a hermeneutical point of view what this comes down to is that there is no understanding the Scriptures from a distance. There is no question of objectifying the text as a document.[47] Just as one cannot approach another person from an impersonal standpoint, so one cannot approach the Scriptures impersonally, that is, one cannot methodically reflect oneself out of the hermeneutical situation

---

[43] Hans-Georg Gadamer, *Truth and Method* (2nd rev. ed.; trans. J. Weinsheimer and D. G. Marshall; New York: Crossroad, 1989), 308.
[44] *In the Time of Nations*, 66.
[45] Ibid., 19.
[46] Ibid., 19–20.
[47] Ibid., 37–38.

but must understand oneself as exposed to and addressed by the text as if it were another person. This is the meaning of Levinas's emphasis on the personal:

> Is the human not the very modality of the manifestation and resonance of the Word? Is not humanity, in its multipersonal plurality, the very locus of interrogation and response, the essential dimension of interpretation, in which the prophetic essence of the Revelation becomes the lived experience of a life?[18]

The Word is not information; it is not doctrine. It is prophecy, and the prophet is the one who studies—"as if, in this study, man were in mystical contact with the divine will itself."[49] "The Scriptures," says Levinas, "have a mode of being that is quite different from the exercise material for grammarians, entirely subject to philologists; a mode of being whereby the history of each piece counts less than the lesson it contains, and where its inspiration is measured by what it inspires."[50]

However, prophecy and inspiration are not modes of levitation or ecstasy. Exegesis is not scholasticism but it *is* an intellectual practice. "Inspiration," says Levinas, "is . . . the exercise of reason itself !"[51] Levinas insists that transcendence is rational;[52] it is not the hearing of voices but giving one's own personal voice to the sacred texts:

> The Talmud upholds the prophetic and verbal origin of the Revelation, but it already lays more stress on the voice of the listener. . . . The Torah is no longer in heaven, but is given; henceforth it is at men's disposal. . . . [The] heavenly Torah has been on Earth since Sinai and appeals to men's exegesis, against which the echoes of heavenly voices can no longer do anything. Man is not, therefore, a "being" among "beings," a simple receiver of sublime information. He is simultaneously him to whom the word is said, but also him through whom there is Revelation. Man is the place through which transcendence passes, even if he can be described as "being-there" or *Dasein*. In light of this situation the whole status of subjectivity and reason must perhaps be revised. In the event of the Revelation, the prophets are succeeded by the *chakham*: the sage, or scholar, or man of reason. In his own way he is inspired, since he bears the oral teaching. He is taught

[18] Ibid., 64.
[19] *Beyond the Verse*, 141.
[50] Ibid., 137.
[51] Ibid., 114.

and he teaches, and he is sometimes called *talmid chakham*: the disciple of a Sage or disciple-sage who receives, but scrutinizes what he receives.[53]

If one participates in Revelation, one nevertheless does not disappear into it as into a divine immanence—Talmud is not Kabbalah. One is never an anonymous amanuensis passively taking dictation. Participating in Revelation means participating in the tradition of talmudic interpretation, which Levinas takes to be a tradition of rational inquiry, a rigorous scrutiny of the details of the scriptural text with a view toward the generation of new meanings.[54] Indeed, it is not so much that Levinas rejects historical criticism and philological hermeneutics as that he appropriates the rabbinical practice of exploring "what is said by the texture of the text."[55] Levinas follows historical method in at least one crucial respect: namely by going back to or remaining with the Hebrew text. But what is important about the Hebrew text is not so much its originality as its polysemy or what Gadamer would call its "open indeterminacy":[56]

> [In talmudic hermeneutics, says Levinas] there is a vital search, throughout, to go beyond the plain meaning. This meaning is, of course, known and acknowledged as plain and as wholly valid at its level. But this meaning is perhaps less easy to establish than the translations of the Old Testament lead one to suppose. It is by going back to the Hebrew text from the translations, venerable as they may be, that the strange or mysterious ambiguity or polysemy authorized by the Hebrew syntax is revealed: words coexist rather than immediately being coordinated or subordinated with and to one another, contrary to what is predominant in the languages that are said to be developed or functional. Returning to the Hebrew text certainly and legitimately makes it more difficult than one thinks to decide on the ultimate intention of a verse, and even more so on a book of the Old Testament. Indeed, the distinction between the plain meaning and the meaning to be deciphered, the search for this meaning buried away and for a meaning even deeper than it contains, all gives emphasis to the specific Jewish exegesis of Scripture. There is not one verse, not one word of the Old

---

[52] *In the Time of Nations*, 148.

[53] *Beyond the Verse*, 144–45.

[54] See David Banon, "Exégèse biblique et philosophie," in *Emmanuel Lévinas: L'éthique comme philosophie première* (ed. J. Greisch and J. Rolland; Actes du colloque de Cerisy-la-Salle, 1986; repr., Paris: Cerf, 1993), 209–27.

[55] *Nine Talmudic Readings*, 68.

[56] Gadamer, *Truth and Method*, 498.

Testament—read as a religious reading, read by way of Revelation—
that does not half-open on to an entire world, unsuspected at first,
which envelops what is easily read. "R. Akiba went as far as to interpret the ornamentation of the letters of the sacred text," says the
Talmud. The scribes and scholars who are said to be slaves of the letter attempted to extract from the letters, as if they were the folded-
back wings of the Spirit, all the horizons that the flight of the Spirit
can embrace, the whole meaning that these letters carry or to which
they awake.[57]

The reference here to Hebrew syntax is important: words are not
integrated into totalities; they "co-exist" within a porous and open-
ended context that extends from Genesis through the whole of the
Talmud and the commentaries on the Talmud. Exegesis consists of
letting one word from anywhere in the whole illuminate any other,
"animat[ing] the text through correspondences and echoes."[58] "What
matters," Levinas says, "is not the explanation of a word [the method
of classical philology]. At issue here is the association of one biblical 'landscape' with another, in order to extract, through this pairing, the secret scent of the first."[59] Levinas calls this echo-principle,
this anachronistic linking of one text with another, *sollicitation*,[60] which
is a pun that entails both the notion of appealing, calling forth, invit-
ing, but also coercion—"forcing the text"; "Do admire the etymologies," Levinas says of the rabbinical delight in puns and wordplay:
"they force [*sollicitent*] the text, they are far-fetched."[61] Hence the
first principle of a "hermeneutics of solicitation" is that the text "is
capable of saying beyond what it wants to say; that it contains more
than it contains; that perhaps an inexhaustible surplus of meaning
remains locked in the syntactic structures of the sentence, in its word-
groups, its actual words, phonemes and letters, in all this materiality of the saying which is potentially signifying all the time."[62] The
materiality of the saying is signifying all the time, not simply in the beginning and not in a way that the "end of time" will reveal once for
all. The process of scriptural signification, if one may say so, is anarchic: before being and without end, it is always at hand.

---

[57] *Beyond the Verse*, 132.
[58] *Nine Talmudic Readings*, 55.
[59] Ibid.
[60] *In the Time of Nations*, 112.
[61] *Nine Talmudic Readings*, 56.
[62] *Beyond the Verse*, 109.

The question is: to whom is it signifying? And at what level of existence? Rabbinical hermeneutics is rashly considered as neglecting the
spirit, whereas the aim of the signified by the signifier is not the only
way to signify; whereas what is signified in the signifier, according to
its other modes, answers only to the mind that solicits it and thereby
belongs to the process of signification; and whereas interpretation essentially involves this act of soliciting without which what is not said,
inherent in the texture of the statement, would be extinguished beneath
the weight of the texts, and sink into the letters. An act of soliciting
which issues from people whose eyes and ears are vigilant and who
are mindful of the whole body of writing from which the extract comes,
and equally attuned to life: the city, the street, other people.[63]

The meaning of the text—"what is signified in the signifier" according to the rules of grammar or of language—"answers only to the
mind that solicits it and thereby belongs to the process of signification."
Of course, one has to ask: why then is not this just mere subjec-
tivism or private invention? The answer is that the one who reads
is not a disengaged punctual ego but is already situated within talmudic tradition, that is, my solicitation of the text goes on within
the context of reading and argument that constitutes the tradition,
part of the give and take of tradition itself, meaning that my reading does not arise independently of the rabbinical teachers who came
before me (it is, after all, these teachers whom I also read). Accordingly
my solicitation is not just my own—not just a method which anyone might pick up or put down—but "issues from people whose eyes
and ears are vigilant and who are mindful of the whole body of
writing from which the extract comes"—Torah, Mishna, Gemara,
and the commentaries on the commentaries. My solitications of the
text are thus not just for myself but are the working out of tradition in its continuing address to the world or attunement to human
life: "the city, the street, other people." Exegesis is not just deci-
pherment; it is prayer—the movement of one for the other, *hermeneia*,
the ethical relation itself.

V. Torah as First Philosophy

Still, the exegete who belongs to tradition does not disappear into
it. "The texts of the Oral Law that have been set into writing should

---

[63] Ibid., 110.

never be separated from their living commentary. When the voice
of the exegete no longer sounds . . . the texts return to their immobility, becoming once again enigmatic, strange, sometimes even ridicu-
lously archaic."[64] "It is not long historical tradition that counts. It is
the personal nature of the person that counts."[65] The basic hermeneutical principle of Talmud is not repetition but freedom of exegesis:

> Tradition, running through history, does not impose its conclusions
> but the contact with what it sweeps along. . . . In written form, it pro-
> duces the diversity of opinions expressed, with extreme care to name
> the person providing them or commenting on them. It records the
> multiplicity and the disagreement between scholars. . . . The page is
> continuously overlaid [with new readings] and prolongs the life of the
> text which, whether it is weakened or reinforced, remains 'oral.' The
> religious act of listening to the revealed word is thus identified with
> the discussion whose open-endedness is desired with all the audacity
> of its problematics.[66]

As Levinas says, "there are crucial reasons why a certain risk of sub-
jectivism, in the pejorative sense of the term, must be run by the
truth,"[67] because the goal of exegesis is to open the Torah to time
and history, to apply it to the present and the future, to allow it to
address "the city, the street, the other person." The actualization of
the Scriptures requires the singular and irreducible voice of unprecedented exegesis.

And this is what we get from Levinas himself, who reads as a
man of reason—a philosopher—searching the text for what reason
will recognize as the truth, which in this case is the truth of ethics
as absolute responsibility for the other. On this point Levinas is
explicit; it is the message of each of his talmudic lectures:

(1) "It is as an ethical kerygma that the Bible is Revelation."[68]
(2) "Religious experience, at least for the Talmud, can only be pri-
    marily a moral experience,"[69] that is, the experience of an absolute
    responsibility for others.

---

[64] *Nine Talmudic Readings*, 13–14.
[65] Ibid., 106.
[66] *Beyond the Verse*, 136–38.
[67] Ibid., 134.
[68] Ibid., 148.
[69] *Nine Talmudic Readings*, 15.

(3) "The religious is at its zenith in the ethical movement toward the other man."[70]

(4) "The Torah demands, in opposition to the natural perseverance of each being in his or her own being (a fundamental ontological law), care for the stranger, the widow and the orphan, a preoccupation with the other person. A reversal of the order of things . . . a reversal of ontology into ethics."[71]

(5) "To follow the Most-High is to know that nothing is greater than to approach one's neighbor. . . . The adventure of the Spirit takes place on earth among men. The trauma I experienced as a slave in Egypt constitutes my humanity itself. This immediately brings me closer to all the problems of the damned on earth, of all those who are persecuted, as if in my suffering as a slave I prayed in a prayer that was not yet an oration, and as if this love of the stranger were already the reply given to me through my heart of flesh. My very uniqueness lies in the responsibility for the other man."[72]

(6) And this responsibility is radical in its absence of limit or qualification and in its absolute dissymmetry. No one can be substituted for me, who can be substituted for everyone: "To bear responsibility for everything and everyone is to be responsible despite oneself. To be responsible despite oneself is to be persecuted. Only the persecuted must answer for everyone, even for his persecutor. Ultimate responsibility can only be the fact of an absolutely persecuted man, having no right to a speech that would disengage or excuse him from his responsibility."[73]

(7) "Nothing is more foreign to me than the other; nothing is more intimate to me than myself. Israel would teach that the greatest intimacy consists in being at every moment responsible for others, the hostage of others."[74] "In the world we are not free in the presence of others. . . . We are their hostages. A notion through which, beyond freedom, the self is defined."[75]

---

[70] *Beyond the Verse*, 5.
[71] *In the Time of Nations*, 61–62.
[72] *Beyond the Verse*, 142.
[73] *Nine Talmudic Readings*, 114–15.
[74] Ibid., 85.
[75] Ibid., 87.

(8) "The entire Torah, in its minute descriptions, is constituted in the 'Thou shalt not kill' that the face of the other signifies, and awaits its proclamation therein. The life of others, the *being* of others, falls to me as a duty. In the *thou* of this commandment, the *me* is only begun: it is for the other in its innermost nucleus."[76]

(9) "The human is the possibility of a being-for-the-other. . . . An anthropology of an already human humanity, with unlimited responsibility, called Israel."[77]

Each of these citations is an allusion to Levinas's later writings in which the ethical subject—the self—is characterized as one who exists in the accusative rather than the nominative case: one whose mode of existence is persecution in the sense of being responsible for what others do and suffer. This is the philosophy of Talmud as Levinas articulates it. My responsibility for the other person, for the suffering and the fault of the other, is not conditional upon my free act of accepting or agreeing to be responsible. It is an unconditional responsibility, a given that constitutes me as a human being. To be is to be in the accusative, responsible before freedom.

The thesis is this: if my responsibility for what the other does and for what the other suffers were not gratuitous—if it were not without compensation; if it were not free; if it were simply *quid pro quo*—there would never be any such thing as *ethical* responsibility, no one would ever act for the good of another, it would all come down to payment for services or fair exchange: ethics for hire. Ethics would have to be mediated by politics in order for the good to be done. And of course that is maybe the way it is.

But however it is, talmudic ethics is opposed to an ethics of bookkeeping or the balancing of accounts in which I am only accountable for what I have contracted to do or not to do as a basically self-legislating subject. In *Otherwise than Being*, Levinas says that, to be sure, "in a meaningful world"—a Kantian world—"one cannot be held to answer for what one has not done."[78] In a meaningful world, Job would not suffer. But this is not a meaningful world. It

---

[76] *In the Time of Nations*, 111.
[77] Ibid., 126–27.
[78] *Otherwise than Being*, 122; *Autrement qu'être ou au-delà l'essence* (La Haye: Martinus Nijhoff, 1974), 195.

is a Holocaust world in which suffering is anarchic, gratuitous, without reason, and without end. So what can relieve it?

In such a world, a world from which God has absconded, human beings have only one another. Substitution, my being for the other, being responsible for the good of the other despite myself, gratuitous sacrifice, is all we have as humans to survive as human. Otherwise our suffering would be unmitigated.

INDEX OF SOURCES

Hebrew Bible

Ancient Near Eastern Literature

Second Temple Literature

Targum

Philo of Alexandria

Flavius Josephus

New Testament

Greek and Latin Authors

Early and Medieval Christian Literature

Ancient and Medieval Rabbinic Literature

Islamic Literature

Renaissance Literature

Modern Literature

Levinas

INDEX OF AUTHORS

Lightning Source UK Ltd.
Milton Keynes UK
UKOW04f2207071215

264259UK00002B/201/P

9 781589 833876